Alter Orient und Altes Testament
Veröffentlichungen zur Kultur und Geschichte
des Alten Orients und des Alten Testaments

Band 22

Orient and Occident
Essays presented to
Cyrus H. Gordon
on the Occasion of his
Sixty-fifth Birthday

Alter Orient und Altes Testament

Veröffentlichungen zur Kultur und Geschichte des Alten Orients
und des Alten Testaments

Herausgeber

Kurt Bergerhof · Manfried Dietrich · Oswald Loretz

1973

Verlag Butzon & Bercker Kevelaer

Neukirchener Verlag Neukirchen-Vluyn

Orient and Occident

Essays presented to
Cyrus H. Gordon
on the Occasion of his
Sixty-fifth Birthday

Edited by
Harry A. Hoffner, Jr.

1973

Verlag Butzon & Bercker Kevelaer

Neukirchener Verlag Neukirchen-Vluyn

Herstellung: Breklumer Druckerei Manfred Siegel
Printed in Germany
ISBN 3 7887 0402 0 Neukirchener Verlag
ISBN 3 7666 8805 7 Verlag Butzon & Bercker

To Professor Cyrus H. Gordon

June, 1973

The contributers to this volume greet and congratulate you on the happy occasion of your 65th birthday! It is a distinct pleasure for us to present to you this collection of essays. The range of subjects it quite broad. The essays deal with areas scattered from Iran on the east to the sea lanes of the Mediterranean and Atlantic on the west. The time period covered stretches from the fourth millennium B.C. to the end of the first millennium A.D. Documents composed in Egyptian, Coptic, Sumerian, Akkadian, Hittite, Hurrian, Ugaritic, Hebrew, Aramaic, Mandaic, Arabic, Greek and Latin have been utilized. The archeological essays employ not only the time-honored traditional methods but also newer ones such as underwater exploration and radiation analysis of ceramics. All the essays are comparative in the sense that data from several neighboring cultures is evaluated together. Often, though not always, biblical literature and history plays a role. Yet amidst the diversity there is also unity. That unity is perhaps symbolized by the fact that you, Professor Gordon, have either personally engaged in research in each of these areas or have furthered them by your interest and the encouragement of your students.

Some of us were once your students, whom you started in the disciplines which we pursue today. Others of us, although we were never your students, consider ourselves your good friends and well-wishers. We work in disciplines where your contributions have often been considerable. Some of the essays in this volume show unmistakably the influence of your ideas. But in no sense do the contributors to this volume consider themselves members of a single school of thought. In many points our opinions diverge not only from yours, but from each other. We are, however, fully agreed in one important matter. We all wish to greet and congratulate you, Professor Gordon, on this your jubilee, and to wish for you many more years of productive scholarship!

The Contributors

PREFACE

The essays in this volume were submitted by invitation to the editor in June of 1972. Invitations were extended to a group of the friends, colleagues and former students of Professor Cyrus H. Gordon. It was impossible to include every friend, colleague or former student who might have wished to contribute an essay.

The essays were edited during the months of July, August and September, 1972. Because the editor was spending a long awaited sabbatical in Germany during the autumn of 1972, it was possible for him to confer personally with Herren Drs. Loretz and Dietrich in Münster in October and to submit the edited manuscripts in person. The editor wishes to thank Herren Loretz and Dietrich for their kind and efficient assistance in producing this volume and keeping its character confidential until the date of presentation.

The essays are arranged in the alphabetical order of the authors' surnames. The sole exception is the large index of passages from Ugaritic texts cited in Gordon's *Ugaritic Textbook*, which has been placed at the end near the other indices to facilitate usefulness.

The abbreviations employed are those used in the more or less standard reference works of the various disciplines. For Assyriology, W. von Soden's *Akkadisches Handwörterbuch* and the Chicago Assyrian Dictionary. For Egyptology, A.H. Gardiner's *Egyptian Grammar*. For Hittitology, J. Friedrich's *Hethitisches Wörterbuch*. For biblical studies, the *Interpreter's Dictionary of the Bible.* For Islamic studies, the *Encyclopedia of Islam.* Supplementary abbreviations can be found at the head of each article.

For reasons of space it was decided to forego the inclusion of a complete bibliography of Professor Gordon's publications, since this would have required a volume almost half again as large as the present one. A complete bibliography to the year 1962 was published in *Studia Mediterranea: a Student Tribute* (Brandeis University, 1963).

Harry A. Hoffner, Jr.
Editor

Christmas, 1972

TABLE OF CONTENTS

To Cyrus H. Gordon V
Preface VII
Table of contents IX
Aharoni, Y., The Solomonic Temple, the Tabernacle and the Arad Sanctuary 1
Artzy, M., The Late Bronze "Palestinian" Bichrome Ware in its Cypriote Context 9
Astour, M. C., Ugarit and the Aegean 17
Bass, G. F., Cape Gelidonya and Bronze Age Maritime Trade 29
Bush, F. Wm., The Relationship between the Hurrian Suffixes -ne/-na and -nni/e /-nna . . . 39
Dahood, M., S. J., Ugaritic and Phoenician or Qumran and the Versions 53
Fisher, L. R., The Patriarchal Cycles 59
Groll, S., Late Egyptian of Non-Literary Texts of the 19th Dynasty 67
Hillers, D. R., The Bow of Aqhat: The Meaning of a Mythological Theme 71
Hoffner, H. A., Jr., Incest, Sodomy and Bestiality in the Ancient Near East 81
Holmes, Y. L., Egypt and Cyprus: Late Bronze Age Trade and Diplomacy 91
Lacheman, E. R., Real Estate Adoption by Women in the Tablets from URU Nuzi 99
Levine, B. A., Later Sources on the *Netînîm* 101
McKeon, J. F. X., Achaemenian Cloisonné-Inlay Jewelry: An Important New Example 109
Neiman, D., The Two Genealogies of Japhet 119
Newby, G. D., *Sūrat al-'Ikhlāṣ* 127
Owen, D. I., Miscellanea Neo-Sumerica I-III 131
Rainey, A. F., Ilānu rēṣūtni lillikū! 139
Sarna, N., Zedekiah's Emancipation of Slaves and the Sabbatical Year 143
Sasson, J. M., The Worship of the Golden Calf 151
Segert, St., Form and Function of Ancient Israelite, Greek and Roman Legal Sentences . . . 161
Silverman, M. H., Syntactic Notes on the *Waw* Consecutive 167
Smick, E. B., The Jordan of Jericho 177
Todd, I. A., Anatolia and the Khirbet Kerak Problem 181
Ward, W. A., Observations on the Egyptian Biconsonantal Root pꜣ 207
Yamauchi, E. M., Cultic Prostitution 213
Young, G. D., Nuzu Texts in the Free Library of Philadelphia 223
Beitzel, B. J., An Index to the Ugaritic Passages in the *Ugaritic Textbook* 235
Indexes 269
Plates . . . . I*-III*

THE SOLOMONIC TEMPLE, THE TABERNACLE AND THE ARAD SANCTUARY

Yohanan Aharoni

Tel-Aviv University, Israel

The reconstruction of the plan of the Solomonic Temple and the question of its architectural origins are problems which occupy archaeological research and biblical exegesis from their very beginnings. Yet no agreement has been reached, even regarding the most basic questions.[1]

Most scholars believe that the building consisted of three adjoining rooms, *ûlam*, *hêkal* and *d^ebîr* in biblical terminology. The reconstructions of Watzinger (Fig. 1:1),[2] Vincent,[3] Albright-Wright[4] and others[5] all are based on this conception. The temple of Tell Tayinât in northern Syria, is usually accepted as its best architectonic parallel. Dated from the ninth-eighth centuries B.C.,[6] it was built a century or two after the Solomonic Temple. The question of its proto-type is heavily debated.

In all examples from Palestine and Syria which may be taken into consideration, the temple buildings have only one room, the *cella*, with a niche for a statue of the goddess. In only a few cases has this niche been replaced by a special inner room, the *adyton.*[7] Several scholars view the 14th-13th century temples of Hazor and Alalakh[8] as proto-types of the Solomonic Temple, a presumption which has been refuted by Busink.[9] In the temples of Hazor and Alalakh, the *hêkal* is a distinct broad room, as opposed to the long room of the Solomonic Temple. Moreover, the function of the various rooms is different. Of the three adjoining rooms, only the third and innermost one acted as a place for ritual, and it was equipped with a central niche. The two first rooms had other functions, as had the one *ûlam* at the Solomonic Temple.

All these reconstructions and comparisons are based on the assumption that the Solomonic Temple consisted of three adjoining rooms, which assumption itself has been disputed by various scholars. The biblical description is ambiguous and may be interpreted as describing only *two* or perhaps only *one* single room. The description opens with the general measurements of *the house* (*ha-bayit*), which are given as "sixty cubits long, twenty cubits wide" (1 Kings 6:2). *Ha-bayit* obviously includes in this description only the *hêkal* and the *d^ebîr*, while the *ûlam* is viewed as an addition, a fact which is clearly stressed in the next verse: "And the *ûlam* in

---

1 Cf. Th.A. Busink, *Der Tempel von Jerusalem*, I (1970) – henceforth: Busink, *Tempel.*

2 C. Watzinger, *Denkmäler Palästinas*, I (1933), Abb. 39.

3 L.H. Vincent, *Jérusalem de l'Ancient Testament*, II-III (1956), Taf. CI.

4 G.E. Wright, *BA*, 18 (1955), Fig. 9.

5 E.G. *Encyclopaedia Biblica*, V (1968), col. 535 (S. Yeivin; Hebrew).

6 C.W. McEvan, *AJA*, 41 (1937), 9, Fig. 4.

7 Busink (*Tempel*, 358 ff.) has assembled the various examples.

8 See plans *ibid.*, 398, 492.

9 *Ibid.*, 591.

front of the *hêkal* of the house was twenty cubits long, equal to the width of the house, and ten cubits deep in front of the house." How can one understand this complicated description? Was the *ûlam* a separate part of the temple, and accepted as an addition which should not be taken into consideration when looking for architectonic comparisons? Some scholars even see in the *ûlam* a separate and free-standing building which served as an entrance to the temple.[10]

The biblical account continues with the description of the side chambers and various constructional details, like the cover of the walls and the floor with cedar and cypress boards. Only after this comes the description of the construction of the *d^ebîr*: "He built twenty cubits of the rear of the house with boards of cedar from the floor to the rafter (Hebrew: *qôrôt* instead of *qîrôt*), and he built this within as an inner sanctuary, as the most holy place (Hebrew: *wybn lw mbyt ldbr lqdš hqdšym*). The house, that is, the *hêkal* in front (of the *d^ebîr*), was forty cubits long . . . The *d^ebîr* he prepared in the innermost part of the house, to set there the ark of the covenant of the Lord. The *d^ebîr* was twenty cubits long, twenty cubits wide, and twenty cubits high . . ." (1 Kings 6:16-20).[11]

This description is perplexing and complicated, and its exact meaning is difficult to make out. Is the intention to stress that in spite of the adjoining rooms, *hêkal* before *d^ebîr*, the *d^ebîr* actually was "prepared in the innermost part of the house" (verse 19) and, therefore, the termini house=temple and *hêkal* are synonymous? Was the *d^ebîr* reckoned as part of the *hêkal*, and if so, did the temple proper actually consist of only one room? The description also does not leave any width for a wall between the *hêkal* and the *d^ebîr*, since their total length of 60 cubits comprises the exact sum of the measurements of those two rooms. Are the measurements only approximate, or was the partition wall a thin wooden screen, as suggested by Busink? [12]

A still more extreme suggestion was advanced by H. Schult, *i.e.* that the *d^ebîr* was a kind of furniture, "ein Kubus aus Zedernholz," which was erected in the *hêkal.*[13] He recalls as evidence the word "*dbr*" which is mentioned with the determinatives "house" and "wood" on an Egyptian writing-board of the 21st or 22nd Dynasty, listing a temple inventory.[14] With this interpretation in mind, Schult arrives at the following conclusion: "Wenn eine gemauerte Wand zwischen *d^ebîr* und *hêkal* tatsächlich nicht vorhanden war, verliert auch die Bezeichnung des salomonischen Tempels als eines *drei*-geteilten Langhauses ihre Berechtigung. Das Gebäude kann, wie sich ergab, im besten Falle *zwei*geteilt gewesen sein, ja, es muß unter Umständen als *ein*teilig klassifiziert werden . . ."[15]

This suggestion was generally accepted by M. Noth in his exegesis of the Book of Kings.[16] As a result both scholars oppose the comparison of the Solomonic Temple with Tell Tayinât and other tri-partial temples. As the only acceptable parallels they point to the "migdol" temples of Shechem and Megiddo. These consist of a single room with a central niche. This room is preceded by an open vestibule flanked by two towers. A. Kuschke agrees in principle with the argumentation of Schult and Noth, but he raises several intriguing questions:[17] Is it legitimate to define a wooden cube 10 by 10 m. large as "furniture? " Where does the description of the

---

[10] F.C. Foester, *Old Testament Commentary* (1948), 419 (cited according to Busink, *Temple*, 164); J. Ouellette, "Le vestibule du temple de Salomon était-il un bit ḫilâni?," *RB*, 76 (1969), 365-378.

[11] For an analysis of the text, see Busink, *Tempel*, 163 ff.; M. Noth, *Könige, Biblischer Kommentar, Altes Testament* IX (1968), 96 ff.

[12] Busink, *Tempel*, 208.

[13] H. Schult, *ZDPV*, 80 (1964), 46-54.

[14] A.H. Gardiner, *Ancient Egyptian Onomastica*, I (1947), 64 ff.

[15] Schult, *ibid.* (note 13), 54.

[16] Noth, *ibid.* (note 11), 105 ff.

[17] A. Kuschke, "Der Tempel Salomons und der 'syrische Tempeltypus'," *Das Ferne und Nahe Wort* (Rost Festschrift, 1967), 124-132.

wall between the *hêkal* and the *d^e^bîr* in the vision of Ezekiel come from? The unusually thick walls of the "migdol" temples of Shechem and Megiddo testify to their towerlike character. They have no comparison in the structure of the Solomonic Temple. No answers have been produced for these questions.

The purpose of this paper is to add to the discussion the recently discovered temple at Arad, the first Israelite temple from the period of the monarchy which has been discovered by archaeology.[18]

The basic facts leave no doubt that we are dealing with a legitimate Yahwistic sanctuary, built by the kings of Israel and Judah: its period, location and contents. It was built in the tenth century as an integral part of the first Israelite fortress erected at the site. It was repaired and reconstructed during the ninth and eighth centuries. It was finally destroyed with the construction of the new casemate wall during the seventh century.[19] The temple occupied an important place in the plan of the Israelite fortress, which acted as an administrative and military centre of the region. The temple's contents stand in complete agreement with the Mosaic law, including an altar of burnt offering, incense altars and offering tables. Not a single figurine nor other pagan votive offerings were found. A stone *maṣṣebah* was found in the *adyton*, whose connection with Yahwistic worship and use at Israelite highplaces is frequently mentioned in the Bible.[20] Hebrew ostraca with the names of the priestly families Meremoth, Pashhur and the Sons of Korah were found in the side rooms of the temple and its surroundings, and the idiom "House of Yahweh" (*byt yhwh*) is mentioned in one of the Eliashiv letters.[21] Here we have a temple built in the days of Solomon (or David?) as part of a royal fortress, which continued to function there during the ninth and eighth centuries, with implements exactly fitting the rules of the Mosaic law. Is there any reason to doubt its legitimate, Yahwistic character? [22]

This is not the place to deal with the *raison d'être* of the Israelite sanctuary at Arad nor with the reason for its being founded just at this site.[23] We shall limit ourselves to the question of the comparison of its plan with that of the Solomonic Temple (Fig. 1:3).

---

[18] Y. Aharoni, *IEJ*, 17 (1967), 247-9; idem, *Archaeology and Old Testament Study* (ed. D. Winton Thomas; 1967), 395 ff.; idem, *BA* 31 (1968), 18 ff.; idem, *Ariel* 24 (1969), 28-36; see also in Hebrew: *Encyclopaedia of Archaeological Excavations in the Holy Land*, II (1970), 472-7; *Encyclopaedia Biblica*, VI (1971), 379-382.

[19] We should stress that the construction of the casemate wall on top of the temple emphazises its complete destruction, but the dates of its various strata were not determined on behalf of this wall. Even if one would doubt with Yadin the date of this wall because of the dressing of its stones (Y. Yadin, *IEJ*, 15 [1965], 180), it is difficult to see the relevency of his arguments to the opinion expressed in the last sentance of the paper regarding the earlier strata. Or would he argue that the Iron Age material found on the floors, including the Eliashiv ostraca, belongs to the Persian period? If the wall had cut these floors without leaving any foundation trench (and without its own floors being preserved), even then only the date of the wall is under discussion without any connection with the earlier ("cut") strata. Two clear floors with Iron Age pottery were found, for example, on top of the altar of burnt offerings. Tenth century pottery of the first temple has been published in *BA*, 31 (1968), Figs. 7-8. It is true that the chronology of the tenth-ninth century pottery is still heavily debated but at Arad we also possess a definite historical datum: The fortress of Arad is mentioned in the list of cities conquered by Shishak five years after Solomon's death. The temple was built, as stated, with the first fortress erected on the tel. If this fortress is later than the tenth century, which fortress was conquered by Shishak?

[20] Cf. *Encyclopaedia Biblica*, V (1968), 221-5 (Hebrew).

[21] Y. Aharoni, *IEJ*, 16 (1966), 5-7. In this ostracon it is probably the Jerusalem Temple that is meant, but its mention in one of the letters sent to Arad is hardly accidental and indicates the connections with the temple.

[22] So far, S. Yeivin is the only scholar who doubts this and assumes that it was built for foreign mercenaries who served in the fortress (*Am. Ac. Jew. Res. Proc.*, 34 (1966), 152 ff.). As arguments he produces the hieratic ostraca and the mention of "Kittim" in the Hebrew ostraca. However, these inscriptions belong to the end of the Iron Age, at which time the sanctuary was already deserted and no evidence for mercenaries exists in the earlier strata. Even if we had evidence for the employment of mercenaries, may we assume that the king of Israel and Judah tolerated the existance of a pagan sanctuary at the royal fortress from the days of Solomon until the reign of Hezekiah, at least?

[23] For first discussions of this question see B. Mazar, *JNES*, 24 (1965), 297-303; Y. Aharoni, *Ariel*, 24 (1969), 30-36; idem, *BA*, 31 (1968), 27 ff.; idem, *Fifth World Congress of Jewish Studies, Proceedings* (1969), 69-74.

At previous occasions we have already pointed to three similar features of the two buildings:

(a) Their east-west orientation, the entrance at the east and the Holy of Holies towards the west. We may note that the Arad sanctuary was built exactly with the direction of the compass, and it is possible that this was taken into consideration with the construction of the fortress.

(b) The straight axis with central openings.

(c) The width of both buildings (*i.e.*, their north-south measurements) are identical: 20 cubits.[24]

In spite of these similarities, one is striken by the apparent differences of their plan. The Arad temple actually consists of only one room, a distinct, broad room. In its centre is a raised recess, serving as an *adyton*. Thus its architectonic conception seems to be completely different from that of the Solomonic Temple.

This also is Busink's conclusion,[25] and it would be difficult to advance any further, if we did not have an additional description, which has much in common with both temples. We mean the Tabernacle, the traditional movable sanctuary of the desert period (Fig. 1:2).[26]

The similarity between the Tabernacle and the Arad sanctuary is most striking. In the courtyard in front of the Tabernacle was the altar of burnt offering, five by five cubits (Ex. 27:1). That is exactly the size of the altar at Arad and probably also of the original altar in the Solomonic Temple (2 Chron. 6:13). Between the altar and the Tabernacle was a bronze laver for the priests to wash in (Ex. 30:18); a basin built of stone was found in the courtyard of the Arad sanctuary opposite the altar. The measurements of the Arad temple were 6 by 20 cubits.[27] The Tabernacle was constructed of boards, each one and a half cubit in breadth, and "there shall be two tenons in each frame (board), for fitting together" (Ex. 26:16-17). Its measurements are given in boards, 6 on one side and 20 on the other. At least the proportions of the Tabernacle therefore were identical with those of the Arad temple. The technical description of the tenons is difficult to understand. We may suppose, however, that they were joined and overlapped half a cubit. It is, therefore, possible that not only the proportions but the actual measurements were identical at both structures: 6 by 20 cubits.

The entrance to the Tabernacle was from the east, as at Arad. It consisted of one room in which a place was reserved by a veil for the Holy of Holies (Ex. 26:31ff.). One should note that no measurements are given in the description for the indication of the place of the veil. Behind the veil was the ark of testimony (Ex. 26:34), and before it an incense altar (Ex. 30:1ff.). At Arad the place of the Holy of Holies was indicated by a raised, central niche before which two incense altars were found.[28]

The description of the plan and contents of the Tabernacle are virtually identical in all details with those of the Arad sanctuary, except for one basic difference: the Tabernacle is described as a long-room structure with its entrance on one of its short sides, in contrast to the distinct broad-room conception of the Arad temple. The long-room shape which distinguishes the Tabernacle from the Arad temple is, as we have seen, also the characteristic feature of the Solomonic Temple. We believe, therefore, that the description of the Tabernacle has provided us with a bridging link between the Arad sanctuary and the Solomonic Temple, which also may help to explain the complicated description of the latter.

---

[24] For details see Y. Aharoni, *Archaeology and Old Testament Study* (ed. D. Winton Thomas, 1967), 395; idem, *BA*, 31 (1968), 22 ff.

[25] Busink, *Temple*, 593-4.

[26] Cf. *Encyclopaedia Biblica*, V (1968), 532-548 (Hebrew); *The Interpreter's Dictionary of the Bible* (1962), 498-506; Busink, *Tempel*, 602 ff.

[27] Later it was slightly enlarged, probably because of the change in the standard of the cubit in Israel from the common to the royal Egyptian cubit hinted at in the bible (2 Chron. 3:3), see Y. Aharoni, *BA*, 31 (1968), 24.

[28] The altars were found lying on the middle step and plastered over; their location in the entrance is only a possibility, see Y. Aharoni, *IEJ*, 17 (1967), 247.

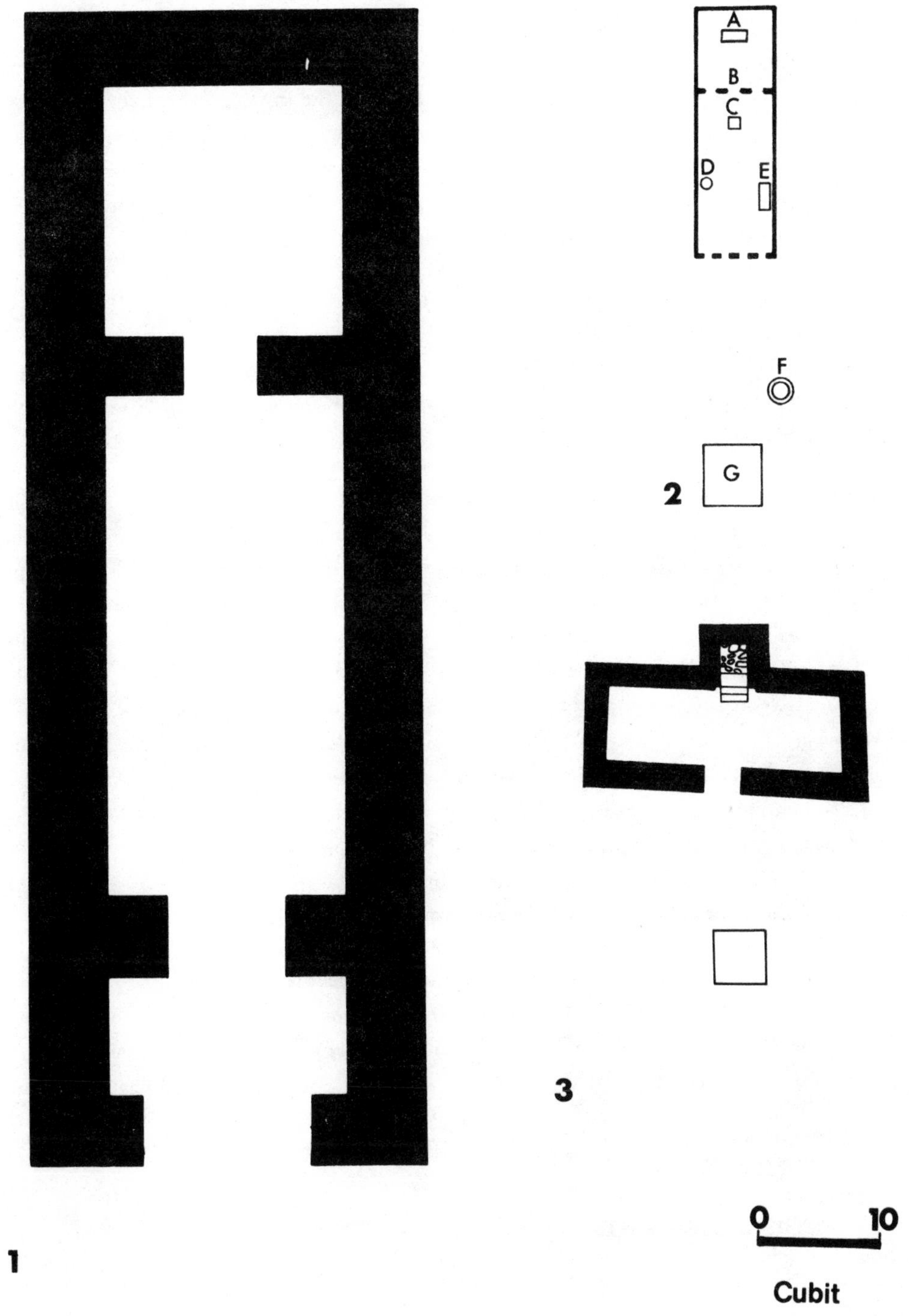

Fig. 1. 1. The Solomonic Temple.

2. The Tabernacle: A. Ark of the Covenant; B. Veil; C. Incense altar; D. Golden Candlestick; E. Table of Showbread; F. Laver; G. Altar of Burnt Offering.

3. The Arad Sanctuary.

Most scholars who dealt with the Tabernacle have pointed to the proximity of its general conception to that of the Solomonic Temple. Some believe that its description is only an artificial projection of the Solomonic Temple into the period of the desert wanderings.[29] Virtually all reconstructions presume that the Holy of Holies behind the veil occupied a third of its length, without, as stated, any indication in the description. This is the case with the *d^{e}bîr* in relation to the *hêkal* in the Solomonic Temple. On the other hand, various scholars have pointed to details which do not fit the Solomonic Temple and which may be taken as evidence for its early and independent tradition. This has led F.M. Cross to the suggestion that the description originated in the tent which David had pitched for the ark of the Lord (2 Sam. 6:17).[30] Busink accepts in principal Cross' view and he writes: "Auch wir halten es für wahrscheinlich, daß der Verfasser des Entwurfs ein Dokument aus Davids Zeit vor Augen gehabt hat. Unter Einfluß des salomonischen Tempels schuf er aber etwas Neues, das überdies gemäß der Funktion eines 'Wüstenheiligtums' zerlegbar sein sollte."[31]

We believe that this approach basically has been confirmed in the light of the Arad sanctuary. The distinct similarities between it and the Tabernacle and their differences from the Solomonic Temple are clear evidences that the description of the Tabernacle is based upon an early tradition, independent from the Solomonic Temple, according to which the Arad sanctuary also was constructed. This tradition evidently was influenced by the Solomonic Temple.

We shall not dwell here on the question of the origin of that tradition and if its roots really were in a movable tent of the desert period.[32] Yet if in the tenth century a sanctuary was built in accordance with that tradition, as was done at Arad, it becomes clear that this is the shape of the traditional Israelite sanctuary, an inheritance of the period of the Judges. It had one room, which was a distinct broad room, with a central niche for the main cult object opposite the entrance. To this simple plan, basic parallels are to be found in the country already in the Canaanite period, like the shrine at Hazor of the 14th-13th centuries,[33] the 12th century stratum VI temple at Beth-shan,[34] and perhaps the recently discovered Egyption miner's temple of the 13th-12th centuries at Timna'.[35] Later examples are the temple at Rawwafah in Midian of the Nabataean period[36] and the Hellenistic "Solar Shrine" at Lachish.[37] The latter is identical in plan with the Arad sanctuary and the proportions of its main chamber are exactly 20 by 6. We believe that it, too, is an Israelite temple, built according to the same ancient tradition.[38] This assumption has been supported by the discovery of a high place and sanctuary from the Iron Age beneath the Hellenistic temple.[39] The early shrine belongs to the tenth century B.C. and it consists of a small broad room with inner measurements of 3.40 by 2.25 m.

Unfortunately, no descriptions of early Israelite sanctuaries are in our possession. However, the few details which may be deduced from the biblical stories well suit a broad-room *cella*. We hear about the Shiloh sanctuary: ". . . Hannah rose (and presented herself before the Lord).[40] Now Eli the priest was sitting on the seat beside the door-post of the temple of the Lord" (1 Sam. 1:9). Hannah was standing outside of the temple

---

29 For the various opinions and references, see *Encyclopaedia Biblica*, V (1968), 540ff.
30 F.M. Cross, *BA*, 10 (1947), 45-68.
31 Busink, *Tempel*, 603.
32 Busink (*Tempel*, 602-3) argues that the construction of the boards as given in the description is impossible from a technical point of view.
33 *Hazor I*, pl. CLXXX.
34 *Beth-Shan II*, pl. VIII.
35 B. Rothenberg, *Bible et Terre Sainte*, 123 (1970), 13.
36 P.J. Parr, S.L. Harding and J.E. Dayton, *Bulletin, Institute of Archaeology, University of London*, 8-9 (1970), 216, fig. 8.
37 *Lachish III*, pl. 121.
38 Y. Aharoni, *IEJ*, 18 (1968), 157-169.
39 Y. Aharoni, *Qadmoniot*, 2 (1970), 131-4 (Hebrew).
40 Only in the Septuagint (*kai katestē enōpion kyriou*).

"before the Lord," thus Busink concludes that the ark of the Lord was in the chamber and that it had no separate *adyton*.[41] This is also indicated in the continuation: ". . . and Samuel was lying down within the *hêkal* of the Lord, where the ark of God was" (1 Sam. 3:3). *hêkal* is usually explained as meaning the temple as a whole,[42] but this only means that the temple and the *hêkal* actually were the same. We hardly may suppose that the temple servant would sleep in the *adyton*, if the temple had one. A broad chamber with a central niche best fits these situations.[43]

No description is given for the temples of Bethel and Dan. Busink assumes that they also had no separate *adyton* because the people saw the calf before them, as indicated in Jeroboam's words: "Behold your gods (Hebrew: Here is your God), O Israel, who brought you up out of the land of Egypt" (1 Kings 12:28).[44]

An illuminating detail for the location of the ark is given at the tent erected by David: "And they brought in the ark of the Lord, and set it *in its place*, inside (*b*ᵉ*tôk*) the tent which David had pitched for it" (2 Sam. 6:17). *b*ᵉ*tôk* in biblical Hebrew means "in the midst of."[45] If the ark stood at its fixed place in the midst of the tent, it seems plausible that the entrance to the tent was across from it on one of its long sides.

It seems, therefore, that the tradition of the early Israelite sanctuary has been preserved in the description of the Tabernacle. However, this is now viewed as a long-room structure under the influence of the Solomonic Temple. This change explains the absence of a measurement for the location of the veil: this originally was in the centre of the Tabernacle, as in both David's tent and the Arad sanctuary. If a measurement of its location existed, it did not fit the rotation of the structure and its contents by 90°.

Hence we return to the Solomonic Temple. Its complicated and apparently contradictory description makes sense, if we suppose that the intention was to dress its new architecture in the traditional termini of the old, venerable sanctuary.

We now may accept that the new temple actually was a tri-partial structure, including an antechamber, a *cella* and a true *adyton*. Yet the traditional description knew only one room, the House of Yahweh, which is also called *hêkal* of Yahweh (*e.g.*, 1 Sam. 1:7, 9).[46] Thus the *ûlam* is no integral part of the temple,[47] but an unessential addition "in front" of the house (1 Kings 6:3). On the other hand, the innermost room, the *adyton* in which the ark was placed, is no true room, but it is the equivalent of the central spot behind the veil in the one-room sanctuary. The word *d*ᵉ*bîr* probably was taken over from Canaanite-Phoenician. Its original meaning apparently was "shrine," as indicated also by its appearance in Egypt as a wooden temple furniture which contained the statue of the goddess.[48] Therefore, it was built "within as an inner sanctuary, as the most holy place . . . The *d*ᵉ*bîr* he prepared in the innermost part of the house, to set there the ark of the covenant of the Lord" (1 Kings 6:16, 19). And in order to avoid any mistake: "The house that is the *hêkal*" (*habayit hû' hahêkal*; 1 Kings 6:17). This is also the solution to the old question regarding the double meaning of the word *hêkal* in the Bible, designating both the entire temple and one of its rooms:[49] the ancient tradition knew in the temple only one room, that is the house = *hêkal*. Solomon built the *ûlam* in front of it and the *d*ᵉ*bîr* inside it, yet the house remained the *hêkal*.

---

[41] Busink, *Tempel*, 594 ff.

[42] *Ibid.*, 595.

[43] Also Busink (*ibid.*) writes that in the light of Arad we may assume that the Shiloh sanctuary was a broad-room structure.

[44] Busink, *Tempel*, 598.

[45] L. Koehler and W. Baumgartner, *Lexicon in Veteris Testamenti Libros* (1958), 1021.

[46] There is no doubt regarding the origin of the word from Sumerian *e-gal* = "great house" through the Akkadian *ekallu* = "palace," cf. Busink, *Tempel*, 180.

[47] Regarding the assumed origin of the word *ûlam* from the Akkadian *ellamu* = "in front of," cf. Busink, *Tempel*, 164.

[48] Busink, *Tempel*, 601 and there references.

[49] Cf. the dictionary of Koehler and Baumgartner, *ibid.* (note 45), 230-1; Busink, *Tempel*, 180-1.
[In Akkadian too *ekallu* could designate either an entire building or its "main room" (*CAD* E, 60; *AHw*, 192). – Ed.]

The practical aspect of this discussion regarding the reconstruction of the Solomonic Temple is not to look for technical termini of construction in the passages which define the relation between the various rooms of the temple.They belong to the sacral traditions which aimed to bridge a gap between old and new. Also the general measurement of "the house" given at the head of the description, which gives the total of the *hêkal* and the *d^e^bîr* as 60 cubits, should not be accepted as an additional, independent datum; it belongs to the ideology of the traditional description in which the *hêkal* and the *d^e^bîr* were one. The size of the building (60 x 20) was ten times that of the ancient sacral tradition (6 x 20); this relation too, may not be accidental.

The new temple was meant to be a monumental royal structure, like the magnificent buildings which adorned the royal capitals of great neighbouring countries in this period. A structure consisting of one broad room was not suitable for that purpose. Evidently a new plan was chosen, probably based on the architecture of neighbouring countries.[50] As its best parallels remain the temple of Tell Tayinât and the widely distributed tri-partial Syrian temple of later periods, as pointed out by Alt[51] and again considered by Kuschke.[52] The question of its proto-type still is problematic, and it is to be hoped that a solution will be found with the discovery of additional temples in the neighbouring countries.

The Solomonic Temple remained the only one of its kind in architectural plan. Other temples built in Israel in this period, like the Arad temple, preserved the traditional sacral architecture. This architecture found its expression in the description of the Tabernacle. However, since the Tabernacle was viewed as a central sanctuary, the spiritual and functional predecessor of the Solomonic Temple, the general outlook of the new magnificent building was impressed on it. It is only natural that the generation viewed and described the Tabernacle under the influence of the general appearance of the Solomonic Temple.

---

[50] Contrary to the assumption of Busink (*Tempel*, 589 ff.), who arrived at the conclusion that the Solomonic Temple is an original Israelite creation, because of the absence of a near comparison.

[51] A. Alt, "Verbreitung und Herkunft des syrischen Tempeltypus," *PJB*, 35 (1939), 83-99; repr. in *Kleine Schriften*, II (1953), 100-115.

[52] Kuschke, *ibid.* (note 17).

THE LATE BRONZE "PALESTINIAN" BICHROME WARE IN ITS CYPRIOTE CONTEXT

Michal Artzy

LBL Univ. of California, Berkeley, California

Recent work on the Late Bronze Palestinian Bichrome Ware, using neutron activation analysis, has shown that most of the Tell el-'Ajjul Bichrome Ware, as well as the Milia Tomb collection assemblage, was not made in Tell el-'Ajjul, or Megiddo, or, for that matter, in Syria. It became clear that the Bichrome Ware was produced in some quantity on Cyprus, specificly the eastern coast of the island.[1]

It seems highly likely that the Ware was already manufactured in Cyprus during the end of the Middle Cypriote Period and reached the Mainland, in sites such as Tell el-'Ajjul, Lachish (Tell ed-Duweir) and Bethel, in the Stratum preceding the Egyptian destruction which marked the end of the Middle Bronze. It continued to be found in Stratum IX of Megiddo and reappeared in time in most of the rebuilt cities. For this reason, it became impossible to accept the theory that the indigenous Palestinian Painted pottery of the Late Bronze is the form predecessor of the Bichrome Ware. The appearance of the Bichrome Ware in both the Mainland and Cyprus preceded that of the Palestinian Painted Ware.

The decoration of the Bichrome Ware included, at times, animal motifs, which were thought by some modern archaeologists to be of Hurrian influence.[2] Arguments which put forth the Hurrian origin recognize the Cypriote influence on the Bichrome Ware, but prefer to ignore the implications of that influence, since the transmission of the Cypriote forms would not have corresponded to the Hurrians' movement and the rise of Mitanni. The reliance of the scholars on the Hurrian migration southward and on the political upheavals caused by the Hyksos' defeat disregards the stratigraphical data of the appearance and reapperance of the Bichrome Ware, which seemed to have been produced regardless of the political situation in the Near East. This suggests the hypothesis that the Bichrome Ware was not produced on the continent but somewhere else. Palestine, itself, had hardly any tradition of expertly painted pottery during its Bronze periods. Cyprus, on the other hand, had a long standing tradition of painted pottery which extended back to the Neolithic Period.[3] Cypriote painted ware of the Middle Bronze Period can easily be shown to be the predecessor of both the form and decoration of the Bichrome Ware assemblage.

The trickle of Middle Cypriote exports to the Levant during the first parts of the Middle Bronze evolved into a developed commerce during the second part of the Middle Bronze Period. There were many factors

[1] The author's forthcoming article "The Origin of the Palestinian Bichrome Ware" in *The Journal of the American Oriental Society.*

[2] Claire Epstein, *Palestinian Bichrome Ware,* (Leiden: E.J. Brill) 1966, 187. See also K.M. Kenyon, *Archaeology in the Holy Land* (1960), 200.

[3] Paul Åström, *The Middle Cypriote Bronze Age* (1957), 206.

which may have contributed to the commercial growth and the dominance of the Eastern coast of Cyprus during the end of the Middle Cypriote Period. Turmoils within Palestine during the Egyptian Second Intermediate Period could have forced some inhabitants from the Levant to leave and settle in Eastern Cyprus, thus promoting the trade between the two areas. Cyprus itself may have suffered from internal conflicts, thus necessitating the new fortified towns which sprang up on the eastern coast at about that time.[4] Still another factor might have been the lull in activity in the Minoan world, which would have caused the eastern ports of Cyprus to grow and sustain a strong trade relationship with the Western ports of the Mediterranean.

The appearance of the Bichrome Ware in Palestine followed that of the White Painted Cypriote Ware. Although most of the White Painted Ware was handmade, there are wheelmade samples which were unearthed not only in Cyprus but also in Palestine. The White Painted Ware in cyprus is a good example of the changes between the early and later parts of the Middle Cypriote Period. While there is no example of the White Painted II Ware or the White Painted III Ware, which are northern in origin, outside of Cyprus, there are quite a few examples of White Painted V Ware, which is eastern in origin, in sites outside of Cyprus. One example is to be found in Megiddo Tomb 3065, Stratum X.[5]

White Painted I Ware, White Painted II Ware and White Painted III Ware were all found in the northern part of Cyprus. White Painted I was found in Philia, which is situated about 15 kilometers inland from the western coast, 12 from the northern coast. White Painted II and White Painted III were found mainly in Lapithos region on the northern shore. Their origin of form and decoration are still in dispute. Although it has some possible northern influence, it seems highly improbable that it was imported to Cyprus. The three Wares have a slip and are painted. Stewart believes that the affiliation between White Painted I Ware and the Chalcolithic Red on White pottery at Erimi and Ambeliko can not be overlooked.[6] The decoration on the White Painted II Ware, which opens the Middle Cypriote Period, was usually placed on the upper half of the body and the neck, a practice which was often found in the later forms as well as in the Bichrome Ware. The pigmentation of White Painted III paint ranged from redbrown to black.

The shapes of the White Painted II Wares are varied. I shall try to present them briefly. Special emphasis will be put on the forms which I believe pertain to this study. We already find the bowls, both the shallow, hemispherical ones and the deep bowls: they appear with a knob handle or with a horizontal one (Fig. 1A). We find beaked jugs with globular bodies (Fig. 2A). The amphorae have oval bodies, squattish necks, flat or rounded bases, and two handles starting below the rim and continuing to the shoulder (Figs. 3A, 3B). The askos which we don't find again until the Late Bronze has a basket handel and a spout, and a flat base (Fig. 4A). The White Painted III followed the steps of the previous White Painted II. There was, however, a new form which is reminiscent of the jug or tankard, as it is called, which became very common in the later stages of the White Painted Ware and the Bichrome Ware (Fig. 5A). It has a globular body, a flat base, slightly carinated rim and shoulder and an almost cylindrical neck; the handle is raised slightly higher than the rim. There may have been a close relationship in forms between the tankards of stage III (Fig. 5A) and the amphorae of stage II (Figs. 3A, 3B).

The next two stages of the White Painted Ware were excavated on Mainland sites. White Painted IV shreds were found both in Megiddo, Strata XII and XI, and at Tell Beit Mirsim, Stratum G. At that juncture we see for the first time the wishbone handles, which are said to have been previously found in Cretan neolithic context.[7] Of the various stages of the White Painted Ware, White Painted V is the most important to our study. It was probably contemporary with the end of the Middle Cypriote Period and the beginning of the Late Cypriote

---

4 H.W. Catling, "Cyprus in the Neolithic and Bronze Age Periods," *CAH*, Rev. ed. I and II, 44-45, fasc. 43.

5 J. Shipton, *Notes on the Megiddo Pottery of Strata VI-XX*, 20; Megiddo II, 170, Plate 41139.

6 J.R. Stewart, "The Early Cypriote Bronze Age," *Swedish Cyprus Expedition*, IV, Part 1a (1962), 254-256.

7 Paul Åström, *op. cit.*, 216.

Period. The White Painted V geographic dispersion is impressive, for not only do we find it in Cyprus, but at Ras Shamra, in several tombs at Megiddo, where handmade and wheelmade specimens were found in Tombs 5050 and 5243 of the XI Stratum and Tombs 3046 and 3065, Stratum X, and at Tell el-'Ajjul, where two White Painted V bowls were found. It is usually handmade, although wheelmade specimens do exist; they are said to have been made exclusively in Palestine for the Cypriote market, which with our present knowledge is most unlikely. The tradition of the previous stages continues, although the corpus is augmented by several new forms. The production of both the shallow and the deep bowls is uninterrupted, as is that of the jugs. The tankards become more common during this phase and their necks when compared with previous ones, are wider. The two new shapes are the jars and storage jars. The jars are squat and have an everted rim with or without a widening neck. Below the rim they have a hole on either side which was probably used for suspension. They should probably be considered as descendants of the squat amphorae. The storage jars appear with two vertical handles below the rim. There is yet another delightful form which appears in the White Painted tradition – the zoomorphic vessel (Fig. 6A). The earliest example of a zoomorphic White Painted Ware is from the third phase of the tradition. Although ornithomorphics and tripeds appeared in the third and fourth stage, the quadrupedic zoomorphic vessels become the potters' favorite zoomorphic form.

Decorational motifs of the White Painted corpora are also of a special importance to this study. The Ware is usually covered with white, off-white, or orange slips. The paint is brown or reddish brown; during the end of the fourth phase and the fifth stage, it is black and brown. There is a certain tendency to decorate the vessels profusely on their upper parts in metope decorations as well as geometric motifs and both vertical and horizontal bands. There are also instances where animal motifs were used in the decoration; one of them is from Tomb 6 at Ayios Iakovos, depicting three horned quadropeds placed above one another in a diminishing size.[8] There is also a lovely jar of the White Painted IV tradition which depicts two winged birds on one side and on the other side two lady-bug-like creatures engaged in a kissing-like position.[9] Another yet is a bird and a quadruped painted on a wheel-made White Painted jar from Ayia Paraskevi.[10]

In juxtaposing the Bichrome Ware with the White Painted Ware, I would like to show the similarities between the two. The bowls of the Bichrome Ware tradition tend to be of the shallow hemispherical type (Fig. 1B). They are decorated in black and red (Hue 5R 2/1 and Hue 7.5R 3/8 in the Munsell Soil Color Chart) with mostly geometric patterns; the metope idea is common and both horizontal and vertical lines are used. They are, no doubt, Cypriote in tradition, for similar types of bowls in the corpus of the Middle Bronze in Palestine can not be found. We can, however, trace the shallow bowls back to the Early Cypriote White Painted corpus. It is quite probable that the Cypriote milk bowl of the White Slip I tradition, with its wishbone handle, is of the same common background as that of the Bichrome Ware bowl.

The Bichrome Ware jugs are globular; they have a flat base, narrow neck and often a beaked mouth (Fig. 2). The beaked mouth is not a popular Palestinian form, at least not during the Middle Bronze; it is, however, a commonly used shape in the Cypriote White Painted Ware corpus. In the Cypriote tradition the beak slowly becomes shorter and levels with the handle and the rim. The decorational motifs of the jugs are often in cross line, which had already become popular in Cyprus in the White Painted V Ware. Among the jugs of the Bichrome Ware there are some which have handles from the base of the neck to the lower part of the shoulder. We already met this particular type among the vessels of the White Painted III Ware. The Palestinian Late Bronze vessel of the similar shape should be considered an imitation of the Bichrome Ware, and its predecessors, therefore, are much the same as those of the White Painted Ware.

---

[8] Paul Åström, *ibid.*, 210.

[9] Vassos Karageoghis, "Chronique des fouilles et découvertes Archeologiques à Chypre en 1967," *Bulletin de Correspondence Hellénique* (1968), 294.

[10] J.M. Cook, "Archaeology in Greece, 1948-1949," *Journal of Hellenic Studies* (1950), 14, Fig. 10.

The tankard which first appears in the fourth phase of the White Painted Ware has a ring base, although at times the base is so thick that it approaches the form of a flat base (Fig. 5). The handle is extended from the rim to the shoulder; it has a cylindrical neck and a flare-out rim. The decoration is usually executed from the neck, or from the junction of the neck down to the middle of the body. The Late Bronze Palestinian Painted tankard should be looked at as an imitation or a variation of the Bichrome Ware family; it is just as in the case of the jugs, a descendant of the White Painted V Ware tradition in Cyprus.

The next few shapes which I would like to discuss are the askos, the amphora, the storage jar (pithos), and the zoomorphic vessel. The askos was losing its popularity during the Middle of the White Painted tradition (Fig. 4). It seems to have survived only partially into the Late Cypriote Period, and the Bichrome Ware askos from Megiddo Level IX is a bit of a relic for its time.

The storage jar of the Bichrome Ware family is extremely similar in its shape to the jar of the White Painted Ware tradition (Fig. 7). It has a rounded base, flowing rims, and vertical handles below the shoulder. While in Palestine the storage jars were common in both habitats and tombs, in Cyprus they were scarce. This fact further suggests the Cypriote provenance of the Bichrome Ware.

The amphorae of the Cypriote Middle Bronze did not survive to the period of the Bichrome Ware *en masse* (Fig. 3). There are, however, two Bichrome pieces of the squat, short-necked amphorae. One is from Tell el-'Ajjul, OM 968; the other from Milia, Tomb 10. It has a squat body, flaring rim, and a hole below the rim for suspension. It is very similar to the amphorae of the Cypriote White Painted V tradition.

The similarity between the Bichrome Ware zoomorphic quadruped from Akhera, Cyprus, which was published by Vassos Karageorghis[11], and the White Painted V Ware quadruped is a continuation of the White Painted Cypriote zoomorphic tradition.

Not all the forms which make up the Bichrome Ware family closely follow the White Painted Ware tradition. Vessels of the krater type have hardly any predecessors during the main part of the White Painted Ware's existence; the krater, however, was a popular form in Palestine. This is not to say that kraters did not exist in Cyprus; among several kraters in Milia Tomb 10, we find not only handmade kraters, but one wheel-made Cypriote White Painted Ware krater.

In juxtaposing the "Palestinian" Late Bronze Tell el-'Ajjul Bichrome Ware and the Cypriote White Painted Ware of the Middle and Late Bronze, it becomes clear that the Bichrome Ware is not Palstinian in its heritage, but Cypriote. The Bichrome Ware was not only the culmination of the White Painted Ware tradition, but was produced by wheel in Cyprus for export to mainland ports. Cyprus at the end of the Middle Bronze and the beginning of the Late Bronze was a major distributor of ceramics. Such pottery as the Basering Ware, the aesthetically pleasing White Slip Ware and the "Palestinian" Bichrome Ware was shipped from Cyprus to Anatolia, as well as Syria, Palestine and Egypt.

---

[11] Vassos Karageorghis, *Bulletin de Correspondence Hellénique* (1961), Fig. 61.

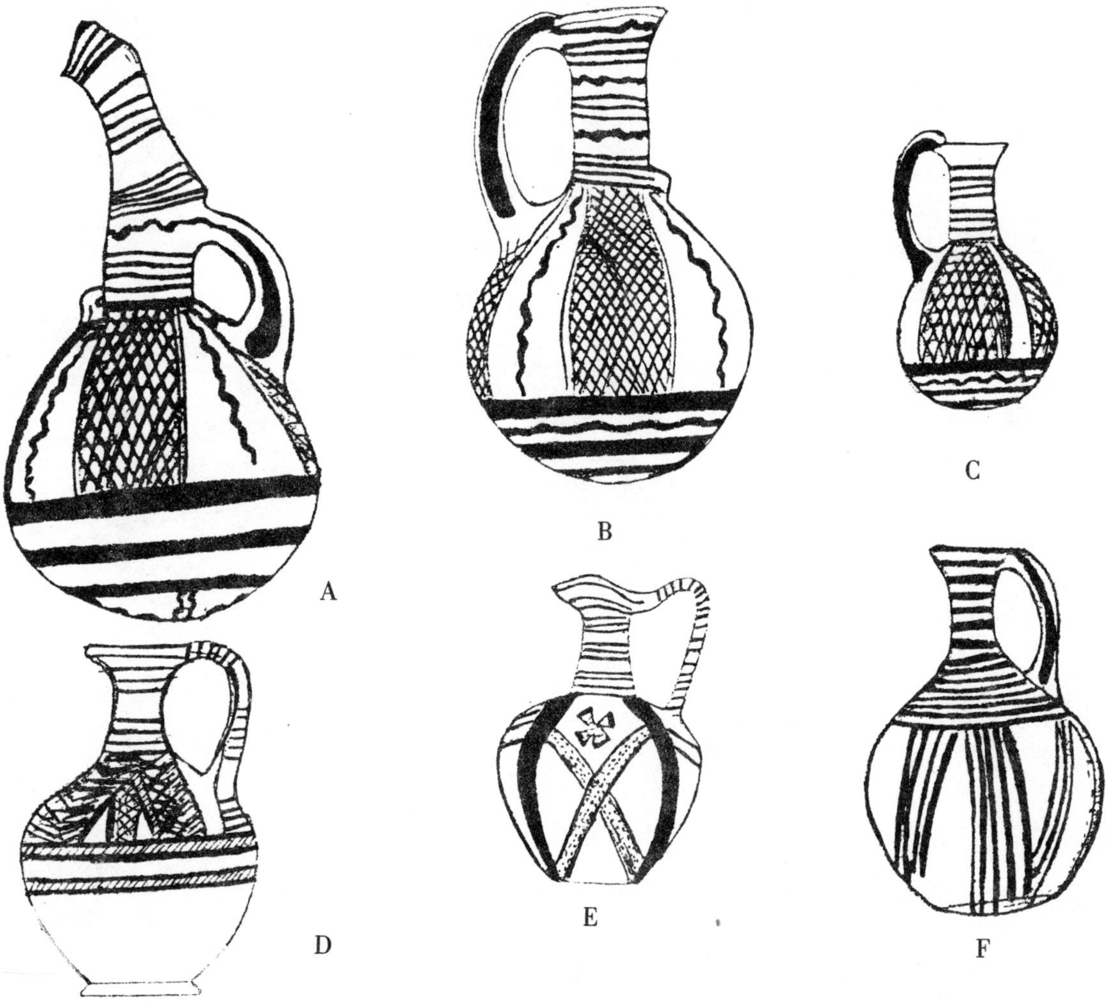

FIGURE 2. Jugs. A-C. White Painted II-V. D-F. Bichrome.

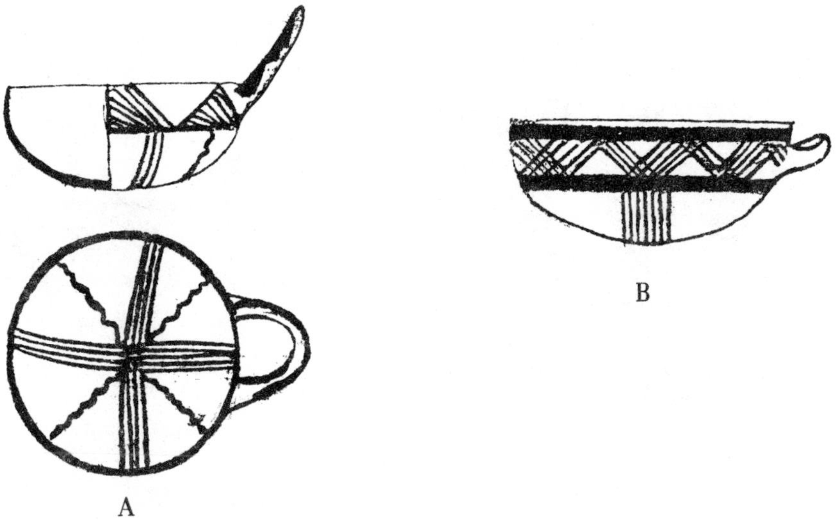

FIGURE 1. Bowls: A. White Painted II. B. Bichrome.

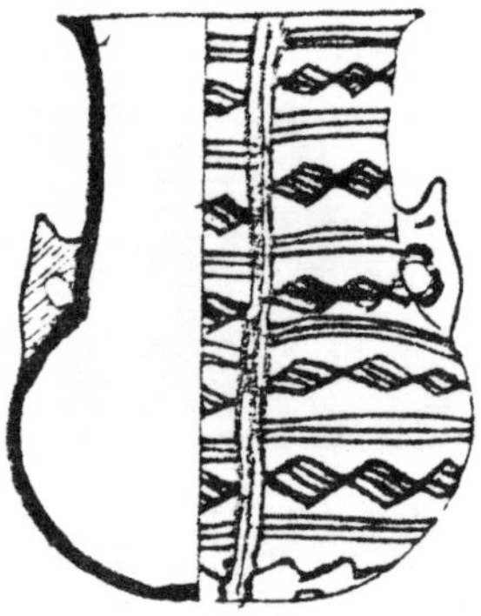

A

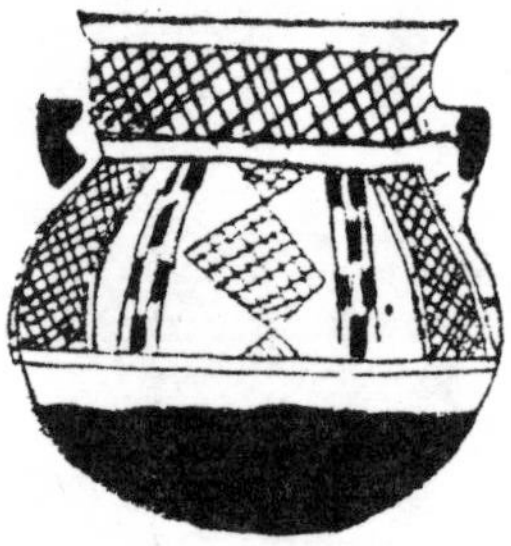

B

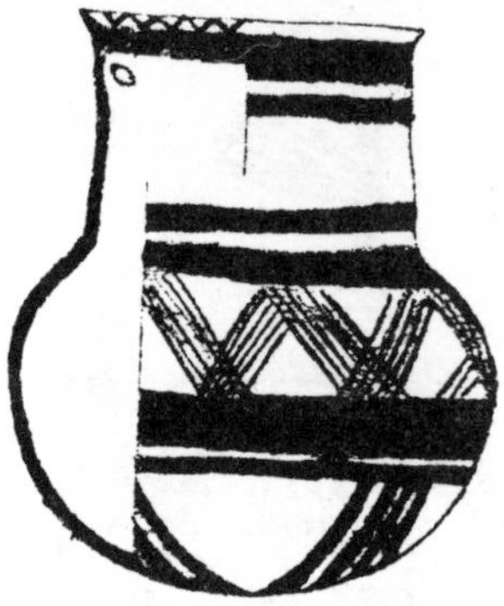

C

D

E

FIGURE 3. Amphorae and jars: A-D. White Painted II and V. E. Bichrome.

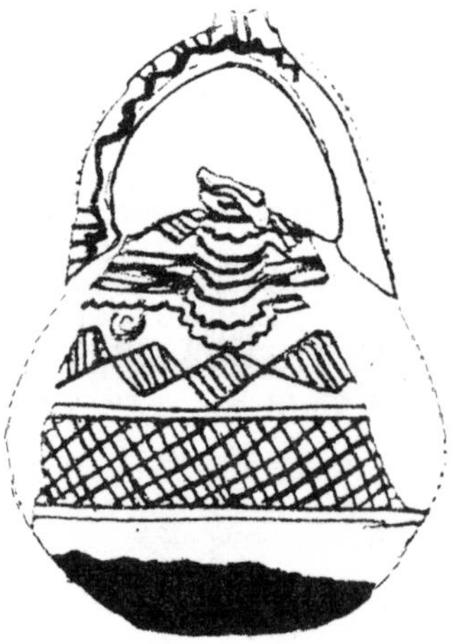

A

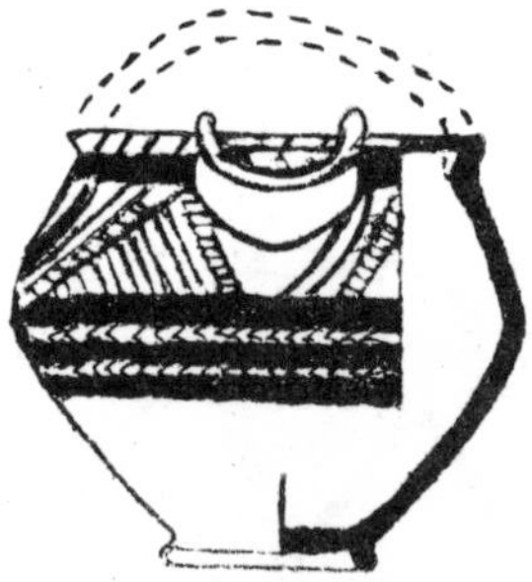

B

FIGURE 4. Askos: A. White Painted II. B. Bichrome.

A B

FIGURE 5. Tankards: A. White Painted III. B. Bichrome.

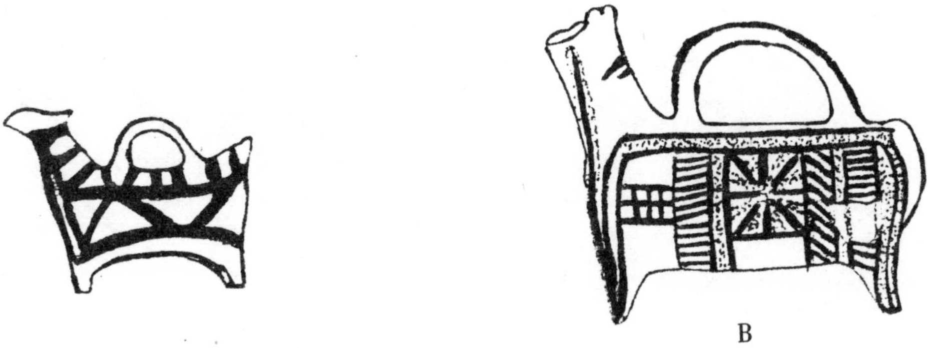

B A

FIGURE 6. Zoomorphic vessels: A. White Painted V. B. Bichrome.

FIGURE 7. Storage jars: A. White Painted V. B. Bichrome.

UGARIT AND THE AEGEAN

A Brief Summary of Archaeological and Epigraphic Evidence

Michael C. Astour

Southern Illinois University, Edwardsville, Illinois, U.S.A.

In speaking about the relations between Ugarit and the Aegean basin, one cannot ignore the Syro-Mesopotamian hinterland, for which Ugarit served as the principal outlet to the Mediterranean Sea during the Middle and Late Bronze Age. Nor was Ugarit culturally isolated from the rest of the geographical complex dominated by what is often called "cuneiform civilization." Besides, written evidence on Ugarit in the Middle Bronze Age – limited but significant – comes from other sites. Ugarit forms the focal, but not the sole, point of the discussion of the reciprocal connections between the Near East and the Minoan-Mycenaean world. This brief and necessarily selective survey deliberately leaves aside the problem of Near Eastern elements in Greek civilization that may have been inherited from the Bronze Age but are only known from their survivals in the religion, mythology, and onomastica of the archaic and classical times.[1] It is limited to such written and material evidence that comes directly from the period under consideration, i.e., in round figures, from 1800 to 1200 B.C.[2]

The earliest oversea links of Minoan Crete were with Libya and Egypt, soon followed by Cyprus during the EM III period.[3] Cyprus was a source of copper, and it became an intermediary in the first contacts between Crete and the cities of the Syrian coast.[4] Bronze daggers were imported from Syria and copied in Crete. Minoan metallurgy of EM III – MM Ia was influenced by Syrian techniques and styles.[5] These influences emanated primarily from Byblos – probably the first Syrian port city to build strong, seaworthy ships, highly renowned in Egypt under the Old and Middle Kingdom.[6] Beside maintaining a steady maritime trade with Egypt, the Byblians were also active in commerce on land: one finds their representatives in Sumer of the Ur III Dy-

---

1 This problem, which in its different aspects has been given considerable attention during the last hundred years, has been recently investigated by Cyrus H. Gordon, notably in *Before the Bible* (1962), and in this author's *Hellenosemitica* (1965, second corrected print 1967).

2 This paper follows the system of "low chronology," i.e., proceeds from W.F. Albright's date for the reign of Hammurapi, 1728-1692. All dates are B.C. [All other articles in this volume employ the "middle chronology" – Ed.]

3 The existence of Early Minoan was denied by Doro Levi, who considered Middle Minoan I as the start of the Bronze Age in Crete, but vigorously defended by K. Branigan; see the latter's *The Foundations of Palatial Crete* (1970), 16-35. It is of secondary importance for the subject of the present paper.

4 K. Branigan, *Foundations,* 182, 187.

5 K. Branigan, *AJA* 70 (1966), 123-26; *AJA* 71 (1967), 117-21.

6 See, e.g., W. Helck, *Beziehungen* (1962), 21-2.

nasty (c. 2000),[7] and some 300 years later, at the court of Mari on the Middle Euphrates.[8] There are reasons to believe that, in late MM I – MM II, a direct contact was established between Byblos and Crete.[9] At that time, however, Byblos had to share its role in Cretan trade with a more northerly coastal city, Ugarit, which soon surpassed its predecessor as a knot of maritime and overland routes.

Ugarit, whose beginnings as a settlement go back to the Neolithic Age, occupied a site (now Ras Shamra) within less than a kilometer from the small bay of Minet el-Beida which still provides good shelter from strong southwestern winds and serves as a refuge for ships when the harbor of Latakia is unsafe to use.[10] A maritime suburb, called Ma'ḫadu in the Ras Shamra texts,[11] existed at the southern shore of the bay. No remains older than the fifteenth century have been found during excavations there,[12] but only one out of the six or seven hectares of the port town's area has been examined so far.[13] It is very unlikely that Ugarit, located so close to the sea, could ever do without a port of its own.[14] Minet el-Beida lies at 105 km from the northeastern tip of Cyprus, which is the shortest distance between the island and the Syrian coast. Ugarit was also the terminal of the highway leading to the Mediterranean Sea from the Euphrates via Halab (Aleppo), at that time a major political center and an intersection of international trade roads. These are the same factors which, in the Hellenistic era and in the contemporary Syrian Republic, brought about the rise of Laodicea (Latakia), 11 km south of Ras Shamra.[15] Halab had another outlet to the sea – the estuary of the Orontes;[16] but if a harbor existed there during the Middle and Late Bronze Age, it was of minor importance.

Ugarit's relative proximity to Cyprus was significant in more than one way. Alashiya, as Cyprus was then called,[17] became in the second half of the eighteenth century the principal source of copper for the countries of the Near East. Earlier, in the period of Old Assyrian trade establishments in Cappadocia, much of the copper supply of Syria and Mesopotamia came from Anatolian mines.[18] But the Assyrian colonies came to a violent end c. 1765,[19] and though communications with Cappadocia were precariously revived at the time of Shamshi-Adad I (c. 1740), this mineral-rich region remained for over a century aloof from the rest of Western Asia. It was at that time that Cyprus entered the Near Eastern copper market. Alashian copper and bronze are mentioned several times in tablets from the archives of Mari,[20] probably from the reign of Zimri-Lim (r.c. 1725-1693). At that time Mari maintained very close relations with Syria in general and Ugarit in particular, includ-

---

7 E. Sollberger, *AfO* 19 (1960), 120-22.

8 G. Dossin, *Syria* 20 (1939), 109, 111.

9 K. Branigan, *AJA* 71 (1967), 119.

10 *B. R. 513: Geographical Handbook Series: Syria* (1944), 58.

11 M. Astour, *JESHO* 13 (1970), 113-27.

12 C.-F.-A. Schaeffer, *Syria* 16 (1935), 168.

13 *Ugaritica I* (1939), 52. The results of more recent excavations at Minet el-Beida have not been published so far.

14 In the LB period, Ugarit possessed several other coastal settlements, at least two of which – Qal'at er-Rūs and Tell Sūkās – existed during the MB period; but the nearest of the two, Qal'at er-Rūs, lays at a distance of 24 km from Ras Shamra as the crow flies.

15 R. Dussaud, *Les découvertes de Ras Shamra (Ugarit) et l'Ancien Testament* (1937), 17; E. Wirth, *Syrien* (1971), 290-91.

16 It was active in trade with Greece from c. 750 to 300: L. Woolley, *A Forgotten Kingdom* (1953), 172, 180; served as the harbor of Antioch during the Crusades: Cl. Cahen, *La Syrie du Nord à l'époque des croisades et la principauté franque d'Antioche* (1940), 133; and still admits light vessels.

17 We assume the identity of Alashiya with Cyprus as definitely established; for the latest survey of evidence see Y.L. Holmes, *JAOS* 91 (1971), 426-9.

18 See P. Garelli, *Les Assyriens en Cappadoce* (1963), 294-8, on copper purchases by Assyrians; add the interesting letter No. 32 in B. Kienast, *Die altassyrischen Texte* etc. (1960), on merchants from Ebla (in Northern Syria) who buy up from a local prince all the available copper, paying for it in Amurru-silver above the market price. On the location of Ebla, cf. M. Astour, *UF*, 3 (1971).

19 P. Garelli, *op. cit.*, 73: c. 1830-1820 (middle chronology); id., *Le Proche-Orient asiatique* (1969), 121: c. 1830.

20 G. Dossin, *Syria* 20 (1939), 111.

ing Zimri-Lim's personal visit to Ugarit.[21] It seems that Ugarit was the principal transshipment point of Cypriote copper to the inner parts of Western Asia. Thus must have considerably enhanced Ugarit's prosperity. Cyprus, a geographical and cultural link between Syria and the Aegean, served as a meeting place between Ugaritians and Minoans, and it was also the first stage on the maritime route to the Aegean along the southern coast of Asia Minor,[22] thence to Rhodes, Carpathos, Crete, Cythera, and the Peloponnese.

Ugarit was the first city in Syria to import genuine Minoan pottery.[23] Fragments of vessels in the Kamares style of the MM IIa period were found at Ugarit in burials datable to the time of the 13th Dynasty of Egypt; one characteristic sherd of that style was associated with local pottery of the Hyksos period.[24] According to the system of low chronology, the closing decades of the 13th Dynasty's control of Lower Egypt and the beginning of the Hyksos domination coincide with the period covered by the Mari archives.[25] It is hardly a coincidence that Mari tablets from the reign of Zimri-Lim contain four references to artifacts from Kaptara.[26] These are the earliest dated occurrences of that geographical name (corresponding to Biblical Caphtor) which was, beyond any reasonable doubt, the Near Eastern appellation of Crete.[27] It is true that the geographical treatise *KAV* 92[28] cites (line 42) "A.NA.KÙ^{KI} (and) *Kap-ta-ra*^{KI}, countries beyond the Upper Sea" among the lands allegedly conquered by Sargon of Akkad who ruled some five hundred years before Zimri-Lim. The tablet is a Neo-Assyrian copy, but its geographical nomenclature unmistakably points to the Old Babylonian period as the time of composition of its original.[29] Sargon of Akkad himself, in his genuine inscriptions, never claimed to have crossed the Mediterranean Sea. This is a much later amplification of his, by then legendary, conquests.[30] Thus the inclusion of Kaptara into the geographical horizon of Mesopotamia coincides with the appearance of Minoan ceramics in Ugarit and of references to imports from Kaptara in the Mari tablets.[31]

---

21 Ch.-F. Jean, *RA* 36 (1939), 112. Ugarit appears five times in the Mari texts; we shall return to a recently published letter which mentions Ugarit.

22 Via Cape Anemurion in Cilicia (45 km from Cape Crommyon on the northern coast of Cyprus), or directly via Cape Chelidonia (now Gelidonya) in Lycia (200 km from Cape Acamas, the northwestern tip of Cyprus).

23 Vases of Minoan style were found in the tomb of Abishemu I, king of Byblos c. 1840-1800, but A. Evans, *The Palace of Minos*, II, pt. 2, 655, and Helene J. Kantor, *AJA* 51 (1947) 19-20, considered them local ware displaying Aegean inspiration. The earliest indubitable specimens of Minoan ceramics at Byblos are two cups of Kamares style: C.-F.-A. Schaeffer, *Stratigraphie comparée et chronologie de l'Asie Occidentale* (1948), 66; W. Stevenson Smith, *Interconnections in the Ancient Near East* (1965), Fig. 19-20.

24 C.-F.-A. Schaeffer, *Ugaritica I*, 54-56.

25 On synchronisms between Middle Minoan Crete, Middle Kingdom and Second Intermediary Period Egypt, and Old Babylonian Period Mesopotamia see C.-F.-A. Schaeffer, *Ugaritica I*, 56-60; W.F. Albright, *BASOR* No. 99 (1945), 9-18; P. Åström, *Krêtika chronika* 1961-1962, 137-50.

26 See n. 33 below.

27 Since the identity of Kaptara/Caphtor with Crete has been accepted by virtually all scholars in the Aegean and Near Eastern fields, there is no need to repeat the mutually corroborative proofs on which it is based.

28 Latest study: E. Weidner, *AfO* 16 (1952-53), 1-24, with further literature.

29 The mentions of the lands of Mari, Edamaruz, Mutiabal, Yamutbal, Turukki, Labnanu (Lebanon, which also makes its appearance in an Old Babylonian fragment of the Gilgamesh Epic), taken together, provide a characteristic picture.

30 This question will be considered separately at a different occasion.

31 As for A.NA.KÙ^{KI}, we agree with E. Weidner, *AfO* 16 (1952-53), 22, that its spelling excludes the reading *anaku*, for *annaku* "tin," and that "the possibility of reading it differently (if the text is in order at all!) can by no means be ruled out." KÙ is an ideogram for *kaspu* "silver" (especially in Old Akkadian and Old Assyrian texts); the first two signs would, in all likelihood, also be ideographic. It is impossible to tell what actual country is hidden under this appellation. Geographically, one would expect to have Cyprus listed along with Kaptara-Crete, but Cyprus had no silver mines. The silver lodes of Laurium in Attica were not exploited even in the Mycenaean Age.

Two of these imports were presented by Zimri-Lim to other Mesopotamian kings: a *katappum kaptarû*[32] to Šarriya of Razamâ, and an object, perhaps a vase, defined as *kaptarītum*, to Hammurapi, probably the famous king of Babylon. The texts also mention a large jar, ^{DUG}GAL *kaptarītum*, and a weapon, *kakkum kaptarû*, with its top and base (covered) with gold, and the top inlaid with lapis lazuli.[33] We see that the beautiful Middle Minoan artifacts were highly valued in Mesopotamia. A suggestion was made that spiral motifs on frescoes of King Zimri-Lim's palace were inspired by decorations on Cretan vases.[34] However, the traffic in expensive goods went both ways. Lapis lazuli which ornamented the Caphtorian weapon at Mari had to be brought to Crete from its place of extraction in Afghanistan, i.e. through the intermediary of Mesopotamia and Syria. Old Babylonian cylinder seals have been found in five different localities of Crete;[35] some or all of them are stylistically attributable to the time of Hammurapi.[36] They were appreciated in Crete as specimens of glyptic art. Many Old Babylonian cylinder seals from the time of Hammurapi were also found at Ras Shamra;[37] this helps to trace down the route by which such artifacts reached Crete.

An Akkadian cuneiform inscription on a stone tablet (which appears to have been the upper part of a stone box) was discovered on the island of Cythera as early as 1849, published in 1853, and subsequently lost. Only the left parts of its five lines are extant. The right parts must have been carved on the lower half of the box which was never recovered.[38] According to the restoration by E. Weidner, the box was dedicated "for his life" to a divinity (whose name is illegible) by Naram-Sin, son of Ipiq-Adad, king of Eshnunna,[39] who ruled till c. 1760, i.e., a generation before the time of Hammurapi or Zimri-Lim. Cythera, a strategically important island between Crete and the Peloponnese, was colonized by Cretans in MM I period;[40] it may thus be considered part of the Minoan domain. There is no compelling reason to assume that Naram-Sin himself dedicated the ex-voto to a deity of Cythera, or even that it was brought there during his reign. As noted by Weidner, it "may well have reached Kythera as a souvenir or as a piece of booty." Eshnunna was destroyed in 1689 by Hammurapi (who at that time was still an ally of Zimri-Lim), and was raided, a few years earlier, by Sheplarpak, king of Elam, who was then congratulated by Zimri-Lim.[41] Any of the two rulers could have sent the inscribed box (with the cylinder seals it apparently contained)[42] as a diplomatic gift to Mari. As we shall see, Eshnunna and Mari were two important stages on the road by which tin from eastern Iran came to Ugarit and thence to Crete.

Already in 1939, the presence of numerous Minoan vessels at Ras Shamra induced its excavator, C.-F.-A. Schaeffer, to assume that Ugarit was one of the principal links of Cretan commerce in Asia.[43] G. Dos-

[32] G. Dossin (n. 33) translated *katappum* "pincers," but *AHw*, 465, sees in it "an implement of wood or metal," without specification. Cf. *CAD* K, 303: "(a container, usually of metal)".

[33] These occurrences are so far known from the summary in G. Dossin, *Syria* 20 (1939), 111-112.

[34] H.J. Kantor, *AJA* 51 (1947), 30-31; W.S. Smith, *Interconnections*, 18.

[35] K. Branigan, *Foundations*, 178.

[36] A. Evans, *Palace of Minos*, I (1921) 197-99; II, 156. The cylinder seal from the burial at Platanos was associated with pottery of the "mature MM Ia class," but it must be taken into account that the MM IIa style was limited only to Cnossus and Phaestus, while elsewhere in Crete MM I ceramics were produced till the start of the MM III period: J.D.S. Pendlebury, *The Archaeology of Crete* (1939), 94 n. 2, 126; F.H. Stubbings, *CAH*³, I (1970) 241, 243.

[37] C.F.A. Schaeffer, *Ugaritica I*, 17.

[38] After partially successful attempts by H. Winckler and E. Unger to decipher the inscription from the very imperfect copy, its time and provenience were correctly determined by E. Weidner, *JHS* 59 (1939), 137-138, on the basis of American excavations in the Diyala Valley, the ancient territory of the Kingdom of Eshnunna.

[39] And, in all likelihood, of Assyria as well. Eshnunna lay east of the Tigris, north of Babylonia proper, southeast of Assyria. It played a major role in the political configuration of Mesopotamia in the eighteenth century.

[40] G.L. Huxley and J.N. Coldstream, *Illustrated London News*, August 27, 1966, 28-29 (excavations at Kastri).

[41] Text published by G. Dossin in *RA* 64 (1970), 97 n. 3 (cf. n. 44 below).

[42] So interpreted by E. Weidner (n. 38 above) on the basis of the description of the stone which had five semicircular grooves on its uninscribed side.

[43] *Ugaritica I*, 22.

sin has recently published a remarkable tablet from Mari belonging to the reign of Zimri-Lim.[44] It lists quantities of tin distributed by the treasury of Mari[45] to its agents in several cities of Syria (including Ugarit, line 8), often for further delivery to Syrian and Palestinian rulers. An entry, which mentions Ugarit for the second time, reads as follows: (28) [*x* M]A.NA AN.NA *a-na Kap-ta-ra-i-im* (29) *1* [+ *x*? MA.N]A AN.NA *a-na* LÚ*ta-ar-ga-ma-an-nim* (30) [*x* MA.NA AN.NA *a-na*] *Zu-ka-ra-i-*[*i*]*m*[46] (31) [*i-na Ú-g*]*a-*[*r*]*i-tim*KI. Thus Ugarit was the place where tin from Mari was delivered to a Caphtorian. On the basis of previously published texts, J. Bottero concluded that "there existed at Mari a truly organized tin commerce, and, remarkably enough, mainly with the West."[47] A Mari letter, published by Dossin,[48] shows that tin arrived to Mari by caravans from Eshnunna.[49] This helps to perceive how an ex-voto from Eshnunna turned up in Cythera, a colony of Minoan Crete.

Another significant detail is the mention, directly after the "Caphtorian," of an "interpreter," to whom over a pound of tin was issued as fee for his services. Since Akkadian was used as the written language in all of Northern Syria, and Mariotes of Amorite extraction spoke practically the same language as the Ugaritians, no interpreter was needed between them. It is evident that the interpreter in question was conversant in the Cretan language of his time, whatever it was, and helped in the transactions between the Mariote seller and the Caphtorian purchaser of tin. The very presence of such an interpreter at Ugarit testifies to the frequency of business contacts with Cretans in that port city. Once the linguistic barrier between Minoan Crete and Semitic Near East was pierced, the exchange of material goods could be accompanied by interpenetration of cultural values.[50]

Western Asia was deeply impressed by the high artistic quality of Cretan vases and bronzes. Ugarit began producing imitations of MM ceramics.[51] There is no need to suppose that this kind of pottery was manufactured by Minoans established as settlers at Ugarit;[52] Ugaritians were quick learners. It was at that time, one may guess, that Kushar-wa-Khasis, the divine architect and artificer of Ugaritic mythology, was given Caphtor as one of his residences, along with Memphis.[53] Both names of the Ugaritic god are purely Semitic;[54] he was not a Cretan deity adopted by Ugaritians and Phoenicians but a West Semitic deity which came to be associated with a remote overseas country because of its artistic renown.[55] Such a high esteem of Crete was due to direct acquaintance with the island rather than to mere admiration of imports. Theres is no reason to believe that only Minoans sailed to Syria, but no Syrians dared to sail to Crete. The Akkadian name for a variety of willow or

---

44 *RA* 64 (1970), 97-106. Beside the tablet in question (A. 1270), the article also includes the fragmentary text mentioned above (n. 41) and the letter A. 16 (n. 48 below).

45 Part of the tin had been received in commission from Hammurapi, king of Babylon, and Sheplarpak, king of Elam (Anshan).

46 Dossin read [*a-na*] *Ka-ra-i-*[*i*]*m* and tentatively interpreted it as "Carian" – another native of an Aegean country. However, *zu* before *ka* is very clear in his own copy. Cf. J.M. Sasson, *RA* 65 (1971), 172.

47 *ARMT* 7, 338.

48 A. 16, *op. cit.* (n. 48 above), 103-06.

49 Its ultimate source, as convincingly shown by Dossin, was the tin-mining district of Drangiana (present-day Sīstān at the border of Iran and Afghanistan), whence it was carried to Eshnunna via the Elamite capital of Susa.

50 "Commercial relations must not be underestimated: most influences from one country to another take place through them," W. Helck, *Beziehungen*, 1.

51 C.F.A. Schaeffer, *Ugaritica I*, 60-67.

52 As believed by C.F.A. Schaeffer, *op.cit.*, 67-69.

53 The Memphite chief god Ptah was identified with Chousoros (Kushar) in the late Phoenician theogony of Philo of Byblos; the Ugaritians had this syncretistic conception some fifteen hundred years earlier. Cf. Th.H. Gaster, *Thespis*[2] (1961), 164.

54 They can be translated "Useful-and-Understanding"; Th.H. Gaster, *op. cit.*, 161, renders them "Adroit-and-Cunning."

55 Thus Th.H. Gaster, *op. cit.*, 163-4; C.H. Gordon, *Ugarit and Minoan Crete* (1966), 23. The extant texts of the Ugaritic mythological poems were written down in mid-fourteenth century or later, but the myths themselves are considerably older and may go back, along with the royal dynasty of Ugarit, to the Old Babylonian period. In the fourteenth century, Crete was no longer what it used to be in the MM period.

poplar was *kaptaru,*[56] and since this kind of timber would not have been imported from as far as Crete,[57] somebody from the cuneiform cultural area must have seen it growing in Caphtor itself.

The next period, MM III, reveals strong Western Asian influences in Crete. Its beginning can be safely dated at c. 1640: an alabaster lid with the name of the Hyksos Pharaoh Khian was found at Cnossus in the stratigraphic context of MM IIIa wares, which cannot thus be much earlier than Khian's reign.[58] This helps to establish priorities. The first figured frescoes at Cnossus ("miniature frescoes") appear during the MM IIIb Phase, which began c. 1600.[59] They are made in a technique resembling that used in the frescoes of the palace of Zimri-Lim at Mari, over a hundred years earlier.[60] Sir Leonard Woolley found in the palace of Level VII of Alalakh the same kind of miniature frescoes as those of the MM IIIb palace at Cnossus, and thought of Northern Syria as the intermediary in artistic transmission from Mari to Crete.[61] His chronology of Alalakh VII was much too high, but if we assume, as it seems probable, that the palace in question was built c. 1650,[62] it still precedes the start of MM IIIb by some fifty years. The recently excavated MB palace of Ugarit[63] turned out to be exactly similar to the palace of Alalakh VII in dimensions and layout.[64] It may have contained frescoes of the same style; already at the time of Zimri-Lim, the king of Ugarit wished to see the palace of Mari.[65] It is possible that the fresco technique came to Cnossus via Ugarit, a coastal city, rather than via Alalakh.

Horns of consecration on altars – a feature of Near Eastern cult going back to the Jamdat Nasr period (late 4th millennium) and familiar to us from the Bible – made their first indubitable appearance in a MM IIb deposit, and became normal from MM III on.[66] A special type of long sword, developed by the Semitic conquerors of Egypt during the Hyksos period, was immediately adopted by the Cretans of MM III.[67] Thus, though exports of Minoan pottery to Syria seem to have stopped after the end of MM II,[68] Crete's connection with the Near East was not interrupted. There are epigraphic indications that a number of Syrians migrated to Crete during the MM III and LM I periods and influenced the written language of the island.

[56] R.C. Thompson, *DAB* (1949), 292. *AHw*, 445 translates "Cretan juniper"; *CAD*, K (1971), 191, "a species of elm" (cf. *ibid.* 504 *s.v. kullaru* A), on the basis of its equation with g i š . m e s . t u and g i š . m e s . a š a l in lexical lists, and the interpretation of m e s as "elm" (Aram. *mayiš*, Arab. *mayis*). However, the element m e s appears in names of several different trees, and both *kaptaru* and *kullaru* are also equated with a š a l = *ṣarbătu* "willow" or "poplar," cf. *CAD*, Ṣ (1962), 108-9. [Note however that *Kaptaru*, as opposed to *Kaptarû*, is not translatable as "from Kaptaru." – Ed.]

[57] H.J. Kantor, *AJA* 51 (1947), 31, surmised that "luxurious products of Crete's first great palatial period may not have formed the main bulk of Cretan cargoes, which could have consisted of raw materials such as, for example, timber from the western part of the island." This is conceivable with regard to Egypt but not Syria which possessed its own extensive forests of highly valued evergreens.

[58] A. Evans, *Palace of Minos*, I, 419; J.D.S. Pendlebury, *Arch. of Crete*, 172; P. Åström (n. 25), 146-47.

[59] R.W. Hutchinson, *Prehistoric Crete* (1962) 178-80.

[60] *Ibid.*

[61] *A Forgotten Kingdom*, 73-4.

[62] Alalakh VII was destroyed by the Hittite king Hattushilish I early in his reign, perhaps c. 1570, and had been ruled by three generations of dynasts after it became the capital of a fief, i.e., during some 80 years.

[63] C.-F.-A. Schaeffer, *AfO* 23 (1970) 134-35; *id.*, *Syria* 47 (1970) 209-13.

[64] As I was kindly informed by J.-Cl. Courtois, member of the Mission de Ras Shamra.

[65] Letter published by G. Dossin in C.-.F.-A. Schaeffer, *Ugaritica I*, 16.

[66] J.D.S. Pendlebury, *Arch. of Crete*, 273-74; R.W. Hutchinson, *Prehistoric Crete*, 225-26. M.E.L. Mallowan, *Iraq* 9 (1947), 184, after describing the clay "Horns of Consecration" of c. 3000, found at Tell Brak (Pl. XXIX, No. 2), remarked: "The constant appearance of this ritual symbol in Cretan religion is further corroboration of the Western Asiatic origin of Cretan civilisation: the sacral horns, the double axe, the spiral, snake worship, the dove, the Mother Goddess, the bucranium and the tholos are in Crete component parts of a mosaic which ultimately derives from Northern Syria, Northern Mesopotamia and Iran." Whatever may be said of the other elements listed by Mallowan, the Near Eastern origin of the "horns of consecration" is certain.

[67] J.D.S. Pendlebury, *Arch. of Crete*, 164; R.W. Hutchinson, *Iraq* 1 (1934) 163-70; N.K. Sandars, *AJA* 65 (1961) 17-29.

[68] C.-F.-A. Schaeffer, *Ugaritica I*, 70: "No object of the brilliant epoch of Late Minoan I has so far been found at Ras Shamra," cf. 72: no Aegean pottery in Ras Shamra graves of the 16th and first half of the 15th century. H.J. Kantor, *AJA* 51 (1947) 36-38, notes only one specimen of LH II ceramics at Ras Shamra, and very few samples of LH I and LH II wares elsewhere in Syria and Palestine.

The transition from MM II to MM III was accompanied by a sudden shift from Minoan hieroglyphic writing to a simplified syllabic script called by Evans Linear A.[69] Most signs of Linear A can be read thanks to their similarity to the corresponding signs of the Linear B script deciphered by Michael Ventris.[70] The controversial problem of the linguistic affiliation of the Minoan language – was it related to Luwian, as believed by L. Palmer,[71] or to West Semitic, as advocated by C.H. Gordon[72] – is beside the framework of this survey.[73] What is beyond reasonable doubt is the occurrence in Linear A tablets of several Semitic words for food staples,[74] condiments,[75] wine,[76] and different kinds of vessels,[77] as well as of Hurrian and Semitic personal names,[78] which also appear in the onomastica of Ugarit and its hinterland. An Egyptian writing board from the early 18th Dynasty,[79] entitled "To make names of Keftiu" (i.e. Cretans), contains fifteen names of which two are Egyptian[80] and the rest are West Semitic, Akkadian, and Hurrian – a linguistic assortment characteristic of Northern Syria and Cyprus of that same general period.[81]

LM I (1550-1450) was the last period of Minoan independence. The advent of LM IIa marks the conquest of Crete by Achaeans from mainland Greece. Mycenaean Greek, written in Linear B, became the official language at Cnossus,[82] and from there the use of Linear B spread to the royal cities of the mainland. These political changes in the Aegean did not sever its cultural ties with the Near East. Geographical terms referring to the Eastern Mediterranean and Semitic loanwords which were believed to have been adopted into Greek not earlier than the eighth century are already present in the Linear B tablets. These include gentilics used as personal names: *A-ra-si-jo* "Alashian," *Ai-ku-pi-ti-jo* "Egyptian" (originally "Memphite"),[83] *Mi-sa-ra-jo* "Egyptian,"

---

69 *Palace of Minos*, I, 612-613.

70 J. Chadwick, *Antiquity* 33 (1959) 269-78, esp. 273: "A further encouraging sign is the appearance of names in A which are known in B" (both personal and geographical); C.H. Gordon, *Evidence for the Minoan Language* (1966), 26.

71 *Mycenaeans and Minoans* (1963), 232-237.

72 The latest and most complete presentation of C.H. Gordon's interpretation of the language of the Linear A texts is given in his *Evidence for the Minoan Language* (1966), 26-39.

73 Cf. M. Astour, *JAOS* 87 (1967), 290-95.

74 *ku-ni-su* (with pictorial determinative WHEAT) = Akkadian *kunāšu*, *kunnišu* "emmer wheat."

75 *ku-mi-na* < Akk. *kammūnu*, Heb. *kammōn* "caraway seed"; *sa-sa-me* < Akk. *šamaššammu*, Ugaritic *ššmn* "sesame"; *sa-mu-ku* < Heb. *ṣimmuqîm* "dry raisins."

76 *ya-ne* (inscribed on a wine pythos) < Heb. *yayn*, Ugar. *yn* "wine"; for the vocalization *yan-* cf. the Ugaritic place name *Yny*, spelled in syllabic cuneiform either *Ya-na* or, ideographically, GEŠTIN-*na* (GEŠTIN = "wine")

77 See C.H. Gordon, *Evidence*, § 115.

78 *Da-ku-se-né* = Hurrian *Taku-šenni*; *Su-ki-ri-te-se-ya* = Hurr. *Šukri-Tešeya; Da-ku-na* = *Daguna* on a seal from the Habur region; *Da-na-ne* = Ugar. *Dnn, Dananu*; *Ku-pà-nu* = Ugar. *Gupanu*; *Ka-du-ma-ne* = *Qdmn*; *Ma-ka-we-te* = Ugar. *Mqwṭ*. See C.H. Gordon, *Evidence*, Ch. 9.

79 Thus dated for palaeographic reasons by T.E. Peet who gave a revised publication of the text, *Essays in Aegean Archaeology, Presented to Sir Arthur Evans . . .* (1927), 90-99.

80 *Sn.nfr* and *Snt.nfrt*. Our earlier attempt (see n. 81 below) to interpret them as Egyptianizing transcriptions of Hurrian names was not warranted. Egyptians may well have been present among foreign residents of LM I Crete. C.H. Gordon, *Evidence* § 127, identified eight Linear A names as Egyptian names ending in *-Re*ʿ.

81 M. Astour, *JAOS* 84 (1964), 240-54.

82 L.R. Palmer's proposed to re-assign the Cnossus Linear B tablets from Evans's date of c. 1400 to early twelfth century because of their palaeographic and linguistic virtual identity with those from Pylos (c. 1200); see L.R. Palmer and J. Boardman, *On the Knossos Tablets* (1963). This view lost much of its attractiveness when exactly similar tablets were found in the Mycenaean palace of Thebes: they date from c. 1300, i.e. stand just halfway between the Cnossus and Pylos tablets. See now W.S. Woodard, *AJA* 76 (1972), 113-125, based on stratigraphic investigation of the site, in which the tablets are assigned to the very end of LM III A 1 or the very beginning of LM III A 2 (i.e., to c. 1350).

83 From Egypt. *Ḥ(t)-k -Ptḥ*, cuneiform *Ḫikuptaḫ*, Ugar. *Ḥkpt*. On the personal names mentioned in the text cf. M. Ventris and J. Chadwick, *Documents in Mycenaean Greek* (1956, second print 1959), 98, 136; O. Landau, *Mykenisch-Griechische Personennamen* (1958), *s. vv.*

from the Semitic name of Egypt (all three at Cnossus); the adjective *po-ni-ki-jo/ja* "Phoenician," referring to dyes and other products imported from Phoenicia, a loanword in Greek;[84] terms for "gold," "chiton," "linen garment," "caraway seed," "sesame," "cyperus."[85] Of greater significance is the similarity of the Mycenaean methods and style of recording to those of the administrative and economic tablets from the archives of Ugarit and its neighbor Alalakh, as this was noted and commented upon by M. Ventris and J. Chadwick in their pioneering work[86] and by T.B.L. Webster.[87] It is interesting that the Mycenaeans replaced the system of weights and measures used in Linear A texts by a new system fashioned after the Mesopotamian metrology, which points to renewed commercial contacts with the Syrian coast.[88] Mycenaean documents are less elaborate than those of Northern Syria, but, as stated by T.B.L. Webster, "If records are largely alike, the civilizations which produce them are likely to have large common elements."[89]

The export of Mycenaean wares to the Near East was very limited during the phases LH I and LH II (1550-1425[90] or 1580-1400[91]) and there was no Mycenaean influence upon the art of Western Asia.[92] An active expansion of Mycenaean trade with the East began in the first quarter of the fourteenth century, during the LH IIIa phase.[93] The earliest Mycenaean vase to be found at Ugarit belongs, according to Schaeffer, to the time between 1410 and 1360.[94] LH IIIa ware appears at Qatna, an inland city of Central Syria which was destroyed by the Hittites in 1366.[95] At Alalakh, three sherds of LH IIIa ware can be securely assigned to Level III (which we date from *ca.* 1410 to 1366), but an import of Mycenaean pottery on a larger scale occured in the following Level II.[96] In Egypt as well, according to E. Edel, "the time of Amenophis III [r.c. 1408-1372][97] marks a milestone of first rank in the history of Egypt's relations with Crete and the Mycenaean world."[98] Among other indications, this is illustrated by the presence of a remarkable list of cities of Crete, Cythera, and the Peloponnese in the funerary temple of Amenophis III at Kom el Hetan.[99] There was a general upsurge of demand for Mycenaean ceramics and works of art in the Eastern Mediterranean countries during the fourteenth and most of the thirteenth century. In Ugarit, a peculiar "Syro-Mycenaean art" was developed, combining Ae-

---

84 M. Ventris and J. Chadwick, 405; cf. M. Astour, *JNES* 24 (1965), 346-50.

85 In that order: *ku-ru-so* (*chrysos*) < Ugar., Phoen. *ḫrṣ*, Heb. *ḫarūṣ*; *ki-to* (*chitôn*) < Ugar. *ktn. ktnt*; *ri-ta* (*lita*) < Assyr. *līṭu*, Heb. *lōṭ*; *ku-mi-no* and *sa-sa-ma* (like in Linear A): cf. n. 75 above; *ku-pa-ro* (*kypairos*) < Heb. *kōpher*, Ugar. *kpr* (?)

86 M. Ventris and J. Chadwick, 106-07, 113, 133.

87 *From Mycenae to Homer* (1958, second print 1964) 7-26, *Antiquity* 29 (1955), 10-14.

88 L.R. Palmer, *The Interpretation of Myceneaen Greek texts* (1963), 101-102 (with further literature).

89 *From Mycenae to Homer*, 7.

90 Chronotomy of A. Furumark, *The Mycenaean Pottery: Analysis and Classification* (1941).

91 Chronotomy of A.J.B. Wace, *Mycenae: An Archaeological History and Guide* (1949), accepted by G. Mylonas, *Ancient Mycenae* (1957), 181.

92 H.J. Kantor, *AJA* 51 (1947), 78; cf. n. 68 above.

93 *Eadem*, 79; F.H. Stubbings, *CAH*³, I, 1, 245.

94 C.F.A. Schaeffer, *Ugaritica I*, 72.

95 F.H. Stubbings, *l.c.*; <R.> du Mesnil du Buisson, *Le site archéologique de Mishrifé-Qatna* (1935), 34. Date of the First Syrian War and destruction of Qatna – according to K.A. Kitchen, *Suppiluliuma and the Amarna Pharaohs* (1962), 42 ("high" date).

96 L. Woolley, *A Forgotten Kingdom*, 151; M.B. Rowton, *CAH*³, I, 1, 230-31.

97 Chronology of E. Drioton and J. Vandier, *L'Égypte*⁴ (1962), 341-343; according to W.C. Hayes, *CAH*³, I, 1 188: 1417-1379; according to K.A. Kitchen (n. 95 above), 39: 1406-1369 ("high" date).

98 E. Edel, *Die Ortsnamenlisten aus dem Totentempel Amenophis III.* (1966), 57.

99 After a first incomplete publication by K.A. Kitchen, *Or* NS 34 (1965), 1-9, pl. I-XIV, followed by his communication *BASOR* No. 181 (1966), 23-24, and M. Astour, *AJA* 70 (1961), 313-17, a corrected and complete list of the toponyms from Kom el Hetan was published and commented upon by E. Edel (n. 98 above); the sector with the Aegean place names (List E_N) is studied on pp. 33-60.

gean and Asian motifs and techniques.[100] A showpiece of that art it the fourteenth century ivory plaque from Minet el-Beida, representing the Aegean "Mistress of Animals" but of unmistakable Syrian production.[101]

The great amount of Mycenaean pottery (both LH IIIa and LH IIIb) at Ugarit evoked the idea that "since the fourteenth and during the thirteenth centuries . . . there was a real Mycenaen colonization of Ugarit"[102] and even its political domination by Mycenaeans.[103] The latter assertion was completely disproved by the publication of the royal archives in the volumes of *Palais royal d'Ugarit*[104] which showed that the native Semitic dynasty remained there in power till the final destruction of the city. But the alleged existence of a Mycenaean colony in Ugarit is still uncritically repeated in some books.[105] Ugarit was indeed a very cosmopolitan city, with many permanent or temporary residents of foreign origin.[106] But their presence is recorded in numerous registers, commercial deeds, and juridical acts. Nowhere in the entire extensive epigraphic material from Ras Shamra can there be found a personal name of Greek Mycenaean type or a gentilic identifying its bearer as a native of any Aegean city of area.[107] Not only does the presumed Mycenaean colony vanish in the light of overwhelming negative evidence, but there is even no record whatever of an Aegean merchant transacting business at Ugarit. For some reason, perhaps political, Mycenaean sailors did not land on the Ugaritian coast. One is compelled to think that the bulk of Mycenaean wares imported to Ugarit came there through the intermediary of Cyprus, one of its chief trade partners, and a certain amount was carried by Ugaritian ships directly from the Aegean.

In 1947, Miss Helene J. Kantor concluded: "After the close of the MM II period, and throughout the later part of the Second Millennium, only the sailors, merchants, and craftsmen of Mycenaean Greece can justifiedly lay claim to the honor of forming the links connecting the Aegean with the Orient."[108] This statement must now be qualified. It is true that the principal areas of Ugarit's maritime trade were Cyprus, the coastal cities of Phoenicia and Palestine, Egypt, and, to an extent, Cilicia. But there is one piece of evidence concerning Crete. It belongs to the "file" of Sinaranu, an extremely rich and influential Ugaritian merchant[109] under the kings Niqmepa and Ammishtamru (first half of the thirteenth century). In the document RS 16.238,[110] King Ammishtamru grants Sinaranu complete tax exemption, which also covers his ship when it returns from a land whose name is written, by the way of ideographic pun rather common at Ugarit,[111] ^{KUR}DUGUD-*ri* (line 10).

100 C.F.A. Schaeffer, *Ugaritica I*, 33-35.

101 *Ibid.*, frontispiece and Pl. XI; cf. the detailed artistic analysis by H.J. Kantor, *AJA* 51 (1947), 86-89.

102 C.F.A. Schaeffer, *Ugaritica I*, 99, cf. 100-05.

103 *Ibid.*, 41-44; already surmised by Ch. Virolleaud, *La légende phénicienne de Danel* (1936), 64-65.

104 Vols. II (1957) and V (1965) by Ch. Virolleaud; vols. III (1955), IV (1956), and VI (1970) by J. Nougayrol.

105 E.g., L. Woolley, *A Forgotten Kingdom*, 151; T.B.L. Webster, *From Mycenae to Homer*, 37, 66, 284-85; D. Page, *History and the Homeric Iliad* (1959), 37 n. 57; F.H. Stubbings in Wace and Stubbings, ed., *A Companion to Homer* (1963), 542; E. Vermeule, *Greece in the Bronze Age* (1964), 255, 265.

106 Among them: Hittites, Assyrians, Egyptians, Alashians, people from Siyannu, Carchemish, Arwad, Byblos, Berytus, Sidon, Tyre, Accho, Ashdod, Ashkelon, and from Ura in Cilicia (the latter restricted to the summer months and subjected to special limitations). Those from the Egyptian possessions in Asia (from Byblos southward) had, apparently, a corporate organizations as "Canaanites" and enjoyed some kind of diplomatic protection from their overlord, the Pharaoh.

107 M. Astour, *JNES* 23 (1964), 193-94; *Hellenosemitica*, 353-55; *JESHO* 13 (1970), 126-27. The existence of a Mycenaean colony at Ugarit was denied by F. Schachermeyr, *MDOG* 9 (1935) 102-07, 108-14, and "Zur Frage der Lokalisierung von Achiava," in E. Grumach, ed., *Minoica* (1958), 377; and by M. Liverani, *Storia di Ugarit* (1962), 52-53.

108 *AJA* 51 (1947), 103.

109 On the merchant class of Ugarit and its social status cf. M.L. Heltzer, *VDI* 1964, No. 2, 3-16, and M. Astour, "The Merchant Class in Ugarit," in the forthcoming Proceedings of the XVIIIe Rencontre Assyriologique Internationale at Munich.

110 J. Nougayrol, *PRU III*, 107-08.

111 E.g., ^{URU}SÍG = *Š'rt*, ^{URU}SAG^{du} = *Riš*, ^{URU}*Ia-ku*-SIG_5 = *Ykn'm*, ^{URU}*Gi_5*-^{d}IM = *Gb'ly*, ^{URU}GEŠTIN-*na* = *Yny*.

This can only be read, with Nougayrol, as $^{m\bar{a}t}$*Kabtu-ri*, "Caphtor," which agrees, of course, with that country's accessibility by ship. We now know that Ugaritian cargo ships had the displacement of up to 500 metric tons,[112] but even small crafts were quite able to sail from Syria, via Cyprus, to the Aegean. One such ship of late thirteenth century, built in Syria and with a Syrian crew, was loaded with copper ingots from Cyprus and bronze scrap and had an ambulant metal shop on board. It did not reach the Aegean and sank off Cape Gelidonya in Lycia, but other similar ships must have been more successful, to judge from the presence in the Acropolis hoard at Athens of bronze tools closely similar to those found in the Cape Gelidonya shipwreck.[113]

If the Eastern Mediterranean countries of the fourteenth and thirteenth centuries were fascinated with Mycenaean ceramics, the Mycenaeans, in their turn, showed an interest in Near Eastern glyptics. Cylinder seals of "Mitannian" and "Third Syrian" styles "are prominent among the various groups of foreign objects found in Greece" and Crete of LH and LM periods.[114] Their imagery seems to have exercised an influence on LH and LM art.[115] The largest hoard of Near Eastern cylinder seals, containing many unusually beautiful specimens, was found in the Mycenaean palace of Thebes which was destroyed at the beginning of LH IIIb period, i.e., *ca.* 1300.[116] Most of the cylinders are of Babylonian style, and those bearing inscriptions are, epigraphically, of Kassite period, but E. Weidner suspects that most or all of them are copies carved in a Syro-Hurrian shop specifically for export.[117] One seal (No. 202), in elaborate "Mitannian" style of fifteenth-fourteenth century, carries the inscription: *Ḫa-am-mi-*^{d}*Id-ra-ap* LUGAL *Ia-ra-qù-úḫ*^{KI} SANGA ^{d}*Id-ra-ap* "Ḫammi-Idrap, king of Yaraquḫ,[118] priest of the god Idrap."[119] The divine name *Idrap* has so far been found only at Ugarit.[120] There are reasons to assume that Yaraquḫ[121] was a small state between Alalakh and Ugarit which was incorporated into the territory of the latter by the edict of the Hittite king Shuppiluliumash c. 1365.[122] The presence of that seal in the Theban hoard may point to Ugarit as the place whence the whole set was shipped to the Aegean.[123] It is possible that the cylinders reached Thebes not directly but through the intermediary of Eastern Crete which maintained a special relationship with Thebes during the fourteenth and thirteenth centuries.[124]

---

112 Cf. J. Nougayrol, *CRAI* 1960, 165.

113 G.F. Bass, *Cape Gelidonya – A Bronze Age Shipwreck* (1967). [Cf. article by G.F. Bass in this volume. – Ed.]

114 H.J. Kantor, *AJA* 51 (1947), 85 n. 29.

115 M.L. Erlenmeyer – H. Erlenmeyer, *Or* NS 30 (1961) 289-291.

116 In addition to the literature listed in *Hellenosemitica*^{2}, 391-392, one may note E. Porada, report in *AJA* 69 (1965), 173; J. Nougayrol, in *Bulletin de Correspondence Hellenique*, 88 (1964), 778-79 and 90 (1966) 848-50; E. Weidner, "Thebai," *AfO* 21 (1966), 193-95; K.M. Kolobova, *VDI* 1970, No. 2, 111-20 (with further literature).

117 E. Weidner, *AfO* 21 (1966), 194.

118 The sign *úḫ* can also be read *uš*$_x$.

119 Transliteration: J. Nougayrol, *Bulletin de Correspondence Hellénique*, 90 (1966) 850 (with hesitation as to whether the first sign of the divine name is to be read *id/t* or *da*). Prof. Nougayrol kindly sent me a copy of the cuneiform text.

120 As an epithet of the god Resheph: *Ršp Idrp*, *Ugaritica V*/3 9 rev. 10; *Ir*[*šp*] *Idrp*, CTA 166:41.

121 I. e., *Yaraqu* "green" (a mountain area west of the lower Orontes known from Neo-Assyrian annals) + the Hurrian formative *-ḫ*, variant of *-(ḫ)ḫe*; if the reading *uš*$_x$ is preferred, the ending would represent the Hurrian formative *-š*, variant of *-(š)še*. Both formatives are extremely common in North Syrian toponymy of the second millennium.

122 This detail was not yet included in our article *Or* NS 38 (1961), 381-414, Pl. LI. It will be discussed elsewhere.

123 The only seal of the hoard to bear a Hieroglyphic Hittite inscription could also have come to Thebes via Ugarit: many such seals have been found at Ras Shamra, cf. E. Laroche in *Ugaritica III* (1956), 97-160.

124 See L.R. Palmer, *Myc. and Min.*^{2}, 203-04; *idem*, *Interpret.*, 275-77, for the Cretan toponyms on the inscribed vases found in the palace of Thebes during earlier excavations; W.A. McDonald, *Progress into the Past* (1967), 355-57, a summary of spectrographic investigation of potsherds from Thebes by H.W. Catling and his associates (with further literature); L.A. Stella, *Atti e Memorie del I Congresso Internazionale di Micenologia*, 517-23.

Ugarit was destroyed, soon after 1200, by the invasion of the Peoples of the Sea which came from the Aegean and was in some way connected with the catastrophe that engulfed at that very time the brilliant palatial civilization of Mycenaean Greece.[125] It took four hundred years before new contacts were established between the Aegean and the Levantine coast. But, to quote the concluding sentence of William Stevenson Smith's *Interconncetions in the Ancient Near East*, "In spite of their intense individuality, the Mycenaeans, and the Cretans before them, seem to have lived in conditions which produced a close understanding with the oriental world which could never be recaptured."[126] We wish we knew more about the exchange of ideas which accompanied the exchange of goods between the two regions, or at least about the concrete, technical circumstances of the East-West trade during the Middle and Late Bronze Age. Perhaps some future campaign of excavations at Ras Shamra will disclose MB tablets (none has been found thus far); perhaps another part of the Mycenaean palace of Thebes will be uncovered and will bring some further surpirses. Our information is incomplete and uneven; but even so, if we ask ourselves: does it provide us with a tangible basis for an assumption of, as L.R. Palmer put it, "an Aegean Oriental religious *koinê*"[127] – the answer would be positive, and we would repeat, with the same scholar, that "for the student of Mycenaean contacts with the Orient, Canaanite Ugarit is of the greatest importance."[128]

---

125 We tried to piece together the pertaining written documentation from Ugarit in *AJA* 69 (1965), 253-8. It may be noted that during the last period of peace before the catastrophe, Syrian-made figurines of a god conventionally called Resheph (but perhaps representing Baal) became popular imports into Crete and Greece; cf. R.W. Hutchinson, *Prehistoric Crete*, 311-12.

126 *Op. cit.*, 185.

127 *Interpret. of Myc. Greek Texts*, 256.

128 *Ibid., l. c.*

CAPE GELIDONYA AND BRONZE AGE MARITIME TRADE

George F. Bass

The University of Pennsylvania Museum

The five years since the publication of a Bronze Age shipwreck at Cape Gelidonya, Turkey,[1] have seen newly discovered or published material, as well as reviews and comments by authorities on Near Eastern and Mycenaean history. The invitation to contribute to this *Festschrift* for Cyrus Gordon provides a fitting opportunity to add to the "final" excavation report, and to evaluate certain aspects of it in the light of new knowledge. I will deal principally with those areas which bear on the mercantile aspects of the study, beginning with:

Chapter V. The Ingots (*CG*, 52-83).*

The ship's preserved cargo consisted largely of copper and bronze ingots, whole and fragmentary. Our original study included a catalogue of previously discovered ingots and ingot representations. Continuing the numbering system used there, we may add to the list of "ox-hide" ingots.

107. Ayia Irini, Kea.[2] Fragment (one quarter) of an ingot of Type 1*b*. Seems to bear a secondary (incised) mark. Dated stratigraphically to the fifteenth century B.C.

108. Teti, Sardinia. H.-G. Buchholz's latest list[3] of "ox-hide" ingots includes this bronze ingot, about which little is now known.

109. Tell al-Abyad, Iraq. While reading through the register books in the Iraq Museum, J.A. Brinkman discovered the description and sketch of what seems to be an ingot of the type under discussion. The actual ingot, which he hopes to locate in the Museum at a later date, seems to be dated stratigraphically to ca. 1200 ± 30 B.C.[4]

---

1 G.F. Bass, *et al.*, "Cape Gelidonya: A Bronze Age Shipwreck," *Transactions of the American Philosophical Society* 57, part 8 (1967), here abbreviated as *CG*.

2 J.L. Caskey, *Archaiologikon Deltion* 24 (1969), 400, with pl. 412b.

3 H.-G. Buchholz, *Schweizer Münzblätter* 16 (1966), 62. To his thorough bibliography of recent writings on ingots may be added the later L. Vagnetti, *Studi Micenei ed Egeo-Anatolici* 3 (1967), 28-30.

4 Dr. Brinkman kindly informs me that he plans to publish all available information in the second volume of his *Materials and Studies for Kassite History*. J.H. Muhly brought this ingot to my attention.

* [Cf. below on p. 92 n. 8 – Ed.]

110. Knidos, Asia Minor. Mehmet Imbat, a Bodrum sponge-boat captain, sketched for me an "ox-hide" ingot which he had netted in very deep water some years earlier, before the antiquity of such pieces was known to him.

111. Enkomi, Cyprus.[5] Miniature ingot of Type 2*a*. Primary signs. Dated stratigraphically to 1300-1190 B.C.

112. Enkomi.[6] Miniature ingot of Type 2*c* (?). Dated stratigraphically to 1190-1125/1100 B.C.

113. Enkomi.[7] Miniature ingot of Type 2*c*. Dated stratigraphically to 1125/1100-1075 B.C.

114. Roman Britain.[8] Miniature silver ingot of Type 1*b*. Stamped EX OF(FICINA) FL(AVII) HONORINI. One of a number.

One ingot from the original list must be removed. G. Cadogan[9] has rightly noted that the example from Sitia, Crete (no. 23 in my original list) is based on a misreading of *Archaiologike Ephemeris* (1912), 220.

Representations of "ox-hide" ingots to be added to the original list in *Cape Gelidonya*, (62-69) are:

30. Gold-leaf plaque of Ay (r. 1353-1349 B.C.) from an unknown tomb at Thebes.[10] The king stands in a chariot (fig. 1), about to shoot an arrow into an ingot of Type 2*c* (or 1*b* ?). The ingot, already pierced with five arrows, is attached to the top of a vertical post to which two foreign captives are fastened, back to back. Two other foreigners, one a Negro and the other probably a Syrian, kneel beneath the rearing horses of the chariot. The target is described as being made from an animal's hide in the early publication, but there can be little doubt that the scene is based on earlier depictions, such as the relief of Amenhotep II at Karnak, where the target is identified as of copper in an accompanying text.[11]

31. Cylinder seal of Ramesses II (r. 1301-1234 B.C.) from Beth-shan.[12] The king shoots arrows into an ingot supported on a post to which two Syrian captives are bound, back to back (fig. 2); also shown is a god wearing a horned, conical crown. I had considered this crudely rendered ingot (roughly Type 1*a*) for my original list, but had rejected it because it did not seem likely that a copper ingot would be supported on a pole; the plaque of Ay (above) proves me wrong.

32. Cyprus. Goddess on an ingot. The piece, in a private British collection, will be published by H.W. Catling.[13]

33. Painting on the Verghi Crater, Cyprus.[14]
Two small human figures carry objects, identified by P. Dikaios as being copper ingots, on Crater No. 36 from the Tomb at Pyla-Verghi (fig. 3). *C.* 1400 B.C.

---

[5] P. Dikaios, *Enkomi Excavations 1948-1958* (Mainz am Rhein, 1969), pl. 138/1 (1995), pl. 148/5, and pl. 171/14.
[6] *Ibid.*, pl. 138/2 (885).
[7] *Ibid.*, pl. 147/35 (774), pl. 148/4, and pl. 176/42.
[8] *Guide to the Antiquities of Roman Britain* (Br. Mus., London, 1966), 46, no. III(b)4, with fig. 21; for other, fragmentary examples see p. 41, nos. 43, 44 with pl. IX.
[9] G. Cadogan, rev. of *CG* in *Journ. of Hellenic Studies* 89 (1969), 188.
[10] T.M. Davis, *The Tombs of Harmhabi and Touatankhamanou* (London, 1912), 127-8, with fig. 3. L. Bell referred me to this.
[11] *CG*, 65 with fig. 73.
[12] J. Pritchard, *ANEP* (Princeton, 1954), 113 and 289, with fig. 338.
[13] H.W. Catling, *Archaeologia Viva* (English ed.) 2, no. 3 (March-May 1969), 86.
[14] Dikaios, *op. cit.* (supra, n. 5), 918-25, with pls. 230/1, 231/1-4, 301/1-2, and 302A/1-2.

34. Painting on the "Zeus" Crater from Enkomi, Cyprus.[15]
One figure carries a possible ingot, while another weighs two "ingots," as identified by Dikaios, with scales (fig. 4). Early 14th century B.C.

35. Painting on a Mycenaean crater from Enkomi.[16]
A figure stands, holding a possible ingot, before a horse-drawn chariot (fig. 5). 14th century B.C.

36. Relief on the throne dais of Shalmaneser III (858-824 B.C.) in Fort Shalmaneser, Nimrud.[17]
The king is approached by a line of North Syrians bearing tribute from "Qalparunda of the land of Unqi." Two of the men carry crudely rendered ingots (fig. 6), which might be considered sacks without the accompanying inscription listing "silver, gold, tin, bronze, bowls of bronze, elephant tusks, ebony, logs of cedar, bright-coloured garments and linen, (and) horses trained to harness," all of which may be identified in the scene.

I originally concluded that "ox-hide" ingots were not a form of currency (*CG*, 71) and agreed with Buchholz that their "legs" were simply handles for ease of porterage rather than being in imitation of cows' limbs. Nothing written since then[18] has caused me to change this first conclusion, but the theories of shape must be reconsidered. We have seen above that miniature ingots in this form existed on Cyprus perhaps as late as the 11th century B.C., and even appeared in Roman times. No "handles" were required for these tiny objects, and it is doubtful that all were in imitation of "full-scale" ingots since there is no evidence, of which I am aware, for large "ox-hide-shaped" ingots in Roman times. Further, the general shape first appears, at Tell Beit Mirsim, in the first half of the 16th century B.C. (*CG*, 57), at least as early as and probably earlier than any representations or actual examples of large ingots have appeared anywhere. It is true that the chronologically more extreme examples do not have very pronounced handles, but there is no question of their being in the peculiar shape which we associate with a certain type of ingot, whatever the origin of its form.

The ingot (no. 109) from just west of Baghdad, and possibly the late representations from Nimrud (about which more below), add significantly to the geographical range of ox-hide ingots, which previously had been restricted to areas easily reached by ships and boats from the Mediterranean (*CG*, 75, map). The spread of large-scale ingots is now seen to extend from Sardinia to Mesopotamia.

Dating of ox-hide ingots and, therefore, their period of manufacture is controversial; in *Cape Gelidonya* I concluded that they ceased being made *c.* 1200 B.C. None of the new evidence changes the fact that we have not a single ingot, from more than one hundred (excluding miniature ingots, found even in Roman times), which can be dated stratigraphically to before 1600 B.C. nor after 1200 B.C., except perhaps by a very few years.[19] Further, we now have eighteen Egyptian representations of ox-hide ingots, which can be dated with some precision, and not one of these is earlier than 1500 B.C. nor later than the 13th century B.C. (the 12th-century relief of Ramesses III at Medinet Habu being almost surely a copy of a 13th-century scene; *CG*, 67). It seems illogical that all such representations would precede 1200 B.C., if, as Catling concludes, ox-hide ingots on Cyprus were introduced by Mycenaean colonists on the island at the end of the 13th century.[20] Cypriot copper was ex-

---

[15] *Ibid.*, with pls. 302/1,2,4 and 302A/3.
[16] *Ibid.*, with pl. 302A/4-5.
[17] M.E.L. Mallowan, *Nimrud and its Remains* II (1966), 446, with figs. a-c on pp. 448-9. O.W. Muscarella brought this to my attention.
[18] N.F. Parise, *Atti del I Congresso Internationale di Micenologia* (Rome, 1968), 117-133, who also quotes from L. Berglia in *Congresso Internationale di Numismatica*, I, *Relazione* (Rome, 1961), 5-17, which I have not seen.
[19] Buchholz, *op. cit.* (supra, n. 3), 67-8, now doubts the 12th-century date assigned earlier to one of the Enkomi ingots.
[20] H.W. Catling, *CAH* 2nd ed., fasc. 43 (1966), 72.

ported before then, and we must wonder what form its ingots took if not the ox-hide shape, especially the generally later Types 2 and 3.

We have presented, however, new secondary evidence for the occurrence of ox-hide ingots after 1200 B.C., much later than deemed possible in *Cape Gelidonya*, and this must also include the statuette of a "god" standing on an ingot at Enkomi (*CG*, 69, no. 29; reviewers mercifully realized that it was not purposely ignored in the discussions which followed the catalogue there; the piece was published[21] when *Cape Gelidonya* was going to the printer, and it was possible to note it, at all, only by condensing other paragraphs on the page).

The latest, by far, is the representation of ingots at Nimrud. No other evidence suggests the manufacture of ox-hide ingots in the 9th century B.C., and I am not sure that they did, in fact, exist. The Nimrud ingots are so awkwardly rendered, both in shape and method of being carried, that one might wonder if the sculptor was familiar with the actual objects. Further, the scene of Syrians bringing tribute looks, in its entirety, curiously familiar.

The scene of Syrians bringing tribute in the 15th-century B.C. tomb of Rekh-mi-rēʿ in Egypt is only the best known of dozens of such scenes examined for the compilation of ingot representations in *Cape Gelidonya.*[22] If there were only a similarity between the types of tribute there and at Nimrud, one could attribute it to a simple similarity of goods produced in north Syria in both the 15th and 9th centuries B.C.: baskets of ring-shaped ingots,[23] ox-hide ingots, elephant tusks, small wood logs, bronze cauldrons, and horses; cloth appears in other Egyptian scenes of Syrian tribute.[24] But the very manner in which these articles are rendered in the processions (except for the cauldrons) suggests the possibility of Egyptianizing influences here as on some of the ivory work from Fort Shalmaneser. This speculation at least deserves more detailed examination: could an artist who had seen earlier Egyptian tribute scenes (not, of course, that in the tomb of Rekh-mi-rēʿ) have influenced the relief at Fort Shalmaneser?

Evidence of ox-hide ingots on Cyprus after 1200 B.C. is more convincing. Two miniature ingots from Enkomi have come from 12th-, and possibly 11th-century levels. Even though miniatures in this shape are not necessarily connected with the manufacture of "industrial" ox-hide ingots (as evidenced by Roman examples), and the possibility of votive miniatures outlasting the manufacture of large ingots exists, it is clearly possible that the people who owned the two Enkomi miniatures were familiar with the larger types.

This brings us to the statuette of a "god" standing on an ox-hide ingot at Enkomi. The 12th-century context in which it was found cannot be doubted.[25] But how can it be explained? C.F.-A. Schaeffer believes that the god was the patron of Cypriot miners and foundry workers and, being identified with Babylonian Nergal and Syrian Reshef, was brought to Cyprus by the Semitic components of the Sea Peoples.[26]

If Catling's thesis that Mycenaean colonization *c.* 1200 B.C. introduced the manufacture of ox-hide ingots into Cyprus is correct, then such a Semitic patron god of copper-working would seem out of place in the 12th century. If my theory that Semitic influence on the manufacture of such ingots in the 13th century was ended *c.* 1200 B.C. by the invasion of Sea Peoples is correct, then a Semitic patron god would seem equally out of place. Is it possible that the statuette was worshipped well into the 12th century, but was cast somewhat earlier, as was the previously discovered horned god at Enkomi (also compared to Reshef) which dates

[21] C.F.-A. Schaeffer, *AfO* 21 (1966), 59 ff.
[22] Norman de G. Davies, *Paintings from the Tomb of Rekh-mi-Rēʿ at Thebes* (Metr. Mus. of Art Egypt. Exped. Publs., vol. X, 1935), pl. XXII.
[23] Their use as ingots is proven by the casting scene in N. de G. Davies, *The Tombs of Menkheperrasonb, Amenmose, and Another* (Theban Tomb Series, 5th Mem., London 1933), pl. XI, bottom register.
[24] *Ibid.*, frontispiece.
[25] *AfO* 21 (1966), 61-2.
[26] *Ibid.*, 63-4, 68-9.

from the "very beginning of the twelfth century," but which was still worshipped in the early 11th century B.C.?[27] This should be considered, but so should Catling's belief that the statue is a blend of Aegean and Near Eastern influences, "a true Cypriote," which would be quite acceptable in the 12th century.[28]

To summarize the dating of ingots, we have no actual examples dated after 1200 B.C., though we do have a couple of miniatures following that date, and we have no positive representations whose date of creation is certain (as is the case with Egyptian tomb paintings) after 1200 B.C., although we do have the existence of a horned "god" standing on an ingot which was at least in use following that date.[29] We have seen that it is possible to "explain away" all of the new evidence pointing to the manufacture of ox-hide ingots on Cyprus after 1200 B.C. Nevertheless, this evidence is so compelling that I should modify the position taken in *Cape Gelidonya*: it does seem probable that some "full-scale" ox-hide ingots continued to be manufactured on Cyprus in the 12th century B.C., but not in the quantity of the preceding centuries.

This does not necessarily disprove the "Semitic" character of the ingots proposed in *Cape Gelidonya*. Levantine as well as Aegean refugees are thought to have fled to Cyprus in the 12th century,[30] and the former could have continued, on a diminished scale, the earlier tradition;[31] perhaps the two peoples worked in concert, explaining the mixed characteristics of the ingot "god" described above. For the earlier periods, it is true that Dikaios sees the representations on the Mycenaean craters from Cyprus (above) as proof that Mycenaeans controlled the copper industry,[32] but the identification of ingots on these vases is not totally convincing. There still exists no certain depiction of Mycenaeans dealing with ox-hide ingots, while unambiguous evidence of Semitic associations is common; the Nimrud relief, the "horned god," and even the two archery scenes may offer further Syrian connections, but none is certain nor, in this case, necessary for the argument.

Bun ingots were also found on the Cape Gelidonya wreck. In the excavation report it was suggested that these round, plano-convex cakes of bronze were possible evidence for early, but still unknown furnaces of a type known in Roman times (*CG*, 80 with fig. 95); the Cypriot stone moulds thought to have been used for casting bun ingots[33] are not convincing on inspection. Recent excavations in the Timna Valley of Israel have now unearthed actual furnaces from the time of the Cape Gelidonya ship, similar to those hypothesized.[34]

Chapter VI. The Bronzes (*CG*, 84-121).

The bronze tools and other objects on the ship, as well as contemporaneous Cypriot bronzes in general, seem to find most of their prototypes in the Near East (L. Åström also reached the conclusion that Catling "seems in some cases a little too willing to attribute bronzes of uncertain origin to the Aegeans."[35]). I still feel that the "very early twelfth century is the latest that they may be dated" (*CG*, 165), but this is not accepted by all.[36]

---

[27] P. Dikaios, *Archäologischer Anzeiger* (1962), 38-9.

[28] Catling, *loc. cit.* (supra, n. 13).

[29] I have not dealt with the bronze stand from Kourion, Cyprus (*CG*, 68, no. 28), which has been assigned a wide variety of origins by stylistic analysis.

[30] Catling, *op. cit.* (supra, n. 20), 67; V. Karageorgis, *The Ancient Civilization of Cyprus* (New York, 1969), 143.

[31] C. Zaccagnini, review of *CG* in *Oriens Antiquus* 10 (1971), 168, cites some of the most recent evidence for continued copper-working in the 12th century.

[32] Dikaios, *op. cit.* (supra, n. 5), 921; n. 789 on 925.

[33] *Ibid.*, 43, with pls. 8/3-4 and 127/48-48a.

[34] *Midianite Timna: Valley of the Biblical Copper Mines* (guidebook publ. in 1971 for a Brit. Mus. exhibit).

[35] L. Åström, *Studies on the Arts and Crafts of the Late Cypriote Bronze Age* (1967), 149.

[36] Catling, *op. cit.* (supra, n. 13), 85, continues to prefer the unequivocal 12th-century dating of the shipwreck given in his *Cypriot Bronzework in the Mycenaean World* (1964), written with knowledge of the Cape Gelidonya material but before *CG*. He has studied the bronzes carefully, and his opinions demand careful consideration.

E. Linder has noted the remarkable similarity between the types of bronzes in the Cape Gelidonya cargo and those on a merchant ship listed in a Ugaritic text (*UT* 2056).[37]

Chapter X. The Weights (*CG*, 135-142).

The study of balance-pan weights on the shipwreck was a particularly frustrating task, which probably consumed more time than the study of any other group of objects. I am not, myself, convinced of all my results, although the general conclusion of a mixture of sets based on Near Eastern standards – qedets of *c.* 9.32 grams, so-called "Phoenician" shekels of *c.* 7.30 grams, neṣefs of 10.30 and 10.50 grams – seems reasonably certain. I was hard pressed to find any convincing parallels from mainland Greece, but the re-publication of lead weights from the Vaphio tomb in the Peloponnese presents evidence of qedets of 9.5 grams (in possible multiples of 6, 14, 25, 50 and 100);[38] such a standard has been found previously in Syria, Cyprus, Palestine, and Crete (*CG*, 139).

Recent excavations on two of the Cycladic islands have yielded additional sets of Late Bronze Age weights, usually lead disks which have suffered weight change due to corrosion. Sp. Marinatos would base the examples from Thera on the Babylonian system, with a shekel of 8.4 grams,[39] but the common occurrence of multiples of 3.50 and 7.25 to 7.5 grams suggests to me stronger evidence of ties with Syro-Palestinian neṣefs and shekels. The lead weights from Ayia Irini in Keos are more difficult to analyze because of their very number (46 weights),[40] but the appearance of fairly close multiples of 10.5 grams points again to the Syro–Palestinian coast.

These newly published weights would seem to strengthen the "Semitic" character I have postulated for much of the trade in the Aegean World prior to 1400 B.C. (*CG*, 166-7). Unfortunately, we still know virtually nothing about Mycenaean weights after that date, but ties between the Cape Gelidonya weights and those of mainland Greece remain the least secure of all known in the eastern Mediterranean.[41]

Chapter XIV. Conclusions (*CG*, 163-7).

I concluded that the ship excavated at Cape Gelidonya was a Syrian[42] merchant vessel which sank about 1200 B.C.; that a Mycenaean monopoly on Aegean maritime trade in the Late Bronze Age had been exaggerated, to the exclusion of an important Near Eastern role; and that copper and bronze trade was largely in Semitic hands from the 15th century until the end of the 13th century B.C.

At this point it is necessary to comment on how these conclusions were reached, although it should not be. When I excavated the wreck and began the study of its remains, I was a graduate student of Classical archaeology with a limited knowledge of the history of the Late Bronze Age. I assumed that the ship was probably Mycenaean, but had no clear idea of its date, and I accepted ox-hide ingots (of which I was completely ignorant before) as being Aegean "Keftiubarren." I was scarcely aware, at that time, of the role of the Sea Peoples or the Aegean settlement of Cyprus, and I did not know of Cyrus Gordon's work on Linear A.

[37] E. Linder, *International Journ. of Nautical Archaeology* 1 (1972), 163-4.

[38] Sp. Marinatos, *Biblotheke tes en Athenais Archaiologikes Etaireias* 64 (1969), 49-50 n. 1.

[39] *Ibid.*

[40] J.L. Caskey, *Archaiologikon Deltion* 24 (1969), 95 ff.

[41] Excavators continue the unfortunate practice of publishing weights without giving their actual weights, as in *Enkomi* (supra, n. 5), *passim.*

[42] Zaccagnini, *loc. cit.* (supra, n. 31), objects to my interchanging the terms Syrian, Canaanite and Phoenician so freely. I realized the dangers involved, but hoped that this might more readily attract the notice of strict Classicists to the significance of our discoveries.

I began my study with the ship's weights, and was surprised that it was so difficult to tie them positively to Mycenaean Greece. I next turned to the ingots, and was again surprised to find them most closely associated, in Egyptian tomb paintings from 15th through the 13th century, with Syrians. In the same vein, I did not expect to find the numerous Near Eastern prototypes for the Cypriot bronzes on board, nor the evidence that the bronzes seemed to be from either the 13th century or, at the very latest, the very beginning of the 12th century B.C. Meanwhile, colleagues were independently studying the seal, scarabs, pottery, stone objects, and basketry. Only when these separate studies of the artifacts had been made, did I try to fit them into a logical picture. The results were not what I might have expected.

I explain this, because some critics have misunderstood my approach: R. de Vaux suggests that I tried to place the date of the wreck before 1200 B.C. because I wished to place it before the arrival of the Sea Peoples on Cyprus;[43] H. Catling writes that I was "concerned to show that the voyage must have preceded the coming of the Aegean refugees to Cyprus;"[44] and A.M. McCann and G. Cadogan believed that I used linguistic evidence, accepting C. Gordon's decipherment of Linear A as Semitic, to bolster my theories of Phoenician maritime trade,[45] whereas I specifically wrote that "I am linguistically incompetent to judge the validity of the decipherment" (*CG*, 77), and only pointed out that independent archaeological evidence pointed to Semitic influences in the Aegean during the Bronze Age (this seemed important, since some scholars had used archaeological rather than linguistic evidence to dismiss Gordon's claims).

It was not I, therefore, who was trying to fit the evidence of Cape Gelidonya to any preconceived historical theories. Several critics disagree with my dating of the ship, feeling that it sank in the 12th century rather than in the 13th.[46] If they are correct, which is possible, then I must obviously modify my theories concerning Cyprus at the end of the Late Bronze Age. I am not convinced that my dating is wrong, but admit that some of these theories now rest on shakier ground than held in *Cape Gelidonya*. What cannot be doubted, however, is the role of Semitic seafarers in the Bronze Age. In fact, my theories there have been strengthened considerably by the written documents which I did not cite.[47]

J.D. Muhly has offered the most serious recent attack on Semitic traders in the Bronze Age Aegean,[48] and this must be dealt with in as much detail as the allotted space of this contribution will allow. His reasoning throughout is curiously one-sided. Why are 34 Mycenaean vases, out of 67 found in the 13th-century B.C. tomb at Sarafand, evidence of "the presence of Mycenaeans in the area" (M., 35), if some 40 oriental cylinder seals at Greek Thebes provide "no evidence for Phoenician traders in Greece" (M., 41)?

M. still believes that "LH IIIA and IIIB pottery in the Near East testifies to the extent of Mycenaean commercial relations in this period, though the other end of this trade is still quite vague" (M., 21-22), whereas the importance of copper from Cyprus to the Mycenaean economy is not vague at all. He admits the possibility that Mycenaeans imported perishable goods, suggesting grain (M., 36; to which I would add raw metals, in the sense that their recognizable shapes perish as soon as they are used); but he stresses that recognizable eastern objects in Greece, such as seals and scarabs, "hardly represent the products brought to Greece by Syrian merchants" (M., 36). This last is so obvious that I wonder why it was mentioned. What is not so obvious is his claim that "such objects represent the bric-a-brac brought back by the Mycenaean trader from his eastern journeys" (M., 36), including that on the Cape Gelidonya ship (M., 36, n. 130). M. shows no evidence, other than pottery, for this hypothetical Mycenaean trader, yet we have at least one trading vessel which carried not only

[43] R. de Vaux, review of *CG* in *RB* 77 (1970), 298-9.
[44] Catling, *op. cit.* (supra, n. 13), 85.
[45] A.M. McCann, review of *CG* in *AJA* 74 (1970), 106; G. Cadogan, *loc. cit.* (supra, n. 9).
[46] R. de Vaux, Zaccagnini, Catling, and probably Cadogan, in works cited above.
[47] J. Sasson, *JAOS* 86 (1966), 126-38; Zaccagnini, *op. cit.* (supra, n. 31), 165-6.
[48] J.D. Muhly, *Berytus* 19 (1970), 19-64. Hereafter cited as "M."

such "bric-a-brac" as a merchant's seal and religious talismans (scarabs and an astragal[49]), but also Near Eastern weights, stone hammers, mortars, a lamp, and bronzes more than half of whose prototypes are found in the Near East; its cargo, of ox-hide ingots, was one associated only with Near Eastern traders, in Egyptian tomb paintings, since 1400 B.C.

As this represents to Muhly a Mycenaean traders, a most serious question is posed for the nautical archaeologist. Are we to do away with all of our archaeological evidence merely to fit preconceived notions? Only a few sherds, none demonstrably from the Greek mainland, suggest that the ship was Mycenaean. Could we call it Sardinian or Egyptian to suit our whims?

The items in question are most similar to those found on other merchant ships of antiquity. We may compare the 7th-century A.D. wreck excavated at Yassi Ada, Turkey.[50] In its galley area were found a merchant's seal, religious items, weights, tools, lamps, a mortar, and coins. As these were all Byzantine, we assume that the ship was a Byzantine merchant vessel, regardless of its cargo. Why do we not suggest that it was an Arab ship carrying Byzantine bric-a-brac?

In moving to a discussion of the nature of Homeric references to the Phoenicians, Muhly questions the "presence of Phoenician ships in the waters of the Aegean and off the shore of Crete" in the Late Bronze Age (M., 42), saying that the scene surely has the world of the Iron Age as its background. But are not most Bronze Age weights on Crete based on Near Eastern weight standards? Did not the only Bronze Age ship excavated carry a partial cargo of bronzes which were largely Near Eastern in type, reflecting the Phoenicians of the *Iliad* who were "known as skilled craftsmen who work in metals and textiles" (M., 21)? And since such bronzes, and also copper ingots, reached the Aegean by ship, would they not possibly have been brought by the same traders who took copper to Egypt? We have not a single representation of a Mycenaean or Minoan fleet in Egyptian art, but we have the clear picture of the arrival of a Syrian fleet.[51] We have only one picture of ox-hide ingots arriving by ship anywhere, and the ship and merchant are clearly Syrian.[52]

One need not pursue this farther. Even if Homeric references to Phoenicians should reflect only the Iron Age, as Muhly believes, it of course proves nothing one way or another about Phoenician activity in the Bronze Age, which should be based on Bronze Age evidence. M.'s paper is thoroughly researched and is useful for its hundreds of footnotes, but careful reading shows that most of his arguments concerning the relations between Greece and the Near East in the Late Bronze Age are irrelevant or illogical. No amount of research has yet produced a Mycenaean trading ship, nor proof of Mycenaean dominance of sea trade. In saying that his paper "is but a detailed elaboration of ideas sketched in the grand manner by Rhys Carpenter" in 1933 (M., 64, n. 329), M. shows that he is still thinking in terms of theories based on evidence four decades old.

There remains the possibility that the Cape Gelidonya ship was Cypriot.[53] Certainly the cargo was Cypriot, and most of the personal possessions, although of Syro-Palestinian origin, were common enough on Cyprus in the 13th century. If it was Cypriot, however, it would only emphasize the strong Semitic influence I have proposed for Cyprus at this time, making Cypriot and Syrian merchantmen indistinguishable. And it would not change the overwhelming evidence of copper being carried to Egypt by Syrians; ox-hide ingots, in fact, are still depicted in Egypt after the reign of Amenhotep IV, when Cypriot contacts with Egypt, as recognized by Cypriot pottery, ceased.[54]

---

49 My suggestion that an astragal might have served as a religious talisman for sailors (*CG*, 133) has since been rendered more plausible by the discovery of ornamental astragals on ancient anchors and ships' stoves.
50 G.F. Bass, *Scientific American* 224, no. 2 (August, 1971) 23-33.
51 Norman de G. Davies and R.O. Faulkner, *JEA* 33 (1947), 40-46.
52 T. Säve-Söderbergh, *Four Eighteenth Dynasty Tombs* (Private Tombs at Thebes, I, Oxford 1957), 25-6, with pl. XXIII.
53 McCann, *loc. cit.* (supra, n. 45); also suggested to me conversationally by W.F. Albright and V. Karageorghis.
54 P. Aström, *Archaeologia Viva* (English ed.) 2, no. 3 (March-May 1969), 80.

Even so, all of my conclusions, both here and in *Cape Gelidonya*, may well give too little credit to the role of Cypriots in the affairs of their own island and the trade of their goods. Did the Cape Gelidonya ship carry "both Phoenician and Cypriote smiths on board," as suggested by P. Aström? [55] Was its crew "as varied as the merchandise it carried and the ports of calls it made," as R.S. Merrillees has written? [56] Is its nationality in some doubt because of the mixed nature of Cyprus, itself, as Catling has suggested, even if for a slightly later period than that to which I would assign the wreck? [57]

All of the evidence from the Cape Gelidonya wreck has been published, so that each scholar can form his own conclusions, which may or may not agree with mine. Clarification of some of the problems raised by the ship will come from the excavation of contemporaneous and slightly earlier ships known to lie on the floor of the Mediterranean.

Addendum:

Only after the above chapter had gone to press was I able to see a number of works which should be consulted by the reader. *Alasia I* (Mission archéologique d'Alasia, vol. IV, Paris, 1971) contains the publication of the statuette of a goddess on an ingot by H.W. Catling (pp. 15-32), mentioned above under representation no. 32; a discussion of ingots and the Cape Gelidonya wreck, by C.F.-A. Schaeffer (esp. pp. 547-560); a chapter on inscribed ingots from Enkomi, by O. Masson (pp. 449-455); and a study of the Cape Gelidonya tools and ingots, by Jaques Lagarce (esp. pp. 428-432).

The joint Boston Museum of Fine Arts – Harvard University excavation of Toumba tou Skourou in Cyprus now strongly suggests the export of Cypriot copper to Crete in the sixteenth century (E. Vermeule, *AJA* 76 [1972] 223-4), strengthening my theories in *CG* on pp. 76-7.

J.D. Muhly, "The Land of Alasia," *Praktikon tou Protou Diethnous Kyprologikou Synedriou*, vol. A (Leukosia, 1972), again dismisses my theories concerning Cape Gelidonya. The article must be read with care, as Muhly seems either not to have read all of the sources he cites, or not to have understood them.

I have not yet seen N.F. Parise, "Un'unità ponderale egea a Capo Gelidonya," *Studi Micenei ed Egeo-Anatolici* 14 (1971) 163-70.

---

55 *Ibid.*, 77.

56 R.S. Merrillees, "Cypriote Relations with the Bronze Age Aegean," in manuscript. Its publication will give a most sensible theory of traders sailing between the Aegean and Egypt (via Cyprus, Syria, and Palestine), "who bought and sold goods and offered services wherever there was a profit to be made . . . Even if the ruler of his homeport exercised some authority over his activities, a merchant would not presumably have had to balance exactly his sales of Mycenaean goods to Cyprus with sales of Cypriote goods to Greece."

57 Catling, *op. cit.* (supra, n. 13), 85.

fig. 1

fig. 5

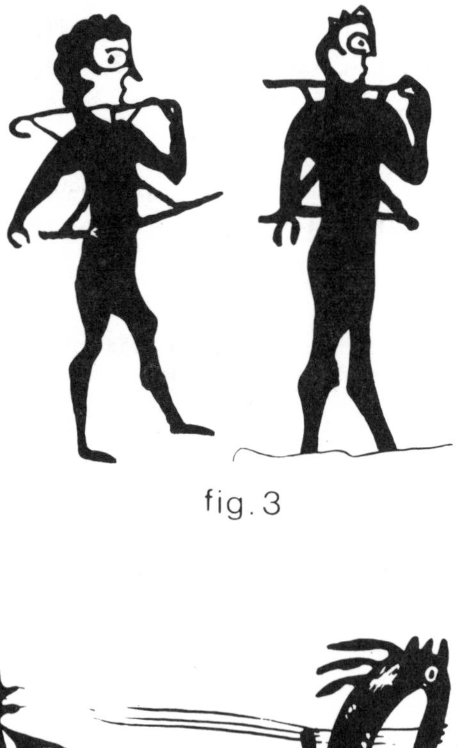

fig. 3

fig. 2

fig. 4

fig. 6

THE RELATIONSHIP BETWEEN THE HURRIAN SUFFIXES *-ne/-na* AND *-nni/e / -nna*[1]

Frederic Wm. Bush

The Hurrian suffixes *-ne-* and *-na-* are among the most ubiquitous suffixes the language possesses. In spite of this prolific use (or perhaps, indeed, because of it), they have not been easy to interpret, and several diverse interpretations have been suggested. F. Thureau-Dangin interpreted them as a definite article, singular

[1] The following symbols and abbreviations have been used in this study:

a) symbols:

– separates suffixal morphemes in morphemic transcription and individual cuneiform signs in normal transliteration.

\+ separates associative morphemes in morphemic transcription.

[. . .] indicates broken or uncertain readings in transliteration and morphemic transcription.

<. . .> indicates scribal omissions in transliteration and morphemic transcription.

! indicates an unusual or noteworthy reading of the cuneiform text.

In the morphemic transcription of Hurrian I have used the most common values of the signs of the various syllabaries (and the Ugaritic alphabet) used, without thereby intending any conclusions of a phonetic nature. Double writing in the syllabary has been represented by double writing in morphemic transcription. To avoid the confusion inherent in the representation of stop phonemes within and among the various syllabaries in use, I have arbitratily used the voiceless variant of the labial, dental, and velar stops in all positions. In order to represent the clear phonemic difference between *u* and *ú* in *ML*, I have represented the former by *-o-* and the latter by *-u-* in morphemic transcription without intending any phonetic conclusions thereby. I have used *-o-* in the morphemic transcription of forms from Nuzi and Boghazköy (where the syllabaries in use make no such distinction) whenever to do otherwise would obscure the comparison between apparently identical morphemes.

b) abbreviations – in addition to the standard abbreviations adopted for this volume, the following have been used:

Bush, *GHL* = F.W. Bush. *A Grammar of the Hurrian Language.* Unpublished Ph.D. dissertation, Brandeis University; Ann Arbor, Mich.: University Microfilms, 1964.

Friedrich, *AS* = J. Friedrich. *Altkleinasiatische Sprache. Handbuch der Orientalistik*, 1. Abteilung, 2. Band, 1. und 2. Abschnitt, 2. Lieferung, "Churritisch," 1-30.

KASD = the transliteration of *ML* by J. Friedrich in *Kleinasiatische Sprachdenkmäler*, No. 163, 1932.

Kronasser, *EhS* = H. Kronasser, *Etymologie der hethitischen Sprache* (Wiesbaden, Harrassowitz, 1963).

Laroche, *PRU* III = "Tablette bilingue accado-hourrite," and "Textes hourrites," in *Le Palais Royal d'Ugari* III. *Mission de Ras Shamra* VI (Paris, 1955) 311-35.

Laroche, *Ugaritica* V = E. Laroche, "Documents en langue hourrite provenant de Ras Shamra," in *Ugaritica* V. *Mission de Ras Shamra* XIV (Paris, 1968), 447-533.

ML = The so-called "Mitanni letter," text 200 in *VS* 12.

Speiser, *IH* = E.A. Speiser. *Introduction to Hurrian. AASOR* XX, 1940-41.

Ug. A-H. Bil. = The Akkado-Hurrian bilingual from Ugarit, published by E. Laroche and J. Nougayrol in *PRU* III (1955), 311-324.

Ug. Quad. Voc. = The Quadrilingual vocabulary from Ugarit, studied by E. Laroche in *Ugaritica* V, 448-62

and plural respectively.[2] In this he was followed by A. Goetze, who noted that these suffixes interchange in identical position with the pronominal suffixes,[3] strongly suggesting a "determining" force. On the other hand, J. Friedrich noted the parallel between the Hurrian *-ne-* suffix and the suffix *-ni-* of Urartean,[4] referring to both as "suffix-joining" particles.[5] E.A. Speiser in his systematic and basic study, *Introduction to Hurrian*, §§ 136-141, departed from all his predecessors by seeing the suffix *-ne-* primarily as a relational suffix in attributive constructions whose function is to mark the relation of the attribute or descriptive adjective to the head noun. Yet the evidence also forced him to acknowledge that "*-ne* seems to have developed in certain instances the value of a derivational element" (i.e., an element that modifies the root meaning of the word rather than relating it to the sentence).[6] Although Speiser's work in *IH* was a masterful synthesis, which has become the standard work in the field and most of which has stood the test of time, his view at this point was seriously defective and has been largely abandoned. In most of the treatments that followed Speiser's work, these particles have been understood as definite articles, sg. and pl., or determining particles, sg. and pl. So it is treated, for example, by Laroche, in both of his articles in *PRU III*, *passim*, and in the grammatical section of his long and useful study of the Hurrian materials from Ugarit in both alphabetic and syllabic cuneiform, published in *Ugaritica V*.[7] Here he introduces the section on the particles *-ne-* and *-na-* with the title "§ 8 L'article," and says: "Le suffixe déterminatif du hourrite, ou article, est au sg. *-(n)ni* 'le/la,' au plur. *-(n)na* 'les, ceux.' "[8] In J. Friedrich's most recent treatment of the subject in *AS*, he seems to have abandoned his former views of these particles and treats them as "eine Art bestimmten Artikels."[9]

The same is true of the systematic examination of the morphology of the Hurrian noun, using the techniques of sequence analysis, attempted by A. Kammenhuber.[10] In setting forth the suffixal sequence of the noun, she places the possessive suffixes in position one and then places in position two: "Artikel *-ne (-n(n)i)* des Sg. oder *-na* des Pl. (die beiden Formen schließen einander aus)."[11] Further on she is more explicit:

> "Der Überblick zeigt deutlich, daß sich *-ne* Sg.: *-na* Pl. mit THUREAU-DANGIN, Syria 12 (1931) S. 254 ff.; RA 36 (1939) S. 19 nur als bestimmter Artikel befriedigend deuten läßt – entgegen SPEISER, Intr. (1941) §§ 136-141, 159, 234 ("attributive particle", Übersetzung "one": "ones"). So erklärt sich unter anderem, daß Possessivsuffix und Artikel (ebenso wie in flektierenden Sprachen) nur selten nebeneinander bezeugt sind (s. schon GOETZE, RHA 39, 1940, S. 200 f.). Unter dem bisherigen Material findet sich eine Ausnahme in Prädikatsstellung Mit. IV 37: "und Asali ist der-mein(ig)e-Schreiber" = *tupšarr-iwwu-nni.*[12]

Now it is important to note that in the interpretations quoted above, Laroche and Kammenhuber identify the particles *-ne* and *-nni*, apparently seeing them as simple variants, with no discussion of the conditions under which either variant may or may not occur. This unexamined assumption is of crucial importance to Frau Kammenhuber, for on the basis of this identification she places the particles *-ne* and *-na* in position 2, following the possessive suffixes, basing her interpretation, apparently, on the single form *tupšarr-iwwu-nni.*[13]

---

2 See *Syria* 12 (1931):254-56.
3 See *RHA* 39 (1940):200 ff.
4 See *An Or* 12 (1935):122, 127, n. 6.
5 "suffixanreihenden Elements *-ni.*"
6 *IH*, § 137, section 5.
7 The grammatical summary is to be found on pp. 527-533.
8 *Ugaritica* V, 530.
9 *AS*, 13.
10 *Münchener Studien zur Sprachwissenschaft* 23 (1968), 49-79.
11 *Ibid.*, 50.
12 *Ibid.*, 57 f. Laroche adopts the same interpretation of *tupšarr-iwwu-nni*, see *PRU* III, 314, n. 2.
13 Cited in the quotation above. Note especially the analysis presented in the synopsis of forms given on pp. 57-58 of her article.

This same identification between *-ne* and *-nni* is also explicitly made by E. von Schuler *passim* in an article in which he interprets one of the uses of *-nni* as the formation of *nomina actoris.*[14]

This identification has regularly been made in Hurrian studies, cf. Speiser, *IH*, §§ 86a, 89, 137(6), 159.[15] It seems at first glance an obvious assumption to make (as we shall show), but there is evidence that seriously calls it into question in specific nominal patterns while there is further evidence that strongly suggests that the two are entirely different morphemes. The whole question needs a thorough investigation both to delineate specifically the dimensions of the problem and to ascertain what solutions can be determined at the present stage of interpretation.[16] Since it was under Dr. Cyrus H. Gordon's tutelage and instigation that I embarked on Hurrian studies, it is a great pleasure to dedicate this study to him.

§ 1 Evidence suggesting that the forms *-ne/-na* and *-nne/-nna* are allomorphs or at least very closely related.

To begin with it must be recognized that there is significant evidence that suggests that these forms function identically or very nearly so. Thus note the alternations:

(1) ^{m}*Tušrat[ta+n]* ^{KUR}*Ḫurwoḫe ewer-ne* [. . . *i*]*š* ^{m}*Immuria+n* ^{KUR}*Mašri[an]ni ewer-ne ML* 4:127-8.
"Tushratta, the Hurrian king, [?] Immuria, the Egyptian king . . ."

and:

(2) *Ište+n* ^{KUR}*Mašrianne-we* [^{KUR}*o*]*min-ne-we ē[wre-nn]ē*[17] *šen-iwwe+nna+an Ḫurwoḫe-ne-we* KUR$_{o}$<*m*>*in-ne-we ew[re-n]ne ML* 2:71-2
"I am king of the Egyptian land and my brother is king of the Hurrian land."

Unfortunately the context in example (1) above in *ML* 4:127-8 is too badly broken to ascertain what the sentence structure is,[18] so we cannot determine if there is a difference in syntactic function between the two forms.[19] Note that the plural of *ewre* in *ML* is uniformly *ewre-nna.*[20] Thus we can establish the pattern:[21]

---

[14] *RHA* 68 (1961), 19-23.

[15] The only exception I have found is the suggestion by A. Goetze that *-anni* should be understood as the suffix *-ni* plus an element *-an-* whose "function has not yet been sufficiently clarified," see *RHA* 54 (1952), 4 and n. 34.

[16] It should be emphasized that we will here be concerned only with the uses of these particles in which they are attached directly to the nominal root (or root + root-complement). (Forms of the type *ašḫošikkonne* are special case, see below.) There are a series of uses of *-ne/-na* in special positions further down in the nominal chain that will not be within the purview of this discussion. It is hoped that a study of these uses will appear elsewhere shortly.

[17] Although the form is broken here, the restoration hardly admits of doubt, cf. the form *ewre-nne-š KUB* XXVII 46 I 20. See Speiser *IH*, 65 and *JAOS* 60 (1940), 266. For *-nne* rather than *-nni* see n. 25 below.

[18] It seems highly unlikely that the phrases in 4:127-8 form an independent sentence. The sentence apparently begins with *anammi+lla+an* in 4:126, with the *lla* anticipatory of the noun phrases in question. The verb is apparently partly preserved in the broken form [. . .]*ú-rak-ki*, 4:127 (this reading, which is the footnote reading in *KASD*, is much more probable as a Hurrian word ending than the [. . .]*ú-gu-ki* of the text of *KASD*).

[19] Speiser suggested that *ewer-ne* was appositional and *ewre-nne* predicative on the basis of the two examples cited above, *JAOS* 60 (1940), 266 n. 5. However, this is not substantiated by the use of the forms with other words. Thus, there is nothing "predicative" about the form *ḫawuru-nne-ra ML* 3:101 (see the evidence below), which further is co-ordinated with *eše-ne-ra*, a form in *-ne*.

[20] Stem case: *ew-ri-en-na ML* 3:120; ergative: *ew-ri-en-na-šu-uš ML* 3:48; dative: *ew-ri-en-na-a-ša ML* 3:72.

[21] For forms and citations see Laroche, *Ugaritica* V, 451, 530 n. 4.

unaugmented	augmented with *-ni/e* or *na*	*-nni/e* or *-nna*
ewre	*ewer-ne*[22]	*ewre-nni/e*
	(ewer-na)	*ewre-nna*

The form **ewer-na* is not attested to my knowledge. However, compare the full pattern of forms from *haw(u)r--* "earth":[23]

unaugmented	augmented with *-ni/e* or *-na*	*-nni/e* or *-nna*
ḫa/uwr-[24]	*ḫawur-ne*	*ḫawuru-nne*[25]
	ḫawur-ra / ḫawur-na	*ḫawuru-nna*

This can also be exampled with the root *muš-*:[26]

unaugmented	augmented with *-ni/e* or *-na*	*-nni/e* or *-nna*
	muš-ni	*mušu-nni*[27]
muš-[28]	*muš-na*	*mušu-nna*

With *papa-* "mountain":[29]

unaugmented	augmented with *-ni/e* or *-na*	*-nni/e* or *-nna*
	papa-ni	*papanni*
(papa-)[30]	*(pap-na)*[30]	*papanna*

And with *eki--* "interior, inner part":[31]

unaugmented	augmented with *-ni/e* or *-na*	*-nni/e* or *-nna*
eki-[32]	*eki-ni*	*eki-nni*[33]
	eki-nni/e	*eki-nna*[33]

---

[22] In *Ugaritica* V, 530, Laroche argues for both *ewri-ni* and *ewir-ni*, citing examples from Boghazköy written *e-eb-ri-ni* or *ib-ri-ni*. However, in the light of the pattern we are establishing here, and the numerous examples at Boghazköy, where double writing of a consonant is not orthographically indicated, (see, e.g., the remarks by von Brandenstein, *ZA* 46 (1940), 85 and esp. n. 3.) these writings are best understood as examples of *ewre-nni/e* (with single writing of the *-n-*) or else as attempts to express orthographically the form *ewr̥ne* (with syllabic *-n*). For a discussion of syllabic *l* and *r* in Hurrian see *GHL*, 81-2.

[23] For citations see the list of forms in von Brandenstein, *ZA* 46 (1940), 86-7.

[24] Whether this form actually occurs is not clear. Von Brandenstein, *op. cit.*, lists the forms *ḫabrae* and *ḫabriaš*, but their relationship to *ḫawur-ne* is unclear. Whether his forms in *ḫubr-* or *ḫu-bur-* are related is also uncertain, but the form *ḫubrušḫe* "brazier, vessel," first deduced by von Brandenstein, *op. cit.*, 89, and now thoroughly confirmed by Laroche, *Ugaritica* V, 506 and esp. 513, suggests that they are. If so, then the stem-case form may be found amoung the forms *ḫubri*, *ḫubra*, and *ḫubru*. The form *ḫubri* could well represent *ḫubr-i* "his earth" (note *ḫubr-iaš* "their earth"), while *ḫubra* could well end in the locative/stative *-a*. This would then leave *ḫubru* as the stem-case. The analogy of *ewre*: *ewer-ne* and *ḫa/uwru*:*ḫawur-ne* is close. Speiser assumes a consonant stem *ḫawur-*, *IH* § 108.

[25] That the form here is *-nne*, not *-nni* is shown by the spelling *ḫa!-a-w -ru-un-ni-e-ra ML* 3:101. For the same conclusion with the forms that pattern as in § 2 below, see n. 36 below.

[26] For occurrences see A. Goetze, *JCS* 2 (1948), 137-8; E. Laroche, "Teššub, Ḫebat et leur cour," *JCS* 2 (1948), 124, n. 51; and F. Thureau-Dangin, *RA* 36 (1939), 22-23.

[27] The writings *mu-šu-ni* etc. at Boghazköy must be understood as single writing of the *-nn-*.

[28] Speiser lists *muš-* as the second example of a consonant stem, *IH* § 108.

[29] For occurrences see von Brandenstein, *ZA* 46 (1940), 89-98; and Thureau-Dangin, *RA* 36 (1939), 9,19.

[30] Neither the unaugmented form nor the form *pap-na* occurs to my knowledge, but derived forms do, e.g., *papaḫḫe*, from which Speiser posits the form *papa*, *IH* §§ 62, 103.

[31] For this meaning see Laroche, *Ugaritica* V, 457-8.

[32] For examples see Laroche, *ibid.*, and von Brandenstein, *ZA* 46 (1940), 98f.

[33] Whether the forms *ekunni/ekunna* cited by von Brandenstein, *op. cit.*, are related is obscure.

These are the only words known to me that exhibit the full pattern that we have examined here.[34] Since most have been known from the beginning of Hurrian studies, they have strongly suggested that the forms *-ni/e* vs. *-nni/e* and *-na* vs. *-nna* are simple variants, perhaps morpho-phonemically conditioned.[35] As noted above, this is the assumption that has regularly been made.

§ 2 Evidence for a different pattern with nouns in *-nni/e*.

Another series of nouns that end in *-nni/e* must, however, be sharply distinguished from the above set on several criteria. These nouns can be grouped in categories as follows:

I. Loan words from neighboring languages that are "hurrianized" by the addition of *-nni.*[36]

1. *Personal nouns.*

a. *Mašrianni* – "Egyptian," *ML* 1:10; 2:69, 71; 3:7, 117; 4:97, 105, 128.
b. *entanni* – "priestess"
c. *marianni* – "charioteer" cf. *mariannarti* – *ML* 3:32
d. *aššuššanni* – "equerry"
e. *šankunni* – "priest"
f. *Milkunni* – a divine name = ᵈISPAK.[37]

2. *Impersonal nouns.*[38]

a. *makanni* – "gift"[39] *ML* 2:15, 54; 3:58.
b. *kirkirianni* – "pine-cone"[40]
c. *maninni* – "collar, neck chain,"[41] at Qatna, Alalakh, and El Amarna.
d. *araššanni* – "a type of pigeon" (*CAD* "wild dove")[42] *EA* 22 I:22.
e. poss. *urukmanni*[43] – "ornament, decoration," at El Amarna. *EA* 22 I:47, II:42, 44.
f. poss. *šarianni* – "shield"[44]

---

34 A full examination of all the forms from Boghazköy would undoubtedly yield others. Unfortunately these are not readily available to me. Note also the two forms of *alummi-*, viz. *šie-ni alummi-ni IBoT* II 51 + *KUB* XXVII 46 I 29-30 vs. *tumuzzi ḫištarami-nni alummi-nni KUB* XXV 42 V 11 = 43:11, cf. Laroche, *RA* 54 (1960), 189.

35 For an attempt at setting forth the conditions, see Speiser, *IH*, §§ 86a, 89.

36 That these forms are properly also *-nne* rather than *-nni* is strongly suggested by forms in *ML* where the *-nne* element is not word-final, e.g., ᴷᵁᴿ*Ma-a-áš-ri-a-an-ni-e-wə*, 2:71 and ᴷᵁᴿ*M[i]-i-it-ta-a-an-ni-e-wə*, 3:104, etc. In the list that follows no documentation or suggested etymologies are given for those forms discussed in E. von Schuler, *RHA* 68 (1961), 19.

37 Possibly borrowed from Semitic *milku* "king, counsellor," see Laroche, *Ugaritica* V, 460.

38 The words listed here, in both the lists of personal and impersonal nouns, are those that seem reasonably certain. There are, however, a number of additional terms that occur in the texts from Hurrianized sites such as Qatna, Alalakh, Nuzi, the lists of gifts in *EA*, etc. Most of these are too uncertain to be included but their number is striking. A thorough study of the forms in *-nni* (most occurring in the Akkadianized nominative *-nnu*) that pertain to colors and attributes of horses has been given by H. Kronasser in *WZKM* 53 (1956-7), 181-192. These are rendered particularly probable by the clear Indo-aryan background of many of the terms having to do with equestrian matters found in texts of Hittite provenance but Hurrian origin (see the literature in Kronasser, *EhS*, 141 (§ 84). Kronasser holds to a Hurrian origin for most of the forms in *-nni* to be found in Hittite and Akkadian sources (*op. cit.*, p. 184). In *EhS*, 136, n. 1, he notes Landsberger's opinion, that all words in *-annu/-innu* in Akkadian are of foreign origin. With further data and greater understanding the list given here will doubtless be greatly expanded. Particularly promising are *paprunni* < Indic *babhru-* "reddish-brown," *pinkaranni* < Indic *piñjara-* "reddish-yellow," etc.

39 A loan word from Indic *magha-* "wealth, riches; gift." See H. Kronasser, *EhS*, 145. The word was in turn borrowed by the Akkadians from Hurrian, see *mag/kannu, mag/kannutu* "gift," von Soden, *AHw*, 574-5. The *-ann(u)* ending clearly shows the Hurrian intermediacy. See also *mgn* at Ugarit.

40 See Laroche, *PRU* III, 331 and *Ugaritica* V, 458; see also von Soden *AHw*, 475. Is the *-anni* ending here influenced by the assonance between the native Hurrian morpheme and the Akkad. form *kikkiriānu*?

II. Native hurrian words:[45]

1. *Personal terms.*[46]

a. (1) *taršu(w)anni* – "man, mankind," *ML* 4:122. See Laroche, *Ugaritica* V, 449 f.
b. (2) *uštanni* – "hero, young man."[47] See *Ugaritica* V, 454 f.
c. *urparinni* – "butcher," at Nuzi, *JEN* 326:8. See C.H. Gordon *Or NS* 5 (1936): 326-327. Note *urpumma epēšu* "to flay."
d. *ittaranni* – "runner, courier," at Boghazköy. See von Schuler *RHA* 68 (1961): 21f. Cf. *Ugaritica* V, 461.

2. *Impersonal terms.*

a. *wantanni* – "right (hand)," at Boghazköy. See *ZA* 46 (1940), 99-103 and Laroche, *RA* 54 (1960), 191f.
b. *urunni* – "behind, rear," at Boghazköy. See Laroche, *RA* 54 (1960), 189-192.
c. *šukkanni* – "distant, future(?)" *ML* 2:84; 3:30, 54, 56, 107, 114, 118; 4:32. See Speiser *IH*, 91.
d. KUR*Mittanni* – "Mittanni–(land)" *ML* 3:104. So also in the Amarna tablets, in the Akkadian texts from Boghazköy, and other Hurrian sites.
e. *ḫutanni* – "fate, fortune(?)" *ML* 1:102, 4:116. For the meaning see Laroche *JCS* 2 (1948), 124-6. For further forms at Boghazköy see *ibid.*, 125, n. 55. This form is especially significant given the related form *ḫute-na* in *Ḫutena Ḫutellura*, a divine epithet at Ugarit and Boghazköy, see *ibid.*
f. Among the divine names and epithets to be found in the *kalutiš* of Teššub and Ḫebat found at Boghazköy, collated and published by E. Laroche in "Teššub, Ḫebat et leur cour," *JCS* 2 (1948), 113-136, are a number that end in *-nni*, most of unknown meaning. Several of them also occur in the lists of gods and the offering lists to various gods found at Ugarit in alphabetic cuneiform, published by E. Laroche in *Ugaritica* V, 497-518. Note the following:

---

41 See J. Bottero, *RA* 43 (1949), 12. Knudtzon, *EA* II, 1462, and Wiseman, *Al. T.* 440:8. H. Kronasser, *EhS*, 145, suggests that it is a loan word from Indic *maṇi* "collar." The phrase *šinamni maninni iḫtumakki* occurs in *Al. T.* 440:8. Does *šinamni* here mean "double (-stranded)," i.e., *šin-am-ni*. Cf. *šin-am-u-na* at Nuzi, (*JEN* 634:23), which Goetze translates "twice," *Lang* 16 (1940), 170. Cf. also *šin-am-ummu epēšu* "to do twice," C.H. Gordon *Or NS* 7 (1938), § 4.17 (175) and *eman-am-umma epēšu* "to do tenfold," E.A. Speiser *JAOS* 59 (1939), 320 ff. For the causative force of *-an/-am*, see Laroche, *RA* 54 (1960), 199-201.

42 *CAD* A/1, 238, takes it as an Akkad. word – a variant of the Akkad. word *amurs/šānu* "type of pigeon." However, since it occurs in *EA* 22, which is a list of the dowry gifts from Tušratta to Amenophis III, it is better regarded as a Hurrian word borrowed from the Akkad. *amurs/šānu.*

43 Kronasser, *EhS*, 146, suggests Indic *rukma* "ornament, decoration."

44 Possibly from Akkad. *siriam/sariam* "shield, coat of mail," see von Brandenstein, *ZA* 46 (1940), 104-5.

45 Obviously such forms as *enni* < *en(e)+ni*, *ominni* < *omin(i)+ni*, *šenni* < *sen(a)+ni*, etc., formed from a stem ending in *-n* plus syncope of the stem-vowel before *-ni*, do not belong here. Neither do forms such as *allanni* < *allai+ni* and *attanni* < *attai+ni*, since the doubled *-nn-* ist most likely due to assimilation, contrary to Speiser, *IH* § 68. In addition forms such as *ḫenni/e* "now" and *anni* "this" obviously involve stems, not the suffix *-nni/e.*

46 Possibly one could add *ušrianni* "crown prince" (?) = *mar šarri* Virolleaud, *Syria* 21 (1940), 253 ff. and *urianni* "marshall"(?) which occur among the Hurrianized titles of Hittite court officials studied by A. Goetze, *RHA* 54 (1952), 1-14.

47 If Laroche, *Ugaritica* V, 454 is correct in identifying the stem as *uštai*, a diphthong stem like *attai* and *allai*, then perhaps it does not belong here, see n. 45 above. However, the context he cites from Boghazköy is not free of difficulty. Since the first two terms are augmented by *-ne*, (*ušḫune ewerne*), one would surely expect *uštanni*, and the **-a* vowel on *šarra* needs explaining. Further, since Ug. Quad. Voc. gives the equation *ewerne* = *šarrum* = *malku*, then are not the two terms *ewerne* and *šarra*, as interpreted, completely redundant? The form *uštan* that he cites from *ML* 4:91 is best understood as *ušta-* plus the associative *-an*, yet note the associative *-màn* on the following word. Further, the form *uštanni-ni-bi* (to be discussed below) makes the development *uštai-ni* > *uštanni* difficult.

(1) *atanni* – *JCS* 2:122, 129.
(2) *Ḫumunni* – *Ugaritica* V, 503, 525 n. 3. *.ḫmn*, *ḫmn-d*, and *ḫmnn-d*.
(3) *šalanni* – *JCS* 2:130; *Ugaritica* V, 503, 523, *šln-d* and *šlnn-št*.
(4) *tu(w)enni* – *Ug. Quad. Voc.* = dUTU = Ug. *ym* "day," *Ugaritica* V, 460. Cf. *JCS* 2:116, 122, 131.
(5) *ušunni* – *JCS* 2:120; *Ugaritica* V, 507. *užn* and *užn-d*.

3. Verbals "nominalized" by the suffix *-nni/e*. A series of forms clearly verbal in origin are nominalized by the suffix *-nni/e*. The following have thus far been noted:[48]

a. *amm-oš-i-kk-o-nne* – *KUB* XXVII 38 III:20.
b. *ašḫ-oš-i-kk-o-nne* – Boghazköy texts, *passim*.
c. *ḫaš-i-kk-o-nne* – *KUB* XXXII 19 I:19.
d. *ḫill-oš-i-kk-o-nne* – *ML* 4:4, 11.
e. *kat-i-kk-o-nne* – *ML* 4:2; *KUB* XXXII 19 I:21.
f. *wirarri-kk-o-nne* – Nuzi *HSS* XV 103:18.
g. *wur-i-kk-o-nne* – *ML* 3:9; *KUB* XXXII 19 I:20.

The verbal base of these forms is patent. The pattern is:

Verbal Root	+	tense marker	+	transitive[49] class marker	+	verbal negative[50]	+	?[51]	+	nominalizing suffix
[R]	–	[*oš* – past / none – present]	–	[*i*]	–	[*kk*]	–	[*o*]	–	[*nni*]

Note that only transitive verbs are so far exampled in both present and past tense forms. That these are nominal forms, however, admits of no doubt whatsoever given their clear augmentation with nominal suffixes in the following forms from *ašḫošikkonne* : *ašḫošikkonne-na*, KUB XX 93 VI:9 etc.; *ašḫošikkonne-ne-we-na-šta*, *KUB* XII 44 II:6; *ašḫošikkonne-we-na*, *KUB* XXVII 14 II:6 etc., and the fact that *wirarrikkonne* is a term descriptive of horses. Their interpretation, however, is yet unclear.[52]

Now, we began this list with the statement that the forms just enumerated must be sharply distinguished from the set whose pattern of forms was set forth in § 1 above, on the basis of several criteria. These criteria are as follows:

---

[48] Another form that could possibly be included is *amumikuni*, *KBo* V 6 II 17. So von Schuler, *RHA* 68 (1961), 23, n. 13.

[49] For an interpretation of these vocalic verbal class markers, see *GHL*, 194-198. There are, of course, still problems to be worked out in the verbal system as a whole, but the identification of the *i*-vowel here as the indicator of the transitive verbal class admits of no doubt, see *GHL*, 197-8.

[50] This suffix proves to negate subject-action constructions, i.e., either the doer of the verbal action or the victim of the verbal action only is present. If both are present the whole morphological pattern is different. See provisionally *GHL*, 201-205.

[51] That this vowel is morphologically distinct (force yet undetermined) can be shown by the fact that it can be present without the *-nni* suffix: *išuḫ-oš-i-kk-o+nna* *ML* 4:92 and that the vowel can vary in otherwise identical construction: *tatuḫḫul-i-kk-i+nna+an* *ML* 3:4. It would seem most probable that the tense suffix *-oš-* would be irrelevant in this connection.

[52] Ever since Speiser, *IH*, § 186, they have been interpreted as "agent-nouns," (see, e.g., von Schuler, *RHA* 68 (1961), 21 and most recently Friedrich, *AS*, 13, § 20). This interpretation was strongly favored by Speiser's proposal to render the suffixal complex *-ošikkonne* "one who has performed a certain act repeatedly," *IH*, 151. However, the discovery that the element *-kk-* was not a state element with a meaning in the range "iterative-durative" as he interpreted it (*IH*, 150), but a verbal negative, has completely changed the picture. See for example Laroche's treatment of the three forms c., e., and f. in the list above in *RA* 54 (1960), 194 and note our brief comments as to function below.

First, although the number of occurrences of the nominals listed in § 2 above is yet too few in most instances to speak with much certainty, they do not seem to exhibit either the unaugmented forms nor the forms with single *-n-* noted for the nouns that exhibit the pattern set forth in § 1 above.[53] Although many of them exhibit plurals in *-nna*, these can be understood as from *-nn(i)* + *na* > *-nna*, especially in view of the sporadic examples of *-ən-ni-ni* and *-ən-ni-na* to be discussed below.

Secondly, there is one instance where the *-nn-* of forms in *-nni* remains before the addition of the collective root-complement *-arti*,[54] a phenomenon totally at variance with the nature and position of the suffix *-ne/na*. This is *mariann-arti+l+an*, *ML* 3:32.[55]

Thirdly, there are an increasing number of examples of these nominals in *-nni* which are augmented by the suffixes *-ne* and *-na*.[56] Note the following examples:

1. with *ašḫošikkonne:*

   a. *ašḫošikkonne-na* – Laroche cites this form in the list of divine epithets published in *JCS* 2 (1948), 113-136, 116 no. 19, and 122 no. 16. There he cites *KUB* XX 93 VI:9; XXV 44 V:9-10; XXVII 8 obv 17; XXXII 93:9, 84 rev 3-4; XXXIV 102 II:23-24.
   b. *ašḫošikkonne-ne-we-[na]* – *KUB* X 27 III:9.
   c. *ašḫošikkonne-ne-we-na-šta* – *KUB* XII 44 II:6.

2. *urunni-na* – *KUB* XXX 26 IV:5, Laroche *RA* 54 (1960), 190.

3. *uštanni-ne-we* – *KUB* XXVII 42 I:23. Laroche *Ugaritica* V, 455.

4. *marianni-na* – at Alalakh, texts 128 and 129.

5. DINGIR.MEŠ-*na-še-ni šelanni-ni* – *KUB* XXIV 13 I:1 cited by Goetze *RHA* 39 (1940), 202 recalls the *šalanni* of Teššub and Ḫebat studied by Laroche *JCS* 2 (1948), 116, 122, 130.

6. The same phenomenon lies behind the writings *šlnndm* 274:5, *šlnnšt* 261:11, i.e., *šalanni-ni-da-ma* and *šalanni-na-šta* as over against *šlnd (šalanni-da)*, *atnd (attanni-da)* etc. in the alphabetic texts at Ugarit, Laroche, *Ugaritica* V, 503, 523, 529, (especially in light of 5.).

7. So also *en-ḫmnnd* 172:5, i.e., *eni-ḫumunni-ni-da*, *Ugaritica* V, 525, nos. (10-11) and n. 3.[57]

8. Finally, note *ḫawurunni-ni* – *KUB* XXIX 8 II 49, which belongs to the nouns in section § 1![58]

[53] Writings of these forms in documents from Hurro-Akkadian and Hurro-Hittite sites such as *EA*, Boghazköy, Mari and Nuzi, etc., such as *entani*, *mariani*, *uštani*, etc., must be understood as single writing of a double *-nn-* in keeping with the widespread practice in cuneiform writing at those sites. This practice is well-known for Akkadian. For the same practice in the material from Boghazköy, see the remarks in n. 22 above. This assumption is obviously open to question and needs much more documentation to be regarded as established. However, in its favor is the whole pattern of the forms in *-nni/e* here being set forth.

[54] See the discussion in *GHL*, 109-10.

[55] The *-nn-* in *irinn-arti+l+an*, *ML* 3:72, must be part of the root, as is shown by *irin<n>!-iwwaš+ša+an*, *ML* 3:123. This form is written *i-i-ri-i-in-iw-wa-aš-ša-ā*[*-an*]. The least familiarity with the orthography of *ML* shows that it must be corrected to *i-i-ri-i-in-<ni->iw-wa-aš-ša-ā*[*-an*]. The form *i-ri-i-in-na-ar-ti-iw-wu-ú-a*, *ML* 3:72, confirms the fact.

[56] The first time these were encountered, the natural explanation was dittography, so Thureau-Dangin, *RA* 36 (1939), 23, n. 3, 24, n. 2. The more frequently they appear, the more difficult does this become.

[57] The remark of Laroche on p. 503, "La gemination *šlnn-* en face du plus fréquent *šln-* s'observe aussi dans l'hapax *en-ḫmnn-d* (172,5), en face de *ḫmn*; elle n'a sûrement aucune valeur morphologique," must be corrected in the light of the above. The uniform practice of the Ugaritic alphabetic orthography is the lack of indication of consonantal length. His comment to the same effect in the grammar section, p. 529, must also be corrected. The form *šlnndm*, 274:5, must be added to the forms of *šln-* in the lexical list, p. 538.

[58] Such augmentations are not exampled in *ML*, but the examples of *-nni* are few there. Since I do not have ready access to the texts from Boghazköy, the examples above have been taken from published transliterations in various articles. Without doubt a careful examination of the Hurrian portions of the Boghazköy texts would increase the above examples considerably.

§ 3 The evidence for the existence of an *associative -nni.*

It has been known since *IH* §§ 216, 221 that an associative element[59] *-nni* also existed in Hurrian as well as the nominal suffix *-nni*. The evidence for such seems decisive given the following passage:

ḫaš-oš-au̯u+n[60] *pisant-oš-i+tta+an*
"I have heard it and I have rejoiced.

ai+ma+nin šen-iww-uš anam tan-oš-i-w-a+lla+nni
if indeed (?) my brother thus has not done them + ?

ḫisuḫ-ul-(i)-l-e+tta+an tiššan ML 4:9-11
then I shall be very grieved."

Whatever problems exist with some of the grammatical details, the basic translation is certain. The 3 pl. pronominal associative *-lla* in all probability refers to the goals of the two previous transitive sentences in lines 6-7, whose subject is the ergative[62] *šen-iww-uš* "my brother." Since the *-nni* element follows the clearly associative *-lla*, it too must be an associative. Unfortunately, all the other possible occurrences of this *-nni* element are either in obscure or ambiguous contexts. These are the following:

a. on verbs:
(1) *ai+n tupp-o+nni ML* 2:86-87 – obscure context
(2) . . .]*+man šar-oš-i+nni ML* 4:79 – totally broken context
(3) . . .] GUŠKIN *šua-šše-na anzukal-la ak-oš-a+nni ML* 2:60 -- broken and obscure context

b. on nouns:
(4) *awe-šše+nin wurra-nni šue anti pis-o+nin ML* 3:3-4 – obscure context
(5) [. . .]*mam turupi-nni ML* 1:15 – totally broken context
(6) ᵐ*Asali+nna+an tupsarr-iwwu+nni kip-oš-u-šš-i*(?) *ML* 4:37-38

c. on particles:[63]
(7) *au̯u+nni+man anni turupi eti-š tar-ra-š(w)a ḫuš-ia-šše ML* 3:121-122 – obscure passage

---

[59] The associative suffix is differentiated by the fact that it can be appended to any of the three types of Hurrian words, i.e., nominals, verbals, or particles, but it does not function on the word level, relating rather to the syntax of the sentence.

[60] The morphemic division of the form *-ša-ú-ú-un* is either *-au̯u+n* or *-au̯+un* (so Speiser, *IH*, 163). In the light of W. Farber, *Or* 40 (1971), 29-66, esp. 42 f., where he shows that the 3 sg. pronominal associative has either the form *-n-* or *-nna-*, the first is preferable. He notes on p. 62 that he does not list the "copula" (i.e., the 3 sg. pronominal associative used as a copula), when it occurs as /n/ at word end.

[61] For the analysis of the form, see *GHL*, 227 ff. and n. 122.

[62] The term "ergative" is preferable to "agentive," not because of some presumed connection with the Caucasian languages, but because, in the interests of precise and unambiguous linguistic terminology, "passive" and "agentive" are best limited to those languages in which a full transformation between "active" and "passive" systems is possible. That is, the "active" statement, consisting of a performer of the activity, an activity, and a recipient of the activity, can be fully transformed into a "passive" statement in which the recipient of the activity becomes the subject of the verb, now in the passive, while the performer of the activity becomes the agentive tagmeme of the passive verb. Since Hurrian is incapable of the "active" statement, the term "passive" is best avoided and "ergative" employed. For a succinct and clear statement on the subject, including a discussion of Hurrian and Urartean, see Francis I. Anderson, "Passive and Ergative in Hebrew," in *Near Eastern Studies in Honor of William Foxwell Albright*, 1971, 1-15.

[63] The only other possibility for a *-nni/e* form on a particle is the word *awe+nne+nin*, *ML* 4:17. However, this cannot be the element *-nni*, for its correlative is *awe+nna+nin*, *ML* 4:24, each introducing contrasting contin-

Only a few comments can be made with any confidence on these forms. In (1) *tupp-o-nni* is probably verbal. The previous sentence is complete and translatable, while the word immediately succeeding seems to introduce the next clause (*kimr-a+tta+an* "and I. . ."). In (3) the form *ak-oš-a+nni* is most probably transitive. The sentence clearly begins with *ai+l+an* "and + if + them" in *ML* 2:58, with the plural nouns that follow expressing the goal. One finds "four (*tumni*) objects of some kind (*iššiḫḫe-na*), two (*šin*) ivory (*šiniperuḫḫe*) objects of some kind (the word is not preserved), and some kind of golden (GUŠKIN) objects (*šuašše-na anzukal-na*)." The sentence immediately following begins *inu+tta+an*, "so I . . .," contains the word "dowry" (*niḫar-*) and ends with "rejoice very much" (*piš-ost-a teonae tiššan*). The *-a*, then, of the form *ak-oš-a* is best understood as the 3 s. ergative morpheme "by him," referring to either "Mane" or "my brother" of the first two sentences in *ML* 2:57-58. However that may be, both *tupp-o-* and *ak-oš-a-* are clearly the verbs of their respective sentences, so that *-nni* here must be the associative *-nni* and not the nominalizing *-nni* of § 2. 3. above.

With the nouns, the forms in (4) and (5) are totally ambiguous as to the character of the *-nni* element. In (5) *turupi-nni* clearly involves a nominal stem, *turupi-* "need, danger,"[64] but the clearly contrasting *turupinn-u-kku* "there is no danger(?)" in *ML* 1:17 suggests that we are here dealing with a root-complement. The form *tupšarr-iwwu+nni* will be dealt with below in § 4, "Conclusions."

Finally, the form *au̯unni* in (7) is most tentative for the *-nni* associative on a particle, suggested by the particle *au̯ (a-u)* at Boghazköy, translated by Speiser "lo, behold."[65]

That an element *-nni* occurs in associative position on verbs, and possibly also on nouns and particles, requires that we posit the existence of an associative *-nni*, meaning yet undetermined. This must be taken into consideration as a possibility when interpreting individual instances of the *-nni* element.

§ 4 Conclusions.

Due to the scarcity of material and the yet uncertain state of the interpretation of Hurrian grammar and lexicography, no definitive solution to the problem can, of course, be attempted. But the following gains can be said to have been made as a result of this investigation. First, there is little doubt that the suffixes *-ne* and *-na* function as a k i n d o f d e f i n i t e a r t i c l e when attached d i r e c t l y to the nominal root (or root + root-complement), especially given the evidence of the Ug. Quad. Voc. where *ewre* = Akk. *bēlu* = Ug. *ba'lu*, "lord," whereas *ewer-ne* = Akk. *šarrum* = Ug. *malku*, "king."[66] What is not clear is whether the type *ewre-nne* is simply an allomorph or imparts some other nuance of meaning (closely related apparently, see the discussion of the forms in § 1 above). It is perhaps significant to note that the alternation *-nne-/-ne-* or *-nna-/-na-* is never clearly attested anywhere else but in the position directly attached to the root (or root + root-complement); in all other positions where the interpretation is clear only *-ne-/-na-* is attested. Hence, in the light of the uncertainty as to what difference exists, if any, between forms in *-ne/-na* and those in *-nne/-nna* in § 1 above, the difference in the nominal patterns set forth in § 1 and § 2 above, and the clear existence of an associative suffix *-nni*, § 3; it seems best to keep these suffixes separate until such time as further evidence can decide the question of rela-

---

gent clauses having to do with the communication of "malicious gossip" (*tiwe šurwe*), about Tušratta or his land to the Pharaoh in the first section, 4:17-23, and the reverse in the second, 4:24-29. Given the alternation *ya+lla+nin* vs. *ya+lle+nin* (e.g., 1:96 vs 1:98, also introducing contrasting statements), *awe+nne+* and *awe+nna+* must contain variant forms of the 3 sg. pronominal associative *-nna* (contrary to *GHL*, 242). This fits Speiser's suggested translation "anyone, someone," *IH* § 115, well. *awe-* may well represent the personal relative as over against *ya-/ye-* impersonal. (This can no longer use Ugaritic *d-* vs. *dt* as support, as in *GHL*, 370, n. 16, given the clearer understanding of these pronouns in C.H. Gordon, *UT*, §§ 6.23-7.

64 See Speiser, *JAOS* 59 (1939), 313 f.

65 Following Forrer, see *IH*, 90, § 127.

66 See *Ugaritica* V, 451, no. 6.

tionship. On this basis alone it is certainly precarious and premature to assign the particles to position 2 in the nominal suffixal sequence as does A. Kammenhuber, on the evidence of *tupšarr-iwwu-nni ML* 4:37.[67]

This is the case on several grounds. Besides the uncertainty of the identification of the nominal suffixes *-ne* and *-nne* just discussed, it is most probable that in this instance we have to do with the a s s o c i a t i v e *-nni,* not the nominal suffix at all. In her interpretation of this passage Fr. Kammenhuber notes that the definite article and the possessive suffixes seldom appear together, but that "unter dem bisherigen Material findet sich eine Ausnahme in Prädikatsstellung Mit. IV 37: 'Und Asali ist der-mein(ig)e-Schreiber' = *tuppšarr-iwwu-nni.*"[68] But, that interpretation does not take into account the whole clause. Apart from the clause involving *tupšarr-iwwu-nni*, the rest of the paragraph in *ML* 4:30-39 is one of the clearest passages in *ML*. Before the clauses in question, it reads "Now then all the things which my brother has declared (and) desires (30-31) these I have done tenfold, and my brother's heart I have not grieved in a single (?) insignificant (?) matter (31-33). I have given my brother's wife, who is pleasing to my brother's heart (3:33-34).[69] Now, Mane is my brother's envoy. Now, Kelia and Artešsupa and Asali are my envoys (3:35-36)." The remaining clauses are:

(1) ᵐ*Kelia+n+an talami*

"Kelia+cop.+conn. chief (?)," i.e., "Kelia is chief (?),"

(2) ᵐ*Asali+nna+an tupšarr-iwwu+nni kip-u/oš-u-šš-i*

"Asali+cop.+conn. scribe-my + ? ? "

(3) *šeniwwa-ta+lla+an niroš-ae tiššan pašš-oš-au̯*

"my brother-to+them+conn. good-adv. very I-have-sent-off"

(4) *šen-iww-u(š)+lla+an wur-et-a*

"my brother+them+conn. will-see.", i.e., "I have sent them off to my brother in a very excellent state[70] and my brother will see them."

First note how clearly clause (2) is set off by the sentence connectives, showing that any interpretation of it *must* take the form *kip-u/oš-u-šš-i* into account. This form must be an abstract noun formed by the suffix *-šš-* and must be related to the form *ki-i-pa-aš-ši-iw-wə ML* 2:114, which is modified by ᴷᵁᴿ*omin-iw[wu]-u̯e-na,* "the *kipašši*'s of my land," clearly revealing the nominal character of the form.[71] *Kip-u/oš-u-šš-i* must contain the nominal root-complement *-u/oš*[72] plus the vowel *-u-*.[73] It cannot be a verbal form, for all clear examples of verbs nominalized by *-šš-* in *ML* end in *-šše* when word final. Its meaning is unkown.[74] Note that it is not augmented by the suffix *-nni* and yet must be descriptive of *tupšarr-iwwu-*. All these facts militate most strongly against Kammenhuber's interpretation of the suffix as the definite article and it must be understood as the associative *-nni.* Hence it cannot determine the relative order of the article and the possessive suffixes. There are,

[67] *MSS* 23 (1968), 50 and esp. 57-59.

[68] *Ibid.*, 58.

[69] The text here must be emended to *še-e-ni-iw-wə-ú-e-ni-e-en<-na> ti-ša-an-na,* cf. the almost identical passage in *ML* 3:13-14. Cf. *IH* § 164 and *GHL*, 147.

[70] See the discussion in *GHL*, 345, n. 170.

[71] Cf. also the form *ḫi[šm]ašš-iw[wə-* in broken context in *ML* 2:115. These three forms seem to be the only examples of abstract nominals in *-šš-* in *ML*. All the other examples of abstract nominals in Hurrian come from other texts.

[72] See *GHL*, 112, no. (9) and *IH*, 132, no. (6).

[73] This vowel occurs with nominalized verbs whose root ends in the complement *-mpu*, cf. *a-lum-pu-ú-uš-še ML* 4:107, [. . . *-š]i-im-pu-ú-uš-še ML* 4:108 etc., as well as the form *ka-na-pu-ú-uš-šu-uḫ-ḫa ML* 2:25.

[74] E. Laroche in *PRU* III, 314, attempts to take it as a nominalized verb in the perfect (*-oš*) from the root *kip-* "to put, place." However, the form he is discussing in the Ug. A-H Bil. is written *kí-e-en,* which is certainly *ke+n* and must be connected with *ML kep+an,* always written GI-*pa-n* -, with the sign GI = ke as always in *ML*, see *GHL*, pp. 20, 22 and 41. Compare this with the *ki-i-* of the form in question. The root-complement *-p-* is well known. (*GHL*, 183) as is the causative *-an-* (*GHL*, 179 f.)

however, several forms in *ML* that very clearly carry both the definite article and the possessive suffix. Thus the phrase ^{d}*e-en-ni-iw-wa-a-še-e-en* ^{d}*Te-e-eš-šu-up-pè* ^{d}*A-m[a-]a-nu-ú-e*, *ML* 2:77, must be ^{d}*en-n(a)-iwwaš-(w)e+n* ^{d}*Teššup-we* ^{d}*amanu-ṷe* "of our gods, of Teššup, of Amanu."[75] With the singular note the following in a fairly clear passage: *inu+me+nin šer-ne-tan* [DINGIR][76] *en-ne-p-tan šeḫar-n(e)-iwwaš*[77] *ḫutann-iwwaš šar-ill-ett-a*, *ML* 4: 115-16, "As indeed our fate (?) (and) our destiny[78] will have been inquired from thy god (and) from the Bull (of Teššub)."[79] The agreement between [d]*en-ne-p-tan* "from thy god" and *šer-ne-tan* "from the Bull (of the weather-god)," both with *-ne*, makes the interpretation virtually certain.[80]

The results clearly show that, when the "article" *-ne/-na* and the possessive suffixes do occasionally occur together on a nominal, the article occupies position 1 and the possessive suffix position 2. Hence, Fr. Kammenhuber's sequential analysis must be corrected accordingly.

Finally, one result can be said to be certain as regards the use of the suffix *-nne/i* on nominals. In a significant number of cases it forms adjectives that pattern fully with the forms in *-ḫe*. Consider the following examples involving the adjectival *Ḫurwoḫe* "Hurrian," and the *-nne* forms *Mašrianne* "Egyptian" and *Mittanne* "Mitannian," in contrast with the clearly substantival *Mizir* "Egypt":

(1) ^{m}*Tušrat[ta+n]* ^{KUR}*Ḫurwoḫe ewer-ne . . .*
^{m}*Immuria+n* ^{KUR}*Mašri[an]ne ewer-ne ML* 4:127-8

(2) ^{KUR}*Mašrianne-we* [^{KUR}*o*]*min-ne-we ē[wre-nn]ē*
Ḫurwoḫe-ne-we ^{KUR}*o<m>in-ne-we ew[re-n]ne ML* 2:71-2

(3) ^{f}*Tatuḫepa+n* ^{m}*Tušratta-we* ^{KUR}*Mittanne-we ewri-we šala* ^{m}*Imurria-we* ^{KUR}*Mizir-ne-we-ne-we ewri-we ašti+nna ML* 3:103-5

"Tatuḫepa is the daughter of Tušratta, of the Mitannian lord, the wife of Immuria, of the lord of Egypt . . ."

(4) *šena -wə-š+an* ^{m}*Nimmuria-š* ^{KUR}*Mizir-ne-we-ne-š ewri-š ML*:84-5

"And by my brother, by Nimmuria, by the lord of Egypt . . ."

Note how *Mašrianne* and *Ḫurwoḫe* pattern identically in examples (1) and (2).[81] Particularly instructive are examples (3) and (4). In (3) ^{KUR}*Mittanne-we ewri-we*, "of the Mitannian lord," contrasts sharply with ^{KUR}*Mizir-ne-we-ne-we ewri-we*, "of the lord of Egypt." When the substantive *Mizir* rather than the adjectival *Mašrianni* is used, it must be placed in the genitive, *Mizir-ne-we*, "of Egypt" in order to express the relationship of appurtenance to the head noun *ewri* "lord." Since the head noun is also in the genitive in (4), the modifier,

[75] Compare the expression of the plural with the determinative in the immediately preceding line: DINGIR. MEŠ *e-e-ni-iw-wə-šu-uš*.

[76] Friedrich, *KASD*, reads [DINGIR.MEŠ]. If Schroeder's facsimile represents the actual tablet, the space involved is not determinative either way. The interpretation, however, excludes the possibility of MEŠ.

[77] This could be *šeḫar-n(a)-iwwaš*, cf. *šeḫar-na+lla+an*, *ML* 1:103.

[78] For *ḫutanni* "destiny, fate," see Laroche, *JCS* 2 (1948), 124-126.

[79] For this meaning, "Bull of the weather-god," see Schroeder, *AfK* 2 (1924), 70 and E. Ebeling, *Or* 23 (1954), 126. Note how Tušratta continues in the next line "Let our gods, Teššup and Aman, our lords (and) our fathers, guide us both, the two of us."

[80] Notice in the two examples just given, how the known morphology of the pronominal suffixes completely fits together with and corroborates the interpretation. With the l.p. sing. suffix *-iwwə*, the vowel of the previous morpheme always elides, as in ^{d}*en-n(a)-iwwaš-(w)e+n ML* 2:77, whereas the 2 sg. suffix *-w/p-* is always added to the vowel of the previous morpheme, as in [d]*en-ne-p-tan*, *ML* 4:16. See *GHL*, 116, Speiser, *IH* 103-4, and Kammenhuber, *MSS* 23 (1968), 51.

[81] So also in *ML* 2:68-9; 3:6-7; and 3:113, 117-18.

Mizir-ne-we, adds the "case" ending of the head noun by the characteristic "suffix-duplication" of Hurrian. The same is true in the ergative in (5). Contrast this with the pattern of *Mittanne* in (3) and *Mašrianne* in (2).[82]

The same pattern is observable with *šukkanni* "far, distant, future."[83] In each context, where the form occurs in *ML*, it stands before the noun (i.e., in attributive position).[84] The passage *šukkanne-wa+n tiw-i-wa+n eti-tan*, ML 2:84, is revealing. If *šukkanne* was substantival it would have to pattern like *Mizir* above, i.e., *šukkanne-we-ne-wa+n*, since the head noun of the phrase is in the dative "case."

Possibly the same pattern is observable with the form *urunni* "behind, after," which functions as the antonym of *api-* "before, in front of," see Laroche *RA* 54 (1960), 189-90, but certainty is not attainable since the ending of the form is broken.[85] However, in the same discussion Laroche presents a section of a ritual giving the ceremony of consecration of a chair or throne to the goddess Ḫebat.[86] Here in successive passages the following phrases occur:

(1) *ana ukri wantanni awantalli*, to the right (*wantanni*), front (*awantalli*) foot (*ukri*)";
(2) *ana ukri wantanni uruntalli*, "to the right, rear (*uruntalli*) foot";
(3) *ana ukri šapḫali awantalli*, "to the left (*šapḫali*), front foot";
(4) *ana ukri saphali uruntalli*, "to the left, rear foot."

In this passage *wantanni* "right (-hand)" is clearly the antonym of and patterns identically with *šapḫali* "left (-hand)".

Finally the verbs nominalized by *-nne*, § 2.3, must be considered. Unfortunately, these are almost all in obscure context. However, note the form ANŠE.KUR.RA *wirrarikkonne* at Nuzi, *HSS* XV 103:18. This form, an attribute of horses, is parallel with Akkadian and Hurro-Akkadian adjectival forms: *ṣalmu* "black," 103:10, 20; *dannu* "large, powerful," 103:5, 16; *amkamannu* "? ,"[87] 103:9, 12, 13, 22, 24; *zilukannu* "? "; and *zirramannu* "very swift (?)"[88] 103:7, 21.[89] The forms in *ML* are all in obscure context,[90] but do not seem to be in the least adjectival in force.[91] The forms discussed by Laroche in *RA* 54 (1960), 194 are also in rather

---

[82] Having not observed this "adjectival" function of *Mittanne*, I had previously emended *Mittanne-we* in *ML* 3: 104 to *Mittanne-we*<*-ne-we*>, to agree with *Mizir-ne-we-ne-we* in the next line, assuming haplography. In the light of this analysis, one must translate the phrase KUR*Mizir-ne-we* KUR*omin-ne-we allai* in *ML* 1:62 as "lady of the land, (lady) of Egypt" or else assume a *lapsus calami* and emend to KUR*Mizir-ne-we*<*-ne-we*> KUR*omin-ne-we allai* "lady of the land of Egypt." Speiser, not having observed the adjectival force of *Maš=rianni-* sought to explain the function by interpreting the **a-* vowel before the *-nni* as the locative case, see *IH* § 137 (c).

[83] See Speiser, *IH*, 91 for the meaning.

[84] For this position of the attributive see Speiser, *IH*, § 232. The examples are: *šukkane-wa+n tiw-i-wa+n ML* 2:84; *šukkanne eše-ni* 3:30; *šukkanne+lla+. . . paššiḫ-iwwə* 3:54, 56-7; *šukkanni+man šue-ni* 3:114, 118; *šukkanne+n pati tiwe-ne+n* 4:32-3.

[85] Laroche restores DINGIR.MEŠ*-na a-bi-e-bi-na* DINGIR.MEŠ*-na u-ru-un*[*-ni-bi-na*], *RA* 54 (1960), 190. In the light of our discussion, it seems entirely possible, if not probable, that the form would have been *u-ru-un*[*-ni-na*].

[86] *RA* 54 (1960), 191. The text is found in *KUB* XXXII 40 + 49a completed by the unpublished pieces 2327/c + 2352/c. [+ *KBo* XXI 33 (cf. *StBoT* 15, 35) – Ed.]

[87] Kronasser, *WZKM* 53 (1956-7), 189, suggests "marked with a brand," < Indic *añka-* "brand-mark."

[88] So Kronasser, *op. cit.*, p. 187, < Indic *jira-ma* "very fast." [But cf. Akkad. *serrēmu* "wild ass" – Ed.]

[89] It is rather striking that each of the Ḫurro-akkadian forms ends in *-ann(u)*, with the Akkad. nominative in *-u*, but *wirrarikkonne* violates Akkadian grammar by ending in *-nni.*

[90] *wurikkonne ML* 3:9, *katikkonne ML* 4:2, *ḫillošikkonne ML* 4:4,11.

[91] To translate *ḫenni+man kuru ḫillošikkonne ḫilloši ML* 4:11, "Now then, furthermore, he who was not speaking has spoken," is, to say the least, forced.

obscure context. Laroche analyses the three forms *ḫašikkonne*, *wurikkonne*, and *katikkonne* as negative verbal adjectives which form the nominal subjects of their respective clauses. If he is correct, these forms also are evidence of an adjectival force for forms in *-nne*, here treated as substantives. However, the whole analysis is yet too uncertain, and too many ambigous and inexplicable forms remain. It is, however, tantalizing to hypothesize that verbs nominalized by *-nne* produce concrete nominals, which describe the performer of the verbal activity (somewhat analogous to the "participle" of the Semitic languages used substantivally), while verbs nominalized by *-šše* produce abstract nominals, which name the verbal action (somewhat analogous to the Semitic "infinitive"). This remains but conjecture, however, for the forms in *-ikkonne* comprise, at this point in our understanding of the language, one of the most puzzling features of the grammar of Hurrian.

UGARITIC AND PHOENICIAN

OR

QUMRAN AND THE VERSIONS

Mitchell Dahood, S.J.

Rome

Ten years ago Professor Gordon wrote: "For understanding the Old Testament, by far the most important literary texts ever discovered are the clay tablets from Ugarit, written between the fourteenth and twelfth centuries B.C. at a north Syrian coastal city and in a language closely related to Hebrew. The Ugaritic myths and epics are a kind of Canaanite Bible, portraying the culture against which the Hebrews rebelled."[1] Granted that by 1963 the flood of studies on Qumran had begun to ebb, it remains to Gordon's credit that he never lost sight of the importance of Ugaritic research amid the excitement created by the Dead Sea discoveries. In 1965 the present writer raised some hackles by claiming that "the Ugaritic usage of prepositions and particles alone sheds more light on the meaning of the text of the Old Testament than do all the Qumran Scrolls."[2] That this claim was not gratuitous[3] may be gathered from the number of notes and formal studies on biblical prepositions in the light of Ugaritic usage that have appeared in recent years.[4] What is the situation today? The following few examples aim to illustrate the current validity of Gordon's high assessment of Ugaritic in 1963.

Familiarity with the Ugaritic-Phoenician manner of writing in *scriptio defectiva* conditions the biblical critic to see a defectively written original under the Masoretic normalization that often conceals the true purport of the text. In MT, Is 33:3 reads:

miqqôl hāmôn nād^e^dû ʿammîm
mērôm^e^mūtekā nāp^e^ṣû gôyīm

---

1 In *JBR* 33 (1963), 208-209.

2 *Ugaritic-Hebrew Philology* (Rome, 1965), 26.

3 J.C. Greenfield, *JAOS* 89 (1969), 176, terms my evaluation "A totally uncalled -for remark, for we are dealing with two different types of text materials, important in two separate fields and *not* mutually exclusive." Though Ugaritic and Qumran are different and separate, both directly impinge on the Hebrew Bible and often suggest mutually exclusive translations and grammatical analyses. On a theoretical plane Greenfield's statement might be acceptable, but in practice students of OT must often make a choice, since the disposable time does not permit the mastering of both disciplines. When faced with such a choice, the student would be well -advised to choose Ugaritic studies over Qumran. Of course, he should ideally learn both Ugaritic and Qumran.

4 To cite but three studies published in the past two years: William Chomsky, "The Ambiguity of the Prefixed Prepositions *m, l, b* in the Bible," *JQR* 61 (1970-71) 87-89; Georg Schmuttermayr, "Ambivalenz und Aspektdifferenz: Bemerkungen zu den hebräischen Präpositionen *b, l* und *min,*" *Biblische Zeitschrift* 15 (1971), 29-51; C.F. Whitley, "Some Functions of the Hebrew Particles *Beth* and *Lamedh,*" *JQR* 62 (1971-72), 199-206.

The chief difficulty resides in the congeries *mrmmtk*, read by IQIs[a] as *mdmmtk*. This interesting variant, not registered in BHK but noted in BHS, suggests, on the one hand, a defectively written original *mrmmtk*. Ugaritic *rm*, "sound", in the phrase *rm tph*, "the sound/roll of his drum" (*UT*, Glossary, No. 2333; *Ugaritica V*, 603), on the other hand, indicates that this suspiciously long sequence be broken up into two words, *mrm* + *mtk*. Hence the entire verse may be vocalized and rendered:

miqqôl hāmôn nādᵉdû ʿammîm	At the voice of your army, may the peoples flee;
mērām (or *mērōm*) *mᵉtêkā nāpᵉṣû gôyīm*	At the sound of your soldiers, may the nations be scattered.

Thus the verse scans into an A:B:C:D || A':B':C':D' sequence: *qôl* matches *rām* (or *rôm*) and recalls the phrase *qôl rām* in Deut 27:14; but cf. Hab 3:10, *qôlô rôm*, so the *scriptio plena* of MT *rôm* may prove sound. Thus the pair *qôl* || *rām* illustrates the breakup of the composite phrase *qôl rām*, or *rām* (or *rōm*) is a substantive synonymous with *qôl*, and identifiable with Ugar. *rm*, "sound". In *hāmôn* || *mᵉtêkā*, the former shares the suffix of the latter, and both elicit the collocation in Is 5:13, *mᵉtê rāʿāb*, "the men of the Hungry One," and *hᵃmônô*, "his throng." Since the metaphor of our verse is military (cf. vs. 2), *hāmôn* assumes the well-attested meaning "army" (e.g., Is 29:5; see *BDB*, 242b) while *mᵉtêkā* bears the same sense as in Is 3:25, "Your soldiers (*mᵉtayik*) will fall by the sword and your warriors in battle." The alliterative perfects *nādᵉdû* and *nāpᵉṣû* parse as precative, stylistically balancing the two imperatives of vs. 2, *ḥonnēnû*, "Have mercy on us," and *hᵉyēh*, "Be!"[5] In other terms, vs. 3 continues the prayer of vs. 2.[6]

The existence of the Phoenician third person singular suffix *-y* in Hebrew is gaining acceptance[7], but it remains to point out the presence of the Phoenician plural suffix *-nm*[8] in Hos 13:2:

wᵉʿattāh yôsîpû laḥᵃṭōʾ	Yet now they sin more and more
wayyaᵃśû lāhem massēkāh	and have made for themselves a cast image;
mikkaspām KTBWNM ᵃṣabbîm	with their silver they engrave idols for themselves,
maᵃśēh ḥārāšîm kullōh	nothing but the work of craftsmen.

MT vocalizes consonantal *ktbwnm* as *kitᵉbûnām*, and those who do not emend to *kᵉtabnît* (LXX *kat' eikona*), seek to explain the ending *-ām* as shortened from *-ātām*, so Gesen-Kautzsch, *Grammatik* § 91e. But the parallelism *kᵉtûbāh*, "engraved" || *ḥᵃrûšāh*, "carved," in Jer 17:1 makes it probable that *ktbwnm* parses as the verb *kātᵉbû* plus the plural suffix *-nm*, here expressing the *dativus commodi* balancing prepositional *lāhem* in the preceding colon.

---

5 For the translation of *hᵉyēh zᵉrōʿām*, see M. Dahood, *CBQ* 20 (1958), 45-46; *Ugaritic-Hebrew Philology*, 34, and C.H.W. Brekelmans in *Oudtestamentische Studiën* 15 (1969), 172 n. 1.

6 It may be noted here that *miqqôl hāmôn*, "at the voice of your army," supports the writer's translation of Is 24:18, *hannās miqqôl happaḥad*, "he who escapes the howling pack," since *paḥad*, like *hāmôn*, is a collective noun. Consult Dahood, *Psalms II*, 331. D.R. Hillers, *JBL* 91 (1972), 92 n. 18, asserts that the translation of *paḥad* by "pack" is in every case unnecessary and unjustified, but he fails to discuss any of the texts where this meaning allegedly occurs. I find it necessary to identify it, say, in Is 24:18, because of the metaphor of the hunt and because traditional "the voice of fear" makes little sense. Hillers' further assertion that "it is far from common or natural that a term for a human social group, such as *faḫid*, "clan", is extended to an assembly of animals," overlooks the neat instance of *ḥebel*, " a band of prophets," in I Sam 10:5,10, but herd of deer," in Job 39:3. Ugar. *ḥbl* is predicated both of women and of birds; *UT*, Glossary, No. 832.

7 See most recently, James L. Crenshaw, *CBQ* 34 (1972), 49, and Wilfred G.E. Watson, *Biblica* 53 (1972), 202.

8 Consult J. Friedrich and W. Röllig, *Phönizisch-punische Grammatik* (2d ed.; *AnOr* 46, Rome, 1970), 49, 128 n. 1; Charles Krahmalkov, *Journal of Semitic Languages* 15 (1970), 181-188, esp. 181-185.

The relative frequency of dative suffixes in both Ugaritic and Phoenician warrant the search for this usage in difficult biblical texts. For example, D.R. Hillers[10] needlessly emends consonantal *tmnw* to *tammû* in Lam 3:22:

ḥasdê YHWH kî lō' TMNW	Yahweh's mercy is surely not terminated for us,
kî lō' kālû raḥamāyw	nor is his pity exhausted.

Consonantal *tmnw* may be vocalized *tammūnû* and the suffix *-nû* parsed as datival. The resultant parallelism *tammū* || *kālû* is now encountered in Is 33:1 if the reading of 1QIsa *kklwtk* is adopted:

khtmk šwdd twšd	When you have finished as destroyer, you will be destroyed,
kklwtk (MT *kannelōtekā) lbdg ybgdw bk*	when you have ended dealing treacherously, they will deal treacherously with you.

Here then would be an instance where Ugaritic and Qumran conspire to clarify a biblical text (Lam 3:22) which contains a dative suffix as well as two emphatic *kî*'s.[11]

Since the infixed *-t-* conjugation is standard in Ugaritic and sporadic in Phoenician, it grows more difficult to question its existence in Hebrew or to admit only exceptional occurrences. Thus S.B. Wheeler ends his article, "The Infixed *-t-* in Biblical Hebrew," with the judgment, "With few exceptions, infixed *-t-* forms do not exist in biblical Hebrew," but he does not explain why 1QIsa reads in Is 50:6, *pny lw' hsyrwty*, "I did not turn away my face," where the received consonantal text offers *hstrty*. Within the Ugaritic-Phoenician framework one can obtain both the preferable meaning presented by 1QIsa and at the same time preserve consonantal *hstrty*, to be parsed as an infixed *-t-* form of *swr*, "to turn aside." In this light the hapax expression in Job 6:9, *ytr ydw*, "Should he point his hand," may be parsed as infixed *-t-* of *yrh*, "to show, point out," and disputed Job 9:12, *hēn yḥtp mî yešîbennû* may reasonably be rendered, "If he surrounds, who can repel him? " where *yḥtp* may well contain the root *ḥpp*, "to surround, enclose," predicated of God in Deut 33:12.

In his discussion of the verbal preformative *t-* with the third dual and plural, Gordon (*UT*, § 9.14) notes that this Canaanitism is sporadically found in Hebrew with third masculine plural subjects, citing Job 19: 15 among his examples: *gārê bêtî we'amhōtay lezār taḥšebūnî.* It is very interesting that 11QTgJb, Col. II:4, reads singular *'mty*, "my maid servant," in place of MT plural *'amhōtay*, "my maid servants."

The editors of this Targum[13] are at a loss to account for the singular reading, but one may surmise that faced with *tḥšbwny*, which looks like a singular verb, the Qumran scribe or translator felt obliged to alter plural *'mhty* to singular *'mty*. Northwest Semitic shows plural *'mhty* and *tḥšb* to be grammatically compatible.

---

[9] Exegetically useful would be a systematic study of the dative suffix balancing a prepositional phrase, a frequent stylistic phenomenon in Job. A.C.M. Blommerde, *Northwest Semitic Grammar and Job* (Rome 1969), 111, correctly renders Job 29:16, *'eḥqerēhû*, "I investigated for him," parsing the suffix as datival, but failed to cite in support of his interpretation the parallelism with the triple *l* in 29:15-16 expressing advantage. This stylistic phenomenon is witnessed in *UT*, 125:25-26, *bn al tbkn al tdm ly*, "My son, cry not for me, shed no tears for me," where the dative suffix of *tbkn* has its counterpart in prepositional *ly*.

[10] *Lamentations* (Anchor Bible 7a; Garden City, N.Y., 1972) 56-57.

[11] For another example, consult *Biblica* 47 (1966), 107-108.

[12] In *Journal of the Ancient Near Eastern Society of Columbia University*, III (Autumn 1970-71) 21-31. See also S.P. Brock in *JTS* 23 (1972), 156-157. Contrast the more positive approach of H. Cazelles, *VT* 21 (1971), 627, who accepts some of the infixed *-t-* forms identified in Proverbs by W. van der Weiden, *Le Livre des Proverbes: Note philologiques* (Rome, 1970).

[13] J.P.M. van der Ploeg et A.S. van der Woude, avec la collaboration de B. Jongeling, *Le Targum de Job de la Grotte XI de Qumrân* (Leiden, 1971), 15 n. 4.

The yiphil causative, characteristic of Phoenician, sporadically occurs in the OT,[14] but the ancient versions seem not to have understood it, if we may judge from Qumranic readings. In 1951 Gordon[15] identified as perfect yiphil the form *yakkîrānû* in Is 63:16; this has been confirmed by 1QIs^a^, which reads hiphil *hkyrnw*, a lection indicating that at the time of Qumran the yiphil conjugation was not appreciated. Another instance of the yiphil conjugation may be recognized in Is 14:30b:

wᵉhēmattî bārāʿāb šoršēk	But I will kill your offspring with hunger.
ûšᵉʾērîtēk YHRG	and your remnant I will utterly slay.

In this context, *šoršēk* bears the Ugaritic sense of *šrš*, "offspring" (|| *bn*, "son"),[16] while consonantal *yhrg* (1QIs^a^ reads qal *ʾhrwg*) may be parsed as the yiphil infinitive absolute continuing the finite verb *wᵉhēmattî*. The causative conjugation is here taken as elative, hence "I will utterly slay." This analysis acquires conviction from the observation that in the next line (vs. 31) *nāmôg* also parses as an infinitive absolute rather than as masculine prefect:

hêlîlî šaʿar zaʿᵃqî ʿîr	Wail, O gate; cry out, O city;[17]
nāmôg pᵉlešet kullēk	melt in fear, O Philistia, all of you!

Though König[18] and Delitzsch[19] in the last century correctly parsed *nāmôg* as a niphal infinitive absolute (cf. Is 59:13 *nāsôg*) continuing the feminine imperative *hêlîlî*, the more recent dictionaries such as Gesenius-Buhl, Koehler-Baumgartner, and its latest edition by W.L. Holladay[20], analyze it as niphal masculine perfect. The one addressed is feminine *pᵉlešet*, so a feminine finite form would be expected.[21] When employing the yiphil infinitive absolute in vs. 30 to continue the finite verb, and the niphal infinitive absolute in vs. 31 as a surrogate for the imperative, the prophet follows the Ugaritic-Phoenician penchant for infinitives absolute. That Qumran did not fully appreciate this usage is further attested in Is 37:19 where 1QIs^a^ reads finite *wytnw* for the infinitive absolute *wᵉnātôn* of MT.[22]

If acquaintance with Northwest Semitic morphology is a *conditio sine qua non* for understanding biblical Hebrew, knowledge of Ugaritic-Phoenician idioms also proves valuable for translating the Hebrew Bible. For example, King Azitawadd claims that he was revered as a father, *bṣdqy wbḥkmty wbnʿm lby*, "because of my justice, and because of my wisdom, and because of the goodness of my heart" (*KAI*, 26:12-13). The idiom *bḥkmty* suggests that the sense of Job 38:37 has eluded translators: *my yspr šḥqm bḥkmh*, "Quis enarrabit caelorum rationem? " (Vulgate). How much more incisive to render "Who is told out by the heaven for wisdom?", the motif of Ps 19:2?

---

14 See the recent, brief discussion by W.G.E. Watson in *Biblica* 53 (1972), 199.

15 *JKF* 2 (1951), 50.

16 On Phoenician *šrš*, "offspring," see C.F. Jean - J. Hoftijzer, *Dictionnaire des inscriptions sémitiques de l'ouest*, 321, and on the parallelism *šrš* || *bn* in Job 5:3-4, Dahood in L. Fisher, ed., *Ras Shamra Parallels*: *The Texts from Ugarit and the Hebrew* Bible, I (*AnOr* 49; Rome, 1972) Ch. II:116, p. 147.

17 NEB's rendition, "Howl in the gate, cry for help in the city, let all Philistia be in turmoil," is grammatically indefensible, distorts the sense of the Hebrew, and destroys the climatic buildup from "gate" to "city" to all of Philistia.

18 *Lehrgebäude*, 473.

19 Franz Delitzsch, *Commentar über das Buch Jesaja* (4th ed.; Leipzig, 1889), 473.

20 *A Concise Hebrew and Aramaic Lexicon of the Old Testament* (Leiden, 1971) 185 b. F. Zorell, *Lexicon Hebraicum et aramaicum Veteris Testamenti* (Rome, 1955), 416a, seems to be the only recent dictionary that understands *nāmôg* as niphal infinitive absolute.

21 One might counter with the objection that in *hêlîlî šaʿar* there is gender discord since elsewhere *šaʿar* is always masculine and the plural is always *šᵉʿārim*, but it should be noted that Ugar. witnesses plural *ṯǵrt*. So we must leave open the possibility of fem. sing. *šaʿar*, as indicated by fem. impv. *hêlîlî*.

22 This interesting variant is inexplicably not registered in BHS, *Liber Jesaiae* (Stuttgart, 1968), edited by the late D. Winton Thomas.

On the strength of a cognate Akkadian formula, Hayim Tawil[23] proposes to translate *b'lmy qmw 'my 'lhw hdd*, "Since my youth the gods of Haddad stood with me" (*KAI*, 214:1-2). This understanding of *b'lmy*, it may be noted, is not without bearing on the disputed translation of Lam 3:27:*ṭôb laggeber kî yiśśā' 'ōl bineʿûrāyw*, "It is good for a man that he bear the yoke from his youth."[24]

In Ugaritic, *yṯb l*, "to sit upon," is well attested; cf. especially *UT*, 67:VI:12-14, *yrd lksi yṯb lhdm wl hdm yṯb larṣ*, "He descended from the throne, sat upon the footstool; and from the footstool, he sat upon the ground." The description of this ritual is important for the text and interpretation of Is 47:1, but here only *šebi lā'āreṣ 'ên kissē'* will be discussed. Apparently unfamiliar with the Canaanite idiom, 1QIs^a reads *šby 'l h'rṣ*,[25] while the LXX, probably not conversant with the ritual involved, simply omits *'ên kissē'*. In these two phrases, Ugaritic manifests its superiority over both Qumran and the LXX as a tool of textual criticism and biblical exegesis.

The recognition of the breakup of composite phrases, especially attested by the Ugaritic practice of splitting up composite divine names, may provide the solution to the longstanding difficulty in Job 19:17:

rûḥî zārāh le'ištî	My spirit is a stranger to my wife,
weḥannōtî libnê biṭnî	and my supplication to the sons of her womb.[26]

Zech 12:10, *rûaḥ ḥēn wetaḥnûnîm*, "a spirit of compassion and supplication," strongly suggests that, when Job puts *rûḥî* in the first colon and *ḥannōtî* in the second, he is splitting up a composite phrase containing *rwḥ* and *ḥnn*. The evidence for *ḥannōtî*, "my supplication," is provided by *UT*, 2 Aqht:I:17-19, *[w]yqrb b'l bḥnth abynt [d]nil mt rpi anḥ ǵzr [mt] hrnmy*, "Then Baal drew near because of his supplication, because of the need of Daniel the Raphite, because of the groaning of the Harnamite Hero." This version follows from construing *b* of *bḥnth* as causal *beth* which extends its force to the two succeeding nouns of the triple parallelism.

In the study of the linguistic and literary interconnections between Ugaritic-Phoenician and Hebrew, the Bible has been the chief beneficiary. The final three examples have been chosen to show that Hebrew can sometimes reciprocate by elucidating disputed Northwest Semitic texts. In his study of the Aḥiram curse, *tḥtsp ḥtr mšpṭh thtpk ks' mlkh* (*KAI*, 1:2), J.C. Greenfield[27] translates *tḥtsp* by "be broken" arguing that the proof for *ḥsp*, "to peel," – the common rendition – is not conclusive. Employing the same parallel pair *hpk* || *ḥśp*, Ecclus 6:8 weighs in with evidence supporting the translation "to peel" and demonstrating that Greenfield's doubts are ill-founded. The text reads:

yš 'whb nhpk lśn'	There is a friend who turns into an enemy,
w't ryb ḥrptk yḥśwp	and to your shame makes public a dispute.

Jer 30:20a contains the breakup of a composite expression that bids fair to clarify *UT*, 51:VII:15-16. The former reads:

---

[23] In *Or* 42 (1973).

[24] Hillers, *Lamentations*, 50, translates *bineʿûrāyw*, "in his youth," with the comment (p. 50), "Some Hebrew MSS and some Greek MSS and the Vulgate have 'from his youth.' Since this is a much more common expression in the Old Testament than *'in* (his, etc.) youth,' it seems preferable to retain MT here, as the less common expression." I fail to follow this reasoning. "What makes better sense? " is the proper question here, and now that we have the cognate expression *b'lmy*, "since my youth," and other instances of *nś' b*, "to take/bear from" (e.g., Job 7:13; Eccles 5:4), we should adopt "from his youth" as the preferable rendering.

[25] [1QIs^a variant missing in BHS. – Ed.]

[26] Of course here, as in Job 3:10, the suffix of *biṭnî* is the Phoenician third person singular *-y*.

[27] In H. Goedicke, ed., *Near Eastern Studies in Honor of William Foxwell Albright* (Baltimore, 1971), 254-257.

wehāyû bānāyw keqedem	His sons shall be as of old,
waʿadātô lepānay tikkôn	and his community shall be established before me.

51:VII:15-16

aštm kṯr bn ym	I will install them, Kothar, son of the sea,
kṯr bnm ʿdt	Kothar, son of the confluence

For the disputed phrases *bn ym* and *bnm ʿdt* a large number of translations have been advanced,[28] but Albright's interpretation "son of the sea" || "son(s) of the assembly"[29] is sustained by the biblical breakup of the composite expression and by the publication in *Ugaritica V*, 564 (607:3), of the text *mbk nhrm bʿdt thmtm*, where *ʿdt thmtm* = "confluence of the Upper and the Lower Flood." In other words, the pairing *nhrm* || *thmtm* substantially equals the brace *ym* || *ʿdt*, since *nhrm* sometimes signifies "ocean currents"[30] and *ʿdt* may well, thanks to the parallelism, connote *ʿdt thmtm*. It may be recalled that Kothar's homeland was the island Crete, so that such epithets as "son of the sea" and "son of the confluence" would be appropriate. Moreover, in Greek mythology Aphrodite, who was widely worshipped as a goddess of the sea and seafaring, was born from the Cypriote sea. Her husband was Hephaestus, now to be identified with Kothar.

Finally, the collocation of the roots *qr'* and *srr* in Prov 7:10-11, *hinnēh 'iššāh liqrā'tô*, "Lo, a woman to call / invite him" . . . *hōmīyyāh hî' wesōrāret*, "She is turbulent and aggressive," may help to identify the second of the parallel verbs in *UT*, 51:VII:47-49:

yqra mt bnpšh	Mot called out from his throat,
ystrn ydd bgngnh	the Beloved cried defiance from his windpipe.

The biblical collocation points to disputed *ystrn* as an infixed *-t-* form of *srr*, "to be rebellious, defiant." And hurl a challenge is precisely what Mot did, as may be seen from the following lines 49-52.

Before concluding this article in tribute to Professor Gordon, I must recount a small incident that illustrates how his openness to new ideas has influenced me. Some years ago, when I was preparing a note on the phrase *hkkbm 'l* in the Pyrgi Inscription,[31] I had the opportunity to discuss the matter with Gordon during the international congress of the Old Testament Society at Geneva in August, 1965. When I explained that, to my mind, *hkkbm 'l* was a construct chain whose construct was accoutered with both the article and the enclitic *mem*, he replied that these presented no inherent difficulty since "the stars of El" made good sense. When I further observed that *kôkebê 'ēl* occurs in Is 14:13, he forthwith accepted the translation and urged publication. This open-mindedness stands in refreshing contrast to the narrow dogmatism of, say, W. Röllig, who writes: "Dennoch soll hier die Deutung von M. Dahood, Or. 37 (1965) 170-172 'die Sterne Els' nochmals zurückgewiesen werden . . . Nichts rechtfertigt hier die Annahme eines enklitischen *-m*, alles spricht aber gegen eine stat.-cstr.-Verbindung gegen alle grammatischen Regeln. Hier wird eine sachliche Schwierigkeit durch eine grammatische Unmöglichkeit erklärt."[32]

[28] For a full listing of views, consult J.C. de Moor *AOAT* 16 (1971) 160-161.
[29] *JPOS* 14 (1934), 129. Cf. also *UT*, 52: 61, *bn ym*, "sons of the sea," as rendered by Gordon, *Ugaritic Literature* (Rome, 1949), 61.
[30] M. Dahood, *Psalms I*, 151; G.M. Landes, *Interpretation* 21 (1967), 6 n. 14.
[31] See M. Dahood, *Or* 34 (1965), 170-172.
[32] *WO* 5 (1969-70), Heft 1, 116 n. 38. The translation "the stars of El" is now being accepted widely; see, e.g., N. Lohfink in G.H.W. Wolff, ed., *G. von Rad Festschrift: Probleme biblischer Theologie* (München, 1971), 283 n. 29; F.M. Cross, Jr., in G.J. Botterweck und H. Ringgren, edd., *Theologische Wörterbuch zum Alten Testament* (Stuttgart, 1971), s.v. *'l*, Spalte 272; S.B. Parker, *UF* 2 (1970), 248.

THE PATRIARCHAL CYCLES

Loren R. Fisher
School of Theology at Claremont
Claremont, California

INTRODUCTION

Cyrus H. Gordon has made so many great contributions to our studies that it is difficult to decide which one should be developed in his honor. Nevertheless, I would like to develop and extend a statement which he made in a very interesting article entitled "Hebrew Origins in the Light of Recent Discovery".[1] In this paper he said:

> " . . . we are obliged to consider the patriarchal narratives as an authentic reflex of the second millennium, specifically of the fourteenth and thirteenth centuries, . . ."[2]

Now, I do not intend to review all of the reasons that Professor Gordon gives for making this statement. Rather, I would like to extend the argument in support of the statement along different lines. I am motivated to do this because of some recent work that I have been doing on the structure of the book of Genesis.[3]

In order to make it very clear, I should say that I accept the Amarna Age dating of the Patriarchs[4], and I will attempt to show why I think that the Patriarchal Cycles were fixed in the time of the Judges. It should be added that I have some special requirements for the use of parallels. It should be clear that an early parallel to the form or content of the Patriarchal Cycles does not secure an early date for them. Such parallels can theoretically only open the possibility for an early date. The opposite position is also true, i.e., a late parallel does not make the material late but only makes that a possibility. Recently, John Van Seters has rightly pointed out that scholars have neglected late parallels to the Patriarchal material.[5] However, it seems that he makes some basic mistakes. First, he demands an exactness of the so-called "early" parallels that seems to be relaxed when he turns his favorite "late" parallels. Also, even though he says that ". . . it is very precarious to use marriage customs for the purposes of dating . . . ,"[6] he goes on to say, "Nevertheless, the form of the customs reflected in the Genesis

---

[1] This appeared in *Biblical and Other Studies*, ed. by Alexander Altmann, *Studies and Texts*, Vol. I (1963), 3-14.
[2] *Ibid.*, 4.
[3] This work was done in 1968, but it remains unpublished. I did report on it in a presidential address in 1969 at the Pacific Coast Section of the Society of Biblical Literature.
[4] This was also the view of H.H. Rowley, Martin Noth, and Yehezkel Kaufmann.
[5] John Van Seters, *JBL*, 77 (1968), 401-408.
[6] *Ibid.*, 407.

stories seem to be late rather than early in this continuum."[7] In a more recent article he shows his basic position, when he points to a late parallel, concerning a different matter, with the words:

> "On the other hand there is a corresponding body of material much closer to hand which has been ignored in this discussion of form."[8]

I am saying that a late parallel does not make the tradition or form late. If we have a letter-form at Ugarit that has an exact parallel in late Hebrew or Aramaic sources that does not mean that the letter-form at Ugarit is late. Yet Van Seters seems to use this kind of reasoning.[9] Early or late parallels are necessary and helpful in order to understand both form and content of biblical traditions. They may show that certain laws and customs last for centuries and they may expand the dating possibilities. However, in order to date material in the Bible one needs more than the date of the parallel literature. Both literary groups have to be carefully studied as to their structure, their intention, and their *Sitz im Leben*. If one can deal with these three things, then it is easy enough to come up with a name for this type of literature. To be able to date when the type was used is not especially helpful, but to be able to answer the question about *Sitz im Leben*may be helpful in dating when a particular group used a certain type in their own history. In other words a particular situation in the history of any people calls for a particular type of literary activity. In order to have royal literature there needs to be a monarchy. Parallels help us to understand the nature of royal literature and how it is used within a monarchy. However, the dates of Israel's monarchy will be the determining factor in dating royal literature in Israel, even if one discovers early or late parallels which existed in other monarchies.

In addition to these remarks on parallels I should add a few on form criticism. Many scholars in our time are skeptical about a form criticism which concentrates on small units and the early stages of tradition. However, more and more there seesm to be an interest in the structure of the final form or the large complexes. Professor James Muilenberg sees his work, in what he calls "rhetorical criticism," as the legitimate heir of form criticism. He says:

> "What I am interested in, above all, is in understanding the nature of Hebrew literary composition, in exhibiting the structural patterns that are employed for the fashioning of a literary unit, whether in poetry or in prose, and in discerning the many and various devices by which the predications are formulated and ordered into a unified whole."[10]

Certainly this is an important task. I would only like to stress that in the first step of our exegesis we should focus such a method on the final form of large complexes or even books.[11] This first step is an obvious one but it is not so easy to accomplish. In many places the structure seems final until one finds some additional element, which was added at a late date. This can change the situation, so that what seemed to be the final form is not final after all. So we must try again and again to find the final form. Only then can we trace the traditions back into their earlier stages.

---

[7] *Ibid.*, 408.

[8] John Van Seters, *JBL*, 91 (1972), 187.

[9] It may be interesting to have a late parallel to an early custom, but it is more important to talk about Gordon's point on the Patriarchal Narratives, when he says: "If they had been invented by later authors they would reflect later Hebrew law and custom." See C.H. Gordon, "Hebrew Origins," *op. cit.*, 6.

[10] James Muilenburg, *JBL*, 88 (1969), 8.

[11] This, by the way, is very close to the main interest of such scholars in the past as Martin Buber, Franz Rosenzweig and Umberto Cassuto.

THE CYCLES

If one attempts to look at the final form of the Book of Genesis, he sees at once that the book has been divided into "histories." It is not divided into a Primeval History and a History of the Patriarchs but rahter into sequential *tôledôt* or "histories." Since these histories seem to be related to a final stage in the tradition, it is important to pay attention to this arrangement. I cannot deal with all of these sections in Genesis in this paper, but I follow Umberto Cassuto's lead in suggesting that usually the subject in the title of each section has already been introduced in the preceding material and what follows the title deals with the descendants of the subject or with subsequent events.[12] Thus in the Patriarchal Histories we find the History of Terah (11:27 - 25:11) which deals with Abram and his sons. Next there is a short History of Ishmael (25:12-18) and then another long history, the History of Isaac (25:19 - 35:29) which deals with Jacob. The pattern is repeated with a short History of Esau (36:1 - 37:1) and then the History of Jacob (37:2 - 50:26) which deals with Joseph.

Now, if we look at the structural arrangement of the three longer "histories" (as we now have them) some interesting things stand before us. When first I divided these three "histories" into subsections, I was amazed that each one had 17 parts. However I would like to emphasize that I am not overly interested in the number 17. You or I could come up with a different number for each one.[13] Claus Westermann divides these three into 19, 21, and 17 sections.[14] The important thing is that *we have essentially the same "bulk" in each* and *there is a similar overall structure for each.* There is also variety and difference in each one, which is the result of different subjects and narrative progression. In a very general way we have in all three "histories" the following:

1) A word about the descendants and promise
2) A section dealing with the success of the central character
3) More material on the descendants and land
4) Similar conclusions.

In the History of Terah, the initial word about descendants and promise is in the form of a geneology and a promise (11:27 - 12:3). In the History of Isaac this first word emphasizes the theme that the "elder shall serve the younger" (25:19-34). This is also the case in the History of Jacob (37:2-36). In the second general section which deals with the success of the Patriarch, it is emphasized that regardless of how difficult the situation is in which the Patriarch finds himself, God is with him. God is with Abram, Jacob, and Joseph, and he grants them success in very material ways. The situations are usually of the same type and involve the Patriarch in at least one of the following:

1) Famine (12:10 - 13:1; 26:1-35; 42:1-38)
2) Seduction (Sarah, Rebekah, and Joseph)[15]
3) Difficulties in the presence of kings or powerful individuals but always with material success.

In the third general section of the "histories," the additional words on descendants and land vary in several ways. With Abram the story of the heir is full blown with much repetition and suspense. Here the heir is the mos

---

[12] U. Cassuto, *A Commentary on the Book of Genesis*, Part I, From Adam to Noah, translated by Israel Abrahams (1961), 99.

[13] In fact, I recently divided them into 17, 19, and 18 sections, and some of my students have seen the structure in yet a different way.

[14] Claus Westermann, *Handbook to the Old Testament*, translated by Robert H. Boyd (1967), 29-53.

[15] In 20:1-18 the seduction scene is used again. At this point there is a new beginning for Abram.

important element. With Jacob God's gift of sons is important, but it does not stand out. In fact it is blended into many other things, among which one very important element is that of obtaining land at Shechem. Certainly, God is also with Joseph. His sons are included within the "twelve" and he receives from Jacob the land at Shechem (48:1-22). In the conclusions to these "histories" there is always:

1) A burial scene (Sarah, 23:1-20; Rachel, 35:16-20; Jacob, 50:1-14)
2) Additional material on the heir(s) (Isaac, 24:1-67; the sons of Jacob, 35:21-26; the brothers and their descendants, 50:15-21)
3) A death scene (Abram, 25:1-11; Isaac, 35:27-29; Joseph, 50:22-26)

These three parts of the conclusions are naturally the last three subsections of any kind of division of these "histories" (i.e., whether the end result is 17 in each or 19, 21, and 17 subsections). There are many other interesting comparisons such as the fifth subsection of both the Abram and Jacob materials deals with the tithe (14:1-24 and 28:10-22).

In the above discussion we moved from remarks about the final form of the book of Genesis to a comparison of three major cycles within Genesis. Now I would like to discuss only the History of Isaac, which deals with Jacob, and compare that to the Kret text at Ugarit. When we try to compare the final form of these two cycles, we face some problems. We do not have the end of the Kret material and the final prose form of the Jacob material covers up many important features. It is probable that if we had all of the Kret text(s), and if we had the texts or traditions which were available to the Genesis editors, we could see a great many structural parallels between the Jacob material and Kret. Perhaps it is more than probable for several reasons. In the first place, in the Jacob materials we can still see an abundance of formulae, which allow one to divide the material into sections like those in the Ugaritic texts.[16] When the material is divided, there are many themes and motifs that are clustered together in such a way that a similar thrust or point may be seen in both cycles. There are also significant differences, which must not be overlooked. However, there would also be great differences in any two cycles at Ugarit. Certainly you will alsways have different names, situations, and side events. Nevertheless when one looks carefully at the structure of the Jacob and Kret cycles, the following is impressive:

1) The purpose of the cycles has to do with obtaining a wife in order to produce an heir. (Also the promise of land is important in the Jacob cycle.)
2) Both men are given instructions for the journey. The instructions are given to Kret by El and Jacob by Isaac. In both cases the instructions precede the journey, however in Kret the dream also precedes the journey and contains the instructions whereas in the Jacob cycle the dream immediately precedes the vow.
3) Nevertheless in both the dream does contain the promise of God which in both cases is not apparently adequate in light of the conditional vows.
4) In both we have the conditional vow with a similar structure (see Gen 28:20-22) set early in the journey,[17] and not dealt with in the instructions.
5) In both cases the vow has to do with the success of the trip. In both cases it is at a shrine and a different God is involved.[18] When we say "a different God," we must ask "different from what?" In Jacob's instructions (not in a dream) it is *'el šadday* who is asked to bless him; in the dream it is Yahweh who makes a promise and it is probably Elohim with whom Jacob makes his vow.[19] Now

[16] As an example of this note Gen 33:1 "and Jacob lifted up his eyes and looked, and behold. . ."

[17] In Kret the place of the vow is after a three-day journey (cf. Ex 5:3 for a three-day journey to a shrine) but in the Jacob cycle the visit to a shrine in the beginning seems to be after one day (see Gen 46:1 for another example). I have given a detailed comparison of these vows in *UF* 3, where this discussion also appears.

[18] Another great difference comes out here. With Kret it is a goddess.

[19] Even if he makes the vow to Yahweh, this means that he is dealing with a different God. But all of this is not so simple. What names were in the original story? *'ēl, 'ēl šadday* or *bêt'ēl*? There are too many divine names. Yahweh may have been added to Jacob's promise. Cf. Gen 31:13.

with Kret it is El who gives instructions in the dream and who probably (though the text is broken) makes a promise of blessing, but it is Asherah to whom he makes his vow. Asherah undoubtedly makes a promise of children, which is mentioned later on (128:III, 25b-26).[20]

6) Both cycles have seven day journeys, but this has to do with epic style.[21]

I will not list any more points in general, since for the Kret story we move on to other texts that are not complete. However, in the latter part of these cycles there are probably structural parallels in that both deal with marriage, children, success, threat, and fear, and apparently both have a bright conclusion.

In the comparison between Jacob and Kret we have not been talking about the final form (more on that below). Nevertheless, at this point it would appear that the similarities in structure, content, and intention are manifold. Cyrus Gordon has pointed to some of these things many times. He says:

> "We are thus confronted with the fact that Ugaritic legends of Aqhat and Kret reflect a pervading element of the patriarchal narratives; to wit, the divine promise of progeny."[22]

Or again:

> "The prevalence of royal epic (the Kret and Aqhat texts) in Canaan has shown us that the Patriarchal Narratives are (among other things!) royal epic. Like Kret, the Patriarchs are plainly described as the founders of a line of kings in Genesis 17:6 and 35:11."[23]

Now, I think that Professor Gordon is right when he calls these cycles royal epics. The type or genre is right, because the place of these cycles within the history of each state is similar. It seems clear that such royal epics or more generally speaking saga materials have their origin in tribal and pre-monarchial times. Martin Buber says,

> "The saga is the predominant method of preserving the memory of what happens, as long as tribal life is stronger than state organisation."[24]

This does not mean that they cannot be used in several ways during the history of a particular nation. The individual narrative is concerned with a small group. Collections or cycles of such stories relate to entire tribes. At a still later point the cycles can provide a "common national tradition," and still later they can be used for a connected history.[25] This is also the case for more cosmopolitan centers such as Ugarit. Kret was a member of the tribe of *ṯ*ʿ, and this "tribal" material was obviously in existence before the time of the scribe *'Il-Mlk* or *Nqmd*, the King of Ugarit, who probably also belonged to *ṯ*ʿ. Regardless of the original use of the cycle it was used in the time of the kingdom of Ugarit as a royal epic. From father Kret came forth kings. Materials used as royal epics precede the kingdom.

DAVID'S USE OF THE CYCLES

At one time the three major "histories" which we have been discussing probably were separate. They were concerned with tribal fathers, who were in a very real sense kings. Each royal epic was put together by a

---

20 Here Jacob was faithful, whereas Kret seems to have paid little attention to his vow. Kret should have been instructed along the lines of Eccles 5:5.

21 In Kret the journey is seven days, and there is also a seven day waiting period, after he arrives. The seven days are not mentioned in conncetion with Jacob's trip, but, as one should expect, it takes Laban seven days to reach Jacob on the return trip (Gen 21:23).

22 Cyrus H. Gordon, *The Ancient Near East* (1965), 294.

23 Cyrus H. Gordon, *Before the Bible* (1962), 285. Also note p. 282.

24 Martin Buber, *Moses* (1958), 15.

25 J.R. Porter, *JBL*, 87 (1968), 23.

minstrel; a known structure was filled with traditional materials. Some material such as Gen 28:1-9 would be very difficult to assign to a late source, since it is so important to the structure. This passage contains the major purpose of Jacob's journey, namely, to obtain a wife. It should not surprise us, if some of the material that is used to fill such a structure is contradictory, or if it is used several times.

Now it is clear that these cycles were later put together, perhaps at Shechem, in the interest of national unity. This happened during the period of the Judges. It is also true that, when they were put together, many transitional phrases were added that are usually assigned to P. Perhaps even the final conclusions were added, because in them we can see a movement toward a united Israel.[26] This can be illustrated in the burial scenes. Isaac and Ishmael buried Abram; Jacob and Esau buried Isaac; the Twelve buried Joseph at Shechem. "The people" or "all Israel" are basically the northern groups. They use these cycles not only as means of unification but as a claim on the land. They establish their identity and their claims.[27]

I think that, when David became king, his own royal epic was too narrow. When I speak of David's royal epic, I am referring to the "History of Judah." This source is not completely hypothetical. I think that we have the beginning of it in Genesis, chapter 38. It has a very common beginning in terms of structure and content. We not only have the seduction scene, but the "elder shall serve the younger." This epic would help to secure the line of David, but it would not help to win Israel, if it was given in its complete form. This is another way in which the David-Zion tradition of Jerusalem was united with the Patriarchal-Exodus-Sinai traditions of the North. In short the David material intrudes into the preceding material. Without overemphasizing the line of David, the materials that separately were once royal epics and then welded into an epic of nationhood are now, via a fragment of the History of Judah, used once again as royal epic.

There are many details which need further discussion, but my main point is that our Patriarchal Cycles have preceded the monarchy.

Many scholars point to the existence of these cycles before the time of the major sources of the Pentateuch. If this is the case, it is some kind of a miracle that they were continued in separate sources and then reunited into their original shapes. I doubt if this is the case at all.

CONCLUSION

The parallels to royal epics of Patriarchal Cycles help to identify this kind of literature. Early and late parallels are welcomed, because they provide us with more details and open up broad possibilities for dating. However we must stress the *Sitz im Leben* within the history of each nation or state in order to date individual epics. The Patriarchal Cycles existed and were used by Israel before the time of David who reused them (with additions) in order to maintain his own line and to unite it with Israel.

Man other things should be discussed at length in this paper. I have not shared my own work in any complete way, and I have not discussed the Greek side of this question, which is so important in the work of Cyrus Gordon.[28]

---

[26] This does not mean that Judah would be included.

[27] I am of course aware that this type of argument is not new. It can be documented among the works of Gordon, Noth, von Rad, and others.

[28] See Cyrus H. Gordon, "Homer and Bible," *HUCA* 26 (1955), 54-57, where he discusses how such material is used for "national union."

Someday I want to relate this kind of work to the kind of historiography that I think we need. The various stages of the Patriarchal traditions are able to help us in various ways in writing Israel's history. In other words, the Patriarchal traditions in their earliest form could theoretically preserve some "observable facts" (what someone would have seen if he had been there) and some "actual facts" (i.e. what the father actually experienced). But there is probably very little left of this stage. When this material was put into the form of royal epic we are probably confronted with the "actual facts" of the minstrels or tribal groups, i.e. their experience of pride in the success of the fathers who are portrayed in exalted epic form. When these royal epics were put together into an epic of nationhood we again have materials that witness to the "observable fact" of some kind of an "all Israel" and their "actual" experience of kinship. When the epic of nationhood, as supplemented by the History of Judah, is used by David, it would seem that we have material which witnesses to the "observable facts" of the existence of the Kingdom, David, the History of Judah, and similar things. Once again the "actual facts" would be the way in which David and the people now experienced their new unity and kinship with "their" fathers. In short, these studies should relate to our historical interest, because these traditions can contribute various kinds of facts to our understanding of a long period in the history of Israel.

LATE EGYPTIAN OF NON-LITERARY TEXTS OF THE 19th DYNASTY

Sarah Groll

Hebrew University – Jerusalem

It is appropriate that in this volume of studies in honour of Professor Cyrus Gordon my contribution should be in both historical grammatical and cultural interconnections.

Late Egyptian is the spoken language of the New Kingdom. It became the literary language during the reforms of Akhenaten. Our main source of information for Late Egyptian is the non-literary texts of the 19th and 20th Dynasties, written in Hieratic. But even in the framework of the 19th and 20th Dynasties one can trace a considerable grammatical development. The ostracon studied below is an example of the non-literary Late Egyptian of the 19th Dynasty. One should, of course, pay attention to the peculiarities of this language, and perhaps describe the grammatical peculiarities of our ostracon by means of historical grammar.

The Ostracon Translation: Černý and *Gardiner, Hieratic Ostraca,* (abbreviation *H.O.*) pl. XLVI, 2 recto 2 verso.

2 Recto:

(1) Year 6, third month of summer, day 10. This day. The workman Nebnūfer, son of Nakhi, (2) approached the Court of the jury, (lit.: the arriving which the workman A did)[a.] and laid[b.] a charge against the citizeness, Ḥeria, and the workman Nebnūfer said, "As for me, I buried[c.] a chisel of mine in my house after the war, and it was stolen[d.] (4) and I caused all the people who are in the town to bind themselves by an oath concerning my chisel.

After (5) many days the citizeness Nubemnahme came, saying to me,[e.] "The power of god exists.[f.] I (6) saw Ḥeria, while she was stealing[g.] your chisel," so she said.

Then the court said[d.] to Ḥeria, (7) "It was you[i.] who stole this chisel; is it true, or is it not? "

Then Ḥeria answered, (8) "No! It was not I who stole it[j.]"

Then the Court said to Heria, "Are[k.] you prepared to take a great oath (9) by (lit.: "of") the ruler concerning the chisel, saying, 'It was not I who stole it'? "

Then the citizeness Heria said, (10) "As Amun endures, and as the Ruler endures, he whose power is worse than death, (namely) Pharaoh, l.p.h., if it be found[l.] that it was I who stole this chisel, - - - - - ."

(12) After a short time, the court started to re-examine her, (lit.: examined her), and the attendant Pešhedu was sent (13) with her, and she brought the chisel being (14) buried[m.] in her possession together with

a . . . *wšb* of Amūn of the Fair Encounter, (15) which she had buried[n.] (them) in her house, after[o.] she had stolen the . . . . *tꜣ*(16) *nnw* of . . . . and *pꜣ-wšb* of Amun, although[p.] she had taken a great oath by the Lord, l.p.h. saying, (*2 Verso*) (1) "It was not I who stole this chisel." Then the Court (2) stated, "A great wrongdoer[q.] is the citizeness, Heria, worthy[r.] of death (is she), righteous is the workman Nebnūfer[s.],(3) and they left her case to the arrival[t.] of the vizier.

The court (5) of this day consisted of the chief workman Penēb, the chief workman Ḥai, the chief workman Pešhedu, (6) the scribe Pesiūr, the scribe Pentwēr, the chief of police Mentmose, the guardian Ipuy, and (7) the crew altogether: And since the greatest abomination of this town is stealing[u.] (8) copper in it, try[v.] this widow!

In order to inform my lord about the customs[w.] (9) of this place[x.]: The Precedence: the citizeness Tanedjemhese stole a small . . . *ṯk* of $1\frac{1}{2}$ *deben,* here in (10) this town, formerly. The vizier, Neferronpet, was alarmed (?), and, although she was a wife of Pešhedu, (11) the son of Haḥ, the vizier sent the scribe Hatiay, and he caused her to be taken to the market (?) (lit.: river-bank).

(12) My lord shall cause[y.] this woman who stole both the chisel and (13) the . . . *wšb* to be punished, so that no other woman will repeat doing it likewise.

Behold, I am (hereby) informing my lord (of the facts), but the vizier is (15) he who has the last say. May he act in (16) any way he wishes. May the facts (lit.: they) be known!

Grammatical notes:

a. *spr iri.n.A:* an infinitive, (*spr*) of a verb of motion followed by an relative form, (*iri.n.A*). (see Gardiner, *Grammar* § 380).

Note that the relative form *stp.n.f* does not occur in the non-literary texts of the 20th Dynasty.

b. *smi.n.f:* a non-initial *stp.n.f* formation, i.e., the Middle Egyptian narrative *stp.n.f* formation. (Gardiner, *Grammar,* §§ 412-18).

Note that the Middle Egyptian narrative *stp.n.f* formation does not occur in the non-literary texts of the 20th Dynasty.

c. *tims.i:* the Late Egyptian perfect active *stp.f,* the negative counterpart of which is *bwpw.f stp.f.*

Note that the perfect active *stp.f* is a specific Late Egyptian formation, i.e., it is the equivalent of the Middle Egyptian *iw stp.n.f,* (see Gardiner, *Grammar* §§ 68. 464.).

Note that the genuine Late Egyptian formations occur, in our ostracon, basically in the framework of the actual trial investigation, and not in the framework of the technical procedure of the trial.

d. *iw.tw ḥr iṯꜣy.f,iw.i ḥr di.t ʿḳꜣ sn rmṯ nb:* are the non-initial *iw.f ḥr stp.f* of the past, which is made negative by *iw.f ḥr tm stp.f,* (see A. de Buck, *JEA* 23 (1937), 161).

Note that the first position of the actual trial investigation is filled by *ir ink tims.i,* and the *iw.tw ḥr iṯꜣy.f* fills the second position.

Note that the *iw.f ḥr stp.f* of the past is a specific Late Egyptian formation. The corresponding Middle Egyptian formation is the narrative *stp.n.f,* the negative counterpart of which is *n stp.f.*

e. *ḥr ir ḥr sꜣ hrw ḳnw iw ʿnḫ-n-niwt* A *ḥr iy.* Note that an adverb of time fills the first position, whereas the second position is filled by the *iw.f (ḥr) stp.f* of the past.

f. *bȝw nṯr ḫpr:* a first present pattern, the second position of which is filled by a stative of the verb *ḫpr*.

Note that it is a specific Late Egyptian form. Its Middle Egyptian equivalent is either *iw bȝw ḫpr* or *mk bȝw ḫpr*. (see Gardiner, *Grammar*, 319-334.)

Note that the first present is used in the framework of the direct speech.

g. *ptr.i* A *iw.s ḥr iṯȝ: ptr.i* the perfect active *stp.f* of a verb of perception. *iw.s ḥr iṯȝ* the circumstantial first present, (indicating the relative present time), which is made negative by *iw bn sw ḥr iṯȝ*, (see *JEA* 23 (1937), 162).

Note that it is a specific Late Egyptian construction.

h. *ꜥḥꜥ.n dd.n tȝ-ḳnbt,* and see also line 9)., *ꜥḥꜥ.n ḏd.n cnḫ-n-niwt* A, and see also the verso, 1-2)., *ꜥḥꜥ.n tȝ-ḳnbt ḥr ḏd.*

*ꜥḥꜥ.n ḏd.n.*A, although being a common Middle Egyptian formation, (see Gardiner, *Grammar* § 478), it can be classified here as a specific formation of the Late Egyptian of the 19th Dynasty:

1. it occurs only with the verb *ḏd,*
2. it is used to indicate a new phase in the actual trial investigation, and a change of personnel,
3. the formation *ꜥḥꜥ.n.tȝ-ḳnb.t ḥr ḏd* (see Gardiner, *Grammar* § 482.) is used to express the last phase of the trial, namely the verdict, i.e., although *ꜥḥꜥ.n ḏd.n.f* and *ꜥḥꜥ.n* A *ḥr ḏd* are morphologically Middle Egyptian formations, as far as syntactic uses are concerned, they are specific 19th Dynasty formations. Note that in the 20th Dynasty they do not occur.

i.  is the independent pronoun *nṯt*.

j. *bn ink r.iṯȝy sw* a negative participial statement, (see Gardiner, *Grammar*, §§ 373-4.).

r.iṯȝy = *i.iṯȝy,* a specific formation of the participle for the 18th and the 19th Dynasties.

k. *n iw.ṯ (r-)rḫ ir.t ꜥnḫ: n* is the interrogative particle *in.*

iw.ṯ (r) rḫ ir.t is a third future pattern, built in with the infinitive *rḫ* + *ir.t*, indicating willingness or ability.

Note that the marked morpheme of the third future, namely the *r*, which precedes the infinitive, is left out.

Note that it is a specific Late Egyptian formation.

l. *mtw.tw gm.t,* the elliptical conjunctive in an oath, (see Spiegelberg, *Rechtwesen des Pharaonenreiches,* 76-81).

Note that it is a specific Late Egyptian formation.

m. *iw.f tims m-di.s* is a circumstantial first present, with the stative of a transitive verb expressing the passive mood.

m-di.s, "in her possession", indicates, here, "by her".

n. *wꜥ-wšb . . . iw tims.s,* a virtual relative clause, indicating absolute past time, and not relative past time. Note that this is a specific Late Egyptian form.

o. *iw iṯȝy.s* = *iw* + the perfect active *stp.f*, indicating plusperfect, (see A. de Buck, *JEA* 23 [1937], 158(h)).

Note that it is a specific Late Egyptian formation.

p. *ḫr iw iri.s* = *ḫr iw* + the perfect active *stp.f*, expressing the notion of "although". (see Gardiner, *Revue D'Égyptologie* 6 (1951) 120).

q. *ꜥḏȝt ꜥ (t) n niwt:* since *ꜥḏȝ* has the ending *t*, one must classify the sentence as a nominal sentence, and not as an adjectival.

r. *ꜥšꜣw mwt* a one membral adjectival sentence, (see Groll, *Non-verbal Sentence Patterns,* [1967] Exx. 141-3).

s. *mꜣꜥty rmt-iswt* is a "*nfr* B" pattern, (see Groll, *ibid,* Ex. 112).

t. *r-iyt ṯꜣty* = *r* + infinitive + a noun in the direct genitive, a Middle Egyptian formation.

u. *tꜣ-bwt . . . ṯꜣwt* a bimembral nominal sentence, *tꜣ-bwt,* being defined, is the subject, *ṯꜣwt,* being undefined, is the predicate.

It seems that *tꜣ*-, the definite article, here expresses the notion of the superlative.

The *tw,* which follows *bwt,* indicates that the final *t* should be pronounced,

v. *ḫr irm tꜣ-hꜣr.t: ḫr* is the imperative of the verb *ḫr,* 'to speak'. *ḫr irm* means 'to try', (see Caminos, *Late Egyptian Miscellanies,* 459).

tꜣ-ḫꜣr.t = this widow. i.e., *tꜣ* is not the Late Egyptian definite article but the Middle Egyptian anaphoric demonstrative (see Gardiner, *Grammar,* § 110).

w. *sḫr* means, in Late Egyptian, a "way", a "custom", i.e., a specific Late Egyptian connotation.

x. *tꜣ-st* is "this place", i.e., here again the *tꜣ*- is the anaphoric demonstrative.

y. *iri.pꜣy.i-nb r dit,* a third future pattern, with a nominal subject, (see *JEA*, 16 (1930), 220-230).

z. *mry.f,* a Middle Egyptian relative form, indicating future time.

Conclusion:

It seems that Middle Egyptian elements still exist in the non-literary texts of the 19th Dynasty. Indeed, since they occur only under specific conditions, which are peculiar to the 19th Dynasty, one is entitled to describe the Late Egyptian of the 19th Dynasty as an independent selfsufficient system, which is neither Middle Egyptian, nor the Late Egyptian of the 20th Dynasty.

As for the common ancient Near Eastern background of our ostracon, it is perhaps worthwhile to mention that, in contradistinction to the biblical law (according to which two witnesses are required in order to accuse a person), the Egyptian law requires only one eye-witness to accuse a person; compare *H.O.* pl. XLVI, 2 Recto, 6 with Deut 19, 15.

The notions which our ostracon and the biblical law share in common are:

1. A local custom is regarded as being as binding as a law; compare *H.O.* pl. XLVI, 2 Verso, 9-10 with Gen 29, 29; "And Laban said, It is not done in our place."

2. A widow is regarded as a specific legal category; compare *H.O.* pl. XLVI, 2 Verso, 10-11, with Deut 10:18; 14:19; 24:19; Prov. 15:25; Lev 21:14; Num 39:9.

3. A punishment is given, to discourage others from doing likewise; compare, *H.O.* pl. XLVI, 2 Verso, 14, with Deut 19:20: "And those which remain shall hear and fear, and shall henceforth commit no more any such evil among you."

THE BOW OF AQHAT:
THE MEANING OF A MYTHOLOGICAL THEME

Delbert R. Hillers

The John Hopkins University

Those passages in the Aqhat epic which deal with the bow of Aqhat are among the clearest and most coherent portions of the preserved text.[1] Most translators would agree on at least the essential points[2] of the following summary of the sequence of events.

Someone, presumably the craftsman-god Kothar, has promised the wise patriarch Danel a bow. Danel is sitting one day as a judge at the city gate, when he sees Kothar coming, bringing a bow and arrows. Danel and his wife hurriedly prepare to entertain the divine guest. Kothar arrives and presents Danel with the bow and arrows, then dines with them and departs. Danel presents the wonderful bow to his son, Aqhat. There is a break in the text, and from the damaged portion which follows it is only certain that the goddess Anath, while dining, sees the bow and covets it. She offers Aqhat gold and silver for it, but he refuses, suggesting that she could have Kothar make her one just like it. Next she offers him immortality, the life of a god, but he spurns this also, accusing her of lying and (apparently) suggesting that she as a female has no business with a bow anyway. She is thoroughly incensed, and flies off to the father of the gods, El. She slanders Aqhat before El, and wins his grudging permission to do as she pleases. From a much-damaged section it seems that she pretends to make up with Aqhat and leads him on a hunt near a place called Abelim. After a long lacuna, we find her securing the co-operation of a henchman, Yatpan, in a plot on Aqhat's life. As Aqhat is dining, eagles will soar over his head, and among the eagles will be Anath and Yatpan; Yatpan will smite and kill him. They carry out this plot; after the murder Anath weeps, and seems to say (the passage is damaged) that she did it just for his bow. On the next tablet the bow is mentioned again, in a mutilated context; it seems to have been broken. The bow receives its

---

1 Throughout this paper I take Aqht to consist of *CTA* 17, 18, and 19 (*UT*: 2 Aqht, 3 Aqht, and 1 Aqht) and disregard *CTA* 20, 21, and 22 (*UT* 121, 122, 123, and 124), whose connection to the Aqhat epic is obscure and problematic.

2 It seems necessary to comment only on the understanding of *l* in *ltḥwy* (18 IV 27), *l.aḥw* (19 I 16), *lt*[*ḥwy*] (18 IV 13) which is assumed in the present discussion. As rendered by Ginsberg (*ANET*, 152-153) and others, the *l* in each case is positive, so that Anath and Yatpan seem to be predicting the resurrection of Aqhat each time they discuss his death. It seems preferable to take this as negative (so C.H. Gordon) in each case, yielding a parallel (19 I 15-16) *mḫṣ* || *laḥw* and (18 IV 13) *tmḫṣh* || *lt* [*ḥwy*] "slay || not let live." For *l* + *ḥwy* = "kill" cf. Ex 22:17; Deut 20:16 *etc.*; cf. also *ḥym* || *blmt* (17 VI 26-27).

final mention in a frightfully obscure passage, from which we can make out only that Anath (or Yatpan?) killed him just for the bow, and says – such are the ambiguities of Ugaritic – that the bow has been (or has not been) or should be (or should not be) given to her. The rest of the extant text is taken up with telling how Danel and his daughter Paghat learn of the murder, and set about avenging it.

Despite the relative intelligibility of this episode concerning the bow, there is still disagreement on two important points in its interpretation: the motivation of the characters, especially the Virgin Anath, and the relation of this story to other Near Eastern and classical tales. As will become apparent the two problems are related. Only the main lines in the history of interpretation of this episode will be reviewed here, for the sake of clarity.

One popular line of interpretation has been to see in the encounter between Anath and Aqhat a seduction scene. Anath is furious because Aqhat refuses, hence she kills him. De Vaux, in 1937, shortly after publication of the text, saw in Aqhat the story of a young hunter to whom the love of a goddess proves fatal, and he adduced as a parallel the story of Eshmun and Astronoe as related in Damascius, and the Adonis legend.[3] W.F. Albright seconded this opinion with customary vigor: "It is perfectly clear that Aqhat . . . has unwittingly aroused the passionate desire of the goddess Anath, because of his strength and beauty. Like Bitis and Joseph in Egypt, like Eshmun and Kombabos in Syria, like Gilgamesh in Babylonia, the chaste hero spurns the advances of the goddess of love and war. A more characteristic specimen of Near-Eastern mythology would be hard to find."[4]

H.L. Ginsberg threw cold water on this notion in an influential article the next year. Aqhat did not die because the goddess was "love-lorn;" it was the bow which aroused the cupidity of Anath in her character as fierce warrior-goddess. Ginsberg argued that sensuality and fecundity are not prominent attributes of Anath; she is "beautiful, youthful, girlish, vigorous, hoydenish, bellicose, even vicious . . . but not ... voluptuous and reproductive."[5] Since on examination there is nothing in the text which says that Anath tried to seduce Aqhat, Ginsberg's argument were hard to meet. In an article of 1949 reviewing interpretation of the Aqhat myth, Andrée Herdner accepted Ginsberg's case as proven,[6] and in 1949 de Vaux withdrew his earlier idea and agreed with Ginsberg.[7]

Ginsberg's refutation of the seduction theory, however convincing it may be on the negative side, cannot be considered a completely satisfying exegesis. Ginsberg does not take into account the parallels to other tales which de Vaux and Albright had noticed. Even if one concedes that Aqhat, unlike these other stories, does not speak of a seduction, there remain features which are strikingly similar. Even if de Vaux and Albright were mistaken in detail, they seem to have grasped something important which Ginsberg leaves out of account. Furthermore, Anath's cupidity and her frustrated wrath are not perhaps completely accounted for by stressing her bellicose nature. If there is one thing clear from the story, it is that she wants Aqhat's bow; she does not just want a bow, nor would she be content with one just like his. Would the goddess of war necessarily take that line? Several interpreters have framed theories, elaborating on Ginsberg, to account for her motives more fully. Driver, who is in general very pessimistic about our chances of understanding the epic, argued very briefly that the magic bow would have made Aqhat equal to a god, hence Anath's envy.[8] In his *Thespis*, T.H. Gaster developed a similar idea at greater length. Aqhat is the story of ". . . how a mortal huntsman challenged the sup-

[3] Roland de Vaux, Review of Virolleaud, *La légende phénicienne de Danel* (1936), *RB* 46 (1937), 441.
[4] *BASOR*, No. 94 (Apr., 1944), 34. Cf. also H. Stocks, *ZDMG* 97 (1943), 126 n. 1 for similar views.
[5] *BASOR*, No. 97 (Feb., 1945), 3-10; quotation from page 9. Cf. also part II of the article, *BASOR*, No. 98 (Apr., 1945), 15-23 esp. p. 19.
[6] *Syria* 26 (1949), 6.
[7] *RB* 56 (1949), 310 n. 3.
[8] G.R. Driver, *Canaanite Myths and Legends* (1956), 8.

remacy of the goddess of the chase and how his subsequent execution for this impiety caused infertility upon earth."[9] Elaborating on this, Gaster would have it that the bow of Aqhat is a divine bow "withdrawn from a stock which the artisan god Kothar was carrying to the gods."[10] Anath would not desire an ordinary bow, since she presumably already possessed a divine one; she is trying to recover a lost divine weapon. By its very fullness Gaster's explication points to a weakness in the argument; none of this is actually there in the text. To sum up, the course of scholarly discussion of the bow episode in Aqhat has not yet led to a completely satisfying conclusion.

A new line of approach, the one to be carried farther here, was suggested by Harry Hoffner in an article: "Symbols for Masculinity and Femininity."[11] Hoffner was primarily concerned with the use of these symbols in rituals, and so alludes to literary texts, among them Aqhat, only in passing. The bow in Aqhat is "a masculine symbol." This, as will be shown below, is an insight of fundamental importance. Hoffner's further comments on Aqhat unfortunately seem to veer off at once from the promising path struck in the original insight into the symbolic value of the bow.[12] It is this line of interpretation which invites our further consideration.

I. The Bow of Aqhat

That the bow is a common, practically unequivocal symbol of masculinity in ancient Near Eastern texts is sufficiently established by passages quoted in Hoffner's article, and in the present writer's collection of curses on the theme "Warriors become women."[13] One may add to the familiar Ps 127:4-5 ("Like arrows in the hand of a warrior, etc.") another biblical passage, where "bow" seems to be a metaphor for masculinity, specifically sexual prowess, Job 29:20. Job is wishing he were in his prime again: *w^{e}qaštî b^{e}yādî taḥ^{a}lîp* "when my bow was ever new in my hand." Note too that, whereas Hoffner holds that the bow becomes a masculine symbol simply because war is a masculine activity, the phallic symbolism of the arrow is rather obvious. It is in fact confirmed by an ancient text called to my attention by J.J. Roberts, Ben Sira (Ecclesiasticus) 26:12. The sage is warning about the evils of a "headstrong daughter." "As a thirsty wayfarer opens his mouth and drinks from any water near him, so will she sit in front of every post and open her quiver to the arrow" (RSV; Gk. *kai enanti belous anoixei pharetran*). The bow itself, and the quiver, are explicitly sexual symbols in a Mesopotamian potency incantation, one of the ŠÀ.ZI.GA texts: "May the [qu]iver not become e[mpt]y, may the bow not be slack!"[14] In the accompanying ritual, and in several other ŠÀ.ZI.GA rituals, instructions are given for making of model bows to be used in potency rites. To sum up, there is ample proof that bow and arrows are symbols for masculinity.

---

[9] Revised edition (1961), 320.

[10] *Thespis*, 341. At another level of his complicated and nuanced reading of the text, Gaster argues that Aqhat is an astral myth, a version of the Orion story, and that the bow episode is designed to account for certain celestial phenomena of the summer months, the Bow being a constellation. The arguments used to prove this, involving a combination of classical myth and Mesopotamian astronomical lore, seem ingenious and unconvincing to me, but in any case Gaster himself also tries to explain the motives of the characters in Aqhat apart from astronomy, so that it seems permissible at present to bypass his astronomical arguments.

[11] Subtitle "Their Use in Ancient Near Eastern Sympathetic Magic Rituals," *JBL* 85 (1966), 326-334. Aqhat is discussed 330.

[12] Hoffner calls the bow episode in Aqhat a "mythological context with no sexual associations" and asserts that "the goddess seeks the bow, not to secure for herself male sexual powers, but rather to enhance her 'quasimasculine' bellicose attributes." As to the first statement, how can a "masculine symbol" have "no sexual associations"? As to the second – a sheerly ad hoc explanation, – see the following discussion.

[13] D.R. Hillers, *Treaty-Curses and the Old Testament Prophets*, (1964), 66-68.

[14] Robert D. Biggs, *ŠÀ.ZI.GA: Ancient Mesopotamian Potency Incantations*, (1967), 37, No. 18, lines 3'-4'.

A less obvious but for our purpose more important point is that the goddess of love and war is explicitly described, in a number of texts, as the one who takes away men's bows, that is, who changes men into women. The point is of such importance for Aqhat as to justify quotation of the texts, some of which were not cited in Hoffner's study.[15] From an 8th-century treaty we have this curse: "As for the men, may the Mistress of Women take away their bow."[16] From an Old Babylonian prayer: "It is within your (power), Ishtar, to change men into women and women into men."[17] The goddess herself is quoted: "[I change] the man into a woman . . ."[18] The Era Epic iv 55-56 refers to ". . . the male prostitutes and sodomites, whom Ishtar, in order to make the people reverent, had turned from men into women."[19] From a curse in one of Esarhaddon's inscriptions: "May Ishtar, mistress of battle and conflict, turn his masculinity into femininity and set him bound at the feet of his enemy."[20] When the Hittites wish to destroy the prowess of their enemies, they appeal in ritual and prayer to Ishtar of Nineveh: "Take from (their) men masculinity, prowess, robust health, swords (?), battleaxes, bows, arrows, and dagger(s)! And bring them to Hatti! Place in their hand the spindle and mirror of a woman! Dress them as women!"[21] In sum, we have, not just the bow as a symbol for masculine prowess, but a whole complex of symbols parallel to the episode of Aqhat under consideration: the terrible goddess of love and war who may confront a virile and capable man and take away his bow, rob him of his manliness. That most of the texts cited explicitly refer to Ishtar, whereas the Ugaritic epic is concerned with Anath, is not an insuperable obstacle in the way of using the texts cited to elucidate Aqhat. There is a sufficient similarity in conception between Ishtar and Anath to justify the connection.[22] Like Ishtar, Anath is beautiful[23] and sexy;[24] that she is also a ferocious warrior is the most obvious part of her character. An Egyptian text adds exlicit evidence for the transvestite nature of Anath; she is called ". . . Anat the divine, thou the victorious, woman acting as a warrior, clad as men and girt as women."[25]

To sum up, at a literal level Aqhat tells of a young man who loses his bow and his life at the hands of the goddess of love and war; at a symbolic level, a sexual meaning is present. Recognition of this last point is important for clarifying the relation of Aqhat to other myths with a similar plot.

II. The Mythological Theme

The term "theme" is used here to describe a narrative pattern which can be abstracted from a number of concrete examples embodying a variety of the pattern. None of the individual concrete examples includes all the elements which make up the full ideal theme. In fact, a considerable part of the interest in this sort of study is to notice which elements are present or absent or distorted in a given story. Aqhat, for instance, is eccentric in interesting ways. Note that the group of parallels cited is doubtless far from exhaustive even if one thinks

---

15 [Not cited were those in which no bow or arrows are mentioned. – Ed.]
16 Hillers, *Treaty-Curses*, 66-67.
17 *Op.cit.*, 66.
18 *Ibid.*
19 *Op.cit.*, 67.
20 *Ibid.*
21 Hoffner, *JBL* 85, 331.
22 [^{d}IŠTAR is employed as logogram for Anat in Elkunirša Myth. Cf. Hoffner, *RHA* 76 (1965), 5-16. – Ed.]
23 *CTA* 14 (*UT* I Krt) 146, 292-293.
24 *CTA* 11 (*UT* 132), 1-7.
25 The translation is that of A.H. Gardiner, *Hieratic Papyri in the British Museum*, Third Series, Vol. I. Text (1935), 63 (Papyrus VII, Verso I, 12 – II, 1). See also Rainer Stadelmann, *Syrisch-Palästinensische Gottheiten in Ägypten*, Probleme der Ägyptologie, Vol. 5 (Leiden, 1967), 131-133. [Cited already by Hoffner, *JBL* 85 (1966), 334 n. 54. – Ed.]

only of Near Eastern and classical literature. It is not the writer's intention to suggest any historical connection between what are presented here as various forms of the same theme, or story. It is not at all unlikely that historical connections might account for some of the resemblances, for example, between Aqhat and Gilgamesh, but on the one hand there is no direct evidence which could raise such suggestions above the level of speculation, and on the other hand, fundamental traits of human sexual psychology might be responsible for recurrence of similar motifs.

Since not all the tales I regard as parallel to Aqhat are widely known, I will first briefly summarize the essentials of the plot of the stories of Adonis, of Attis, of Stratonice and Kombabos, of Eshmun and Astronoe, of Anubis and Bata, and of the Ishtar episode in Gilgamesh. Thereafter I will discuss the essential theme common to all, and the details found in varying treatments of the theme.

Leaving aside stories of the birth of Adonis, we turn directly to versions of his love and death.[26] In all versions he is the favorite of the goddess of love: Aphrodite, Venus, or in Pseudo-Melito, Balti of Gebal, and in Theodor bar Koni, Balti, also called Estra (presumably a corruption of Astarte). All versions agree that he died a violent death. That made classic by Ovid, who followed Alexandrian predecessors, and attested in many other authors and artistic representations, is that he was killed by a boar (*Metamorphoses*, x 708-716). This version is at least as old as Apollodorus (iii 182ff.; 2nd century B.C.), but just how much older it may be is uncertain. In other, less well-known versions, Adonis is killed by Persephone, or the muses, for grievances against Aphrodite. In Nonnos of Pamphilus (5th century A.D.), Pseudo-Melito, and Theodore bar Koni, he is killed by the love-goddess's jealous husband, Hephaestos. In an eccentric tale preserved in Suidas, Apollo transformed himself into a boar and killed the handsome youth.

The story of Attis also exists in various versions;[27] again that of Ovid is best known (*Fasti*, iv 223-244). Attis, a handsome Phrygian boy, was beloved by Cybele. He promised fidelity to her, and to remain a chaste boy forever. But he broke his vow, and she drove him mad, so that in the end he emasculated himself. In a Phrygian version reconstructed by Hepding the wonderfully fair Attis is loved by the androgynous monster Agdistis, who interferes just when Attis is about to be wed and sets the wedding party all raving mad. Attis himself runs beneath a pine-tree and emasculates himself. In an Lydian version, Attis, a Phrygian, was born without sexual powers. When he grew up he moved to Lydia where he initiated the people into the cult of the Great Mother. She so loved him that Zeus became jealous and sent a boar which killed many Lydians and Attis himself. Herodotus (5th century B.C.) shows the antiquity of the Attis story and of the death through a boar; he transforms elements of the legend into a tale of the Lydian royal house: Croesus' son Atys is tragically killed on a boar-hunt by a Phrygian whom Croesus had offered hospitality.

Lucian's story of Stratonice and Kombabos is told in De Syria Dea 19-27. Stratonice, wife of the king of Assyria, is bidden in a dream to build a temple of Juno in Hierapolis (Bambyce). Her husband sends her with a great company of builders and soldiers, and gives command to a young and very handsome man, Kombabos, to watch over her. Kombabos is very afraid, for he is young and she is fair, so he emasculates himself, puts his member in a little pot with honey and spices, and commits the pot to the king to keep. In Hierapolis, Stratonice falls madly in love with him, but he resists, until finally he must tell her the truth. They continue to keep company and are accused before the king. Summoned by the king, Kombabos proved his innocence and the king gives him gold and vengeance on his slanderers. Kombabos then finished the temple, and his image in

---

[26] For details see W.W. Graf Baudissin, *Adonis und Esmun* (Leipzig, 1911) and Wahib Atallah, *Adonis dans la littérature et l'art grecs* (1966).

[27] For details see Hugo Hepding, *Attis, seine Mythen und sein Kult* (1903) and cf. M.J. Vermaseren, *The Legend of Attis in Greek and Roman Art* (1966).

bronze is set up in the sanctuary, "in shape like a woman, but dressed like a man." His best friends also geld themselves, out of sympathy, or others say, Hera put it in men's minds to do so, so he need not mourn alone. The custom survives until this day.

The tale of Eshmun and Astronoe is told only by Damascius, as transmitted in Photius' *Bibliotheca* (Migne, SG, Tomus CIII cols. 1303-1304).[28] "He (Eshmun) being exceeding fair of face and an admirable young man to look at, was beloved, as the story goes, by Astronoe, a Phoenician goddess, the mother of the gods. He used to go hunting in the wooded glades. Once he saw the goddess lying in wait for him, and fled. She gave chase and had just about caught him, when he cut off his own sexual organ with an axe. She, grieved at this, called the youth Paian, and restored the warmth of life to him and made him a god, called by the Phoenicians Eshmun on account of the warmth of life."

The Egyptian New Kingdom story of Anubis and Bata , the "Story of Two Brothers," is long and full of details; only the barest essentials can be retold here.[29] It is presented as a tale about mortals, but from the names Anubis and Bata, both names of gods, and from other evidence it seems to have been originally a tale about gods. Two brothers lived together, the younger, Bata, as a man of all work for the older, Anubis. The older brother's wife tried to seduce him, but he refused her, and she in revenge accused him to his brother. His brother pursued him with a spear, but miraculously a river full of crocodiles appears between them. The younger man swears to his brother that he is innocent and to confirm his oath cuts off his phallus and thows it into the river. After a complicated series of episodes the story reaches a happy ending.

Only those elements of the Gilgamesh Epic need be recalled which are related in theme to the mythological pattern being considered, Gilgamesh (at the beginning of Tablet VI; *ANET* 83-85) has washed and adorned himself after his victory over the monster Ḫumbaba. Ishtar sees his beauty, and offers rich gifts if he will be her husband. Gilgamesh refuses in a lengthy tirade, in which he recites her cruelties to her former lovers. Isthar is enraged and flees off to heaven, where she bullies Anu into making the Bull of Heaven to ravage the earth. But Gilgamesh and his friend Enkidu kill the Bull of Heaven, and Enkidu tears off its right thigh and tosses it in her face.

As stated above, more stories might have been included (e.g. Actaeon, Hippolytus and Phaedra, Joseph),[30] but these should suffice to permit statement of the essential theme, and comparative study of some details. The basic theme involves the man to whom the attentions of the goddess of love – the embodiment of all that is feminine – prove fatal or at least harmful. Gilgamesh departs farthest from this pattern in that he, the mature hero, is triumphant, not defeated. Otherwise all embody the same pattern. Several have transferred it to the human level, so that the fatal female is not a goddess, but this does not obscure the theme, it only de-mythologizes it.

Details will now be examined, to call attention both to resemblances and divergences. The confrontation of the male by the female is usually depicted as a sexual approach. This is true of all the versions quoted above except for Aqhat. Only in Aqhat is the goddess's initial approach so undisguisedly hostile and threatening. The sexual theme is present (discounting the broken passage *CTA* 18 I 24) in symbolic form, but only emasculation is stressed.

The male is almost always a young man – only Gilgamesh seems to be different – hence this seems to possess considerable importance. In many of the tales, of course, his youthful beauty serves to explain the goddess's ardor, but especially in view of Aqhat, there seems to be more involved. It seems important that he be shown as immature and inexperienced compared to the older and wilier woman.

---

[28] Cf. Baudissin, *Adonis und Esmun*, 339-40.
[29] See *ANET*, 23-25, and literature cited there.
[30] [Cf. also the Elkunirša myth, where ʿAnat solicits then assaults Baʿl. – Ed.]

The youth is a hunter in a significant number of the stories. This is true of some versions of the Adonis and Attis stories, and in Eshmun and Astronoe, and in Aqhat. The reason for this feature is most obvious in Aqhat, where it permits very natural and obvious use of the bow symbol. It seems probable that in the other stories hunting symbolizes and emphasizes the masculine character of the hero.

The hero resists in most versions of the theme, in one fashion or another. In Gilgamesh and Aqhat, where the approach of the goddess is soon felt to be threatening, the hero's resistance is well motivated. In other stories, the youth initially consents, and becomes her lover, but is subsequently unfaithful. In two cases where the story is transferred to a completely human plane, the resistance motif is rationalized and moralized: Kombabos and Bata resist because she is a married lady, the wife of the hero's brother or overlord. This seems from one point of view an obviously secondary development, less primitive than the versions which more openly represent the feminine as a threat to man. But from another point of view, the incest motif introduced in the Bata story may represent a genuine and important component of the sexual tension which gives rise to this sort of tale.

It is interesting to consider the degree to which the goddess is made responsible for the death of the hero, or for seeking his death in cases where he escapes. There is least uniformity here. Instead there is a continuum running all the way from the classical Adonis myth, where there is not the slightest explicit ascription of blame to the goddess, through the version where it is her jealous husband who kills the youth, through the version where the goddess herself causes his death out of jealousy or vengeance for some slight, to Aqhat and Gilgamesh, where she is presented as hostile, deceptive, and threatening to man from the beginning. As a representative of the theme under discussion, the Adonis story in Ovid's telling seems very tame and Aqhat by contrast much bolder and more open. On reflection, however, the Adonis story is perhaps only more subtle.

Emasculation is a feature of a significant number of the stories; it is present as a major feature of Attis stories, in Eshmun and Stratonice, in Anubis and Bata, and in the Kombabos story. It is in Aqhat, under the symbol of the bow, and it is hinted at in versions of the Adonis story. In Ovid, the boar gores Adonis in the groin (*totosque sub inguine dentes abdidit*; as Shakespeare renders it, "And nuzzling in his flank, the loving swine / Sheath'd unaware the tusk in his soft groin"). The wound in Adonis' thigh, familiar from artistic representations, may be taken as the pictorial counterpart of a euphemism.[31] In view of the persistence of this motif, it is scarcely correct to suppose that it is an aetiological intrusion, intended to account for the existence of castrated priests,[32] or to assume that where it occurs, in Eshmun and Astronoe for instance, it has been borrowed from the Attis myth.[33] It comes close to being an essential, constant feature of the theme.

Death through the agency of a beast is present in various versions of the Attis and Adonis myths (the boar); in Gilgamesh (the Bull of Heaven); and in Aqhat (the eagles). This seems worth pointing out, through the significance is not clear to me.[34] The goddess Anath is closely associated with eagles, which play a role in her murder plot. This is clear from the story itself (*CTA* 18 iv 21 "Among the eagles I will soar") and seems to be indicated by her title in a recently-published text *di.dit.rḫpt* "who flies on soaring wings" (*Ugaritica* V 2:8).[35]

---

[31] In Malory's *Morte d'Arthur* Book XIV Sir Perceval nearly yields to temptation in the form of a beautiful woman. Saved in the nick of time, he punishes himself: "and therewith he rooff himselff thorow the thygh."

[32] So J.G. Frazer, *Adonis, Attis, Osiris*, 3rd ed. (London, 1914) I, 265.

[33] So Baudissin, *Adonis und Esmun*, 340.

[34] The boar in the Adonis myth has been explained by Frazer, *ibid.*, as aetiology of a food-taboo, but this seems hardly sufficient to explain all the occurrences.

[35] [In Elkunirša 'Anat transforms herself into a ḫapupi-bird (owl or hoopoe?) and flies into the desert. – Ed.]

The resurrection of the slain youth is not a universal feature. Eshmun is said to have been revived, but otherwise, if we consider only the tales and leave out of account the cult which may have been connected with the myth, the stories end with the tragic death. It is therefore unwarranted to conclude, as some have done, that the incompletely preserved story of Aqhat must originally have ended with his restoration to life.

III. The Meaning of the Theme

As a preliminary to a statement of the meaning of this mythological theme, note that I do not wish to suggest that the explanation to be proposed will serve as a key to everything in mythology. On the contrary, it seems to me axiomatic that there is no single key to everything in mythology, and that we must distrust any universalist principle.[36] Beyond a certain point the more a theory explains, the less credible it becomes. Doubtless some myths, or episodes in myths, arise out of rituals, others are nature myths, or are motivated by concern over social structure, or by astronomy, or by intellectual curiosity, and so on. Whatever in ancient man's life was a significant source of tension, of malaise, could be a source of myth.

The theme which concerns us seems to arise from psychological tension, particularly male sexual tension. The mythological theme springs from man's experience of woman as attractive, yet threatening to his sexuality and his life. We cannot go altogether wrong in mythology, if we occasionally take things at face value. If our story is of rain and crops, we may suppose it to be a nature myth, but if it is of an attractive, menacing woman, of castration and death, then we ought with equal alacrity to recognize that this is a human-nature myth.

There is sufficient evidence outside of myths to show that ancient man was intensely concerned about problems of his potency and his sexuality. Hoffner quite aptly cites the extant Hittite potency incantations in this connection;[37] Bigg's edition of the ŠÀ.ZI.GA texts amply proves that the mind of the ancient Babylonian was not totally preoccupied with whether the grain would rise again. The self-mutilation of the devotees of the great goddess, the pathetic, transvestite Galli, shows, at least for Hellenistic times, the pathological form of the sexual tension which in less extreme form worked on the minds of the mythographers. The essential rightness of the present reading of the bow episode in Aqhat seems to me to be demonstrated by the recurrence of the same theme in so much later misogynist literature. Katherine M. Rogers, in *The Troublesome Helpmate: A History of Misogyny in Literature*, sums up the stereotype: "Woman is mindless and heartless, but all-powerful; sexual involvement with her is irresistible, but dreadfully dangerous; man had better defend himself by attacking her before she attacks him; yet, no matter what he does, she will survive him because of her animal insensitivity and unawareness of morals."[38]

---

[36] This view is well argued at various points in G.S. Kirk, *Myth: Its Meaning and Functions in Ancient and Other Cultures* (1971). Something similar was argued by W.F. Albright in an early article, "Historical and Mythical Elements in the Story of Joseph," *JBL*, 37 (1918), 111: "No one brush will suffice to reproduce the variegated coloring of Truth." Though Albright later rejected much in it, his paper is still of value in consideration of the mythological theme discussed here.

[37] *JBL*, 85, 326 n. 3.

[38] (Seattle and London, 1966), 252. Note also Gilbert Highet's discussion of Catullus' Attis, in *Poets in a Landscape* (1957) 26, where, after treating the surface meaning of the poem, he continues: "But it has another hidden significance, which has not been noticed. That is that it is a translation into mythical terms of Catullus's relation to Clodia. It is the desperate complaint of a young man who was once happy and normal, but who has been seized and dominated by a female demon. The demon does not stand for comfort and satisfaction, not even for the ecstasies of sexual fulfilment. She is a primitive spirit, living in dark jungles and served by fierce animals. The man can have no peaceful and balanced relationship with her. Although she is feminine and he is (or was) masculine, he must be utterly subservient to her. Her aim is to take away his manhood, to destroy him and yet to keep him alive as a slave and a symbol of her power. (In his farewell poem to Clodia, written much later, Catullus said she treated all her lovers in the same way, 'leaving their loins limp,' almost unmanning them.)"

It must be left to the professional psychologist or psychiatrist to go farther into the springs of human nature which give rise to this mythological theme. Beyond this point the philologian runs too great a risk of dilettantism. In fact, one may justly ask whether a Semitic philologian has any business exploring this aspect of mythology at all. Certainly some psychiatrists and theoreticians of mythology have a wider perspective, and offer more penetrating insights into mythology, than is possible for someone who starts from the narrow base of an acquaintance with Ugaritic myths in the original. There are, I believe, two considerations which help justify such a venture outside one's proper field as the present. The first is that a philologian may occasionally offer some control to the more speculative postulations of thinkers in other disciplines. That is perhaps true in the present case. What a speculative psychiatrist like Erich Neumann, for instance, might have said about the figure of Anath and the bow episode in Aqhat, to judge from his extant writings,[39] finds explicit confirmation in Near Eastern texts. The second contribution a philologian may hope to make in this field is to help break down a kind of unexamined orthodoxy which has grown up in the study of Near Eastern mythology[40] and more particularly, in biblical studies. Scholars in biblical studies inevitably reflect on the nature of myth, one principal motive being their desire to compare Israelite thought with the thought of contemporary polytheism. In this interesting area, however, the theory of myth which prevails is practically unrelieved Frazer. In the popular and influential work on Near Eastern religion and mythology of Henri Frankfort and others, *Before Philosophy*, myths are presented as ". . . natural phenomena . . . conceived in terms of human experience."[41] Here nature is not taken to include man's own nature, but is rather the material world, or even the rural landscape as opposed to urban life.[42] In another influential work, G. Ernest Wright's *The Old Testament Against Its Environment*, polytheism is presented entirely as arising from "ancient man's experience of power and force in nature" – nature understood as made up of thunderstorms, the sky, the stars, the earth, and so on through the macrocosm with the microcosm, man, left out of account.[43] A similar criticism may be leveled against the view of myth presented in Brevard Child's *Myth and Reality in the Old Testament*. Although Childs alludes to "psychological stimuli" as a source for myth alongside "impressions from nature", in the development of his work the psychological avenue is left unexplored.[44] Such a narrowing of one's notion of what myth may be about is in danger of underestimating the spiritual concerns of ancient man, and distorts the relation between the thought of ancient polytheism and Israelite thought.

IV. The Meaning of the Aqhat Epic

Enough has already been said about the writer's interpretation of one episode within the Aqhat epic. At this point it would be in place to give some account of how a new understanding of the bow episode would

---

[39] See, for instance, *The Origins and History of Consciousness*, Bollingen Series XLIII (Princeton, 1954), 39-101.

[40] Ugaritic mythology is so widely held to be concerned with fertility that G.S. Kirk, *Myth*, 223, rates Canaanite myths as uninteresting in comparison to Greek, for "the Canaanite merely repeat *ad nauseam* the themes of succession and the disappearance of fertility." Wolfgang Helck, *Betrachtungen zur großen Göttin und den ihr verbundenen Gottheiten*, Religion und Kultur der alten Mittelmeerwelt in Parallelforschungen, Band 2 (Munich and Vienna, 1971), deserves credit for stressing that the great goddess represents aggressive sexuality. At the same time, one may criticize Helck's one-sidedness; in refusing to recongnize motherly traits and fecundity as part of the conception of the goddess he not only seems to neglect some of the evidence, but misses the point that ancient man, like man since, experienced ambivalent feelings about the feminine. Moreover, his derivation of fear of the female from a hypothetical stage of society where the sexes ran in separate bands seems implausible at best.

[41] Henri Frankfort, Mrs. H.A. Frankfort, J. A. Wilson, and Thorkild Jacobsen, *Before Philosophy* (1949), 12.

[42] *Op. cit.*, 238.

[43] Studies in Biblical Theology, No. 2 (London, 1950), 17.

[44] Studies in Biblical Theology, No. 27 (Naperville, Illinois, 1960), 17.

affect interpretation of the epic as a whole, in so far as that is possible in view of the fragmentary state of the text. The writer prefers to defer this discussion. One would have to take up the question of whether the epic is in any important way concerned about fertility, or a seasonal cycle of fertility and infertility, and this would in turn involve giving attention to the same question about Attis and Adonis and the rest, a process which would unduly lengthen this paper. Leaving that major question aside, one may nevertheless point out that also in other episodes the epic is concerned with sexuality and the feminine. The first preserved episode depicts the patriarch Danel's anguish over his sterility, his lack of a son and heir, a problem in the sexual sphere. In the final tablet of the three which make up the epic as we have it, after the death of Aqhat a new character makes an appearance, Aqhat's sister Paghat (the name means, apparently, "girl, maid"). Her stock epithets, in so far as we understand them, stress her knowledge of astrology, and the fact that she is able correctly to interpret the meaning of the vultures over her father's house is consistent with seeing her as a wise-woman, someone skilled in divination. This is not, of course, enough to maker her a full-fledged Athena figure, yet it is legitimate to point out the contrast to the irrational, violent Anath. The end of the preserved story is especially interesting. Paghat sets out saying: "I'll slay the slayer of my brother," and to do this she arms herself as a warrior. (The preserved text is unclear as to just how she is clothed; one line asserts that she clothes herself as a man, *CTA* 19 IV 206; another seems to have her put on woman's clothing over it, 208.) Before we find out if she succeeds in killing her brother's murderer, the text breaks off, but if we assume, as most have, that she does, there is a nice balance in the feminine types presented in Aqhat. One is the Virgin Anath, deceiving, violent, emasculating, the one who turns a man into a woman; opposing her and perhaps victorious in the end is Paghat, the sister, wise, compassionate, and loyal, who turns herself into a man in the cause of justice.[45]

---

[45] Neumann, *Origins and History*, 201-202 has a good discussion of this feminine type.

INCEST, SODOMY AND BESTIALITY IN THE ANCIENT NEAR EAST

Harry A. Hoffner, Jr.
Yale University – New Haven, Conn.

I. Old Testament Legislation.

That a human male should have sexual relations with any other than a human female who herself was born outside the circle of his own immediate blood kin was regarded as a moral outrage in ancient Israel. Thus sexual relations with animals (bestiality), with humans of the same sex (homosexuality), or with one's own immediate blood kin (incest) made an individual liable to the death penalty.[1]

Although other passages indirectly express the same resolute hostility toward the coupling of man and animal,[2] the most forthright and direct statement of condemnation is to be found in Lev. 18:23 ("And you shall not give your semen to any beast to defile yourself with it, neither shall any woman give herself to a beast to copulate with it: it is perversion [Heb. *tebel*].") and Lev. 20:15-16 ("If a man lies with a beast, he shall be put to death; and you shall kill the beast. If a woman approaches any beast and lies with it, you shall kill the woman and the beast; they shall be put to death, their blood is upon them."). In each of the formulations just cited it is explicit that the human partner has initiated the cross-species mating.[3] The action brings an automatic blood guilt upon both the human and the animal, which must be resolved by execution.

Homosexual relations were also regarded as a crime worthy of death (Lev. 18:22; 20:13). Wages earned by homosexuals could not be accepted in the temple as payment for a vow (Deut. 23:18; Judg. 19:22). Various terms were current in ancient Israel for the homosexual: *keleb* "dog" (Deut. 23:19), and *qadeš* "sacred male (prostitute)".[4] Houses of male prostitutes were destroyed by King Josiah (2 Kings 23:7). No distinct terms have survived in the OT to designate the dominant as opposed to the passive homosexual, although the Greek term *malakos* "effeminate" is employed by St. Paul (1 Cor. 6:9; Rom. 1:27) to designate the latter type.

Incest (Germ. *Blutschande*) is defined as sexual intercourse between two persons too closely related for marriage according to the mores of the community. Each community determines the degrees of kinship permitted. A number of forbidden couplings are enumerated in Lev. 20:11-12, 17-21. One was forbidden to copulate with his father's wife, whether or not she was only a step-mother (Gen. 35:22; 49:4; Ezek. 22:10-11; 1 Cor. 5:1). One was forbidden to copulate with one's sister, whether paternal or maternal (Lev. 20:17; Ezek. 22:10-11), even though the patriarch Abraham was alleged to be paternal brother of his wife Sarah (Gen. 20:2 and 12). This crime formed the subject of the story of Amnon and Tamar, who were both children of King David but from different mothers (2 Sam. 13). One was forbidden to lie with his daughters or daughters-in-law (Lev. 20:12; Ezek. 22:10-11). This crime formed the subject of the story of Lot and his two daughters, who deemed themselves to be the sole survivors of the human race after the destruction of Sodom and Gomorrah

---

1 Whereas in English one distinguishes "bestiality" from "sodomy" (homosexuality as the practice of Sodom, cf. Gen 19), in German "Sodomie" includes both homosexuality and bestiality.

2 Thus in Gen. 2:18ff. the search for a mate (Heb. *ʿēzer* k^{e}*negdô*) appropriate for the first man led first to the animal kingdom (verses 19-20) before it became apparent to God that no suitable partner for the man could be found there. Having rejected the animal solution, God created woman (2:21-24).

3 By contrast Hittite law § 199 envisages the possibility of the animal taking the initiative, on which see below.

4 Perhaps, however, the clients of the *qadeš* were females.

and thus justified their act (Gen. 19:31-35). An exception to this rule was the patriarch Judah, who was obliged to fulfil the duty of the *levir* (Heb. *meyabbem*) to Tamar on his sons' behalf (Gen. 38). The penalty for committing incest was death (Lev. 20:11-13), by fire if a man cohabited with a wife and her mother also (Lev. 20:14).

II. Syro-Palestine and Mesopotamia.

Among the ancient Syro-Palestinian cultures we cannot determine with certainty the attitude toward such acts. It has often been supposed that the Israelite legislation was in response to the practice of these acts by the surrounding peoples, and in fact this notion is attested in the OT itself (e.g. Lev. 20:23).[5] The story of the Syro-Palestinian god Ba'al copulating with a heifer seems to have been told with no trace of disapproval.[6] This does not mean, of course, that adult human males and females within the community in which these myths were told had no scruples against copulation with animals.[7] Unfortunately we have no corpus of laws for the communities living in Syro-Palestine other than the Isrealites.

In Mesopotamia bestiality is not mentioned in any corpus of laws. It is only a supposition that in the Gilgamesh Epic the man Enkidu copulated with animals until his first encounter with a woman, namely the harlot, who introduced him to human sexual intercourse and thus alienated him from his animal friends.[8] It must be a supposition, for nothing in the text explicitly says that he ever mated with the animals. Yet one must admit that it is not an improbable supposition, since Enkidu was raised among the animals and might well have imitated the mating activities which he observed. There are few laws regarding homosexuality in Mesopotamian legal corpora.[9] It has been suggested that male cult figures such as the *assinnu*, the *kulu'u*, the *sinnišānu*, and the *pilpilû*, some of whom are said to dress as women, were homosexuals, but there is no agreement among scholars on this point.[10] With regard to incest the Code of Ḫammurapi §§ 154-158 enumerate several forbidden degrees of relationship: father – daughter, father – daughter-in-law, son – mother, son – foster-mother.

III. Hittite Asia Minor.

It would seem that aside from the OT the only ancient Near Eastern culture in whose legal literature the copulation of humans and animals is mentioned is that of the Hittites. In laws §§ 187-88 and §§ 199-200A it is stated that, if a man has sexual relations with a cow, a sheep, a pig or a dog, he has become guilty of *ḫur=kel* and must die. If on the other hand he has sexual relations with a horse or a mule, there is no offence. I cannot offer a solution to the problem of the distinction between the cow, sheep, pig and dog on the one hand and the horse and mule on the other. C.H. Gordon has expressed the opinion that these laws are a manifestation of the "varying degrees of kinship with the different animal species" felt by the ancients.[11] The same kind of distinction is implicit, he thinks, in modern western man's willingness to eat beef, pork, and mutton, but his reluctance to eat horse or dog meat. One might seek a distinction between the other animals and the

---

5 For example see C.H. Gordon, "A Note on the Tenth Commandment," JBR 31 (1963), 2-8 and 209, and O.J. Baab, IDB, I, 387 s.v. "bestiality".

6 C.H. Gordon, UT, 196, text 132:1ff. (cf. ANET, 142).

7 See the remarks about the Bena, Dahomeans, Kiwai, Lakher, Penobscot, etc. in C.S. Ford and F.A. Beach, *Patterns of Sexual Behavior* (New York, 1951), 146f.

8 O.J. Baab in IDB, I, 387, basing his observation on Gilgamesh, Tabl. I, iv 1-41 (cf. ANET, 75, and R. Labat, in *Les religions du proche-orient* [1970], 153-54).

9 Only in Middle Assyr. Law § 20, on which see G. Cardascia, 133-5.

10 *assinnu* "Buhlknabe" (AHw, 75), *kulu'u* "Kultprostituierter, Buhlknabe" (AHw, 505), *kurgarrû* "ein Kultdiener" (AHw, 510), *pilpilû* "Buhlknabe, Kinäde" (AHw, 863), and *sinnišānu* "effeminate man" are some of the relevant terms. A negative verdict on association with homosexuality is given by the CAD A^2, 341 on *assinnu*, and CAD K, 529, 557ff. on *kulu'u* and *kurgarrû*.

11 *The Ancient Near East* (3rd ed., 1965, in paperback of *Introduction to Old Testament Times*, 1953), 242 with note 8a.

equids in the more recent date of domestication of the horse and the mule. But I confess that I do not see in this a ready and workable solution.

In Hittite law § 199 an allowance is made for cases in which a sexually aroused animal might initiate the relationship, in which instance no guilt accrues to the human. As strange as such a situation might appear to some readers, especially readers whose life-locus is distinctly urban, there is ample attestation in the annals of anthropology of animal-human sexual relationships initiated by the animal partner. Several of these instances are recorded by Clellan S. Ford and Frank A. Beach, including an account by A.W. Yerkes in *The Mind of the Gorilla* of sexual solicitation directed at himself by an immature female gorilla named Congo. I quote only particularly relevant lines from Yerkes: "Congo came close to me . . . [and] throwing herself on her back she pressed her external genitalia against my feet and repeatedly and determinely tried to pull me upon her . . . In this activity she was . . . vigorously aggressive, and it required considerable adroitness and strength of resistance on my part to withstand her attack. . . . Her insistence on sexual contact was . . . somewhat dangerous because of her enormous strength, but throughout the period of observation she was unusually gentle and friendly, although determined in her efforts to satisfy her desire."[12] Such behaviour is by no means limited to primates, but can be and has been observed in other species. Incidence is particularly high, however, when the animal has been denied normal sexual contacts with members of its own species.

There is no indication in the Hittite laws that the life of the animal involved was ever spared, when the human was executed. Thus Hittite (and ancient Hebrew) law stands in contrast to the derivative law of the Christian societies of medieval Europe and colonial America, in which a court could find the animal partner innocent.[13]

In Hittite those couplings which were illegal were called *ḫurkel*. As *ḫurkel* the Hittites designated sexual relationships with most animals (§§ 187-88, §§ 199-200A),[14] with one's mother, daughter or son (§ 189), with one's stepmother while one's father was alive (§ 190), with one's sister-in-law while one's brother was alive (§ 195), with a free woman and her mother (§ 195), or with a free woman and her sister (§ 195). Aside from the coupling with animals it is clear that the definition of *ḫurkel* always takes into account the degree of kinship. Stating it another way, those couplings which are condemned are incestuous, in that they involve partners who are too intimately related by blood or by marriage to allow sexual intercourse. Homosexuality as such is not termed *ḫurkel*. A man who sodomizes his son is guilty of *ḫurkel* because his partner is his son, not because they are of the same sex. It is not out of the question that one should regularly translate *ḫurkel* as "incest" (*Blutschande*, *inceste*). The principal apparent exception would be in the cases involving animals, and these would be no exception, if Gordon's theory were accepted. There is no case to my knowledge in published Hittite texts were *ḫurkel* describes a crime which does not involve a sexual combination which is condemned by social mores. One would need such an example, it would seem, in order to reject the translation "forbidden sexual relationship" in favor of the more general "abomination" or "detestable act".[15]

One can subdivide the translations of Hittite *hurkel* which have been offered up to the present into two groups: (1) those which concern the nature of the act, and (2) those which specify the mode of punishment. Those of A. Goetze ("capital crime", *ANET*, 196f.) and S. Alp ("Räderung", *JCS* 6 [1952], 95f.) fall in the second category

12 R.M. Yerkes cited by Ford and Beach, *Patterns of Sexual Behavior*, 148-49.

13 "E.P. Evans states that at Vanvres in 1750 one Jacques Verrons was hung for copulating with a she-ass. The animal was acquitted on the grounds that she was a victim of violence and had not participated of her own free will. The prior of the local convent and several citizens of the town signed a certificate stating that they had known said she-ass for four years, and that she had always shown herself to be virtuous both at home and abroad and had never given occasion of scandal to anyone. This document was produced at the trial and is said to have exerted a decisive influence upon the judgment of the court." Ford and Beach, *Patterns of Sexual Behavior*, 144-45.

14 H. Hoffner, *Tyndale Bulletin* 20 (1969), 41-42.

15 HWb, 76, and Friedrich, HG, 112-13.

and can be disallowed by virtue of the variety of responses available to the community toward the act of *hurkel*: it could executed, banish, or – as we shall see below – purify the offender. In category one fall the translations "Greuel, abscheuliche Tat, unerhörte Tat" offered by Friedrich (e.g., *HWb*, 76). These translations lack the precision which the available evidence now allows. In the majority of the occurrences in ritual texts the word simply denotes an evil to be removed from the man who committed the deed (IBoT II 117+ 1'-3'; KBo XXI 35 i 4'; KBo XIII 104+ Bo 6464 15'; Bo 2968 obv? 5'-10'; Bo 69/900 10'-11'; 254/d 15'; 173/q 4'-5'), from his house or city (KUB XXX 34 iv 15-18), or from the king who is indirectly defiled by the misdeeds of his subjects (KBo XIII 109 iii 4-11 (with dupl. Bo 898 rt. 1'-7'). In these passages *ḫurkel* is associated with such other terms as *paprātar* "defilement" (KBo XIII 109 iii 10), (*idālu*) *alwanzātar* "(evil) sorcery" (Bo 2968 obv? 8'; 173/q ii? 5'; Bo 6464 13'-14'(?)), *lingāiš* "(evil) oath, perjury" (Bo 2968 obv? 9') *eš*[*ḫar*?] "bloodshed" (Bo 2968 obv? 8'; rev? 5'; KUB XXX 34 iv 17), *inan* "disease" (KUB XXX 34 iv 17), *mūlatar*/*mulātar* (KBo XIII 109 iii 10; Bo 898 rt. 7'), and the Akkadiogram *AN-ZE-EL-LU* (KBo XIII 109 ii 10', iii 9; Bo 898 rt. 6') "tabu, forbidden food, forbidden deed".[16]

Like these terms *ḫurkel* should be allowed a general meaning but distinct from each of the accompanying terms. That general meaning I would propose was "forbidden sexual combination, incest" (German "unerlaubte Geschlechtspaarung, Blutschande"). Friedrich's "Greuel, abscheuliche Tat, unerhörte Tat" overlaps too much with the meaning of the other terms in the lists. Nor can one adduce a single example from the cases in the Hittite laws (or elsewhere in Hittite texts) in which an act other than a sexual one is called *ḫurkel*.

The passage from Bo 6464 11'-14' is strikingly similar to the entry in the catalogue text KUB XXX 67 7'-9' (cf. Laroche, CTH, p. 40 n. 1, pp. 171-72):

[I *ṬUP-PU nu-uš-š*]*a-an* III SISKUR *a-ni-ya-an* INIM *ᶠḪu-un-ta-ri-it-ta-a*
[*ma-a-an* . . . . . *.na*? *-a*]*ḫ-ḫu-wa-i na-aš-ma-an-kán* DINGIR.MEŠ *pár-ra-an-da* ḪUL *-lu*
[. . . . . *n*]*a-aš-ma ḫur-ke-el i-ya-an ḫar-zi*

The same phrases may have stood in the text of which we now have only a very small piece, the as yet unpublished Yale Hittite fragment YBC 3991, which reads:

. . . . *ma-*]*a-an-za* UN*-an* [*ku*? *-iš*? *-ki*? . . . .
. . . . *na-aš-m*]*a kur-ke-el* [*i-ya-an ḫar*? *-zi*? . . . .
. . . .]x ᴰU*-aš* Ù [. . . . .
. . . .]*-i*? *ku-it-ki* [. . . . .

Bo 2968 obv? 5'-10' reads as follows:

ka-a-aš-wa-kán GIM*-an* . . . . . . [. . . . .
É IN.NU.DA IN.NU.DA *pa-ra-a* [. . . . .
zi-in-na-a-i ki-nu-un-na-wa ke[*-e-da-ni*]
[U]N*-ši* ḪUL*-lu al-wa-an-za-tar e-eš-*[*ḫar*? . . .]
[*l*]*i-in-ga-a-en ḫu-ur-ki-il* [. .*QA*? *-TAM*? *-MA*?]
[GAM]*-an ar-ḫa ze-en-ni-eš-d*[*u*]

"As this . . . .[17]. [. . . .] the straw barn (and?) straw . . [. .]
makes an end, now [for] th[is ma]n [in like manner] let [. .]
make an end of evil sorcery, bloo[dshed, . . .], perjury (and) *ḫurkel*!"

[16] (*AHw*, 56; *CAD* a/2, 153; on the Sumerian word an-zil see *MSL* 12, 165 and 183 [lú-an-zil-kú-kú], and ZA 57, 101. A related Sum. word may possibly be written zi-lá = Akkad. *ebīru ša usukki* "offence of the sex-criminal" [Delitzsch, *Sum.Gloss.*, 225; Th. Jacobsen, *Image of Tammuz*, 207].).

[17] It would appear that E. Forrer (*BoTU*, I, p. 16, number 8) read the configuration of wedges which I have left untransliterated as ᴳᴵˢAGA. H.G. Güterbock (*JCS*15 [1961], 68-69, n. 19) suggested that this as yet unpublished tablet be checked in order to compare Forrer's "AGA" with the sign in KBo VI 2 ii 57, which is problematic. It seems to me purely from a contextual viewpoint that AGA (i.e., "crown") is out of place in Bo 2968 obv? 5'-10'. The item is the grammatical subject of the verb *zinnai*, the direct object of which appears to be É.IN.NU.DA (and) IN.NU.DA. One thinks of an agricultural implement of some type, but not a crown.

Since it would appear that homosexuality was not outlawed among the Hittites, we can proceed to the question of punishments only with regard to bestiality and incest, and perhaps, since mating with equids was permitted, only with regard to incest itself. In the Hittite laws, whose formulation in the main version dates to the very beginning of the Old Kingdom (c. 1650 B.C.), if not earlier, the normal punishment for *ḫurkel* was execution. However, the king might spare the life of his subject, in which case the one guilty of *ḫurkel* was banished from his city.[18] In another text, whose period of composition probably falls in the 15th or 14th century B.C.,[19] it is stated that various cities and towns within the Hittites' sphere of control had different traditions regarding punishment of *ḫurkel*. Some executed the offender(s), others banished. From the 17th through the 14th century no Hittite document records any option for the city other than executing or banishing.

These punishments render it apparent that such a law does not belong to the category of torts and personal offences, such as do the bulk of the laws in the corpus. *ḫurkel* constitutes an offence against the culprit's city. By committing such an act he has brought impurity upon his fellow townsmen and made them liable to divine wrath. Thus the townsfolk must protect themselves by eradicating the cause of divine wrath, i.e., either by executing the offender(s) or removing them permanently from the town.[20] Thus is explained the attending actions associated with purification. In the laws the offender(s) may not approach the king (§§ 187-88, 199-200A).[21] Even the man whose coupling with an equid is deemed "no offence" may not approach the king nor ever after become a priest.[22] Townsfolk who banish one guilty of *ḫurkel* must afterward bathe themselves.[23] Such purification rites as transpired, therefore, would have been for the city and its residents rather than for the banished man.[24] His departure from the city would lose its significance, if the impurity could be removed from him by a ritual. Like the scapegoat the banished man carried his impurity with him far away from the city (Lev 16:20ff.).

It is therefore highly interesting that there have recently turned up tablets and library catalogue entries for tablets containing rituals to remove the impurity of bestiality and incest from a man.[25] For this constitutes primary evidence for a further development in the religio-legal attitude toward incest and bestiality among the Hittites. During the Old Kingdom and the earliest years of the Empire period it would seem that either execution or banishment was practiced in the towns of the Hittite empire and purification rituals were performed for the town(sfolk) after the offender's departure. The present copy of the ritual *KUB* XLI 11 may be dated to the reign of Ḫattušili III or that of one of his two successors (second half of the 13th century B.C.),[26] while the

[18] Law § 196. Two offenders (slaves) are involved. Each is removed to a different town. Both are banished from the town in which they committed the offence. Even in §§ 187-88 and 199, where "the king may spare his life" (*huišnuzi-an* LUGAL-*uš*), the offender was not allowed to stay in the town in which the crime was committed (see also below).

[19] KUB XIII 2+ iii 9ff. (von Schuler, *Dienstanw.*, 47; ANET, 211; Güterbock, JAOS Suppl. 17 [1954], 18).

[20] See the societies enumerated in Ford and Beach, *Patterns*, 146-47, in which death or banishment are the preferred courses of action taken by the citizens. Note also that in the Code of Hammurapi the man guilty of incest is either executed (§§ 155, 157) or banished from home and city (§§ 154, 158).

[21] Goetze's translation (ANET, 196-97) "he must not appeal to the king" is unlikely. One must remember the sacred person of the king and the need to scrupulously protect him from men bearing impurity. A. Goetze, *Kleinasien*[2] (1957), 89ff.; J. Friedrich, MAOG 4 (1928), 46-58; ANET, 207 (KUB XIII 3).

[22] Goetze's (ANET, 197) "nor shall he become a case for the priest" would require: *ŠA* LÚSANGA *Ú-UL ki-i-ša*, instead of what the text offers: LÚSANGA-*ša* *Ú-UL ki-i-ša* "he shall not become a priest".

[23] XIII 2+ iii 14 (von Schuler, *Dienstanw.*, 47; ANET, 211): *nam-ma-za* URU-*aš* EGIR-*an-da wa-ar-ap-du*, "furthermore afterwards let (all) the city bathe itself."

[24] A sample ritual designed to remove the taint of *ḫurkel* from a town is KUB XXX 34 (iv 15ff.).

[25] Only the newly published KUB XLI 11 explicitly pertains to bestiality. The library catalogue entry is KUB XXX 67 7'-9', which ritual is designed to purify a man who has committed *ḫurkel*. Presumably this applied to all types of *ḫurkel*, including bestiality. But the catalogue entry does not specify. A ritual to purify from incest is KBo XII 115 with dupl. IBoT II 117 (CTH 445). Note too the association of the *nakkuššiuš* with *ḫurkel* in 254/d ii 1' and 15'.

[26] Specific linguistic clues are the following datable spellings: UN-*aš* (line 29') as replacement for older *an-tu-uḫ-ša-aš* generally not earlier than Mursili II; GAM and GAM-*an* (lines 2' and 32') for older *kat-ta-an* not be-

time of the ritual's written composition may go back to the reign of Mursili II.[27] It is highly unlikely that this ritual was composed as early as the reign of Šuppiluliuma I much less during those of his predecessors. The ritual has a pronounced Kizzuwatnaean cast and compares strikingly with other Hittite rituals of Kizzuwatnaean origin composed during the empire period (14th and 13th centuries). As in other Kizzuwatnaean rituals the offering of birds is prominent (lines 4 and 6ff.) including the bird whose name is usually written MUŠEN *ḪUR-RI* but in this text MUŠEN *ḫur-ri-li-in* ("Hurrian bird"; line 4)![28] As in other such rituals each bird is offered not to a deity but for an aspect of the sin or its effect: for sin, for the curse, for anger, for weeping; or for some aspect of the hoped-for reconciliation: for peace (*takšul*).[29] The location of the offerings is specified by the two locative forms *ambašši* (8', 11') and *kutruešni*.[30] Like other Hurrian rituals one or more animals (in this case a sheep and a bird, line 12) are released as scapegoats (*nakkušši-*, in this text, line 12, the unique spelling *nakkuššan*) to carry away the defilement to a remote and unoccupied place.[31] The ritual is probably late therefore and belongs to a period when Hurrian religious influence from Kizzuwatna was particularly strong (perhaps the reign of Muwatalli or Hattusili III).

KUB XLI 11

TRANSLITERATION

§ 1 2 [*ma-a-an* LÚ-*a*]*š* UDU-*i na-aš-ma* ÙZ-*i* GAM *w*[*a*]-*aš-t*[*a-i nu* UDU? *-un da-an-zi*]
3 [*na-an-kán* MÍ].É.GE$_4$.A-*aš i-wa-ar an-*[*d*]*a ka*[*-ri-ya-an-zi* x x x][32]
4 [x x x x L]Ú-*LIM* I MUŠEN *ḫur-ri-li-in* SUM-*an-z*[*i* x x x x x x]
5 [x x x x -*š*]*i*? *-kán še-er ap-pa-an-zi*

---

§ 2 6 [*nu-za* x x *k*]*u-up-te-uš wa-al-ḫa-an-zi* I UDU I MUŠEN *wa-aš-t*[*úl-aš*]
7 [I UDU I MUŠE]N *ḫur-ti-ya-aš* I MUŠEN NA$_4$-*i* RA-*an-zi*
8 [I UDU I MUŠEN-*y*]*a ták-šu-la-aš* I MUŠEN *am<-ba-aš>-ši ḫur-ti-ya-a*[*š* x x x]

---

fore Muršili II; SUM-*an-zi* (line 4') for older *pí-(ya-)an-zi* probably no earlier than Tudḫaliya IV; RA-*an-zi* lines 7', 10') for older *wa-al-ḫa-an-zi* or GUL-*an-zi* not before Tudḫaliya IV; DÙ-*at* (22', 30') for older *i-ya-at* rare in Muršili II becomes more common in Muwatalli and Ḫattušili III; KAR-*zi* (26') for older *ú-e-mi-ya-zi* appears first in Ḫattušili III; *me-ma-an-zi* (21') for older *me-mi-an-zi* probably no earlier than Muršili II; *kiš-an* (21') for earlier *ki-iš-ša-an* first becomes common in Ḫattušili III, although rare in Muršili II. The accumulated evidence indicates a date for the copy in the reign of Ḫattušili III or more likely Tudḫaliya IV (late 13th century B.C.). As regards the script, nothing on the tablet contradicts the late dating supposed above on the basis of the spellings. The following signs are typical of the documents from the reign of Ḫattušili III and Puduḫepa: ID (rev 16', 33'), AL (rev 6'), ŠAR (rev 14'). The following are typical of the documents written during the reign of Šuppiluliyama (Šuppiluliuma II): RU (rev 11', 12'), NA (rev 12', 31'), BI (rev 19', 31'). The following are typical of documents written during the entire period from Ḫattušili III to Šuppiluliuma II: ḪA (rev 6', 19', 20', 22'), LI (rev 4', 15'), DA (rev 9', 20', 25'), URU in URU+URUDA (= BANŠUR) (rev 13'). For the sign shapes cf. now Christel Rüster, "Hethitische Keilschrift-Paläographie" (StBoT 20 [1972]).

[27] The form *pé-en-ni-an-zi* (19') is an archaic vestige of the earlier copies, for this form was generally replaced by *pé-en-na-an-zi* during the reign of Muwatalli.

[28] Unless, of course, we are to read: 1 MUŠEN <1> *ḫur-tal-li-in* (cf. HWb, 77).

[29] Cf. for example KUB XV 31 iii 54-59, iv 32-35; KBo II 9 iv 24-25; XII 27+ i 31-39 (Muršili II); KBo V 1 ii 2, iii 5ff., iv 27ff.

[30] The cultic site *kutruessar* "(place of divine) witness" recalls Heb. *'ēdût* (Ex 25:16, etc.).

[31] On the *nakkušši-* see N. van Brock, RHA f. 65, 126ff., 136ff. Laroche (private talk) denies the Hurrian origin of *nakkušši* and derives it from the Old Hittite neuter noun *nakkuš* "noxa" (Hitt. laws § 98).

[32] For a restoration *ka-*[*ri-ya-an-zi*] see below.

9 [I UDU I MUŠE]N *wa-aš-túl-aš* I UDU I MUŠEN *ša*? *-a-an-da-aš* [x x x]
10 [x x I MUŠ]EN NA_4*-i* RA-*an-zi* I [MUŠE]N *ḫur-ti-ya-aš*
11 [I MUŠEN *am-b*]*a-aš-ši ták-šu-la-aš* I [UD]U? ? I MUŠEN *ku-ut-ru-e-eš-ni*
12 [I MUŠEN *iš-ḫ*]*a-aḫ-ru-wa-aš* [I U]DU I MUŠEN *na-ak-ku-uš-ša-an tar-na-a*[*n-zi*]

---

§ 3 13 [III GÍN KÙ.BABBAR III GÍ]N GUŠKIN I[II GÍ]N AN.NA III GÍN URUDU I TÚG^{TUM}
14 [x x x x x x x] I TÚG ŠÀ.GA.DÙ I ^{TÚG}*ku-re-eš-šar* SÍG.BABBAR SÍG.G[E_6]
15 [x x x x x x x] *QA-DU* ^{TÚG}*KA-PAL-LI* I ^{DUG}*tal-la-i* x [x x]
16 [x x x x x *TU-T*]*I-IT-TÙ* KÙ.BABBAR I *a-šu-ša-aš* KÙ.BABBAR x[x x]
17 [x x x x x x G]ÍN.GÍN KÙ.BABBAR I PA ŠE I PA ZÍZ I BÁN GÚ.x[x x]
18 [x x x x x x LÀ]L I DUG GEŠTIN *i-wa-ar-wa-an-ni*[*-eš*?*-kán*?*-zi*?][33]

---

§ 4 19 [x x x x x x] x *pé-di ar-ḫa pé-en-ni-an-zi ki-i* [x x x]
20 [x x x x x x]x *pé-e-da-an-zi nu* UDU *ar-ḫa tar-na-*[*a*]*n-zi*
21 [x x x x x x] *kiš-an me-ma-an-zi ka-a-ša-wa-ra-aš a-pa-a-aš*
22 [x x x x UN-*aš w*]*a-aš-ta-aš-wa ku-iš ḫa-ra-tar-wa ku-iš* DÙ-*at*
23 [x x x x x x *-a*]*n-kán ka-a-ša i-wa-ru-wa-za IŠ-TU* KÙ.BABBAR GUŠKIN
24 [AN.NA URUDU *ḫu-u-ma-an-d*]*a-za aš-ša-nu-nu-un* NUMUN.ḪI.A-*wa-aš-ši a-ni-ya-nu-un*
25 [x x x x x x]-x-x-*uš pa-iz-zi* DINGIR^{LUM} *pa-ra-an-da-aš-ša-an* x[x x]
26 [x x x x x x]x *nu-za ku-iš ka-a-aš*[34] UDU-*un* KAR-*zi*
27 [x x x x x x] *ḫa-ra-tar wa-aš-túl a-pa-a-aš da-a-ú* EN.SISKUR-*m*[*a-* x]
28 [*ke-e-da-az wa-aš-tú*]*l-az pár-ku-iš e-eš-du*

---

§ 5 29 [x x x x x x x] x UN-*aš nu-za wa-ar-ap-zi* [x x x x x]
30 [x x x x x x x] UN-*aš nu-za* EGIR-*ŠÚ* SISKUR.MEŠ DÙ-x[x x x]

---

§ 6 31 [*ke-e-da-ni-iš-ša-an*] *A-NA ṬUP-PÍ* II SISKUR *a-ni-ya-an* [I SISKUR]
32 [*ma-a-an* LÚ-*aš* UDU-]*i*?[35] *na-aš-ma* ÙZ GAM-*an wa-aš-ta-i*
33 [I SISKUR *ma-a-an* UN-*š*]*i*? *an-da pa-ap-ra-tar ku-it-ki* [x x x]
34 [x x x x x x x x x x] x GIM-*an pár-ku-nu-uz-zi* [x x x x]

(Remainder of the colophon is broken away.)

A connected translation of the entire text would not justify the space it would require. I content myself with the translation of selected portions and with comments thereupon. As can be seen from the colophon, this tablet is a *Sammeltafel*, on which two rituals have been set down. The colophon lists the two in the opposite order from which they occur on the tablet, naming first the ritual for sodomy, "[When a man] sins together with [a sheep] or a nanny goat." The ritual actions are described in verbs of the present-future tense with third person plural subject (verbs in *-anzi*). Within the ritual a formula is quoted, which a single priest or magician recites, as he send the scapegoats out of the town. It is phrased with past tense verbs with a first person singular subject (lines 21ff.: *aššanunun, aniyanun*), followed by a section whose principal verbs are third person singular imperatives (*dau, ešdu* in lines 26-28). The plural subjects in the first and principal portion of the ritual doubtless represent the village elders, who acting for the village purify the offender. The single in-

---

[33] For a restoration *i-wa-ar-wa-an-ni-*[*eš-kán-zi*] see below.
[34] Perhaps scribal error for *ku-u-un*?
[35] One expects *-i* here, but the trace does not fit. What could it be?

dividual who sends away the scapegoats cannot be the offender himself, since he would be referring to himself in the third person in lines 22 and 27-28. Rather it is a priest or magician. Line 3 is tantalizing. Should one restore *ka-[ri-ya-an-zi]* at the end? If so, whom do they "veil like a bride"? [36] The animal? To the man they give a "Hurrian bird" and hold [it? ?] over him. In the second paragraph (lines 6-12) a number of birds are offered for various aspects of the offence, the bad consequences and the hoped-for purification (see above). At the end of that paragraph "[one she]ep (and) one bird they dispatch as a scapegoat."

Paragraph 3 (lines 13-18) appears to detail the items in the *iwaru* alluded to again later in § 4, line 23. It would seem that the animal with whom the offender has copulated must be treated like a bride. It must first be veiled as a bride (§ 1, line 3), and when it is sent away from the city, its dowry (*iwaru*) must be paid back (but to whom and how?), just as in a human marriage the husband who divorces his wife gave back her dowry (*iwaru*) to her to go with her back to her parents' home.[37] No Hittite text of which I have knowledge ever describes the items which made up a typical dowry. And although this is to say the least a *very* atypical case, it is interesting to see what the items were.

> "[Three shekels of silver, three sh]ekels of gold, t[hree she]kels of tin, three shekels of copper, one garment, [. . .], one *šagadu*-garment,[38] one woman's headdress, white wool, bla[ck] wool, [. . .], together with stockings, one *tallai*-jar[39] (for cosmetics?) [. . . pec]toral of silver, one silver *ašušaš*,[40] [. . .] shekels of silver, one *parīsu* of barley, one *parīsu* of wheat, one BAN of l[entils? ?, . . hon]ey, one jug of wine." The verb, which comes at the end of the paragraph, is probably to be restored as *i-wa-ar-wa-an-ni-[eš-kán-zi]* "they customarily give as a dowry", although theoretically it could be *i-wa-ar-wa-an-ni [pí-an-zi]* "they give for (i.e., 'as') a dowry (**iwarwatar*)."

Paragraphs 4 and 5 (lines 19-30) describe the ritual formula and ritual ablutions which accompany the sending off of the animal laden with impurity. The formula is introduced by "thus they say" (line 21), yet the speech is in the first person singular (line 24). "Lo, that one [is the offender? ?.] He who sinned, he who committed the offence [. . .], and I have 'made it good' for him by (the payment of) [al]l (this) dowry of silver gold, [tin and copper]. I have sown seed for him. [. . .] . . . . Whoever shall encounter this (*ka-a-aš* is error for *ku-u-un!*) sheep, let him take on [all the . . ,] offence (and) sin! And let the sacrificer (here) from [this si]n be purified!" Then the man washes himself and performs other rites.

Fragments of two copies of a ritual to treat a man who has committed incest have been identified by E. Laroche in CTH 445. On the basis of the two duplicates the entire colophon can be restored, which reads:[41]

> DUB.1.KAM! *QA-TI*
> *ma-a-an* UN-*aš* *ḫ*[*(ur-ki-il i-ya-zi)*]

[36] For *kariya-* "zudecken, verhüllen, – verstecken" see *HWb*, 100.
For the specific meaning "to veil" see KUB XXXII 115++ (Maštigga 2nd vers.) i 25-26: 2 ALAN GIŠ TÚG *wa-aš-ša-an-da na-at-kán* SAG.DU-*ŠU-NU ka-ri-ya-an-te-eš*; and KUB XXXIX 9 obv 2-3 (Otten, *Tot.*, 52f.); *Babyloniaca* 4 (1911) 225, text ≠3, obv 6; KUB XXV 37 ii 24. Also see Goetze's remarks on the TÚG*kariulli*: "It must be concluded that it [the *kariulli*] is a garment which drapes the head of women and covers their whole figure to the feet." (*Corolla linguistica*, Wiesbaden, 1955, 61).

[37] The disposition of the *iwaru* in cases of divorce does not seem to have been determined in the Hittite laws (§§ 26-27). Compare Ḫammurapi's Code §§ 137 and 142 requiring repayment of the wife's dowry (cf. RLA 2:284).

[38] Goetze (*Corolla linguistica*, 54-55 interprets these spellings as Akkadian *šaggatu* and proposes the translation "waistband." The Hittite equivalent of the Akkadian word is apparently TÚG*maššiya-*.

[39] In KUB XXIX 4 iii 24 and 31 the *tallai*-jar contains perfumed oil (Ì.DÙG.GA), as also in KBo VII 44 obv 8. The traces of the sign following *tallai* conform to neither Ì or KÙ, although one would expect either Ì[.DÙG.GA] or K[Ù.BABBAR]. For one of these made of silver see KUB XXXVIII 1 iv 12.

[40] The *ašuša-* was a piece of woman's jewelry (H. Otten, *Tot.*, 112[1]; ZA 54 [1961], 150; HWb Erg. 2, 9).

[41] KBo XII 115 rev 1'-5' with restorations from IBoT II 117 IV 1'-3'.

nu-za DUMU.MÍ-*ŠU* NIN[-*Š(U* AMA-*ŠU da-a-i)*]
nu-za ki-i da[*-aḫ-ḫi* . . .]
ŠU ^{m}*Ma-d*[*a-* . . .]

"First tablet, complete, (of the ritual) 'If a man commits incest (in that) he takes sexually his daughter, his sister (or) his mother, I take (the following steps).' Written by (the scribe) Mad[a- . . .]." The body of the ritual is almost completely lost. Comparison with the ritual treated above for bestiality allow a partial restoration of the three lines of column III whose initial words are preserved on IBoT II 117 iii 1'-3':

ḫa-r[*a-tar-wa ku-iš* DÙ*-at* . . . .]
*pa-ra-*x[. . . . . EN.SISKUR*-ma wa-aš-túl-az*]
pár-ku-i[*š e-eš-du* . . . .]

"[As for him who has committed] the off[ence . . . .] . . [. . may the sacrificer be] purif[ied from this sin!]"

One of the interests of this text is that it includes the sister (NIN-*ŠU*), which was omitted from the formulation in the Hittite laws (§ 189), although clearly stated in KBo V 3 iii 28ff. (*Hukk.* § 29). The text is also of interest in that it shows that all types of *ḫurkel* (bestiality and human incest) were handled in this fashion during the 14th and 13th centuries B.C.

Still another fragment, which seems to deal with the case of incest, is 827/z, which contains the first nine lines of a ritual to deal with a case of incest.

1 *ma-a-an* UN*-aš IT-TI* AMA-[ŠU	If a man [sleeps] with [his] mother, [his daughter? ,]
2 *na-aš-ma ḫa-aš-ša-an-na-aš ši*[-	or one of (his) immediate family [. . . . .],
3 *na-aš ma-a-an* EGIR*-zi-iš*[	if he be a low-ranked [person or a high-ranked one? ? ,]
4 UN*-aš ku-iš wa-aš-da-i n*[*a-an*? -	The man who has committed the offence [. . . . . . .]
5 *nu* URU*-aš ḫu-u-ma-an-za an-d*[*a*	And all the city [shall] a[ssemble? . . . .]
6 *a-pé-da-ni* URU*-ri* EGIR*-a*[*n*?	to that city . . . . . . [. . . . .]
7 MÍ.ŠU.GI *a-ni-ya-ta-*x[	the "old woman" [her] ritual [. . . . .]
8 *i-ya-an-zi n*[*a-*]x[	they perform [. . . . .]
9 *nu* LÚ.^{D}U x[	And the man of the storm god [. . . . .]

Either at the end of line one or line two one should restore the verb *šešzi* "sleeps" or *wašdai* "sins". Compare line four. The traces on the photo do not allow that the sign after *ḫaššannaš* be read as the first sign in *wa-*[*aš-da-i*] "sins". There is just enough space between this *si* and the preceding word to preclude that it is the enclitic pronoun *ḫaššannaš-ši* (or *ḫaššanna-šši*). Line three must contain a nominal sentence, of which EGIR-*zi-iš* (*appezziš* "latter, last, low-ranked person") is either the entire, or the first half of the predicate. At the end of line five restore perhaps [*ta-ru-up-pa-an-za e-eš-du*] "let it be gathered together". Thus the entire village assembly takes part in the purification and/or banishment. From the preserved parts of the ritual it is not clear whether it deals with the purification of the village only, in which case the man would have been banished, or if it deals with the purification of both village and culprit, in which case the man could remain there. The two functionaries, whose names are preserved in connection with the ritual are the "old woman" (MÍ.ŠU.GI) and the "man of the storm god".

The word *ḫu-ur-ke-el* also occurs in the fragmentary text KBo XXI 35 obv i 4', where seven lines later (11') there occurs the word ^{MÍ}*an-na-ni-ku-uš*. This word, which was translated "Dirne, Prostituierte(?)" by Friedrich (*HWb*, 21), "sister(s) of the same mother" by Goetze (*ArchOr* 17 [1949], 289f.), and "sister" by the present writer (*Or* NS 35 [1966], 391f.), has been reconsidered recently by H. Otten (*ZA* 61 [1971], 239ff.) in the light of a newly identified duplicate to Hittite laws § 199-200. Otten's new evidence suggests that an independent word *nega-* denoting a female blood relative ("sister" or "daughter") may in fact exist in Hittite. Quite another question is the relationship, if any, between the words *nega-* and *annanega-*. As I noted in *Or* NS 35 (391f.), the sister relationship of the *annanikuš* in law § 194 is clear already from *annaš-šman-a* "and their mother", so that there is no reason why *annanega-* could not be the syllabic writing of MÍKAR.KID-*aš* in the same law (also paired with GEMÉ). The Hittite word underlying MÍKAR.KID is an *a*-stem common gender noun; it cannot therefore be MÍ*karšant-* as was suggested by Laroche in Ugaritica V, 783. Besides in Bo 5622 left 7'-8' the two (MÍ*kar-aš-ša-an-ti*[-. .] and MÍKAR.KID-*aš*) are kept distinct. The employment of the determinative MI in KBo XXI 35 does not exclude a term of family relationship (cf. MÍ*annawanna-*, MÍ*anninniyami-*), but its employment with professional designations is also frequent (cf. P. Reichert, *RHA* XXI, fasc. 73 [1963], 136f.). If MÍ*annanikuš* is a term for blood (or family) relationship, then its presence in the same context with *ḫurkel* in KBo XXI 35 recalls Hitt. law § 191 and supports the translation "incest".

Let us now summarize. From the evidence of the Hittite laws (§§ 187-88, 199-200A) and the early 14th century instructions to the commanders of the border garrisons it seems clear that persons found guilty of *ḫurkel*, i.e. having sexual relations of a forbidden (perhaps incestuous) type were either executed or banished, while the town in which the offender lived was purified. During this early period it is unlikely that any known offender avoided either death or banishment. The phrase *ḫuišnuzi-an* LUGAL-*uš* "the king may spare his life" (§§ 187-88, 199) means he would be banished instead of executed. In the course of history, after the intensification of Hurrian religious influences on the Hittite court and society during the reigns of Muwatalli and Ḫattušili III, a third option developed. The human offender need not be killed or banished. The animal could be sent away from the city, bearing the impurity of the act, and a kind of fine, which took the appropriate form of a "dowry" (*iwaru*), was paid perhaps to a deity. In this way the human offender could continue to live in the city without bringing the wrath of the gods upon it.

From ancient written sources of Israel, Canaan, and Hatti we have long known that bestiality was practiced and that at least in Israel and in Hatti it was considered an improper combination (Heb. *tebel*, Hitt. *ḫurkel*). In Israel the only disposition of such a case known to us was execution. But now for the first time we can see how in Hatti the earlier and more rigorous treatment of the offender was ameliorated, giving way to a purification ritual and the payment of a fine.[42] There is no evidence regarding the punishment for bestiality in Israel. But the deed continued to be viewed along with homosexuality as a dishonorable and unnatural passion (see St. Paul's Epistle to the Romans 1:24-27).

---

[42] The same pattern of ameliorating older and more rigorous penalties and replacing them with simple fines can be seen again and again in the Hittite laws themselves.

EGYPT AND CYPRUS: LATE BRONZE AGE TRADE AND DIPLOMACY

Y. Lynn Holmes

West Georgia College – Carrollton, Georgia

Because of its modern connections with the West, and in particular Greece, the island of Cyprus has seldom been considered part of the Near East and has generally been neglected when one studies this area, even though it is much closer to Syria and Turkey than to Greece. This is certainly true of the Late Bronze Age, because numerous Minoan and Mycenaean finds have been made on the island and thus it has been thought that most of its ties were westward. My purpose here is to show that Late Bronze Age Cyprus was an intricate part of the ancient Near East and that it played a most important role in the trade and diplomacy of this area. Such a purpose can be accomplished by showing what type of relationship Cyprus had with the most important power of the Late Bronze Age – Egypt. Thus I will attempt to evaluate the commercial and diplomatic relationship which existed between these two countries and thus show how Cyprus fitted into the ancient Near East.

It is quite certain that trade and diplomacy were intricately related in the ancient world and that it is impossible to understand one without the other. Perhaps it would be proper to see what indications of commerce between Egypt and Cyprus emerge from the textual and archaeological evidence and then try to evaluate the possible diplomatic connection on the basis of this data and that from diplomatic texts.

Although in the Middle Bronze I period there is little or no contact between Egypt and Cyprus, in Middle Bronze II Cypriot pottery occurs in Egypt and Egyptian faience in Cyprus. Trade became even stronger in Middle Bronze III and reached its peak in the Late Bronze Age.[1]

---

1 H.W. Catling, "Cyprus in the Neolithic and Bronze Age Periods," *CAH*,[43] (Cambridge University Press, 1966), 44. In this paper the Late Bronze Age will cover the periods from 1550 to 1075 B.C. This will generally be represented in the paper as LB. As for the breakdown during this period, LB I will be from 1550-1400, LB II from 1400-1200, and LB III from 1200-1075.

During the Late Bronze Age, the textual evidence clearly indicates that the main export of Cyprus was copper.[2] In the Amarna Letters it is only copper which is sent in such large quantities as 200 talents[3] and 500 talents[4] and that is referred to in numerous passages.[5] On one occasion the Cypriot king even apologized about sending such small amounts of copper and then promised to send the Egyptian king "all the copper that you desire."[6] In an Egyptian text from the Temple of Ramses II at Luxor, which gives a list of mining regions, Cyprus appears as a place which produced copper "in millions in endless masses, in hundreds and thousands."[7] In Cyprus itself there is quite adequate proof of the mining and smelting of copper which is referred to in these texts.[8]

Another important Cypriot export was wood. According to the Amarna Letters the king of Cyprus sent to the Egyptian Pharaoh wood,[9] and the Cypriot official sent to Shumitti and the Egyptian official two ships loads of wood and a piece of boxwood.[10] Along with this wood, the Cypriot king also promised to make ships in great number for the Egyptian ruler.[11] These passages indicate that Cyprus was not only exporting timber, but was likewise manufacturing and exporting ships. This may well denote that Cyprus was a sea power with vessels going to and from Egypt and that it was one of the ship building nations of the Late Bronze Age.[12]

---

2 It should be noted that the Late Bronze Age textual evidence will come from the so-called "Alashiya texts," since these texts have been shown to refer to either part or all of the island of Cyprus. See Y. Lynn Holmes, *JAOS*, 91 (1971), 426-429.

3 EA 33:16.

4 EA 35:10.

5 EA 33:16, 18; 34:18; 36:5-7; 40:7, 13.

6 EA 35:12-17.

7 W. Max Müller, *Egyptological Researches* (1910), 19. It should also be noted that this text includes silver as a product of Cyprus. As Wainwright has observed, "The scribe who composed this text has shown himself a somewhat unsafe guide in his allocation of the various materials mentioned by him." See G.A. Wainwright, *Klio*, 14 (1914-15), 26. Thus this reference to silver from Alashiya may well be put into question, since the Amarna Letters show the Cypriot king asking Egypt for silver and since Cyprus has no good silver deposits.

8 From Late Bronze Age Cyprus archaeologists have discovered slag heaps of copper at eleven sites, moulds for copper from two sites, and copper workshops with tools and fragments of furnaces and crucibles from four sites. There is even evidence of Late Bronze Age mining at the site of Apliki. See Porphyrios Dikaios, *Journal of Historical Studies*, (1967), 41-49; Vassos Karageorghis, *AA*, (1963), 521 and 528; Kyriakos Nicolaou, *AJA*, 74 (1970), 73; H.W. Catling, *Cypriot Bronzework in the Mycenaean World* (Oxford: Clarendon Press, 1964), 20-25; Porphyrios Dikaios, *A Guide to the Cyprus Museum* (1961), 117-118.
There is also the possibility that some of the copper ingots scattered around the Mediterranean came from Cyprus. The origin of the ingots is a rather difficult thing to figure out, but Catling has suggested that they probably developed in Crete as an administrative measure in the palaces and were then adapted by the Mycenaeans who brought them to Cyprus, when they came in LB III. Catling's Type III ingot is not found anywhere except in Cyprus, and its date was after 1200. It is quite possible that these ingots may have been made in and exported from Cyprus. See Catling, *Cypriot Bronzework in the Mycenaean World*, 266-272 and George F. Bass, *Cape Gelidonya: A Bronze Age Shipwreck* (Philadelphia: The American Philological Society, 1967), pp. 52-83. [On these ingots cf.above, on pp. 29-36 – Ed.]

9 EA 35:28.

10 EA 40:6-8, 12-15.

11 EA 36:13.

12 Later Hittite texts clearly show that Cyprus had a fleet, which fought with the Hittite fleet. See Hans Guterbock, *JNES*, 26 (1967), 73-81. It should also be noted that three model ships, and probably a fourth, of clay are known of LB I or II dates. They were made in Plain White Hand-made Ware and came from Maroni, Kazaphani and Enkomi. There are some factors which speak in favor of identifying at least three, possibly all four, of the Cypriot ships as seagoing crafts. See R.S. Merrillees, *The Cypriote Bronze Age Pottery Found in Egypt* (1968), 188-189.

Oil is a promised item in the Amarna Letters,[13] while Papyrus Anastasi mentions "*Fidi* liquid," "*Inbu* liquid"[14] and "oil of *Aoupa*"(?)[15] as Egyptian imports from Cyprus. Other products indicated as Cypriot exports to Egypt include elephant's tusks[16] and horses.[17]

Although archaeological evidence is lacking to prove most of these textual assertions, materials is available to show that Cyprus was exporting vast amounts of pottery to Egypt during the Late Bronze Age. This pottery included Base-ring I and II wares, White Slip I and II wares, Black Slip II ware, White Painted Pendent Line Style ware, and White Painted VI ware.[18] Varying quantities of these Cypriot wares have been found at some fifty sites scattered all over Egypt.[19] These pottery imports were at their peak in LB I, dropped considerably in LB II and stopped altogether in LB III.[20]

Since there is no basic shape, size or decorative differences in these vessels over a long period of time, perhaps the Cypriotes were exploiting sales potential in Egypt based on known preferences.[21] Such consistency of demand and necessarily of supply, along with the great quantities, geographical distribution and social setting argues for a regularized commercial traffic which was based on a well defined cooperation between manufacturer and merchant in Cyprus and Egypt.[22]

Having discussed this vast amount of Cypriot pottery which was exported to Egypt, one should be reminded that the Base-ring I and II vessels, the types which appear most often in Egypt, are not extremely well-made and that their decorations are far from beautiful, so it seems rather strange that vessels would be valued for their own sake.[23] It is more likely that value came from their contents.[24] Sjöqvist has suggested

[13] EA 34:51.

[14] Papyrus Anastasi IV, Pl. 15 lines 2-4. These are mentioned in connection with liquids from Hatti, Babylon, Amurru, Naharayim and an unidentified place (*thys*). For the text and discussion of this passage, see G. Maspero, "Le Pays d'Alasia," *Recuil de travaux relatifs*, 10 (1888), 209.

[15] Papyrus Anastasi IV Pl. 17 lines 7-9.

[16] EA 40:7, 12-15. It is interesting that although ivory is sent to Shumitti and the Egyptian official, in the same letter ivory is requested from the Egyptian official. See EA 40:11.

[17] Papyrus Anastasi IV, Pl. 17 lines 7-9. In EA 34:22 and 37:9 the Cypriot king requests that horses be sent to him.

[18] For the description and quantities of these wares, see Erik Sjöqvist, *Problems of the Late Cypriote Bronze Age* (Stockholm: The Swedish Cyprus Expedition, 1940), 34-43, 156-161, 174-175 and 179-180; and R.S. Merrillees, *op. cit.*,

[19] Places where Cypriot pottery were found in Egypt include Sinai, El-Arish, Nabesha (Tell Farun), Saft el-Hinna, Ali Mara, Tell el-Rataba, Tell el-Hahudiya, Heliopolis, El-Giza, Zawyet el-Aryan, Abusir, Memphis, Saqqara, Mazghuna, Tarkhan, El-Riqqa, Maidum, Abusir el-Malaq, El-Haraga, El-Lahun, Kahun, Gurob, Sidmant, Dishasha, Zawyet el-Maiyitin, Beni Hasan, El-Amarna, Deir Rifa, Dei Tasa, Qaw el-Qebir, El-Sawana, El-Balabish, Abydos, Hu, Dendera, Deir el-Ballas, Qift (Koptos), Thebes, Esna, El-Shallal, Moalla, Aman Daud, El-Dakka, Quban, El-Maharraqa, Aniba, Quadrus, Buhen, Semna, Amarna West.

[20] Eric Sjöqvist, *op. cit.*, 190. Merrillees also notes that Cypriot pottery abruptly ceased occurring in Egypt after the reign of Akhenaten. See *The Cypriote Bronze Age Pottery Found in Egypt*, 186 and 202.

[21] See Merrillees, *op. cit.*, p. 157.

[22] *Ibid.*, p. 168.

[23] It should be mentioned that the Egyptians were impressed with these Cypriot vessels to such an extent that they imitated them in alabaster, glass, paste, faience and pottery. *Ibid.*, 148-154 and 161-166.

[24] Additional evidence for this theory has been given by Merrillees who points out that in Egypt one can distinguish a gradual development from Base-ring I to Base-ring II. Since the same shape was continually used despite the transformation of its external appearance, Merrillees concludes that it was the contents which remained unaltered and desirable on the Egyptian market. See R.S. Merrillees, *Antiquity*, 36 (1962), 288.

that these contents were scents or ointments,[25] but Merrillees believes that it was opium.[26] Based on the fact that oil and other liquids were known exports from Cyprus and on the fact that oily substances have been found in some of these vessels in Egypt,[27] the writer is more inclined to support Sjöqvist's theory. It is therefore quite probable that one of the prime Cypriot exports was some type of oil or ointment which was shipped in Cypriot vessels.

Attention should also be turned to what Cyprus imported from Egypt. According to the Amarna Letters the Cypriot king and official request from Egypt such luxury items as fancy furniture,[28] a chariot,[29] horses,[30] linens,[31] ebony,[32] oil,[33] silver,[34] an ox[35] and ivory.[36] To find archaeological evidence in Cyprus for the importation of these luxury goods is of course almost impossible, but if one regards the jewelry, ivory and stone products, glass, faience, glyptics and ostrich eggs which have been found in Late Bronze Age Cyprus, it is clear that these Egyptian luxury items would not be out of place.[37] Perhaps it would be worthwhile to mention some of the luxury items which have been designated as Cypriot imports from Egypt.

Suggested Egyptian jewelry imports include an engraved ring with the cartouche of Thutmose III;[38] a massive silver finger ring with a scaraboid bezel;[39] a plain finger ring with oval, engraved bezel;[40] bronze decorated rings;[41] the Enkomi pectoral;[42] and some scarab-shaped and frog-shaped beads.[43]

It should be mentioned that much of the above jewelry is made from gold and that much more of the Cypriot jewelry of supposedly local manufacture is also of gold. Where did Cyprus obtain all this gold? Even though a Hittite text includes gold as an item of tribute from Cyprus,[44] there are actually only a few

[25] Sjöqvist, *op. cit.*, 79.

[26] Merrillees states that the form of the Base-ring I and II vessels in Egypt is very much like the head of an opium poppy whose dried out shell could easily have been used in its own right as a container. With this theory as his basis, he goes on to mention that opium was introduced into Egypt during the time that Base-ring I was being imported and that the decline of Base-ring II corresponds with the emergence of faience copies of poppy heads in Egypt. Merrillees hints that the opium was grown in Cyprus, but he never really says so nor does he offer any other origin for the opium. He likewise never produces evidence that opium was found in these vessels. See Merrillees, *op. cit.*, 288.

[27] Merrillees, *The Cypriote Bronze Age Pottery Found in Egypt*, *op. cit.*, 180.

[28] EA 34:20, 28.

[29] EA 34:21.

[30] EA 34:22; 37:9.

[31] EA 34:22-23, 25, 47.

[32] EA 34:21.

[33] EA 34:24; 35:24-25.

[34] EA 35:19-20, 43-44; 37:18.

[35] EA 35:24.

[36] EA 40:11. There are also five talents of something merely written as 5 *biltu*. It is very interesting that while horses, oils, linens and ivory were being sent from Cyprus to other countries, the Cypriots also requested that these things be sent to them. Perhaps these things were thought to be royal gifts which should be exchanged between all courts.

[37] See Lena Åström, *Studies on the Arts and Crafts of the Late Cypriote Bronze Age* (1967).

[38] This comes from the sanctuary at Dhima. See Einar Gjerstad, *et al.*, *The Swedish Cyprus Expedition: Finds and Results of the Excavations in Cyprus 1927-1931* (1934), I, 360.

[39] On the bezel is engraved in hieroglyphs, "Nefer-Kheperu-Ra (Amenhotep IV), beloved of Ra and Ptah, lord of vigor and truth." See H.R. Hall, *Catalogue of Egyptian Scarabs, etc. in the British Museum* (1913), I, 276.

[40] There are several of these in Cyprus and Åström suggests that they are Eighteenth Dynasty Egyptian. See Åström, *op. cit.*, 93.

[41] All of these are from Enkomi. See Catling, *Cypriot Bronzework in the Mycenaean World*, *op. cit.*, 235.

[42] Åström, *op. cit.*, 107.

[43] *Ibid.*, pp. 134-135.

[44] KBo XII 38 i:5ff. In addition to the gold, the text includes copper and an unclear tribute called *gayatum*. [Read here: 3 PA(!) *GA-YA-TUM*; the PA = Akkad. *parīsu*, the Akkadian *gayatu* (= Sum. ŠE.SA.A; cf. *MSL* 13, p. 121, l. 246) denoting roasted grain. – Ed.]

poor gold deposits known in the island.[45] Therefore, the great quantities of gold jewelry which have been found in Cypriot tombs, mainly of the LB II period, must have been imported either as manufactured items or raw material to be worked by Cypriot craftsmen. Since Egypt was decidedly the main supplier of gold in the Near East at this time,[46] and since Cyprus was carrying on extensive trade with Egypt during this period, the writer would suggest that the raw gold, if not much of the jewelry itself, was imported from Egypt.

Glass was also an item which appears in Cyprus and which is often specified as an Egyptian import. Examples include pomegranateshaped jars, glass jugs of base-ring shape, two-handled flasks, a footed flask and several unusual vases.[47] As this evidence shows, frequent glass imports came into Cyprus from Egypt, so it is not surprising that Flossing would affirm that all glass found in Cyprus was of Egyptian origin.[48]

Another luxury import was alabaster. Although there is alabaster of fair quality in the lowland parts of Cyprus and in most Mediterranean coastlands, the fine quality alabaster came only from Egypt. It is therefore not unexpected that many alabaster jars, jugs and amphorae from Cyprus have been classified as Egyptian products.[49]

Other probable Egyptian objects include scarabs,[50] faience jars[51] and ostrich eggs.[52]

Considering all this evidence, the writer has been led to believe that there were close commercial contacts between Cyprus and Egypt during the Late Bronze Age. It should be noted, however, that numerous scholars do not agree with this conclusion. Lena Aström, who believes that there are not many Cypriot objects of Egyptian origin, postulates that even most of the original Egyptian objects spread to Palestine and came from there to Cyprus, sometimes in a modified form.[53] In agreement with Aström, Karageorghis related to the writer in a personal conversation that the many Egyptianlooking objects in Cyprus probably did not come from Egypt but rather from Palestine.[54] Unfortunately neither of these scholars has published evidence to verify their theories. The origin of such beliefs may have come from Sjöqvist, who suggested that in LB II Cypriot trade

---

[45] This was related to the writer by Dr. Vassos Karageorghis, the Director of the Department of Antiquities of Cyprus.

[46] For information about this see the Amarna Letters from the kings of Assyria, Mitanni and Babylon in which they ask for much gold. See also Wolfgang Helck, *Die Beziehungen Ägyptens zu Vorderasien im 3. und 2. Jahrtausend v. Chr.* (1962) and Vassos Karageorghis, *The Ancient Civilization of Cyprus* (1969), 145.

[47] Aström, *op. cit.*, 125.

[48] Paul Flossing, *Glass Vessels before Glass Blowing* (1940), 30. Dan Barag agrees that most Cypriot glass was of Egyptian derivation with slight local variation. See Dan Barag, "Mesopotamian Glass Vessels of the Second Millennium B.C.," *Journal of Glass Studies*, 4 (1962), 27.

[49] John L. Myres, *Handbook of the Cesnola Collection of Antiquities from Cyprus* (New York: 1914), p. 274; Aström, *op. cit.*, 144; and Karageorghis, *The Ancient Civilization of Cyprus, op. cit.*, 145.

[50] There are many scarabs, that appear to be of authentic Rameside origin, and numerous others which bear the name of Egyptian rulers of earlier periods. It is quite possible that these may have been imported from Egypt. There are also many scarabs that are certainly non-Egyptian, but at the same time show great Egyptian influence. See Gjerstad, *op. cit.*, II, 626, 825 and 845-850; Hall, *op. cit.*, I, 195, 235 and 274; and Arne Furumark, "A Scarab from Cyprus," *OA*, 1 (1953), 55.

[51] Aström, *op. cit.*, p. 121.

[52] Such eggs have been found in tombs at Enkomi and Kition. It is known that these eggs were used as vases at Abydos in the Eleventh and Twelfth Dynasties and in shaft graves in Mycenae. See Aström, *op. cit.*, 144 and Karageorghis, *The Ancient Civilization of Cyprus, op. cit.*, 145.

[53] Aström, *op. cit.*, p. 150.

[54] In contrast to his personal statement, Karageorghis in an article ("Excavations at Kition 1963," *RDAC*, 1963, 9) points out that the quantity of Egyptian goods in Tomb 9 at Kition suggestes that there were relations with Egypt from the 13th if not the 14th century. He likewise suggests that the copper which was smelted in Kition was mainly shipped to Egypt.

with Egypt was largely in the hands of the Cypriot emporium at Ras Shamra.[55] Since no evidence has been presented to validate this indirect route and intermediary merchants, the writer is more inclined to interpret the substantial Cypro-Egyptian trade and the appearance of Cypriot merchants in Egypt in the Amarna Letters as evidence of direct trade between these two countries through Cypriot and perhaps some Egyptian merchants.

All of this is clear evidence of the extensive trade contact between Cyprus and Egypt, but one must now ask how this commercial contact is related to the diplomatic association between these two countries. It is necessary to understand that much trade between these two countries took the form of the exchange of "gifts" between the royal courts and that this was handled by the messengers who acted as diplomatic envoys.[56] These messengers were employed not only for communication but also to carry and distribute gifts to foreign rulers, thus making them the middle men in royal trade.[57] This dual function of merchant and diplomat is distinctly spelled out in *EA* 39:10-16: "my brother, my messengers very quickly send them, so that I may hear of your greeting. These men are my merchants, my brother, very quickly send them." This equation of merchants and messengers explains why the king of Cyprus was so interested in exchanging messengers with Egypt and why he wanted them to return quickly. These men were handling the trade between Cyprus and Egypt, and thus the greater frequency of their visits meant a larger volume of trade. If the frequent mention of the exchange of messenger-merchants in these texts is a representative one, then there must have been immense trade between these two countries.[58]

These elements of messenger exchange and royal trade seem to have brought the royal houses of Cyprus and Egypt close together. The Amarna Letters indicate that these monarchs not only wrote one another about the regular diplomatic matters of important state occasions,[59] alliances,[60] state debts,[61] the messenger service[62] and foreign intrigues[63] but also about such things as the death of a newborn son,[64] transference of

---

[55] Sjöqvist, *op. cit.*, 186. The fact that numerous anchors were found at the LB ports of Hala Sultan Tekke and Kition and that four ships were found at LB sites in Cyprus indicates that the people of Cyprus had some knowledge of the sea. This could well imply that they had the ability to sail to Egypt. See K. Nikolaou and H.W. Catling, *Antiquity*, 42 (1968), 229.

[56] During the Amarna Age the messenger was a multipurpose position which not only served as a bearer, reader, interpreter and defender of his master's message, but also as a diplomat, and more importantly, a merchant.

[57] From the Amarna Letters it is clear that the exchange of letters was suppose to be accompanied by gifts, and that the sender expected to receive in return presents of equal or superior quantity and quality. To make certain that presents were brought, the foreign kings were not adverse to bribing the Egyptian king or requesting specific gifts or quantities. This type thing is well exemplified in the correspondence of the Cypriot king with the ruler of Egypt; see EA 34:16-19; 35:17, 41; and 37:13-16.

[58] Wainwright has also interpreted this messenger service as pointing to much intercourse between Egypt and Alashiya. See Wainwright, *op. cit.*, 28.

[59] EA 33:9-11 and 34:9-15. One of these texts speaks about the beginning of a sacrificial feast in Egypt and the other notes that a new king has been enthroned in Egypt. Wainwright has thought that the relationship between Cyprus and Egypt was so intimate that the Pharaoh had taken it for granted that the king of Alashiya would know that he was celebrating a sacrificial feast and had felt hurt at Cyprus's ignorance. See Wainwright, *op. cit.*, p. 28.

[60] There is a discussion about Cyprus's cooperation with the Lukki on Egypt's part and a concern on the part of Cyprus that Egypt not make alliances with Shanhar and the king of Hatti. See EA 38:13-22 and 35:49-50.

[61] In EA 35:27-29 the Cypriot ruler says that his people are talking about some wood the Egyptian king took, so the Egyptian leader should pay him for it.

[62] One big problem centered around initiating an exchange of messengers. Although the Egyptians seemed to have had little concern about this matter, the Cypriot king was most interested in establishing regular messenger contact and made it a frequent subject in his letters. Egypt is simply asked to send messengers on some occasions (EA 33:27-32 and 34:42-46), while at other times the Cypriot king asks the Egyptian ruler to send couriers so that "they may bring my brother's *šulmānu*." (EA 37:14-16 and 39:12-13). In close conjunction with the trouble of initiating this messenger exchange, there is also a problem of quickness. The reason for this is that Egypt has gained a very bad reputation for the retention of foreign messengers (EA 38:23-24).

the estate of a deceased Cypriot[65] and the mentioning of Cypriot messenger-merchants to the Egyptian king by name.[66] Certainly these things would not have been mentioned, unless these courts had intimate diplomatic relations.

This close diplomatic contact should be indicative of a position of equality between Egypt and Cyprus, and the texts concur with such a hypothesis. There are seven letters from the king of Cyprus to the king of Egypt and one from the LÚ*rābiṣu*[67] of Cyprus to the LÚ*rābiṣu* of Egypt. It is remarkable that in the beginning of *EA* 33-35 and 37-39 the letters are addressed to *šarri* KUR*Mi-iṣ-ri aḫi-ya*, "the king of Egypt, my brother," and is from *šàr* KUR*A-la-ši-ya aḫu-ka*, "the king of Cyprus, your brother."[68] Although the use of *aḫi-ya* and *aḫu-ka* is one of the stylized salutations of this period, it takes on significance, when one looks at the other letters from the Amarna archives, in which the king of Egypt is called *aḫi-ya* by a foreign ruler. Such an appellation is only given to the king of Egypt by the Kassite kings Kadashman-Enlil I[69] and Burnaburiash II,[70] Ashur-uballit of Assyria,[71] Tushratta of Mitanni,[72] and an unknown Hittite king.[73] In the case of other letters addressed to the king of Egypt, the term applied to the Egyptian ruler is *bēli-ya*, "my lord."[74] While the city-states of Palestine and Syria are forced to admit their subservience to the Egyptian ruler even in the salutation of their letters, the kings of Babylon, Assyria, Mitanni, Hatti and Cyprus place themselves as equals to the Egyptian Pharaoh. It is thus clear that Cyprus was grouped with the major powers of this era and that it was classified on an equal level with Egypt in the protocol of the Late Bronze Age.

Additional evidence for this hypothesis comes from the fact that the king of Cyprus shows his extreme interest in communicating with Egypt and, at the same time, shows his independence by withholding gifts until messengers arrived,[75] complaining about the slowness of messengers[76] and by keeping an Egyptian messenger for three years.[77] It is interesting that the city-states of Syria and Palestine, while asking for troops and mentioning the exchange of messengers, never complain about the slowness in the messenger service or the keeping

---

Thus the Cypriot ruler constantly orders the Egyptian king not to retain his messengers (EA 33:25 and 37: 19-27), and reminds him that he should send the messengers back quickly (EA 33:19-26; 35:40-41; 37:13-14; 39:10-12).

63 There is a discussion about Cyprus's cooperation with the Lukki on Egypt's part (EA 38:13-22).

64 EA 35:37-39.

65 In EA 35:30-34 the Cypriot king points out that a citizen of Cyprus has died in Egypt with his possessions, but that his wife and child are still in Cyprus. The Cypriot king then requests that the deceased man's things be sent back to Cyprus by his messenger.

66 EA 37:21-27.

67 This is EA 40. LÚ*rābiṣu* is a title simply meaning a high official. [Cf. A.L. Oppenheim, *AOS* 53, 178f.; A.F. Rainey, *Or* NS 35 (1966) 426f. – Ed.]

68 The sequence of *aḫi-ya* and *aḫu-ka* likewise occurs in EA 40 with LÚ*rābiṣu*. It should also be noted that EA 36 is not included in this list because the salutation is broken and no idea is given as to how it began.

69 EA 1, 2, 3 and 5.

70 EA 6, 7, 8, 9 and 11. There is also one letter from Amenhotpe IV to Burnaburiash II in which this phrase appears – EA 14.

71 EA 16.

72 EA 17, 18, 19, 20, 23, 24, 27, 28, and 29.

73 EA 42.

74 There is also one occasion in which the term *a-bi-ya*, 'my father' appears – EA 44:2.

75 He seemingly tries to bribe the king of Egypt into sending messengers by promising to send copper (EA 35:17) and gifts (EA 35:42) only when the Egyptian messengers come.

76 EA 38:23-30.

77 EA 35:35-36.

of their messengers in Egypt. It is only the great powers such as Babylon,[78] Assyria,[79] Mitanni,[80] and Hatti[81] who join Cyprus in quarreling with Egypt about the return of messengers.

This same sense of equality is shown by the Cypriot ruler when he tells the Egyptian king: "As for my merchants and my ship, do not allow the man in charge of your affairs to come near them."[82] The Cypriot king does not speak here as a lowly king or vassal but rather as one who is equal to the great king of Egypt.

From this material, one can discern the extensive commercial contact between Egypt and Cyprus which brought copper, wood and oil to Egypt and gold and luxury goods to Cyprus. This need for luxury goods on the part of Cyprus and raw materials by Egypt pulled Cyprus into the arena of the Late Bronze Age East not only commercially but also diplomatically. In this position it acted not as an insignificant island but rather as an important power, participating fully in the commercial and diplomatic activities of the ancient Near East. This role was played by Cyprus during the LB I and LB II periods, but during the turbulence of the LB III the trade routes were disturbed, Cyprus was invaded by Aegean people, and its position as a great Eastern power passed away, as it became an ally and frequent colony of the West.[83]

---

[78] EA 7:18, 50-52 and 9:46-47.

[79] EA 15:7-22 and 16:35-52.

[80] EA 17:46-53; 19:71-73 and 28:17-24.

[81] EA 41:14-15.

[82] EA 39:17-20. An almost verbatim passage is given in the letter of the official of Cyprus to the official in Egypt (EA 40:25-26).

[83] For information about the Aegean conquest and settlement of Cyprus see the following: Einar Gjerstad, *Opuscala Archaeologica*, 3 (1944), 107-123; Vincent Desborough, *The Last Mycenaeans and Their Successors: An Archaeological Survey c. 1200-c. 1000 B.C.* (1964); Sara A. Immerwahr, *Archaeology*, 13 (1960), 4-13; H.W. Catling, *BSA*, 58 (1963), pp. 94-115; H.W. Catling, *Cypriot Bronzework in the Mycenaean World* (1964); Arne Furumark, "The Excavations at Sinda: Some Historical Results," *OA*, 6 (1965), 99-116; Jean du Plat Taylor, *PEQ*, (1965), pp. 22-37.

REAL ESTATE ADOPTION BY WOMEN IN THE TABLETS FROM URU *NUZI*

Ernest R. Lacheman
Brandeis University

C.H. Gordon has written two papers on the role of Women in the tablets from URU *Nuzi*[1] : The Status of Woman Reflected in the Nuzi Tablets," in *Zeitschrift für Assyriologie*, 43, 146-169 and: "Fifteen Nuzi Tablets Relating to Women", in *Le Muséon*, 48, 113-132. The purpose of this paper is to go one step further in analyzing the legal status of women in these tablets. I have chosen purposely what I now call "Real Estate Adoption" (instead of the awkward "Fake, or False Adoptions"), not only because this type of contract is found in the largest number of tablets from this ancient city, but also because it is unique in the whole Mesopotamian literature. These documents also raise the question whether they were really very different from the "Real Adoption" contracts.

Concerning the Real Estate Adoption documents in general it should be observed that the terminology changed noticeably from the earliest to the latest texts. Thus what I believed to be the three oldest tablets found in Yorghan Tepe, i.e., SMN 3082, 3094 and 3101, have a very interesting terminology: "Tablet of sonship of PN (the adopting father), PN_2 into sonship he has made, and PN_3, his (adopter's) brother has given M of field, and PN_2 (adopted son) has given NN shekels of silver. Whoever changes (the contract, *i-nu-ú*) NN minas of gold, NN minas of silver shall give." (One text has *a-na ki-zi* ^{d}*adad* Ì.LÁ.E) At the end of the contract, in each case, there is an unusual clause: "PN_2 (the adpoted son) is the big one (i.e., the older son) and Wantiia, the brother (of the adopted son) is the small one (i.e., the younger brother) and according to his "hand" (i.e., his rank) he shall receive (his inheritance share). This terminology indicates very clearly that these Real Estate adoptions are formulated according to the real adoption contracts. In view of the fact that in several lawsuits it is stated that the adopting father and/or his descendants had kept the real estate property from the adopted son and/or his descendants, it would be tempting to say that in the Real Estate Adoption contracts, the implication is that the real estate will pass on to the adopted son only after the death of the adopting father – which would also explain why the adopting father in nearly all cases continues to bear the *ilku*. Another possibility would be to say that in the real adoption contracts the adopted son takes over at the time of the adoption what is promised to him in the contract as inheritance share.

An interesting fact is that there is no real adoption of women in the contracts called *ṭuppi martūti*. All these documents deal with marriage. The conclusion is therefore obvious that women could not inherit real estate.

---

[1] In view of the controversy concerning the proper transcription of the name of this city, I use the most common cuneogram found in these documents.

To circumvent this law the Hurrians adopted a legal device which I think is unique in the history of ancient Mesopotamia. In order to acquire real estate, a woman had herself adopted as a "son". This custom goes back to at least the third generation of the tablets from URU *Nuzi.*[2]

fWinnirki[3], the wife of Puḫi-shenni, son of Turi-shenni is known to have been adopted as a son in four contracts: JEN 82, 560, 561 and 562. Again here the terminology is different from later Real Estate Adoptions. But what is obvious is that she is adopted as a "son."

Later on we have especially the Real Estate Adoption contracts of the woman Tulpunnaya, daughter of Sheltunnaya.[4] In every case she is adopted as a "son."

In his paper published in *Le Muséon*, 48, 124-125, Gordon transliterated and translated *JEN* 160. In this contract a certain woman is "adopted as a son" (*ana marūti ipussu*). In a note Gordon states: "lit. '(for) sonship had made him' instead of l.c. '(for) daughtership had made her'. Such violations against rules of gender are not rare in the Nuzi texts." The latter part of this statement is correct. For instance the possessive pronoun of the third person feminine singular is seldom used. Instead the scribes almost invariably use the masculine pronoun. But I believe that this is not the case here. My opinion is strengthened by the fact that we have two unpublished *ṭuppi šimti*, one in the Iraq Museum, the other in the Yale Babylonian collection. In both cases a father adopts his own daughter as sons so that they can inherit his real estate. In the second text, the father even wills to his daughters his *ilānī u etemmī.*

This, of course, reminds us of the analogue in Num 27. The five daughters of Zelophehad had asked Moses to give them "a possession among our father's brethren", because their father had no son. The answer given was a law, which states that "if a man dies and has no sons, then you shall cause his inheritance to pass to his daughter."

---

[2] I date as the first generation the texts SMN 3082, 3094 and 3101; the second generation is that of Turi-shenni the father of Puḫi-shenni; the third generation is that of Puḫi-shenni, son of Turi-shenni and of his wife Winnirki; the fourth generation of Teḫip-tilla, son of Puḫi-shenni, and so on.

[3] I normalize the personal names according to Gelb, Purves, MacRae, *Nuzi Personal Names.*

[4] The scribes who write documents for fTulpunnaya belong to the late part of the life of Teḫip-tilla, son of Puḫi-shenni, who used scribes of four generations of scribes of the same family. Therefore fTulpunnaya cannot be considered as belonging to an early period.

LATER SOURCES ON THE *NETÎNÎM*

Baruch A. Levine

New York University

Our first researches into the Hebrew term *netînîm* as a survival of Ugaritic *ytnm* were initiated under the direction of Cyrus Gordon, and it is therefore appropriate that a further discussion of the history of the *netînîm* appear in a volume dedicated to our masterful teacher.

In our earlier study on the biblical *netînîm* we noted that according to Neh 10:29, they were among the principal signatories of the *'ammānāh*, the new covenant enacted in Jerusalem during the last half of the fifth century B.C. Their status at that time could hardly have been stigmatized, for only full-fledged Israelites would have been considered part of the covenant community and listed so prominently among the framers of the *'ammānāh.*[1]

How, then, do we explain the assignment of a socio-religious stigma to persons designated as *netînîm* in early Talmudic times, as epitomized in the provisions of *M. Qiddûšîn* IV:1? In that section of the Mishnah, a delineation of ten genaeological ranks, *netînîm* are grouped with *mamzērîm* "bastards" and other grades of declassed Jews, and are forbidden to marry within the proper community[2]. This general classification is main-

---

[1] A full discussion is provided in B.A. Levine, *JBL* 82 (1963), 207-212. See ns. 5 and 7 for additional bibliography.

[2] In the "ten genealogical ranks" (*'asārāh yôḥāsîn*) the *netînîm* are placed in the lowest of three levels. The highest level includes those of priestly and Levitical lineage, and "Israelites", whose parents are both Jewish. The second level includes those born of a union expressly forbidden to priests, i.e., *ḥalālê*, and those whose immediate parentage was non-Jewish, such as proselytes (*gērê*) and emancipated slaves (*ḥarûrê*) who became Jewish upon manumission. The lowest level includes those whose parentage is recognized as being stigmatized, like *mamzērîm* and *netînîm*, and persons of unidentifiable parentage, such as *šetûqê*, a term given to those whose fathers are not identifiable, and *'asûpê* "foundlings", neither of whose parents can be identified. Persons in this category may not marry with proper "Israelites". Cf. *Tos. Qidd.* V:1, *TP Qidd.* IV, end of *hal.* 1; *Qidd.* 72^b, 74^a. and *Sifre*, ed. Friedman, *kî-tēṣē'* 119^b, par. 347.

tained quite consistently throughout Talmudic legislation[3], and is buttressed by an Aggadic theory on the lowly origins of the post-exilic *netînîm*, alleged to be descendants of the pariah Gibeonites of early biblical times[4].

Scholars dealing with the problem have generally assumed a degree of fluctuation in the history of the *netînîm* whereby the descendants of temple slaves, captives, and other foreigners, were accepted into the community at the time of Ezra and Nehemiah, and possibly prior to the returns, while still in Babylonia; but were subsequently rejected. They would regard the Talmudic *netînîm* as later descendants of essentially the same, early group.[5]

Historically speaking, this interpretation projects a problematic situation, since the acceptance of the *netînîm* would have occurred at the least probable time, precisely when efforts were underway to weed out of the community all persons of unestablished lineage.[6] It also fails, of course, to provide an explanation for the rejection of the *netînîm* in the Talmudic period.

For us, the two poles of Neh 10:29 and *M. Qiddûšîn* IV:1 represent a major discrepancy. We had proposed that the biblical *netînîm* were, from their beginnings in the pre-exilic period, a guild-like group of cultic practitioners, whose acceptability in socio-religious terms was *never* a problem.[7] Chronic fluctuations in status seem to us improbable, and we must therefore search for another solution to our central problem.

---

3 See *M. Qidd.* III:12, which delineates four categories of forbidden unions and the corollary status of offspring. The *nātîn* belongs to the second category, which includes marriages specifically forbidden to persons of priestly lineage, whose offspring bear the stigma of the inferior parent. Cf. *M. Yeb.* VIII: 8 which states that the ban on marriage with *netînîm* is permanent, like that pertaining to *mamzērîm* and cf. *ibid.* II:4, and VI:2; *Ket.* I:8, XI:6; *Giṭṭîn* IX:2, *Makkot* III:1. The statements relevant to *netînîm* in *M. Sotah* IV:1 and VIII:3-5 may be theoretical.

4 Principal sources are *TP Qidd., hal.* 1, and *TB Yeb.* 78-79. See L. Ginzberg, *Legends of the Jews* VII (1946), Index, 181, s.v. "Gibeonites" (8 entries), and especially sources cited in IV, 1947, 443, n. 40.
Joshua reduced the Gibeonites to the status of "hewers of wood and drawers of water for the congregation and the altar of the Lord-" (Josh 9:27). The verb *nātan* is there taken to connote reduction to slavery (cf. 1 Kings 9:22), which serves the Aggadah as the etymology of the term *netînîm*. This lowly status was not intended to be permanent, until during David's reign the Gibeonites, in their vengeful demand for retribution against the house of Saul, demonstrated that they were unworthy to be accepted as Israelites. (They had previously converted under duress). David rejected them (Hebrew: *riḥḥēq*) permanently, as is written: "For the Gibeonites are not of the children of Israel" (2 Sam 21:2). Ezra, in his time, repeated this rejection with respect to the *netînîm*, taken to be the descendents of the Gibeonites. The statement: "The *netînîm* reside in the *'Ôpel*." (Neh 3:26, and cf. 11:21) is understood to mean that the *netînîm* were segregated, so to speak, and prohibited from marrying within the community. See n. 33 for further discussion c.f. the verb *riḥḥēq*.

5 Essentially this is the view of M. Haran in *Encyclopaedia Biblica* (Hebrew) V (1968), 983-86, s.v. *netînîm*, and note literature cited here.

6 See, *inter alia*, Ezra 2:62-63 on the questionable lineage of certain priestly families at the time of the first return, under Zerubabel, and of *ibid.* 6:21, 8:1 f, 9:1-2 f., and ch. 10. It is interesting that according to one Talmudic tradition, Ezra's rigorism on questions of family status commenced, while he was still in Babylonia. Thus, *TB Qidd.* 69b: "Ezra did not 'ascend' from Babylonia until he had rendered it (i.e., the Babylonian Jewish Community) as fine flour, and only then did he 'ascend'." (The imagery of "dough" (*'issah*) as questionable lineage and "fine flour" (*solet*) as pure lineage is well attested).

7 See B.A. Levine, *op. cit.* 211-12, idem., *IEJ*, (1969), 49-51: idem., *Encyclopedia Judaica* 1972, VII, 522-4, s.v. "Gibeonites and *Nethinim*;" *ibid.* XV, 116-17, s.v. "Solomon, Servants of." Note that in *Tos. Qidd.* V: 2 *'abdê melākîm* "royal slaves" are associated with the stigma of *netînût* (See n. 29). This is a traditional formulation refelcting the biblical connection between the *netînîm* and *'abdê šelōmô* "the servants of Solomon." See B.A. Levine, *Encyclopedia Biblica* (Hebrew) VI (1972), 25-26, s.v. *'abdê šelōmô*.

I.

M. Qiddûšîn IV:1 is predicated on a tradition which traced the contemporary *netînîm* of the early Talmudic period to the biblical group by that name, especially to the period of Ezra, and which posited that Ezra had already rejected the *netînîm* and prohibited them from marrying proper Israelites.[8]

Does this tradition reflect in any significant way the actual history and origins of those persons who were the subject of Tannaitic legislation? We think not.

It is fairly obvious that the Sages saw Ezra as the prototype of the rigorous, religious leader who dealt forcefully with some of the problems which they, themselves, faced regarding intermarriage and those abrogations of Jewish family law which affected the status of future generations of Jews. This similarity of concern makes the ideological link between Talmudic legislation regarding the latter-day *netînîm* and Ezra's religious policies understandable, yet this same identification violates the context of the biblical sources in Ezra, Nehemiah, and Chronicles; since there is, in those sources, no indication whatsoever that the *netînîm* of the post-exilic period were in any way stigmatized or rejected by the community of returning exiles.[9] That aspect of the later tradition is certainly unhistorical.

That the later *netînîm* were not descendants of the post-exilic *netînîm* is further suggested, albeit indirectly, by the following considerations:

1) In epigraphic sources dating from the period between the 5th and 2nd centuries B.C. Hebrew *nâtîn*, and Aramaic *netînā'* were used in a positive, even honorific sense. Thus, *nātîn* occurs as a personal name in the Elephantine onomasticon, in documents dating from c. 400 and c. 300, B.C.[10] The mere fact that *nātîn* could serve as a personal name indicates that it conveyed a positive, religious nuance; that of "devotion."

   In an Aramaic statuary inscription from Hatra, dated in the second pre-Christian century, or later, Aramaic *netînā'* (sing. det.) means "the devoted one, the devout", and is one of a series of laudatory epithets applied to a king of Hatra, dressed and coiffed as an Arab.[11]

   This sparse evidence allows for the suggestion that usage of the designation *nātîn* up until early Talmudic times was not derogatory, as one would deduce from Talmudic etymologizing on this term; where the verb *nātan* is taken to convey reduction to a pariah status, or to temple slavery.[12]

---

8 The use of the indeterminate Aramaic pl. *netînê* (cf. *gērê*, *ḥalālê*, etc.) is archaistic, evoking the atmosphere of Ezra's day. Cf. *netînayyā'* in Ezra 7:24. We doubt if such usage demonstrates the antiquity of this section of the Mishnah (*pace* J.N. Epstein, *Prolegomena ad Litteras Tannaiticas* (Hebrew) [1957], 54, 414). In fact, Epstein, himself, attributes this Mishnah passage to a later Hillel, not to Hillel the Elder, as some had suggested. On the traditions of the Aggadah, see n. 4.

9 Ezra 8:20 at least implies that the *netînîm*, like those families listed in 8:1-19, had an established lineage, for "they were all designated by name." Intermarriage is an offense most often associated with priestly and Levitical families (*ibid.*, 9:1 f.) but never with *netînîm*. See literature cited in n. 7.

10 See A.E. Cowley, *Aramaic Papyri of the Fifth Century B.C.* (1923), 158, S.V. 53:2: *ptysy br ntyn*, in a papyrus dated 410-400 B.C. I am informed by Professor M. Silverman that the reading is clear and the date fairly certain. In *ibid.*, 194, S.V. 81:90 we have: *'byty ntyn*, with the word for "son" omitted. The text contains Greek names, and is consequently dated c. 300 B.C.

11 See A. Caquot, *Syria* 29 (1952), 101, no. 21, and comments. The inscription, broken at the end, reads:

ṣlm' dy 'tlw mlk' ntyn'
šry' plḥ 'lh' bryk 'lh' dy [. . . . .

"The statue of *'tlw* the king, the devoted one, the generous one (?), worshipper of God, blessed of God, who/which [. . . . . ". On *pḥ 'lh'* cf. Ezra 7:24. On other aspects of the text, see B.A. Levine, *JAOS* 87 (1967), 185-87.

12 See n. 4 for sources.

2) To our knowledge, Talmudic literature never mentions the *netînîm* in connection with any actual role in the cult of the second temple during the early Talmudic period, or as being in any real sense associated with the priesthood functioning at that time. Nowhere in the expansive and detailed descriptions of cultic activity preserved in the early Tannaitic compilations *Yômā*, *Middôt*, *Tāmîd*, or *Ta'anît*, for example, do we read of cultically functioning *netînîm*.[13]

The same silence is evident in other sources on the cult of the Second Temple and in the writings of Josephus.[14] In fact, Josephus was probably familiar with the Aggadic tradition identifying the *netînîm* of Ezra, Chapter 2, with the Gibeonites, since in refering to them he calls them *hierodouloi* "hierodules, temple-servants."[15] The Septuagint, on the other hand, never so renders the word *ne=tînîm*, which it usually transcribes into Greek, untranslated; and in one instance renders it literally by Greek *hoi dedōmenoi*.[16] One may suggest that the Seputagint writers were no longer aware of the real identity or function of the *netînîm*, and had no special tradition about them, which means that the Aggadic tradition is probably later than the Septuagint.

II.

The character of Talmudic legislation relevant to persons designated as *nātîn*, *netînāh*, etc. allows for the conclusion that an actual class of contemporary Jews was involved, and that such legislation was not essentially anachronistic or merely theoretical, despite the literary interrelatedness with Aggadic traditions.[17] According to Tannaitic sources, one was a *nātîn/netînāh* if he or she was born of a union involving at least one *nātîn* parent. In such a case, *qiddûšîn* "connubium" had taken effect, as a legal fact, since the offense involved, like that involved in the marriage of one of priestly lineage to a divorcee, for example, was not of the order that would nullify the fact of marriage, as would have been the case had a *mamzēr* been involved as parent.[18] Nevertheless, the *nātîn/netînāh* bore some of the disabilities of the *mamzēr*, at least in theory. Whereas violations of priestly law limited proper marriage only within the priestly society, the *nātîn/netînāh* was not per-

---

[13] Actually, the terms *nātîn*, *netînāh*, etc. never occur in any of the truly early tractates or compilations of the Mishnah, unless we accept Epstein's view that *M. Qidd.* IV:1 is part of an ancient code on prohibited unions (*ibid.* III:12 - IV:14, with interpolations), a view which we doubt. (See n. 8).

[14] Sources on the ritual praxis of the Second Temple are summarized by S. Safrai in *Encyclopaedia Judaica* (1972), XV, 969-70 f, s,v, "Temple, Ritual". They include the works of Josephus, especially *Antiquities of the Jews*, books 3, 5, 20, and his polemic, *Contra Apionem*; as well as apocryphal and pseudoepigraphic writings.

[15] See: *Josephus, with an English translation by Ralph Marcus, (Loeb Classical Library)*, VI, 1937; *Jewish Antiquities* XI, 128, 134. Also see R.H. Charles, *The Apocrypha and Pseudepigrapha of the Old Testament* (1965), I, 21, *ad loc.* I Esdras I:3, where *hierodouloi* refers to the *netînîm*.

[16] In 1 Chron 9:2 the Septuagint has *hoi dedōmenoi* "the devoted ones" (cf. *ta didōmena* "things offered" in (Liddell-Scott, *A Greek-English Lexicon*, [8th ed.], 366, s.v. *didōmi*). Elsewhere, we find only transcriptions. Cf. *hoi nathinaioi* (*ad* Ezra 2:43, Neh. 11:3); *hoi nathinin* (Ezra 2:58); and most often: *hoi nathinim.*

[17] See n. 3 for some theoretical statements in the Mishnah regarding *netînîm*. The tradition on the attempt to remove the ban against marriage with *netînîm* contains Aggadic elements, at the very least. *TB Yeb.* 79b places it in the time of Judah the Prince and *TP Qidd.* IV, *hal.* 1 in the time of Eleazar ben Azariah, about a century earlier. Also see *Tos. Qidd.* V:4. (See n. 29 on the term *netînût*). Most legislation concerning *ne=tînîm* is built into the fabric of family law as presented in the order *Nāšîm*. It has no hermeneutic basis in the Torah. In part, such legislation represents an extension of principles applied to *mamzērîm*. One could, of course, question why all Aggadah about the *netînîm* is projected into the biblical period if, indeed, an actual group of contemporary Jews was intended in the Talmudic legislation.

[18] See *M. Qidd.* III:12. "Wherever *qiddûšîn* does not obtain (as a legal fact) for the woman *vis à vis* this particular man, but where she has the right of *qiddûšîn* with respect of others, the offspring is a *mamzēr*. Which case is this? This applies to one who has sexual relations with any of the *'ārāyôt* specified in the Torah" (Lev. 18:6ff.). In other words, a *mamzēr* results from incest or adultery. Also see S. Lieberman, *Tosefta Ki-fshuṭah* (Hebrew) VI, 1967, 58-59, *ad loc. Tos. Yeb.* VI:9.

mitted to marry any proper Jew.[19] In practical terms, this restriction may not have been very consequential. A *netînāh* improperly marrying a Jew nevertheless received a *ketûbāh*, the document of settlement.[20] The legal classification embracing all the diverse applications of family law to *netînîm* is *'issûr qedûšāh* "prohibition [based on] sanctity", the same classification as was applied to unfit priests.[21]

Tannaitic literature gives ample evidence of the contemporary concern with personal status and family lineage. The fourth chapter of *M. Qiddûšîn* illustrates how the *netînîm* question related to this larger area of concern. There we observe the nexus of priestly lineage and personal status. Priestly lineage continued to serve as an index of acceptability long after the cessation of the temple cult. One way of determining that a woman was fully acceptable was to establish that she came from a family that could marry or had married into the priesthood.[22] The real concern underlying the use of priestly records for establishing lineage, certainly in post-temple times, was to achieve effective control over the execution of marriage and divorce, and for the prevention of intermarriage. Simeon ben 'Azzai, a sage of the Hadrianic period, claimed to have discovered in Jerusalem a genaeological register (*megillat yôḥāsîn*) which listed a certain person as a *mamzēr*.[23] *M. Qiddûšîn* IV:4-5 spells out how parentage was investigated and specifies certain backgrounds which required no further investigation.[24]

It would appear that *netînîm* families, like those of *mamzērîm* were, at certain periods, at least, identifiable in the Jewish communities of Palestine.[25] Questions persistently arose, nevertheless, and undoubtedly it became progressively more difficult to establish clear family lineage.[26] Nevertheless, *netînîm* and *memzērîm* were apparently distinguishable from one another.[27]

---

19 See n. 2 *à propos M. Qidd.* IV:1, and cf. *ibid.* IV: 6-7.

20 See *M. Yeb.* IX:3, *Ket.* XI:6. Also see *Tos. 'Arākîn* IV:18, relevant to the estate rights of a *nātîn* (or a *mamzēr*, for that matter), which were protected.

21 See *M. Yeb.* II:3-4, IV:13, VI:4, and S. Lieberman, *op. cit.* VI, 49-50, *ad loc. Tos. Yeb.* VI:5. A comparable classification is *pesûlê mišpāḥāh* "[types of] unfitness [based on] family (status)" (*TP Qidd.* IV, *hal.* 1; *Ket.* III, hal. 1): "Rabbi Yose said: 'They were concerned about the *netînîm* only as regards [types of] unfitness [based on] family (status).' " (One could take *pesûlê* not as the pl. const. of *pesûl* "unfitness", but as the pl. const. of the adj. *pāsûl* "unfit".) Also see *Tos. Niddah* V:1, parallel in *Tos. Yeb.* VIII:1-2, in S. Lieberman, *op. cit.*, 64-65, *ad loc.*, where the *nātîn* is referred to as one whose "seed" is *pāsûl* "unfit". Here, again, notions of unfitness affecting persons of priestly lineage were applied to *netînîm*.

22 See *M. Qidd.* IV:4-5, *Ket.* I:10. and cf. *'Arākîn* II:4, and also *San.* IV:2, where it is stated that only one from such families as could marry into the priesthood may serve in a court adjudicating capital cases. See *Tos. Ket.* II:3 (S. Lieberman, *op. cit.* VI, 215-217, especially 217, no. 38) on the matter of valid objections to priestly status, one of which was to state that a person had been born of a *nātîn*-parent.

23 See *M. Yeb.* IV:13.

24 Investigation of a woman about to be married proceeded on the maternal line. The Mishnah exempts from special investigation persons whose ancestors had performed priestly or Levitical functions in the temple, had been members of the Sanhedrin or officials in charge of communal instutitions and funds. Also mentioned as exempt are those who were registered as witnesses "in the ancient archive of Sepphoris" or "conscripted" in the *stratia* (Mishnaic: *'istratîā'*) "army" of the king. On archives of the Hellenistic cities in Palestine, see G. Alon, *A History of the Jews in Eretz Israel in the Period of the Mishnah and Talmud*, [Hebrew] (1952), I, 346-47, and *ibid.* II (1955), 106 on the *stratêgia* (= *'istratîā'*?), possibly an appointment to civic office. Also cf. *Tos. 'Eduyot* III:2.

25 See *Tos. Qidd.* V:2, *TP Ket.* I, *hal.* 9, *TB Ket.* 10a-b: "On what basis did they say that an *'issāh* woman is unfit for the priesthood? (See n. 6), It is because possible *ḥalālîn* were mixed into her lineage. Jews can identify the *netînîm* and *mamzērîm* in their midst, but they cannot identify the *ḥalālîn* in their midst."

26 See the discussion by I.M. Ta-Shma in *Encyclopaedia Judaica* (1972), VIII, 379-382, s.v. "Genealogy", and literature cited, *ibid.*, 383.

27 This may be deduced from the provision that a marriage could be voided if a man had misrepresented himself as a *nātîn* when he was, in fact, a *mamzēr*, or *vice versa* (*M. Qidd.* II:3). In *TP Qidd.* II, hal. 2, it is stressed that especially in matters affecting personal status it makes no difference whether the misrepresentation was ameliorative or prejorative. See J.M. Baumgarten, *Revue de Qumran* 29, 1972, 87-97. Writing on problems of *4Q Florilegium*, Baumgarten confuses the differences among *gērîm*, *mamzērîm*, and *netînîm*. The term *netînîm* is not attested in *4Q Florilegium*.

From *M. Hôrāyôt* I:4, we may deduce that a *nātîn* could not properly serve as a member of a court, which may suggest that *netînîm* were subject to certain civic disabilities.[28] It also implies, however, that they might have otherwise been qualified for office on cultural or socio-economic grounds had they not borne the religio-legal stigma of *netînût*.[29]

Some light can be shed on procedures used in determining the family background of *mamzērîm*, *netînîm*, and those of priestly lineage by reference to records from Uruk, and elsewhere, pertaining to devoted persons, some of them temple slaves, known as *širkūtu*. The disposition of cases involving *širkūtu* in certain documents dating from the Neo-Babylonian and Persian periods strongly resembles Mishnaic dicta on the taking of evidence, the status of offspring, and recourse to official records in acertaining personal status. The offspring of some classes of *širkūtu*, like those of the Talmudic *netînîm*, inherited the restricted status of their parents. In addition to revealing parallels with the biblical *netînîm*, the *širkūtu* documents illustrate the relatedness of Talmudic legal processes to older Near Eastern practices.[30]

III.

Who were the so-called *netînîm* of the Talmudic period? They were not *gērîm* "proselytes" in the usual sense, despite some confusion evident in the Talmudic discussions, which sometimes lump *netînîm* and *gērîm* together.[31] Talmudic legislation never considers the immediate parentage of the *nātîn*/*netînāh* as anything

[28] The Mishnah stipulates that a court with a *nātîn* as one of its members, like a court otherwise improperly constituted, does not come under the legislation of Lev 14:13 requiring a sacrificial offering in the event a court inadvertantly issued an incorrect edict, thus incriminating the entire *ʿēdāh* "community".

[29] For the abstract term, connoting stigmatized status, see *Tos. Qidd.* V:1, and *TB*, *Ket.* 14[a-b] (*à propos* Ezek 36:25). The term *netînût* is semantically equivalent to Akkadian *širkūtu* where it connotes membership in the order and the assumption of the consequent status. (See n. 30). *Tos. Makkôt* I:7 states that persons who conspired to testify that a man was a *nātîn* or *mamzēr* were subject to corporal punishment, since such an allegation constituted a slur, damaging to a person's standing in the community.

[30] For a discussion of parallels between the biblical *netînîm* and the *širkūtu* see B.A. Levine, *JBL* 82 (1963), 207, 210 and R. Dougherty, *YOSR* V:2 (1923), 90-91, and notes. In his study on the *širkūtu* Dougherty refers only to *M. Qidd.* III:12 and *Yeb.* II:4. There is much more: a) *REN* 224 (Dougherty, 36-38) concerns a charge that a man belongs to the *širkūtu*, i.e., that he was a temple slave; because his grandmother, a slave-woman, had been a *širkatu*. The man being charged produced a female witness, a niece of his grandmother's owner, who testified that she had never seen the star-brand of the temple order on the hand of his grandmother, and on that basis the man was set free. This is precisely the type of investigation into one's lineage prescribed in the Mishnah (*Ket.* II:8-10, *Qidd.* IV:4), b) *REN* 57 (Dougherty, 39-40) concerns the testimony of one who had seen the star-brand of the *širkūtu* order on the hand of a female slave eighteen years prior to the case in question, and on that basis the slave was declared a member of the order. In similar matters the Mishnah allowed one to testify in adulthood to what he had witnessed as a child (*M. Ket.* II:10). c) *REN* 116 (Dougherty, 42-43) concerns a controversy as to whether or not two brothers were *širkē*. Two records were consulted. Although the royal record contained no listing of these brothers as *širkē*, the temple record did, and they were consequently declared temple property. Cf. *YBT* VII, 91 (Dougherty, 45) for a further instance of recourse to records. We have already referred to the genaeological record mentioned in *M. Yeb.* IV:13. The documents pertaining to the *širkūtu* have even greater relevance to the practice of cultic devotion, but this goes beyond our concern here, which centers upon family status. A restudy of the *širkūtu* is required, and we are informed that unpublished documents await treament. D. Weisberg, *Guild Structure and Political Allegiance in Early Achaemenid Mesopotamia* (1967) has clarified some problems of temple organization at Uruk, having a bearing on the *širkūtu* (See *ibid.* 44).

[31] The discussion in *TP Qidd.* IV, *hal.* 1, is in the context of proselytizing. Also see L. Ginzberg, *op. cit.* IV, 110-11, and also n. 4, above.

but Jewish, and takes care to distinguish between the status of the *gēr* and the *nātîn*.[32] Despite observable differences of opinion on the advisability of seeking converts, the Sages would not have rejected those whose conversion to Judaism took effect under their own auspices.

One may question whether the Sages themselves knew the exact origin or background of those whom they called the *netînîm*. If they did, they have not disclosed such information in their literature. The sages were antagonistic in their feelings towards such Jews, although they were careful, as we have seen, not to infringe on their essential legal rights, while endeavoring to ostracize them. The term *riḥḥēq* ("to reject") used to characterize the actions of the Sages *vis à vis* the *netînîm* was also used with respect to certain families or clans whom they would not "accept" (*qārēb*) into the Jewish community.[33] Tannaitic statements on these matters are cryptic and do not reveal precisely what was involved in such actions except for the prohibition of marriage. There is even an indication that the power to "reject" or "accept", whatever it connoted in practical terms, was occasionally abused.[34]

Speculation on the precise identity of the Talmudic *netînîm* is not likely to produce very much of historical value. Were they the descendants of Hellenizing families, with a history of heterodoxy dating from the Maccabean or post-Maccabean periods?

It is strange that, whereas the Sages had good things to say about *Kûtîm*, presumed to be the descendants of the post-exilic Samaritans, and showed compassion for the *mamzēr*, in certain regards, they never have a good word for the *netînîm*, which suggests that it was not primarily their ethno-religious origin which determined official attitudes toward the *netînîm*, but rather their persistent behavior and relationship to the community, and to Jewish religious leadership.[35] We cannot rule out the possibility that the Talmudic *netînîm* were descended from earlier proselytes, whose subsequent behavior aroused opposition. This would account for the Aggadic projection of contemporary hostility into the biblical period, epitomized in the identification of the *netînîm* with the Gibeonites, as if to say that no good could come from the likes of those!

IV.

This is as far as we can go in identifying the *netînîm* of the later sources. We have sought only to disallow the identification of the latter-day *netînîm* with those of the post-exilic books of Ezra, Nehemiah, and Chronicles, and to place the Aggadic traditions in proper perspective, in relation to the contemporary character of Talmudic legislation. Such legislation was not addressed to cultic servitors or their descendants, but to contemporary Jews whose social intermingling with the Jewish community the Sages sought to prevent, out of concern for the status of the Jewish family and the coherence of the larger community.[36]

32 *TP Qidd.* IV, *hal.* 1 cites as proof of the fact that the *netînîm* had no problem of immediate foreign parentage, as did proselytes and emancipated slaves, the law of *M. Ket.* III:1 which stipulates that one who rapes or seduces a *netînāh* while she was a *na'ărāh* "pubescent maiden" is liable to the penalty imposed by the Torah (Ex 22:16, Dt. 22:29). This indicates that there is no suspicion of non-Jewish status, since, as a legal fact, non-Jewish females were not presumed to retain their virginity until puberty.

33 See *M. 'Ēdûyôt* VIII: 2-3, 7 and *Tos. ibid.* III:4. Here, again priestly considerations were often involved in "acceptance" or "rejection". Also cf. *M. 'Ēdûyôt* V:7 on acceptance as one of the fellowship of scholars. Of possible relevance is *M. Nedārîm* I:7: *meruḥḥāqānî mimmāk* "I will keep myself apart from you".

34 See *M. 'Ēdûyôt* VIII:7 which refers to those forcibly accepted and rejected from the community.

35 According to *M. Hôrāyôt* III:8, a *mamzēr* ranks higher than a *nātîn* in terms of respect due him, and we have the hyperbolic statement that a *mamzēr* who is a student of the wise ranks higher than an unschooled High Priest! Also cf. *Tos. Hôrāyôt* II:10 and see G. Alon, *op. cit.* I, 350-52 and sources cited there on the varying attitudes of the Sages toward the *kûtîm*, and also *ibid.* II, 1955, 248-251.

36 As a fitting postscript, we note the contemporary Hebrew term *nātîn* "subject, citizen", and related *netînût* "citizenship". See E. Ben-Yehuda, *Dictionary and Thesaurus of the Hebrew Language*, (Hebrew) V, 1960, 3870, s.v. *nātîn*, b. and *ibid.* 3871, s.v. *netînût*. Also see A. Ibn-Shoshan, *Hammillôn Heḥḥādāš* [Hebrew], (1969), II, 889, s.v. *nātîn* and *netînût*. Modern Hebrew usage has thus restored the original, positive connotation of the ancient term.

ACHAEMENIAN CLOISONNÉ-INLAY JEWELRY: AN IMPORTANT NEW EXAMPLE[1]

John F.X. McKeon

Museum of Fine Arts, Boston, Mass.

The Achaemenian Empire was established by the Persian King, Cyrus the Great, upon his defeat of Astyages, King of the Medes in 550 B.C. The cultural history of pre-Achaemenian, First Millennium, Iran, has been the subject of much study in recent years. Interest in this fascinating period has been stimulated by the archaeological excavations carried out at sites at Marlik, Hasanlu, and Susa and also by hoards such as Ziwiye and Hamadan.[2]

The cross fertilization which took place during this period as a result of the inter-influence of Assyrian, Urartian, Scythian, Median, Mannean, and Elamite traditions is evident in the material from these sites. One need only read the various studies of the Ziwiye material to understand how difficult it is to discern the direction and extent of the cultural influences which took place at the time.[3]

Achaemenian art, developing gradually from the reign of Cyrus, absorbed many of these Ancient Near Eastern traditions at a point after they had already lost much of their original vitality within their native culture. One can discern *two major traditions* within Achaemenian arts. One, the more *formal*, official empire style, is

---

[1] The writer would like to express, from the start, his indebtedness to those who have assisted him in this study. In addition to her fine drawings, Suzanne Chapman, his associate in Boston, has contributed helpful insights in regard to ancient jewelry. The writer was able to profit by the advice of Professor Porada, Columbia University, regarding some of the points discussed in this article, although she is in no way responsible for the conclusions expressed here (except as cited). W.J. Young, Head of the Research Laboratory, shared the fruits of his technical study of the earring, soon to be published in the *Boston Museum Bulletin*. Valuable references were kindly offered by D.G. Mitten, Havard University, and R.D. Barnett of the British Museum. The writer would also like to thank the editor, Prof. Harry A. Hoffner, Jr., for allowing him the honor of contributing to this volume dedicated to our respected mentor.

[2] See E. Porada, *The Art of Ancient Iran*, New York, Crown Publ., (1956), (see 264-5 for an extensive bibliography); R.H. Dyson, *JNES* 24 (1965), 198ff. for a thorough analysis of the archaeological evidence; for a specific study of the jewelry of this period, K.R. Maxwell-Hyslop, *Western Asiatic Jewellery*, 232-69.

[3] Porada, *op.cit.*, 137-41; H. Kantor, *JNES* 16 (1957), 1-23, stresses the Scythian element while R.D. Barnett "Median Art," *Iranica Antiqua* II (1962), 77-95, portrays the Medes as transmitters of both Urartian and Scythian elements. For what is perhaps the best discussion of styles in Achaemenian minor arts see P. Amandry, *Antike Kunst* (1958), 9-23, esp. 15.

best represented in the Persepolis reliefs, but is also apparent in the minor arts. It can be said with sufficient justification, that this style is most indebted to the arts of Assyrian empire. The other, an *"animal style"* is most characteristically expressed in the minor arts, although its traces can also be discerned in major works of sculpture. This style is perhaps most intimately linked to Median and Scythian traditions which themselves are not yet clearly isolated.[4]

One aspect of Achaemenian artistic taste which is not always apparent to the modern viewer is a strong penchant for *polychrome decoration* of their works. The monochrome, polished surface of the Persepolis reliefs today conveys nothing of the striking impression which Herzfeld, who excavated Persepolis in 1923, so vividly describes in regard to the original condition of the sculptures.[5] He states "On a deep black background the colours stand out, luminous and almost transparent, like cloisonné enamel. Turquoise blue changes with a light scarlet red, the yellow has an orange or gold shade; deep purple or lapis blue." He also notes that certain parts of the sculptures had inlays of precious materials, such as lapis lazuli, or were overlaid with gold. This latter observation ties in well with the famous inscription of Darius I from Susa[6] where the Medes and Egyptians, who are listed first as goldsmiths, are then described as "decorating the sculptures". The fact that these craftsmen, whose work as goldsmiths involved them in the production of objects on a minor scale, were also involved in the decoration of major works of sculpture, underlines the cohesion of Achaemenian art which has been already noted.[7]

Turning, then, from the monumental to the miniature, the same taste for color is perhaps best illustrated by an Achaemenian earring in the Museum of Fine Arts, Boston (pl. Ia,b).[8] This splendid example of the jeweler's art sums up many of the characteristic features of Achaemenian decorative art. The materials used in the production of the earring once again relate intimately to the inscription of Darius noted above.[9] The circular earring is made of gold cloisonné with inlays of lapis lazuli, carnelian and turqoise. A large central roundel contains a bust of what is probably Ahuramazda, the supreme god of the Achaemenians, upon a winged crescent moon. One hand is raised in a gesture, and the other holds a lotus blossom. Encircling this central roundel, in a prefectly balanced symmetry, are seven smaller roundels. Six of them contain a similar figure, here seated upon a simple crescent, who perhaps represents the king. The last of the small roundels contains a lotus blossom and is positioned at center bottom as a counter balance to the clasp-opening at the top. The arc of the clasp completes the full circle formed by the cloison band with triangular designs, which separates the roundels from the encircling palmette forms on the outer edge. The obverse and reverse of the earring are identical, but the obverse has better preserved inlays.

---

4 See G. Borovka *Scythian Art*, London, Ernest Benn Ltd. (1928), for what is still the best survey of Scythian Art.

5 E.E. Herzfeld, *Iran in the Ancient East*, (1941), 255; quoted by Porada, *op.cit.* 154.

6 R.G. Kent, *AOS* 33 (1950), 144; H. Frankfort, *The Art and Architecture of the Ancient Orient*, 214; Porada, *op.cit.*, 156. Darius also mentions that the Babylonians were responsible for baking the bricks, i.e., the polychrome glazed bricks like those found at Susa. This is another example of polychrome decoration on a monumental scale.

7 Amandry, 15; H. Kantor, *op.cit.*, 2. Porada, *op.cit.*, 160. Both also note the relation between the gold appliqués and the figurative decoration of garments on the sculptures. This later relation may have exsited in Neo-Assyrian art as suggested by J.V. Canby, *Iraq* 33 (1971), 31-53.

8 MFA 1971. 256. Edward J. and Mary S. Holmes Fund. 5 cm. diameter. The companion piece, less completely preserved, is in a private collection. W.K. Simpson, *Conoisseur*, 179 (Feb. 1972), 119-120, fig. 8. No author, "Treasures of Massachusetts," *Boston Globe*, 5 March 1972, 34-35. "The Rathbone Years", exhibit catalogue, Museum of Fine Arts, (Boston, 1972), 30, pl. 16 (color) W.J. Young, *BMFA*, Vol. 70, No. 359 (1972).

9 Footnote 5; Darius states, "The gold from Sardis and from Bactria was brought, which was used here. The stone – lapis lazuli and carnelian – which was used here, this from Sogdiana was brought. This stone – turquoise – this from Chorasmia was brought, which was used here." An interesting technique employed on the Boston earring was brought to the writer's attention by W.J. Young, Head of the Museum's Research Laboratory. The base of the cloisons containing carnelian inlays was painted with cinnabar in order to deepen the color of the translucent stone. This technique is still in use today.

In addition to the choice of materials, the static repetition of forms reminds one of the Persepolis reliefs and is a basic characteristic of this formal, official style of Achaemenian decorative art.[10] The iconographic details of the earring underline the already mentioned dependency of Achaemenian art upon the earlier Assyro-Babylonian traditions. The central figure is identified as Ahura Mazda because of the prominent place which this representation holds in all forms of Achaemenian art. (fig. 1)[11] Such a premier position could only be held by the supreme god himself, whose patronage was so often sought by the king in royal inscriptions. This manner of representing a supreme god is taken from the earlier Mesopotamian traditions of the Assyrian supreme god, Assur, and the moon god Sîn, whose cult was especially favored by the last Neo-Babylonian king, Nabonidus. Assur was depicted as a bust-figure upon a winged sun-disc, while Sin was represented upon a simple crescent moon. The Achaemenian portrayal of Ahuramazda on the Boston earring shows an adaptation of these traditions. The wings of the disc on the central roundel being upturned in a characteristically Persian fashion.[12] The bust figure rests upon what seems to be a composite sun disc-crescent moon like that found above the fire altar at the entrance to the tomb of Artaxerxes I and, perhaps, other tombs at Naqsh-i-Rustam. On the obverse of the earring the turquoise inlay of the crescent is preserved, while on the reverse the carnelian inlay between the crsecent and the gold bust figure remains. Another distinctive feature is the carefully engraved, incredibly minute form of an earring worn by the god. It is an attested Achaemenian earring form, crescentic in shape, thereby differing from the one upon which it is engraved. That the artist should bother to include this detail is a sign of his precision. It is interesting to note, in relation to the smaller roundels here, that the Mesopotamian moon god, Sîn, is sometimes depicted upon his crescent in conjunction with a lotus blossom.[13] The bust figure upon a simple crescent in Achaemenian art could also be the god, Ahuramazda, as has been suggested, or it may be the king.[14]

fig. 1
Achaemenian stamp seal – Louvre
(Drawing by Suzanne Chapman)

In order to give this important piece its proper place within the context of Ancient Near Eastern jewelry, we shall consider it under two general aspects: technique and form.

The *technique* of cloisonné inlay, which attained such magnificent heights in Egypt, was included in the repetoire of the Ancient Near East craftsmen from the earliest times.[15] Examples can be found in the Jemdat

---

[10] G. Richter, *Hesperia* Suppl. VIII, 295; H. Frankfort, *op.cit.*, 232; R. Ghirshman, *The Arts of Ancient Iran* (1964), 237.

[11] H. Kantor, *op.cit.*, 14ff., pl. VI, fig. 10; also E.F. Schmidt, "Persepolis II," Chicago, *O.I.P.* 49 (1957), 8 pl. 16-18; *Encyclopédie photographique de l'Art*: The Louvre Museum II, (1936), ≠ 134 and others; also B. Segall, *Art Bulletin*, XXXVIII/2 (1956), 75-80.

[12] E.F. Schmidt, *op.cit.*, p. 8.

[13] Several cylinder seals: Walters Art Gallery 42.802 see C.H. Gordon, *Iraq* 6 (1939), pl. XIII, no. 105; B. Segall, *op.cit.*, Pl. 2; Boston Museum of Fine Arts, 36.216, Seth K. Sweetser Fund. (unpublished)

[14] See note 11 above.
Both were represented identically and one would like to understand the reason for the subordination and differentiation of the smaller figures, as on the Louvre seal (fig. 1). Another intriguing representation pertinent to the problem is the seated figure upon a crescent above the altar of the tomb at Qyzqypan which may date to the Achaemenian period. The figure here seems to be a man, perhaps a king, rather than a god. The significance of this representation cannot be estimated until the monument as a whole can be properly interpreted. See Porada, *Iran*, 138; C.J. Edmonds, *Iraq* I (1934) 186, fig. 2.

[15] We distinguish here cloisonné inlay from cloisonne enameling ("true" cloisonne). The former denotes that stone or paste was cut to fit the cloisons of gold and set into them. The latter refers to powdered glass which

Nasr Period at Tepe Gawra[16] and during the Sumerian Early Dynastic Period among the fabulous riches of the Royal Tombs at Ur.[17] Akkadian jewelry of any type is rare, due to the small number of excavated sites of this period.[18] The absence of examples of cloisonne inlay in Akkadian jewelry may be due to the accidents of discovery, but this type of decoration does not seem entirely to suit the character of Akkadian art. Future excavations, however, may prove the contrary.

The survival, or continuation, of this technique during the *Ur III Period* is dramatically witnessed by the handsome necklace of the priestess Abbabashti, discovered in the Eanna Temple at Uruk.[19] Sumerian goldwork, since the Early Dynastic Period, seems to have had widespread influence. It is particularly true in the Ur III period where connections with Troy, Trialeti and Byblos have been strongly suggested.[20] The last mentioned site was a great metallurgical center as attested by the numerous examples of metalwork and its associated paraphanalia known from there. The influence of her workshops seems to have stimulated the rise of lesser centers at Megiddo and Tell-el-Ajjul. At both sites the technique of cloisonné inlay is well attested, but it is at Tell-el-Ajjul that we find the first real parallel to the form of the circular Achaemenian earring under discussion. (fig. 2)[21] This important site, whose role in international trade relations is so well evidenced by the archaeological record, may have been the channel for the introduction of the earring into Egypt during the Second Intermediate Period (MB II)[22].

fig. 2
Tell Ajjul Earring
(Drawing by Suzanne Chapman)

During this same period in Mesopotamia and Iran neither cloisonné inlay nor earrings of similar shape are known to this writer. However, Babylonian terracottas depict men and women adorned with elaborate jewelry, one example seeming to suggest cloisonné work.[23] During the 15th century B.C., however, the technique was practiced by the rather sophisticated goldsmiths at Alalakh, on the Orontes, North Syria.[24]

---

is fused in place. Champlevé is yet another allied technique, perhaps best typified by the Nimrud ivories. Here the cells are hollowed out rather than soldered onto the ground. The earliest example of cloisonné enameling known to the writer is the finger rings from Kouklia, Cyprus (13th century B.C.) cited by Maxwell-Hyslop, 120, pl. 84. Champlevé enameling is known at Ziwiye. A Godard, *Le Tresor de Ziwye*, (1950), fig. 90; Maxwell-Hyslop, 214; for studies of the history of these techniques see E Margulies "Cloisonne Enamel" in A.U. Pope (ed), *Survey of Persian Art*, IV, text 779ff.; R.A. Higgins, *Greek and Roman Jewellery*, (1961), 28-30.

[16] Maxwell-Hyslop, 1; A.J. Tobler, *Excavations at Tepe Gawra II*, (1950), pl. LVIII, LIX.

[17] Maxwell-Hyslop, 13-14, pl. 11 c.

[18] Ibid, 17-34.

[19] Ibid, 65.

[20] Ibid, 64-52. The presence of a gold cloisonne pin at Troy, a stunning gold cup with polychrome inlays at Trialeti and a gold pendant set with cloisons at Byblos are among the possible connections. Byblos seems to have been a contact point for the spread of numerous artistic impulses at this time.

[21] Ibid, 112 ff.

[22] The earring was unkown in Egypt in the Old and Middle Kingdoms. It first came into use during the Second Intermediate Period when West Asiatic influence was so strong. Examples from the 18th Dynasty, eg. those from Tutankhamun's tomb resemble the form of the Ajjul earrings, with elaborate additions. See, A. Wilkinson, *Ancient Egyptian Jewellery*, (1971), 12, pl. XLV B and C; C. Aldred, *Jewels of the Pharaohs*, 142, pl. 121, 122; M. Vilimkova, *Egyptian Jewellery*, (1969), pl. 56-59. The use of the earring seem to have continued through Dynasty 25, when it disappeared until Hellenistic times (Wilkinson, 194).

[23] Maxwell-Hyslop, 84ff., Fig. 53-56.

[24] Ibid., 136; L. Wooley, *Alalakh*, (1955), 272.

The magnificent hoard of jewelry discovered in tomb 45 at Assur is dated to the *Middle Assyrian Period*, specifically to the reign of Tukulti-Ninurta I (1244-1208 B.C.).[25] Here we see the brilliant effloresence of Near Eastern jewelry traditions. Surely this should not be considered a freak occurence which must be explained by means of positing outside influences. It should rather point out to us the paucity of excavated 2nd millenium sites in Mesopotamia and stimulate the search for important First Dynasty of Babylon, Kassite and Middle Assyrian centers. The strength of communication between Egypt and the Near East during the slightly earlier *Amarna Period* is well attested by texts. We know that raw materials, finished works and even craftsmen were exchanged between courts. While Egyptian influence may be evident in Late Kassite glyptic,[26] the hoard of jewelry from Assur fits comfortably into the Near Eastern traditions we have already discussed. The interesting relationship between the jewelry of tomb 45 and the elaborate description of that worn by Ishtar in the "Descent of Ishtar" underlines the indigenous nature of the hoard. It is the chance discovery of Tut-Ankh-Amun's sealed tomb and its fabulous contents which has skewed the evidence. One need only subtract the contents of this single tomb from the recent books on Egyptian jewelry to realize the way it has influenced our judgment. Perhaps the future discovery of an unplundered royal tomb of Babylonia or Assyria might restore the balance.

Included in the material from Assur tomb 45 is a superb cloisonné inlay pectoral ornament, which formed part of an elaborate necklace.[27] The circular gold disc was set with cloisons of gold, which were inlaid with lapis lazuli and white shell, with, perhaps, other materials not preserved. The importance of this piece in relation to an Achaemenian button from a hoard of jewelry excavated at Pasargadae has already been noted.[28] The similarity of material, form and technique emphasizes the continuity of the deeply entrenched artistic traditions in West Asiatic jewelry.

In *Iran*, the earliest known example of cloisonné inlay jewelry, an earring excavated at Susa, is probably datable to the early part of the Second Millennium B.C.[29] From the mid-Second Millennium, the site of Gök Tepe (Geoy Tepe) yielded a pair of double hollow lunate earrings decorated with cloisonné inlay of lapis lazuli.[30] At Marlik, in the earlier tombs which are tentatively dated to 1350-1150 B.C., were discovered a ceremonial dagger having a blade inlaid with lapis lazuli and a pair of gold pendants decorated with delicately patterned cloisons which originally must have held inlays.[31] The Marlik dagger may be the prototype for a spectacular knife handle excavated at Hasanlu and dated to the 9th Century B.C.[32] The latter is the earliest known use in Iran of cloisonne-inlay for representational art, the handle containing the figure of a man outlined by cloisons of gold. Perhaps the presence of this object at Hasanlu, in the light of other evidence, may represent the eastern extension of the use of polychrome inlay in figurative decoration so lavishly employed by the Neo-Assyrians at Nimrud. While the Nimrud ivories are decorated with inlays similar in shape to later Achaemenian jewelry under discussion, the forms of Neo-Assyrian earrings are quite different from the Achaemenian circular examples, and the use of cloisonné-inlay for their decoration is rare.[33]

At Tepe Sialk, a pair of gold earrings with granulated decoration were discovered in cemetery A, tomb V.[34] These, being crescentic rather than circular in shape, are of a different, more common type. However, in

---

[25] Maxwell-Hyslop, 169ff; A. Haller, *Die Gräber und Grüfte von Assur*, (1954), 123ff.

[26] E. Porada, "Kassite Art,", *Archaeologia Orientalia in Memoriam Ernst Herzfeld*, (1952), 179-88. Professor Porada has suggested in conversation that the flat shape of the inlaid stones both in the Middle Assyrian and Achaemenian periods are characteristic of Egyptian workmanship.

[27] Maxwell-Hyslop, 173, fig. 106; Haller, *op.cit.*, 126, Taf. 34(x).

[28] R. Stronach, "Excavations at Pasargadae," *Iran* 3, 39.

[29] Maxwell-Hyslop, 84, pl. 59 c.

[30] Ibid., 159, pl. 121.

[31] Ibid., 192; E.A. Negahban, *Marlik*, (1964), fig. 67.

[32] Porada, *Iran*, 118, pl. 31.

[33] Maxwell-Hyslop, 244; Porada, *Iran*, 110 for reference to Assyrian influence in 9th century Hasanlu.

[34] Maxwell-Hyslop, 187, fig. 112, pl. 133.

Sialk cemetery B, tomb 3, the excavations discovered a number of silver ornaments, decorated in repoussé, which adorned the individual's temple or forehead. The form and decoration of one of these ornaments strongly resembles a distinctive type of earring which was the immediate precursor of the later Achaemenian circular gold earrings.[35]

The earrings to which we refer were found in North Syria, Mesopotamia and Iran and seem to date to the 6th/5th cent. B.C. Their form, like the somewhat later Achaemenian gold examples, consists, basically, in a series of concentric circles, the outer one being decorated with a row of globules. The first example, in the British Museum, is part of a hoard of silver from Mesopotamia, possibly from Babylon. (fig. 3)[36] While some of the material in the hoard (coins and a vase handle) suggest a 5th Century B.C. dating for it's deposition,[37] the earring may be somewhat earlier. Both the Sialk repoussé ornament and the British Museum earring have the characteristic outer row of globules attached to a narrow circular band. Within this, there is a band of triangular shaped cloisons, followed by further concentric circles. It is particularly interesting to compare the British Museum earring with the Boston inlaid earring. The outer row of globules of the former are transformed on the latter into palmettes, a most prominent Achaemenian motif[38].

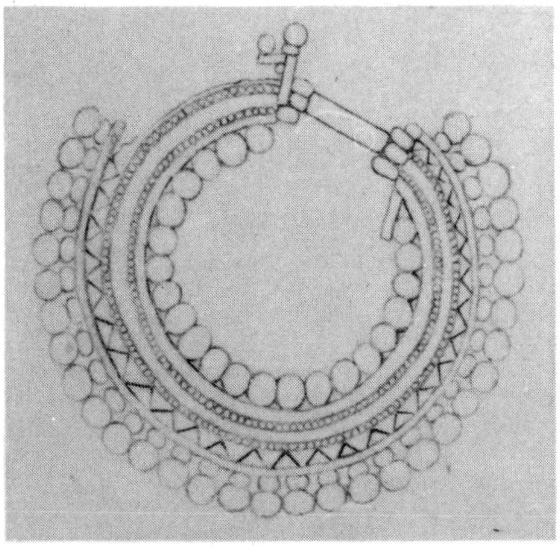

fig. 3
Silver Earring – British Museum
(Drawing by Suzanne Chapman)

Next, the band of triangular shaped cloisons compares most closely with the Boston earring. However, the British Museum example seems to terminate at center in a row of globules, while that in Boston has a solid central roundel, closer in this aspect to the Sialk B ornament.

The British Museum earring has been compared with a group of earrings excavated at *Neirab* near Aleppo, Syria.[39] Here we find a series of three closely related pairs of earrings of the type under discussion. The tombs have been dated to the late Neo-Babylonian/Early Achaemenian periods, i.e., the 6th century B.C. The reasons for the including these earrings in this group are obvious – the concentric circles with outer row of globules and characteristic clasp.

---

[35] R. Ghirshman, *Sialk II*, Paris (1939), pl. L (S 545 B). 6 cm. diam.; Maxwell-Hyslop, 265ff. The author rightly associates it with the Assur earring, but misunderstood the latter; W. Culican, *The Medes and the Persians*, (1965), 127. The author cites, without a reference, an eigth century example from near Antioch.

[36] E.S.G. Robinson, *Iraq* 12, (1950), 44-8, pl. XXIV. (5.3 cm diameter). These may be related to certain simple bronze "hoop" earrings with globules on lower edge which are said to come from Luristan and Kurvin and would be more or less contemporary with the Sialk B example. See P.R.S. Moorey, *Catalogue of the Ancient Persian Bronzes in the Ashmolean Museum*, Oxford, Clarendon Press, 1971, 229, pl. 60, no. 407-409; A. Godard, *Les Bronzes du Luristan*, Paris (1931), pl. XXIX, no. 98. Two silver earrings in Ashmolean Museum Catalogue (pl. 73, no. 537-8) seem to be more specifically related to the "mulberry" type of earrings best known from Syria – Palestine – see Maxwell-Hyslop, pl. 200.

[37] P. Amandry, *Antike Kunst* (1959-2), 46-7.

[38] Ghirshman, *Iran*, 289, 290, pl. 217.

[39] M. Abel, *Syria* 8 (1927), 211, pl. LIV; ibid, *Syria* 9 (1925), fig. 2 (a. b. c), pl. LVI C. The pair of silver earrings from tomb 28 (Pl. LV b) called "Anneaux" by the excavators were found in association with a late Neo-Babylonian chalcedony stamp seal. These are simple circular hoops with globules on outer edge like the earlier Luristan bronze examples, but having a distinct clasp. Maxwell-Hyslop, 268.

W.J. Young, *BMFA* (1972). The fact that the gold comes from Sardis does not actually tell us anything about its provenience. As Darius states, the gold was brought from there to be worked at Susa.

A broken pair of silver earrings of this same type was discovered at *Assur* but were not recognized by the excavator or subsequent writers.[40] It was described as "Schmuckstück" (a piece of jewelry) by Haller and even called a "broken bracelet" by Maxwell-Hyslop. However, a careful comparison with the British Museum earring is sufficient to convince one of its identity. There remain only a few of the inner row of globules of the wholly preserved earring, while more can be seen on the partial fragment of the second earring. The identification of this pair of earrings strongly suggests that the grave, originally dated by Haller to Middle Assyrian Period on the basis of some pottery found therein, should be dated rather with the "post Neo-Assyrian" graves in the same cemetery. The excavator notes the difficulty in dating the individual graves and many objects are common among them.

At a site in North Syria, Deve Hüyük, one each of two different pairs of earrings of this type were discovered, along with scabbard chapes in the form of stylized animals.[41] These latter are well known from the illustrations on the Persepolis reliefs and elsewhere. This fact underlines the parallels between certain objects at Deve Hüyük and Persepolis. These include, in addition to earrings of the type under discussion, godrooned bronze bowls and bridle bits.[42]

Further west, at Lydian *Sardis* in Asia Minor, there came to light a fine illustration of the use of a similar type of circular earrings. (fig. 4).[43] Adorning the ear of an ivory statuette, which is related to the ivories at Ephesus, we see such a jewel. Here also we see additional material to illustrate these formative stages of Achaemenian arts. An early example of a sheet gold applique depicts Ahura Mazda as a bust figure upon a winged disc, like other examples to be discussed later. However, an early feature of this piece is the fifth wing at the bottom which is shown as if in side view. A large number of actual gold earrings were also discovered. While some are simple gold rings like those illustrated on Persepolis reliefs,[44] others are more elaborate. Several have clasps of similar construction to the Late Neo-Babylonian and Achaemenian types. Some are crescentic in shape like the more common, earlier examples. Of those circular in shape, some are decorated with uniform ribbing or lion's head terminals. Several examples are decorated with sweated globules of gold and are identical with one found in a Neo-Babylonian context at Uruk. These must be somehow related to the type under discussion but they do not seem to be their source, as suggested elsewhere.[45] They seem, more probably, to be a contemporary variation.

fig. 4
Ivory head with circular earring from Sardis
(Drawing by Suzanne Chapman)

---

[40] Haller, 59, grave 715. 5 cm. diam. The size itself would eliminate it from the bracelet category. It fits perfectly with the size of the other earrings cited. The pottery from this tomb is not illustrated, so the strength of the resemblance to Kassite wares cannot be judged. Maxwell-Hyslop, 265.

[41] L. Woolley, *AAA* 7 (1914-16), pl. XXIII No. 7 is actually shown in reverse as Maxwell-Hyslop, pl. 256. The stylized animal form of the chapes is of Scythian type, generally considered to have been transmitted by the Medes and dated to the 5th century B.C., cf. Ghirshman, *Iran*, Pl. 287-8, Porada, *Iran*, 138; W. Culican, *op. cit.*, 131.

[42] Deve Hüyük, Pl. XXIII, no. 547 = Persepolis II, pl. 45, no. 27; Deve Hüyük, pl. XXI = Persepolis II, pl. 67, no. 3; Deve Hüyük, pl. XXIV = Persepolis II, pl. 78, no. 2,4.

[43] C.D. Curtis, *Sardis XII*, Jewellery and Goldwork Part I (1910-14), pl. VIII, no. 87; gold applique, pl. I, fig. 8 (8), gold earrings, pl. VII.

[44] Ghirshman, *Iran*, pl. 215, 218, 226, etc.

[45] Maxwell-Hyslop, 268.

That Sardis should be an early focal point is particularly fitting in regard to the Boston earring. The Late Neo-Babylonian/Early Achaemenian examples which we have discussed were almost all of silver. Upon the defeat of Croesus, the riches of Lydia fell into the hands of Cyrus.[46] Recent studies of inclusions in the gold of the Boston earring, in Lydian coins and in another Achaemenian piece have established that this metal came from the Pactolus River Valley around Sardis.[47] This coincides perfectly with the inscription of Darius as we have seen above.

After considering these early examples we can mention one other pertinent object of this period before approaching the "classical" Achaemenian jewelry. This is a gold cloisonné-inlay pectoral ornament from *Armavir*, in Urartu.[48] The ends are decorated with swans' heads and the outer border with a row of alternating lotus flowers and lotus buds. When viewed along with the inner band of triangular cloissons, these forms can be seen as yet another translation of the "globules", as are the palmettes on the Boston earring. While cloisonné-inlay is attested as early as the 9th century B.C. in Urartu,[49] this piece would seem to date to the 6th/5th Century. This would place it in the period of either Median or early Achaemenian control over the area.

Within the more "classical" repertoire of *Later Achaemenian* jewelry we find some striking comparisons to the Boston earring. The closest parallel is found within a rich cache of Achaemenian jewelry from a sarcophagus burial at Susa.[50] This cache, like that from Middle Assyrian tomb at Assur already discussed, gives us only a tantalizing glimpse at the wealth of jewelry which was current in each period. The skeleton was bedecked with bracelets, torques, necklaces and earrings. These earrings, like much of the other material, are gold with cloisonné-inlay but, however, are without figurative decoration. Their general shape conforms to the concentric circle type, and the technique of construction is the same, including the clasp. However, the center is empty and the cloisons are set into geometric patterns. Other objects here, this time gold cloisonné buttons inlaid with turquoise provide us with our iconographic parallel (fig. 5). Here we see representations identical to the smaller roundels on the Boston earring. The button's roundels, one central and five encircling, are identical in size and detail. Can we here follow our reasoned attribution of this figure to the king, rather than the god? There is no new evidence here, and the lingering doubt remains. The triangular dividers between the roundels and the outher row of granulated globules further heighten is identity. Individual such roundels were used as spacer beads on necklaces within this cache. Another example, unrecognized by the excavator, was found at Persepolis.[51] The form of the Susa button, combined with that of a gold medallion in the Vidal Collection (fig. 6),[52] which provides the palmette border, would then closely approximate the Boston earring.

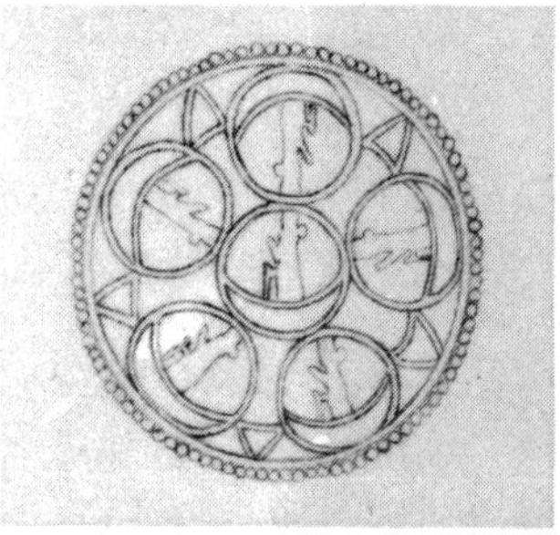

fig. 5
Cloisonné-inlay Button from Susa (Louvre)
(Drawing by Suzanne Chapman)

fig. 6
Gold Medaillon in Vidal Collection
(Drawing by Suzanne Chapman)

The material from the Susa burial has already been intensively studies in relation to the other known groups of Achaemenian jewelry.[53] The strongest links are with the famous *Oxus treasure*, which is now partially collected in the British Museum.[54] Here are found brilliant examples of cloisonné-inlay gold armlets, much like certain examples at Susa. There are also gold appliqués representing the king and/or Ahuramazda. These once again remind us of the two-dimensional nature of the bust-figures on the Susa button and the Boston earring. These latter are both flat plates, soldered onto their base and having engraved details. One particular Oxus example shows Ahura Mazda upon a winged crescent in the same manner as the Boston earring. This is seen as a late feature in contrast to the earlier Sardis example already noted.[55] These along with the Chicago applique, have been dated to the 4th Century B.C.[56]

The "classical" Achaemenian earrings have recently been re-studied by Stronach following the discovery of the new examples from Pasargadae.[57] The purpose of the excavations at Pasargadae was to shed light on early development in the Achaemenian Period. It was hoped that material such as the jewelry might be found in a scientifically datable context. Unfortunately, the jewelry was discovered in a coarse-ware pottery vessel having no stratigraphic relationship. The excavator was therefore forced to rely upon stylistic analysis to date this material. Noting the difficulties involved in such an analysis, he suggests a dating in the 4th century B.C., possibly even the second half of that century, for the jewelry. The late features such as openwork and attached pendants, found on the Pasargadae earrings would seem to confirm this dating.[58]

Having thus considered the major groups of Achaemenian jewelry, we can now make a suggestion regarding the date of the Boston earring. As we have seen, the closest iconographic parallels are with the Susa burial, dated to the 4th century B.C. However, the Boston earring retains a resemblance to the earlier, silver earrings not found among the Susa jewelry. It would then seem to be characteristic of an intermediate stage, probably during the second half of the 5th century B.C. or the very beginning of the 4th century B.C. Its excellent state of preservation has enabled us to better understand the development of cloisonné-inlay jewelry during the Achaemenian Period.

---

46 M. Mallowan, *Iran* 10 (1972), 5, 6; Maxwell-Hyslop 268-9.

47 W.J. Young, *BMFA* (1972). The fact that the gold comes from Sardis does not actually tell us anything about its provenience. As Darius states, the gold was brought from there to be worked at Susa.

48 C. Burney and M. Lang, *The Peoples of the Hill*, London, Weidenfeld and Nicolson, 1972, pl. 72. The lotus border must be related to the Neo-Assyrian earrings classified as type V by T.A. Mahdloom, *The Chronological Development of Neo-Assyrian Art*, London (1970); Maxwell-Hyslop, p. 243ff, fig. 127, 31. She mentions specifically an earring from Ur (U. 460 A & B) which was inlaid with lapis lazuli and may have originally had pendants in shape of lotus buds and flowers. (pl. 223). For a Phoenician earring from Aliseda related to Neo-Assyrian type V see D.B. Harden, *The Phoenicians*, New York, Praeger, 1962, 212ff, pl. 97. This reference was kindly located by Dr. Vaughn Crawford.

49 Ibid, 199ff. Another example from Kamir Blur datable to 7th-6th century B.C. is decorated with gold cloisons.

50 J. De Morgan, *MDP VIII*, Paris (1905), pl. II, sarcophagus; 51, fig. 79, pl. IV, button; 52, fig. 80, spacer beads; 50, fig. 79, pl. V, earrings.

51 Schmidt, *Persepolis II*, 76, pl. 43, no. 10.

52 *Illustrated London News*, July 17, 1948, 59, fig. 7; L. Van den Berghe, *Archeologie de L'Iran ancien*, Leyden (1959), 109, pl. 135f (left); Kantor, *op.cit.*, 15, fig. 11 c.

53 Amandry, 11ff; Kantor, 15; Porada, *Iran*, 170-72; Stronach, *op.cit.* 36.

54 Dalton, *The Oxus Treasure*; Porada, *Iran*, 168ff.

55 Dalton, pl. XXI, no. 35, Ghirshman, *Iran*, 264.

56 Kantor, 20. All share a common feature with the Boston earring: the circular forms on the sleeve of the candys which are understood as representing appliques themselves. This is the same sort of 'twist" as the earring engraved on the central figure on the Boston earring.

57 Stronach, 38-40.

58 Ghirshman, *Iran*, 265. The situation regarding the early development of these earrings is more complex than Ghirshman suggests.

THE TWO GENEALOGIES OF JAPHET

David Neiman

Boston College

The Table of Nations found in Gen 10 has been the subject of countless studies, commentaries, and analyses. It is an intriguing document, filled with volumes of interesting and puzzling data, confusing to the interpreter, yet tantalizing in its suggestions. Reams have been written attempting to substantiate, to contradict, and to understand the material found in this chapter, and many theories have been advanced and rejected trying to create a reasonably logical and consistent system out of the materials included in this early attempt to categorize and classify the nations and peoples of the earth.[1]

While attacks upon the problem of Gen 10 have been many and varied, the nature of the Table of Nations in its entirety is not the subject of this paper. The objective of this limited study is to clarify the identity of the figure of Japheth, to determine its position in the original context from which it was taken, and to analyze its transformation in the process of being adopted and transplanted into the biblical setting of the Table of Nations.

The author of Gen 10 divides his world into three parts.[2] Herodotus in his description of the world he knew also uses a tripartite division. But while Herodotus, in keeping with his world view as an Ionian living in the middle of the classical phase of Athenian civilization, defines his world by geographical divisions, drawing his map of the world as Europe, Asia, and Libya (Africa),[3] the writer of Gen 10, because he has an infixed sense of patriarchal classification and thinks in genealogical terms, divides his world into "families,"[4] or groups of related "descendants" of primary ancestors. Both of these writers, the Greek and the Hebrew, keep a threefold division as fundamental to their systems.

While Herodotus of the 5th century B.C. views relationships spatially, the writer of Gen 10 views them in terms of family relationship, or genealogically. The tribal nature of his society, the strong patriarchal basis of

---

1 There are literally hundreds of commentaries on Genesis, and many of them have dealt at some length with the problems presented by the Table of Nations. John Skinner's "ICC" *Commentary* (New York, 1925), devotes thirty-five closely printed pages to it, and is quite comprehensive. A. Reubeni's *Shem, Ham, ve-Yafet* [Hebrew], (Tel-Aviv, 1932), is a complete volume devoted to this one subject. Speiser's *Genesis* commentary in the "Anchor Bible" is brief, but his references to former studies of his own as well as of others, are valuable.

2 Shem, Ham, and Japhet. Gen. 9:19 and 10:32.

3 Herodotus, II, 16; IV, 36, 42.

4 Genesis 10:5, 20, 31, 32.

early Israelite history, lead him naturally to think in terms of family relationships, among nations as among individuals. This genealogical view was also characteristic of Greek civilization and society, but at a period much earlier than that of Herodotus, and closer in time to the writer of the Genesis narratives. If we examine the sense of relationship of the early Greeks – those of the Homeric Age – whose stories were recorded at about the same time as were the Genesis accounts, we find that they too tend to be patriarchal in attitude and in mode of identification.[5]

According to the author of the Table of Nations, and following his general scheme of the prehistory of Israel, all of humanity is descended from one man, Noah, who with his wife and three sons and their wives survived the universal flood. Noah is represented as the father of these three, the ancestors of the three subfamilies of mankind.[6]

While all the nations and tribes mentioned in the genealogies are presumably nations and peoples of the world known to the compiler of the Table, a reading of the three lists reveals that in each case the attention of the author concentrates on a specific area or on a particular group of nations. Thus, while the genealogy of the children of *Shem* includes Elam, Arpachashad, Lud and Aram,[7] the attention of the compiler turns to the area of Arabia and to the descendants of *Joktan*, to whom he devotes more attention than to any of the others.[8]

The same pattern is followed in the case of *Ham*, where Cush, Mizraim, Put and Canaan are mentioned but one's attention is then drawn to *Mizraim* and *Canaan*, whose descendants are enumerated in greater detail.[9]

One might view this approach as natural on the part of the biblical writer, for surely Canaan and Egypt [Mizraim] are close to biblical Israel, and their interaction with the people of Israel was intimate and of long duration. This concentration of attention on the nations with which he was most familiar is to be expected, and reveals his primary area of interest and of familiarity.

In the genealogy of the descendants of *Japheth* too the author of the Table seems to display a greater knowledge of one area as against another. While he mentions nations by name as children of Japhet who inhabit areas of Central Asia,[10] his primary interest is focused on the region of the Aegean Sea and its surrounding coastlands and islands, and the nations that interest him most are the Hellenes and those that fall within the geographical-cultural area of Greece.[11]

The descendants of Japheth, according to the genealogy of Gen 10, comprise a group of tribes and nations that constitute a geographical continuum, which stretches from the Aegean Sea eastward to Persia, northward to the steppes of southern Russia and to the mountains north of Iran. While some of the names in the list are not clearly recognizable, and their identity from extra-biblical sources cannot be determined beyond a doubt,[12] the majority of the names in the list are well known from sources external to the literature of the

[5] Almost every person in the *Iliad* and the *Odyssey* is identified at one time or another by his patronymic, rather than his personal name. Thus, Peleides, Atreides, Tydeides, and Laertiades refer to the more familiar Achilles, Agamemnon, Diomedes, and Odysseus. Even Zeus is referred to as Cronides! [Cf. C.H. Gordon, "*Homer and Bible*," HUCA 26 (1955), 66, par. 46.]

[6] Gen. 9:19; 10:32.

[7] Gen. 10:22.

[8] Gen. 10:26-30.

[9] Gen. 10:6, 13-19.

[10] Gen. 10:2-3; Gomer, Ashkenaz, Madai, and the doubtful Tubal, Riphath, Magog, and Togarmah.

[11] Gen. 10:2, 4-5; including Tiras, Javan, Elishah, Tarshish, Kittim, Dodanim, *'iyye hagoyim*, and the doubtful Meshech.

[12] Magog, Riphath, Tubal, and Togarmah.

Old Testament; from Greek, Phoenician, Babylonian, Hittite and Egyptian writings.[13]

Thus, while we cannot be certain as yet of the identity of Magog, Tubal, Riphath, and Togarmah, there is little doubt of the validity of the equations that can be made between the rest of the names in the list and their counterparts from the extra-biblical sources mentioned above.

Gomer is Cimmeria, Madai is Media, Javan is Ionia in particular and Greece is general, and Tiras is Tyrsenia/Tyrrhenia. Ashkenaz is correctly identified as Scythia and closely related to Gomer, for we know from Greek sources that the Scythians and the Cimmerians are paired in most instances, and are identified as related nations who came into the near eastern region from central Asia.[14]

That the children of Javan are listed as Elishah, Tarshish, Kittim and Dodanim is an accurate observation on the part of the author of the Table, for all of these tribes or nations are generally identifiable to us from Greeke as well as other sources, and can logically be considered as "related" to the Greeks. Elishah is Alashiyah on the island of Cyprus,[15] Kittim is preserved in the name of Kition on the same island, and the name Kittim was still used as a designation for the Greeks in later Jewish literature.[16]

The Dodanim are to be identified with the Dodonoi, the people of Dodona, the most ancient oracle in Greece, and one of the most revered.[17] That some scholars prefer to correct *ddnym* here to *rdnym* as the name appears in LXX, Sam. Pent., and 1 Chron 1:7 and to identify the Rhodanim with the island of Rhodes necessitates but a very minor scribal emendation of the *textus receptus.*[18] I fee, however, that this is incorrect view. Although Rhodes is closer to Asia, and offers the opportunity to shorten the limits of perspective of the author of the Table of Nations in keeping with a generalized prejudice in favor of limited horizons for the peoples of antiquity, I believe that Dodanim is the more plausible reading. Dodona was a most significant name in the traditions of ancient Hellas, and is probably the original name we have in the designation of the children of Javan in the Table of Nations.

The *'iyyê haggôyîm*, which is to be translated simply as "the islands of the nations," can refer only to the islands of the Aegean Sea area as well as to Cyprus itself. That *'iyyîm* can be found in contexts where the word designates "coastlands," does not change the force of its meaning in this passage, where it clearly refers to the "islands of the nations," given its antecedents. *'Iyyê haggôyîm* also strikes a harmonic chord, when sounded together with the designation of "the peoples of the islands in the sea," of the Egyptian inscriptions of the 5th year of Merneptah and the 8th year of Raamses III, where the "sea peoples" certainly designates the populations of the Aegean area.[19]

---

[13] *Elishah* = *Alašiyah* of the cunieform sources, which is the island of Cyprus, mentioned in the Amarna tablets. [Cf. Y.L. Holmes, *JAOS* 91 (1971), 426ff. – Ed.] *Tarshish* is the name of several places founded by the Canaanites/Phoenicians around the shores of the Mediterranean Sea and beyond. One Tarshish has been located on the island of Sardinia (BASOR, No. 83, 1941). Another, in Spain, is known from Greek sources: Herodotus I, 163; IV, 152; Strabo, III, 151; and Pliny, *Hist. Nat.*, III, 7, iv, 120. See also W.F. Albright, "Role of the Canaanites in the History of Civilization," in *The Bible and the Ancient Near East*, ed. G.E. Wright (1961), 328-362; and my article in JNES 24, 113ff. Tiras = Tyrsenioi/Tyrrhenioi. See JNES 22 (1963), 128ff.

[14] Hebrew Ashkenaz [read *'škwz* instead of *'šknz*?] is equivalent to Assyrian *Aškuza*/*Ašguza*, to be equated with the *Skythoi* of the Greek sources. Hebrew *Gomer*, Assyrian *Gimmiray(a)*, to be equated with Greek *Kimmerioi*. *Odyssey*, XI:14; Herodotus, I, 15, 103; and Book IV, 1-142. In Esarhaddon's inscriptions, in E. Schrader, KB, II, 128f., D.D. Luckenbill, *Ancient Records of Assyria and Babylonia* (1927), vol. II, 206-207.

[15] Alashiyah is Elishah. See note 13 above.

[16] I Maccabees 1:1; 8:5. Babylonian Talmud, *Ta'anith*, 5b.

[17] Dodona is mentioned in the most ancient of Greek sources. *Iliad*, II:750; XVI:233, 234; *Odyssey*, XIV:327, XIX:296. Apollodorus, *Library*, I, 9, 16, in which "a timber from the oak of Dodona," could speak, suggestive of the oracular power of the sacred region.

[18] [Another suggests emending both *dnnym* and *rdnym* to **ddnym* "Danunaeans, Danoi" (*BHS*, page 14, note on Gen 10:4). – Ed.]

[19] The "Sea Peoples" are mentioned in the inscriptions of Merneptah, in the "Great Karnak Inscription," and in the "Athribis Stela." See *Ancient Records of Egypt*, ed. J.H. Breasted (1906), III, 249, 255; in *Historical Re-*

It is apparent from an examination of the "prehistory" in Genesis, which is found in the etiologies of the first eleven chapters, that the authors of these stories are universalistic in their *Weltanschauung*. The Genesis "Introduction to the History of Israel" is not narrowly nationalistic and certainly far from parochial. The view of the authors and redactors of the stories found at the beginning of the Book of Genesis are broad and ecumenical. Israel is not mentioned in the early chapters of the book. Even Eber, the eponymous ancestor of the Hebrews is not mentioned until chapter 10, and then only as one of the many progenitors of the families of man. The origins of mankind are not placed in the land of Israel, nor is the rise and growth of civilization. On the contrary. The Genesis tradition quite accurately places the cradle of civilization in the Tigris-Euphrates Valley.[20] It is clear that the writers of Genesis were presenting a universalist view of the world and its inhabitants as prolegomena to the story of Abraham and his descendants. All of the problems dealt with in the beginning of Genesis concern the world and mankind as a whole. Gen 10 retains the same attitude as do the preceding stories and accounts. There is no tendentious quality about the Table of Nations, although many biblical scholars insist on seeing the genealogical chart of mankind as compiled by the author of the Table of Nations as an expression of ephemeral political attitudes and prejudices; a supposed portrayal of existing friendships and hostilities.[21]

A close study of Genesis 10 convinces the objective student that we have in the Table of Nations an honest attempt on the part of the compiler to draw an accurate chart of the genealogies of mankind, a table of the relationships among the many nations that make up the family of man, based on the assumption that all men are descended from one set of parents and constitute, therefore, one family.

The world of the Table of Nations extends, evidently, from Greece in the west to the Iranian highlands in the east, from the Black Sea and Armenia in the north, to the southern shores of Arabia on the Indian Ocean, and to Nubia and Ethiopia in the south.[22]

On drawing up the Table of Nations, the author classified his information based on the traditions that he knew. Except for some names which pose problems of identification, we need not question the traditions relating to Shem and his family, since the author was himself a member of one of the nations descended from Shem. We cannot be certain of the sources he used in his compilation of the list of the children of Ham, although it is obvious that Egypt [Mizraim] and Canaan are the nations that dominate this family from his point of view. It is a distinct probability that the name Ham is an Egyptian appellation of their land. Ham is often used in synonymous parallelism with Egypt in the Old Testament,[23] and it may be a form of the native Egyptian name for the "Black Land," the fertile soil of the land of Egypt, or by extension, the land of Egypt as a whole. This name appears in Coptic as *Khēmi.*[24]

When we come to the family of Japheth's descendants, we find the area of primary interest and attention to be the region of Hellas and the islands of the Aegean Sea.[25]

---

cords of Ramses III, ed. W.F. Edgerton and J.A. Wilson, (1936), 42, 53-55, and in *Ancient Records of Egypt*, IV, 37-40; also in ANET^2, 262-263.

20 Gen. 2:14 and 11:2-9.

21 John Skinner, in *Commentary on Genesis* (1925), 184-187 and 202; Gerhard Von Rad, *Commentary on Genesis*, (1961), 138.

22 Geographical limits of the world of Genesis 10 are shown in verse 2 ("Javan" to "Madai"), v. 3 ("Gomer" and "Ashkenaz") vv. 6, 26 ("Kush" and "Hazarmaveth"). In v. 2 we have the east to west limits (Greece to Iran), and in vv. 3, 6, 26, we have the north to south limits (Scythia and Cimmeria to Nubia and Hadhramawt).

23 Ps 78:51; 105:23, 27; 106:22.

24 *Khēmi* is the standard form of the word in the Bohairic dialect of Coptic. [Hieroglyphic Egyptian ancestor of the Coptic word begins with consonant *k*. – Ed.]

25 Gen. 10:4-5.

Who is the figure of Japheth, and from what source were his name and identity derived? Our concern here is not solely with the identity of Japheth and the source of his name, but equally significant is the transformation of his nature brought about by translating him from his native context to the biblical world and to the particular role he fills in the classification system of the Table of Nations. What we see here is not only a cultural adaption by adoption, but a conscious transformation of the nature of a significant figure on religious or theological grounds; the viewpoint of the writer of Genesis 10 based on his own concept of the nature of man.

Japheth of the Old Testament is, in origin, Iapetos of the Greek mythology.[26] Iapetos is the Titan, the father of Prometheus, who is the forerunner, the creator, and the progenitor of man.[27]

Many biblical scholars have for many years rejected the identification of Japheth with Iapetos, for reasons which were never stated.[28] The reasons are, however, not difficult to surmise. It had been the view of biblical scholars for over a century (and many have still not rid themselves of this view) that ancient Israel had no knowledge of ancient Greece and that the two worlds, of Hellas and of Israel, knew nothing one of the other.[29] To find, therefore, a figure from Hellenic literature in the Old Testament was dismissed as highly improbable. This view is completely erroneous. Israel and Greece had intimate contacts from the moment that both of these nations entered upon their historical encounter in the eastern Mediterranean world at the end of the 13th century B.C.[30]

The biblical writer knew the traditions of the Greeks and utilized this information in his complilation of the family tree of the world's peoples in his Table of Nations in Gen 10.

The Titan Iapetos was, according to the Greek tradition as preserved in its mythology, the ultimate ancestor of the Greek peoples. He was the father of Prometheus. Prometheus was not only the forerunner of man, the prototype of man striving to rise above his earthbound condition; he was also the actual progenitor, the physical forefather of man. Prometheus was the father of Deucalion, who is protrayed in the Hellenic tradition as the one man who, together with his wife, Pyrrha, survived the universal flood.[31] Deucalion fathered Hellenos,[32] the eponymous ancestor of the Hellenic peoples, and Hellenos begat the eponymous ancestors of all the Hellenic nations.[33]

Iapetos is the ultimate father of all men. But since the Hellenic tradition concerns itself solely with Greeks, he is, for all purposes, the ultimate ancestor of the Greek peoples. This is precisely the role that he plays in the genealogies of Gen 10. There he is portrayed as the ancestor of the Greeks and of the nations related to them.

---

[26] *Iliad*, VIII:479; Hesiod, *Theogony*, 507-616; Apollodorus, *Library*, I, 5, 13.

[27] Hesiod, *Theogony*, 48, 50-58, 507-510, 614. Apollodorus, *Library*, I, 7, 1.

[28] E.g., G. Von Rad, *Genesis, A Commentary* (1961), 134.

[29] E.g., *The Abingdon Bible Commentary*, ed. F.C. Eiselen, (1929), 227: "The geographical knowledge of the day evidently did not extend as far as continental European Greece."

[30] As pointed out by C.H. Gordon in "Homer and Bible: The Origin and Character of East Mediterranean Literature," in HUCA 26 (1955), 43-108; in *Before the Bible* (1962), and in *Ugarit and Minoan Crete* (1966); and by David Neiman, in "The Date and Circumstances of the Cursing of Canaan," in *Biblical Motifs: Origins and Transformations* (1966), 113-134.

[31] Hesiod, *Catalogues of Women*, 1; Apollodorus, *Library* I, 7, 2.

[32] *Ibid.*

[33] Hesiod, *Catalogues of Women*, 4. "Hellenos, the war-loving king, was the father of Dorus, and Xuthus and Aeolus." Apollodorus, *Library*, I, 7, 3. Hellenos was the father of the Greek nations. "Those who were called Greeks, he named Hellenes, after himself, and divided the country among his sons." These were then known as Achaeans, Dorians, Ionians and Aeolians.

Let us examine the relationship between the Iapetos of the Hellenic tradition and his descendant Hellenos. Iapetos was a Titan, an immortal, a divine figure. Hellenos was man, the father of mankind, the ancestor of the Greek peoples. Iapetos was divine and immortal. Hellenos was mortal and human.

In the pagan tradition, the creation of man involves a descent from a god or the gods. It requires a transference of the essence of divinity, of the quality of immortality from the immortals to the epehmeral creature of earth. Man, in this tradition, is the result of the interaction between the divine and the material, between a god or gods and the earth. Man is, therefore, portrayed in pagan traditions – and this is especially clear in the Greek tradition – as descending from the gods in a physical sense, as a son is begotten by a father of flesh and blood. There are scores of examples of this idea in Greek mythology.[34] It is also, apparently, the same in the Babylonian tradition which has come down to us directly as well as by transmission through intermediate Greek sources.[35]

In most pagan mythologies there is a generation of transition between god and man (between god the creator or begetter of man and the first human creature). The intermediate generation, that of the figure of transition, is of a proto-human type, the archetype of man. He of the intermediate generation is possessed of human qualities, yet is in some measure closer to the gods than are ordinary men, his historical descendants.

In the Babylonian tradition of the first generation of man as transmitted to us by Berossus in his *Babyloniaca*, we have this very interesting genealogy of the generation of man.[36]

Aruru, the creator of man, a goddess, brings forth Adapa.

Adapa is human, yet he is specially favored by the gods, is intimate with them, and stands at the very borderline between mankind and the immortals. This middle figure, the transition figure, is the child of the god(dess), but the father of man. Adapa begets Awelu.

Awelu is all man. He is "Man," human, mortal, one of us.

This genealogy of man (Awelu), as the child of god-man (Adapa), the grandson of god (Aruru) is paradigmatic for the pagan concept of the creation of man as a descendant of god or the gods.

Exactly the same pattern is found in the Iapetos-Hellenos genealogy. Iapetos is the divine immortal, father of gods. But these immortals, Prometheus and Epimetheus, are prefigures of man. Prometheus is immortal, but proto-human, possessed of human propensities, characteristics, and inclinations. He is very like his Babylonian counterpart, Adapa. The third generation from Iapetos, Deucalion, is all human, the father of men. His son Hellenos is man, the father of all the Hellenic peoples.

The author of Gen 10, in choosing the individual names for the fathers of the nations of man, chose the names that represented, in each tradition, the ultimate progenitor of that particular branch of the family of man. In classifying the genealogy of the Greeks and the peoples related to them, he chose the ultimate ancestor in the Greek tradition. But he chose, for his own reasons, neither Hellenos nor Deucalion, nor Prometheus,

---

[34] E.g., Achilles, son of mortal Peleus and of immortal Thetis. Hesiod, in *Theogony*, Lines 963ff., has many examples of this myth.

[35] *Epic of Gilgamesh*, I, ii, 1; and IX, ii, 16. describes the nature of Gilgamesh as "Two-thirds of him is god, and one-third man." See *ANET*^{2}, 73, 88; A. Heidel, *The Gilgamesh Epic and O.T. Parallels* (1945), 18, 66.

[36] Berossus' *Babyloniaca*, in *Fragmenta Historicorum Graecorum*, ed. Carolus Mueller (1878), II, 499; and Felix Jacoby, *Die Fragmente der Griechischen Historiker* (Leyden: 1958), Dritter Teil, C, pp. 374-377.

but the father of Prometheus; namely, Iapetos. Why he chose the first name in the genealogy can be surmised. He preferred to trace the genealogy back to its very beginning. He preferred the very first ancestor in the Greek story of the descent of man, rather than the figure of a later generation.

But the author of the Table of Nations did not present Iapetos in his original role. This he would not do. What he did was to bring Iapetos down from his divine position, humanize him, and make him a son of Noah and the progenitor of the Greeks and the peoples related to them.

But this treatment accorded to Iapetos by the author of Gen 10 was not a unique treatment. It was consistent with the treatment he meted out to the divine Aruru in his recreation of the Babylonian genealogy of the first generations of men which he transformed into the fifth chapter of Genesis, of which he was also the author.[37]

The genealogy of Gen 5 bears a striking resemblance to the early genealogies of the first generations of man according to the Babylonian mythology as transmitted by Berossus.[38] In the Babylonian genealogy of man, the creation of man is pictured as a descent from the gods. The first name in the genealogy is that of Aruru, the goddess, creatress of man.[39] The second name in the genealogy is that of Adapa, the man who was privileged to sit in the presence of the great gods.[40] The third name is that of Awelu, which is the normal name for "Man" in Babylonian.

It is clear from this list that the Babylonian account of the descent of man is identical in theory as well as in form with the Greek genealogy of first man. Just as the Hellenic genealogical chart of man has a three-generation scheme in which the first is divine, the second is god-man and the third is fully human and the ancestor of men, so too does the Babylonian pattern of the descent of man have the first three generations arranged in the same order: god, god-man, and man.

In the following chart, the first column on the left gives the first three generations of the descent of man according to the tradition preserved in Hellenic mythology. The second column contains a description of the nature or *physis* of the individual named. The third column gives the name of the first three generations of the descent of man according to the traditions preserved in the Babylonian mythology as transmitted by Berossus in his *Babyloniaca.*

Hellenic Genealogy	*Physis*	Babylonian Genealogy
Iapetos	Divine	Aruru
Prometheus	God-Man	Adapa
Hellenos	Human	Awelu

But the writer of Gen 5, in compiling his list of the first ten generations of man from the Creation to the Flood, while he relies on the Babylonian genealogy and its scheme – with which he was quite familiar – does not accept the pagan element in the Babylonian genealogy. It is evident that the Hebrew idea of the re-

[37] Gen. 5 and most of Gen. 10 are generally conceded to be the work of one author, the so-called P-source.
[38] Berossus, see note 36 above.
[39] Aruru, goddess, creator of man. ANET^2, 74; 437b.
[40] Adapa. See "The Legend of Adapa," in ANET^2, 101-103.

lationship between God and man had already been clearly defined in Israelite thought. God in the Hebrew view, created man. Man is not a physical descendant of the Creator of the universe.[41]

Thus, while borrowing many elements from the original Babylonian genealogy of the antediluvian ancestors of man, the writer of Gen 5 rejected the Babylonian idea of the divine descent of man, and changed the character and the *physis* of the first two names in the list, in order to destroy the pagan pattern. Thus, instead of God – God-Man – Man that we see in the Babylonian and especially in the Greek patterns of man's origin, the author of Gen 5 changes the names in the Babylonian list to Man – Man – Man.

That is why the list in Gen 5 has the name "Man" in two positions; the first and the third.[42] Gen 5 has *Adam, Seth, Enosh,* which must be understood as "Man," "Seth," "Man." What the name "Seth" means, I cannot fathom, but the substitution of "Man" for "God" in the first position on the list is a clear indication of the Hebrew attitude on man and his relationship to God in contrast to the pagan parallel.

Iapetos, the divine figure of Hellenic mythology was taken by the compiler of the Table of Nations in Gen 10 as the ancestor of the Hellenic peoples and those related to them. He was reduced from his divine position in Greek mythology to the human position of father of one of the families of man, and son of Noah. In like manner the same author, who compiled the list of antediluvian patriarchs in Gen 5, did the same to the divine ancestor of men found in Babylonian mythology, and reduced him to the level of mortal man, to conform to the Hebrew concept of man, creature of God, but not physically descended from Him in a father-son relationship.[43]

That the author of Gen 5 knew Babylonian sources, was never questioned by biblical scholars. We have also to recognize that the author of the earliest stories in the Bible was familiar as well with the people of the Aegean world, and with their literature and traditions. It would be fatuous to believe that the ancient Greeks and Hebrews lived in isolation from each other. They were both active participants in the very daramatic, history-making events that transformed the eastern Mediterranean world at the end of the Bronze Age. Both were instrumental in bringing to the ancient world the Iron Age at its beginning, and in setting the patterns that gave rise to the history of western civilization.[44]

---

[41] Gen. 1 and 2.

[42] Gen. 5:1-3, 6-7.

[43] N.W. Porteus, "Man, Nature of," in *Interpreter's Dictionary of the Bible*, III, p. 242. "Man's nature is determined entirely by his relation to God, a relation which preserves the distance between the Creator and the creature . . . . He cannot claim divine descent, . . . "

[44] C.H. Gordon, *Before the Bible;* D. Neiman, in *Biblical Motifs* (1966), 113ff.

SŪRAT AL-'IKHLĀṢ

A Reconsideration

Gordon D. Newby
Brandeis University. Waltham, Mass. USA

bismi -llāhi -r-raḥmāni -r-raḥīmi
qul huwa -llāhu 'aḥaduni
-llāhu -ṣ-ṣamadu
lam yalid wa-lam yūlad
wa-lam yakun lahu kufu'an 'aḥadun

Sūrat al-'Ikhlāṣ, normally numbered Surah 112, is usually reckoned as the most important single chapter of the Qur'ân, since the recitation of the entire chapter is equal to the recitation of a third of the whole Qur'ân.[1] Its statment about the unity of Allah and the denial of His paternity has made this Surah one of the chief scriptural definitions of Islam's attitude toward Allah. Yet, there has been considerable disagreement about the proper interpretation of this Surah, especially the first two verses.

The first major point of discussion concerns the word *'aḥadun* in verse one, after the *basmalah*, and in verse four. The word can be used in two distinct ways, and it is so used here. One way is as an indefinite noun meaning "one", "anyone", like the german "man". Thus one could say, *mā ra'aitu 'aḥadan* "I did not see anyone" or, as in the fourth verse of *Sūrat al-'Ikhlāṣ*, *wa-lam yakun lahu kufu'an 'aḥadun* (lit.: "And one was not to Him as an equal."). In this sense, *'aḥad* cannot be substituted for *wāḥid*, for one can say, *rajulun wāḥidun* but not *rajulun 'aḥadun*.[2] This is so, even though the grammarians understand the root of both *'aḥad* and *wāḥid* as *prima wāw*.[3] In the second sense, *'aḥad* is understood as an attribute, *ṣifah*, of Allah.[4] Thus *al-'aḥad* is one of the ninety-nine names of Allah and is the primary attribute indicating divine perfection. *al-wāḥid* as a *ṣifah* indicates the singularity of Allah.[5]

---

1 Fakh. ar-Râzî, *Mafâtîḥ al-Ghaib 'aw at-Tafsîr al-Kabîr*, Cairo, s.d., vol 32, p. 174, in a tradition from his father.
2 E.W. Lane, *An Arabic-English Lexicon*, (1863), Book I, Part I, 27
3 Abû-l-Q. J. Maḥ. b. 'Amr az-Zamakhsharî al-Khawârizmî, *al-Kashshâf* (1966), vol. 4, 298.
4 *Ibid.*
5 L. Gardet, "Al-'Asmâ' al-Ḥusnâ", *Encyclop. Islam*², (1960), vol. I, 716.

It has been primarily the grammar of the first two verses that has caused differences of interpretation. az-Zamakhsharī, whose grammatical discussions are still widely respected in the Arab world, states in his *Kash=shāf* that *huwa* is a pronoun of fact in verse one, *ḍamīr ash-sha'n*, citing the example, *huwa zaidun munṭaliqun*.[6] The first verse would then be translated, "It is a fact that Allah is One," as though the fuller *huwa 'anna -llāha 'aḥadun* were written. Other commentators regard *huwa* as the *mubtada'* of a nominal sentence, with *Allāhu* as the *khabar* and *'aḥadun* as either a *badal* or a second *khabar*, yielding the translation, "He is Allah, One."[7] A third interpretation, where *Allāhu* is in apposition to *huwa*, would translate as, "He, Allah, is One."[8] No matter which explanation is selected, however, it remains clear that *Allāhu* is equated with *'aḥadun*, and some readings of this verse even eliminate *qul huwa*, thereby simplifying the grammatical problem.[9]

In his article, "His Name is 'One' ", Cyrus H. Gordon demonstrates that the use of the word *'ḤD* in Zech 14:9 and in the *Shema'* should be understood as meaning the numeral *'ḤD* (1).[10] Thus ". . . *'ḤD* means not only that there is but one God, but also that his name is *'ḤD* "One": *šm' yśr'l yhwh 'lhynw yhwh 'ḥd* (Deut. 6:4) "Hear, O Israel, Yahweh is our God, Yahweh is 'One' ".'[11] This association of a deity with his special number was a common practice in the ancient Near East, and the Greeks, concerned as they were with first things and causes, identified "The Good" or the "Prime Mover" with the "One". Plotinus' statement that everything that exists does so by reason of the One[12] becomes the basis for much philosophical discussion, but it is the extension of that formulation, The One equals the Creator equals The God, that allows the use of Greek philosophical thought to be used as the basis of the orthodox theologies of the major Semitic monotheistic religions.

This use of *'ḤD* has had an important impact on Islam, primarily through two lines of influence. When Islam expanded into former Byzantine territory and faced the need of developing a rational system of apologetics acceptable to the intellectual tastes of the Medeterranean world, it took over those aspects of Greek thought that had been partially predigested, chiefly by Syrian and Egyptian Christians.[13] The link between the Semitic God and a Greek explanation of Him having already been made, it remained for Muslim apologists and theologians to recast the concept into specific Islamic forms.

The association of Allah and *'aḥad* in the pre-theologic period of Islam, during Muhammad's lifetime, is of primary importance. Without Qur'ânic sanction it would have been more difficult, if not impossible, to accept Greek forms of thought so easily. Even with this, there was much resistence, as the numerous anti-rationalist movements show. But further, the equation of Allah with *'aḥad* tied Islam to its Judaic antecedents. Islam's debt to the Judaeo-Christian past makes it not surprising that the first verse of this Surah is reminiscent of the *Shema'*.

The second verse, "*-llāhu -ṣ-ṣamadu*", complicates our understanding of the Surah. It presents fewer grammatical problems to the commentators, and most all agree that the two words form a unit, a noun and its adjective, *ṣifah*, which functions as a second predicate, *khabar thānī*, to the subject of the sentence in verse one,

6 az-Zamakhsharî, *op. cit.*, 298. For a discussion of the grammatical problems in this Surah, but without conclusions and representing very closely the *'ijmâ'*, see E.E. Calverley, *Studia Islamica* 8 (1957), 5-14.

7 Jalâladdîn 'Abd ar-R. b. a. Bakr as-Suyûṭî and Jalâladdîn Muḥ. b. 'Aḥ. al-Maḥallî, *Tafsîr al-Jalâlain* (1969), vol. II, 309.

8 ar-Râzî, *op. cit.*, 178.

9 *Ibid.*

10 Cyrus H. Gordon, *JNES* 29 (1970), 198-9.

11 *Ibid.*, 198.

12 *Ibid.*

13 While this is generally true, there is no reason to suppose that the urban centers of Arabia around the time of Muhammad were entirely innocent of Greek thought, since there was contact both through trade and missionary activity

that is, either to *huwa* or to *Allāhu*. It is also possible to regard the unit as a *badal* to *'aḥad* or to *Allāhu*.

While the grammar of the second verse seems relatively well understood, the meaning of *aṣ-ṣamadu* has caused considerable speculation. It is *hapax legomenon*in the Qur'ān, so definitions must rely either on this Surah alone or on pre-Islamic sources, but transmitted through the *'asānīd*. Most of the accepted explanations of the word seem to be derived from the context of this one Surah, even though evidence from poetry or traditions allegedly from Muhammad are cited. Thus we get the general sense that *aṣ-ṣamadu* is an adjectival noun from *ṢMD* referring to a *ṣayyid* to whom everyone turns and upon whom everyone depends for their needs.[14] On the basis of this, M.M. Pickthall translated the verse as "Allah, the eternally Besought of all."[15] Other definitions are advanced only to be rejected as unsatifactory by the commentators. The word can mean a place raised up,[16] something with no hollow in it,[17] something firm with no softness,[18] the smoothness of a stone with no dust, that neither takes anything in nor gives anything off,[19] to strike or beat, with *'aṣā*,[20] and the name of an idol of the tribe of *'Ād*, but in the form *ṣumūd*.[21] The consensus, *'ijmā'*, that the word means the relied upon *sayyid*, obviously presents a barrier to our understanding, and the first task is to seek a definition of *aṣ-ṣamadu* before the syntactical problems of verses one and two can be solved.

Harris Birkeland has demonstrated that a careful examination of the *'asānīd* will often allow us to determine the development of the *'ijmā'* and approximate the original interpretation of Qur'anic passages by comparing both the content of the traditions and their chains of authority.[22] Following Birkeland's method, an examination of the traditions on this Surah in the commentaries of ar-Rāzī, aṭ-Ṭabarī, and az-Zamakhsharī yields an interesting interpretation of *aṣ-ṣamadu*. az-Zamakhsharī quotes only the opinion of the *'ijmā'* with no *'isnād*, saying that it is a *fa'al* in the meaning of a *maf'ūl* adding a gloss of *QṢD*.[23] aṭ-Ṭabarī presents seventeen traditions saying that *ṢMD* means not hollow, two saying that nothing issues from Him, three saying that he did not bear and was not born, four saying that He is a *sayyid* who had decided His sovereingty, and two that depict Allah as the Everlasting.[24] Ibn 'Abbās appears as the authority in sets one and four, and 'Ikrimah appears in one and two.[25] This is a good indication that these definitions are not original, but represent various stages in the development of the consensus. Of the two remaining sets of traditions, one fails to define *aṣ-ṣamadu*, since it quotes the third verse of this Surah as the explanation. The fourth definition is an obvious etiological definition based on the name of the Surah as *Sūrat al-'Ikhlāṣ*.[26]

---

[14] as-Suyūṭī, *op. cit., loc. cit.*; ar-Rāzī, *op. cit.*, 181; az-Zamakhsharī, *op. cit., loc. cit.*; Muḥ. b. Ya'qub al-Firuzabadī, *al-Qāmūs al-Muḥīṭ* (1330 A.H.), vol. I, 308.

[15] M.M. Pickthall, *The Meaning of the Glorious Koran*, 454.

[16] Muḥ. b. Mukkaram b. Manẓur, *Lisān al-'Arab* (1300 A.H.), vol. 4, 246f.

[17] Abū Ja'far Muḥ. b. Jarīd aṭ-Ṭabarī, *Jāmi' al-Bayān 'an ta'wīl 'āy al-Qur'ān* (1954), vol. 30, 344f.

[18] ar-Rāzī, *op. cit.*, 181.

[19] *Ibid.*

[20] Lane, *op. cit.*, Book I, Part IV, 1726f.

[21] *Ibid.*

[22] Harris Birkeland, *The Lord Guideth: Studies on Primitive Islam* (1956, no. 2.). The application of this method corroborates the conclusions of F. Rosenthal on the use of *aṣ-ṣamadu*. See F. Rosenthal, "Some minor Problems in the Qur'ān", *The Joshua Starr Memorial Volume* (1953), 72-83, for a complete discussion of this word. In light of these conclusions and my own analysis of the material, I feel, however, that Muhammad and his audience well understood the import of this Surah. If this were not the case, one would expect the more usual pattern of explanatory comments.

[23] az-Zamakhsharī, *op. cit., loc. cit.*

[24] aṭ-Ṭabarī, *op. cit.*, 344-7.

[25] *Ibid.*

[26] *Ibid.*, 346.

ar-Rāzī quotes the various stages of the *'ijmā'* and then two traditions not found in aṭ-Ṭabarī or az-Zamakhsharī. The first is a philological comment on the authority of Qatadah b. Di'āmah that substitutes a *T* for the third consonant, *D*, giving *ṢMT*, meaning of even composition and having no hollow.[27] The next is on the authority of an unnamed late lexicographer and is, ". . . the smoothness of a stone that admits of no dust and is impervious."[28] The tradition of Qatadah that gives the reading of *aṣ-ṣamat* comes at the time of the development of the consensus or after it, quoted by aṭ-Ṭabarī in seventeen traditions. On stylistic grounds it is unlikely as an original reading, for it would spoil the *saj'*. Without corroboration, the second tradition is suspect because of its lateness.

Outside of the dogmatical commentaries, we find that *ṢMD* is defined in the *Lisān al-'Arab* as the "head of a mountain raised up in the sky as if it were a column," or "the high place of anything," or "the top of a rock sticking up from the surface of level ground."[29] From the examples of the *ka'bāt* at Najrān, Ṣan'ā', and Mecca, we know that it was the practice of the pre-Islamic Arabs to venerate stones, especially a meteorite stone as in Mecca. We also know that the root of this word was used as the name of an idol of the tribe of 'Ād.[30] In Ugaritic and Phoenician, *ṢMD* is associated with divine names, most commonly referring, in the dual, to the two clubs of Ba'al, and as the second element of a divine compound name.[31]

When we compare these definitions with the late definition advanced by ar-Rāzī, but not part of the *'ijmā'*, we are drawn to the conclusion that *aṣ-ṣamadu* somehow refers to a stone idol and/or a divine epithet usually associated with Ba'al. Ba'al's characterization as the Striker is well known, but an interesting passage in *Sūrat Yūnus* (v. 107) characterizes Allah in the same manner: *wa-'in yamsaska-llāhu bi-ḍurrin fa-lā kāshifa lahu 'illā huwa wa-'in yuridka bi-khairin fa-lā rādda li-faḍlihi yuṣību bihi man yashā'u min 'ibādihi wa-huwa -l-ghafūru -r-raḥīmu.* "If Allah afflicteth thee with some hurt, there is none who can remove it save Him; and if he desireth good for thee, there is none who can repel His bounty. He striketh with it whom He will of his bondmen. He is the Forgiving, the Merciful."[32] Here Allah is shown as striking (lit.: hitting the mark) His subjects. Since both Ba'al and 'Il show their power by striking, it is hardly surprising to find Allah similarly characterized.

This interpretation of *aṣ-ṣamadu* requires a re-examination of the first two verses of the Surah. We know that Muhammad's first religious experience was with that divine historical presence associated with the *Ka'bah* first named *rabb*. It was not until later that Muhammad made the permanent association of *rabb* with Allah, the name of a pre-Islamic deity, and with *ar-Raḥmān*, another pre-Islamic deity.[33] This Surah seems to be the formal statement of Muhammad's intent to establish worship of a deity that would supersede all other forms of worship in Arabia. The verse must mean, "Say, He, Allah (the Islamic deity), is (the same as) 'Aḥad (the Judaeo-Christian deity), (that is, the same as) *Allāhu-ṣ-ṣamadu* (the pre-Islamic deity)." After it is clear about whom the Surah is talking, it then goes on to reject all former associations customarily made before Islam. *Sūrat al-'Ikhlāṣ* must be one of the earliest Surahs of Muhammad's public career and one of the earliest definitions of Islam separate from Judaism, Christianity, and polytheism. As the *'ijmā'* crystallized, first assuming Muhammad to have been divinely guided from childhood and then from conception, any notion of development in Muhammad's religious experience was necessarily rejected, if recognized at all. Islam preserved traditions contrary to the *'ijmā'* when those traditions were not dogmatical, and it is through these non-dogmatical traditions that we are able to glimpse behind the period of the formation of the consensus.

---

[27] ar-Rāzī, *op. cit.*, 181.
[28] *Ibid.*
[29] Ibn Manẓur, *op. cit., loc. cit.*
[30] Lane, *op. cit., loc. cit.*
[31] C.H. Gordon, *Ugaritic Textbook* (1965), 474. Note the use of *ṣmd 'il*; and W.F. Albright, *Yahweh and the Gods of Canaan* (1969), 233.
[32] Trans. from Pickthal, *op. cit.*, 164f.
[33] Toufic Fahd, *Le Pantheon de l'Arabie . . .* (1968), for an extensive discussion of pre-Islamic deities commonly recognized in the literature.

MISCELLANEA NEO-SUMERICA I-III

David I. Owen
The Dropsie University

It is an honor and a pleasure to present the following studies on the occasion of the 65th birthday of Professor Cyrus H. Gordon, teacher and friend, who first introduced me to the study of cuneiform.

I: A New Ensi of Nippur in the Reign of Šū-Sîn

The University Museum of the University of Pennsylvania has in its Babylonian Collection a number of casts of tablets excavated during the first Nippur excavations,[1] the originals of which are now kept in the Nippur Collection of the Archaeological Museum of Istanbul[2]. As part of a long-term project to catalogue and copy the neo-Sumerian archival texts in the University Museum[3], the cast collection was studied and sorted in search of texts from this period[4]. The resulting discovery of the following text and the nature of its contents prompted its advance publication[5].

(cast CBS 9766)

Tablet[6]: obv.

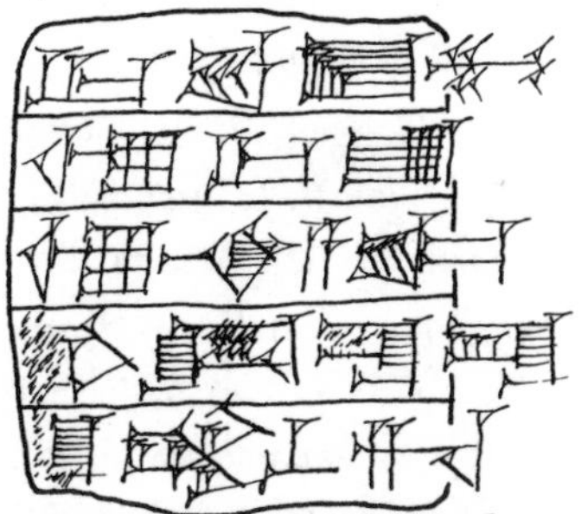

Ur-ni$_x$-g̃u$_{10}$
ù Ur-sukkal(a)
ù-na-a-du$_{11}$
[g]u$_4$ *Á-la-la*
šu ḫé-bar-re

rev. uninscribed

---

1 The original tablet was excavated by J. Haynes at Nippur during the season of 1890. The catalogue states that it was excavated on Temple Hill.

2 Cf. M. Çığ and H. Kızılyay, *Neusumerische Rechts- und Verwaltungsurkunden aus Nippur* I, 1965 [= *NRVN*], p. xiii.

3 This project is in part supported by a grant from the American Philosophical Society.

4 Most of the original neo-Sumerian tablets in the Nippur Collection of the Istanbul Archaeological Museum of which the University Museum has casts have now been published in M. Cıg and H. Kızılyay, *NRVN*.

5 Texts in the University Museum are published with the permission of Å.W. Sjöberg, Curator of Tablet Collections.

6 The copy was made from a cast catalogued as CBS 9766. The number of the original tablet in the Istanbul Nippur Collection is not available.

Envelope:

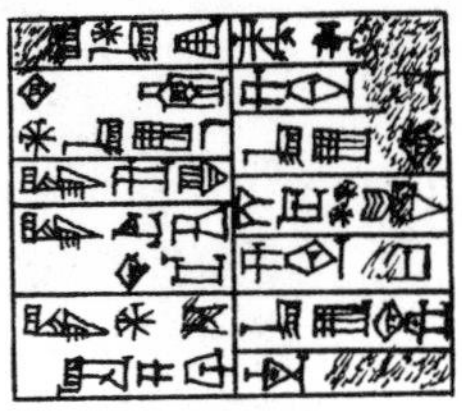

[d]Šu-^{d}Sîn
ki-ága-^{d}En-líl-lá
lugal-kala-ga
lugal-Urí^{ki}-ma
lugal-^{d}Uba-da-limmu-ba

Nam-z[i-tar(a)]
en_5-si
Nibru^{ki}
dumu Ur-^{d}Nanibgal(a)
en_5-si
Nibru^{ki}-ka
ìr-[zu]

Translation:

"Say to Ur-nig̃u and Ur-sukkala that they should release Allala's ox! (Seal:) Šū-Sîn, beloved of Enlil, king of Ur, king of the Four Quarters, Namz[itara], ensi of Nippur, son of Ur-Nanibgala, ensi of Nippur, (is) [your] servant."

Comments:

Letter-orders[7] of this type have been collected and studied by E. Sollberger, *TCS* 1 (1966). Additions to this corpus have been appearing regularly.

line 1:
For the reading ni_x = NIG̃ÌN, cf. J. Krecher, *Sumerische Kultlyrik*, 128 and Å.W. Sjöberg, *TCS* 3, 92. Ur-nig̃u may be a short form of the PN Ur-nig̃ara[8] who is well known in the Nippur archive[9] as well as in the published corpus of letter-orders. Cf. E. Sollberger, *TCS* 1, glossary no. 644 1D 12 and D.I. Owen, *Or* NS 40 (1971), 396.

line 2:
Ur-sukkala appears on a tablet sealed by Namzitara, son of Ur-Nanibgala, ensi of Nippur, before Namzitara himself became ensi.[10] The son of Ur-sukkala, Adada, occurs on another letter-order from Nippur where Allal is to receive a large calf[11].

line 4:
For a possible Akkadian interpretation for the PN Allal, cf. E. Sollberger, *TCS* 1, glossary no. 41, where he cites the possible equation with I.J. Gelb, *MAD* 3, 41 s.v. '$_x$LL *allalum*? . In support of the Akkadian interpretation of the name is the writing Al-la-la in M. Çığ and H. Kızılyay, *NRVN* 2:24. For a possible Sumerian etymology for the name, cf. H. Limet, *Anthroponymie Sumérienne*, 109 and 218. In the published neo-Sumerian Nippur texts Allala occurs in M. Çığ and H. Kızılyay, *NRVN* 58 (no date), 74 (AS 5), 91 (AS 4), 215 (ŠS 5), and in D. Myhrman, *BE* 3 I (ŠS 5), 18 (IS 4), 35 (AS 3). It does not necessarily follow that all these citations are of the same individual. Additional references to this name are also available from unpublished Nippur material as well as from texts from other sources[12].

[7] For this designation, cf. A.L. Oppenheim, *AOS* 32 86 sub H 24 and W.W. Hallo, *BiOr* 26 (1969), 172.
[8] Cf. H. Limet, *Anthroponymie Sumérienne*, 208.
[9] Cf. H. Limet, *ibid.*, 553 sub Ur-nigìn-gar(a).
[10] Cf. E. Sollberger, *op. cit.*, no. 73.
[11] E. Sollberger, *ibid.*, no. 44.
[12] Cf., for example, H. Limet, *op. cit.*, 372 sub Á-la-la .

line 5:
On the use of šu-bar, 'to release,' cf. E. Sollberger, TCS 1, glossary no. 97 1B. It should also be noted that the verb in this letter is in the singular, although it is addressed to two persons. Note the similar remarks by E. Sollberger, *TCS* 1, 24 no. 59, as well as in other letter orders such as nos. 19 and 314.

seal:
The seal of Namzitara, ensi of Nippur, is impressed on an otherwise uninscribed envelope. Of the envelopes from letter-orders that are preserved, a number of them occur without any inscription except for the impression of the sender's seal[13]. We must imagine that many of the letter-orders which are not sealed originally were encased in evelopes that contained only the sender's seal which were then broken in order to read the letter-order. It is probably for this reason that so few envelopes are preserved[14].

The epithet ki-aĝa-^{d}Enlila is not otherwise known from any other dedicatory seal inscription to Šū-Sîn but does occur in a hymn to Šū-Sîn[15]. However, longer epithets incorporating ki-aĝa are known[16].

The owner of the seal and the sender of the letter-order, Namzitara, was a member of a prominent priestly and administrative family at Nippur, the subject of a recent study by W.W. Hallo[17]. Hallo had correctly placed Namzitara in his proper setting at Nippur as the son of Ur-Nanibgala[18], but did not have any evidence available for his official status in the city[19]. On Namzitara's seal he is designated ensi of Nippur, the son of Ur-Nanibagala who was also ensi of Nippur in the reign of Šulgi[20]. Namzitara's tenure in office must have been brief perhaps lasting no longer than a few months. No documents attesting his official status at Nippur have so far been published and none are known to the writer from the unpublished Nippur texts at the University Museum. He must have followed the ensi-ship of Lugal-melam who was known to have held his office at least until AS 9/XI/27[21]. Evidence for the next ensi at Nippur does not occur until ŠS 5, by which time Dada was in office[22]. From Dada's seal inscriptions it is known that he inherited the office of ensi from his father, Ur-saga, who preceded him as ensi of Nippur[23]. This would leave only a four year period, from Šū-Sîn 1-4, into which we must fit the reigns of both Namzitara and Ur-saga. The evidence at hand does not allow any further conclusions beyond this. We can perhaps surmise that the reign of Namzitara was a last ditch effort by the "House of Ur-Meme"[24] to reasert its former dominance over the political scene at Nippur after the death of Amar-Suena who seems to have altered the fortunes of the family at Nippur[25]. Perhaps it was under Šū-Sîn, who restored the

[13] Cf. E. Sollberger's comments on the sealing of letter-orders, *op. cit.*, 2ff.
[14] A few envelopes with just seal impressions are preserved. Cf. E. Sollberger, *op. cit.*, nos. 61, 125, 142, 281 and D.I. Owen, *Or* NS 40 (1971), 392 n. 6.
[15] Cf. A. Falkenstein, *WO* 1 (1947-1952), 43 and M.-J. Seux, *Épithètes Royales*, 416.
[16] Cf. M.-J. Seux, *ibid.*, 416 sub ki-áĝa and 433 sub pà.
[17] "The House of Ur-Meme," *JNES* 31 (1972), 87-95.
[18] The reading ^{d}Nanibgal = DINGIR.DINGIR.NISABA is based on the unpublished Nippur text 3 NT 299 (forerunner to Diri VII) communicated by B. Landsberger apud Å.W. Sjöberg, *TCS* 3 [1969], 147 and by T. Jacobsen apud W.W. Hallo, *Actes de la XVIIe Rencontre Assyriologique Internationale*, (1970) 131 note 1.
[19] Cf. the genealogical chart compiled by W.W. Hallo, *JNES* 31 (1972), 89 and his comments, *ibid.*, 93.
[20] Little is known of the career of Ur-Nanibgala. He may have died on or close to the year ŠS 7. Cf. W.W. Hallo, *ibid.*, 94 note 61.
[21] *Ibid.*, 94 note 62.
[22] *Ibid.*, 94 note 68.
[23] *Ibid.*, 94.
[24] However, the father of Ur-saga is not yet known. It would be interesting to speculate that the father of Ur-saga was in fact Namzitara who passed on the office of ensi to his son maintaining the hereditary character of the office reinstituted by Šū-Sîn.
[25] W.W. Hallo, *loc. cit.*

hereditary character of the office of ensi at Nippur[26], that Namzitara tried, albeit without lasting success, to regain the coveted office for himself and for the "House of Ur-Meme"[27].

II: Additional Evidence for the Reading of MAR.TU

H. Sauren[28] and S. Lieberman[29] recently proposed the reading Mar-dú for MAR.TU[30]. They based their suggestions on M. Çığ and H. Kızılyay, *NRVN* no. 215, where the year name of Šš 5 was restored as mu ú[s-sa bàd] Mar-du$_8$ ba-[dù][31], and on the unpublished Old Babylonian Susa text quoted by J. Krecher, which reads: Mar-du = *A-mur*!(AH)*-ri-i*[32]. This reading, long ago proposed by A. Poebel[33], should now be seriously reconsidered. In a fragmentary neo-Sumerian archival text from Nippur in the University Museum[34] a complete example of the above quoted year name is preserved substantiating the restorations proposed by M. Çığ[35], H. Kızılyay[36] and H. Sauren[37] and accepted by S. Lieberman[38]. The text, UM 29-13-268, reads: [m]u ús-a bàd Mar-du$_8$ ba-dù[39]. Another phonetic writing for MAR.TU was kindly brought to the writer's attention by Prof. W.G. Lambert[40]. In his forthcoming edition of the lexical series AN = Anum he reports the writing, ^{d}Mar-du$_{10}$-edin-an-[na] = =𒌋𒌋[=^{d}MAR.TU] (tablet VI:231)[41]. These two additional phonetic writings for MAR.TU add to the growing evidence for the true reading of MAR.TU and perhaps indicate the direction to follow in seeking the etymology of the term[42].

(UM 29-13-268)

rev.

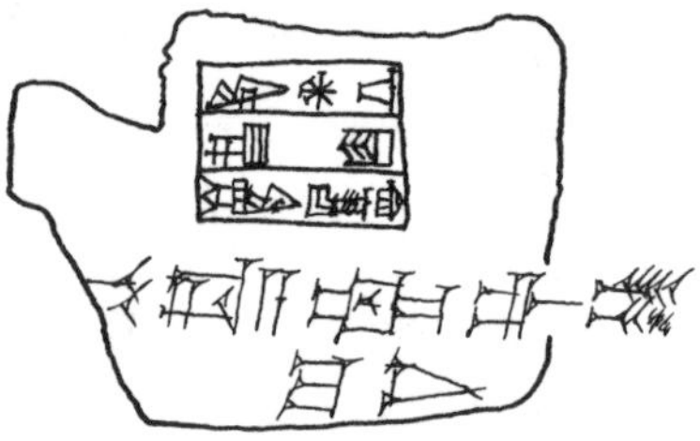

obv. destroyed

---

[26] W.W. Hallo, *ibid.*, 94.

[27] I would not exclude the possibility that Namzitara, ensi of Nippur, is, in fact, to be identified with Namzitara, ensi of Gudua in the first year of Amar-Suena. W.W. Hallo, *ibid.*, 93, would rather keep the two separate. But perhaps this is yet another instance of an individual holding the office of ensi at different cities at different times during his lifetime. Cf. C.E. Keiser, *Patesis of the Ur Dynasty.* (1919), 10 and W.W. Hallo, *The Ensis of the Ur III Dynasty* (Unpublished Master's Dissertation, Department of Oriental Languages and Literatures, The University of Chicago, 1953), 74ff.

[28] *BiOr* 24 (1967), 337.

[29] *JCS* 22 (1969), 55.

[30] The reading Mar-dú was also adopted by C. Wilcke, *Das Lugalbandaepos*, 205.

[31] Cf. *NRVN*, 56 and *BiOr* 24 (1967), 337.

[32] *HSAO*, 94. Note Krecher's suggestion for the reading of MAR as g̃ar$_7$, *ibid.*, 94. However, M. Civil cautions us against the use of such peripheral data, cf. *JNES* 31(1972), 222.

[33] *JNES* 1 (1941), 256 note 17; reference courtesy of Dr. Sol Cohen.

[34] The text is published with the permission of Prof. Å.W. Sjöberg, Curator of Tablet Collections.

[35] M. Çığ and H. Kızılyay, *NRVN*, 56.

[36] *Ibid.*

[37] *BiOr* 24 (1967), 337.

[38] Not Šš 4 as stated by S. Lieberman, *JCS* 22 (1969), 55.

[39] The writing ús-a occurs periodically in the Nippur texts and in at least one instance, CBS 9178, the tablet has mu ús-a ... whereas the envelope has mu ús-sa ...

[40] I wish to thank Prof. Lambert for making this information available to me and allowing me to quote it. Prof. Lambert is preparing a new edition of the Assyro-Babylonian god list AN = ^{d}*A-nu-um* originally edited by R.L. Litke in his unpublished and unavailable dissertation, *A reconstruction of the Assyro-Babylonian God-Lists AN: ^{d}A-NU-UM and AN: ANU ŠÁ AMĒLI* (Yale Dissertation, 1958).

III: A Campaign Against Mardu[43] in the Third Year of Ibbī-Sîn*

The recent study on the Amorites-Mardu of the Ur III period by G. Buccellati[44] followed by the excellent review article by C. Wilcke[45], has placed at our disposal nearly all the available source material, both archival and literary, bearing on the history of the Amorites-Mardu in this period. Since their studies have all but exhausted the available sources, it is all the more welcome when new evidence relating to the Amorites-Mardu comes to light.

In the Wilson Library of the University of North Carolina there is a small collection of cuneiform tablets, part of which has been placed at the writer's disposal for publication[46]. Among the Ur III tablets in the collection is UNC 7[47], a perfectly preserved archival text written in an elegant script (cf. photo below Pl. II* a), the subject of our study.

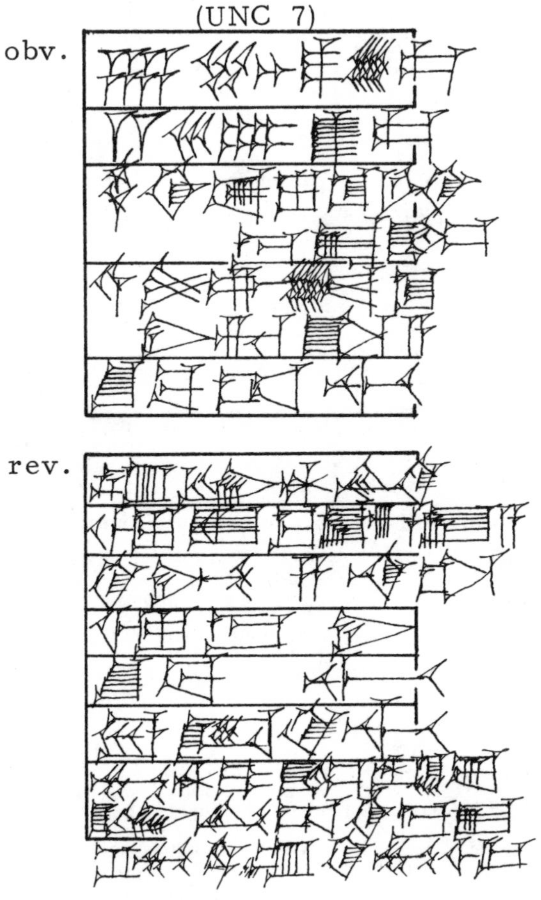

Transliteration:

1) 532. 0. 3. še gur
158. 0. 0. zíz gur
erín Ugnim^{ki}-ma-ke$_4$$^{!}$-ne
u$_4$ kaskal Mar-dú-šè ì-re-ša-a
5) šu ba-ab-ti
kišib Lú-^{d}Nanna
ù *Iš-ku-un-É-a*
ki Gu-za-na-ta
Ù-ma-né
10) šu ba-ti
iti *Á-ki-ti*
mu ^{d}*I-bí-*^{d}*Sîn* lugal Urí^{ki}-ma-ke$_4$
Si-mu-ru-um^{ki} mu-ḫul

---

[41] Based on YBC 2401 IX. Cf. R.L. Litke, *op. cit.*, 237, reference courtesy of Prof. H.A. Hoffner, Jr.

[42] A. Poebel, *JNES* 1 (1941), 256 n. 17, proposed that Mardu was a plausible etymology for Akkadian *(w)ardum*, 'slave.' This was followed by S.N. Kramer in *Genava* NS 8 (1960), 273 n. 4. S. Lieberman, *op. cit.*, 55 also maintains that Mardu is a Semitic word, although he does not suggest an etymology for it. Dr. S. Cohen informs me that he will devote a future article on this term supporting the etymology proposed by A. Poebel.

[43] For this reading, cf. above Part II.

* The substance of this paper was read before the 83rd annual meeting of the American Oriental Society, Washington, D.C., March, 1973.

[44] *The Amorites of the Ur III Period* (1966).

[45] *WO* 5 (1969), 1-31.

[46] The writer wishes to thank Prof. J.M. Sasson for bringing the collection to his attention. He would also like to acknowledge his debt to Dr. Lawrence F. London, Curator of the Rare Book Section of the Wilson Library for arranging for the extended loan of the tablets and for the permission to publish these texts.

[47] The sigla UNC = University of North Carolina.

Translation:

"The troops of Ugnim received 532 gur, 3 ban of barley (and) 158 gur of emmer, when they set out on an expedition against Mardu. Receipted by Lu-Nanna and Iškun-Ea. Umani received (the grain) from Guzana (in the) month of Akiti, the year Ibbī-Sîn, the king of Ur, raided Simurum."

Comments:

line 1-2:

The quantities are expressed according to the system used in E. Sollberger, *TCS* 1, 7. The amount of emmer and barley, nearly 700 gur, which was received by the troops indicates a rather sizeable contingent was involved in the campaign. I.J. Gelb has shown that the average monthly barley ration for a man (guruš) in the Ur III period was about sixty quarts (silà)[48]. If this can be compared to what might be needed for the avergage soldier of the same era, 700 gur would be sufficient to feed 3500 troops for a month. Unfortunately, there is no indication from the text, or from any other source, how long this campaign took or, for that matter, how far the troops had to travel. In any case the quantity of provisions involved indicate a large number of troops in the field possibly for a prolonged period of time.

line 3:

Ugnim^{ki} occurs in E. Chiera, *STA* 10 I 9', H. Sauren, *WMAH* 115 13, 176 passim and in H. Waetzoldt, *Textilindustrie*, no. 16 V 2. These texts are from Lagaš. The exact location of Ugnim^{ki} is not known.

line 4:

For temporal clauses governed by u_4 . . . a (*inūma*), cf. E. Sollberger, *Système Verbal*, 206ff.
For the verb *ere = *alāku*, 'to go,' cf. *CAD* A/1 206 s.v. *alāku*, lexical section and J. Krecher, *WO* 4 (1967), 3-7, where J. Krecher points out that *ere is used exclusively with plural subjects and with the *ḫamṭu* aspect.
For the phrase *ana* KASKAL *alāku*, 'to go forth on a military campaign,' cf. *CAD A*/1, 313a and *CAD* Ḫ, 111b.

line 6:

Lu-Nanna, one of the two individuals who receipted this document is probably to be identified with the šakkana[49] Lu-Nanna, who was the source of booty from Mardu in Š 48[50], as well as the Lu-Nanna who was also the source of booty from Mardu again in Š 48 in the text discussed by S. Lieberman[51]. Lieberman is certainly correct in equating the Lu-Nanna of CT 32 pl. 19-22 iii 1 with the above mentioned individual[52], and we would add our own citation to the growing amount of evidence for the career of this individual[53].

line 7:

Iškun-Ea[54], the second individual who receipted this document, is no doubt to be identified with Iškun-Ea, šakkana of *UET*3 719 (no date), with Iškun-Ea of *ITT* 3 5255 (IS 3/I, Drehem calendar), where he receipts a large quantity of barley (33.3.2. gur) and with the Iškun-Ea of *ITT* 2 976, where he is designated šakkana

48 *JNES* 24 (1965), 230-243.

49 For the reading šakkana = GÌR.NITÁ, we follow A. Goetze, *JCS* 17 (1963), 7-8. Cf. also, E. Sollberger, *op. cit.*, glossary no. 656.

50 G. Buccellati, *Amorites*, no. 12.

51 *JCS* 22 (1969), 57.

52 *Ibid.*, 60.

53 It should be pointed out that YBC 7149 (Lieberman, *ibid.* 60 n. 60) has Lú-^{d}En-ki and not Lú-^{d}ŠEŠ.KI as ensi of Zimudar (collation thanks to Mr. Piotr Michalowski). However, this must be a scribal error in view of the duplicates (YBC 4672 reads Lú-^{d}ŠEŠ.KI) and the contemporary references for Lu-Nanna as ensi of Zimudar in the reign of Šū-Sîn. I have recently discovered a small envelope fragment in the University Museum collection containing the seal of Lu-Nanna. N-798 is dated to SS 1 and the seal inscription reads: [^{d}Šū]-^{d}Sîn / lugal-kala-ga / lugal Urí^{ki}-ma / lugal ^{d}Uba-da-limmu-ba / Lú-^{d}[Nanna] / GÌR.[NITÁ] / Zi-m[u-dar^{ki}] / ìr-[zu].

54 For this name, cf. I.J. Gelb, *MAD* 3, 268 sub *škn*.

and where his seal, dedicated to Ibbī-Sîn, is preserved. His father's name on the seal is *Kur-bi-la-*[*ag*][55]. ITT 2 976 is dated early in the third year of Ibbī-Sîn (mu ús-sa date).

line 8-9:

Guzana[56] occurs at Drehem in IS 3 representing the sukkal-maḫ and dispensing barley[57], dispensing barley at Drehem in ŠS 9/X[58], dispensing barley at Drehem in ŠS 9[59], and dispensing sesame at Drehem in ŠS 6[60], the last mentioned text containing the seal of Umani[61]! Guzana is probably the same individual who occurs on the seal published in *PBS* 13 13 (IS 1, but upon opening the envelope we found that the inner tablet contained a mu ús-sa date, i.e. IS 2!) where *ᵈŠu-ᵈSîn-nu-úr-ma-ti-iš-sú* is designated the servant of Guzana.

line 12:

According to T. Jacobsen[62], it was in Ibbī-Sîn's second year that trouble began in the northeastern area of Mesopotamia, when Ešnunna ceased using Ibbī-Sîn's year formulae. Early in the third year of Ibbī-Sîn he undertook a punitive raid against Simurum in the far northeast, an event which gave its name to the third year. By the sixth month of that year, i.e. Akiti, he undertook yet another campaign against Mardu. Although the direction of the campaign is not recorded in our text, it is, in all probability, to be sought in the same general northeastern area. It is not fortuitous that Simurum is mentioned as an ally of Mardu in the Šarrum-bānî-letter[63], or that Susa breaks off from the control of Ibbī-Sîn also in his third year[64]. S. Lieberman has collected an impressive amount of data indicating the direction from which the main thrust of the Mardu infiltration into Mesopotamia must have come[65]. Our text appears to support his conclusions. It is likely that the campaign recorded in our text was but one of many punitive expeditions carried out by Ibbī-Sîn[66] in his repeated attempts to stem the Mardu-tide which was rapidly engulfing his kingdom. That these efforts were to be in vain is now history[67].

---

55 For this name, cf. *ibid.*, 149 sub *krb.*

56 For the Sumerian name Guzana, cf. H. Limet, *Anthroponymie Sumérienne*, 251.

57 A.L. Oppenheim, *AOS* 32, P 2.

58 *Ibid.*, P 3.

59 *Ibid.*, P 4.

60 *Ibid.*, S 1.

61 I.J. Gelb, *op. cit.*, 45 sub *'mm*, considers *Ummānî* an Akkadian name. Cf. also, E. Sollberger, *TCS* 1, glossary no. 757. However, H. Limet, *op. cit.*, 312 proposes a plausible Sumerian etymology for the name, which we follow here.

62 *JCS* 7 (1953), 38.

63 Cf. for now, S. Lieberman, *op. cit.*, 62 n. 83. Mr. P. Michalowski of Yale University is preparing a complete edition of the Šarrum-bānî letter and the associated correspondence.

64 T. Jacobsen, *op. cit.*, 38.

65 S. Lieberman, *op. cit.*, 60ff. Cf. also Buccellati, *op. cit.*, 247ff. On the strategic location and importance of Simurum, cf. the comments of A. Goetze, *JNES* 12 (1953) 123 and J.J. Finkelstein, *JCS* 9 (1955) 4.

66 T. Jacobsen, *op. cit.*, 37.

67 *Ibid.*, 38ff.

ILĀNU REṢŪTNI LILLIKŪ!

Anson F. Rainey – Jerusalem

In response to the very lucid and comprehensive exposition by Pat Miller of the various proposals to find a Hebrew root *ʿzr* II as a cognate to Ugaritic *ǵzr*,[1] it may be worthwhile to re-evaluate this material in the light of both old and new evidence. The semantic concepts involved in this discussion fall into three categories: (1) "helpers" of deities, who actually stand in the same relation to their god as do the human "helpers" in the next class to their leader; (2) human "helpers" in battle who are followers, i.e. vassals, of some human ruler; and (3) the deity as "helper" who aids his faithful followers, especially in combat or in time of distress.

The most cogent piece of evidence pertains directly to category (1) but is therefore valid for (2). It is the parallel, the Ugaritic version of which is noted by Miller,[2] between Akkadian and Ugaritic entries on deity lists in *Ugaritica* V. There one finds that the syllabic entry, *ilānu*(DINGER.MEŠ) *til-la-at* ^{d}*Baʿla* (IŠKUR),[3] corresponds to the alphabetic *il tʿḏr bʿl*,[4] and the clear meaning of both passages is "the gods of the support troops of Baʿl," i.e. "Baʿl's helpers." This of course confirms the fact that the *ʿôzᵉrê rāhab* (Job 9:13) are from Hebrew *ʿzr* I which is cognate to Ugaritic *ʿḏr*, "to help in time of trouble," and Arabic *ʿḏr*, "to excuse."[5] Miller[6] has also noted the helpers of Marduk in *Enuma Eliš*, viz. *ilānu*(DINGIR.MEŠ) *re-ṣu-šu a-li-ku i-de-šú*, "the gods, his helpers, who go at his side."[7] Human allies were depicted in like terminology. Sennacherib in his first campaign defeated Merodach-baladan *a-di ummānāt*(ERÍN.ḪÁ) *Elamti*(ELAM.MA)^{ki} *re-ṣi-šú*, "with the troops of Elam his ally."[8] Hezekiah and his confederates had sent for the kings of Egypt and Ethiopia who *il-li-ku re-ṣu-su-un*, "came to their aid."[9] To these we may compare passages such as that in the Yakhdunlim inscription when several neighboring kings gathered together against him and *a-na ti-lu-ti-šu-nu ṣa-ab Su-mu-e-pu-uḫ ša ma-at Ia-am-ḫa-ad*^{ki} *il-li-ka-am-ma*, "to their aid the army of Sumu-epuʿ of the land of Yamkhad came forth . . ."[10] It is not surprising, therefore, that Rib-Haddi speaks

---

[1] Patrick D. Miller, "Ugaritic *ǵzr* and Hebrew *ʿzr* II," *UF* 2 (1970), pp. 159-175.

[2] *Ibid.*, p. 164.

[3] RS 20.24:25 (U 5 N, 18, pp. 45, 379).

[4] UT 609:8 (U 5 V, 9, pp. 579, 580).

[5] And not Arabic *ʿzr*, "to censure, rebuke," as stated in the older edition of *KBL*, p. 695; cf. *GB*, p. 578 and *BDB*, p. 740.

[6] *Loc. cit.* (*supra*, n. 2).

[7] *Enuma eliš* IV, 69; cf. also with reference to Tiʾāmat, *ilānu*(DINGIR.DINGIR) *re-ṣu-šá a-li-ku i-de-šá*, *ibid.*, 107.

[8] *OIP* 2, I, 21-22.

[9] *Ibid.*, II, 81.

[10] G. Dossin, *Syria* 32 (1955), pp. 7, 14, Col. III, 12-15.

now of ERÍN.MEŠ *til-la-ti*[11] and then of ERÍN.MEŠ *re-ṣú-ti*[12]; he is asking for support troops, or reinforcements, i.e. "helping forces." In another letter he combines his terms; first he says: *ù i-nu-ma ia-nu-um* LÚ. MEŠ *ti-la-ta*$_5$ *ša a-ṣa-at a-na ia-a-ši*, "and that there is no support force that has come forth to me . . . ,"[13] and later regarding support troops (*a-*⌜*na*⌝ *ti-*⌜*la*⌝*-ti*)[14] from the neighboring coastal rulers he claims: *ù aš-*⌜*tap*⌝*-*⌜*par*⌝ *a-na ša-šu-nu a-na re-ṣí-ia*, "and I have frequently written to them to help me."[15]

Now at Ugarit the fact that most able bodied citizens, especially those who received land grants from the king, were required to do military service is demonstrated by the rare instances when someone was given an exemption: ⌜*ù*⌝ I*ʿAbdu*(ÈR-*du*) [*a*]*-na re-ṣú-ti la i-*⌜*lak*⌝, "and ʿAbdu will not serve with the support troops."[16] On the basis of this semantic evidence, the present writer had pointed out that the vassals of Ben-Hadad were really "the thirty-two *kings who helped him*" (*melek ʿôzēr ʾôtô*), in the literal sense.[17] Another passage cited by Miller contains, as he has observed, allusions to both *sômᵉkê miṣrayim*, "the supporters of Egypt,"[18] and *kōl-ʿôzᵉreyhā*, "all her helpers"[19]; the obvious parallel between these two expressions (note that Kush is also explicitly referred to)[20] simply proves that these allies are really defined by *ʿzr* I. Finally, the much vaunted *ʿôzᵉrê hammilḥāmāh*[12] is paralleled *in the same chapter* by the "Aramaicised" reflex, *kōl-ʾēlleh ʾanšê milḥāmāh ʿôdᵉrê maʿᵃrākāh*, "all these are the men of war, the *helpers* in battle."[22] The semantic and phonetic evidence all points to *ʿzr* I as the only possible root for "help(ers)" in battle, both human and divine.

The parallel in Ugaritic between *ǵzrm* and *ṣbim*, *mhr* and *ḏmr* is surely secondary and not basic to its meaning.[23] The administrative texts show the term only on lists of members of families[24] and not among the many rosters of military personnel. Its function as an epithet for legendary characters like *Dnil* and his son *Aqht*,[25] of Keret's son *Ilḥu*,[26] or Mōt the god of death,[27] can usefully be compared with Sumerian g u r u š = Akkadian *eṭlu*,[28] which means "grown young man," then "man" and also serves as

---

[11] EA 82-18.

[12] EA 126:44.

[13] EA 92:22-23; W.L. Moran had recognized that the spelling *ti-la-ta*$_5$ could not be an ideographic writing, TI.LA-*ta*$_5$, for *balāṭa* (CAD B, 46 ff.) but must refer to *tillatu*-troops, *A Syntactical Study of the Dialect of Byblos as Reflected in the Amarna Tablets* (dissertation, Johns Hopkins Univ., 1950; Univ. Microfilms, Ann Arbour, 1970), pp. 15, 67, 161.

[14] EA 92:36; in accordance with the correct interpretation of line 22 (cf. n. 13, *supra*), the plain syllabic reading is to be preferred here over the ideographic. As we noted in *AOAT* 8, p. 60, the examples that J.A. Knudtzon interpreted as writings of (non-existant) *bilaṭu*, *VAB* 2, II, p. 1392, must be read *tillatu*; we should have added that his first example cited there must either be read ERÍN.MEŠ *pí-ṭá*!(LA/AT)-*ti*, EA 104:35, or better yet (with Moran, *op. cit.*, p. 164), ERÍN.MEŠ *til*!(BI)-*la-ti*, since the troops were posted in Ṣumur.

[15] EA 92:44-45.

[16] RS 16.239:14-15 (*PRU* III, p. 80); cf. also RS 16.132:17 (*PRU* III, p. 140).

[17] *JNES* 24 (1965), p. 17 n. 6.

[18] Ezek. 30:6; Miller, *op. cit.*, p. 167.

[19] Ezek. 30:8.

[20] Ezek. 30:9.

[21] I Chron. 12-1; Miller, *op. cit.*, p. 166.

[22] I Chron. 12:38; I was reminded of this parallel by Shmu'el Ahituv; the reading is certainly to be preferred as being the more difficult, *contra* LXX *et. al.*

[23] UT *ʿnt*: II, 20-22 (*CTA* 3); Miller, *op. cit.*, p. 164.

[24] UT 119:16, 18, 20, 23 (*CTA* 80); UT 2081:1 (*PRU* V, No. 81); Miller, *op. cit.*, pp. 162-3.

[25] Cf. Miller, *op. cit.*, p. 162 for text references.

[26] UT 125:46, 58, 83, 95 (*CTA* 16); Miller, *op. cit.*, p. 163.

[27] Miller, *loc. cit.* for references.

[28] This obvious parallel had not struck me until pointed out by my colleague, Dr. R. Kutscher of Tel Aviv University.

an epithet for gods, demons and kings.[29] In fact, *eṭ-lu* on one of the vocabulary lists from Râs Shamra is translated by Ugaritic ⌈*ba*⌉*-aḫ-ḫu-rù*, i.e. **baḫḫūru* = Hebrew *bāḥûr*.[30] The total range of usage for Ugaritic *ǵzr* certainly bears a striking resemblance to that of Hebrew *bāḥûr*; the normal meaning of the latter term is "youth,"[31] and the *derived* meaning can be seen in the expression *'îš bāḥûr*, "elite soldiers."[32] For that reason, one may accept the one lone passage: *šiwwîtî 'ēzer 'al-gibbôr, hᵃrîmôtî bāḥûr mē'ām*, "I exalted a youth over the man of war, I raised up a young man from the people."[33] Here the point of the passage is the *contrast* between the experienced warrior, *gibbôr*, and the healthy youth on the threshold of manhood. Thus, we may have an isolated example of Ugaritic *ǵzr* appearing in Hebrew dress. But the function of *ǵzr* as an epithet in Ugaritic for heroic personages is no justification for seeking this root in biblical passages pertaining to warfare. On the contrary, the evidence is overwhelmingly in favor of the view that the correct concept in military contexts is that of "help(ers)" in the literal sense, i.e. the Hebrew passages all contain *'zr* I!

Though the Ugaritic *ǵzr* was evidently a strong person, there is no proof that the root means "strong," or "to have/give strength."[34] Neither Sumerian g u r u š and Akkadian *eṭlu* nor Akkadian *ba=tūlu*, nor even *bāḥûr* in Hebrew signified strength in the specific sense. Yet *eṭlu* became an important epithet. Therefore, it need not disturb us that the cognate Arabic *ǵazîr*, *et. al.*, do not express strength but mainly "(one) abundant (in)," etc.[35] For example, it might indicate an abundance of facial hair or some other characteristic. Note the equation m è $^{\check{s}mi\text{-}i\check{s}\text{-}su\text{-}l\acute{a}}$s u_6 - l á = *ba-tù-lu* EME.SAL, "man-with-beard = *batūlu* (EME.SAL)."[36] For the transitive D stem *uṭṭulu*, one also finds: s a t e - n a b í - i n - m ú d a m i n - n i - i n - t u k = *ú-uṭ-ṭi-il-*[*šu*] *aš-ša-tu*$_4$ *ú-šá-ḫi-i*[*s-su*], where the Akkadian entry explains that the adoptive father brought his foster son to maturity, "he caused him to reach manhood, he had him take a wife." However, the Sumerian reads: "he let beard grow on his cheek and had him take a wife."[37] The position of Ugaritic *ǵzr* in the family registers mentioned above and the secondary parallel with various military terms, suggests that *ǵzr* can also be defined very well by adopting Thorkild Jacobsen's definition of g u r u š /*eṭlu*, viz. "the young adult man of marriageable age and particularly fit for military service."[38]

It follows, therefore, that there is no sense in looking for the root *ǵzr* behind expressions reflecting the "help" given by the deity to man. In cuneiform literature one could multiply examples of *rēṣūtu* and cognates expressing the idea that the god(s) came to the aid of someone, especially in time of war or distress.[39] Sennacherib says that he prayed to the gods and they *ur-ru-ḫi-iš iš-mu-ú il-li-ku re-ṣu-ti*, "quickly

---

29 *CAD* E, pp. 407-11; *AHw*, pp. 265-6.

30 U 5 N, 137: II, 24'; for the corrected reading, cf. A.F. Rainey, *IEJ* 19 (1969), p. 107; this was noted independently by J. Blau and J.C. Greenfield, *BASOR*, No. 200 (Dec., 1970), p. 17.

31 As seen in its parallelism with *bᵉtûlāh*, e.g. Dt. 32:25, *et al.*

32 Judges 20:15, 16. 34; I Sam. 24:3; II Chron. 13:3, 17, *et. al.*

33 Psalms 89:20; Miller, *op. cit.*, p. 165.

34 Miller, *op. cit.*, pp. 160-1, has argued in a circle; he takes for granted that the passages he intends to cite further on that deal with "strength", etc. are valid indicators for the Ugaritic word, and then he defines the Ugaritic *ǵzr* as "hero, valiant one, warrior." In fact nothing in the Ugaritic contexts gives any clue at all to the nuance attached to this vocable! A better explanation for the "strength" passages will be given further on.

35 Cf. M. Held, *JBL* 84 (1965), pp. 278-9 n. 31, cited by Miller, *op. cit.*, p. 160 n. 8.

36 Lu III iii, 83; *MSL* XII, p. 126; cf. *CAD* B, 174.

37 Ai VII iii, 20-21; *MSL* I, p. 101; *CAD* E, 397a; Th. Jacobsen, *JNES* 12 (1953), p. 179-80 n. 41, now *idem.*, *Toward the Image of Tammuz and Other Essays on Mesopotamian History and Culture* (ed. by W.L. Moran; Cambridge, 1970), pp. 342-3.

38 Jacobsen, *loc. cit.*

39 Cf. *CAD* A-1, pp. 319-20.

heard and came as my help."[40] Furthermore, the "help" given by the deity was frequently expressed in West Semitic proper names. It is most remarkable that in Ugaritic one finds *y'ḏrd*[41] meaning "(May) Hadad help," and other names from this root[42] but *never once* does *ǵzr* appear as an element in personal names! We may compare the biblical *hᵃdad'ezer* of the tenth century B.C.[43] with the ᵈ*Adad*(IŠKUR)-*id-ri* of the ninth century B.C.[44] The later form shows the Aramaic shift of *ḏ* > *d* and proves that *'ḏr* is the root. Such biblical names as *'azrî'ēl*[45] paralleled by *'adrî'ēl*[46] and *'ēzer*[47] by *'ēder*[48] also show that *'ḏr* is the root expressing the divine concern.

As for the various passages proposed by differant scholars and assembled by Miller in which the idea of "strengthening" or "being strengthened" is expressed, a very natural and convincing solution has been proposed by Gershon Brin.[49] He has gathered an impressive array of passages to support the thesis that *'zr* I had become attracted to the root *'zz* in various semantic contexts. Perhaps the most relevant point in his essay for the present discussion is his demonstration that *'zz* and *'zr* have a common family of synonyms including forms from the root *yš'*.[50] Certainly "salvation, deliverance," reflect the kind of assistance meant by Akkadian *rēṣūtu*, Ugaritic *'ḏr*, Hebrew *'zr* and Aramaic *'dr*!

We may summarize our conclusions as follows:

(1) those who support a leader, human or divine, in combat were truly "helpers" and no other semantic concept such as "forces, strength," etc., is applicable.

(2) The deity gave real "help" to his faithful follower; this "help" included "strength/strengthening" to the degree that that semantic coloring had become attached to *'zr* I through attraction to *'zz*.

(3) Ugaritic *ǵzr* is primarily a familial qualifier that developed into an epithet for people distinguished by heroic qualities.

(4) Only the passage Ps. 89:20 has any legitimate claim to possessing a Hebrew reflex of Ugaritic *ǵzr* and there it is precisely in the sense of a "young man." However, this would justify a lexical entry for *'zr* II.

Though the basic viewpoint expressed herein is largely opposed to that of Miller and those whom he cites, it was his meticulous presentation of the evidence that helped this present writer to focus his own thoughts on the problem.

---

40 *OIP* 2, V, 66-67; for the adverbial accusative cf. R. Borger, *BAL*, par. 147b, p. XXIX.

41 *PTU*, pp. 41, 190; the Amurrite names cited by Miller, *op. cit.*, p. 160 and n. 6, can hardly derive from any root other than *'ḏr*; *APNM*, p. 193.

42 *PTU*, p. 113.

43 II Sam. 8:3 *et al.*; 10:16-19; I Ki. 11:23.

44 K. Tallqvist, *APN*, p. 8.

45 I Ch. 5:24; 27:19; Jer. 36:16.

46 I Sam. 18:19; II Sam. 21:8.

47 I Ch. 4:4; 12:9.

48 I Ch. 23:23; 24:30; Shmu'el Ahituv placed at my disposal the proofs of his articles on this and the name in n. 42, *supra*, from *Encyclopaedia biblica* (Hebrew), VI (Jerusalem, 1971), s.v.

49 *"Hašerašim ' 'zr–'zz' bamikra,"* *Lešonenu* 24 (1960), pp. 8-14 (Hebrew; "The Roots ' *'zr–'zz'* in the Bible).

50 *Ibid.*, p. 10.

ZEDEKIAH'S EMANCIPATION OF SLAVES AND THE SABBATICAL YEAR

Nahum Sarna

Brandeis University, Waltham, Mass. USA

Cyrus H. Gordon was one of the first scholars in modern times to express the view that the institution of the sabbatical year may go back to pre-Israelite origins.[1] He pointed to the well established and widely diffused seven year cyclical pattern in the ancient Near East and noted that the narrative of Jer 34:12-16 attests to an attempted revival of the sabbatical obligations which had fallen into disuse.

Gordon's interpretations of some of the Ugaritic texts (e.g. *UT* 52) as having been connected with the inauguration of a new septennial cycle[2] have both won support[3] and encountered challenge.[4] Of greater importance to his thesis are recent studies in the institution known as the *mīšarum* which was practised in Mesopotamia in the old Babylonian period. J.J. Finkelstein has forcefully argued for the recurrent character of the *mīšarum*, if only for the reason that this economic reform, which involved the remission of debts and other obligations, must have occurred at predictable intervals, if economic chaos was to be avoided.[5]

The problem of the antiquity of the calculation of the sabbatical year in Israel is complicated by the silence of the sources. Lev 26:34f., 43 and 2 Chron 36:21 testify only to the neglect of the obligations of the sabbatical laws, not to the complete ignorance or abandonment of the septennial calculations. Since Jer 34 can be located in a historic context, it is worthwhile re-examining the relationship of the narrative there to the sabbatical institution.

---

1 C.H. Gordon, *Or* 22 (1953), 79-81.
2 *Ugaritic Literature* (1949), 4, 57.
3 Cf. J. Gray, *Archaeology and the Old Testament* (1962), 111.
4 J. C. de Moor, *Seasonal Pattern in the Ugaritic Myth of Ba'lu* (1971).
5 J.J. Finkelstein, *JCS* 15 (1961), 91-104; in *Studies in Honor of B. Landsberger* (1965), 233-46, esp. n. 38; *ANET* (Suppl., 1969), 526; on the need to re-evaluate the antiquity of the sabbatical and Jubilee institutions, cf. M. Weinfeld, *Deuteronomy and the Deuteronomic School* (1972), 153, n. 1.

Jer. 34

At some period during Nebuchadnezzar's siege of Jerusalem, King Zedekiah issued a proclamation of emancipation for male and female Hebrew slaves. The mass manumission, apparently initiated by the king and accepted with some reluctance[6], was put into effect through a solemn covenant contracted within the Temple (Jer. 34:8-10, 15, 18-19)[7]. However, during a temporary lifting of the siege, misinterpreted by the men of Jerusalem (Jer. 34:21-22), the former owners violated their commitments and pressed the liberated slaves back into their service (vv. 11, 16, 18).

The historical background

Although these events are not precisely dated by the Book of Jeremiah, the historical background can now be reconstructed with a goodly measure of confidence[8].

Nebuchadnezzar began the siege of Jerusalem on the 10th of Teveth in the 9th year of King Zedekiah of Judea (2 Kings 25:1; Jer. 52:4; Ezek. 24:1-2; Jer. 39:1). This date may now be fixed as Jan. 15th, 588 B.C. It is clear that most of Judea had already fallen by the time the emancipation of the slaves took place; only the fortress towns of Lachish and Azekah still held out (Jer. 34:7). This fact presupposes that quite some time must have elapsed by then since the start of the siege. This would place the mass manumission of slaves toward the end of 588. It cannot be later than December of that year because soon after this, as will be seen, the slave owners found reason to reconsider their decision.

It is beyond doubt that what occasioned the rescission of the emancipation was the entry of an Egyptian relief force into Judea[9]. Nebuchadnezzar had no option but to raise the siege in order to deal with a serious threat to his flanks from the southwest. Jeremiah (34:21-22) specifically mentions the departure of the Babylonian army at this time. Elsewhere the prophet reports the Egyptian intervention and denounces it as a false hope, predicts its defeat and foresees the Babylonian resumption of the siege (37:5-11). A further reference to Zedekiah's appeal to Egypt for military support is to be found in Ezekiel's denunciation of the king's violation of his oath of loyalty to Nebuchadnezzar (Ezek. 17:11-18)[10]. He too scoffs at the Egyptian ability to aid Judea and, in another prophecy (29:1), this time dated to the 12th of Tebeth in the tenth year of Johoiachin's exile (= 7th Jan. 587), Ezekiel warns against reliance upon Egyptian help. This oracle comes almost exactly one year after Nebuchadnezzar had arrived at the walls of Jerusalem and its wording (vv. 6-7) strongly reflects the optimism that now pervaded the city[11]. It is thus certain that by Jan. 587 the Egyptian relief operation was imminent. Three months later, however, on the 7th of Nisan 587 (= 29th April), the same prophet could proclaim that the

---

[6] This is possibly hinted at in v. 10. *wayyišmeʿû*.

[7] On this ratification of covenants by sacrifice, see M. Weinfeld, *op. cit.*, 102-04.

[8] See E.R. Thiele, *The Mysterious Numbers of the Hebrew Kings* (1965), 167-9; A, Malamat in *Jerusalem Through the Ages* [Hebrew] (1968), 42-5; *IEJ*, 18 (1968), 137-56.

[9] It should be noted that no formal abrogation of the covenant took place. Rather, it would seem that, with the raising of the siege, the need for manpower to work the neglected fields led many individual owners to pressure their erstwhile slaves back into their service. It is not unlikely in view of the prevailing conditions that many slaves required little persuasion. For a theological interpretation of Zedekiah's measure, see M. Kessler, *BZ* 15 (1971), 104-08.

[10] See 2 Chron. 36:13; cf. Jos. *Ant.* x.7 (102). On vassal oaths of this type, see M. Tsevat, *JBL* 78 (1959), 199-204; A. Malamat, *IEJ op.cit.*, 145 n. 18; *Jerusalem, op. cit.*, 36 n. 17.

[11] Lam. 4:17 most likely reflects this state of affairs.

arm of Pharoah had been broken (Ezek 30:20-21). The brief and ineffectual intervention of Pharoah Hophra (Apries: 589-570) took place, therefore, between January and April 587, just about one year after the Babylonians had first invested Jerusalem[12]. It was sometime in the course of these few months that the sorry events which earned the fierce denunciation of Jeremiah occurred.

To sum up: Nebuchadnezzar invested Jerusalem from the middle of Jan. 588. Toward the end of that year an emancipation of Hebrew slaves, male and female, was effected within Jerusalem. This was rescinded, however, with the raising of the siege following the arrival of the Egyptian expeditionary force sent by Pharoah Hophra to relieve the city early in 587.

If the historical circumstances surrounding these events are more or less clear, the actual nature of the social institutions involved and their legal basis are far from being so.

Jer. 34 and Deuteronomy

A close examination of the vocabulary and style of Jer 34:8-22 leaves no room for doubt that the literary formulation of the episode there described has drawn its inspiration generally from the Book of Deuteronomy[13], and specifically from ch.15 therein.

The opening declaration of the prophet which refers to the covenant at the time of the Exodus (v. 13) corresponds almost word for word to Deut 29:24. Indeed, the covenant at Sinai is a recurrent theme of the Deuteronomist (cf. 4:23; 5:2,3; 9:9; 28:69; 29:11, 13, 21; 31:16). The description of Egypt as the "house of bondage" (Jer. 34:13) is more frequent in D (5:6; 6:12; 7:8; 8:14; 13:6, 11) than in the rest of the Pentateuch (Ex 13:3, 14; 20:2). The expression "to do what is right in God's eyes" (Jer 34:15) is characteristically Deuteronomic (6:18; 12:25, 28; 13:19; 21:9) occurring elsewhere in the Pentateuch but once (Ex 15:26). Similarly, the phrase "transgressing my covenant" (Jer 34:18) occurs in the Torah only in Deut 17:2. The maledictions of D seem especially to have left their mark on this chapter for the threat of Israel becoming "a horror to all the kingdoms of the earth" (Jer 34:17) has its source in Deut 28:25. Likewise, Jer 34:18 was inspired by Deut 27:26, while the dire punishment of Jer 34:20 that the carcasses of those who transgressed the covenant would "become food for all the birds of the sky and the beasts of the earth," has been drawn directly from Deut. 28:26.

These many stylistic parallels reinforce the inescapable conclusions to be derived from a detailed comparison between the legal material of Jer 34 and Deut. 15. In the aggregate they exclude any possibility of the direct dependence of the events of Jer. 34 upon Ex. 21:1-11[14]. The evidence may be subsumed as follows:

(i) Jeremiah's characteristic phrase for manumission is *šillaḥ ḥofšî* (34:9, 10, 14, 16. cf. v. 10). This is precisely the term employed in Deut. 15:12, 13, 18. In Ex. 21, however, this formula is restricted to the release of a slave in compensation for the infliction of permanent bodily injury (Ex. 21:26f.), whereas the standard technical term for manumission is *yaṣa' (l)ḥofšî* (*ibid.*, vv. 2, 5; cf. 3, 4, 7, 11).

---

[12] For the importance of Ezekiel's anti-Egyptian prophecies as a historic source, see Malamat, *Jerusalem*, 42f.; *IEJ*, 152f. The relevant dates are also to be found in M. Greenberg, *Encyclopaedia Judaica*, 6, 1081f.

[13] For an exhaustive listing of characteristically Deuteronomic phraseology, see Weinfeld, *op. cit.* 320-65, esp. 359-61.

[14] The contrary thesis of A.F. Puuko, *BWAT* 13 (1913), 126-53, esp. 146f., has been effectively refuted by Y. Kaufmann, *Tôledôt Hā'Emûnāh Hayisre'ēlît* (1947), III, 437, esp. n. 39.

(ii) In Jer. 34:14 the previously discussed phrase is followed by *me'immak* which is the characteristic style of Deut. 15 (vv. 12, 13, 18).

(iii) The narrative refers to *ha'iwrî wᵉha'iwrîyāh* (Jer. 34:9) exactly corresponding to *ha'iwrî 'ow ha'iwrîyāh* of Deut. 15:12 and in contrast to Ex. 21:2 which provides only for the *'ebed 'iwrî.*

(iv) Even through the prophet's citation of the law mentions only the male Hebrew slave (Jer. 34:14), vv. 9, 10, 11, 16 leave no doubt that the law in its operation made no discrimination between the sexes. This is the situation that exists in Deut. 15:12, 17. On the other hand, the legislation in Ex. 21:7-11 sharply differentiates between the fate of the male and female slave.

(v) The Hebrew slave is several times designated "brother" (Jer. 34:9, 14, 17^2). This corresponds exactly to the formula of Deut. 15:12. In fact, the use of this appellation is one of the distinguishing features of D, where it appears more than twenty-five times in legal contexts.

(vi) Jeremiah's citation of the law begins with the phrase *miqqēṣ šeba' šānîm*[15] (Jer. 34:14). The same words head the chapter in D (15:1), in which the emanicpation of slaves is dealt with and its only other occurrence is also in that book (31:10).

(vii) Jer. 34:14 expresses the means of enslavement by *'ašer yimmākēr lᵉkā* and Deut. 15:12 has *kî yimmākēr lᵉkā*. Ex. 21:2, on the other hand, has *kî tiqneh* regarding a male slave and *kî yimkōr iš 'et bittô* (v. 7) in respect of a female slave.

(viii) Both pentateuchal sources limit the term of service to six years. However, while the formulations of Jer. 34:14 and Deut. 15:12 coincide (*wa'abadᵉkā šēš šānîm*) the word order of Ex. 21:2 differs (*šēš šānîm ya'abōd*).

(ix) Both Jeremiah (34:13) and D (15:15) associate the emancipation of slaves with the redemption from Egypt, a connection that is wholly absent from Ex. 21[16].

Deut. 15

The literary analysis as well as matters of substance demonstrate conclusively that the events that occurred in Jerusalem during the Babylonian siege, as detailed in Jer. 34:8-10, were grounded in D. This conclusion, however, raises serious problems of exegesis, for at first glance there would seem to be no way of reconciling the action of Zedekiah with the legal provisions of Deut. 15.

The relevant material of that chapter naturally divides into two parts. The first eleven verses deal with the remission of debts in the septennial release; the subsequent seven verses (12-18) restrict the service of the Hebrew slave, male and female, to six years. The two institutions would seem to be wholly unrelated. The cancellation of debts took place within the context of a fixed seven-year cycle of universal application. This interpretation is certainly assured by the initial formula *miqqēṣ šeba' šānîm* (v. 1), more closely defined as the "seventh year, the year of the release" (*šᵉmiṭṭāh* v. 9), as well as by the employment of the same expression

[15] This is the text in all the ancient versions except G in which "seven" has been "corrected" to "six". The meaning of *miqqēṣ* here is not pertinent to the present discussion.

[16] For the emphasis on the redemption from Egypt in D, cf. 5:15; 16:12; 24:18, 22 *et al.*; cf. Weinfeld, 326f.

and definition in Deut. 31:10 in a passage that unambiguously points to the fixed, cyclic and national nature of the institution referred to. On the other hand, the manumission of the slaves would seemingly have had to occur on an individual basis, since each bondman's six year period of service would naturally be completed at a different time.

In contrast to the apparently plain intent of Deut. 15:12-18, the action of Zedekiah took no account of the individual slave's term of service, but involved the general and simultaneous emancipation of Jerusalem's entire slave community. Appropriately, the royal edict is repeatedly designated *d^erôr* (vv. 8, 15, 17), a technical term that, to judge from its other biblical usages and ancient Near Eastern analogies[17], is applicable only to an institution administered on a community-wide basis (Lev. 25:10; Is. 61:1-2; Ezek. 46:17). How is this to be reconciled with the indubitable fact that the legislation of Deut. 15 in its substance and literary formulation constituted the legal and theological foundation upon which rested the events that took place during the Babylonian siege of Jerusalem? This problem is exacerbated by another fact. Jeremiah himself acknowledges that Zedekiah's enactment was in fulfillment of, and in accord with, the provisions of the Sinaitic covenant, which earlier generations had honored more in the breach than in the observance (vv. 13-14). He cites directly from the original law code, the quotational form being confirmed by the introductory *le'môr* and by the presence of the 2nd. pers. sing. – *l^ekā, w'abad^ekā, w^ešillaḥtô* – in contrast to the use of the plural in the rest of his oration. Significant, because it is not in D, is the absence of the term *d^erôr* despite its prominence otherwise in the chapter. The question then remains as to the nature of Zedekiah's edict and its relationship to the legislation of Deut. 15.

The release of slaves and the sabbatical year

In actual fact, no real contradiction between the Deuteronomist and Jer. 34 need be assumed, if the latter be understood to be reflecting an ancient interpretation of the intent of the former.

The phenomenon of debt-bondage in Israel is attested in several sources[18]. The institution is presupposed by Lev. 25:39, which must be understood in the light of the preceding legislation referring to the impoverished Israelite who is not to be subjected to usury (vv. 35f.)[19]. Similarly, the sale into slavery of the thief who lacks the means to make restitution for his theft (Ex. 22:2) is nothing but a form of debt-bondage. That the seizure of the defaulting debtor by his creditor was indeed practised in life is clear from the narrative of 2 Kings 4:1 and from the fulminations of Amos (2:6; 8:6) and Deutero-Isaiah (50:1). In the time of Nehemiah people in financial straits were driven to press their sons and daughters into slavery (Neh. 5:5). The proverbial observation that "the borrower is the lender's slave" (Prov. 22:7) certainly reflected a sad reality of life, even if the enslavement of a debtor is not officially explicated in biblical legal texts. Although the sources do not say so outright, it is obvious that there must have been an inextricable connection between the remission of debts and the manumission of slaves[20]. Lev. 25:47-54 provides for the possible early redemption of an Israelite

---

[17] On the *andurāru*, see G.R. Driver and J.C. Miles, *The Babylonian Laws*, I (1952), 224; II (1955), 207; J. Lewy, *Eretz-Israel*, 5 (1959) 21*-31*.

[18] See I. Mendelsohn, *Slavery in the Ancient Near East* (1949), 14-19, 23-33; cf. E.E. Urbach, *Papers of the Institute of Jewish Studies London* (1964), 4.

[19] A distinction must be made between a social phenomenon on the one hand and the acceptance or rejection of the same in the codified law on the other; cf. the remarks of M. Elon, *Freedom of the Debtor's Person in Jewish Law* [Hebrew] (1964), 2, n. 9.

[20] This was noted by S.R. Driver, *Deuteronomy* (1902), 177-8; Mendelsohn, *op. cit.*, 147, n. 257; cf. also R.H. Pfeiffer, *Introduction to the O.T.* (1948), 222; R. de Vaux, *Ancient Israel* (1961), 83. A. Menes, *BZAW* 50 (1928), 79-80, also interpreted Deut. 15:12-18 as referring to the manumission of enslaved debtors and explained 31:10ff as presupposing the equality, i.e., the freedom, of all Israel following the sabbatical year. It is likely that Jer. 17:4 *w^ešāmaṭṭāh ... w^eha'abadtîkā* reflects the close connection between the *š^emiṭṭah* and release from slavery.

driven by poverty to sell himself to a resident alien. In 2 Kings 4:1-7 the peonage of the sons of the impoverished widow is ended after the miracle performed by Elisha enables her to pay off her creditors. Since the law codes, biblical and Mesopotamian,[21] limit the terms of bondage, they must have looked upon the service as simply a distraint of the debtor's person for the purposes of liquidating the debt.

It is difficult to believe that one who entered into slavery for debt should have had to continue in bondage beyond the cancellation of the original financial obligation. If, as is certain, insolvency constituted the prime cause of Hebrew slavery, then it is self-evident that the major portion of the slave population would automatically and simultaneously have gained its freedom with the general nullification of indebtedness[22]. For this reason, the juxtaposition of the septennial remission of debts and the manumission of slaves forms a perfectly natural and logical nexus. This is precisely the situation that exists in Deut. 15 and it is not surprising that Jeremiah should quote the legislation of Deut. 15:12 in connection with the mass liberation of slaves and that the entire pericope of Jer. 34 should be saturated with the language of that chapter[23].

It is apparent, therefore, that in Zedekiah's day the provisions of Deut. 15:12 were interpreted in the context of the sabbatical year. The prescribed six year limit on debt-bondage was regarded as a maximum that would be reduced by the incidence of the sabbatical year[24].

Evidence for the existence in ancient times of such a correlation between the *š^e^miṭṭah* and the manumission of slaves is provided by the Targum Pseudo-Jonathan to the Pentateuch[25]. This version has preserved traditions to this effect in its exegetical amplifications of its renderings of Ex. 21:7 and 22:2. In the former passage, the release of a slave-girl is differentiated from that of a bondman. "She shall not be freed as male slaves are" says the text, to which the Palestinian Targum adds ". . . but in the year of the *s^e^mittah.* The second passage legislates concerning the thief who, lacking the means to make restitution, must be sold into slavery. The Targum again specifies that the term of service lasts "until the *š^e^miṭṭah* year."

Now this exegesis of the Pseudo-Jonathan is in direct contradiction to the Tannaitic *halakhah*[26]. For this reason it must represent a much earlier legal stratum and reflect a tradition of great antiquity, one that is in direct line with that of Jer. 34 in its interpretation of the legislation of Deut. 15, namely, that the remission of debts in the sabbatical year automatically carries with it the freeing of slaves sold because of insolvency.

---

[21] Cf. Code of Hammurapi, § 117 on which see Driver & Miles, *op. cit.*, I, 217-221.

[22] Thus, the *mīšarum* edict of Ammiṣaduqa makes clear provision for the automatic release of citizens in debt-servitude; see F.R. Kraus, *Ein Edikt des Königs Ammi-ṣaduqa von Babylon* (1958), 40, 41, § 18 (= *ANET*, 528, § 20). For the relation of this clause to CH § 117, see Kraus, 167-72.

[23] The contention of W. Rudolph, *Jeremiah* (1947), 189, that the connection between Jer. 34 and Deut. 15 is "secondary" cannot possibly be maintained; cf. J. Bright, *Jeremiah* (1965), 223-4.

[24] It is not necessary to assume with M. David, *OTS* 5 (1948), 63-79, that a socio-legal development took place whereby the original Deuteronomic individual manumission after six years yielded to a general one in a fixed year in the time of Jeremiah. In fact, the evidence seems to show that the reverse process took place, namely that the earlier interpretation of Deut. 15:12 which connected the "seventh year" with the sabbatical was later abandoned.

[25] *Pseudo-Jonathan*, ed. M. Ginsburger (1903), 136, 138. On the remnants of the earlier *halākhāh* in this Targum, see B.J. Roberts, *The O.T. Text and Versions* (1951), 203f. and the literature there cited. It is remarkable that as late as the 12th century, the Jewish Bible commentator Joseph b. Isaac Bekhor Shor (of Orleans) explained the "seventh year" of Ex. 21:2 in terms of the *š^e^miṭṭah* rather than the seventh year of service.

[26] Cf. Mekilta d. R.Y., *Mishpaṭim* I, ed. H.S. Horovitz & I.A. Rabin (reprint of 1960), 249; Sifra, *Behar* II, 6, ed. A.H. Weiss (1862), 107b; Sifrei, *Re'eh*, § 111-12, ed. M. Friedmann (1864), 97^a-b^; P. Kid. 1:2; b Arak. 18^b^; Nid. 48^a^.

The sabbatical year 588-587 B.C.

It has been shown earlier that Zedekiah's proclamation of emancipation must have taken place late in the year 588 B.C. The most likely time would have been the Autumn New Year festival[27]. Lev. 25:8-10 indicates a Fall to Fall cycle for the sabbatical year. Deut. 31:10 provides for a septennial national assembly in the Fall in connection with the year of release. The national conclave held in Jerusalem in the time of Nehemiah took place in the seventh month (Neh. 8:2; 9:1) and, significantly enough, the provisions of the covenant then drawn up included the fulfillment of the sabbatical year legislation requiring the fallowness of the land and the remission of debts (Neh 10:32). This last item was directly connected with the distraint of persons for reasons of insolvency (Neh 5:1-13).

It follows from the above that the year 588-587 would have been a sabbatical year in Judea. The Temple would then have fallen in a post-sabbatical year (586)[28]. This fact exactly accords with rabbinic tradition[29]. The previous sabbatical year would have been 595-594. From the Babylonian Chronicle we now know that Zedekiah came to the throne soon after Nebuchadnezzar's capture of Jerusalem on 2nd Adar in his seventh regnal year, i.e., 15/16 March, 597[30]. His accession year covered Nisan-Tishri 597. This period was known in Akkadian as the *rēš šarrūti*[31] for which the Hebrew equivalent is *rēšît mamlākāh*[32] (Jer. 27:1; 28:1). The accession year of Zedekiah would then have fallen within the fourth year of the sabbatical cycle 595-594. This indeed provides a satisfactory explanation for the otherwise obscure superscription of Jer. 28:1 which equates the "beginning of the reign of Zedekiah" (*bᵉrēšît mamleket Ṣidkiyāhû*) with "the fourth year."[33]

In the light of the evidence here presented it seems clear that Gordon's original suggestion that Jer. 34 reflects the sabbatical legislation is correct. We now have a fixed date 588-587 B.C. as a base for the determination of some other sabbatical calculations[34].

---

27 It should be noted that the *mīšarum* of Ammiṣaduqa formally took effect on Nisan 1st, the Babylonian New Year Festival (§ 3); cf. J.J. Finkelstein, *RA* 63 (1969), 49, 55; cf. S. Mowinckel, *The Psalms in Israel's Worship*, I (1962), 128f.

28 For the date 586, see Malamat, *op. cit.*; Thiele, *op. cit.*

29 b. Arak. 11b, Ta'an. 29b.

30 D.J. Wiseman, *Chronicles of the Chaldean Kings* etc. (1956), 32-35, 48, 72-73.

31 On the *rēš šarrūti*, see H. Tadmor, *JNES*, 15 (1956), 227 n. 11; *Encyclopaedia Miqrāʾît* 4, col. 258, n. 6 & cols. 267-8; in *Studies* in Honor of B. Landsberger (1968), 352 & n. 13; R. de Vaux, *op. cit.*, 194.

32 Cf. also Jer. 26:1; 49:34. In 27:1, MT "Jehoiakim" must certainly be corrected to "Zedekiah" (so Syriac) in the light of vv. 3, 12 and the reference to the exile in vv. 16-22; cf. also 28:1. In 49:34ff. the reference to Elam can have nothing to do with the Babylonian Chronicle's report of the defeat of an Elamite army (Wiseman, *op. cit.*, 72-73, cf. 36, 48) since that document says nothing about the utter destruction of Elam and the exile of its people which are the themes of Jeremiah's prophecy. Hence there is no reason to understand *bᵉrēšît malkût* other than the equivalent of *rēš šarrūti.*

33 On Jer. 28:1 see the present writer's study in *Hagut Iwrît b'Amerika* [Hebrew], ed. M. Zohori, *et al.*, I (1972), 121-30.

34 The computation is complicated by the question as to whether the Jubilee year constituted a blank year or the first of the next sabbatical cycle. The lack of explicitness in the biblical formulation gave rise to a difference of opinion among the Tannaim; cf. b. R.H. 8^{b}-9^{a}; Ned. 61^{a}; Arak. $12^{a\text{-}b}$, 32^{b}.

THE WORSHIP OF THE GOLDEN CALF

Jack M. Sasson
Univ. of North Carolina, Chapel Hill, North Carolina, U.S.A.

Whether among the rabbis of old or the scholars of today, there has always been a fascination with the "golden calf" episode. The reasons are quite fathomable. The narrative that unfolds in Ex 32 contains elements which invariably arouse strong unrest. An indignant protagonist with right on his side is challenged by a willful people eager to sample forbidden fruits. Another leader, otherwise thoughtful and wise, abandons caution to join a popular cause. To such materials are added colorful, if not dramatic, vignettes: a festival before an idol, a trial by ordeal, a fervent appeal for clemency, and a spectacularly bloody massacre. All this within the compass of 35 verses.

The following remarks should be prefaced by what will not be attempted. We will not judge whether this narrative is to be considered a unity or a composite.[1] Nor shall we speculate on the possibility of it being a post-Jeroboamic polemic against bovine cults as opposed to a historical tradition that might have affected the cults of early Israel.[2] This paper will not decide on the identity of the deity, symbolized by a calf, be it Ba'al, Sin, YHWH, or a divinized Moses.[3] Finally, it will not delve into the mysterious acts of grinding the golden calf, and concocting a portion from its chars.[4] We will simply focus on the act of adoration which the Hebrews presented before the calf.

---

1 On the problem of unity for this chapter the debate is still raging. Beyerlin (*Origins and History of the Oldest Sinaic Tradition*, 18-22) finds mostly "E" material, with a touch of "D". In general Eissfeldt (*The Old Testament, an Instruction*, 195, 201) holds similar views, but assigns vs. 17-18, 25-29, to "L." I. Lewy (*JBL* 9(1959), 318-319) thinks of "J" as a basic narrator upon whom relied three other annotators, "E_1," "E_2," and "D." G.W. Coats (*Rebellion in the Wilderness*, 188) unravels Aaronic additions (vs. 1-6, 21-29), "D" (7-14), "E" (?) (1-6), in addition to the basic "J." And so forth . . .

2 Much has been written concerning the dating of the "Golden Calf." S. Lehming in *VT* 10 (1960), 16-50; R. DeVaux, *Bible et Orient*, 151-163; H. Aberbach and L. Smolar in *JBL* 86 (1967), 129-40; G.W. Coats, *op. cit.*, 185-186; H. Beyerlin, *op. cit.*, 126-133; Y. Kaufman, *Religion of Israel*, 270-273; W.F. Albright, *Yahweh and the Gods of Canaan* (1968), 171-172.

3 See J.M. Sasson, *VT* 18 (1968), 380-387; Lloyd R. Bailey, *HUCA* 42 (1971), 97-115.

4 Some scholars have commented upon this episode's relationship to Num. 5:11, either to claim or to deny possible connections (cf. R. DeVaux, *Ancient Israel*, 150; U. Cassuto, *Commentary to Exodus*, 249-250; Beyerlin, *op. cit.*, 131). Others have brought the evidence of Ugaritic texts to bear. In this, Loewenstamm has the most complete exposition in *Biblica* 48 (1967), 481-490 (note also Fensham, IEJ, 16 (1966), 191-193 and P.L. Watson, JAOS, 92 (1972), 60-64). He compares the fate of the calf in the hands of Moses to that of Mot in those of 'Anat: "With sword she doth cleave him / with fan she doth winnow him – / with fire she doth burn him – / with hand-mill she grinds him – / In the field she doth sow him. Birds eat his remnants / consuming his portions. / Flitting from remnant to remnant." UT 49:ii:31-37 (Translation Ginsberg *ANET*^{2}, 140; cf. Gordon, *UT*, §§ 9.11, 9.52, 10.4). Note that, in the variant 49:v:19, Mot's remains were cast upon the sea. The text breaks before we learn whether these waters were drunk. It is interesting,

Scholars have displayed impressive imagination when moved to describe this worship. With few exceptions, they would conjure orgiastic images worthy of Hollywood at it most inventive moments. Despite the absence of any significant evidence from actual texts, this sexual licentiousness is attributed to Canaanite influence. As random examples of this position, one can quote in quick succession, the following authorities:

1) Martin Noth: "Special emphasis is laid on the extravagant celebrations at the cult feast which inaugurate the new divine worhsip (v. 6). True, eating (and drinking) form part of the rite of communal sacrifice. Here, however, they are expressly mentioned with a purpose; "and rose up to play' doubtless refers to sexual orgies (see Gen. 26:8) such as played a part in the Canaanite fertility cults."[5]

2) Umberto Cassuto: "But the people, who had already broken down every barrier, were beyond control . . . ; *and the people sat down to eat and drink and rose up to play* [means:] in accordance with the custom obtaining at the feasts of the people addicted to the worship of the gods of fertility and the unchastity connected therewith."[6]

3) Johannes Pedersen: "The day began with burnt offerings and peace offerings, and the people sat down to eat and drink. They then arose to abandon themselves (*l^e ṣaḥḥeḳ*). A noise heard as from a singing people, which reached the ears of Moses and Joshua, and when they approached they saw the people abandoning themselves to an ecstatic tumult without restraint or self-control . . ."[7]

4) J.P. Hyatt: "This suggests a fertility ceremony probably with obscene rites. In Gen. 26:8; 39:14, 17, the verb *ṣaḥaḳ* (piel) has a sexual connotation."[8]

Hopefully, the following lines will show that such descriptions are not legitimate and that the Hebrew text displays no such intent. Rather than wild abandoned acts, the scene that unfolds before the calf was probably an orderly ritual that followed practices will known to the ancient Near East, festivals that consisted of a (ritual) banquet followed by sports, miming, and antiphonal singing to honor the gods.[9]

---

in this respect, to note that Deut. 9:21 speaks of the calf's remains as strewn upon a stream that descended from the holy mountain. R. Gradwohl, *ThZ* 19 (1963), 50-53 considers the Deut. passage as primary over Ex. 32:20. If true, we would have here a strong remembrance of the role that divine rivers played in ordeals (*Contra*, see Beyerlin, *op. cit.*, 131).

5 *Exodus*, 248, *Contra* H. Schmid, *Mose*, 82-83.

6 *Commentary on Exodus*, 413-414.

7 *Israel*, IV, 468.

8 *Exodus* (New Century Bible, 1971), 305.

9 It might be worth quoting a generous portion of a ritual which was presented before Ishtar in Mari of the Middle Bronze Age. Because better preserved Akkadian documents – to say nothing of Egyptian or Hittite texts – could have been equally *à propos*, it should be stated that this choice is made for the following reasons. First, the text, published by Dossin in the early days of Mari scholarship (*RA* 35 [1938], 2-3), deserves a newer rendering. Secondly, the "Amorite" milieu of Mari seems to be, as research increasingly shows, seminal to the history of the Hebrew people.

"(I.) [. . . . . .] will be collected [. . . . .] he places in Ishtar's own temple. According to the king's wish, he [the king] lies down in the bed of Ishtar. In that early morning, the banquet of Ishtar will be set out earlier than usual. The temple of Ishtar is continually purified, while (?) they place Nin-(i)gizibbara before Ishtar [. . . .] on the left side of Nin-(i)gizibbara [. . . .] are standing right and left. The brewer, the carpenter, the leather-worker, the cord-maker, the fuller, all the skilled craftsmen deposit their instruments. The barbers stand beside the other craftsmen and, when this is done, they deposit their razors and pans (?) of roasted flour before Ishtar. The roasted flour and *sasqum*- flour which has been wetted with water, is spread out in the pans (?) of roasted flour. They fill with water the bronze *sahum*-cauldron and place (it) on the ground [. . . . . .]

(II.) [. . . . .] and [. . . .] Latarak and the Angubbi-deities take their places. The emblems of the goddesses are brought out from their shrines and placed in the temple of Ishtar, to the right and the left. When this is done, the king wears a *lulumtum* – garment and, behind the *kalū* – singers, sits on a sailor's seat. One of the king's followers, who is liked by the king, sits beside the king on a lower chair. No one can sit in front of the king. *girseqû* – bodyguards stand to the right and the left. The

The Hebrew text contains the following verses to describe the worship of the calf.

Verses 5-6: "Aaron saw [the calf], and built an altar before it. Aaron proclaimed: 'Tomorrow shall be a feast to YHWH.' They awoke early the next day, presented burnt offerings and brought up sacrifices of well being (*wayyaʿalû ʿōlôt wayyaggīšû šelāmîm*). The people sat to eat, drink, and *wayya=qûmû leṣaḥḥēq.*"

Verse 8: YHWH tells Moses to join with his people for "they have made for themselves a molten calf,[10] prostrated themselves before it, and sacrificed to it (*ʿasû lāhem massēkāh wayyištaḥawû-lô wayyizbeḥû-lô*).

Verses 17-18: Upon returning from the mountain, "Joshua, hearing the uproar the people were making, said to Moses, 'Listen! there is fighting in the camp.' Moses replied;

> 'This is not the clamor of warriors *(qôl ʿanôt gebûrāh)*
> nor the clamor of a defeated people *(qôl ʿanôt ḥalušāh)*
> it is the sound of singing *(ʿannôt)* that I hear.' [NEB].

Verse 19a: "As soon as Moses approached the camp, he saw the calf and the *meḥōlôt.*"

---

kalū – singers sing . . . . at the beginning of the month. If (at) the beginning of the month, the *muḫḫûm*-ecstatic has departed, and (thus) could not [. . . .] for ecstasy, out of prison [. . . .] they reach (?) [. . . .] they release [. . . . .] prison.
(III.) The *kalū*-priests sing the song I.GI.IT.TE.EN.DI.BA (and) after the race for [. . . . .] he (?) has arrived (?), they sing AN.NU.WA.ŠE the song of [. . . . .] . As they begin to sing AN.NU.WA.ŠE, the king begins to stand, (thereupon), one of the *kalū*-priests begins to stand and sings ER.SI.MA.ŠE to Enlil (accompanied by) a *ḫalhallatu*-drum. At the beginning of the ER.SI.MA.ŠE, the *ākilu* performer sits down and performs. After the performance, the juggler juggles. After the juggler, the wrestlers approach. After the wrestlers, the acrobats tumble. After the acrobats, the (female) masqueraders (?) masquerade [cf. CAD K, 172-183; 184]. As they finish the AN.NU.(W)A.ŠE, the king sits . . ."
In this ritual, note the following sequence: An early meal – presentation of divine offerings before the gods and their emblem – chanting with musical accompaniment – displaying acrobatic feats and dramatic performances –. Libating and provisioning before the deities occurs in the unquoted segments.

[10] The literature concerning the fabrication of the idol has also been quite large. One of the difficulties concerns the destruction of the calf, some scholars remaining unconvinced that a "golden" calf could be burnt. Another deals with the casting of the calf. On these, see Noth, *VT* 9 (1959), 419-22 (Petuchowsky, *VT* 10 (1960), 74); Gradwohl, *op. cit.*, 50-53. Cassuto, *op. cit.*, 412-413 thinks of gold plating over wooden material. In this he could be supported by ARMT 13: 2, 4, 9; *Syria* 20 (1939), 107.
Two further suggestions can be made in this regard. It is possible to think of the calf as produced from wood with gold encrustation throughout the body. A bronze calf similarly decorated from the neighborhood of Tell Dan, has been published by Schaeffer (*Syria*, 43 [1966], 14-19). At Mari, it is to be observed, sacrificial bull were adorned with horn-sheaths and pectoral of gold (see the convenient illustration of the "sacrificial scene" in Parrot's *Sumer: The Dawn of Art*, 276-277). Thus the calf could have been almost totally a wooden product with golden embellishments only.
More radical is a suggestion made by many scholars (Bailey, *op. cit.*, 97³), among whom Eissfeldt (*Kleine Schriften* [1963], 282), which is followed by Schaeffer in his above-quoted article. The god "who will go before [the Hebrews]" (Ex. 32:1) is thought of as a statue of a calf mounted atop a portable standard (cf. *Yahweh-nissî* of Ex. 7:15 and the emblems and standards brought out in the Mari ritual). A representation of a bull on his pedestal can be found in Gurney, *The Hittites*, 149. See also the many depictions collected by Schaeffer, *ibid.* Should this be true, then one could understand the difficult *massēkāh* of Ex. 32:4, 8; Deut 9:16, Ps. 106:19, not as an adjective usually translated "molten," but as the word for "platform pedestal" upon which was fixed the deity. As it is, the dictionaries (e.g. *BDB*, 650-651) recognize two meanings for this word. One with the rendering "molten;" the other denoting "woven stuff, web." An Akkadian *mapras* or *mapris*, masculine formation of the root *nsk* is known (*AHw*, 619) as a "rug" destined for temple use. One text however (*AOTU*, I, 120, 31) speaks of a goddess who awakens in heaven on a *massiku* of gold. Perhaps it is important to note that, when according to v. 20, the furious Moses approaches the scene of worship, *only the calf* is mentioned as pulverized, indicating the *massēkāh* to have been a separate, golden, entity. Impossible to pulverize, it was left untouched.

From these passages one can extract at least eight terms used to describe the ritual as it unfolded. Of these, the following will not occupy our attention as they have been widely studied, more or less precisely explained, and elicited little or no controversy.

A) *lĕhaʿălôt ʿôlôt* (verse 6): 'to present burnt offerings.'

B) *lĕhaggîš šĕlāmîm* (verse 6): 'to bring forward sacrifices of well-being.'

C) *lĕhištaḥăwôt* (verse 8): 'to prostrate oneself (so as to strike the forehead on the ground).'

D) *lizbēăh* (verse 8): 'to offer sacrifice.'

It is to be noted at this point that both Hebrew and Canaanite cults share the above mentioned terminology.[11] Requiring further elucidation, however, are the following terms:

E) *(lāqûm) leṣaḥḥēq* (verse 6).[12]

F) the infinitives *ʿanôt (qal)* and *ʿannôt (piʿʿel)* (Verses 17-18).

G) the noun *meḥōlāh* (verse 19).

The *qal* of *ṣḥq*, 'to laugh' is found 6 times in the O.T. Not surprisingly, all the biblical occurrences are found in the Isaac narrative, where the obvious word-play on the name of the protagonist obtains. Two of the seven OT attestations of the *piʿʿel* of this verb are also embedded in the same narrative. In its usage, the *piʿʿel* of *ṣḥq* denotes the amusement one derives either from observing or in joining an act which involves physical exertions.

Most suggestive, for the prupose of confirming this interpretation, is its attestation in Judg 16:25, where it parallels the verb *śḥq*, also in the *piʿʿel*: "the tyrants of the Philistines were gathered to offer a great sacrifice to their god Dagon, and to rejoice; for they said: our god has delivered Samson, our enemy, in our hands' . . . when they became happy, they said: 'Call Samson out and have him sport before us [*wiyśaḥḥēq* . . . *lānû*].' So they summoned Samson out of prison and he performed gymnastics before them [*wayyĕṣaḥḥēq lipnēhem*]." This translation, by the way, could explain the Philistines' utter lack of suspicion when Samson placed himself between the pillars. No doubt they had expected a superior acrobatic display.

Gen 21:9 describes Sarah's fears, when she notices Hagar's son, Ishmael, *meṣaḥḥēq*. It is doubtful that the rendering "laughing at him [NEB]," mocking [AV, RV] or "playing [*Torah*]" could have furnished an offense serious enough to merit the consequent events. This is one reason why most modern translators turn to the readings of the Septuagint and the Vulgate: "*paizonta meta Isaak tou uiou autēs*", *ludentem cum Isaac filio suo*, and offer "playing with her son Isaac" (*Jerusalem, Anchor, Donay, RSV*).[13] That chronology would have Ishmael a teen-ager while Isaac a mere child, was not easily dismissed either by Talmudic Rabbis or by St. Paul (Gal. 4:29). In general, they opted for sensational solutions to justify Sarah's ire.[14]

The compiler of Genesis, however, shows definite prejudice against hunters, (over)-violent behavior, and outdoorsmen (e.g., Nimrod, Simeon & Levi, Esau). According to Gen. 16:12 and 21:20, Ishmael was to become known for his physical strength and for his talent in archery. It is probable, therefore, that what Sarah observed with disdain, if not fear, was Ishmael performing athletic feats, a deed that went against the matriarch's approval. The event, it should be noted, occurred during a weaning ceremony, when ritual sacrifices were includ-

---

[11] In general, see the remarks of R. DeVaux, *Ancient Israel*, 438-440, H.H. Rowley, *Worship in Ancient Israel* (1967), 125 ff.

[12] Beyerlin, *op. cit.*, 127, wonders whether this passage is secondary.

[13] Latin *ludō* sometimes, Greek *paizein* hardly ever, denotes athletic gaming.

[14] For bibliography, see Driver, *Genesis*, 210[1].

ed among various festivities (cf. 1 Sam 1:24). A similar rendering arrived at unintentionally, the JPS's 'making sport', could be adopted for *meṣaḥḥēq* in Gen. 21:9.

"To sport," with its wide range of meaning is also usable in translating another attestation of *ṣḥq* in the *piʿʿel* associated with Isaac's saga. With the preposition *ʾēt*, 'alongside, beside,' followed by a PN (Rebekkah), *meṣaḥḥēq* could more accurately be equated with "to banter" or with the slang expression "to horse-around."

This verb is construed absolutely in Gen. 19:14. Lot is having trouble convincing his sons-in-law of his earnestness: "*wayyĕhî kimĕṣaḥḥēq bĕʿēnēy ḥătānāyw.* To his sons-in-law, he seemed as if he were clowning." A translation such as "joking (*Anchor*), "jesting (*RSV, ICC, JPS,* Torah)," or "mocking (Driver, *Genesis*)" would hardly do justice to a scene where tension was carefully nurtured. Here was Lot, sitting at the gate, minding his own business. When unusual beings approach him, he offers them his hospitality. In quick succession, his guests are pounced upon by lecherous crowds, perform a wondrous act, reveal the doom of Sodom, and advise him to immediately pack and abandon his home. In rushing to save his married daughters' family, is is unlikely that Lot's warnings were delivered calmly. No doubt, a certain amount of huffing and puffing, punctuated by gesticulations must have aroused his in-law's suspicions. Hence, the use of *meṣaḥḥēq* is understandable.

Joseph's story contains the last two examples of *piʿʿel ṣḥq*, construed with the preposition *b(a)*, "in the presence of, before." Potiphar's wife is fabricating an alibi to blame Joseph for her foiled seduction attempt. She calls a large group of servants and bitingly states (Gen. 39:14): "Look here! He brought us a Hebrew fellow to sport in our presence; (instead) he came to tup me, but I screamed my head off . . ." In this verse, the accusation of sexual abuse is found in *bāʾ ʾēlay liškab ʿimmi* and not *leṣaḥḥēq bānû*. Speiser's (*Anchor*) 'to make love to us' reduces the sarcasm to a mass orgy. Redford's 'to insult us' is interpretation rather than translation.[15] Other renditions have the standard 'to mock.' Upon Potiphar's return, the accusation is repeated again, but in a shortened form:[16] "The Hebrew servant whom you brought for us to sport in my presence . . .". An etc., . . . is presumed at this point.

The equation of *ṣḥq* with *śḥq*, both in the *piʿʿel* in the above-quoted passage from Judges permits consideration of one more Old Testament example. 2 Sam 6, repeated in 1 Chron 15-16 with some important variations such as inclusion of a role for the Levites, contains a description of the jubilations accompanying the ark's introduction with a tent erected by David. Since this passage preserves one of the oldest descriptions of early Hebrew festivities, it might be worth while quoting a generous passage:

> "David and all the people who were with him proceeded from Baʿale-yehudah, to bring up from there the ark of God which was called by a name, a name (written) upon it [the ark]; 'YHWH Sebaoth, who sits upon the cherubim.'[17] They loaded the ark of God upon a new cart, and brought it out from the house of Abinadab which is in the hill . . . And David and all Israel *performed* before YHWH, (accompanied) with all manner of wooden-instruments (made of) cypress, and with cythers, psalteries, timbrels, sistra, and cymbals . . .[18] And David went to bring up the ark of the Lord from Obed-Edom (into) David's city with joy. As soon as those who carried the ark of God made six paces, [David] sacrificed an ox and a fatling. And David was whirling with all his might before God [*mĕkarkēr bĕkol ʿōz*] while he was girded with a linen ephod only.[19] So David and all Israel (proceeded) to bring up the ark of the Lord with shouting and (with) the blast of the ram's horn. When the ark of God was entering David's city, Michal saw David the King leaping [*mĕpazzēz*] and whirling [*mĕkarkēr*] before God, so she despised him in her heart. They brought in the ark of YHWH and set it in its place, in the midst

---

[15] D.B. Redford, *A Study of the Biblical Story of Joseph* (1970), 78.
[16] Note *wattĕdabbēr ʾēlāyw kaddĕbārîm hāʾēlleh*, "she told him something like the following words."
[17] Difficult text. See J.P. Ross's version in *VT* 17 (1967), 82.
[18] But see 1 Chron. 13:8 "with all (his) might and with songs." Cf. J.A. Soggin, *VT* 14 (1964), 374-377.
[19] I cannot agree with A. Phillip's conclusion as set in *VT* 19 (1969), 485-487.

of the tent which David had pitched for it. David, then, presented burnt sacrifices and offerings of well-being before YHWH."[20]

Upon blessing the populace and distributing baked products, David returned to his household only to be criticized by his wife. That his acrobatics, consisting of leaping, whirling, and dancing, were considered quite acceptable to YHWH is clear; for Michal was was struck with barrenness, a most heavy punishment, for daring to criticize the king's behavior.[21]

Now were the Hebrews, and Canaanites for that matter, alone in presenting ritual sports before the image of deities. A passage from a neo-Assyrian text (*KAR* 119:6ff) declares that "the young men, the strong men, fight one another in wrestlings and athletics for you [Ninurta]." Another tablet confirms this type of activity. *OECT* 6:pl.16:4:10ff records that "wrestlers [shall perform at a goddess' festival] with [acrobatic feats]."[22]

Among the Hittites, dancing, psalmodizing, and dervish-style whirling took place during the festival of the war-god.[23] At times, full dress war games were presented as part of the worship.[24] In Egypt, even the pharaohs were wont to be involved in a ritual ball-game before the goddess Hathor, while acrobatics, music, and dancing played a role in the jubilee of Amenhotep III, a celebration in which Hathor was also worshipped.[25] Evidence for Mycenean Greece are remembered in the well-known passages from, respectively, the twenty-third and eigth books of the Iliad and the Odyssey.[26]

---

[20] This translation is influenced by A. Caquot's rendering in *Les Danses sacrées*, 126-127 and 140 n. 13. For David the 'dancer' in his Near Eastern setting, see C.H. Gordon, *Yehezkel Kaufmann Jubilee Volume*, (1960), 46-49. Although not stemming from a cultic or festival context, one other episode is worth mentioning here. Ever since Yadin [then Sukenik] studied 2 Sam. 2:12-17, it has been fairly well accepted that a combat of champions took place between the followers of Joab and those of Abner (JPOS, 21 [1948], 110-116; *Act of Warfare* II, 266-267). In v. 14's: "*Yāqûmû nāʾ hannĕʿārîm wiyśaḥḥăqû lĕpāneynû*, let the warriors rise to perform before us," the *piʿʿel* of *śḥq* is obviously intended to connote an activity more strenuous (and dangerous) than mere "playing" [RSV, JPS]. For further on the subject, see C.H. Gordon, *HUCA* 23 (1900), 132[6] ("For the early Hebrew and Greeks, sport and bloodshed were not naturally exclusive"); 26 (1955), 87 (109); R. DeVaux *Bible et Orient*, 225f.

[21] In the absence of any "Jebusite" epigraphic or cultic remains, it becomes difficult to accept the often repeated hypothesis, which has David practicing a non-Yahwist ritual. The fact that Yahweh himself approved of it should be reason enough to reject the over-complex theorizing built around this enigmatic people. For background, see H.H, Rowley, *Worship in Ancient Israel* (1967), 77-78 and 192[3].

[22] Further Mesopotamian evidence can be gleaned through perusal of an article by B. Landsberger, *WZKM* 56 (1960), 115-117. See also *CAD* A/1 *sub. abāru B* and *ša abāri*, 38.

[23] A. Goetze, *ANET*^{2}, 358-359; H.G. Güterbock, "Religion und Kultus der Hethiter" in *Historia, Einzelschrift* 7 (ed. G. Walser), 63-64, n. 49.

[24] A. Goetze, *Kleinasien*, 163-166. Mock battles, in full martial dress, were not limited to the Hittite world. In his *Anabasis* (VI:1) Xenophon writes of a mock armed dance which was performed after a sacrifice and feast. For this, and other such performances (e.g., the "Pyrrhic" dances), see F. McD. Cornford, *Origin of Attic Comedy*, (1934), 65-66; J.E. Harrison, *Themis*, (1912), 22-27. Rome knew of an association of minor priests (*sodales*), the *salii* who were dedicated to Mars. On certain days during the months of March and October, marking the beginning and the end of the campaign season, they proceeded through the city, halting at certain sections to perform a war dance characterized by leaping (*salire*), beating on shields with small daggers, and shouting ancient, and half understood songs (*Carmen saliare*). Further, see Plutarch, *Lives: Numa*, XIII. 3-7; K. Latte, *Römische Religionsgeschichte*, (1960), 115ff.

[25] C.E. DeVries on pp. 25-35 and E.F. White on pp. 83-91 of *Studies in Honor of John A. Wilson* (*SAOC*, 35).

[26] For Greece of the first millenium, see M. Wegner, *Musik und Tanz* (*Arch. Hom.* III/4), 65-68. Note especially his Attic Kantharos of pl. VIa, p. 65-66 which shows boxers, lute players, a jumping acrobat, whirlers (?) veiled (?) dancers, duelers, and horse tamers all in the same band. For more evidence, see E.N. Gardiner, *Athletics of the Ancient World*, 28-52.

Plastic representations for the Near East afford additional evidence that sporting activities, in a variety of ways, and dancing were incorporated into well-regulated religious observances. Those from Mesopotamia have been conveniently collected in Marie-Therèse Barrelet's recent encyclopedic work *Figurines et reliefs en terre cuite de la Mésopotamie antique*, I, 409-410.

Verse 18 contains three examples of the root *ʿānāh*. The first two are *qal* infinitive in form, the last appears to be a *piʿʿel* infinitive. Some scholars, exemplified by Albright in his *Yahweh and the Gods of Canaan*, would emend all these examples to the *piʿʿel*, this, to bring it in harmony with Greek and Syrian recensions.[27] Often, the last colon is considered defective since, as contrasted to the *qal ʿanôt* of the first two cola, the *piʿʿel ʿannôt* is not succeeded by any vocable. The text, therefore, is emended to include one more word in that last colon.

Other explanations have been offered to explain this peculiarity. E. Edelmann prefers to see in the third *ʿannôt* a misvocalization of the Canaanite goddess Anat's name.[28] In this, he is supported by R.N. Whybray.[29] F.I. Andersen connects *ʿannôt* with Ugaritic *ʿnn*, a word which appears in difficult Ras Shamra passages and which seems to be a technical term for a divine attendant. Hence, Andersen suggests the Ugaritic term refers to one who orders chanting.[30] Köhler - Baumgartner (*LVTL*, 1034) records a suggestion that *tannôt*, "to celebrate, to praise," is to be read.

The *qal* of *ʿānāh*, is often found in festive contexts, in which singing played a role. For this reason, most lexicographical sources separate and organize these attestations under a specific rubric, usually labelled *ʿānāh* IV (eg. BDB, p. 777; LVTL, pp. 719-720). One wonders, however, whether such a step is legitimate. As has been noted by a number of scholars, all the examples cited clearly indicate that the main idea is that of "returning," of "answering", a given lyric. In other words, the verb *ʿānāh* is employed to emphasize the antiphonal or the responsive quality of a chant. A similar situation obtains in Akkadian where the verb *apālu*, "to answer, to respond" – never meaning "to sing" – is employed. As examples culled from the *CAD* (A/2, 164), unfortunately derived from non-ritual texts, we have the following: "*ilsû šamê qaqqaru īpul* (Gilgamesh VII: IV:15), the heaven roared and the earth echoed"; "*ana rigmiya danni etanappalā šadû u nāru* (Lambert, *BWL*, 192:18), mountain and stream echo to the powerful sound of my voice."

It must be admitted that a satisfactory explanation for the use of the *piʿʿel* in the third colon eludes us. This form of *ʿānāh* occurs in two other biblical passages. In Is 27:2 the text reads: "on that day [of slaying Leviathan, there will be] a vineyard of frothing wine. [So:] *ʿinnû lāh.*" What follows is a striking verse of four cola, each of which ends in the feminine singular pronomial suffix *āh*. Ps 88, a lament, is labelled: "A Song, a psalm of the sons of Korah, for the choirmaster, *ʿal māḥalat lĕʿannôt*, a *maskîl* of Heman the Ezrahite." Some authorities (e.g., *RSV*, *JPS*, *Anchor Bible*) ignore the basic problem and render *māḥalat lĕʿannôt* as a place name. With *BDB*, 318, LVTL, 513 perhaps *māḥalat* is to be connected with *meḥōlāh*, for which meaning see presently. *lĕʿannôt* would then be a particular way in which a chant is presented at the time of a *meḥōlāh*. One more speculation before scampering toward firmer ground: should one distinguish between the *qal* and *piʿʿel* of *ʿānāh* by translating, respectively, "responsive" and "antiphonal" singing?

Even a hurried look into the biblical passages which contain the word *meḥōlāh*, and the masculine *māḥôl* for that matter, is enough to suggest that the common and usual translation "round-dance" is, at best, imprecise. Such a meaning, it is suspected, depended more on etymologising from a *ʿayin-waw* root *ḥwl*, a root which connotes "circling around," than on contextual exegesis.[31]

---

27 Albright, *op. cit.*, 19[53].
28 *VT* 16 (1966), 355.
29 *VT* 17 (1967), 122.
30 *VT* 17 (1967), 108-112. G. Beer, *Exod.* (HAT), 1939, p. 154 reads "*ʿinnug*, sound of Joy."
31 One can even suppose that Judg. 21:21, *laḥûl bimḥôlôt* may have rendered such etamylogizing very tempting.

Benno Landsberger has convincingly argued that Hebrew *meḥōlāh* and *māḥôl* should be derived from a *ʿayin-ʿayin* root **ḥll.* He also posited the existence of an Akkadian verb **elēlu* (B), and distinguished it from the well-attested *elēlu* (A), "to become pure, to be free (of debts)." As it is, *elēlu*, an infinitive of the posited **elēlu* (B) is known, from first millenium B.C. texts, to mean 'jubilation, festivities.' Landsberger translated this **elēlu* (B) by 'to play', and insisted on separating it from the usual Akkadian verb for dancing *raqādu* and for circle-dancing, *sâru.*[32] Accepting Landsberger's position, von Soden's *Handwörterbuch* gives the meaning "*Spielen*" to the irregular verb *mēlulu*, a derivation of this posited **elēlu* (B).[33] A formation of this irregular verb is *mēlultu*, a noun which may very well be cognate to Hebrew *meḥōlāh*. With its Sumerian equivalent KI.E.NE.DI, *mēlultu* is not, in itself, an activity that is confined to cultic moments. The same authorities that are listed in footnotes 32-33 preserve examples to show that the term was applied to a variety of games: rope-skipping (*keppû*), gambling with knucklebones (*kiṣallu*), board-gaming, hunting, and puppetry (*passu*). Often, the wars and bloodbaths of the goddess Inanna/Ishtar are likened to a *mēlultu*. There are, however, instances where the term is used in contexts recording ritual festivities. Lexical texts (*Diri, Antagal*) speak of the 'festi-val-games of Ishtar.'"[34] A Sumero-Akkadian *bilingual*, in fact, urges one never to shirk his duties at such events.[35] Hemerological texts suggests that the 27th day of Nisan was devoted to "ritual-games for Nergal."[36] Unfortunately, we still laek the evidence which would give details concerning the various activities that were scheduled at these festivals.

The Hebrew verses where the term *meḥōlāh/maḥôl* occur clearly show that musical instruments ac-companied festivities. But consider the following examples: Ps 149:3: "May they praise his name in the *māḥôl*"; 1 Sam 21:12b: "Did they not echo for [David] in the *meḥōlôt*: Saul has slain his thousands, while David his ten thousands? " [also 29:5]; Song 7:1 "Come back, come back, Shulammite; come back, come back so that we can gaze upon you. But what will you see in the Shulammite, as if (she were) a *meḥōlāh* of a double com-pany? "; Jer 31:3: "I will once more build you, and you will be built, maiden of Israel. You will be adorned (with) your tambourines, and will go forth in the *māḥôl* of those that perform ritual games [*bimḥôl mĕśaḥ=ḥăqîm*]." From these, rather than a mere round-dance, the *mĕḥōlāh/māḥôl* appears to consist of antiphonal singing, a double group of performers which include females and musical accompaniement, and ritual sporting.

All this permits the cautions suggestion that *mĕḥōlāh/māḥôl* could be favorably compared with the Greek *hyporchēma.* Since later classical authors and scholiasts were rather inexact in their use of the term, much ink has been spilled by modern scholars in their attempt to arrive at an exact definition.[37] A specialist on the dance in ancient Greece, Lilian B. Lawler offers the following:

> "The *hyporchēma* . . . was a combination of instrumental music of lyre or flute or even both together. It could be performed by men or women, boys or girls. Writers repeatedly stress the fact that it was lively, rapid, flashing, joyous, fiery. Sometimes a musician both played his instruments and sang, as the chorus danced. At other times a musician or musicians furnished the instrumental accompaniment,

---

32 *Op. cit.*, p. 119[30] and 120[31], *WZKM* 57 (1961), 22-23.

33 *AHw*, 644. On the verb *mēlulu*, 'to game, play, sport,' see von Soden, *Or* 20 (1957), 265-266; Th. Jacobsen, *Toward the Image of Tammuz*, 338[21]. Bibliographical data on the verb *mēlulu* and its Sumerian equivalent E.NE.DI is found in W.H.Ph. Römer, *SAKIZ* (1965), p. 173; C. Wilcke, *Das Lugalbandaepos* (1969), 167; A. Sjöberg, *TCS*, 3 (1969), p. 107. I thank Prof. H.A. Hoffner for calling my attention to many of the above discussions of *mēlulu* and E.NE.DI. Note that the performer listed between *zammirum*, 'singer,' and *raqqidu* "dancer" (*MSL* 12, 136:236) is *mu-um-mé-lu*! (Landsberger, *WZKM*, 57 [1961], 22). Von Soden, *AHw*, 671, connects with *mēlulu* and translates" (Schau?-)Spieler." Earlier, Jacobsen, *op. cit.*, 338[21], understood this vocable as "'foredancer,' the person who leads the dance and the singing."

34 Landsberger, *op. cit.*, 123 and 123[42].

35 Cited by Landsberger, *op. cit.*, 23; *CAD* I/J, 11 (1, a, 2); Römer, *op. cit.*, 173; *AHw*, 783 (*nêʾu(m)*, 2 a).

36 R. Labat, *Hémérologies* (1939), 65:6 (and p. 65[6]); B. Landsberger, *Kultische Kalender* (1915), 14-15; 141.

37 The problem was complicated by an attempt to contrast the *hyporchēma* with the *stasimon*, a term which, erroneously, has been rendered as "a motionless dance;" see A.H. Dale, "Stasimon and Hyporcheme," *Collected Works* (1969), 34-40.

while the chorus sang and used gestures or simple movements, and a smaller group of dancers preformed spiritedly without taking part in the singing at all."[38]

Witnesses, both ancient and modern seek the origin of this form of ritual presentation, so characteristic of worshippers in the Mediterranean world, in Crete. It is thought that the practice is datable to the Bronze Age. During the 7th century B.C., mythographers allege, Thaletas (Thales) of Gortyn accepted an invitation to migrate to Sparta to stave off Apollo's anger against its citizenry.[39] There he introduced the *hyporchēma*, along with other new genres of choral dances. By the 6th and 5th century some of Greece's most talented lyricists were "composing" *hyporchēmata*. Among others, Pratinas of Phlius, Pindar, and Bacchylides of Keos presented examples to the gods: the first to Dionysus, the second to the Sun.[40] Plato (*Ion*, 534C) considered the *hyporchēma* to be an accepted form with which to approach the deities.

Rather than a distinct innovation, the *hyporchēma* that was brought into the mainland must have been considered an elaboration, an expansion of older forms of choral-dances which were familiar to Greeks everywhere. Such an hypothesis would help to explain its seemingly easy acceptance in the usually conservative cults and festivals. Indeed, rudiments of the *hyporchēma* are to be found in Homer's works. On the shield of Achilles the following scene is described (Iliad 18:593-605): "And there were young men on it and young girls sought for their beauty with gifts of oxen, dancing, and holding hands at the wrist . . . And the girls wore fair garlands on their heads, while the young men carried golden knives that hung from sword-belts of silver. At whiles on their understanding feet they would run very lightly . . . At another time they would form rows, and run, rows crossing each other. And around the lovely chorus of dancers stood a great multitude happily watching, while among the dancers two acrobats led the measures of sing and dance revolving around them."[41]

---

[38] *The Dance in Ancient Greece* (1964), 101. See also her *The Dance of the Ancient Greek Theatre* (1964), 30-31. Ms. Lawler's definition agrees substantially with Theodore Reinach's explanation written, at the turn of the century, for the Daremberg-Saglio, *Dictionnaire des Antiquités grecques et romaines*, III, 352. Reinach's article came to my attention after this portion of my paper was completed. I mention it only because this *savant*, who was familiar both with Hellenic and Hebrew cultures, to my pleasant surprise, connected the *hyprochēma* with the *meḥōlāh* (p. 352[6]).
Dale, *op. cit.*, 39 believes that one cannot go much beyond defining the *hyporchēma* as "characterized by dancing of especial speed, vigour and expressiveness." Basing herself on a fragment written by Pratinas, she also holds that the *hyporchēma*'s form was non-responsive. In these ideas, she is followed by her husband, T.B.L. Webster, in *The Greek Chorus* (1970), 62-63.

[39] For the *hyporchēma*'s odyssey from Crete toward the mainland, see the evidence collected by E. Diehl, Pauly-Wissowa, *Real-Encyclopadie d. Klass. Altertums Wiss.*, III, 338-339; Reinach, *op. cit.*, 353; R.F. Willetts, *Cretan Cults and Festivals* (1962), 311.

[40] Consult the first two authorities cited in preceeding note.

[41] Lattimore's translation is quoted. cf., also Odyss. IV:17-19; VII:262 ff; the *'Homeric' Hymn to Phythian Apollo*, 182-206. Athenaeus of Naucrates (ca. 200 A.D.) writes in his *Deipnosophists*, I:15: ". . . and in the Forging of the Arms a boy played the lyre while others opposite him "frisked about to the music and the dance." Here there is an allusion to the style of the hyporcheme, which became popular in the time of Xenodemus and Pindar. This variety of dance is an imitation (*mimesis*) of acts which can be interpreted by words." It is interesting, by the way, that the *hyporchēma* as described by Athenaeus – cf. also, Plutarch *Quaest. Conviv.* IX:152; Lucian *The Dance*: 16 – includes a mime. As it was known and practiced in classical days, the mime itself, originating at religious festivals, consisted of ritualized dancings accompanied by musical instruments, and was punctuated with by spoken dialogue. It often included antiphonal singing, and acrobatic displays. An example of the mime is to be found in Xenophon's *Symposium*. See A. Nicoll, *Masks, Mimes, and Miracles*, (1963), 17-79.

FORM AND FUNCTION OF
ANCIENT ISRAELITE, GREEK AND ROMAN LEGAL SENTENCES

Stanislav Segert
University of California, Los Angeles

Many important studies were devoted to the Israelite law, its form and its relations to the laws of other nations[1]. The aim of the following short contribution is to bring into the discussion some material from ancient Greece and Rome which shows substantial structural affinities to Israelite, Mesopotamian and Anatolian laws.

Two pioneering attempts to distinguish the sentences in Israelite law according to their form were published in 1927 by A. Jepsen[2] and A. Jirku[3]. Since the study about the origin of Israelite law by A. Alt[4]

---

1 Books quoted by authors' names or abbreviations:
[Alt] – A. Alt, *Die Ursprünge des israelitischen Rechts* (1934) Reprint: *Kleine Schriften zur Geschichte des Volkes Israel*, I (1959), 287-332. English translation by R.A. Wilson: *Essays on Old Testament History and Religion* (1966), 79-132.
[Bruns] – *Fontes iuris Romani antiqui*, G. Bruns, ed. (1879).
[DHR] – *Recueil des inscriptions juridiques grecques.* R. Dareste, B. Haussoulier, Th. Reinach, eds., (1892-1904, Reprint: 1965) I-II.
[Gerstenberger] – E. Gerstenberger, Wesen und Herkunft des "apodiktischen Rechts" (1965).
[Gortyn], see Willetts, 39-50.
[Hentschke] – R. Hentschke, Erwägungen zur israelitischen Rechtsgeschichte. *Theologia Viatorum* 10 (1966), 108-33.
[Jolowicz] – H.D. Jolowicz, *Historical Instruction to the Study of Roman Law* (1954).
[Paul] – M. Paul, *Studies in the Book of the Covenant in the Light of Cuneiform and Biblical Law* (SVT, XVIIII) (1970).
[Riccobono] – *Fontes iuris Romani antejustiniani.* Pars prima: Leges. S. Riccobono, ed. (1941).
[Willetts] – *The Law Code of Gortyn*, R.F. Willetts, ed. (Kadmos, Suppl. I) (1967).
[XII tab], – see Riccobono, 21-75.

2 *Untersuchungen zum Bundesbuch.*

3 *Das weltliche Recht im Alten Testament.*

4 V. supra, n. 1.

(1934) the division in casuistic and apodictic legal sentences is generally accepted. But the discussion concerning the apodictic sentences, especially the delimitation of apodictic law and its origin is not closed. Besides several articles, dissertations by G. Heinemann[5] (1958) and E. Gerstenberger[6] (1961; 1965) were devoted to these questions; more recently (1970) Sh. Paul[7] conveniently summarized the results.

One contribution, not contained in the very rich bibliography presented by Paul, "Considerations to Israelite history of law" by R. Hentschke[8] deserves to be especially mentioned, as it presents new relevant view-points.

While the casuistic and apodictic legal sentences were earlier distinguished according to the formal criteria, continuing research, using also Mesopotamian and Hittite legal material, stressed more the function and setting of the legal sentences.

The transformational approach[9] can be applied to delimit the boundary between apodictic and casuistic legal sentences in a more exact and in the same time more functional manner than the rather formal approach accepting the use of jussive or of similar verbal form as the main criterion for the apodictic type[10].

It is quite clear that the sentences introduced by *kî* or *ʾim* "if" are casuistic, as are the relative constructions. The participial constructions were considered by A. Alt as belonging to the apodictic type[11], but many scholars dealing with them after, ascribed them more or less to the casuistic type[12]. This standpoint is to be confirmed, as the participial constructions in biblical Hebrew can be – and in several cases actually were – transformed into hypothetic and/or relative constructions. The participle in the Book of Covenant (Ex 21:12) *makkê ʾîš wāmēt* – in English it is hard to keep the participle in translation "Whosoever strikes a man, so that he dies"[13] – can be compared with the later formulation expressed by a hypothetical construction (*wĕʾim*) . . . *ʾō beʾêbâ hikkāhû* . . *wayyāmōt* (Num 35:20-21) "if . . . or . . . he struck him . . . so that he dies", or by a relative sentence: *ʾăšer yakkê ʾet-rēʾēhū* . . . *wāmēt* (Deut. 19:4-5) "if anyone kills his neighbor . . . so that he dies." Another participial construction of the Book of the Covenant (Ex 21:17) *umqallēl ʾābîw* "whosoever curses his father" is reflected in Lev. 20:9 as *kîʾîš ʾîš ʾăšer yeqallēl ʾet- ʾābîw* "for everyone who curses his father".[14]

The participial constructions and the relative sentences belong together with the conditional sentences to the casuistic type. This type is most frequently represented in Israelite, Mesopotamian, Hittite, Greek and Roman laws. The primary element is the case, the action can begin after the case happens. All these three formal expressions fit completely the exhausting characteristic of the casuistic law as presented by R.A.F. Mackenzie[15].

Many parallels to the casuistic formulas in the Israelite laws were found in ancient Mesopotamian and Hittite collections of laws; some apodictic formulas were also found there[16]. For more parallels to the apodic-

---

5 *Untersuchungen zum apodiktischen Recht.* Diss. Hamburg.
6 V. supra, n. 1.
7 V. supra, n. 1.
8 V. supra, n. 1.
9 For a first information cf. J. Lyons, *Introduction to Theoretical Linguistics* (1969), 247-70.
10 This approach underlies some statements by Alt, Engl. transl., 105, 107, 109-110, 112; cf. Paul, 113-14.
11 Alt, Engl. transl. 109, 111.
12 Cf. Hentschke, 111-13; Paul, 118, n. 1.
13 The English translations according to the RSV.
14 Cf. Hentschke, 111, n. 7.
15 The formal aspect of ancient Near Eastern Law. *The Seed of Wisdom: Essays in Honor of T.J. Meek* (1964), 31-44, esp. 35-37; cf. Paul, 116.
16 Cf. Hentschke, 114, n. 12.

tic formulas it is necessary to take into consideration the royal edicts[17], where the apodictic sentences expressing the will of the king are relatively more frequent. The same is true for Hittite instructions for different categories of personnel and officials[18].

The Israelite tradition also contains relatively more apodictic formulas outsides of the collections of law[19]. Some ordinances of the kings – like David's instructions for distributing of booty (1 Sam. 30:24), – and of other authorities (cf. Esd. 6:11; Neh. 5:13) are quoted in the historical books.

It is possible to consider the dependence of Israelite legal sentences on similar formulas in ancient Mesopotamian law or on a common tradition underlying both Israelite and Mesopotamian law[20]. In some cases there are rather structural similarities.

While it is not excluded that there could be some similarities in content between Hittite and Israelite law[21], rather their structural similarities will here be pointed out[22]. The same approach is appropriate in using ancient Greek and Roman laws in studying the form and function of Israelite legal sentences[23].

As an appropriate counterpart to the ancient Israelite law, the Greek Law Code of Gortyn[24] and the Roman Twelve Tables[25] can be used. Both these collections are rather "codification not of law, but of laws"[26], they combine the traditional law with innovations[27]; in both these respects they are comparable especially to the Israelite Book of the Covenant[28]. The social structure of the Cretan city and of ancient Rome, according to both these codifications made in the 5th century B.C. exhibit some similarities with that of ancient Israel. We will not dwell on the similarity of individual legal regulations, like the female heiresses in Gortyn[29] or the punishment for burglary at night in Rome[30]. Besides these corpora, the other laws of Gortyn[31], the Draconian law on murder in Athens[32], and the laws about the burials[33] and mourning[34] provide some interesting parallels, as well as also some ancient Roman royal laws[35] and local sanctuary rules[36].

---

17 F.R. Kraus, *Ein Edikt des Königs Ammi-ṣaduqa von Babylon* (1958); cf. ANET, Suppl. (1969), 526-8; E. von Schuler, *Festschrift J. Friedrich* (1959), 435-72; Hentschke, 114-24; K. Koch, *Was ist Formgeschichte?* (1964), 24.

18 ANET, 207-211; for formulas in Hittite treaties cf. G. Mendenhall, Ancient Oriental and Biblical Law (1954), *Biblical Archeologist Reader* 3 (1970), 3-24, 7-8. [Cf. E. von Schuler, *Dienstanw.* for the editions of the texts. – Ed.]

19 Cf. Hentschke, 125-8.

20 Cf. Paul, 42, 99-105, 112-17.

21 Cf. Koch (supra n. 16); Paul, 98, 103-104. – For not yet explained relations between Hittite and late Palestinian literary motives cf. ArOr. 25 (1957), 505. – For Hittite law in general, cf. Friedrich, *Heth. Gesetze* (1960), J. Puhvel, "Hittites" (III,4), *Enc. Britannica* (1964), F. Imparati, *Le leggi ittite* (1969), and for similarities with Israelite laws see H. Hoffner, *Tyndale Bulletin* 20 (1969), 39ff.

22 Cf. Mendenhall, supra n. 18.

23 For problems of relation cf. E. Volterra, *Diritto romano e diritti orientali* (1937).

24 V. supra: Gortyn. – The quotations are given here in simple transliteration of the inscription written in Doric Cretan dialect. – For the role of Crete as a connecting link between the Near East and Greece cf. C.H. Gordon, *Introduction to Old Testament Times* (1953), 289; and ArOr 22 (1954).

25 V. supra: XII tables.

26 Willetts, 29.

27 Willetts, 8; Jolowicz, 113, 106-111.

28 H. Cazelles, *Études sur le Code d'Alliance* (1946); Paul 43. Of course, Mesopotamian and Hittite legal corpora also combine tradition with innovation.

29 Col. VII 15 - IX 24; Willetts, 45-47, 23-27, esp. 24, n. 19-23; cf. Num. 27:8; 36:1-12.

30 XII tab. VIII 12; cf. Exod. 22:1, Hammurapi 21.

31 DHR, I, 392-404.

32 DHR, I, 2-5.

33 DHR, I, 10-13.

34 DHR, I, 19-20.

35 Riccobono, 1-20.

36 Bruns, 44-45.

Most laws in the above mentioned Greek and Roman sources belong clearly to the casuistic category. They are expressed in hypothetical sentences introduced mostly by typical hypothetical conjunctions[37], but also by relative pronouns[38] and adverbs[39].

In so far as participial constructions occur in Greek (Gortyn I 56 - II 2)[40] and Roman (XII Tab. I 8)[41] laws, they have the participle as the dative object, and therefore cannot be compared with Hebrew constructions in which the participle serves as subject[42].

The apodictic independent sentences are expressed both in Greek and Latin mostly by peculiar forms of imperative, extended by *-tō*[43].

In Greek, these forms indicate the third person imperatives[44], in Latin they are so-called future imperatives[45] extending the validity of command or prohibition to unlimited time.

These "apodictic" formulations are relatively frequent in Roman laws, but limited to instructions concerning sanctuaries[46], burial[47] and mourning rites[48], and to rather arbitrary regulations determining the functions of the magistrates[49].

Some ancient Roman laws are formulated in second person singular: "Hominem mortuum in urbe ne sepelito neve urito" (XII tab. X I)[50] "Do not bury nor burn a dead man in the City"; "Vino rogum ne respargito" (Numa Pompilius, I)[51]; "Do not sprinkle the (burial) stake with wine".

An apodictic prohibition is sometimes followed by a casuistic sentence determining the punishment for the transgression of the apodictic legal rule[52]. Such combinations are of course known in ancient Near Eastern laws[53] and also in later Jewish tradition as quoted in the Sermon on the Mountain (Mat 5:21)[54]: "You shall not kill and whoever kills shall be liable to judgment".

In the mentioned Greek laws, the independent apodictic formulations occur only in the third person imperative ending in *-tō*. But also the much more frequent construction with infinitive in Greek laws belongs definitely to the apodictic type.

---

37 Si nox furtum faxsit, si im occisit, iure caesus esto, XII tab. VIII 12.
38 Cui testimonium defuerit, . . . II 3; Qui malum carmen incantassit . . . VIII 1a.
39 Uti legassit . . . V 3.
40 Gortyn, I 56 - II 2 *[t]on de nenikamenon ka[i ton ka]takeimenon agonti apaton emen*, "but one who seizes a man condemned or who has mortgaged his person shall be immune from punishment".
41 XII tab. I 8, post meridiem praesenti litem addicito.
42 Cf. Exod. 21:12, 17.
43 For the ancient Indoeuropean juridic style cf. C. Watkins, Studies in Indo-European Legal Language, Institutions and Mythology; G. Cardona et al., edd., *Indo-European and Indo-Europeans* (1970), 321-54.
44 J.M. Stahl, *Kritisch-historische Syntax des griechischen Verbums der klassischen Zeit* (1907, reprint 1965).
45 Ch.L. Bennett, *Syntax of Early Latin*, I, The Verb (1910), 320.
46 Houce loucom ne quis violatod, Lex Spoletina, Bruns, 44.
47 XII tab. X 1, 5; cf. n. 50.
48 Mulieres genas ne radunto, XII tab. X 4.
49 V. n. 47.
50 V. n. 47.
51 Numa Pompilius, 13, Riccobono, 13.
52 Paelex aram Iunonis ne tangito; si tanget, Iunoni crinibus demissis agnum feminam caedito, Numa Pompilius, 3, Riccobono, 13; Lex Lucerina and Lex Spoletina, Bruns, 44-45.
53 Cf. Ex 21:17, 20-21.
54 E.G. Gortyn, II 27-31: *proveipato de anti maityron trion . . .*, "let (the captor) proclaim in the presence of three witnesses . . .".

There are infinitives in Homeric poetry[55], comparable to Hebrew absolute infinitives in imperatival function, but in the Greek laws the infinitives are dependent on an introductory formula of law expressing the authority of the legislative body or the individual legislator, like "the Gortynians decreed this by voting"[56], "The council and the people decreed"[57], "Alexon, the son of Damon, said"[58]. The gods are mentioned in the beginning of the Law Code of Gortyn[59], but this is rather an invocation than ascribing of the following laws to a divine authority[60].

The basic types of formulations known from Israelite, Mesopotamian and Hittite legal sources can be found also in ancient Greek and Roman juridical texts: Casuistic formulas are expressed by hypothetical and relative sentences. They occur mostly in collections of laws.

In all these areas apodictic formulations in third person were used, mostly in edicts and laws promulgated by an authority, king, ruler, council, people's assembly.

The apodictic sentences in second person can be found in Israelite laws[61], in Hittite instructions[62], and in ancient Roman laws where they are limited to the prohibitions of sacral character[63]. For the general apodictic formulas of ethical character known from the Israelite decalogue no comparable sentences were found[64]. Basic presupposition of apodictic formulas is an authority promulgating them; while the formally comparable Hittite and Roman formulations mention a king or a legislative body, the Israelite formulas are presented as based on the authority of God[64].

Sentence form:	hypothetical / relative (Israel only: participial)	jussive
Type of legal sentence:	casuistic	apodictic
Function:	law	edict
Basis:	case	authority[65]

---

[55] Cf. Stahl (supra n. 44), 599-600.
[56] *Tad evade tois Gortyniois psapidonsi*, DHR, I, 403.
[57] *[e]dochsen tēi boulēi kai tōi dēmō[i]*, Dracon's Law, DHR, II, 2.
[58] *Alexon Damonos eipen*, Law of Gambreion, DHR, I, 19.
[59] Gortyn I, 1, *thioi.*
[60] Cf. Gerstenberger, 70-76.
[61] Limited to a definite person only, the singularic expression does not possess general validity.
[62] Not limited to definite person, in general validity closer to similar Israelite formulations. For the general validity of some Israelite apodictic sentences cf. S. Herrmann, "Das apodiktische Recht", *MIO* 15 (1969), 249-261, esp. 260-261.
[63] Cf. Paul, 124.
[64] In their Biblical setting; for the hypothetical attribution of some of them to the head of clan cf. Gerstenberger, 55-61, 110-117.
[65] Some parts of this paper were presented to the VIIth Congress of the International Organization for the Study of the Old Testament, Uppsala, August 11, 1971: "Remarks to Forms and Function of Apodictic Formulas in Israelite Law". – A summary was presented to the meeting of the Society of Biblical Literature, Pacific Coast Section, Los Angeles, April 28, 1972: "Apodictic Sentences in Israelite Law: Form, Function, Parallels". – The author wishes to express his thanks to the participants in the discussions of these papers, especially to Prof. R. Hentschke (Berlin). For friendly advices the author is indebted to his colleagues at the U.C.L.A., Professors G. Buccellati, J. Puhvel and A. Rosett, and to Rev. R.W. Meyer (Pacific Palisades).

SYNTACTIC NOTES ON THE *WAW CONSECUTIVE**

Michael H. Silverman

State University of New York at Buffalo

I

The phenomenon of the so-called *waw conversive* or *waw consecutive* has posed a special problem to students of biblical Hebrew grammar. While discussion of it begins in the earliest lessons given to the beginner, it remains little understood and problematic.

This *waw consecutive* or *conversive* appears, on the surface, to convert an apparently past-tense verb to the future and *vice versa.* Thus, e.g., the past-tense *hēnîăḥ*, "he placed," becomes, with the addition of this *waw*, the future-tense *wĕhēnîăḥ*, "he will place"; just as the future-tense *yĕdabbēr*, "he will speak", becomes, with a like addition, the past-tense *wayyĕdabbēr*, "he spoke".

The Hebrew verb-system consists of two tenses, two finite verb conjugations: *qāṭáltî, qāṭáltā*, etc. (named from the third person masculine singular, *qāṭal*) and *'eqṭōl, tiqṭōl*, etc. (named from the third person masculine singular, *yiqṭōl*). The exact nature of these forms is disputed: some believe that they denote differences in aspect, while others are of the opinion that they indicate differences in time and are true tenses. According to the former, the distinction is between completed action–*qāṭal–versus* incomplete action–*yiqṭōl*; according to the latter, it is between past action–*qāṭal–versus* future action–*yiqṭōl*. These forms are even given different names depending on the view that is accepted:

(1) if they denote aspects, *qāṭal* is perfect, and *yiqṭōl*, imperfect;

(2) if they are tenses, *qāṭal* is past and *yiqṭōl*, future.

The problem of tenses *versus* aspects is very complicated and truly cannot be resolved at present. For now, the forms will be termed "tenses," *qāṭal*, "past", and *yiqṭōl*, "future", without prejudicing the ultimate resolution of this issue.[1]

---

* Presented at the Joint Regional Meeting, Southern and Southwestern Sections, *Society of Biblical Literature*, and Southeastern and Southwestern Sections, *American Academy of Religion.*
The following abbreviations are used: GKC = A.E. Cowley (rev.) - E. Kautzsch (ed.), *Gesenius' Hebrew Grammar*[2] (Oxford, 1910 [1960]); Rosén, *Proceedings* = H.B. Rosén, *Proceedings of the International Conference on Semitic Studies* (Jerusalem, 1965); Rabin, *Taḥbîr* = Ch. Rabin, *Taḥbîr Lĕšōn Ham-Miqrā'* (Biblical Hebrew Syntax) (Jerusalem: Akademon, 1966); and *UT* = C.H. Gordon, *Ugaritic Textbook* (AnOr 38; Roma, 1965). Additional bibliography (*not* cited in the following notes): H. Bauer - P. Leander, *Historische Grammatik der hebräischen Sprache des Alten Testamentes,* (Halle, 1922 [Hildesheim, 1966]), 1-26; F.R. Blake, *JBL*, 63 (1944), 271-295; C.H. Gordon, *JBL*, 57 (1938), 319-325; A.S. Hartum, *World Congress of Jewish Studies*, Proceedings (Jerusalem, 1952), 81 [1]ff. (Heb.); R. Hetzron, *JSS,* 12 (1967), 178-193 and 14 (1969), 1-21; G.M. Schramm, *General Linguistics*, 3 (1957) 1-8; J.F.X. Sheehan, *Biblica*, 51 (1970), 545-548 and 52 (1971), 39-43; E.A. Speiser, "The Pitfalls of Polarity", *Oriental and Biblical Studies: The Collected Writings of E.A. Speiser* (Philadelphia, 1967), 433-454; and P. Jouon, *Grammaire de l'hebreu biblique* (Rome, 1923), 319-320.

1 On the matters discussed up to this point, see GKC, §§ 40, 49, and for the debate on tenses *versus* aspects, see Rabin, *Taḥbîr*, 30-31, citing S.R. Driver, *A Treatise on the Use of Tenses in Hebrew* (Oxford, 1874) and F.R. Blake, *A Resurvey of the Hebrew Tenses* (Rome, 1951). See also Rosen, *Proceedings*, 1-23.

The tenses with *waw consecutive* are constructed from these two basic forms in accordance with the following rules:

(a) The verb in the basic tenses usually occupies second position within the clause. It is taken from this position and placed first.

(b) Then, the *waw* is prefixed to it.

(c) When the *waw* is prefixed to the future, it assumes the vocalization of *wa* plus gemination of the first consonant of the verb. In addition, the word accent usually, through not always, drops back one syllable, with attendent shortening of the final vowel of the word. This form is distinct, and cannot be confused with other verbal types.[2]

(d) When it is prefixed to the past, it is vocalized like the morpheme *wĕ*-, "and," the conjunction. Here again, there is usually, though not always, a change in accent: if it originally stood on the penult, it may shift to the ultima. When this change in accent does *not* occur, this form, the past with *waw consecutive* cannot be distinguished from the regular past with the conjunction "and." The reason for this is that the conjunction *wĕ*-, "and", may be joined directly to the verb with no change in accent.

Thus, while the future with *waw consecutive* always has a separate and distinct form, the past with *waw consecutive* cannot always be distinguished from other verbal types. When this ambiguity exists, semantic or contextual criteria are employed in order to decide which *waw*, conjunctive or consecutive, is intended.

If the basic tenses and those with *waw consecutive* are joined together, a system of four tenses emerges:

1. *qāṭal*, etc. –past
2. *wĕqāṭal*, etc. –past with *waw consecutive*
3. *yiqṭōl*; etc. –future
4. *wayyiqṭōl*, etc. –future with *waw consecutive*

The names for (2) and (4) indicate only their morphological relationships. Their functions are the opposite: *wĕqāṭal* is past in form, but future in meaning; *wayyiqṭōl* is future in form, but past in meaning. For this reason, it seems best to choose names for these tenses according to their function:

a. *qāṭal*– simple past (abbreviated sp.)
b. *wayyiqṭōl–waw* past (abbreviated wp.)
c. *yiqṭōl* – simple future (abbreviated sf.)
d. *wĕqāṭal–waw* future (abbreviated wf.)

Wayyiqṭōl and *wĕqāṭal*, the *waw* past and *waw* future, together will be termed the "consecutive tenses" in the following discussion. They are to be opposed to *qāṭal* and *yiqṭōl*, the simple past and simple future, the "simple tenses."

I propose to investigate the syntactic relationships among these four tenses, and to determine under what conditions each one is apt to occur. In this examination I propose to study the uses of the simple *versus* the consecutive tenses in the present text of the Bible rather than to engage in speculations on the origin of the *waw consecutive* and the history of its development. In my opinion, the two questions of its present usage *versus* its historical origin ought to be kept separate. To use linguistic terminology, this study is *synchronic*, dealing with the phenomenon at the present or at a fixed point in time, rather than *diachronic*, dealing with the phenomenon in its historical development. Finally, in order to exclude extraneous issues, the inquiry is restricted to the usage of these tenses in biblical Hebrew prose.

[2] [Not therefore to be confused with *wĕyiqṭōl*, whose function is quite different. – Ed.]

II

The two past and the two future tenses occur in sequence: simple past is followed by *waw* past, and simple future, by *waw* future. In such cases the *waw* past or future indicates the logical or temporal consequence attendent on the preceding simple past or future. This fact has long been recognized, and is explained in *Gesenius' Hebrew Grammar* as follows:

> The *imperfect* with *wāw consecutive* [= *waw* past] serves to express actions, or states which are to be regarded as the temporal or logical sequel of actions, or states mentioned immediately before . . . As a rule the narrative is introduced by a perfect [= simple past] and then continued by means of imperfects with *wāw consecutive* [= waw past.]
> . . . The perfect . . . is used with *wāw consecutive* [= *waw* future] to express actions, events, or states which are to be attached to what precedes, in a more or less close relation, as its *temporal* or *logical* consequence. And, as according to [the preceding paragraph], the narrative which begins with a perfect, or its equivalent [simple past], is continued in the imperfect consecutive [*waw* past], so vice versa, the perfect consecutive [*waw* future] forms the regular continuation to a preceding imperfect, or its equivalent [simple future].[3]

The *Grammar* then lists many specific uses of the *waw* consecutive, all having to do with this idea of temporal or logical consequence following upon the preceding narrative.[4]

This conception is certainly valid. Nevertheless, I should prefer to reduce the several specific uses of the consecutive tenses listed in the *Grammar* to two main varieties:

1. Logical consequence, i.e., the reason or result of the preceding verb. For example, Gen. 2:24: *ʿal kēn yaʿăzōb (sf.) ʾîš ʾet ʾābîw wĕ-ʾet ʾimmô wĕdābaq (wf.) bĕʾištô* . . . , "therefore, a man will leave (sf.) his father and mother, and, as a result, will cling (wf.) to his wife."

2. Change in time, i.e., the action of the verb is seen as occurring either earlier or later than that of the preceding verb. Sometimes, the force is merely "in addition". For example, Gen. 27:16-17: . . . *wĕʾet ʿōrôt gĕdāyê hāʿizzîm hilbîšāh (sp.) . . . Wattittēn (wp.) ʾet ham-maṭʿamîm* . . . , ". . . and the goatskins she put (sp.) . . . Afterwards, she gave (wp.) the choice foods . . ."

In addition, a consecutive tense verb may rather serve to indicate one special aspect that has hitherto not been discussed:

3. A break in the narrative or the expression of an antithesis to the preceding verb in the sentence. This verb is sundered from the preceding one, and is to be considered by itself. For example, Ex. 13: 18-19: *waḥămūšîm ʿālû (sp.) bĕnê Yiśrāʾēl mēʾéreṣ Miṣrāyim. wayyiqqaḥ (wp.) Mōšeh ʾet ʿaṣmôt Yōsēp ʿimmô* . . . , "Israel went up armed (sp.) from Egypt. Now, Moses took (wp.) Joseph's bones with him." This aspect will be termed "break in the narrative/antithesis."

All, or almost all, consecutive tense verbs express either (1) logical conseqeunce, (2) change in time, or (3) break in the narrative. Now, the Bible contains many hundreds of occurrences of such verbs and nevertheless almost all may be subsumed under one of these three headings.[5] The few exceptions will be noted in due course.

---

3 GKC, §§ 111a, 112a. This view is followed by many grammars, such as J. Weingreen, *A Practical Grammar for Classical Hebrew*[2] (Oxford, 1959), *ad loc.*

4 GKC, §§ 111a-x, 112 a-uu, See also Rosen, *Proceedings*, 5-9, for a different analysis of these forms which still follows the traditional view of the consecutive tenses.

5 Approximately one-sixth of the Pentateuch was examined closely for these phenomena, and over 300 examples were collected. Besides the few exceptions to be noted in due course, all 300 examples follow the rules being set forth.

The examples cited above all consist of a simple verb followed by a consecutive one. In this sequence, the fact that the second verb, the consecutive one, expresses one of the three varieties of meaning just listed is not a new discovery. What is new, what has not been noticed hitherto, is that the reverse sequence, i.e., a consecutive verb followed by a simple one, also indicates one of these three varieties of meaning: Not only the sequence of simple past followed by *waw* past or simple future followed by *waw* future, but also that of *waw* past followed by simple past or *waw* future followed by simple future express one of these three aspects.[6] Note the following passages which, for each variety of meaning, comprise two examples, one *waw* past followed by simple past, and the other, *waw* future followed by simple future:

a. *Logical consequence*: (i) Ex. 15:19: *wayyāšeb (wp.) YHWH ʿălêhem ʾet mê hay-yām uběnê Yiśrāʾēl hālěkû (sp.) bay-yabbāšāh bětôk hay-yām.* "The Lord turned back upon them (wp.) the waters of the sea, and, as a result, the Israelites marched (sp.) on dry ground in the midst of the sea." The fact that the Israelites marched on dry ground *in the midst of the sea* results from the fact that God had already turned back upon the Egyptians *the waters of the sea.*[7,8] (ii) Ex. 14:4: *wěḥizzaqtî (wf.) ʾet lēb Parʿōh wěrādap (wf.) ʾaḥărēhem wěʾikkābědāh*[9] *(sf.) bě-Parʿōh uběkol ḥêlō . . .*, "I shall stiffen (wf.) Pharoah's heart and he he will pursue (also wf.) them, and, consequently, I shall gain glory (sf.)[9] through Pharoah and all his host."

b. *Change in time*: (i) Num. 11:30-31: *wayyēʾāsēp* (wp.) *Mōšeh ʾel hammaḥăneh hûʾ wěziqnê Yiśrāʾēl. wěrûăḥ nāsaʿ mēʾet YHWH . . .*, "Moses withdrew (wp.) into the camp, both he and the elders of Israel. Later, a wind went forth (sp.) from the Lord . . ." (ii) Lev. 26:5: *wěhiśśîg* (wf.) *lākem dáyiš ʾet habbāṣîr ubāṣîr yaśśîg (sf.) ʾet zāraʿ . . .*, "Your threshing shall overtake the vintage (wf.), and later your vintage shall overtake (sf.) the sowing."

c. *Break in the narrative*: (i) Ex. 13:18: *wayyassēb (wp.) ʾĔlōhîm ʾet hāʿām dérek hammidbar Yam Sûp waḥămûšîm ʿālû (sp.) běnê Yiśrāʾēl mēʾéreṣ Miṣrāyim.* "Consequently,[10] God led (wp.) the people round about by way of the Sea of Reeds. Now, the Israelites went up armed (sp.) out of the Land of Egypt."[11] (ii) Lev. 19:18-19: *wěʾāhabtā (wf.) lěrēʿăkā kāmōkā . . . ʾet ḥuqqōtāy tišmōrû* (sf.) . . . , "You shall love (wf.) your neighbor as yourself . . . You shall observe (sf.) my laws." In both of these verses, the new Jewish Publication Society translation of the Torah begins a new paragraph with the second clause, the one with the simple tense verb. This shows that the translators were conscious of the break in the narrative at this point in each case.[12]

---

[6] "Aspect" is being used here and in the sequel to denote all three of the main uses of the consecutive tenses that were described on p. 169. This is the case even though only the third type is a true aspect in the technical sense.

[7] [But perhaps this verse exhibits the sequence: sp (*bāʾ*) + wp (*wayyāšeb*) + sp (*hālěkû*). – Ed.]

[8] A second example of the sequence of *waw* past followed by simply past which expresses consequence may be found in Deut. 32:15. This example is unsure since the passage belongs to a poem, and our rules apply to prose in the first instance:

wayyišman Yěšurūn wayyibʿāṭ	"So Jeshurun grew fat and kicked –
šāmantā ʿābītā kāśītā	" Consequently you grew fat and gross and coarse."

That is, because Jeshurun (the personification of the people of Israel) grew fat and kicked, you (the individual member of the people of Israel) also grew fat and gross and coarse, etc.

[9] The *waw* prefixed to this word is the conjunction "and." If it were consecutive, the form would be vocalized *wāʾikkābědāh*, and not *wěʾikkābědāh*. Thus *wěʾikkābědāh* is not a consecutive form at all.

[10] "Consequently" is added here because *wayyassēb* follows a simple past. This shift in tense, not cited here, expresses consequence.

[11] Besides normal full verbs, the same phenomenon may occur when the auxiliary verb *hāyōh*, "to be," is employed. It is true that this verb is sometimes considered a "bound morpheme" whose use, in and of itself, cannot be taken as evidence of anything having to do with tenses. Nevertheless, as is shown by the following example, the tense in which *hāyōh* occurs is meaningful, and corresponds to the rules being set forth. Gen.

These six examples are illustrative of the phenomenon; they are in no way exhaustive. For, many dozens of examples may be found in the Pentateuch in which the sequence of a consecutive tense followed by a simple one expresses one of these three varieties of meaning. It is clear, then, that both sequences — i.e., a simple tense followed by a consecutive one *or* a consecutive tense followed by a simple one — indicate one of these three aspects. In other words, it does not matter which type of tense — whether simple or consecutive — is placed first; what is required in order to express one of these aspects is merely the change from either type to the other.

In connected prose passages, several changes in aspect, each indicated by shifting from a simple tense to a consecutive one, and *vice versa ad infinitum* may occur in one narrative section, or even in one verse. For example, in the introduction to the "Covenant between the Parts," Gen. 15:1-8, most of the verbs are *waw past* since they are used to relate an event on one level. Such is the character through v. 5b: *wayyō'mer (wp.) lô kōh yihyeh zarékā* . . . "He said (wp.) 'So shall be your offspring.'" Suddenly, in v. 6, the tense changes twice, first from *waw* past to simple past (vv. 5b-6a), and then from simple past back to *waw* past (v. 6a-b): *wĕhe'ĕmîn* (sp.)[13] *ba-YHWH wayyaḥšĕbehāh (wp.) lô ṣĕdāqāh.* "Consequently, he trusted (sp.) in God, and for that reason, He [God] reckoned (wp.) it to his merit." Both of these changes in tense express the consequence of the immediately preceding action:

1. *wĕhe'ĕmîn*, "he trusted" (sp.) following *wayyō'mer*, "He [God] said" (wp.) — because God assured him of bounteous offspring, he trusted in Him.

2. *wayyaḥšĕbehāh*, "he [God] reckoned it" (wp.) following *wĕhe'ĕmîn*, "he trusted (sp.) — because he trusted in Him, God reckoned it to his merit. Afterwards the narrative continues on the same level, and therefore the following verses contain verbs in the same tense as *wayyaḥšĕbehāh*, "he reckoned it" — *waw* past.

With this example, the analysis of the regular rules for changing from consecutive tenses to simple ones and *vice versa* may be concluded.[14]

III

Like most grammatical rules, these governing the use of the consecutive tenses have their exceptions or special cases. They are: (i) the needs of the poetic structures embedded in the prose narrative; and (ii) negation. Both of these are external, non-meaningful factors which by themselves cause the verb to be shifted from a consecutive to a simple tense. More specifically, they require, in some way, that the consecutive tense verb be moved from its clause initial position to another place in the sentence. However, a consecutive tense verb, as explained above,[15] must stand first in its clause, and once its position is changed, it must revert to a

---

27:30: *wayĕhî (wp.) ka'ăšer killāh Yiṣḥāq lĕbarrēk 'et Ya'ăqob wayĕhî (wp.) 'ak yāṣō' yāṣā' Ya'ăqob me'et pĕnē Yiṣḥāq 'ābîw wĕ-'Ēsāw 'āḥîw bā' (sp.) miṣṣēdō.*
"It was (wp.) when Isaac finished blessing Jacob; yea, it was (wp.) when Jacob had just left the presence of his father Isaac — Esau came back (sp.) from his hunt." Here the change from *waw* past (*wayehî*) to simple past (*bā'*) expresses the absolute shift in perspective, interrupting the previously flowing narration. Note that *killāh* and *yāṣā'* are syntactically, though not logically, subordinate to *wayĕhî*.

[12] See *The Torah, The Five Books of Moses, A New Translation* . . . (Philadelphia: The Jewish Publication Society of America, 1962), 122, etc.

[13] There is no need to emend *wĕhe'ĕmîn* (*wh'mn*) to *wayya'āmēn* (*wy'mn*), as is suggested in Kittel's *BH*[3], if our interpretation is valid.

[14] It has sometimes been suggested that the *waw consecutive* is used to introduce a dependent clause. This is true, to the degree that a clause containing a consecutive tense-verb is equivalent to an *English* dependent clause. However, it remains syntactically in *Hebrew*, an independent one.

[15] See p. 168.

simple tense verb. In such cases, the actual change in tense need not necessarily express one of the three aspects noted above.

The first group of such cases occurs as a by-product of poetic structures. Now, in prose passages some poetic structures may have been introduced in order to evoke a solemn or festive mood, or may simply occur because the passage was originally composed in poetry, and only later rewritten in prose.[16] In such contexts, some changes in tense may result innocently from the requirements of the poetic structures themselves. One common art of the poet is chiasmus, which is the reversing of the order of the words in the two parallel lines of a poetic distich. Often the chiasmus is obtained by changing the position of the verbs in the two parallel stichs. Whereas a simple tense may be placed in any position within the clause, a consecutive tense must come first in its clause on account of the very nature of the *waw* that is prefixed to it. Therefore, if one wishes to use a consecutive tense verb in the first parallel stich, and to change its position in the second one, he would also have to change the consecutive tense verb to a simple one. The reason, again, is that the consecutive tense verb must stand first in its clause, and as soon as its position is moved, it must revert to a simple tense verb. In such cases, this shift in tense does *not* indicate one of three varieties of meaning elaborated earlier. This fact is illustrated by the following four examples. In each one, the consecutive tense verb occurs in the first stich in initial position whereas the simple tense verb is placed in second position in the second stich:[17]

(i)	Gen. 1:5:	
	wayyiqrā' (wp.) 'Ĕlōhîm lā-'ôr yôm	"Called God (wp.) the light day
	wĕlāḥōšek qārā' (sp.) laylāh.	"And the darkness he called (sp.) night."
(ii)	Ex. 12:8:	
	wĕ'ākĕlū (wf.) 'et hab-bāśār bal-laylāh haz-zeh ṣĕlî-'ēš umaṣṣôt	"They shall eat (wf.) the flesh that night roasted over the fire with unleavened bread,
	'Al mĕrōrîm yō'kĕluhû (sf.)	"Over bitter herbs they shall eat (sf.) it."[18]
(iii)	Ex. 12:14:	
	wĕḥaggōtem (wf.) 'ōtô ḥag la-YHWH	"You shall celebrate it (wf.) as a festival to the Lord
	lĕdôrōtêkem ḥuqqat 'ôlām tĕḥagguhû (sf.)	"Throughout all generations as an institution for all time shall you celebrate (sf.) it."[18]
(iv)	Ex. 14:6:	
	wayye'ĕsōr (wp.) 'et rikbo	"Hitched he (wp.) his chariot
	wĕ-'et 'ammô lāqaḥ (sp.) 'immō.	"And his people he took (sp.) with him."

In these four examples the change in tense does not express any of the aspects described above. Nevertheless, once the new tense is determined by the requirements of chiastic parallelism, it is continued or shifted in accordance with the usual rules. In the four examples just cited, the following occurs:

(i) The creation narrative, Gen. 1:1-5 immediately changes to the *waw* past in order to express later time: *wayĕhī* (wp.)[19] *'éreb*, "later it was (wp.) evening."

---

[16] On the matter of poetic originals for currently prose narratives, cf. U.M.D. Cassuto, *From Adam to Noah* (Heb.) (Jerusalem, 1959), x, 3ff., *et passim; idem, A Commentary on the Book of Exodus* (Heb.) (Jerusalem, 1959), vii, 3, 108f.; *idem, Tarbiṣ*, 13 (1941-42), 197-212, ibid., 14 (1942-43), 1-10; and *idem, Kenesset le-Zekher H.N. Bialik*, VIII, 126, etc.

[17] The translations of these couplets are intentionally stilted for effect and clarity.

[18] The two halves of these verses may be divided differently without affecting the fact of the chiasmic parallelism.

[19] See n. 11.

(ii) The first commands for the Passover, Ex. 12:8ff., continue in the same tense until v. 11b, where the verb shifts to the *waw* future to express consequence: *wa'ăkaltem (wf.) 'ōtô bĕḥippāzôn*, "consequently you shall eat (wf.) it in haste."

(iii) The later commands for the Passover, Ex. 12:14ff., also continue in the same tense, this time until v. 17. There, it changes to the *waw* future to express the result of the preceding series of commands: *ušĕmartem (wf.) 'et hammaṣṣôt*, "therefore, you shall observe (wf.) [the Feast of] Unleavened Bread."

(iv) The Exodus narrative, Ex. 14:6ff., immediately changes to the *waw* past to give the force of "in addition": *wayyiqqaḥ (wp.) šēš mē'ôt rékeb bāḥûr*, "In addition, he took (wp.) six hundred of his picked chariots."

Thus, it is clear that even if a change in tense is initially caused by the requirements of poetic structures, once it has been so shifted, it is immediately thereafter brought into alignment with the normal rules for sequence of tenses. It is continued in the same tense, or is changed, as is needed to express one of the three aspects.

The second group of cases in which the shift from a consecutive to a simple tense is determined by external factors is negation. The particles which directly negate the verb, *'al* and *lô'*, must immediately precede the verb which they govern.[20] That is, they assume first position in relation to the verb, while it stands in second position relative to them. However, a consecutive tense verb, as we have seen, must stand first in its clause. Therefore, it cannot be directly negated, but a simple tense verb must be used instead.

Yet, even though this shift from a consecutive to a simple tense is caused by this external rule of word order, the change itself is still meaningful. It expresses one of the three aspects described above, as in the following examples:

1. *Logical consequence*: Gen 27:22-23: *wayyĕmuššēhû (wp.) wayyō'mer (wp.) haq-qôl qôl Ya'ăqōb wĕhayyādayîm yĕdê 'Ēsāw wĕlô' hikkîrô (sp.)* . . . , "He felt (wp.) him and said (wp.): 'The voice is the voice of Jacob, but the hands are the hands of Esau'; therefore, he did not recognize (sp.) him . . ."

2. *Later time*: Ex 21:18: . . . *wĕhikkāh (wf.) 'îš 'et rē'ēhû bĕ'ében 'ô bĕ'egrôp wĕlô' yāmût* (sf.) . . . , "and one strikes (wf.) the other with stone or fist, and later he does not die. (sf.) . . ."

3. *Break in the narrative*: Ex. 14:28: *wayyāšûbû (wp.) hammayim wayĕkassû (wp.) 'et hārékeb wĕ'et hap-pārāšîm lĕkol ḥêl Par'ōh hab-bā'îm 'aḥărêhem bayyam lô' niš'ar (sp.) bāhem 'ad 'éḥad.* "The waters turned back (wp.) and covered (wp.) the chariotry and the horsemen belonging to all of Pharoah's army that had followed them into the sea: not one of them remained (sp.). While it does summarize the preceding, the last clause interrupts the narrative.

IV

On the basis of these observations it is possible to formulate the rules for sequence of tenses in prose as follows:

1. There are two possible sequences and two tenses in each:
a. past sequence – 1. simple past, as *dibbēr*; 2. *waw* past, as *wayyō'mer.*
b. future sequence: – 1. simple future, as *yĕdabbēr*; 2. *waw* future, as *wĕ'āmar.*

2. *In independent clauses*, in either sequence, the first verb may be placed in either of the two tenses.

[20] Cf. GKC, § 152e.

3. Further verbs occur in the same tense as the first until there is a change in aspect.

4. The tense of the verb is changed from that of the preceding one, either from simple to *waw*, or from *waw* to simple, in order to express one of the following aspects:

a. consequence or result
b. later time or logically additional matter
c. break in the narrative, or an antithesis to the preceding matter.

Remark 1: Sometimes poetic devices embedded in the prose narrative, such as chiasmus, may by themselves cause a change in tense without expressing one of these three aspects. In such cases, the sequence of tenses immediately thereafter continues according to the regular rules.

Remark 2: Even though negation requires the use of simple tenses following *waw* ones, such changes in tense still express one of these three aspects.

5. In one narrative there may be several changes in tense, but each one expresses one of these three aspects. A narrative may be continued in one tense for several verses, then be shifted to the other and be so continued for several verses, before it is finally changed back to the first; or, it may shift back and forth several times within a verse or two; or its number of changes may be midway between these extremes. The amount of such changes in tense depends solely on the nature of the narrative.

6. In analyzing the sequence of an *independent clause*, only it is to be taken into account. A neighboring *dependent clause* is to be disregarded because it has a sequence of its own (see § 7). For example, in the consecution: (i) independent clause – (ii) dependent clause – (iii) independent clause, one takes into account only (i) and (iii).

7. *In dependent clauses*, there are also two sequences and two tenses in each. However, such a clause requires that the verb assume second position since the subordinate conjunction occupies first place. Consequently, as in negation, the first verb in a dependent clause must occur in a simple tense.

8. Further coördinate verbs in a dependent clause may appear either in a simple or in a *waw* tense following the rules of §§ 3-5.

9. While a subordinate clause ordinarily depends directly on an independent one, it may instead depend on a second subordinate clause, which itself depends on an independent one. That is, in one sentence there may be several different orders of subordination. In such cases, one must analyze the sequence of each order of subordination separately.[21]

V

From the preceding analysis, one fact emerges clearly; the simple tenses do not signify anything inherently different than the consecutive ones: it is rather the juxtaposition of the one *versus* the other that expresses the several aspects. In fact, it is conceivably possible to change a simple tense to a consecutive one anywhere in a passage without changing the meaning, so long as *all* the verbs are correspondingly shifted from their

[21] In order to illustrate the application of these rules, I have prepared a graphic analysis of Ex. 12:1-42. Because of its length it cannot be printed here. However, readers desiring it may obtain a Xerox copy by writing the author.

original tenses. The change from a simple tense to a consecutive one and *vice versa* is what counts – not the inherent nature of the two tense types.[22] In a word, the two have exactly the same function.

To use phonetic terminology, the two possible sequences (simple followed by consecutive or consecutive followed by simple – see p. 173 f, §§ 1-4, especially 4) may be compared to two allophones of one phoneme. Just as the two allophones express the same phonemic value and are only differentiated by their position within the word, so either sequence signifies the same syntactic value and is only differentiated by its position within the sentence. That is, either tense type may occur first, to be followed by the other tense type according to the rules given above. Therefore, since either 'allophone' may precede, the tenses involved in the two 'allophonic' sequences' are truly identical.

In summary, the simple and the consecutive tenses may be defined as two functionally equivalent tense-systems which occur, one following the other, according to the rules for indicating the three aspects of consequence, later time, or break in the narrative/antithesis.

This discovery, that the two tense types are essentially the same, is significant for understanding the nature of biblical Hebrew verbs. For, we may conclude that, whatever the situation may have been in Proto-Semitic or in Proto-Hebrew, the tenses in biblical Hebrew prose do express some sort of time. On our system, it is possible to interpret every biblical Hebrew prose verb-form as a *true tense*, one indicating *the time of the action*. The simple past and the *waw* past always refer to past time in the broadest sense, and may be interpreted, in terms of English tenses, as simple past, past progressive, perfect, pluperfect, etc. The simple future and the *waw* future, correspondingly, always refer to present or future time in the widest sense, and may be understood, in terms of English tenses, as present, present progressive, future, future progressive, future perfect, etc. The three aspects listed above, on the other hand, are indicated by the juxtaposition of the two tense-types. It is then conceivable that the more widely studied aspects of completeness (perfect) *versus* incompleteness (imperfect) would also be indicated by the placement of the verb within the clause, and not by its morphology. If this is correct, it would add weight to the findings of F.R. Blake (cited above)[23] that the biblical Hebrew finite verb forms are true tenses expressing some sort of time, and would contradict the assertion of S.R. Driver (also cited above[24]) that the biblical Hebrew finite verb forms signify aspects rather than true tenses. However, this determination applies only to *prose*; it has no bearing on this issue in other strata or literary types (especially poetry) in the language.

This discovery is also important for understanding the origin of the consecutive *versus* the simple tenses. That is, the preceding synchronic discussion is highly relevant to the historical, diachronic issue of the development of the consecutive tenses including the *waw consecutive* itself. This is a subject to which Professor Cyrus H. Gordon and his student G. Douglas Young have made a great contribution.[25] However, on account of the space required to expound this matter, it must be deferred to another occasion.

---

[22] The distinction is not between a *waw*-tense and a non-*waw*-tense, but rather between the actual tenses as described on p. 168.

[23] See p. 167 and n. 1, esp. Rabin, *Taḥbîr*, 30-31, citing Blake, and recently J.A. Hughes, *JNES*, 29 (1970), 12-24.

[24] See p. 167 and n. 1, esp. Rabin, *Taḥbîr*, 30-31 citing Driver.

[25] See Gordon, *UT*, 110, § 12.9, citing his study in *Or.*, N.S. 22 (1953), 231, and that of G.D. Young, *JNES*, 12 (1953), 248-252.

I should like to acknowledge the helpful criticism of earlier drafts of this paper given by my colleagues Profs. B.A. Levine of New York University, and J. Mey and R.L. King, both of the University of Texas at Austin, and to express my thanks to Prof. R. Hetzron of the University of California at Santa Barbara, for references to some of the current literature.

THE JORDAN OF JERICHO

Elmer B. Smick

For centuries the derivation of the term Jordan has been a challenge to Hebrew scholars. The most popular explanation derives it from the root *yrd* (descend) as the "river that goes down." But this derivation fails to explain the last letter, not to speak of the vocalization. The Greek form *ho Iardanēs*[1] and the Egyptian *Iarduna*[2] imply that all four letters *yrdn* are part of the root. Some scholars have looked for a non-Hebrew origin. Koehler and Baumgartner in their Hebrew Lexicon cite von Soden's negative reaction to an Iranian explanation which posits two Indo-European words, *yar* = year and *don* = river, thus the "always flowing river," similar to the meaning of the Sumerian word for the Tigris, *idigna* = "always streaming river."[3] A good explanation is C.H. Gordon's interesting suggestion, based on Homeric references to *ho Iardanos* as rivers in Crete and Elis, that *yardēn* is an East Mediterranean word for "river."[4]

The early Aegean contacts with the Bible World are now more than ever appreciated, as new studies in Homer and Minoan documents strengthen the view that the East Mediterranean peoples of the second millenium were interdependent. It is now reasonable to look toward the west as well as toward the east for an understanding of biblical terminology. C.H. Gordon points out regarding Gen 10 that ". . . the very first group is the Japhethite branch including the Ionians and the inhabitants of Cyprus and the islands of the Aegean (vv 2-5). . . . When the Hebrews themselves see fit to place the populations of the East Mediterranean at the very head of the list, we may safely conclude that the area was of prime importance in the Bible world."[5] In the Bible from the Patriarchal times on we find not only the East Mediterranean Philistines, who bequeathed their name to the land

---

1 As in the Septuagint.

2 *ANET*, 242, as taken from J. Simons, *Handbook for the Study of Egyptian Topographical Lists Relating to Western Asia* (1937).

3 Koehler - Baumgartner, *Lexicon in Veteris Testamenti Libros.*

4 Cyrus H. Gordon, *World of the Old Testament*, 122, n. 19; Koehler - Baumgartner also notes this link.
New Horizons in Old Testament Literature, p. 21; [cf. above, pages 119ff.].

of Palestine, but their cousins, the Cretim and the Caphtorim, who are also mentioned in Egyptian and Ugaritic sources.[6] It is also common knowledge that some Hebrew common nouns have an Aegean origin.[7] These Sea peoples played a significant role in the cultural continuum throughout the East Mediterranean littoral from the early second millenium.[8] Jerome suggested that the "Jor" of Jordan was from *ye'ōr* (stream, used of the Nile and other rivers), which he says is equivalent to Greek *hreithron* (stream); and the second half of Jordan, "dan," he takes as the city Dan near one of the river's sources. While this etymology is highly questionable, it appears that the Homeric usage of *Iardanos* has affinity with the word *hreethra* (streams). It is therefore most interesting that *ho Iardanos* (cf. LXX *ho Iardanēs*) is used in Homer to designate two rivers, one in Crete and the other on the Peloponnesus.

In the *Iliad* (7:135) Nestor recalls his youth, when he fought beside the swift flowing Celadon beneath the walls of Pheia about the streams of Jardan, written *Iardanou amphi hreethra.* Pheia was in Elis, a district on the northwestern corner of the Peloponnesus. In the *Odyssey* (3:292) Menelaus, caught in a storm, brings half his ships to Crete, "where the Cydonians dwelt about the streams of Jardan"; again the phrase *Iardanou, amphi hreethra* is employed. Homer's use of the same expression to describe two different rivers, especially when in the *Iliad* the name of the river is already mentioned, adds weight to the view that *Iardanou amphi hreethra* means "on both sides of the streams of the river," *Iardanos* being an old East Mediterranean word for "river."

Though we are still without an etymology, it must be noted that consistent use of this word in Hebrew with the definite article, *hayyardēn*, marks *yardēn* as a common noun. It is not characteristic of Hebrew to use the definite article with a proper name. The Lexicon by Brown, Driver and Briggs notes this fact with the statement that the Hebrew article is "Never, however (as in Greek e.g. *ho platon*), before true proper names, though it is used with certain terms, chiefly geographical of which the original appellative sense has not been lost."[9] Thus, *habba'al* = the lord, *haśśāṭān* = the adversary. It is significant that the only two passages where *yardēn* is used without the definite article are poetry.[10] We attribute this to the archaizing tendency of poetry. Hebrew in its early stages did not use the article at all. So despite these two poetic usages of the word, *yardēn* was understood by the people as a common noun employing the article to mean "the river."

A most interesting Old Testament usage of *yardēn* is found in a series of passages in Numbers, Joshua and 1 Chron where we find the expression *yardēn yerēḥô*. For example, in Num 33:50 the plains of Moab are located *'al yardēn yerēḥô*, which most take to mean "by Jordan near Jericho."[11] But several other passages using *yardēn yerēḥô* have made Old Testament scholars question the text, notably Num 34:15, Jos 16:1, 20:8, and 1 Chron 6:63 (78). Here the Hebrew expression is *mē'ēber lᵉyardēn yerēḥô*, which is regularly translated "beyond the Jordan at Jericho" in the RSV. But the territory described is not limited to the region near Jericho and that is why the texts are questioned.

Likewise, Jos 20:8 locates the eastern cities of refuge from Bezer in the plain of Reuben to Ramoth in Gilead and Golan in Bashan as adjacent to (*mē'ēber*) the Jordan at Jericho (cf. also I Chron 6:63 (78)). How could all this territory possibly be opposite Jericho? At this point the problem centers around the two words in juxtaposition, *yardēn yerēḥô*. In the three passages, Numbers 34:15, Joshua 20:8 and 1 Chron 6:63, the He-

---

6 Cf. Gen 10:13, 14; Deut 2:23; Amos 9:7; II Sam 8:18; Ezek 25:16; Zeph 2:5; *ANET*, 241, n. 39; Cyrus H. Gordon, *Ugarit and Minoan Crete*, 28, 30, 49, n. 10.

7 *kōba'*, helmet; *seren*, lord (tyrant) are words brought to Palestine with the sea people.

8 Gordon, *Ugarit and Minoan Crete*, 14.

9 *BDB*, 207, Ia.

10 The two passages are Ps 42:7 and Job 40:23. Poetry in any language tends to preserve archaic grammar. So even a common noun which otherwise might carry an article, in old Hebrew poetry would fail to have it.

11 "At Jericho" (RSV); "near Jericho" (KJV).

brew text is identical (*mē'ēber yardēn yerēḥô*) and the Alexandrinus Septuagint of Jos 20:8 has *peran tou Iordanou Iericho.* But in Num 34:15 the Septuagint translators struggled with the meaning and saw fit to add *kata* (toward, by) between *Iordanou* and *Iericho*, as we also have in our English versions. On Num 34:15 G.B. Gray in the *International Critical Commentary* says, "'at Jericho' is an unsuitable limitation in describing the frontier line of two or two and one-half tribes: The phrase has perhaps been mechanically written or added under the influence of 22:1 and other passages where the limitation is suitably used." *The Interpreter's Bible*, following this lead, says, "The sentence is written as from Canaan itself, for Jericho is said to be eastward,[12] and the mention of Jericho is not exactly a full description of the territory asked for by the tribes of Reuben and Gad."

It is difficult to believe that all these references to *yardēn yerēḥô* were "mechanically written." In my opinion the evidence converges on the point that *yardēn yerēḥô* means exactly what it says in Hebrew: "the river (or Jordan) of Jericho," as distinguished from other Jordans (rivers). Jericho, being one of the world's oldest cities and for so long a time the most commanding fortress in that valley, was employed in this old appellative for the river in days when the root meaning of *yardēn* as "river" was widely understood.

Thus Josh 16:1 makes sense and may be translated: "The lot of the children of Joseph went out from the 'river of Jericho,' east of the waters of Jericho, going up through the wilderness from Jericho to the hill country of Bethel." Here "the river of Jericho" (*yardēn yerēḥô*) refers to the whole eastern border of Ephraim and Manasseh, while "the waters of Jericho" may be a specific reference to Ein es-Sultan, the spring at Jericho. The southern boundary began at the Jordan and went by Jericho up through the barren slopes to Bethel.

1 Chron 6:63 (78), giving the eastern cities of refuge, would go as follows: "And opposite the river (*yardēn*) of Jericho, that is, on the east side of the river (*yardēn*) . . ."

Num 34:15 would read: "The two and a half tribes took their inheritance adjacent to the river (*yardēn*) of Jericho, eastward toward the sunrising."[13]

Since the Jordan Valley was the earliest area in Palestine to have an established urban settlement, some consideration should be given to the notion that this was the river of the moon (god) in very early times. If names mean anything, Jericho in the south and Beth Yerah (Khirbet Kerak) in the north, where the river Jordan leaves the Lake of Galilee, were originally "moon" cities. Their names being derived from the Canaanite word for "moon" (*yeraḥ*) may indicate that they were great centers of moon worship. The Canaanites also worshiped the moon farther north on the edge of the Huleh valley at Hazor.[14] A term such as *yardēn yerēḥ(ô)* (the river of the moon) may be behind the terminology dealt with in the passages above.

---

[12] In numerous places where *'eber* (usually translated "beyond" or "opposite") is used in relation to the Jordan the author specifies which side he means. Thus Josh 1:5 speaks of the west, but Num 34:15 explicitly speaks of the east. *'Ēber* itself simply means "a side" or just "opposite" or "adjacent" and has no reference to which side. For example, in Ex 32:15 the tablets of the law were written *miššnê 'ebrēhem*, "on both their sides." The force of *'ēber* as "adjacent to" or "opposite" reminds us of the New Testament use of the preposition *peran* in the phrase translated "Bethany beyond Jordan." The Greek phrase says nothing about which side Bethany was on. *Peran*, when not used with verbs of motion, denotes "across from," "opposite" or "over against." (Cf. Pierson Parker, "Bethany beyond Jordan," *JBL* [December 1955]). This also explains the Matthew 4:15 quotation from Is 9:1, 2, where Galilee seems to be placed "beyond Jordan"; both the Old and New Testament should be translated" over against (adjacent to) the Jordan in Galilee of the Gentiles." This also dissolves the old notion that Jericho was being considered east by the writer while he was pretending to be Moses in Transjordan.

[13] The city of Jabesh (Gilead) either gave its name or received its name from the wady Yabis. The same is true of Nahr el-Leddani (the Dan stream) and the city of Dan.

[14] Cf. Yigael Yadin, *Hazor* 1:89.

ANATOLIA AND THE KHIRBET KERAK PROBLEM[1]

Ian A. Todd

Department of Mediterranean Studies, Brandeis University, Waltham, Massachusetts

The Khirbet Kerak Problem has exercised the minds (and imaginations) of numerous scholars over the past thirty-five years or so, and widely scattered material has been assembled to form a seemingly coherent picture of wide ranging contacts, possibly involving the movements of people. The determination of interconnections amongst prehistoric East Mediterranean cultures is of the greatest importance for a true understanding of the history of the region, but archaeologists must attempt to ensure that their framework of relationships is based upon solid foundations. Too often in the past sweeping movements of people and interconnections have been based on the flimsiest evidence, and the writer is in full agreement with the present trend to re-examine many of the proposed "migrations" in the light of the currently available archaeological evidence.

Where possible, theories of movements of people and artifacts must be substantiated by the application of scientific analytical techniques to the artifacts in question; such analyses have been undertaken with apparent success on obsidian from Anatolia and the Aegean, and it has been possible to assemble a coherent, if incomplete, picture of the mechanics of the obsidian trade in the prehistoric East Mediterranean area.[2] Neutron activation and other forms of analyses are also of the greatest value in determining the actual movement of artifacts.

Although the movement of ideas is much more difficult to document, scientifically proven movements of materials such as obsidian may indicate the existence of routes of communication along which other ideas

---

[1] The following abbreviations are used in this paper:

AfO	Archiv für Orientforschung
AJA	American Journal of Archaeology
AnSt	Anatolian Studies
IEJ	Israel Exploration Journal
OIP	Oriental Institute Publications
PPS	Proceedings of the Prehistoric Society
TAD	Türk Arkeoloji Dergisi

Also see select bibliography which follows.

[2] C. Renfrew, J.E. Dixon and J.R. Cann, *PPS* 34 (1968) 319ff. and G.A. Wright, *Obsidian Analyses and Prehistoric Near Eastern Trade: 7500 to 3500 B.C.*, Anthropological Papers 37, Museum of Anthropology, University of Michigan, Ann Arbor (1969).

may have passed.[3] Suggestions of migrations must be supported by a sizable body of archaeological evidence rather than a few approximate similarities of artifact types occurring in widely separated regions, often with no similar material being found in the intervening area. Known historical events must be taken into consideration, but the historian must beware of forcing archaeological fact to fit his interpretation of such events. If the Mycenae Shaft Graves are to be attributed to the expelled "Hyksos" rulers of Egypt, for instance, a great deal more evidence must be presented than a number of legends supported by a small number of similarities in artifact types in Greece and Egypt.[4] The same may also be said for the proposed Hyksos presence in the Karpass Peninsula of Cyprus in the Middle Cypriot period.[5] Similarly, it is unsatisfactory to propose the "arrival" of the Sumerians in Mesopotamia from outside on the basis of philological arguments, when the Mesopotamian archaeological evidence strongly indicates continuity, and when there is no clear candidate for the country of origin for the proposed migration.[6] In brief, archaeologists must avoid attributing changes in material culture to movements of people unless their evidence is sufficiently conclusive. Due attention must also be paid to the circumstances governing the availability of information; apparent changes may be due to gradual development not yet visible in the archaeological record, rather than to actual population movements. Many variables must be considered to account for a given set of circumstances. The purpose of this paper is to sound a cautionary note in the discussion of the Khirbet Kerak Problem, and to make available some pertinent information derived from a recent survey of Central Anatolia.

In essence, the Khirbet Kerak Problem centres on the connection of the dark burnished wares found in Eastern Anatolia, Northwest Iran and the Trans-Caucasian area with the Red-Black Burnished Ware of the 'Amuq Plain and with the Khirbet Kerak ware found in the Syro-Palestinian region (Fig. 1).[7] Many authors see close similarities between the pottery types, and additional evidence has been cited in the form of the occurrence of circular architecture at Beth Yerah, Yanik Tepe and the Trans-Caucasus. The distribution of certain types of portable hearths and stands has also been considered to add weight to the proposed connections. This combined evidence is often taken to indicate a movement of people southwestward from Eastern Anatolia and beyond to the 'Amuq Plain, and then southward to Syria, Lebanon, Israel and Jordan. In a recent publication, Charles Burney has reiterated his earlier opinion that the people involved in this movement must be the Hurrians.[8]

Central Anatolia and its Relationship to Eastern Anatolia

The relationship of Central Anatolian Early Bronze Age wares to those of the Trans-Caucasus and Syro-Palestine needs to be clarified in view of recent statements. Professor Ruth Amiran views the "great affinity, indeed almost homogeneity of the pottery, both shapes, surface treatment and decoration, which unifies the whole wide range of separated regions, from Transcaucasia, . . . through Eastern and Central Anatolia, to the whole length of the Levant" as one phenomenon suggesting an ethnic movement emanating from the Trans-Caucasian regions.[9] However, both Mellaart and Burney have pointed out that ceramic connections between Central and

---

[3] G.A. Wright, op. cit., 81f.

[4] cf. F.H. Stubbings, *Camb. Anc. Hist.*, rev. ed., fascicle 18.

[5] cf. E. Sjöqvist, *Problems of the Late Cypriot Bronze Age*, Stockholm (1940) 198f.

[6] J. Oates, *Iraq* 22 (1960) 44ff.

[7] For a detailed site distribution map of the Early Trans-Caucasian Zone, see C.A. Burney and D.M. Lang, *The Peoples of the Hills*, London (1971) map II. For the 'Amuq, see R.J. Braidwood, *Mounds in the Plain of Antioch*, *OIP* XLVIII, Chicago (1937), especially Map XXII. For Palestine, see J.B. Hennessy, *The Foreign Relations of Palestine during the Early Bronze Age*, London (1967) pl. LXII.

[8] Burney and Lang, *The Peoples of the Hills*, London (1971), 49.

[9] R. Amiran, *AnSt* 15 (1965), 165.

Eastern Anatolia in the Early Bronze Age are not as close as Amiran's observations imply.[10] This latter view is certainly correct, and is reinforced by material discovered by the writer on a survey of Central Anatolian sites undertaken during the years 1964 to 1967.[11]

The area covered by the survey is bounded approximately by the modern towns of Ankara, Yozgat, Kayseri, Niğde and the Tuz Gölü. Although the survey did not extend quite as far north as the Alaca Hüyük area, much of the pottery discovered shows clear parallels with excavated material from the sites of Alaca Hüyük, Büyük Güllücek and Alişar Hüyük. The area is of geographic importance in that it lies between the West and East Anatolian regions, and it is now possible to correlate the ceramic sequences of these various regions as a result of the field surveys of David French, James Mellaart, Gavin Brown, Charles Burney and the writer. It has also been possible, at certain periods, to divide these large areas into a number of smaller units on the evidence of ceramic distribution. Not surprisingly these ceramic units can often be equated with geographical divisions.

The chronology and ceramic variations within the Trans-Caucasian group have recently been discussed in detail by Burney, and a brief summary will suffice here.[12] Hand-made dark burnished wares are characteristic throughout the period termed Early Trans-Caucasian by Burney;[13] common shapes are jars with everted rims and various types of bowls (Fig. 2). Features[14] such as the "rail rim", the Nakhichevan lug and incised or relief decoration are common in various localities during the Early Transcaucasian period. Although the exterior colour is often dark-black, grey or brown – interiors are commonly light. It should be stressed here that, unlike the pottery of Central Anatolia, dark burnished wares remained characteristic in Eastern Anatolia in all three phases of the Early Trans-Caucasian period apart from a small group of painted wares which occur in the Malatya-Elazığ region. Painted wares have been known in this area for some years and were dated Early Bronze III by Burney in his 1958 survey report (Fig. 8:12-20).[15] These have been re-named Early Trans-Caucasian III in his latest work. However, it would appear from the most recent excavations in the Keban Dam area near Elazığ that local painted wares may occur there as early as Early Bronze I in association with Reserved Slip ware.[16] This latter ware occurs at several sites in the area – Norşun Tepe, Tepecik and several unexcavated sites.

[10] J. Mellaart, *The Chalcolithic and Early Bronze Ages in the Near East and Anatolia*, Beirut (1966) 81. C.A. Burney and D.M. Lang, *op. cit.*, 51.

[11] For preliminary reports, see the writer's articles in *AnSt* 15 (1965) 13f, 34ff, 95ff; *AnSt* 16 (1966) 15f, 43ff, 139ff; *TAD* 15 No. 2 (1966) 103ff; *AnSt* 17 (1967) 11f; *AJA* 72 (1968) 157f; *AfO* 22 (1968/9) 142. The Neolithic material found on the survey will be published in the series *Studies in Mediterranean Archaeology* and the post-Neolithic material is currently being written up for publication.

[12] C.A. Burney and D.M. Lang, *op. cit.*, chapter 3.

[13] For a discussion of the problem of terminology, see C.A. Burney and D.M. Lang, *op. cit.*, 44. In this paper I have adopted Burney's terminology of Early Trans-Caucasian I-III when referring to the whole of the East Anatolian, Northwest Iranian and the Georgian and Armenian areas of Russia. When speaking specifically of Eastern Anatolia, the terminology originally proposed by Burney in *AnSt* 8 (1958), 157ff (Early Bronze I-III) has been retained. For Central Anatolia, the conventional Early Bronze I-III terminology is used. Although only few C14 dates are available, Burney has suggested the following dates for the phases of the Early Trans-Caucasian culture:

I-II: starts c. 3000 B.C. or just before and ends c. 2300 B.C.

III: c. 2300 B.C. to c. 2000 B.C.

[14] See description of illustrated pottery in the Catalogue which accompanies each figure.

[15] C.A. Burney, *AnSt* 8 (1958), 205ff and figs. 244-85.

[16] U. Esin, *1968 Summer Work*, Middle East Technical University, Keban Project Publications, Serial No. 1, Publication 1, Ankara (1970), 168f. The same situation occurs at Norşun Tepe according to a personal communication from Dr. H. Hauptmann.

Another significant feature of the Elazığ area is the occurrence in quantity of southern imports – not only Reserved Slip ware but also a form of 'Amuq Plain Simple ware;[17] at Korucu Tepe a small quantity of wheel-made grey to orange ware occurs which seems to precede the 'Amuq Simple ware imports at that site. Van Loon suggests a North Mesopotamian or Northeast Syrian origin.[18]

It is also clear that the area as far west as Kültepe-Kayseri participated in this trade with the South. Reserved Slip ware and 'Amuq Simple ware both occur in the Elbistan Plain, while Syrian wheel-made jars and Tarsus EB II type corrugated cups are found at Kültepe.[19] However, it would appear that these imports do not penetrate further west than Kültepe. Although Kültepe, in common with the Elazığ region, shared in this trade with the South, no recognizable East Anatolian dark burnished wares have yet been found there; in fact, the local Kültepe wares clearly belong to the Central Anatolian ceramic province, although the site is close to the southeastern boundary with the East Anatolian region (Fig. 1).[20]

The ceramic dividing line between the Eastern and Central Anatolian provinces is more clearly visible in EB II and III than in EB I, although the similarities between the dark burnished EB I material in Central Anatolia and the Early Trans-Caucasian wares are by no means extensive. On the evidence of the surveys of Gavin Brown and the writer, the dividing line may be drawn east of Kayseri and west of the Elbistan Plain; it would seem to run approximately northeast to southwest in the area south of Pınarbaşı on the Kayseri-Malatya route.

A serious problem in Central Anatolia is the lack of a well stratified and published pottery sequence, but some information is available from Alaca Hüyük, Alişar Hüyük, Eskiyapar, Suluca Karahüyük-Hacıbektaş, Has Hüyük, Kültepe-Kayseri and a number of sites in the Ankara region. The material from Alaca and Alişar is most relevant in discussion of Central Anatolian EB I types.

The EB I period in Central Anatolia is best represented by the "Chalcolithic" material in levels 19M-12M at Alişar Hüyük.[21] The wares are predominantly black or grey burnished with only a few examples of red pottery. Some of the larger vessels have a dark burnished exterior with a light interior, similar in effect to the East Anatolian types. The shapes of the two regions, however, do not display the same similarity. "Fruitstands" occurred comparatively frequently amongst the small amount of EB I material recovered from Alişar (Fig. 3), but this shape is not paralleled in Eastern Anatolia. In fact, few "fruitstand" sherds were found by the writer on survey, and this type would seem to have a more northern than southern distribution within Central Anatolia. Other EB I shapes include large jars with small ring bases and everted rims as well as various jar, cup and bowl shapes, some with handles (Fig. 4). Black Topped ware occurs in the "Chalcolithic" levels at Alişar and is also common in the succeeding phases of the Early Bronze Age in Central Anatolia, especially at Kültepe (Fig. 5: 1-6).[22] The characteristic shape in this ware is a small open bowl, but some handled jugs also occur. The interior of the bowls is usually black burnished with the dark colour sometimes extending over the rim onto the exterior. The rest of the exterior is normally a light to medium brown burnished. Isolated sherds of this type have been found in Eastern Anatolia, but they are clearly not at home there, and should probably be regarded as Central Anatolian imports rather than Cilician.[23] A glance at the Alaca Hüyük reports will show that the

---

[17] U. Esin, op. cit., 168.

[18] M. Van Loon, *1968 Summer Work*, 91f.

[19] G. Brown, *AnSt* 17 (1967) 132, 134f (Elbistan) and M.J. Mellink in *Chronologies in Old World Archaeology* (1965), 113.

[20] Observations at the site.

[21] H.H. von der Osten, *The Alishar Hüyük, Seasons of 1930-32, Part I*, OIP 28 (1937), 28ff.

[22] H.H. von der Osten, *op. cit.*, 52 and pl. I:5
See also, G. Brown, *op. cit.*, 133 and fig. 12.

[23] C.A. Burney, *AnSt* 8 (1958) 195 and fig. 226-28.

same basic shapes occur at that site in the "Chalcolithic" level as in the "Chalcolithic" levels at Alişar.[24] Decoraction on these wares apart from burnishing and the differential colouring of the interior and exterior of vessels is not particularly common; some examples of parallel fluting occur, but these are the exception rather than the rule. In no case is there a very close parallel to the ribbed and fluted vessels of the Trans-Caucasian zone.[25] Incised decoration also occurs, especially on the pedestals of fruitstands.[26]

A type of pottery which has been the subject of much discussion is the incised ware found at Büyük Güllücek (Fig. 6).[27] Similar material occurs in the earliest levels at Alişar and Alaca.[28] Clearly related pottery occurs further south in the Tuz Gölü region, but the full pattern of distribution is as yet uncertain.[29] Small dark burnished jars with incised, sometimes white-filled, patterns on the exterior are characteristic. A less common form of decoration consists of matt white painted lines on a dark ground. Parallels for the Central Anatolian white painted wares are found in Western Anatolia, at sites such as Beycesultan, but in no case are they specific enough to allow positive chronological deductions.[30] However, undecorated wares are predominant at Büyük Güllücek, including some examples of a Heavy Black Burnished ware, with black exterior and light interior. Horned handles also occur, having parallels in the more westerly areas of Anatolia, but again little reliance can be placed on these similarities. The chronology of the Büyük Güllücek wares is extremely uncertain: they have often been dated to Late Chalcolithic, but more recently W. Orthmann has classified them as EB I.[31] The writer would prefer the term Late Chalcolithic since there are some indications that these wares occur earlier than the "fruitstand" types characteristic of EB I.

The origin of the Central Anatolian incised wares is completely unknown. Amiran has suggested that the decoration should be considered as a derivative from the incised patterns found at Yanik Tepe.[32] Considering the lack of similarity both in shapes and designs of the pottery in these two areas, this suggestion would seem to be without foundation, and a local Central Anatolian origin is far more likely. Any consideration of the origin of the Late Chalcolithic wares in Central Anatolia must take into account the incomplete nature of our knowledge of the earlier prehistory of the region. Although a number of Neolithic sites are now known in Central Anatolia south of the Kızılırmak, none have been located north of the river despite intensive field survey work.[33] Furthermore, the Early Chalcolithic wares of the whole region are still little known; painted sherds with a possible affinity to Çatal Hüyük West in the Konya Plain have been found at Elemenli Hüyük in the Şereflikoçhisar peninsula on the east side of the Tuz Gölü, and also at Totak, about 65 km south of Ankara, but their date is uncertain, and they are few in number.[34] It would seem likely that the majority of the Early Chalcolithic pottery of Central Anatolia was undecorated and has remained so far unrecognized.

---

24 H.Z. Koşay and M. Akok, *Ausgrabungen von Alaca Hüyük, 1940-48*, Ankara (1966) Lev. 60 lower and Lev. 148.

25 With the exception of the sherds published in H.Z. Koşay and M. Akok, *op. cit.*, Lev. 61:1 72 and 1 73, which Koşay and Akok suggest are imports of Karaz type

26 H.H. von der Osten, *op. cit.*, 54 and fig. 65.

27 H. Koşay and M. Akok, *Ausgrabungen von Büyük Güllücek*, Ankara (1957).

28 See H.Z. Koşay and M. Akok, *Ausgrabungen von Alaca Hüyük, 1940-48*, Lev. 62, top right.

29 I.A. Todd, *AnSt* 17 (1967), 12.

30 J. Mellaart, *op. cit.*, 118f; S. Lloyd and J. Mellaart, *Beycesultan I* (1962) 104ff.

31 W. Orthmann, *Die Keramik der Frühen Bronzezeit aus Inneranatolien*, Istanbuler Forschungen 24, Berlin (1963), Tabelle 9, 98-99.

32 R. Amiran, *AJA* 72 (1968), 318.

3′ See note 10 for references to the results of the writer's survey in Central Anatolia.

34 Elemenli Hüyük: I.A. Todd, *AnSt* 16 (1966), 44 and fig. 4:35 Totak: D.H. French, *AnSt* 14 (1964), 35 and figs. 1-2.

Considering the origin of the dark burnished wares of Central and Eastern Anatolia, Burney has suggested that the wares of the two regions may have descended from a common ancestor, but, in view of the scanty nature of our knowledge of the earlier prehistory of Eastern as well as Central Anatolia, it would seem somewhat premature to opt for either region.[35] A comparison of the Central Anatolian EB I wares with those of Eastern Anatolia reveals certain similarities, but the differences in shape and form of decoration are more marked. The technique of dark burnished ware with light coloured interior occurs in both regions, and the writer's survey has shown that the Heavy Black Burnished ware is widespread over Central Anatolia, occurring in large quantities as far south as the Niğde region (Fig. 5: 7-9). The black burnished bowls which seem to be associated with this ware are also paralleled at Tarsus in EB I levels.[36] The technique of the dark burnished ware in Central Anatolia does suggest a general relationship to the material of Eastern Anatolia, but the shapes are dissimilar and the elaborate relief decoration of the Early Trans-Caucasian area is entirely missing.[37] A few sherds of Heavy Black Burnished ware found at Köşk Pınar, 15 km south-southwest of Niğde, bear traces of relief decoration, but this is limited to a line curving out along the body of the vessel on each side of the point at which the handle is attached to the body. In summary, Central Anatolian EB I wares bear no close resemblance to the Early Trans-Caucasian dark burnished wares although a common origin is possible.

Unlike the Trans-Caucasian zone where dark burnished wares continue through all three phases of the Early Period, the EB II phase in Central Anatolia is marked by a change to predominantly red burnished pottery, a feature also common in Western Anatolia at this time.[38] Apart from scattered earlier painted sherds, painted wares begin to occur in EB II, but they are more characteristic of the succeeding EB III period. Black Topped ware continues, but other dark burnished wares seem to be rare. Consequently most, if not all, of the Heavy Black Burnished ware should be dated to the EB I phase. Common red ware shapes are bowls with or without handles, together with various jar forms (Fig. 7). As is the case in Western Anatolia in the EB II period, regional ceramic variations also exist in Central Anatolia. Thickened rims and high raking handles are characteristic of the Nevşehir region bowls. Other forms of thickened rims are found in the Alişar and Kültepe regions, and it would seem on present evidence, that both of these sites lie within the same ceramic group.[39] Not only do shapes vary from group to group, but the surface colouring and techniques of manufacture also display a certain variety, and it is possible to assign some wares to their correct group even when the preserved section of the profile is too small to aid in identification. Decoration apart from slip and burnish is again rare; some ribs and fluting occur, but these are not widespread. Pattern burnishing and incision also constitute uncommon forms of decoration.[40]

Comparison of Central Anatolian types with those of Eastern Anatolia again shows there to be little similarity between the two pottery groups; the shapes are different, and the ribbed or fluted decoration of Central Anatolia is not closely paralleled in the more easterly region. This situation continues in the EB III period where the Central Anatolian EB III painted wares bear no relation to the East Anatolian painted pottery of the Malatya-Elazığ-Adıyaman area (Fig. 8).[41] It is thus clear that, despite the possibility of a common ancestry for both the Central and Eastern Anatolian dark burnished wares, the Central Anatolian wares should not be included in a discussion of the Khirbet Kerak problem.

---

[35] C.A. Burney and D.M. Lang, *op. cit.*, 51.

[36] H. Goldman, *Excavations at Gözlü Kule, Tarsus, II* (1956) 95 and figs. 239-40.

[37] With the exceptions cited in Note 24.

[38] For details of the Western Anatolian pottery groups, see D.H. French, *Anatolia and the Aegean in the Third Millennium B.C.*, unpublished Ph.D. dissertation, University of Cambridge (1969).

[39] Examples of thickened rims of Alişar type: H.H. von der Osten, *op. cit.*, fig. 165:6 (= pl. III:3) and some sherds illustrated in fig. 175.

[40] *Ibid.*, pl. III:3.

[41] A detailed analysis of all the Central Anatolian EB painted wares will be presented by S.A. Todd in her doctoral thesis for the University of Ankara.

The Khirbet Kerak Problem

The core of the problem lies in the possible connection between the pottery types of Eastern Anatolia and the Trans-Caucasus area, on the one hand, with those of the 'Amuq and Syro-Palestine, on the other. If the connection is found to exist it must then be decided whether the similarities represent the influence of one area on another, or whether a movement of objects or people is involved. If the last view is taken it is then necessary to examine the possible types of migration and the routes which were available to the migrating peoples. Further the archaeological data from sites located on or near these routes must be analysed for evidence of their passage. A movement of people, rather than of artifacts or ideas, can only be safely postulated when all of the considerations listed above clearly point to this end.

Although certain similarities do exist in the form and decoration of the pottery in the Trans-Caucasian/ East Anatolian, 'Amuq and Khirbet Kerak areas, these similarities do not suggest to the writer that the groups are "so close as to be almost indistinguishable" as Mellaart suggests.[42] As might be expected from geographical considerations, there are close similarities between the material from Syro-Palestine and the 'Amuq, and between Eastern Anatolia and the Trans-Caucasus area. But between these two major areas, there are definite differences. Mellaart points out that "the East Anatolian pottery has sharper and more metallic profiles than the Khirbet Kerak pottery which is more rounded", and that the jar shape is not common in the 'Amuq or Palestine.[43] However, it is this angular jar shape which is particularly characteristic of Eastern Anatolia and the Trans-Caucasus area.[44] Furthermore, the potstand shape of the southern region does not occur in the northern area.[45] There are also differences in the colouring of the wares in the various regions; unfortunately, a full technical study of the methods employed in the pottery manufacture of these regions has never been undertaken.

In the light of our present knowledge, it seems clear that the Red-Black Burnished ware of the 'Amuq and the Khirbet Kerak ware itself cannot be considered as direct imports from Eastern Anatolia, and two alternatives remain if the similarities between the pottery groups are to be considered other than fortuitous: either the southern area was influenced by the north (the evidence seems to point rather more strongly to this direction than to the opposite), or there was a southward migration of people. The latter course of events is generally favoured, but there are major obstacles to be overcome before the picture can be presented in a sufficiently convincing fashion. There is no trail of destruction on sites from Eastern Anatolia to the 'Amuq, and theories of a massive wave of barbarians descending on the 'Amuq and putting the inhabitants to the sword are unwarranted excursions into the realm of fantasy.[46] Unfortunately for the "migrationists", neither is there a clearly indicated route for the proposed migration with suitable pottery types occurring in the intermediate areas.[47] The dark burnished wares of Early Trans-Caucasian type occur in the Malatya-Elazığ regions and spread as far west as the Elbistan Plain.[48] To the south of Malatya, Bahadır Alkım reports the discovery of Khirbet Kerak type ware at Maraş and south-east of Gaziantep.[49] If such a ware occurs at Maraş, it is indeed strange that it is not found in quantity in the Islahiye region which lies on the main route from Maraş southward to the

---

[42] J. Mellaart, *op. cit.*, 83.
[43] *Ibid.*, 81.
[44] Cf., C.A. Burney, *AnSt* 8 (1958), figs. 77-87 on p. 183.
[45] J. Mellaart, *op. cit.*, 83.
[46] Cf., S. Hood, *AnSt* I (1951) 118 and Sir Leonard Woolley, *A Forgotten Kingdom*, Baltimore (1953) 32f.
[47] For a suggested route, see J.B. Hennessy, *The Foreign Relations of Palestine during the Early Bronze Age* pl. LXXIV.
[48] Malatya: C.A. Burney, *AnSt* 8 (1968) 195.
Elazıg: *1968 Summer Work*, passim.
[49] B. Alkım, *Anatolia I*, Archaeologia Mundi, Cleveland and New York (1968) 98. The writer has not seen these sherds himself.

'Amuq Plain.[50] Alkim suggests that the "invaders" followed a route from Maraş south-eastward to the east of Gaziantep – a seemingly unnecessarily circuitous route when the main route lies direct from Maraş down the valley of the Hopnik Çayı into the 'Amuq Plain.[51] Another roundabout route from Eastern Anatolia into the 'Amuq follows the route Elazığ-Diyarbakır and then approximately west-southwest through the Urfa region. However, it should be noted that no pottery which is relevant to this discussion was found in the deep sounding at Harran, nor has it been found in the upper Balikh and Habur river areas in the east, nor in Cilicia in the west.[52] In short, there are obstinate gaps in the archaeological record which do not aid in the identification of the route followed by any suggested migration. For the present, until the most southerly occurrences of relevant pottery types have been fully published in quantity, it seems safest to draw the southern boundary just to the south of Malatya. Further survey and excavation may change this picture, but the current difficulties inherent in the migration theory must be fully recognized. Gaps in pottery distribution cannot be explained by the speed of a folk migration covering a distance of at least four hundred kilometers.[53]

Other forms of evidence have been adduced to support migration theories. Circular architecture has been commonly discussed, an architectural type which occurs frequently in the Trans-Caucasus area with an isolated example at Yanık Tepe in Iranian Azerbaijan.[54] Amiran draws a parallel between the round houses of Yanık Tepe and the well-known building at Beth Yerah which consists of at least eight circular "rooms" sunk into the ten meter wide outer wall of an almost rectangular building.[55] The lack of close similarity between the plans of the architecture of the two sites and the distance of approximately eleven hundred kilometers (as the crow flies) which separates them render the comparison somewhat unattractive. It should be added that there are no instances of approximately contemporary circular buildings in Eastern Anatolia or in the 'Amuq, and that the Beth Yerah occurrence is unique in Palestine. In view of this, the writer suggests that circular architecture should be divorced entirely from the Khirbet Kerak Problem.

Various forms of hearth features have also been introduced into the discussion. These are the horseshoe shaped clay andirons or potstands which often bear incised and relief anthropomorphic decoration. The area of distribution covers both the Trans-Caucasian/East Anatolian area, the 'Amuq and Palestine. Other examples are known from Central and Western Anatolia as well as Cilicia. A notable gap in the distribution map of these features occurs in Syria, Lebanon and Jordan, and the same gap is present between the East Anatolian region and the 'Amuq as was noted above in the discussion of pottery distribution.[56] An examination of the distribution map of Diamant and Rutter's class II types suggests that these hearth features should be considered rather as an Anatolian feature which only occurs but rarely further south.[57] It is quite possible that the Central Anatolian andirons as well as the dark burnished wares are descended from the same ancestor as the East Anatolian and Trans-Caucasian types. If the occurrence of these features is to be used as evidence in favour of a migration, the apparent gap between the 'Amuq and the Israeli sites must be satisfactorily filled.

---

50 *Ibid.*

51 *Ibid.*

52 See K. Prag, *Levant* 2 (1970) 63ff for the Harran report.

53 S. Hood, *AnSt* I (1951) 118.

54 C.A. Burney and D.M. Lang, chapter 3 and references.

55 R. Amiran, *AnSt* 15 (1965) 167 and *AJA* 72 (1968) 318.
For a description of the Beth Yerah building, see B. Maisler, M. Stekelis and M. Avi-Yonah, *IEJ* 2 (1952) 165ff and 218ff.

56 For discussion, see S. Diamant and J. Rutter, *AnSt* 19 (1969) 147ff.

57 *Ibid.*, fig. 46. Note that Tabara el Akrad is wrongly located on the map. S. Hood, *AnSt* I (1951) 113, gives the location as "about a twenty minute walk east of Atchana". The writer visited the area but was unable to locate the site which was covered by the cotton crop.

The conclusion to be drawn from the preceding examination of the problem is that a movement of people has not yet been established beyond doubt, and that the Khirbet Kerak ware can scarcely be described as "probably the most obvious instance of a pottery associated with ethnic movements".[58] Much further work remains to be done before such an assertion can be generally accepted; for the present, the similarities of pottery and other artifact types may be attributed just as plausibly to influence of one culture on another and the interchange of ideas, as to an actual ethnic migration.

The imported southern pottery found at Kültepe and in the Keban Dam area points clearly to strong contacts between the 'Amuq-North Syrian region on the one hand and the Kültepe region and Eastern Anatolia on the other. But this connection is clearly not in one direction only, and it is hard to envision southern pottery types being taken northward in the face of a large scale migration moving southward. At this period there was clearly wide-spread international contact between Anatolia and Northern Syria just as there was between the Aegean, Anatolia and Mesopotamia. Viewed against the wider background of the whole of the East Mediterranean world in the Third Millenium B.C., it seems less necessary to postulate a movement of people to explain the phenomena preserved in the archaeological record.

It may be objected that the appearance in the 'Amuq Phase H of the Red-Black Burnished ware in large quantities (52-55% of selected sherd bulk) must indicate the arrival of new people.[59] However, this ware occurred for the first time late in Phase G, and the transition between the two phases may not be accurately documented in the areas excavated.[60] Braidwood states that continuity between the two phases is also displayed in other types of pottery and the chipped stone.[61] It must also be remembered that the size of the Phase H area excavated at Çatal Hüyük, Judaidah and Ta'yinat was small (169.5 sq.m., omitting the excavation at Dhahab which is stratigraphically unreliable) and may not be representative of the period as a whole.[62] Furthermore, the question posed by the sudden disappearance of the Red-Black Burnished ware from the 'Amuq must also be answered. In Phase I, the ware constitutes 35-40% of the total selected sherd bulk, but in Phase J only a few sherds an one reconstructible bowl of true Red-Black Burnished ware were found. These appear to Professor Braidwood "more likely to be extrusive than in proper context."[63] Is this another example of the incomplete nature of the archaeological record in the 'Amuq Plain or must another explanation be sought? The "migrationists" may feel compelled to suggest that the "bearers of the Red-Black Burnished Ware" left the 'Amuq as suddenly as they had arrived! The frequently implied, but ill founded, concept that each new pottery type indicates a new people must be finally laid to rest. Fashions in pottery change, especially in a period of expanding trade relations, and are often totally unconnected with any population movement. In the case of the Khirbet Kerak question, the arguments for migration must be considerably strengthened before such a population movement can be allowed to enter the record as accepted historical fact.

It is to be hoped that a re-examination of the problem in the light of the various archaeological and anthropological techniques currently available will result in its solution. This re-examination should include problem-oriented excavation programs throughout the area in question from the Caspian to Jericho, but especially along the routes of the proposed migration; anthropological studies will also be of assistance to aid in the archaeological identification of migrations. Such work on an international basis will be of great value in determining the nature of the possible interrelationships within the region in the Early Bronze Age. Such interconnections have long formed an important part of Professor Gordon's studies, and I am happy to offer this paper in his honour.

---

[58] R. Amiran, *AJA* 72 (1968), 317.
[59] R.J. Braidwood and L. Braidwood, *Excavations in the Plain of Antioch* I, *OIP* LXI, Chicago (1960) 358.
[60] *Ibid.*, 294.
[61] *Ibid.*, 518.
[62] *Ibid.*, 345.
[63] *Ibid.*, 431 n. 1.

KEY TO MAP: FIGURE 1

1. Totak
2. Elemenli Hüyük
3. Büyük Güllücek
4. Alaca Hüyük
5. Alişar Hüyük
6. Kültepe-Kayseri
7. Tarsus
8. Beycesultan
9. Tabara el Akrad

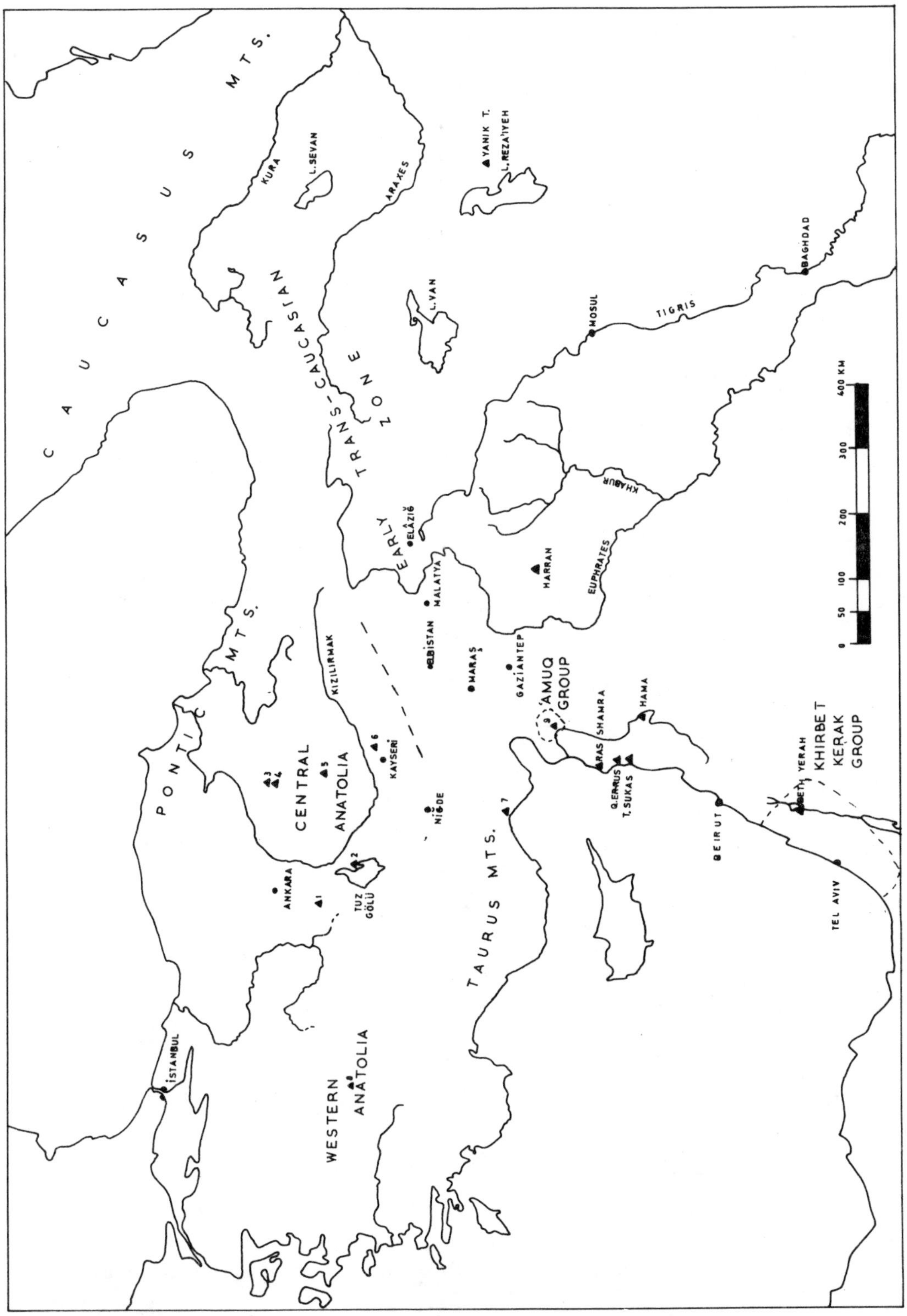

Fig. 1. Map of Areas discussed in the text.

CATALOGUE OF ILLUSTRATED POTTERY[64]

All pottery is handmade unless otherwise noted.

Figure 2.

1. Ernis; light red ware, red burnished slip with black burnished patches; top part above carination possibly turned on slow wheel; after Burney, *AnSt* 8, 189, fig. 114.

2. Hankendi; inside black to brown, exterior light grey to black burnished; after Burney, *AnSt* 8, 197, fig. 202.

3. Könk; black burnished; after Burney, *AnSt* 8, 197, fig. 200.

4. Ernis; black ware, exterior burnished; Nakhichevan lug; after Burney, *AnSt* 8, 185, fig. 91.

5. Ernis; black with burnished exterior; after Burney, *AnSt* 8, 183, fig. 77.

6. Hinsor; black ware with high burnish; after Burney, *AnSt* 8, 197, fig. 198.

7. Ernis; black ware, interior plain, exterior burnished; after Burney, *AnSt* 8, 183, Fig. 83.

8. Ernis; dark grey interior, black exterior, slightly burnished inside and out, Nakhichevan lug at rim; after Burney, *AnSt* 8, 189, fig. 102.

9. Yaycı; dark grey ware, exterior black burnished, with grooved decoration; after Burney, *AnSt* 8, 191, fig. 130.

10. Yaycı; black and red-brown ware, interior plain red-brown, exterior black burnished, grooved decoration on exterior; after Burney, *AnSt* 8, 191, fig. 128.

---

[64] A more technical description of the Central Anatolian pottery will be published in the author's final report.

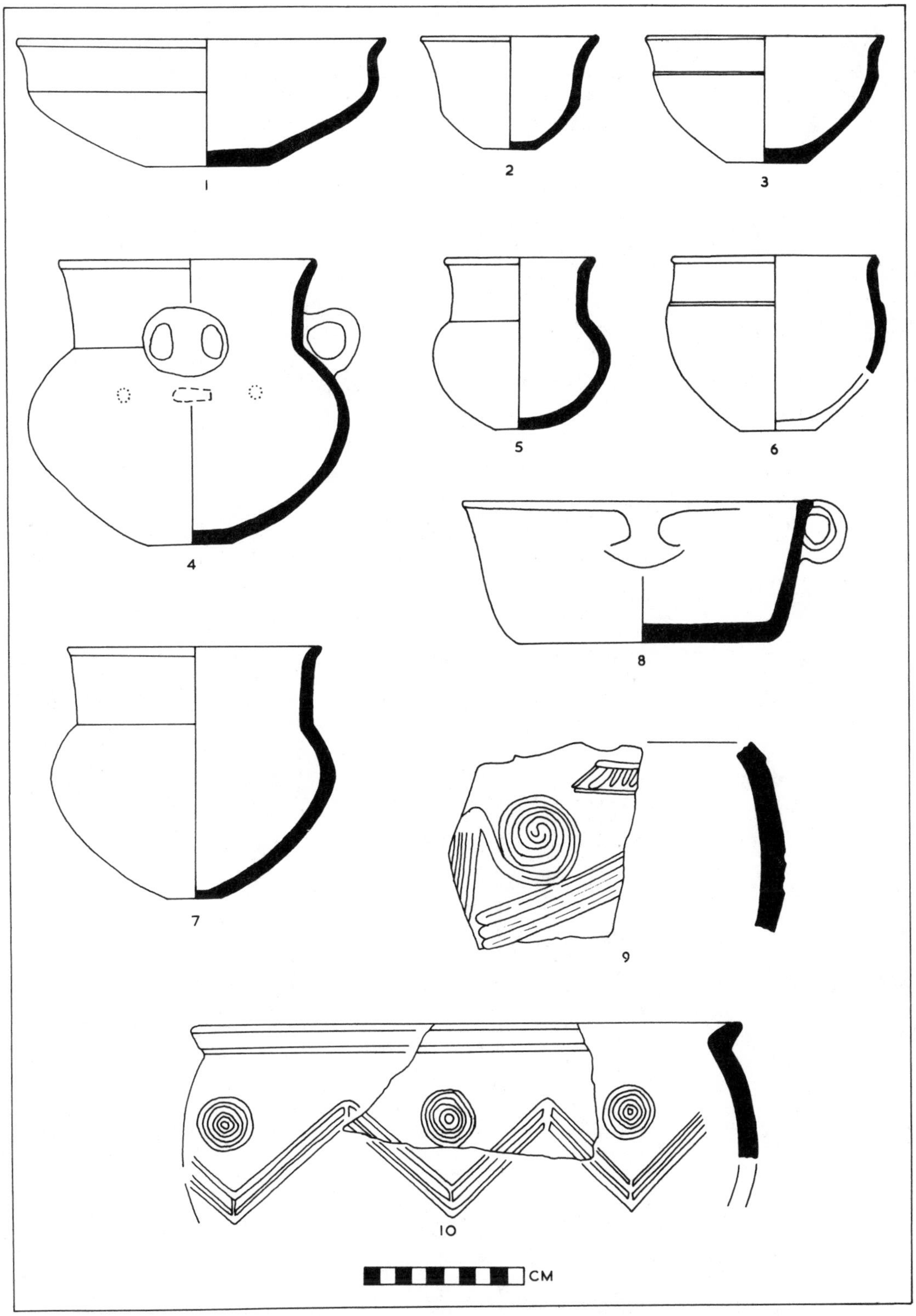

Fig. 2. Early Trans-Caucasian type pottery from Eastern Anatolia.

Figure 3.

1. Alişar; bowl of fruitstand, interior and exterior black with black-brown slip, burnished; after Orthmann, *Die Keramik der Frühen Bronzezeit aus Inneranatolien*, Tafel 4 2/09.

2. Alişar, Level 15; from fruitstand, light brown with grey-black slip on exterior, burnished; after Orthmann, *Keramik*, Tfl 4 2/11.

3. Alişar, 13 M; from fruitstand, black slip inside and out, and burnished; after Orthmann, *Keramik*, Tfl. 4 2/10.

4. Alişar; from fruitstand, grey-brown interior, yellow-brown exterior with grey-brown slip on exterior; after Orthmann, *Keramik*, Tfl. 4 2/13.

5. Alişar; interior brown-grey, exterior black with black burnished slip; after Orthmann, *Keramik*, Tfl. 4 2/14.

6. Alişar 12 M; exterior black with well burnished slip, horizontal grooved decoration; after Orthmann, *Keramik*, Tfl. 4 2/15.

7. Alişar 12 M; exterior red-brown burnished slip with grooved decoration; after Orthmann, *Keramik*, Tfl. 7, 2/29.

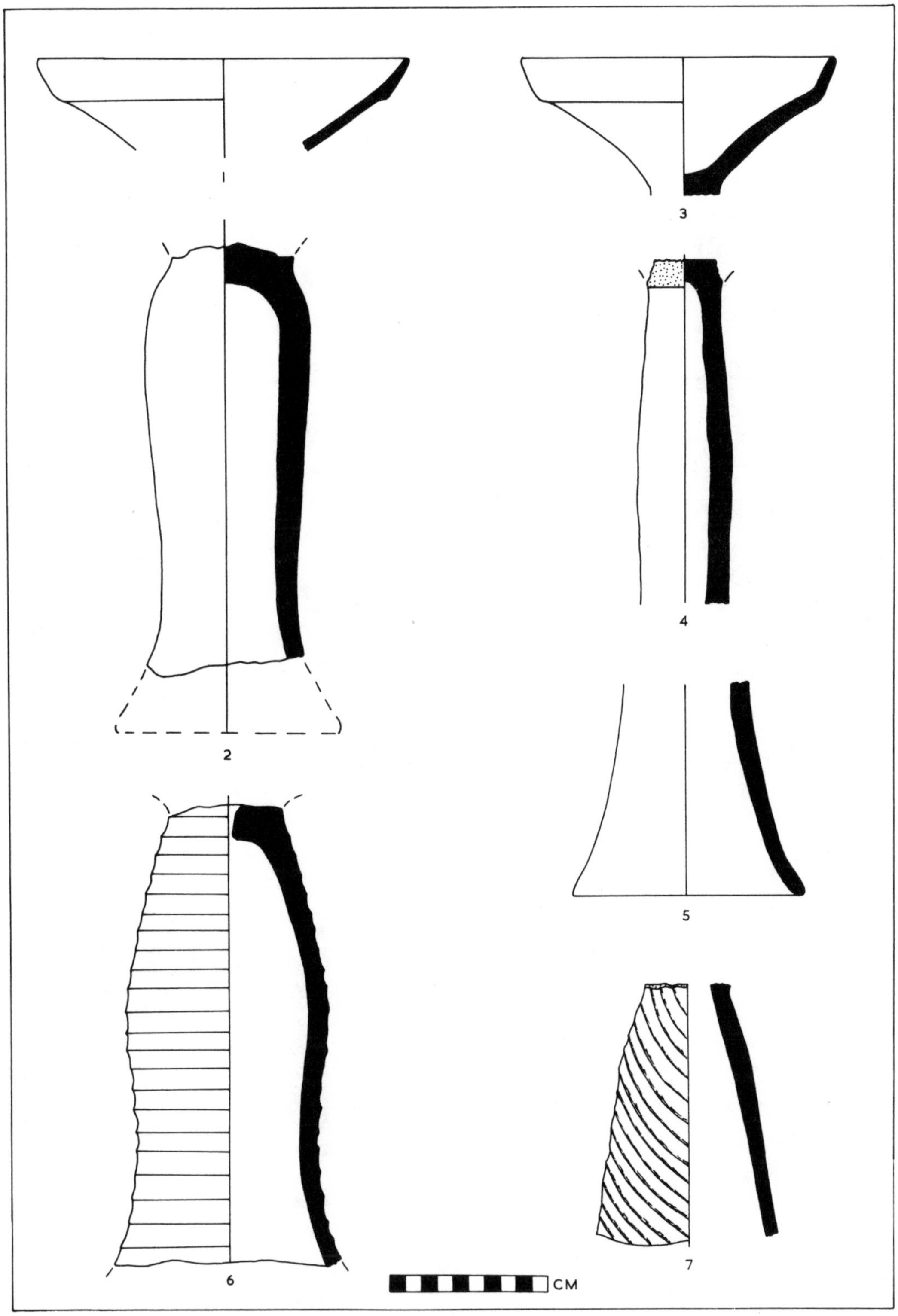

Fig. 3. Central Anatolian EB I "Fruitstands" from Alişar Hüyük.

Figure 4.

1. Alişar 13 M; small jug, brown to black-brown slip on exterior; after Orthmann, *Keramik*, Tfl. 3 2/04.

2. Alişar 14 M; two-handled cup, yellow-brown with light red burnished slip on exterior; after Orthmann, *Keramik*, Tfl. 7 2/31.

3. Alişar 12 M; large jug, red burnished slip on exterior, after Orthmann, *Keramik*, Tfl. 7 2/32.

4. Alişar 12 M; large jar on short pedestal base, with grey-brown slip; after Orthmann, *Keramik*, Tfl. 6 2/25.

5. Alişar 12 M; large jar, black burnished slip on exterior; after Orthmann, *Keramik*, Tfl. 6 2/23.

6. Alişar 12 M; large jar, black burnished slip on exterior; after Orthmann, *Keramik*, Tfl. 6 2/21.

7. Alişar Level 13 M grave eX12; large jar, yellow-brown with black burnished slip; after Orthmann, *Keramik*, Tfl. 6 2/26.

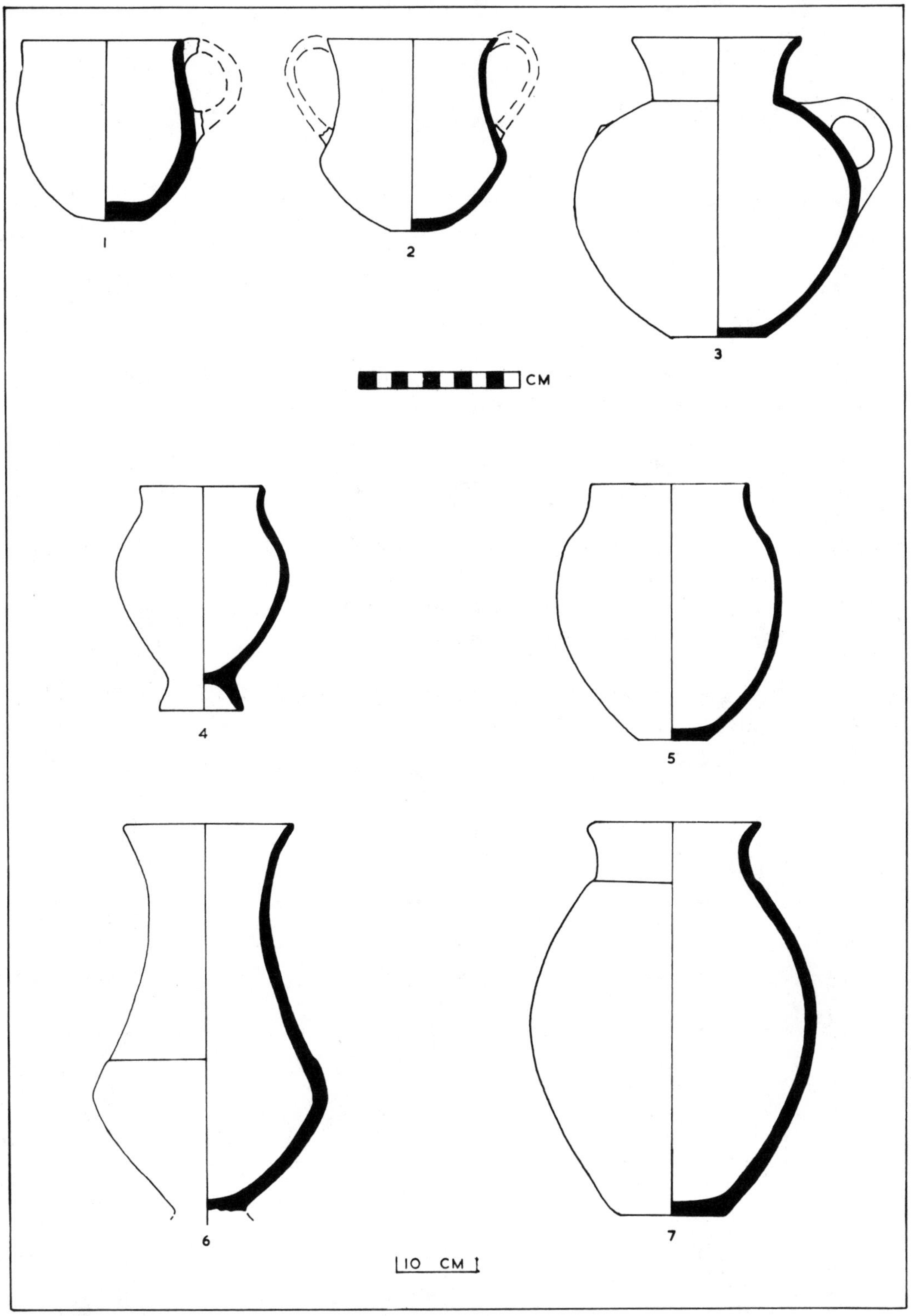

Fig. 4. Central Anatolian EB I wares from Alişar Hüyük.

Figure 5.

Black Topped Ware sherds are tempered with fine grits and straw, and Heavy Black Burnished Ware with fine to coarse grits and straw.

1. Karaoğlan; black core, interior and over rim on exterior black burnished; rest of exterior streaky dark brown burnished; after Brown, *AnSt* 17 (1967), fig. 12:103.

2. Kara Elbistan; core reddish-brown near exterior and dark grey near interior; interior black burnished, exterior reddish-brown burnished with darker mottling; after Brown, *AnSt* 17 (1967), fig. 12:110.

3. Emirilyas; grey core, interior black burnished, exterior brown burnished with darker band below rim; after Brown, *AnSt* 17 (1967), fig. 12;105.

4. Poskoflu; darf grey core, interior black burnished, exterior reddish-brown burnished turning darker near rim; after Brown, *AnSt* 17 (1967), fig. 12:106.

5. Ahlatlıbel; black core, interior and over rim on exterior black burnished, rest of exterior reddish-brown burnished; after Brown, *AnSt* 17 (1967), fig. 12:108.

6. Beydeğirmeni; dark grey core, interior black burnished near rim only, exterior reddish-brown burnished.

7. Köşk Pınar; core dark greg to light brown; interior light brown with light streaky burnish on interior of neck, exterior black burnished; survey 1965, M.L. Ramsden.

8. Köşk Pınar; core buff to black, interior buff burnished; exterior black burnished with buff mottling; rim diam. 50 cm.; survey 1965, M.L. Ramsden.

9. Amas; light brown core, interior light brown, exterior black burnished.

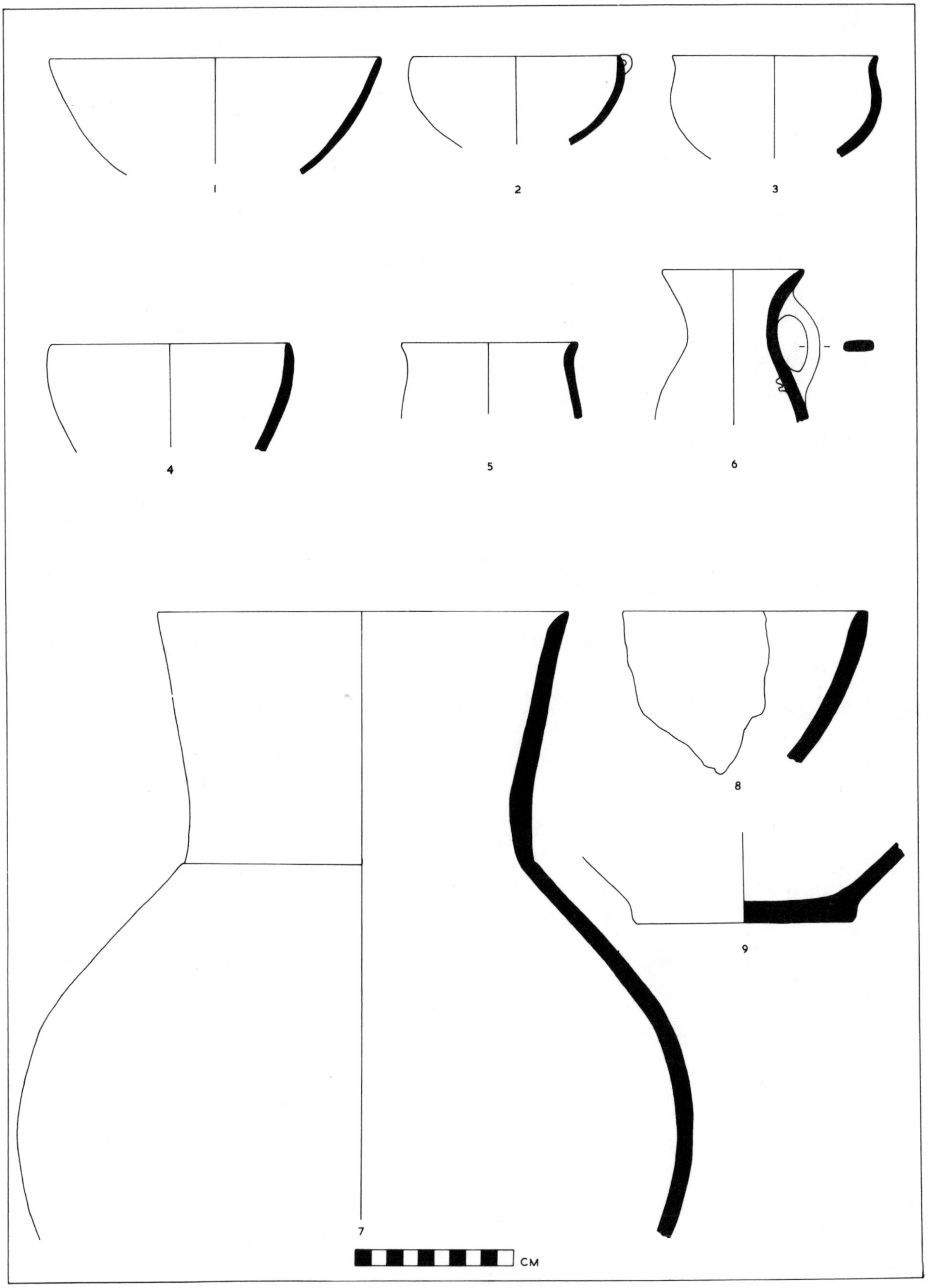

Fig. 5. Black Topped Ware (1-6) and Heavy Black Burnished Ware (7-9) from Central Anatolia and the Anti-taurus Region.

Figure 6.

1. Büyük Güllücek; horned handle with incised decoration; after Koşay and Akok, *Ausgrabungen von Büyük Güllücek*, Tfl. XIX.

2. Büyük Güllücek; jar rim sherd with impressed pattern on exterior; after Koşay and Akok, Tfl. XVI.

3. Büyük Güllücek; from large jar, horned handle with incised decoration, fabric from light brown to black, burnished on exterior; after Orthmann, *Keramik*, Tfl. 52 12/10.

4. Büyük Güllücek; from large bowl, variation of horned handle with incised design, interior brown, exterior dark brown burnished slip; after Orthmann, *Keramik*, Tfl. 53 12/13.

5. Büyük Güllücek; from large jar, brown with incised decoration; after Orthmann, *Keramik*, Tfl. 52 12/07.

6. Büyük Güllücek; jar rim sherd, black-brown fabric, no slip, incised decoration; after Orthmann, *Keramik*, Tfl. 52 12/06.

7. Büyük Güllücek; from large jar, brownish black burnished exterior with incised design; after Orthmann, *Keramik*, Tfl. 52 12/03.

8. Büyük Güllücek; jar sherd, interior brown, exterior dark brown with incised decoration; after Orthmann, *Keramik*, Tfl. 52 12/02.

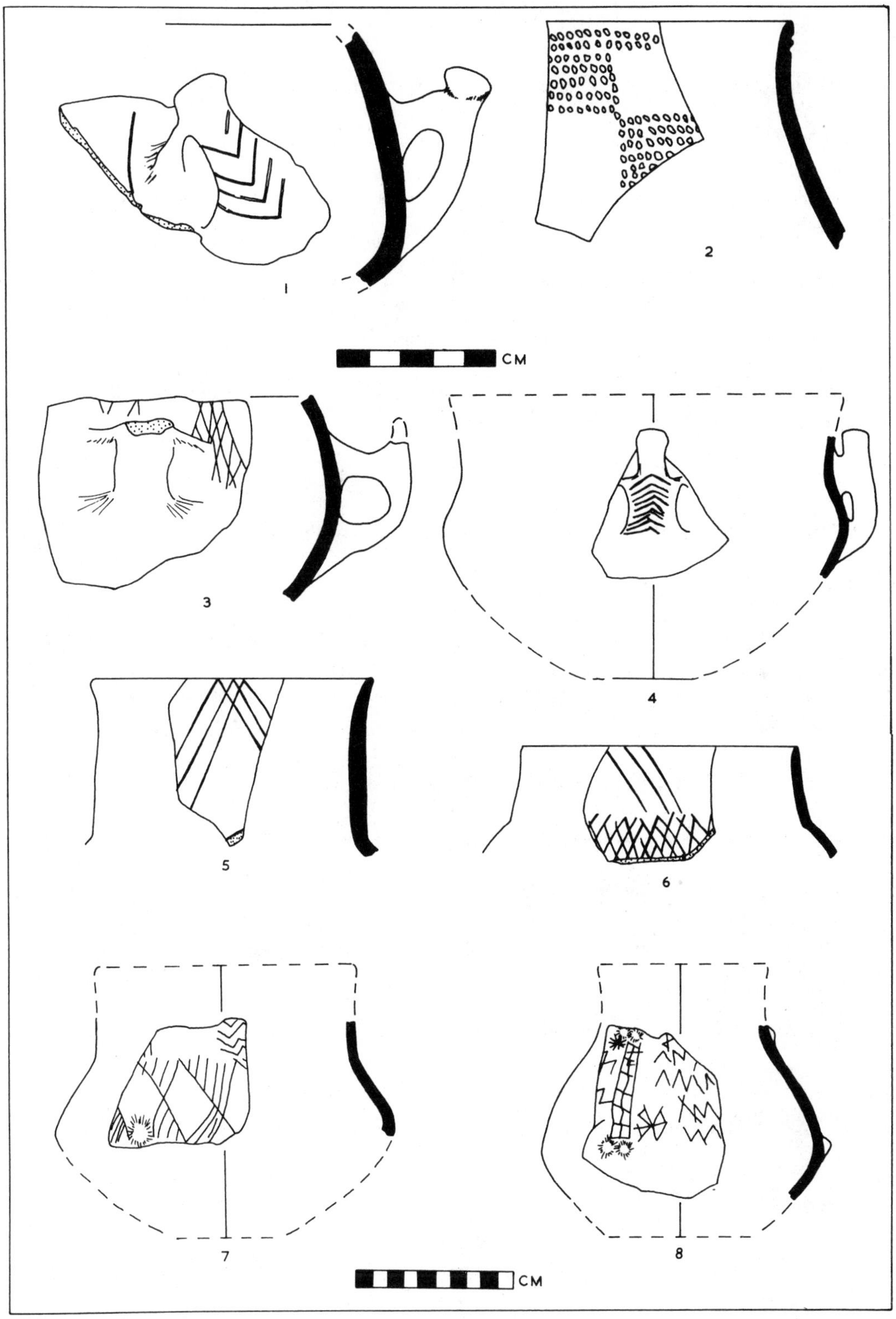

Fig. 6. Pottery from Büyük Güllücek.

Figure 7.

1. Yazıhüyük K.T.; bowl, pinkish-buff ware, red slipped and burnished; from Nevşehir-Kirşehir area.

2. Ömerhanlı; bowl, pink ware, exterior light red-brown burnished.

3. Ömerhanlı; bowl, pink ware with light brown burnished exterior.

4. Karipli B.H.; bowl, interior pinkish-buff slip, exterior light buff slipped and burnished; from Nevşehir-Kirşehir area.

5. Ağzıkarahan S.W.; bowl, reddish-brown slipped and burnished interior and exterior.

6. Ömerhanlı; bowl, red-brown slipped and burnished.

7. Büyük Kale Tepe Harmandalı; interior unslipped buff ware, exterior light reddish-brown slipped and burnished; Nevşehir-Kirşehir region.

8. Aflak; pink ware with grey core; Nevşehir-Kirşehir region.

9. Ulukısla N; pink ware with light reddish-brown slip, burnished; Aksaray area.

10. Kiledere; buff ware with red slip, burnished.

11. Çimeliyeniköy; bowl with handle attached beneath rim, light reddish-brown slipped and burnished; from Aksaray region.

12. Hacafer Tepe; bowl of typical Nevşehir type, reddish-brown slipped and burnished.

13. Hacafer Tepe; Nevşehir region bowl, reddish-brown slipped and burnished.

14. Ömerhanlı; unslipped pink fabric on interior, exterior pinkish-buff burnished.

15. Ömerhanlı; jar neck, pinkish-buff ware.

16. Ömerhanlı; from jar, interior brown slipped and burnished, exterior reddish-brown slipped and burnished.

17. Ömerhanlı; from fine jug, light reddish-brown slipped and burnished on exterior.

18. Hacafer Tepe; Nevşehir ware bowl fragment with typical high raking handle, exterior dark reddish-brown slipped and burnished.

19. Hacafer Tepe; Nevşehir ware bowl rim with high raking handle, reddish-brown to light red slipped and burnished.

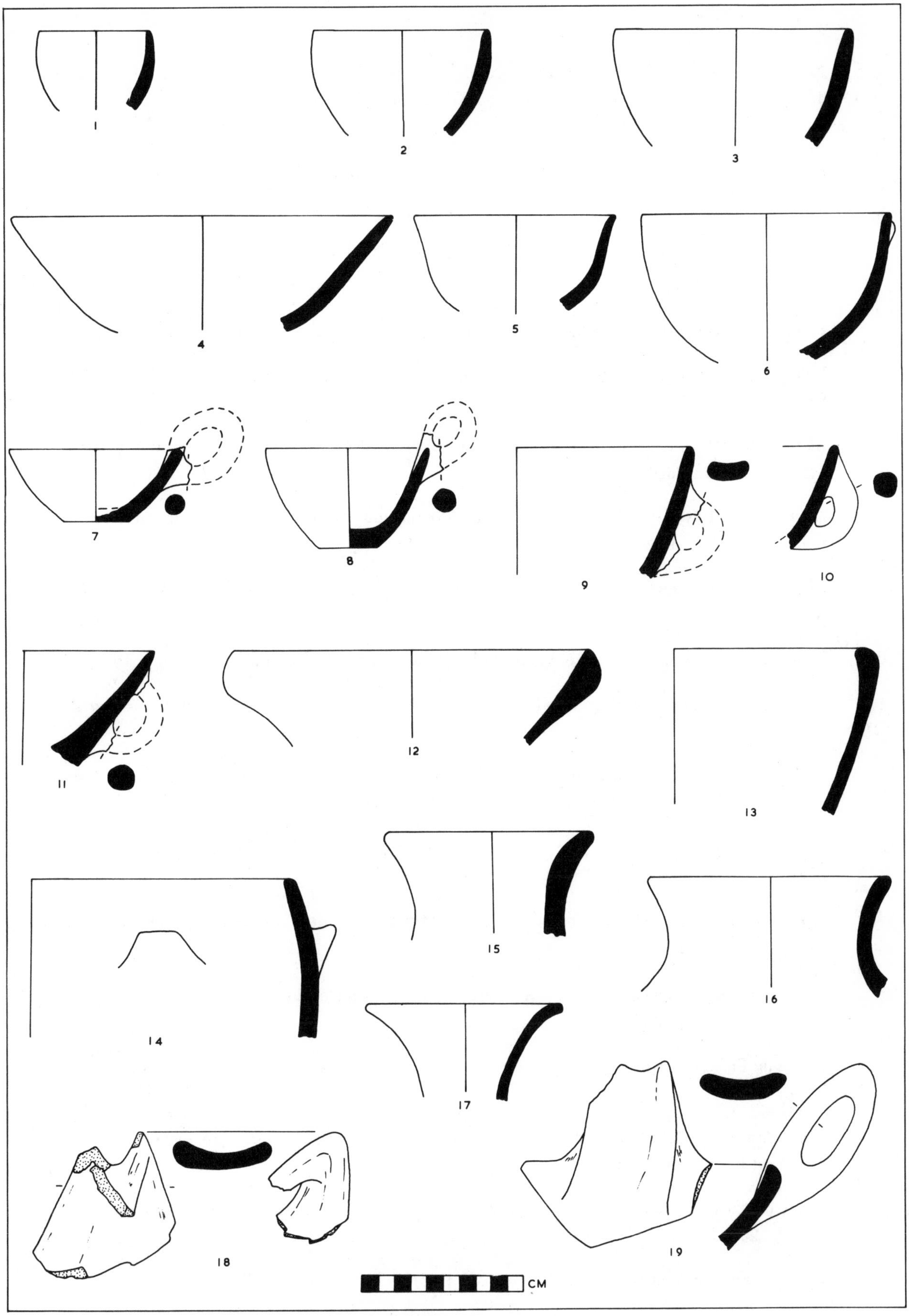

Fig. 7. Central Anatolian EB II red burnished wares.

Figure 8.

1. Alaca Hüyük Al c. 497; Ankara Museum No. 7372; Çıradere type painted sherd, dark brown painted decoration on orange-buff ground, well slipped and burnished.

2. Alaca Hüyük Al b/D. 79, Grave D; Çiradere type painted bowl, brown paint on yellow-brown slip, burnished.

3. Alaca Hüyük Al b/D. 70, Grave D; Çiradere ware, red painted decoration on orange-brown highly burnished slip.

4. Alişar b 742/9, from Terrace; dark red paint on orange-brown highly burnished slip.

5. Eğriköy; Intermediate painted cup, pinkish-white slip over exterior, paint red-orange.

6. Kültepe, mound; Intermediate painted ware, orange-tan slip over exterior, paint dark red, surface well burnished.

7. Kültepe Nr. 315, Kayseri Museum; Intermediate ware, orange slip with dark red painted decoration, exterior well burnished.

8. Karipli Büyük Hüyük; Intermediate bowl type, interior and exterior rim red slipped and burnished, exterior below rim yellow-white ground.

9. Gâvur Hüyük; inturned rim bowl, interior and exterior rim red slipped and burnished, exterior below rim white slipped.

10. Eğriköy; Cappadocian ware inturned rim bowl, red-brown painted design on orange slipped ground, burnished.

11. Battal II; Cappadocian ware inturned rim bowl sherd, black painted decoration on red-brown slip, surface burnished.

12. Karahüyük; Eastern Anatolian painted ware, interior buff, exterior dark brown paint on buff ground; after Burney, *AnSt* 8, 203, fig. 265.

13. Karahüyük; Eastern Anatolian painted ware, light red paint on cream yellow slip, unburnished; after Burney, *AnSt* 8, 203, fig. 264.

14. Samanköy; Eastern Anatolian painted ware, dark brown paint on unburnished buff ground; after Burney, *AnSt* 8, 203, fig. 267.

15. Fethiye; Eastern Anatolian painted ware, dark brown paint on unslipped, unburnished buff ground; after Burney, *AnSt* 8, 203, fig. 269.

16. Hankendi; Eastern Anatolian painted ware, black-brown paint on orange-white slip, unburnished; after Burney, *AnSt* 8, 203, fig. 274.

17. Könk; Eastern Anatolian painted ware, black-brown painted decoration on thin whitish slip; after Burney, *AnSt* 8, 203, fig. 262.

18. Tülüntepe; Eastern Anatolian ware, purple-brown paint on yellow-white slip, unburnished; after Burney, *AnSt* 8, 203, fig. 263.

19. Karavenk; Eastern Anatolian painted ware, black paint on buff ground, unslipped, unburnished.

20. Saracık; Eastern Anatolian painted ware, red-brown paint on yellow-buff slip, slipped only on exterior, unburnished.

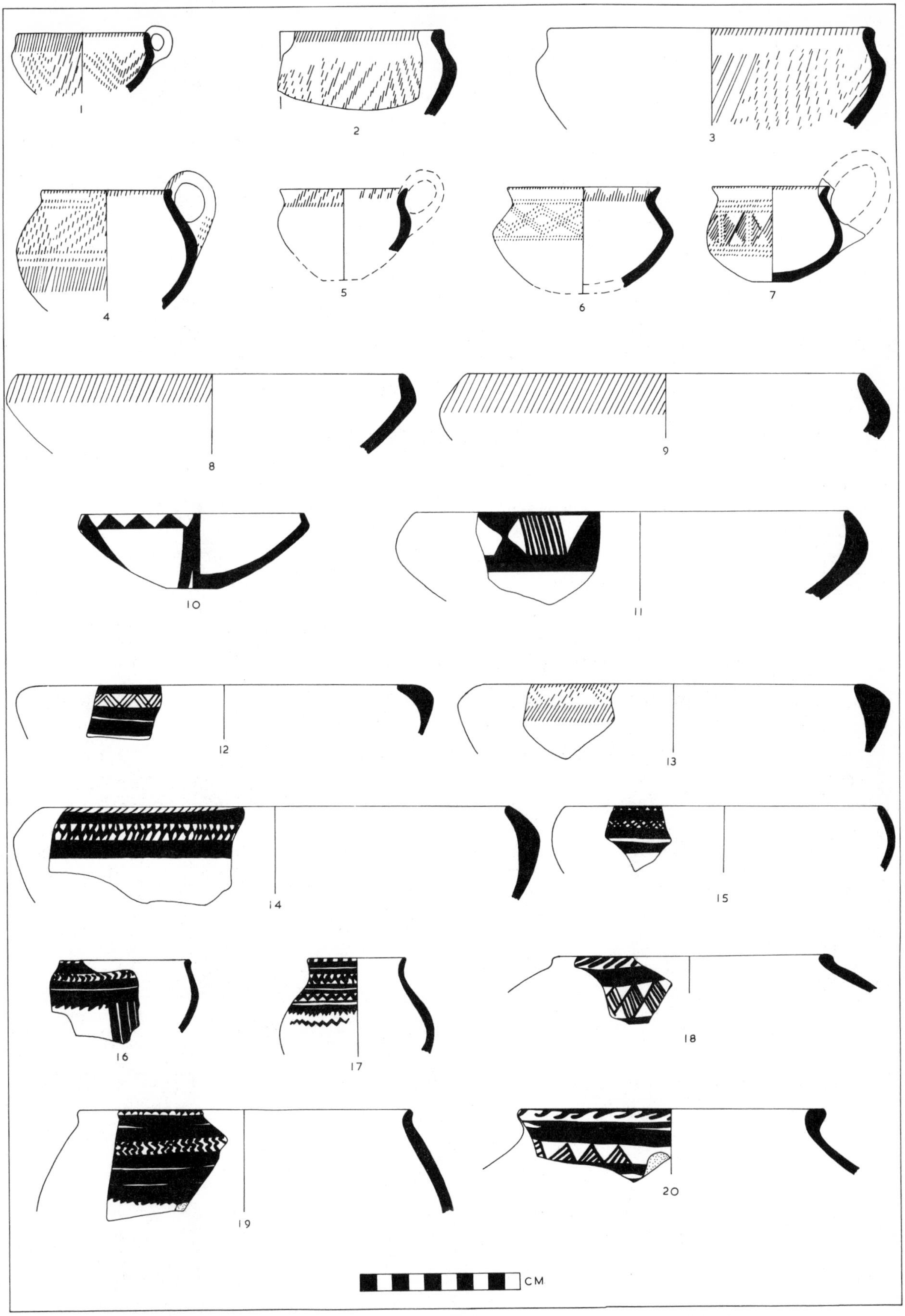

Fig. 8. Central Anatolian EB II-III painted wares (1-11) and Eastern Anatolian EB II-III painted pottery (12-20).

SELECT BIBLIOGRAPHY

Alkım, U.B.	*Anatolia I*, Cleveland and New York (1968)
Amiran, R.	"Connections between Anatolia and Palestine in the Early Bronze Age", *IEJ* 2 (1952) 89ff
	"Yanik Tepe, Shengavit, and the Khirbet Kerak Ware", *AnSt* 15 (1965) 165ff.
	"Chronological Problems of the Early Bronze Age. Early Bronze I-II: the City of Arad. Early Bronze III: the Khirbet Kerak Ware", *AJA* 72 (1968) 316ff
	Ancient Pottery of the Holy Land, Rutgers University Press (1970)
Braidwood, R.J. & Braidwood, L.	*Excavations in the Plain of Antioch I*, OIP LXI, Chicago (1960)
Burney, C.A.	"Eastern Anatolia in the Chalcolithic and Early Bronze Age", *AnSt* 8 (1958) 157ff
Burney, C.A. & Lang, D.M.	*The Peoples of the Hills: Ancient Ararat and Caucasus*, London (1971)
Diamant, S. & Rutter, J.	"Horned Objects in Anatolia and the Near East and Possible Connections with the Minoan 'Horns of Consecration' ", *AnSt* 19 (1969) 147ff
Hennessy, J.B.	*The Foreign Relations of Palestine during the Early Bronze Age*, London (1967)
Hood, S.	"Excavations at Tabara el Akrad", *AnSt* 1 (1951) 113ff
Lamb, W.	"The Culture of North-East Anatolia and its Neighbours", *AnSt* 4 (1954) 21ff
Mellaart, J.	*The Chalcolithic and Early Bronze Ages in the Near East and Anatolia*, Beirut (1966)
Woolley, C.L.	*A Forgotten Kingdom*, Baltimore (1953)

OBSERVATIONS ON THE EGYPTIAN BICONSONANTAL ROOT *p3**

William A. Ward

During preparation of a study on the hitherto unrecongized Egyptian root *b3*, "tremble, flutter,"[1] it became evident that this is a doublet of the root *p3*, long known as cognate to Semitic *pr*, "flee, escape." It also became clear that the semantic range of Egyptian *p3* can be defined much more clearly than heretofore. Thus, new meanings can be adduced and it can be shown that the customary rendering "fly, *fliegen*, *voler*," is, by and large, incorrect. To show this, however, we must begin by summarizing the semantic range of its Semitic counterpart.

I. Semitic *pr*, "flee, escape."[2]

Arabic[3] *farra*, "escape, run away," *ʾafarra*, "chase away," carry the inherant notion of quick, hasty movement, hence *ʾiftarra*, "flash, glitter," describing lightning or a star when it rises, *furrat*, "restlessness, confusion," and *farīr*, "the place of the pulse in horse-lore." *Farfara*, reduplicated from the original biconsonantal root,[4] means "tremble, shake; be unsteady, confused." Among its derived nouns are *farfarat*, "haste," and *fur=fur*, "small bird, sparrow, oriole."

In the more recent Semitic dialects: Syriac[5] *par* "flap the wings, flee, escape; be disturbed, confused," *parpar*, "flap the wings, shake the body, tremble, be restless," and modern colloquial Aramaic *purpiri*, "flutter, flap the wings"; Late Hebrew *pirpēr*, "move convulsively, restlessly," *pirpûr*, "writhing"; Ethiopic *farra*, "flee, escape," *farara*, "fly, run," and Harari *firfir bāya*, "shiver, tremble, be in convulsions."[6]

---

* Abbreviations for Egyptological texts and studies follow A.H. Gardiner, *Egyptian Grammar* (3rd ed., 1957) and R. Faulkner, *A Concise Dictionary of Middle Egyptian.* The abbreviation *Gr. Med.* is for H. Grapow, et al, *Grundriß der Medizin der alten Ägypter.* 8 vols. (1954-62).

[1] This study, to be published elsewhere, includes the evidence for the *b/p* interchange in Egyptian.

[2] Semitists are divided as to whether there is a single root *pr* or several. Those proposed are *pr* I, "escape," *pr* II, "yield fruit," *pr*. III, "break." The present study deals only with *pr* I.

[3] Ibn Manẓur, *Lisānu-l-ʿArab*, ed. Dar Sader (1968), V, 50ff. As usual in Arabic dictionaries, *pr* I, II and III are treated here as a single root.

[4] On Semitic biliteral roots, the key studies are H. Fleisch, *Traité de philologie arabe* I (1961), 252ff.; S. Moscati, *Biblica* 28 (1947), 113ff.; J. Greenburg, *Word* 6 (1950), 162ff.; J. Macdonald, *Leeds Or. Soc. Ann.* 5 (1963-65), 63ff.

[5] See especially ʾal-Kaldāni, *Dalīlu-l-Raġibīni fī Luġati-l-ʿArāmiyyīni* (1900), 604.

[6] On the latter, see W. Leslau, *The Verb in Harari* (1958), 72.

The root is not nearly as widespread in earlier dialects.[7] One clear example occurs in Ugaritic in the legend of Aqhat where Baal commands a flight of eagles: *tpr wdu*, "take off and fly!"[8] It is also possible that the personal name *Prpr*[9] might be the Ugaritic equivalent of Arabic *furfur*, "small bird." The three examples of this root which supposedly exist in biblical Hebrew[10] are ambiguous and translations vary. The lament in Job 16:12 should perhaps be rendered: "my life was restful, but he (God) shook me (*way^{e}parp^{e}rēnī*)," that is, Job's peaceful life was convulsed.[11] One might also see a similar meaning in Isa. 24:19 where it is said "the earth is smashed, the earth is violently agitated (*pōr hitpōr^{e}āh*), the earth staggers."[12]

While there is no clear example of this root in Old South Arabic, one possible occurrence is in a text concerning the rules of pilgrimage to a temple in Marib: "He has banned ʿLB from idle talk (about) women on the seventh day of Dhusarar until the pilgrims of Taʾlib move away (*ltfr qsd tʾlb*)."[13]

Semitic *pr* thus has the basic sense of agitated escape and convulsive or fluttering motion. Since the Egyptian cognate is frequently used in reference to birds, it is of particular interest to note that, when Semitic *pr* defines the action of birds, it means the fluttering motion of the wings, as the bird takes off in flight, that is, "escape by rapid beating of the wings." It does not denote the actual act of flying (with rare modern exceptions), which is expressed by different verbs: Arabic *ṭāra*, Syriac *ṭar*, Ugaritic *dʾy*, Hebrew *ʿûp*, etc.[14]

In the light of the Egyptian cognates discussed below which show an *n*-prefix (*npꜣ*), it is worth noting the possibility that equivalent augmented forms exist in Semitic. It is now recognized that many *primae nun* verbs are in reality biconsonantal roots with an *n*-prefix, not to be confused with the passive-reflexive prefix such as the Hebrew *nifʿal*, Arabic *ʾinfaʿala*.[15] We may therefore ask if those Semitic words with the consonantal structure *npr* are in any way related to the root *pr*, "escape."[16]

It seems likely that Arabic *nafara*, "disperse, flee, scatter in haste," *ʾanfara*, "frighten away," *nafrat*, "escape," and related words should ultimately have derived from *farra*, "escape." Similarly, it is difficult not to relate Syriac *n^{e}par*, "run away," *ʾapar*, "put to flight," which is defined in Syriac-Arabic dictionaries by Arabic *hariba*, "escape," exactly as is its biconsonantal counterpart *par* (see above).[17] Here may also be noted Tigrinya *nefere*, which "only applies to the scaring away of birds, and from this meaning the now current sense of 'to fly' has evolved."[18]

---

[7] That is, *pr* I is not common. Akkadian *parāru* is a widely-used verb though its fundamental sense is "break, scatter about" = *pr* III. *parāru* seems never to have the precise meaning "flee, escape," nor does it appear to be used in connection with birds; cf. W. von Soden, *AHw*, 829f.

[8] 1 Aqht 120, 134, on which see A. Herdner, *Corpus*, 89, notes 9-10. J. Aistleitner, *WUS*, no. 2259, adds other examples but confuses *pr* I, II, III. [Cf. also Gordon, UT, 471 no. 2120, who translates "flee".]

[9] F. Gröndahl, *St Pohl* 1 (1967), 174, "unsicher".

[10] *KBL*, 782, *prr* II.

[11] Though the context also supports *pr* III, "break."

[12] Here perhaps a description of earthquakes? The third occurrence in Ps 74:13 is doubtless better rendered "shatter, smash," with M. Dahood, *Psalms* II (1968), 205.

[13] A.F.L. Beeston, *Sabaean Inscriptions* (1937), 76, 7. In spite of Beeston's remarks on *tfr*, Prof. M. Ghul, who pointed out this reference to me, believes a derivation from *farra* is likely.

[14] *pr* was borrowed into other languages with essentially the same meaning: Nubian *firri*, "fly, flit, whir"; Masai: *ivirivir*, "shake," *ivirri*, "fly, hurry." E. Zyhlarz, *ZÄS* 70 (1934), 109, compares Berber *ẹffi*, "flee, escape."

[15] S. Moscati (ed.), *Introduction to the Comparative Grammar of the Semitic Languages* (1964), 163f.; W. von Soden, *GAG* (1952), 136; G. Botterweck, *Der Triliterismus im Semitischen* (1952), 55.

[16] We face here the same difficulty noted above (note 2) for the root *pr*, namely, that more than one root is probably involved. On *pr/npr*, "flee, escape," see Th. Nöldeke, *Neue Beiträge*, 185f.

[17] Also used to translate Hebrew *dahār*, "hurry, rush away," in Nah 3:2.

[18] E. Ullendorff, *Or* NS 20 (1951), 273f. C.C. Torrey, *JAOS* 54 (1934), 32f., suggests a unique occurrence of *npr* in Aramaic; *DISO*, 182, regards this as doubtful.

This root occurs very rarely in Ugaritic. The noun *npr*, "birds, fowl," found once used parallel to *ʿṣrm*, "birds,"[19] is in general considered cognate to the words just mentioned, hence distinct from the simplex *pr*.[20] Aistleitner, however, suggests it is a *nifʿal* participle from *pr*, "escape."[21] I rather suggest that *npr* is related to the root *pr* just as Arabic *nafara* appears to be closely linked with *farra*; instead of a *nifʿal* form, this is the biconsonantal root with the *n*-prefix. The only other occurrence of the root in Ugaritic is unfortunately in a broken context[22] so that both the meaning and morphology are unclear. This example is usually treated as a verb and, when translated at all, is rendered "shatter, break."[23] However, Rin prefers to treat this as a *nifʿal* form of *pr*, equivalent in meaning to Hebrew *barāḥ*, "flee, escape."[24]

With the exception of the last example the evidence indicates that Semitic verbs with the structure *npr* which fall within the general semantic range "escape, frighten away," may be derived from the simplex *pr*, "escape," by the addition of the *n*-prefix. This is supported by the series of Semitic roots based on *pr* plus a "determinant" third radical,[25] by the cognate of other morphological variants of the root, for example, Arabic *fāra*, "be roused (anger), throb (blood vessel)," Hebrew *pûr*, "frustrate, confuse"; etc.

II. The Egyptian Root *pꜣ*

A detailed examination of the occurrences of Egyptian *pꜣ* (Late Egyptian *py*) shows that its usage conforms precisely to the semantic range of Semitic *pr*. Since the discussion of this root in the Berlin Dictionary is incomplete and many key references are not listed, it is useful to give translations of selected passages here arranged according to the primary meanings of the root.

A. *"escape, run away, take off."*

1) "He *escapes*, he *escapes* from you as (do) ducks; he wrests his hand from you as a falcon" (*Pyr.* 1484a). Of this, Faulkner states: "The allusion is to the Egyptian habit of carrying live birds by their wings; the king is envisaged as a bird escaping from the hand of the fowler."[26]

2) "He (the soldier) has *run away* and gone forth among the deserters" (*P. Lansing* 10, 7).

3) "I have attained the state of *escaping* (*ʿ n py*) to you from the net" (*BD* 153A, 6; *Nu*); the figure is of a fish escaping the fishing-net, not a bird escaping the fowler's trap.

4) "Their hearts are carried off, their spirits are *run away*," said of defeated enemies (*Medinet Habu* I, pl. 37, 15-16; cf. II, pl. 90, 10).

---

19 C. Gordon, *UT*, 168, text 49:II:37.

20 C. Gordon, *UT*, Glossary, no. 1680; J. Gray, *Legacy*, 57 n.2 (though his translation "wild creatures" is incorrect); A. Freyha, *Malāḥīm wa-ʾAsāṭīr min ʾUgarit* (1967), 677; S. and Sh. Rin, *ʿAlîlôth Hāʾēlîm* (1968), 221.

21 J. Aistleitner, *WUS*, no. 2259. J. de Moor, *AOAT* 16, 211, believes the meaning of the term is still unclear.

22 C. Gordon, *UT*, 197, text 137:12.

23 C. Gordon, *UL*, 13; G. Driver, *CML*, 79; A. Freyha, *Malāḥīm wa-ʾAsāṭīr*, 350, translates by Arabic *ḥaṭṭama*, "shatter." A. van Selms, *UF* 2 (1970), 258f., treats the word as a noun, "break" of the teeth (= Arabic *ʾiftarra*, "show the teeth when laughing"). The word would thus be akin to *pr* III, "break" (see note 2).

24 *ʿAlîlôth Hāʾēlîm*, 53.

25 S. Moscati, *Biblica* 28 (1947), 135; W. von Soden, *GAG*, § 73b.

26 R. Faulkner, *The Ancient Egyptian Pyramid Texts* (1969), Utt. 573, n. 5. See also *Pyr.* 463d, 890a; Faulkner regularly translates "fly, flier," etc.

5) "*Take off, take off*! Rise up, rise up! Lift up your face, O rapid falcon, and spread, spread your wings"; said of Re.[27]

6) The previous examples explain the common idiom *pꜣ r pt* found throughout the history of Egyptian literature[28] which means "escape (from earth) toward the sky," an allusion to the agitated fluttering of a bird's wings as its takes flight. While this idiom is universally translated "fly to the sky," it is better rendered "take flight," as its Semitic counterpart.[29]

7) The verb *pꜣ* is sometimes used in apposition to *ḫnỉ*, "alight": "This N *takes off* as a bird, he alights as a beetle";[30] or as a compound meaning all types of birds; "those which *take off* and those which alight."[31] The idiom does not express the act of flying, but the beginning and ending of flight.

B. "*flap the wings, flutter, tremble.*"

8) "Birds which are in (their) nest *flap wings* with joy, their wings which had been folded (now) being spread in praises of the living Aton."[32] Here there is no question of flying, but rather the fluttering of birds which have been aroused while in their nests.

9) In a series of phrases directed toward an unknown person, it is said: "your body is like a sparrow; it is good for you the calling out of your name, and you *tremble* quickly, making the movements of a millstone . . ."[33]

10) A hymn to the Aton states he is the creator of all creatures, including "what hovers in the air *flapping* with their wings."[34]

11) In a late legend, Isis seeks for the child Horus and, on finding him, describes him in part as follows: "his body was weak, his heart was weary, and the vessels (*mtw*) of his limbs did not *pulsate*" (*Mett.* 170). Here *pꜣ* is a clear parallel to Arabic *farīr*, "place of the pulse," *fāra*, "throb (blood vessels)," and underlies the usage of *npꜣ* and *npꜣpꜣ* discussed below.

C. "*leap, jump, flit away.*"

12) This derived meaning of *pꜣ* is well known from *Harris* 500, Vs 6, 2-5, where the prince and his competitors must "jump" to a castle window to win the hand of the princess.

[27] M. Alliot, *IFAO Bib. d'et.* 20 (1954), 623, from Edfu.

[28] *Pyr.* 459a-b, 1948a; *CT* IV, 52g = *BD* 76, 2-3 (*Nu*); Amenemope X, 5; H. Gauthier, *Ann. Serv.* 27 (1927), 8; B. Gunn, *Ann. Serv.* 26 (1926), 89; *P. Beatty* V, Vs 6, 1; F. Ll. Griffith, *Antiquities of Tell el Yahudiyah* (1890), pl. XXV, 9. A Demotic example in F.Ll. Griffith, *Stories of the High Priests of Memphis* (1900), I Khamwas 4, 33.

[29] Also used as a synonym for "die" (king); Orb 19, 3; Ost. Cairo 25515, Vs II, 25; J. Černý, *ZÄS* 72 (1938), 110.

[30] *Pyr.* 366a-b; E. Drioton, *Ann. Serv.* 52 (1952), 118; *CT* VI, 196b-d.

[31] *Amarna* VI, pl. XXVII, 5; *P. Beatty* IV, Rt 7, 8; *P. Beatty* XIII, 10; A. Gardiner, *AEO* II, 256*. M. Alliot, *Rev. d'Ég.* 5 (1946), 72 n. 3, makes an unnecessary distinction between birds that customarily fly (*pꜣ.wt*) and fowl which customarily stay on the ground (*ḫnn.wt*). See further the similar usage with *hꜣỉ*, "descend," in *P. Turin* A, Vs 1, 10; R. Caminos, *L.-Eg. Misc.*, 508.

[32] *Amarna* VI, pl. XVI, lower text, 19-20; see also *Amarna* VI, pl. XXVII, 5, and Ost. Cairo 25212, 11. A similar passage using *ksks*, "dance," in A. Gardiner, *ZÄS* 42 (1905), 19.

[33] J. Černý and A. Gardiner, *Hieratic Ostraca* I (1957), pl. XXXVIII, I, Vs 3-4.

[34] *Amarna* VI, pl. XXVII, 8. This sense may also be intended in the phrase "I *flutter* as a falcon (swallow), I cackle as a goose"; *BD* 149, xi, 7 and *BD* 82, 2 (*Nu*); *Nav.* 82, 2.

13) Several new examples can now be quoted which refer to a male (gods and animals) "leaping" on a female in a sexual sense.[35]

14) In Orb 18, 4, while the queen stands by watching a tree being cut down: "one of the wood-chips *flitted away* and entered into the mouth of the noble lady."

15) In a late mythological text, it is said that the king "jumps" into a pool.[36] It is this sense which is preserved in later times: Demotic *pꜣỉ*, "run, leap," Coptic *pēi*, "leap, jump."

D. *"rush, hurry."*

16) "Don't *rush* to fill that one," that is don't be anxious to pass on information to the gossip (Amenemope XIII, 8).

17) While having a conversation with someone, if he is talking "don't *rush* to enter against him," that is, don't break in and interrupt (Amenemope XXII, 22).

18) "If an orphan who is weak petitions you, and another is after him who would ruin him, *hurry* to him and give him something" (*P. Beatty* IV, Vs 2, 3).

19) The idiom *py ḥr ḫrw*, "*hurry* at (someone's) voice," occurs several times with the sense "act promptly."[37]

E. *"flash, glitter."*

20) In texts at Medinet Habu and Luxor recording an ancient ritual for the foundation of temples, there is the obscure phrase "when the white bird has not yet *pꜣ*." Barguet, following Moret, suggests this is "une image expriment le jaillissement du soleil au matin."[38] While Barguet renders *pꜣ* as "*envoler,*" the imagry rather suggests this is equivalent to Arabic *ʾiftarra*, "flash, sparkle," said of lightning and stars. This phrase would thus mean "before the sun has *flashed*," that is before it has risen, which is precisely the sense of the Arabic term.

21) In the Leiden Magical Papyrus: "I have outfaced thee, O *smn*-disease . . . like he who *glitters* and stands firmly established on a high place just as Parēʿ *glitters* when he rises."[39] The analogy with the preceeding example is obvious; both refer to the flashing of the sun at sunrise.

* * *

The preceding discussion shows that Egyptian *pꜣ* has as its basic sense the idea of hasty escape and agitated movement. In reference to birds, it does not connote the action of flying, but rather "take flight, flap the wings, flutter," and the like. Especially interesting is the rare sense "flash, glitter." Thus, it is quite evident that the use of this verb is much broader than previously thought, covering the entire semantic range of its Semitic counterpart.

[35] Incorrectly listed separately in *Wb.* I, 497, 13-14. To the examples given there may be added: A. Gardiner, *Hier. Pap. Brit. Mus. 3rd Series* I, 62 n. 8 (ostracon from Ramesseum); *P. Beatty* VII, Vs 1, 6; F. Haikal, *Bibl. Aeg.* 14 (1970), 63; J. Goyon, *BIFAO* 65 (1967), 147. For parallel semantics, cf. *nhp*, "leap, beget," *mnhp*, "begettor"; J. Yoyotte, *BIFAO* 61 (1962), 140f.; *sṯp*, "jump up, leap on female," B. Gunn, *ZÄS* 57 (1922), 71 n. 6.

[36] F.Ll. Griffith, *Antiquities of Tell el Yahudiyah*, pl. XXVI, 22.

[37] R. Caminos, *L.-Eg. Misc.*, 351; F.Ll. Griffith, *JEA* 13 (1927), 205, lines 116, 118.

[38] P. Barguet, *Rev. d'ég.* 9 (1952), 9 n. 7.

[39] A. Masaart, *The Leiden Magical Papyrus* (1954), 71.

III. Verbs Derived from Egyptian *pꜣ*

The verb *npꜣpꜣ* appears only in *Sm.*, where the physician is instructed to palpate a head-wound and seek "something there throbbing and *fluttering* (*nhdhd npꜣpꜣ*) under your fingers like the weak place of an infant's crown."[40] Breasted rightly points out that *npꜣpꜣ* must be a reduplicated form of *pꜣ* with the *n*-prefix.[41] Its meaning is thus established beyond doubt as "pulsate, tremble."

This explains the unique *npꜣ* found once in a gloss in *Eb.* on a condition of the heart: *ỉr ḥꜣty.f npꜣ.f ꜥꜣ ꜥḏt ḫr mnḏ.f ỉꜣby*, which the editors of *Gr. Med.* render tentatively: "Was anbetrifft; sein Herz, es flattert übermäßig; die Fettmasse ist unter seiner linken Brust."[42] Their suggestion[43] that *npꜣ* may be related to *npꜣpꜣ* is certainly correct, and *npꜣ* should be considered a derivative of the simplex *pꜣ* plus the *n*-prefix with a meaning "tremble, palpatate."

The causative *spꜣ* has heretofore been listed only for the Pyramid Texts,[44] though I believe it is also to be recognized in a unique verb in *Eb.* In a remedy for constipation, the patient is instructed to take the prescribed medicine for four days *r mḥ ḫt.f r zpꜣ ḳꜣb.f*, "in order to fill his stomach so that his bowels *zpꜣ*."[45] This verb thus indicates movement of the bowels to cure constipation. Because it is spelled *zpꜣ* and is determined with a centipede-sign, it has heretofore been related to *zpꜣ*, "centipede, worm."[46] But since the distinction between *z* and *s* was already becoming vague in Old Egyptian,[47] and *Eb.* itself may write the same word with either sign (e.g., *znf, snf*, "blood"), I suggest the word should be read *spꜣ*, is a causative of *pꜣ* and that *r spꜣ ḳꜣb.f* should be rendered "to make his bowels shudder, move convulsively," an apt description of the effect of an emetic. The centipede determinative is by analogy to *zpꜣ*, "centipede," which by this time would have been pronounced in much the same way and with the same sibilant. Precisely the same situation prevails with other words whose consonantal structure is *zpꜣ/spꜣ*.[48]

Finally, as Westendorff has noted,[49] Demotic *ppỉ* and Coptic *papoi*, "small bird," suggest an earlier, still unattested, **pꜣpꜣ*, the Egyptian equivalent of Arabic *furfur*, "small bird." This reduplicated form may likewise be preserved in personal names. Preisgke lists a rare name *Papaei* which Crum takes as the Greek equivalent of Coptic *papoi*.[50] Since personal names are derived from names of birds in both Coptic and Egyptian,[51] it is possible that some Egyptian names written *Pꜣ, Pꜣpꜣ, Pỉpỉ, Ppỉ*, etc., are from this root.[52] But this must remain a doubtful suggestion as I can quote no example of the latter with a bird determinative.

---

[40] *Sm.*, 165f.

[41] *Ibid.*, 168. Verbs of the *n-abab* form have been studied by P. Montet, *Sphinx* 14 (1910), 201ff., M. Feichtner, *WZKM* 38 (1931), 221ff., and M. Cohen, *MIFAO* 66 (1935-36), 705ff. See also my remarks in *ZÄS* 95 (1968), 70ff., and *ZÄS* 98 (1972), 155f. S. Yeivin, *Kemi* 6 (1936), 72, noted the connection with Late Hebrew *parpēr*, "struggle, tremble," through he erred in suggesting that *npꜣpꜣ* is a *nifꜥal* form.

[42] *Gr. Med.* IV, i, 6 (Eb 855q).

[43] *Gr. Med.* IV, ii, 30 n. 1 on Eb 855q; *Gr. Med.* VII, 456.

[44] *Wb.* IV, 100, 21.

[45] Text in *Gr. Med.* V, 162 (Eb. 204d); translated in *Gr. Med.* IV, i, 93.

[46] *Gr. Med.* VII, 743.

[47] E. Edel, *Altägyptische Grammatik* (1955/1964), I, § 116.

[48] The cult-place of Anubis is spelled *Spꜣ* in the Old Kingdom, but *Spꜣ* or *Zpꜣ* in the Middle Kingdom, sometimes with the centipede-det.; *Aeg. Inschr. aus den K. Mus. zu Berlin* I (1913), 77, 133, 134, 214, 229, 231, etc. Similarly, the centipede-deity *Zpꜣ* appears as *Spꜣ* already in the Coffin Texts; H. Kees, *ZÄS* 58 (1923), 84f.

[49] W. Westendorff, *Koptisches Handwörterbuch*, 149.

[50] F. Preisigke, *Namenbuch* (1922), col. 275; Crum, *Dictionary*, 266.

[51] G. Heuser, *Die Personennamen der Kopter* (1929), 73f.; H. Ranke, *Personennamen* II, 183ff.

[52] H. Ranke, *Personennamen* I, 130ff. For *Pꜣ*: *ibid.*, I, 99, 22; for *Pꜣpꜣ*: *ibid.*, I, 129, 13; II, 286, 5.

CULTIC PROSTITUTION

A Case Study in Cultural Diffusion[1]

Edwin M. Yamauchi

Miami University, Oxford, Ohio

Professor Cyrus H. Gordon, who has been a bold pioneer in adducing cases of cultural diffusion, notes that it would be an error "to insist that a similar feature in two parts of the world must be due to diffusion. Isolated details may prove little or nothing *in any specific case*, though cumulatively a thousand such details might prove much."[2] It is certainly not always easy to decide whether similarities are due to diffusion or to independent invention.

I would like to survey the evidences for a phenomenon of considerable interest for biblical studies whose distribution in the ancient world is by general consent attributed to cultural diffusion – namely "cultic or sacred prostitution." Cultic prostitution is a practice involving the female[3] and at times the male devotees of fertility deities, who presumably dedicated their earnings to their deity. One of the motives of the practice, particularly in Mesopotamia where the king engaged in an act of *hieros gamos* or "sacred marriage" with a temple prostitute, was to insure the fertility of the land and people through sympathetic magic. Other practices of temporary temple prostitution seem to have involved the ritual defloration of virgins by strangers before their marriage to their husbands.

Sacred prostitution quite independent of Near Eastern practices and of a relatively recent date existed in west Africa and in India. In Dahomey numerous girls were trained before puberty to be the devotees of the gods.

> At the end of their noviciate they become public harlots. But no disgrace attaches to their profession, for it is believed that they are married to the god, and that their excesses are caused and directed by him. . . . As the wives of a god, these sacred women may not marry. But they are not bound to the service of the divinity for life.[4]

In southern India girls known as *Dēva-dāsi* served as temple prostitutes as late as the twentieth century. It is estimated that in Madras in 1927 they numbered as many as 200.000.[5]

---

[1] I would like to thank Professor Harry A. Hoffner, Jr., for a number of suggestions with respect to the cuneifrom evidence.

[2] C.H. Gordon, *Before Columbus* (1971), 143, 145.

[3] Note: the Greek word *hierodoulos*, transliterated "hierodule," literally means "sacred slave." As it is used in some classical passages to designate (female) sacred prostitutes, it is used in this sense.

[4] J.G. Frazer, *The New Golden Bough*, (ed.) T.H. Gaster (1959), 54. For a general discussion see E. Westermarck, *The History of Human Marriage* (1925), I, 207-35.

[5] F. Henriques, *Stews and Strumpets: A Survey of Prostitution* (1961), I, 177.

A. Mesopotamia

In the ancient biblical world our fullest – though quite complex and far from satisfactory – evidence for sacred prostitution comes from Mesopotamia. Cultic prostitution was listed by the Sumerians along with kingship, justice, truth, etc. as one of the divinely ordained institutions.[6] The Mesopotamian goddess of fertility and love was the Sumerian Inanna,[7] who was identified with the Akkadian Ishtar. An unpublished Old Babylonian hymn describes Ishtar as a hierodule whom 120 men cannot exhaust.[8]

In the Sumerian city of Uruk the sacred marriage rite was probably repeated annually between a hierodule who represented Inanna and the king who represented Dumuzi.[9] We have a number of sensuous songs celebrating the love between Inanna and Dumuzi.[10] From a text of Iddin-Dagan of the Isin dynasty we learn that the rite in Isin was performed on New Year's eve.[11] There are possible illustrations of the rite on some cylinder seals. A most striking depiction is a plaque from Elam dated to the early second millennium depicting a nude couple on a bed.[12]

Several categories of priestesses may have functioned as hierodules, though explicit references to their functioning as such are lacking.[13] The term often translated "hierodule" is the Sumerian NU.GIG,[14] and one of its corresponding Akkadian terms[15] *qadištum* (and its variants *qadiltum, qaššatum*), a word which means "tabooed," "dedicated" or "holy". From legal texts we learn that the *qadištum* could marry and bear children, or if unmarried could adopt children. An Old Assyrian text permits an Assyrian merchant assigned to Cappadocia to marry a *qadištum* in Ashur.[16] The Middle Assyrian Laws stipulate that a *qadiltum* who is married must veil herself on the street.[17] Some have assumed that marriage ended the *qadištum*'s role as a sacred prostitute.[18] Although we have numerous texts concerning the *qadištum* serving as a wet-nurse, a mid wife, etc., no reference to prostitution is explicit apart from the *ana ittišu* series and a special relationship to the Ishtar cult cannot be demonstrated.[19]

---

6 H.W.F. Saggs, *The Greatness That Was Babylon* (1962), 36.

7 In the prayer of Enheduanna, Inanna is called NU-GIG-AN-NA "the Hierodule of An." Cf. W.W. Hallo and J.J.A. van Dijk, *YNER* 3 (1968), 14-15.

8 W. von Soden, *Die Religion in Geschichte und Gegenwart* (1961), V, 643.

9 See Herodotus I.181-2. Cf. S.N. Kramer, *The Sacred Marriage Rite* (1969); T. Jacobsen, *Toward the Image of Tammuz*, (ed.) W.L. Moran (1970), 28ff.

10 S.N. Kramer, *Expedition*, 5 (fall, 1962), 25-31; *idem, Proceedings of the American Philosophical Society*, 107 (1963), 485-527; *idem, Iraq*, 31 (1969), 18-23, as well as Kramer's work cited in the preceding note. Cf. also W.G. Lambert, *JSS*, 4 (1959), 1-15.

11 As Sidney Smith points out the *hieros gamos* of Gudea did not fall on the New Year, but in May or June when the flood was in spate. S.H. Hooke (ed.), *Myth, Ritual and Kingship* (1958), 42.

12 Louvre SB 5888, illustrated in P. Amiet, *Elam* (1966), 329. [Many further examples and discussion in R.D. Biggs, *TCS*, 2 (1967), 10. – Ed.]

13 M. Jastrow, *The Civilization of Babylonia and Assyria* (1915), 272, 307-8. Cf. M. Astour, *JBL*, 85 (1966), 185-96.

14 This Sumerian term has been explained as "not sick" by E. Dhorme and P. Jensen, as "tabooed" by B. Landsberger, and as "not dirty" by H. Lewy. According to J. Renger, "Untersuchungen zum Priestertum in der altbabylonischen Zeit," *ZA*, 58 (1967), 178 f., a satisfactory translation of the Sumerian word is not possible.
E. Dhorme, *RA*, 11 (1914), 107.
P. Jensen, *ZDMG*, 67 (1913), 508.
B. Landsberger, *MSL* IV, Emesal II, 78-80.
H. Lewy, *JAOS*, 76 (1956), 202 f.

15 [Other Akk. terms employed to translate Sum. nu-gig are *ištarītu* and *kulmašītu* (Deimel, *ŠL*, II, 75:90).– Ed.]

16 J.B. Pritchard (ed.), *The Ancient Near East: Supplementary Texts and Pictures* [abbreviated *ANE*] (1969), 543.

17 *ANET*, 183.

18 Renger, 184.

19 *Ibid.*, 180.

Women devoted to Ishtar known as *ištarītum* appear in numerous texts, which are unfortunately not very informative.[20] One significant text which suggests that they would not make good wives indicates that they were hierodules:

Do not marry a prostitute (*ḫarimtu*), whose husbands are legion (literally "3600"),
A temple harlot (*ištarītu*) who is dedicated to a god,
A courtesan (*kulmašītu*) whose favours are many.[21]

Another class of women who have been identified as sacred prostitutes are the *nadītu* women.[22] For example, Theophile Meek has rendered this term by "hierodule" in his translation of the Hammurabi Law Code.[23] More recently C.J. Gadd has suggested that "there is some indication that they belonged at the same time to the class of temple-prostitutes . . . ."[24] This interpretation has been opposed by B. Landsberger, and in more detail by R. Harris, who maintains that chastity was required of these cloistered women.[25] A vocabulary list, however, gives as the equivalent of the Sumerian LUKUR not only *nadītum* but also *qadištum.*[26]

W.G. Lambert summarizes our state of knowledge as follows:

No one doubts its (cultic prostitution's) prevalence, especially with the cult of ISHTAR, but little is known of its functioning. The names of various categories of priestesses are known, all highly respectable persons since kings even dedicate their daughters, but it is not known if all, or some, or even none of these were especially religious prostitutes. Money was presumably paid for favours received despite its being a glorification of a goddess.[27]

---

[20] Cf. W.C. Gwaltney, Jr., "The *Qadištum* and the *Ištarītum* in Mesopotamian Society" [unpublished dissertation, Hebrew Union College] (1964), 68-78.

[21] W.G. Lambert, *Babylonian Wisdom Literature* (1960), 102-3. The Sumerian signs rendered *kulmašītu* are sometimes rendered, especially in earlier studies, *zêrmašītu*. But the latter reading must now be rejected on the basis of spelling *ku-ul-ma-ši-tum* (Tell Asmar 1931, 463:12; *CAD* K 526). See Renger, 185ff.

[22] The Sumerian signs SAL-ME are now read as a ligature LUKUR.

[23] In *ANET* the translation of the Code of Hammurabi (CH) by Theophile Meek has the following renderings: CH § 40 *nadītum* "hierodule"; so also CH § 137, §§ 144-46; CH §§ 178-79 *entum, nadītum, zikrum* "a nun, a hierodule, or a votary"; CH § 180 *nadīt gagîm ù zikrum* "a hierodule in a convent or a votary"; CH 181 *nadītum, qadištum ù kulmašītum* "a hierodule, a sacred prostitute, or a devotee"; CH 182 *nadītum Marduk* "a hierodule of Marduk"; CH § 187, §§ 192-3 *zikrum* "votary." Cf. D. Luckenbill, "The Temple Women of the Code of Hammurabi," *AJSL*, 34 (1917), G.R. Driver and J.C. Miles, *Iraq*, 6 (1939), 66-70, made the suggestion that the "SAL-ZIKRUM" was a eunuch dressed as a woman!

[24] C.J. Gadd, *Hammurabi and the End of His Dynasty* [*CAH*, II, ch. 5] (2nd ed., 1965), 32.

[25] R. Harris, "The *NADĪTU* Woman," in R.D. Biggs and J.A. Brinkman (eds.), *Studies Presented to A. Leo Oppenheim* (1964), 106-35.

[26] *Ibid.*, 107. Late lexical equivalences as this, however, may only show that long after the institution, which flourished in the Sumerian and Old Babylonian periods, scribes simply guessed at the meaning of the Sumerian term. [Also = *šugītu, tēlītu, saḫiptu* (MSL 12, 129:23f.) – Ed.]

[27] W.G. Lambert, *JEOL*, 15 (1957-58), 195. The significance of other categories as the *kezertu, šamḫatu*, etc. is rather obscure, See Renger, 180 ff. The *CAD* K, 314, on *kezertu*, lit. "woman with curled hair" suggests that she was a "prostitute." [Professor J.J. Finkelstein in his 1972 AOS paper at Chapel Hill, N.C., proposed that the OB *kezertu* women were hair-dressers, whose line of work occasionally earned for them the reputation of "available women." – Ed.]
The *assinnu*, cult personnel "whom Istar had changed from men into women," are sometimes regarded as male cultic prostitutes. Cf. Lambert, *JEOL*, 15 (1957-58), 195, and H.B. Huffmon, *BA*, 31 (1968), 105. The *CAD*, A 2, 341-42, cautions, however, that "there is no specific evidence that he was a eunuch or a homosexual." [Their identification as male cultic prostitutes has been denied by B. Landsberger, in the W. Baumgartner Festschrift (Supplements to VT, XVI), 202-3; A.L. Oppenheim, *Or* 19 (1950), 135, n. 1, thinks that they were priestly actors in cult drama. Cf. also above on p. 82. – Ed.]

In the Gilgamesh Epic VI.165 ff. Enkidu is tamed by a *ḫarimtum*, a cult prostitute of Ishtar. Gilgamesh had apparently been taking liberties with the women of Uruk. Lambert and others have interpreted the Gilgamesh Epic IV. 34-36, "He will have intercourse with the destined wife: he first, the husband afterwards," as a reference ot the practice of *ius primae noctis*, the ritual defloration of virgins by a ruler.[28] This interpretation of the Gilgamesh passage has been challenged by I.M. Diakonoff,[29] and B. Landsberger,[30] but has been reaffirmed by J.J. Finkelstein.[31]

Lambert interprets the famous passage in Herodotus I.199 as related to this practice rather than to cultic prostitution proper. Herodotus (5th century B.C.) wrote:

> The foulest Babylonian custom is that which compels every woman of the land once in her life to sit in the temple of Aphrodite (i.e. Ishtar) and have intercourse with some stranger . . . But must sit down in the sacred plot of Aphrodite, with crowns of cord on their heads . . .

Strabo (63 B.C. – post A.D. 21) XVI.i.20 makes a similar statement. The Apocryphal Epistle of Jeremiah (c. 300 B.C.) 6:43 states: "The women also with cords about them, sitting in the ways, burn bran for perfume; but if any of them, drawn by some that passeth by, lie with him she reproacheth her fellow, that she was not thought as worthy as herself, nor her cord broken."[32] The most explicit texts describing sacred prostitution in Mesopotamia are these late texts which associate the institution with the ritual defloration of women by strangers in contrast to the association of the rite with temple personnel found in the earlier texts.

B. Egypt

According to Albright sacred prostitution was "apparently not known in native Egyptian religion . . . . ."[33] Attempts to prove its presence in Egypt rest on either dubious or late evidence. Henriques interprets certain inscriptions of Ramesses III referring to female prisoners and of Osorkon referring to female temple servants as references to sacred prostitution.[34] His reference to the celebrated passage of Hatshepsut at Deir el-Bahri describing the union of the god Amon and her mother may be evidence of a type of *hieros gamos*, but proves nothing about sacred prostitution since no hierodule is involved.[35]

---

[28] *JEOL*, 15 (157-58), 195 f.; cf. F.M.Th. de Liagre Böhl, *Het Gilgamesj Epos* (1958). [T. Jacobsen, *Acta Orientalia*, 8 (1930), 62-74 suggested that Enkidu's prime mission was to satisfy some of Gilgamesh's excessive sexual drives. The matter is also discussed by Dr. Jeffrey Tigay in "Literary Critical Studies in the Gilgamesh Epic" (unpublished Yale dissertation, 1971). – Ed.]
According to K. Birket-Smith, *The Paths of Culture* (1965), 233, "For many years the Russian peasants maintained a custom called *snokhachestvo* (from the Russian *snokha* – daugther-in-law) whereby the father-in-law or his brother initiated the bride in marriage. There were rumors that "King Benjamin" Purnell, the founder of a sectarian colony at Benton Harbor, Michigan, early in the twentieth century exercised this *droit de seigneur* with the young girls of the community. Cf. E.T. Clark, *The Small Sects in America* (1949), 153-4.

[29] I.M. Diakonoff in *BiOr*, 18.1-2 (1961), 62f.

[30] B. Landsberger, in J.A. Ankum, R. Feenstra and W.F. Leemans (eds.), *Symbolae Iuridicae et Historicae Martino David Dedicatae* (1968), I, 41-105.

[31] J.J. Finkelstein, *JAOS*, 90 (1970), 251-2.

[32] A curious feature of all three of these texts is the mention of cords about the women or on their heads. Is this possibly related to the placing of the "rope of Šamaš" on the hand of the *nadîtu* women? See Harris, 115.

[33] W.F. Albright, in G.E. Wright (ed.), *The Bible and the Ancient Near East* (1961), 338.

[34] Henriques, 330; J.H. Breasted, *Ancient Records of Egypt* (1906), IV, 75 and 373.

[35] Henriques, 332; Breasted, II, 80-81.

There were, of course, numerous women serving in the temples of Egypt. Some of them were called *mrt* and were musician priestesses. From the early XVIIIth Dynasty an office of the *ḥm.t nṯr* "god's wife" is known, an office fulfilled for a time by the queen. Other women were called the *ḫnrwt* or "concubines" of Amon; we even read of the concubines of goddesses![36] The duties of all of these priestesses involved primarily the performance of music before the deities.[37]

In the New Kingdom a number of Semitic deities became popular in Egypt. Astarte first appears under Amenophis II. According to the Amarna letters Ishtar of Nineveh visited Egypt during the reign of Amenophis III, but in the role of a healing deity. Anath is prominent in the reign of Ramesses II as a martial goddess.[38]

It is especially the nude goddess *Qudshu* among the imported Syrian goddesses who has maintained her association with love and fertility.[39] Of thirteen depictions of this goddess, four examples name her specifically as *Qudshu.* One important example of a Qudshu relief in the Winchester College collection bears an inscription in which she is identified as "Qudshu-Astarte-Anath."[40] She is flanked by the ithyphallic Egyptian god Min and by the Syrian god Resheph in the Louvre stele C. 86.[41] It is significant that both Min and Resheph are associated with fertility, but the prayers that we have addressed to Qudshu are for health rather than for fertility.[42] The center of the worship of Qudshu in Egypt was the temple of Ptah in Memphis, where she was viewed as the god's consort. One monument of Qudshu, a stele of *T3kr.t* from Memphis, names her as "the Prostitute." Whether this is evidence for cultic prostitution is a proposition which Helck doubts,[43] but which Stadelmann leaves open.[44]

There are a number of festivals in Egypt in which some kind of sacred marriage is involved. We learn about the great festival of the fertility god Min which took place in the first month of summer from the reliefs of the XIXth Dynasty at Medinet Habu.[45] H.W. Fairman speculates that during this festival "there is a possibility that the king and queen may have had intercourse."[46] There is also a so-called "sacred marriage" in the festival of Hathor and Horus at Edfu described in Ptolemaic texts.[47] But what seems to be involved here are the statues of the god and the goddess and not the participation of a hierodule.[48]

It is once again the late classical texts that give us unambiguous references to cultic prostitution in Egypt. Herodotus I.182 describes a woman who has intercourse with the Theban Zeus (Amon) but not with men in a way which, according to Herodotus, is analogous to certain Babylonian practices.[49] In contrast to Herodotus' statement, Strabo XVII.i.6 maintains:

---

[36] A.M. Blackman, *JEA*, 7 (1921), 8-30.

[37] A. Erman, *A Handbook of Egyptian Religion* (1907), 72-3.

[38] W. Helck, *Die Beziehungen Ägyptens zu Vorderasien im 3. und 2. Jahrtausend v. Chr.* [Ägyptologische Abhandlungen 5] (1962), 482-514.

[39] R. Stadelmann, *Syrisch-palästinensische Gottheiten in Ägypten* (1967), 110-22.

[40] I.E.S. Edwards, *JNES*, 14 (1955), 49-51, pl. 3; also illustrated in *ANE*, fig. 830.

[41] C. Boreux, *Mélanges syriens offerts à M. René Dussaud* (1939), II, 673-87.

[42] Stadelmann, 122.

[43] Helck, 499: "Auch der geäußerte Gedanke, in den weihenden Frauen Tempelprostituierte zu sehen, entbehrt jedes Beweises und wird geradezu durch Louvre C. 86 widerlegt."

[44] Stadelmann, 116: "Dürfen wir deshalb annehmen, daß es die Stiftung einer, dann sicher asiatischen Tempelprostituierten an ihre Göttin im Tempel des Ptah war? . . . Diese Frage soll noch untersucht werden."

[45] J. Vandier, *La religion égyptienne* (1949), 183-7, 202-3; C.J. Bleeker, *Egyptian Festivals* (1967), 49 and *passim.*

[46] H.W. Fairman in Hooke (ed.), 85.

[47] H.W. Fairman, *Bulletin of the John Rylands Library*, 37 (1954), 196ff.

[48] Vandier, 193 ff. In the festival of Opet, Amon visits his harem – perhaps to celebrate a *hieros gamos*. Cf. Bleeker, 78.

[49] Other passages in Herodotus are rather dubious evidence. In II.60 women at a festival of Bastet at Bubastis "pull up their clothes," and in II.126 we are informed that Cheops prostituted his own daughter in order to obtain funds and stones for his pyramid!

As for Zeus (Amon), whom they especially revere, a maiden of exquisite beauty and most illustrious family serves him as priestess, (one of those maidens) whom the Greeks designate concubines (*pallakas*). She acts as concubine (*pallakeuei*) to, and has intercourse with, whom she will, until her (first?) menstrual purgation takes place (*hē phusikē genētai katharsis tou sōmatos*). After the purgation she is given to a man in marriage.

C. Palestine

In the Old Testament the feminine *q^e^dēshâh* and the masculine *qādēsh*, translated by the KJV as "harlot" or "whore," and "sodomite," are now generally interpreted as female and male cultic prostitutes. In Gen. 38:21-2 Tamar is described as a *q^e^dēshâh* – though there is no reference to a cult; in Gen. 38:15, however, the common word for harlot, *zônâh*, is used of Tamar. In Hosea 4:14 *q^e^dēshôth* and *zōnôth* are used in parallel lines in a cultic context.

Some scholars such as H.G. May came therefore to the conclusion that the word *zônâh* and its derivatives refer not just to prostitution but to cultic prostitution.[50] In the 1930's it became quite common for scholars to find allusions to cultic prostitution everywhere in the Old Testament. B. Brooks remarked that "an increasing list of OT personages are regarded by some as being the offspring of sacred prostitution, if not votaries themselves: so Joseph, Shamgar-ben-anath, as well as Jephthah and his daughter, Samson, Samuel and his parents, Tamar, Jeroboam's mother, Gomer, I Isaiah's 'prophetess,' and Ruth."[51] Related trends were the tendency to postulate a common myth and ritual pattern involving the sacred marriage rite,[52] and the attempt to interpret various books of the Old Testament, such as the Song of Solomon, on the basis of an alleged Tammuz cult.[53]

Clear references to cultic prostitution are to be found in the following passages: In Deut. 23:17-18 the contemptuous phrase "dog" evidently refers to a male cultic prostitute.[54] In Rehoboam's time according to 1 Kings 14:23-4 the presence of male prostitutes was one of the abominable practices which became prevalent. 1 Kings 15:12 relates how Asa put away the male prostitutes from the land. Still later Asa's son, Jehoshaphat, had to repeat this cleansing (1 Kings 22:46). According to 2 Kings 23:6-7 Josiah pulled down the houses of the *q^e^dēshîm* (a plural which may refer to both male and female prostitutes), where women wove vestments in honor of Asherah.[55]

The following passages may contain possible allusions to sacred prostitution: Num. 25:1-3; I Sam. 2: 22; Jer. 13:27; Ezek. 16 and 23:37-41; Amos 2:7-8.

Numerous female figurines, usually nude, found in excavations may be related, indirectly at any rate, with the glorification of sexuality in cultic prostitution. For Palestine J.B. Pritchard in analyzing 294 examples has discerned six basic types:[56] 1) An archaic type with earflaps derived from Mesopotamia. 2) A figure holding her hands up to her breasts – type imported from Mesopotamia and appearing in Palestine from the Middle to the Late Bronze periods. 3) A figure with arms hanging to the side, associated with Hyksos scarabs. 4) The "Qadesh" (cf. Qudshu) type in which the figure with arms extended holds lotus blossoms or serpents. 5) A

[50] H.G. May, *AJSL*, 48 (1932), 73-98.
[51] B. Brooks, *JBL*, 60 (1941), 228. Cf. J.P. Asmussen, *Studia Theologica*, 11 (1957), 167-92.
[52] S.H. Hooke (ed.), *Myth and Ritual*; cf. the criticisms of H. Frankfort, *The Problem of Similarity in Ancient Near Eastern Religions* (1951); and S.H. Hooke (ed.), *Myth, Ritual and Kigship* (1958).
[53] Cf. E. Yamauchi, "Tammuz and the Bible," *JBL*, 81 (1965), 283-90.
[54] R. Patai, *The Hebrew Goddess* (1967), 296, suggests that barren women may have made use of the male prostitutes in order to become pregnant.
[55] W.L. Reed, *The Ashera in the Old Testament* (1949); R. Patai, *JNES*, 24 (1965), 37-52.
[56] J.B. Pritchard, *Palestinian Figurines in Relation to Certain Goddesses . . .* (1943).

figure holding a disc dating from the 11th-7th cent. B.C.[57] 6) A pregnant figure also from the 11th-7th cent. B.C.

Inasmuch as the prototypes of these figures can be found in prehistoric Mesopotamia and in Sumer,[58] there can be no doubt that the iconographic form was diffused from Mesopotamia. In Albright's view:

> However, the Canaanites lost no time in substituting carnality for the grace of the Babylonian originals. Both in these plaques and in later ones the female organs are accentuated in various ways, nearly all of them more direct and less restrained than was true of Babylonia. Moreover, in Mesopotamia the plaques nearly all obviously represent a mother-goddess, whereas in Canaan most of them just as clearly portray a sacred courtesan.[59]

D. Syria and Phoenicia

It is generally assumed that the worship of the major Ugaritic goddesses – Ashera, Astarte, Anath, Qudshu (at times listed as the Qudshu of Asherah, etc. perhaps as a special expression of the fertility granting power of the goddesses) – involved sacred prostitution though there are no explicit texts which can prove this.[60]

In the Ugaritic texts[61] of temple personnel we find listed second after the *khnm* "priests" the *qdšm*, who are probably male cultic prostitutes. According to A.F. Rainey, "In the light of the various biblical passages about the priests of this type (esp. Deut. 23:17-18; Num. 4:14), there is no reason to doubt their sexual activities."[62] Though numerous plaques of nude Astartes, etc. have been found at Ugarit,[63] thus far no references to female sacred prostitutes have yet appeared in the Ugaritic texts.

The most explicit references to sacred prostitution in Syria and Phoenicia are to be found in later texts. Lucian (2nd cent. A.D.) in *De Dea Syria* 6 informs us that in ceremonies in memory of Adonis at the temple of Venus at Byblos all women who would not shave themselves had to prostitute themselves to strangers. The practice of the prostitution of women in the service of Venus at Heliopolis (Baalbek) is attested as late as the 4th cent. A.D. by the historians Socrates, Eusebius, and Sozomen. Constantine destroyed the temple there and erected a church upon its ruins. Ephrem Syrus (A.D. 306-73) refers to the prostitution of virgins, and Augustine, *City of God* IV.10 writes: "To her (Venus) also the Phoenicians offered a gift by prostituting their daughters before they united them to husbands."

E. Cyprus and Cythera

There is good reason to believe that Phoenician influence is responsible for the importation of cultic prostitution as part of the Greek worship of Aphrodite by way of Cyprus.[64] and by way of Cythera, an island

---

[57] Cf. D.R. Hillers, *Concordia Theological Monthly*, 41.9 (1970), 94-107.

[58] Cf. A. Parrot, *Sumer* (1960), pp. XVII, XIX-XX, 56, 245, 299, 367.

[59] W.F. Albright, *Archaeology and the Religion of Israel* (1956), 76.

[60] *Ibid.*, 75. Cf. Stadelmann, 99: "Ihre Dienerinnen im Fruchtbarkeitskult waren die Qedešim, die 'Heiligen.' Offenbar verlangte der Kult vieler kanaanäischer Göttinnen die sakrale Prostitution und es scheint so, als ob in älterer Zeit sogar jede Frau sich diesem Brauch vor ihrer Verheiratung unterwerfen mußte."

[61] C.H. Gordon, *Ugaritic Textbook* (1967), 81:2; 113:73; 114:1; 169:7.

[62] A.F. Rainey, "The Kingdom of Ugarit," *BA*, 28 (1965), 124. [Cf. also *idem*, *A Social Structure of Ugarit* 72, 106 (Hebrew). – Ed.]

[63] Cf. A. Parrot, *Le Musée du Louvre et la Bible* (1957), 66-69.

[64] Cf. H. Herter, *Éléments orientaux dans la religion grecque ancienne* (1960), 61-76; O. Masson, *idem*, 129-42; R.D. Barnett, *idem*, 143-53. In a passage describing the Scythian sack of the temple of Aphrodite at Askalon, Herodotus I.105 says:

This temple, as I learn from what I hear, is the oldest of all the temples of the goddess, for the temple

just off the southeastern Peloponnesus.[65] The association of Aphrodite with Cyprus and Cythera was already recognized by Homer in the 8th cent. B.C., e.g. in the Odyssey VIII.288 and 362.[66]

The worship of Aphrodite had its center at Old Paphos in southwestern Cyprus. Cinyras, the father of Adonis, was said to have instituted the custom of religious prostitution there. According to numerous writers (Herodotus I.199, Athenaeus, Apollodorus, Justin, Clement of Alexandria, Arnobius, Lactantius, Firmicus Maternus) women had to prostitute themselves to strangers at this temple. Tacitus (*Histories* II.i.2) records how Titus visited the shrine of the Paphian Venus. Excavations at the end of the 19th century investigated the area of the famous building.[67]

F. Corinth[68]

According to legend Aphrodite first arose from the foam of the sea at Cythera but then passed on to Cyprus. Her associations with Cyprus may be a recognition of her foreign origins.[69] Farnell points out that Aphrodite was nowhere regarded as a divine ancestress except at Thebes, which had very strong Phoenician associations.[70] She was closely related to Cadmus, the founder of Thebes, who hailed from Phoenicia.[71] There were also very strong Phoenician elements at the main center of her worship in Greece – Corinth.[72]

Aphrodite, the goddess of love, who also bore the titles *Hetaira* and *Pornē*, was the patroness of both secular and sacred prostitutes. Strabo VIII.vi.20 asserted that the temple of Aphrodite on the Acrocorinth had more than a thousand *hierodoulous* "sacred slaves" or *hetairas* "courtesans," whom both men and women had dedicated to the goddess. He claimed that the prosperity of Corinth was in no small measure dependent upon these hierodules. Sacred prostitution had been established at Corinth before the 5th cent. B.C. at any rate as we have a record of the prayers of the hierodules during the Persian invasion. Xenophon of Corinth, a participant in the Olympian games of 464 B.C., vowed that if he won he would dedicate a hundred girls to the temple

---

> in Cyprus was founded from it, as the Cyprians themselves say: and the temple on Cythera was founded by Phoenicians from this same land of Syria.

Likewise Pausanias I.xiv.6 writes:

> The Assyrians were the first of the human race to worship the Heavenly One; then the people of Paphos in Cyprus, and of Phoenician Askalon in Palestine, and the people of Cythera, who learnt her worship from the Phoenicians.

[65] Pausanias III.xxiii.1 describes the temple for Aphrodite in Cythera as the oldest of her sanctuaries in Greece. Recent excavations have been conducted on Cythera by G.L. Huxley and J.N. Coldstream. For a bibliography, see J.D. Muhly, "Homer and the Phoenicians," *Berytus*, 19 (1970), 61, fn. 313.

[66] No reference has yet been found to Aphrodite in the Mycenaean Linear B texts. The greatest number of slaves at Pylos are called *te-o-yo do-e-ro*, i.e., *theoio doelos* "slave of god," but there is no description of their function. Cf. M. Ventris and J. Chadwick, *Documents in Mycenaean Greek* (1956), 124.

[67] D.G. Hogarth, M.R. James and R.E. Smith, "Excavations in Cyprus, 1887-88," *JHS*, 9 (1888), 147 ff. The excavators seem to have misinterpreted the evidence and no trace of the actual sanctuary seems to have been unearthened. The German Archaeological Mission under F.G. Maier has just completed its fifth season at Palaipaphos, but no evidence of Aphrodite's temple has yet been found. Cf. reports in *AJA* and *Archäologischer Anzeiger*.

[68] The cult of Artemis at Ephesus had numerous *hierodouloi*, but it is not certain that these functioned as prostitutes in spite of statements by modern authors, e.g. C.F. Pfeiffer and H.F. Vos, *The Wycliffe Historical Geography of Bible Lands* (1967), 362. According to L.R. Farnell, *The Cults of the Greek States* (1896), II, 481: "We hear of hierodulae serving in the precincts of the Artemision as in the worship of Mylitta and Ishtar, but we are *not* told that temple-prostitution was a religious rite at Ephesus."
The only other Hellenic community where an allusion is made to cultic prostitution is Locri in southeastern Italy.

[69] *Ibid.*, II, 618; M.P. Nilsson, *Geschichte der griechischen Religion* (1950), II, 519 ff.

[70] Farnell, II, 620.

[71] Cf. M. Astour, *Hellenosemitica* (2nd ed., 1967), *passim*; for the Near Eastern seals found at Thebes in 1963-64, see 391-2.

[72] T.J. Dunbabin, *JHS*, 68 (1948), 66 ff.

of Aphrodite. The charms and the wiles of the Corinthian hierodules are described by Pindar, Aristophanes, and Athenaeus.[73] When Paul warned his congregation in Corinth against immorality (I Cor. 6), he was warning them not only against ordinary prostitutes but against hierodules.[74]

A thorough investigation of the Acrocorinth by C.W. Blegen in 1926 revealed some finely worked poros blocks, probably of Aphrodite's temple which had been displaced by an early Christian church.[75] Classical sources speak of the temple as a small building so the hierodules must have lived elsewhere. Coins offer contradictory evidence for the appearance of the temple, but agree in depicting the statue of the goddess as nude to the waist.

Artistic confirmations of the eastern affinities of the Greek Aphrodite may be seen in ivory inlays of an alluring goddess peering out of a window, which in Mesopotamia were ascribed to Ishtar and in Greece to Aphrodite.[76] Astarte plaques imported from the east into Corinth served as the models for figurines of Aphrodite.[77]

G. Carthage and Sicily

It is of more than passing interest that Dido of Phoenicia, the legendary founder of Carthage, stopped off at Cyprus on her way to north Africa. There the high priest of the goddess Astarte and 80 maidens destined for sacred prostitution joined her. Evidence from Carthage, however, is scanty. Warmington suggests that this is because the worship of Astarte was supplanted by the worship of Tanit.[78] In view of the strong links between the religious practices of Canaan-Phoenicia and Carthage in other areas,[79] such as in infant sacrifice,[80] the lack of evidence for sacred prostitution is surprising. Representations of "temple boys" on stelae at Carthage have been interpreted as male temple prostitutes.[81]

Several miles inland from Carthage at Sicca Veneria in Numidia women took part in prostitution at the temple of Venus. Sicca was founded by colonists from Eryx in western Sicily, which had earlier been established by Phoenicians. The numerous hierodules at the temple of Astarte-Aphrodite-Venus at Eryx were, no doubt, engaged in temple prosititution.[82] In Strabo's (VI.ii.5) time their numbers had declined. It is interesting to note that the importation of the worship of Venus Erycina into Rome in 215 B.C. did not bring with it the practice of sacred prostitution.[83] To be sure, according to Juvenal,[84] there were numerous prostitutes available in the temples of the Near Eastern goddesses.

[73] J.G. O'Neill, *Ancient Corinth* (1930), I, 50-2; H. Licht, *Sexual Life in Ancient Greece* (1932), 340 ff.; C. Seltman, *Women in Antiquity* (1962), 130-1.

[74] O. Broneer, *BA*, 14 (1951), 77-96.

[75] B.H. Hill, "Excavations at Corinth 1926," *AJA*, 31 (1927), 70-9.

[76] R. Herbig, *OLZ*, 30 (1927), 917-22; H. Zimmern, *OLZ*, 31 (1928), 1-3; cf. D. Harden, *The Phoenicians* (1962), plate 61 for an example from Arslan Tash, and E. Yamauchi, *Greece and Babylon* (1967), fig. 37 for an example from Khorsabad.

[77] J. Boardman, *The Greeks Overseas* (1964), 94.

[78] B.H. Warmington, *Carthage* (1960), 157. For the diffusion of the Astarte cult in the Mediterranean, see: J. Plessis, *Étude sur les textes concernant Ištar-Astarté* (1921); J.M. Solà-Solé, *RSO*, 41 (1966), 97-108; M. Delcor, *MUSJ*, 45 (1969), 320-41; F.M. Cross, Jr., *HTR*, 64 (1971), 189-95; G. Colonna, *Archaeology*, 19 (1966), 11-23; J.A. Fitzmyer, *JAOS*, 86 (1966), 285-97.

[79] Cf. Y. Yadin, in J.A. Sanders (ed.), *Near Eastern Archaeology in the Twentieth Century* (1970), 199-231.

[80] W.F. Albright, *Yahweh and the Gods of Canaan* (1968), 234 ff.

[81] Harden, p. 103 and fig. 25q.

[82] Cf. Diodorus Siculus IV.83. Excavations have uncovered remains of the temple at Eryx. Cf. U. Zanotti-Bianco, *JHS*, 56 (1936), 218-20; cf. S. Moscati, *OrAnt*, 7 (1968), 91-94.

[83] R. Schilling, *La religion romaine de Vénus . . .* (1954), 237-8.

[84] Juvenal IX.24: *Nam quo non prostat femina templo?* , which R. Humphries, *The Satires of Juvenal* (1958), 114, renders as: "Any such temple, it seemed, was full of available women." Our English word "prostitute" is etymologically linked with *prostare* "to stand outside" brothels, etc. Cf. J.P.V.D. Balsdon, *Roman Women* (1962), 224 ff. The notorious seduction of a Roman matron by a man masquerading as Anubis took place in a temple of Isis in the reign of Tiberius. Josephus, *Antiquities* XVIII.65-80.

H. Armenia and Anatolia[85]

We are told by Strabo II.xiv.6 that the Armenians at Acilisene honored the Persian goddess Anaitis by dedicating their daughters to her for sacred prostitution before their marriages.

Herodotus I.93 describes how young girls in Lydia in western Anatolia practiced prostitution to earn their dowries. Ramsay cited an inscription of the 2nd cent. A.D. as evidence of the continuation of cultic prostitution at Tralleis in Phrygia.[86] Large numbers of sacred prostitutes plied their vocation in honor of the goddess Ma at two sites named Comana and at other sites in Cappadocia in eastern Anatolia (Strabo XII.iii.36).

Whether cultic prostitution in Armenia and Anatolia was rooted in indigenous practice or imported from Mesopotamia or Persia is a moot point.[87]

The Persian goddess Anaitis (i.e. Anahita) was the goddess of water and of fecundity. According to R. Ghirshman she is the nude goddess grasping her breasts with her hands depicted in the Luristan bronzes.[88] The Persians under Cyrus conquered Armenia and Anatolia in the 6th cent. B.C. Artaxerxes II promoted the cult of the Anahita from Bactria to Damascus and to Sardis. In Hellenistic and Roman times she was identified with Ishtar,[89] with Ma[90] and with Cybele, the Magna Mater.[91]

Conclusions

If we recognize that our available evidence is quite fragmentary[92] and somewhat contradictory, it may still be plausible to maintain that the practice of sacred prostitution owes much of its distribution in the biblical world through cultural diffusion. In view of the traditional, linguistic, and iconographic evidence this may be affirmed with some confidence for Palestine, Syria-Phoenicia, Cyprus, Cythera, Corinth, Carthage and Sicily. Diffusion may have been involved in Armenia and in Anatolia. On the other hand, cultic prostitution did not seem to accompany the importation of Venus Erycina into Rome and appears to be of dubious attestation in Egypt. As Professor Gordon has noted, "Cultural elements are never borrowed unchanged. Indeed the changes are often so great that they obscure the borrowed essence."[93]

---

85 I confess that I do not understand Asmussen, 179: "Auch zu den Hittittern gelangten der Ischtarkultus und die damit verbundenen Riten. § 194 des hittischen Gesetzes scheint nämlich sakrale Prostitution anzudeuten." [The Hittite texts mention both the MÍ.SUḪUR.LÁ (= Akkad. *kezertu*) and the MÍ.KAR.KID (= Akkad. *ḫarimtu*), but offer little basis to conclude that temple prostitution was practiced. Nor is there unambiguous evidence for a *hieros gamos* rite. – Ed.]

86 W. Ramsay, *Cities and Bishoprics of Phrygia* (1895), I, 95.

87 According to D.M. Lang, *Armenia: Cradle of Civilization* (1970), 148, cultic prostitution in Armenia was practiced "doubtless in imitation of Babylonian and Syrian custom." Cf. also C. Burney and D.M. Lang, *The Peoples of the Hills* (1971), 216. But the counterpart of Ishtar in Armenia was not Anahita but the "voluptuous goddess of maternity" Astghik.

88 R. Ghirshman, *Iran* (1954), 102-3, and pl. 8.

89 F. Cumont, *Oriental Religions in Roman Paganism* (1911), 146.

90 *Ibid.*, 54.

91 *Ibid.*, 65, 227.

92 Cf. E. Yamauchi, *Christianity Today*, 13 (Feb. 14, 1969), 432-4, 436-7.

93 Gordon, *Before Columbus*, 139.

NUZU TEXTS IN THE FREE LIBRARY OF PHILADELPHIA

Gordon Douglas Young

Department of History, Purdue University

It is appropriate that the tablets published herein appear in a volume dedicated to one of the pioneers of Nuzu scholarship. His efforts have resulted in one book, nineteen articles, and the supervision of several doctoral dissertations on various aspects of the language and culture of Nuzu. It is with a great deal of pleasure that this article is presented to Cyrus Herzl Gordon, teacher and friend.

These tablets are part of the John Frederick Lewis Collection of the Free Library of Philadelphia.[1] Nothing is known of the circumstances of their discovery, or the date of their purchase. Internal evidence shows that they are from the Nuzu area, but not necessarily from Yorghan Tepe itself.[2] It may very well be, however, that these tablets do derive from the site of Nuzu.[3]

FLP 1281[4]

(Copy p. 232, Foto pl. II*b)

FLP 1281 is a list of twenty witnesses attesting to the fact that one Adad-nîšū, a leather worker, turned over to Teḫip-tilla a man, Ili-iddina, and a woman, Paššišše. This text is testimony that most likely was read into the proceedings of litigation.[5] Over thirty such tablets are mentioned in the extant proceedings of the Nuzu

1 The Lewis Collection numbers nearly 3000 pieces which range in date from the pre-Sargonic to the Seleucid eras. Under the direction of E.V. Leichty, preliminary work on a complete catalogue has begun.
Thanks are offered to Mr. Howell J. Heaney, curator of the Rare Books Department of the Free Library of Philadelphia for permission to publish these texts, and to his staff for their most cordial assistance during the summer of 1971. Thanks are also offered to A. Sjöberg, E.V. Leichty, and B. Eichler of the University of Pennsylvania Museum staff for the generous use of their facilities and for many helpful observations.
The procedure used in copying these texts is a modification of that described in E.R. Lacheman, *JAOS* 55 (1935), 429-31. It is felt that this results in the most accurate copy possible. Thanks are due also to D.I. Owen of Dropsie University, and R.A. McDaniel of Purdue University for photographic assistance. Work in the Lewis Collection was made possible by a grant from the Purdue Research Foundation, for which the author is very grateful.

2 The script, grammar, and proper names clearly point to the Nuzu orbit. FLP 1282 explicitly states that the transaction concerns property in the city of Arrapha, the provincial capital of which Nuzu was a dependency.

3 See note 9 below, and "Observation on Origin."

4 Currently, these two tablets bear no identification number. In the numbering system to be employed in the proposed catalogue, they have been assigned these FLP (*F*ree *L*ibrary of *P*hiladelphia) numbers.

5 See R.E. Hayden, *Court Procedure at Nuzu*, (Ann Arbour, 1962) for a discussion of the legal procedure of Nuzu.

courts.[6] This is the first known instance of association between the various principals. Teḫip-tilla is a well known figure, of course, and no stranger to the Nuzu courts.[7] All that is known of Adad-nîšū is that he was the father of two men, Ḫašia (*JEN* 281:4) and Urḫia (*JEN* 514:12). Ili-iddina is known only as the father of Ḫaip-šarri (*JEN* 47:19), while the woman Paššišše is known from *JEN* 507:11. Of some interest in this text are the new filiations.[8] There is, as well, a high degree of correlation to names from Kirkuk.[9]

	Transliteration[10]	Translation[11]
		(21-25) These twenty men (are the) witnesses of Adad-nîšū, the leather worker, that Ili-iddina and Paššišše were given to Teḫip-tilla:
	Obverse	
1	m*ḫa-na-a-a* DUMU *na-⸢al⸣-*[tukka?]	(1) Ḫanaya, son of Na (. . .);
2	m*ar-ti-ir-wi* DUMU *ta-⸢i⸣-*[šenni?]	(2) Ar-tirwi, son of Tai (. . .);
3	m*tù-ra-ša-a-a* DUMU *a-ri-*[x - x]	(3) Turašaya, son of Ari (. . .);
4	m*e-ša-ku* DUMU *še-el-la-pa-i*	(4) En-šaku, son of Šellapai;
5	m*ḫu-lu-uk-ka*$_4$ DUMU *zi-in-na-a-a*	(5) Ḫulukka, son of Zinnaya;
6	m*it-ḫa-a-pu* DUMU *ta-e-na*	(6) Itḫ-apu, son of Taena;
7	m*a-kip-ša-at-na* DUMU *ar-te-ya*	(7) Akip-šatna, son of Arteya;
8	mEN*-ya* DUMU *pu-un-ni-tù-ra*	(8) Bêliya, son of Purni-turu;
9	m*še-pè-ya* NU.KIRI$_6$*-bu*	(9) Šêpiya, the gardener;
10	m*ku-bi-*LUGAL DUMU *ta-e*	(10) Kûbi-šarri, son of Tae;
11	m*šum-mi-ya* DUMU *it-ḫa-a-pu*	(11) Šummiya, son of Itḫ-apu;
12	m*e-šúk-ru(m)* DUMU *a-ku-še-ni*	(12) En-šukru, son of Aku-šenni;
13	m*it-ḫi-ip-*LUGAL DUMU *ta-e*	(13) Itḫip-šarri, son of Tae;
14	mdEŠ.DI.KU$_5$ DUMU *pur-na-pí-ḫé*	(14) Sîn-dayyan, son of Purn-apihe;
15	m*pu-ḫi-ya* DUMU *šúk-ri-ya*	(15) Puḫiya, son of Šukriya;
	Reverse	
16	m*tar-mi-til-la* DUMU *te-ḫi-ip-*LUGAL	(16) Tarmi-tilla, son of Teḫip-šarri;
17	m*a-ki-ya* DUMU *ak-ku-le-ni*	(17) Akiya, son of Akkul-enni;

[6] *Ibid.*, 195, n. 51.

[7] He was involved as a litigant in at least 20 cases. *Ibid.*, 263.

[8] Prof. Lacheman kindly informs me that these filiations are not to be found in his files of personal names of tablets published or copied since *NPN*. See "Commentary" for the new filiations.

[9] By Kirkuk is meant the modern city occupying the ground of ancient Arrapha. In the early years of Nuzu studies, the names of Nuzu and Kirkuk were bandied about somewhat indiscriminately. Of the many supposedly Kirkuk tablets, only 51 can be shown with any degree of certainty to have come from there. Many may very well have been taken from Yorghan Tepe (Nuzu) itself, prior to the start of formal excavations by Dr. Chiera in 1925. See C.J. Gadd, *RA* 23 (1926), 50-52. Comparatively speaking, not many of the tablets from the Nuzu area are to be found in private collections, hence some of the interest of FLP 1281 and FLP 1282.

[10] The method of transliteration employed herein is that long established for Nuzu texts, based upon etymological considerations. Since the Nuzu scribes employed a system of sign values that often diverged from normal primary values, any transliteration of Nuzu texts based upon other systems can often result in substantial confusion. Sumerograms, however, are transliterated according to their primary values, and are not translated into their hypothetical Akkadian forms.

[11] The personal names have been normalized according to the system of *NPN*, with the exception that the phoneme /i̯/ of NPN has been rendered /y/, and /u̯/ has been rendered /w/.

Translation

18 ^{m}*zi-in-ni* DUMU *ḫa-ma-an-na*
19 ^{md}UTU.AN.DUL DUMU *ta-a-a*
20 ^{m}*a-kip*-LUGAL DUMU *a-ri-ḫur*-GUB.BE
21 20 LÚ.MEŠ *an-nu-tù ši-bu-tù*
22 *ša* ^{md}IŠKUR-*ni-šu aš$_x$-ka$_4$-a-pu*
23 *ki-i-me-e* ^{m}AN.SUM-*na*
24 *ù* ^{f}*pa-aš-ši-iš-še*
25 ⌈*a-na*⌉ ^{m}*te-ḫi-ip-til-la* ⌈SUM⌉-*nu*

Transliteration

(18) Zenni, son of Ḫamanna;
(19) ^{d}UTU-ANDUL, son of Taya;
(20) Akip-šarri, son of A-ri-ḫur-GUB.BE.

Commentary

1. The father of the Ḫanaya mentioned here may have been Naltukka. This filiation is attested several times at Nuzu (see *NPN*). It is possible that the sign following NA is AL. No other attested filiation for the PN Hanaya fits these traces.

2. The filiation Ar-tirwi, son of Tai-šenni is attested twice at Nuzu (see *NPN*). The traces of the sign following TA best fit I. No other attested relationship seems to fit here.

3. Turašaya is a new PN. Prof. E.R. Lacheman informs me that he has found this name in another unpublished tablet, but the filiation is not known.

7. KIP is clearly written. *JEN* 510:6 seems to read ^{m}*a-rip-ša-at-na* DUMU *ar-te-ya*. P.M. Purves preferred KIP to RIP in *NPN* (p. 15). This text makes it mandatory.

8. This is a new filiation.

9. NU.KIRI$_6$, *nukaribbum*, "gardener," following E. Sollberger, *TCS* 1, 160, sub ≠550. See also D. Edzard, *ZA* 55 (1960), 92f.

11. This is a new filiation.

14. This is a new filiation. ^{md}EŠ.DI.KU$_5$, Sîn-dayyān, read following E. Sollberger, *TCS* 1, 108, sub ≠144.

15. This is a new filiation.

19. ^{md}UTU.AN.DÙL read following H. Limet, *l'Anthroponymie Sumerienne* (1968), 565. [Cf. *NPN*, 168 s.v. UTA-ANDUL. – Ed.]

20. This is a new filiation. KIP is clearly written. The last two signs of this line are clearly GUB.BE, thus ruling out the suggestion of P.M. Purves that the name be treated as *A-ri-ḫar*-PA ŠI-BI (*NPN*, 25). See C.J. Gadd, *RA* 23 (1926), 143, text 3: 37 for the other occurrence of this name.

22. The use of AZ instead of the more common AŠ or ÁŠ in the spelling of *aškāpu* is previously unattested. Thus the reading AŠ$_x$ is offered for AZ.

23 At Nuzu, *kīmē* is used consistently for the conjunction *kīma*, and thus should not be confused with the preposition meaning, "like, in the manner of, according to, corresponding to, instead of, in lieu of, etc." See *CAD* K (1971), 370, citing W. von Soden, *ZA* 41 (1932), 139.

FLP 1282

(Copy p. 233, Foto pl. III*)

FLP 1282 is a property transfer belonging to that class of Nuzu documents known as *ṭuppi šupe'ulti*, "tablet of exchange."[12] A substantial number of these texts are published, but a detailed study of them has not yet appeared.[13]

The standard exchange text may be outlined as follows:

I Introductory phrase naming the principals and nature of property exchanged (houses, lands, etc.).

II Description of the quantity and kinds of property to be exchanged, often located with much precision in relation to important landmarks.

III Specification of balance payment necessary to render the transaction equitable or to serve as an inducement to bring it about, if necessary.[14]

IV Specification that all claims to the land must be cleared before transfer.

V Penalty clause specifying fines for breaking any stipulations of the transfer.

VI List of witnesses.

VII Seal impressions of the witnesses.

The actual exchange of properties seems to have involved two steps, each resulting in the execution of a document. After an agreement between the contracting parties had been reached, a *ṭuppi šupe'ulti* was drawn up. After some delay to clear up prior claims to the properties involved,[15] a declaration was made before the judges that all was in order, and a tablet drawn up to that effect.[16] This declaration tablet was, then, the equivalent of a quitclaim deed, since stated therein was a renunciation of all title claims. That law suits could develop over these exchanges may be seen by texts such as *JEN* 668, where a suit requiring the presentation of a *ṭuppi šupe'ulti* as evidence is recorded.[17]

The primary purpose of these property exchanges seems to have been the consolidation of scattered holdings. P.M. Purves suggests that, ". . . false adoption for sale of land apparently was coordinated with the

---

[12] The noun *šupe'ultu* is derived from the verb *šupêlu*. See E. Chiera and E.A. Speiser, *JAOS* 47 (1927), 45-6. This is the regular NB term for exchange which replaced OB *peḫû*. See C.J. Gadd, *RA* 23 (1926), 102. F.R. Steele, *AOS* 25 (1943), 62-4, has demonstrated that the *ṭuppat pûḫâti* or simply *pûḫ* texts of OB are the parallel documents which illustrate the Babylonian background of Nuzu real estate transactions.

[13] The greater number are published in *JEN* 3, a few more being scattered about in other publications. See F.R. Steele, *AOS* 25 (1943), 78 for a list of those published prior to 1943. His chapters 5 and 6c (pp. 50-4, 62-4, and table 8, p. 78) remain the most comprehensive treatment of the genre. See also the brief treatment of P. M. Purves, *JNES* 4 (1945), 71-3.

[14] See the commentary to line 14 for a discussion of this point.

[15] Note that the verbs *zakû* and *nadānu* which call for the clearing of title are consistently expressed in the so-called present-future tense.

[16] These are the so-called *lišānšu*, lit. "his tongue," texts. Note the pairs of texts *JEN* 260 and 157, *JEN* 266 and 131, and *JENu* 529a and 152. The former in each case is a *ṭuppi šupe'ulti*, the latter a *lišānšu* for the same transaction. See. P.M. Purves, *JNES* 4 (1945), 71-2, where the point is made that the *lišānšu* text lacks a penalty clause, but does contain a renunciation of claim. Thus the *ṭuppi šupe'ulti* is an executory contract, and the *lišānšu* a quitclaim deed.

[17] See also *JEN* 399, 361, 373, 699 and *TCL* 9, 15 which are cases involving *šupe'ultu* transfers.

process of land exchange for the purposes of consolidating many small holdings of peasant families into large estates owned by a minority of wealthy families."[18]

FLP 1282 is in rather poor condition. The upper right corner of the obverse, and the entire bottom edge have broken away. There are several deep and wide cracks on the surfaces of the tablet which result in lost or damaged signs. In addition, the central part of the obverse has been worn nearly smooth, further obscuring several lines. Because of the stereotypical nature of the *šupe'ultu* texts, however, it has been possible to reconstruct many lost passages. In this text, Tehip-tilla, who figures prominently in many *šupe'ultu* transactions, has drawn up an executory contract with two individuals to transfer houses in the towns of Arrapḫa and (?)-zilakku. Unfortunately, the corresponding declaration tablet, as in most cases, is not extant.

Transliteration		Translation
Obverse		
1	*ṭup-pí šu-pè-ul-ti* [*ša*	(1-4) Tablet of exchange of Teḫip-tilla, son of Pu(ḫi-šenni), together with Nai-tilla, son of . . . , and with Wantip-šarri, son of . . . .
2	^{m}*te-ḫi-ip-til-la* DUMU *pu-*[*ḫi-še-en-ni*	
3	*it-ti* ^{m}*na-i-til-la* DUMU [?	
4	*ù* ⸢*it*⸣-*ti* ^{m}*wa-an-ti-ip-* [LUGAL DUMU ?	
5	É.ḪI.A ⸢*i-na*⸣ URU ⸢*ar-ra*⸣-*ap-*[*ḫi*	(5-6) They have exchanged houses in the city Arrapḫa.
6	*uš-te-pì-i-lu* ⸢É.ḪI.A⸣ ^{m}*te-*[*ḫi-ip-til-la*	(6-9) (Here in a damaged passage is given the location of the houses, apparently located in relation to the property of one Uzzuke, which Teḫip-tilla) . . . gave Nai-tilla and Wantip-šarri.
7	*a-šar* [. . . . . .] ⸢*i-na*⸣ [	
8	^{m}*ú-*⸢*uz-zu-ki*⸣[.] ⸢*a-na*⸣ ^{m}*na-i-til-la*	
9	*ù a-na* ^{m}⸢*wa*⸣-*an-ti-*⸢*ip*-LUGAL⸣ *it-ta-din*	
10	*ù* É.ḪI.A *i-na* ⸢URU *ki*⸣ -[x]-*zi-la-ak-ku*	(10-13) And (in return) Nai-tilla and Wantip-šarri gave houses in the city (Ki?-x)-zilakku, in the palace quarter to Teḫip-tilla.
11	*i-na* ⸢*bá-ab* É.GAL⸣ ^{m}*na-i-til-la*	
12	*ù* ^{m}*wa-an-*⸢*ti-ip*-LUGAL⸣	
13	*a-na* ^{m}*te-ḫi-*⸢*ip*⸣ *til-la it-ta-ad-nu*	
14	*u* ^{m}*te-ḫi-*⸢*ip-til-la a-na*⸣ Ú-*ti*	(14-16) In addition, Teḫip-tilla gave Nai-tilla and Wantip-šarri 10 homers of grain (and) 8 sheep for a balance payment.
15	10 ANŠE ŠE ⸢8 UDU⸣.MEŠ *a-na* ^{m}*na-i-til-la*	
16	*ù a-na* ^{m}*wa-an-ti-ip*-LUGAL *it-ta-din*	
17	*ša ma-an-ni-im-me-*⸢*e*⸣ É.ḪI.A-*šu*	(17-19) Whoever has a claim against his houses shall clear (it), and give (the houses to the other party).
18	*pí-ir-qa i-ra-aš-*⸢*šu*⸣-*ú*	
19	*ú-za-*⸢*ak-ka*$_4$⸣-*ma i-*⸢*na*⸣-*an-din*	
20	*šum-ma* ^{m}*na-i-til-la* ⸢*ù*⸣ ^{m}*wa-an-ti-ip*-LUGAL	(20-22) If Nai-tilla and/or Wantip-šarri break the agreement, they shall give 2 minas of silver and 2 minas of gold to Teḫip-tilla.
21	⸢KI.BAL⸣-*tu*$_4$ 2 *ma-na* KÙ.BABBAR 2 *ma-na* GUŠKIN	
22	⸢*a-na*⸣ ⸢^{m}*te-ḫi*⸣-*ip-til-la i-na-an-dì-nu*	
23	[IGI *ar-zi-iz-z*]*a* DUMU *zi-gi* IGI *ta-a-a* DUMU *a-*⸢*ri-ip*-LUGAL⸣	(23-34) witnesses
24	[IGI *zi-li-ya* DUMU *tup-k*]*i-ya*	
25	. . . . . . broken away	
Bottom edge		
26	[. . . . . .]*nu-ma*[	

[18] *JNES* 4 (1945), 71. Note that *JEN* 662 records land bought for the purpose of future exchange rather than immediate cultivation.

Reverse

27 [. . . DUMU.MEŠ]? *a*? -*ta*? [

28 [. . .]*še-el*-[x]-*ú*

29 IGI *ḫu-un-ni-ya* DUMU *ḫa-ma-an*-[*na*]

30 IGI *ar-te-šup* DUMU *ḫa-ni-ku* ⌈DUMU⌉ [DUMU *ta*]-*iš-še-ni*

31 IGI *ni-im-ki-ya* DUMU *ar-ru-pa*

32 IGI *a-kip*-LUGAL DUMU *ar-ru*-⌈*um*⌉-*pa*

33 IGI *ḫa-ši-pa-ra-al-la* DUMU *pa-li*$^{!}$/-*ya*

34 ⌈IGI⌉ *ta-a-a* DUMU ⌈*a*⌉-*pil-sin* DUB.SAR

Seal ≠1

35 [NA$_4$ ^{m}]*mu-uš-te*-[. . .]ŠI
[. . .] ⌈*ar-še*⌉ [. . .]

Seal ≠2

[NA$_4$]^{m}*ta-a-a* DUMU *a-rip*-LUGAL (35-41) seals

Seal ≠3

36 NA$_4$ KIŠIB ^{m}*ar*-⌈*zi*⌉-[*iz*]-*za* DUMU *zi*-⌈*gi*⌉

Seal ≠4

37 ⌈NA$_4$⌉ KIŠIB ^{m}⌈*ḫu-un*⌉-[*ni*]-⌈*ya*⌉ DUMU *ḫa*-⌈*ma*⌉-[*an-na*

Top edge

Seal ≠5

38 ⌈NA$_4$ KIŠIB⌉ ^{m}*ar-te-šup* DUMU ^{m}*na*-[

Seal ≠6

39 ⌈NA$_4$ KIŠIB⌉ ^{m}*ta-a-a* ⌈DUMU⌉ [*a-pil-sin*

Left edge

Seal ≠7

40 NA$_4$ ^{m}*a*-⌈*kip*⌉-LUGAL
DUMU *ar-ru-um-pa*

Seal ≠8

NA$_4$ ^{m}*zi-li-ya*
DUMU *tup-ki-ya*

Seal ≠9

NA$_4$ ^{m}*ni*-⌈*im*⌉-[

Commentary

2 The restoration of the name of the father of Teḫip-tilla is based on the plethora of *šupe'ultu* texts where this filiation is operative. Further, no other man's name beginning Pu- is known to have had a son Teḫip-tilla.

5 *ḫi* or *ḫé* are the characteristic signs used in the spelling of this name. Rarely is it spelled *ar-ra-ap-ḫa*. Further, though the grammar of Nuzu scribes is notoriously bad, the genitive is required by context.

6-8 Unfortunately, this critical passage is worn so smooth as to render exact reading impossible. A few faint traces suggest that line 5 may contain after *a-šar* the signs É.GAL. Between that and *i-na* there seem to be three missing signs, the last of which may be NA. *i-na* appears relatively clear, but the possibility of reading RA exists. One expects that after *i-na* will be found a phrase pointing direction – to the south of, to the north of, on the border of, etc. – to the property of Uzukke. What follows Uzukke is difficult to determine. It appears that no more than two, and most likely just one sign is missing. *NPN* cites an Uzukke in *RA* 23, 7:24, who was an *aššabu*, "tenant" (Sumerian LÚ.KU). See *CAD* A/2 (1968), 460-462. This does not appear in Gadd's copy, but may have emerged in the collation of those tablets by Purves in the summer of 1937. Traces which can fit KU are present, but not LÚ.

It is interesting to note that one Uzukke, the father of one Puḫi-šenni is mentioned in *TCL* 9 44:21. Can it be that Teḫip-tilla was exchanging ancestral properties?

10 *zi-la-ak-ku* is clear. URU is fairly certain from the traces. KI best fits what's left of the sign following URU. The sign between KI and ZI is indistinguishable to me. To my knowledge, no similar town name exists in the Nuzu documents. The divine element *silakku* occurs elsewhere in Nuzu in three personal names: Ḫaip-zilakku, Ḫap-zilakku, and Ḫazip-zilakku (see *NPN*).

11 The traces after AB strongly suggest É.GAL. A phrase locating the houses is in order at this point in the text. For *bābu* meaning city quarter, see *CAD* B (1965), 22.

14 The Ú-*tu* was a "balance payment" that was made for either of two reasons. If the properties being exchanged were of unequal value, an Ú-*tu* made up the difference. F.R. Steele (*AOS* 25, 51) notes seventeen cases where properties of seemingly equal value were exchanged and a balance payment was made nonetheless. Perhaps then, the Ú-*ti*, also served as an inducement for the exchange. As Steele notes, however, many factors not mentioned by the scribe may have been involved so that what appears to have been an equal transfer may not have been so. In this case, neither the number of houses, nor their condition, is given in the tablet. It is still uncertain whether Ú-*tu* is to be read phonetically or ideographically. Note in *CAD* Z (1961), 45, sub *zāninu*, "provider," the references Ú.A = *za-ni-nu e-pi-ru*, "provider," Lu IV, 365f and Izi E, 281f.

19 *zakû* and *nadānu* are a hendiadys here. See B. Landsberger, *ZA* 39 (1928), 288ff.

20-22 Note, in common with other exchanges of Teḫip-tilla, the penalty clause is aimed at the other party.

23 The restoration is based on seal ≠3 (l. 36).

24 The restoration is based on seal ≠8 (l. 40).

25-28 It is difficult to fill in the gaps here. The horizontal wedge after the break at the beginning of line 28 certainly seems to be the end of IGI, which should be expected. No filiation for that name is given, however, which is unusual. Seal ≠1 suggests that a witness, *Mu-uš-te-* . . . should be found in this gap, together with the name of his father. The few clear signs offer no help, however. To make the damaged sign after EL in l. 28 read LU requires some imagination. It is easier to see MU. Perhaps a reference to a *mušelwû* witness is involved. It is best left alone at this point, however.

30 Ar-tešup, son of Ḫaniku, is a previously unattested filiation. Ḫaniku, son of Tai-šenni is attested elsewhere, however. This listing of three generations is somewhat unusual. Note that seal ≠5 (l. 38) is of Ar-tešup, son of Na-. . . . Presumably this is the Naltuya of *JEN* 25:20. No other extant text to my knowledge links a PN beginning Na- to any of these individuals, however.

31 Nimkiya, son of Arrupa, is previously unattested. Note, however, Nikkia, son of Arrumpa in *JEN* 14:15. The fact that line 23 of the obverse has continued over onto the reverse has apparently dictated the shorter form Arrupa.

32 This filiation is previously unattested.

33 Note that a seal impression for Ḫašip-paralla is missing. It may have followed ≠9 and extended into the bottom edge.

35 Seal ≠1 apparently belongs to a witness lost in lines 25-28. It is tempting to link the traces of the second line of this sealing to the signs El-x of line 28.

Note the use of RIP instead of the RI-IP of line 23. Cp. *JEN* 459:18 where the same filiation and spelling occurs, and Purves' decision in *NPN*, 15 and 29, to read the name *A-rip**-šarri. This text lends support to his speculation.

38 See note to line 30 above.

Observation on Origin

It is unfortunate that not one shred of evidence can be found to ascertain when and from whom these tablets were purchased by Mr. Lewis. The Free Library received the complete collection from Mr. and Mrs. Lewis in 1930, five years after the excavations at Nuzu had begun. It would seem unlikely, but not impossible, that these were spirited away from the dig. More likely these were among the tablets whose appearance initially attracted interest in Yorghan Tepe. Yet, the presence of Teḫip-tilla as a principal in both texts is suggestive of a Nuzu origin.

In the introduction to *HSS* 16, E.R. Lacheman states unequivocally that all the Teḫip-tilla documents came from the western suburban area, northwest of Yorghan Tepe, in rooms 15 and 17 of the western building. They were probably transferred there from another storage area after the completion of the central building of this complex.[19]

Teḫip-tilla, son of Puḫi-šenni, does occur on one of the tablets not recovered in the excavations, however.[20] According to Dr. Gadd, this text belongs to those excavated by natives at Yorghan Tepe itself, prior to Dr. Chiera's first season.[21]

The group of texts which derive from Kirkuk are concerned largely with the activities of one Wullu, son of Puḫi-šenni. Taken at face value, it would seem that he should be Teḫip-tilla's brother. The name Puḫi-šenni, however, was quite common. It was borne by no less than 38 men with different parentage.[22]

In FLP 1281, the majority of the witnesses and their fathers bear names attested in Gadd's "Kirkuk" texts, but only one of the filiations is attested therein.[23] Further, with the exception of *A-ri-ḫur*-GUB.BE, all of the names and most of the filiations are attested at Nuzu. Indeed, ^{d}UTU.ANDUL, son of Taya, belongs to a famous family of Nuzu scribes. None of the principals is to be found in the "Kirkuk" texts except Tehip-tilla.

In FLP 1282, none of the filiations of the witnesses can be linked to the "Kirkuk" texts. Indeed, the scribe of the tablet, Taya, son of Apil-Sîn, father of 1281's ^{d}UTU.ANDUL, was one of Nuzu's most famous.

All of this points to the fact that these are indeed Nuzu Tablets.

---

[19] E.R. Lacheman, *HSS* 16, v-vi. "Not a single document of Teḫip-tilla was found elsewhere (p. vi)." Prior to becoming a storage area, room 15 was a bathroom!

[20] *RA* 23, text 59. Here he was taken into "sonship" by one Taya, son of Wat-nini. See also *JEN* 105 and 106 for this filiation.

[21] C.J. Gadd, *RA* 23 (1926), 52.

[22] See *NPN*, 116.

[23] Line 18, Zenni, son of Ḫamanna.

Personal Names

Adad-nīšū (^{d}IŠKUR-*ni-šu*), *aškāpu*, 1281:22.
Akip-šarri, s. *A-ri-ḫur*-GUB.BE, 1281:20.
Akip-šarri, s. Arrumpa, 1282:32, 40.
Akip-šatna, s. Arteya, 1281:7.
Akiya, s. Akkul-enni, 1281:17.
Akkul-enni, f. Akiya, 1281:17.
Aku-šenni, f. En-šukru, 1281:12.
Apil-sîn, f. Taya, 1282:34, [39].
A-ri-ḫur-GUB.BE, f. Akip-šarri, 1281:20.
Arip-šarri, f. Taya, 1282:23, 35.
Arrumpa, f. Akip-šarri, 1282:32, 40.
Arrumpa, f. Nimkiya, 1282:31, [40].
Arteya, f. Akip-šatna, 1281:7.
Ar-tešup, s. Ḫaniku, 1282:30.
Ar-tešup, g.s. [Ta]i-šenni, 1282:30.
Ar-tešup, s. Na-[ ], 1282:38.
Ar-tirwi, s. Tai[-šenni?] 1281:2.
Ar-zizza, s. Zike, 1282:[23], 36.
Bêliya (EN-ia), s. Purni-tura, 1281:8.
En-šaku, s. Šellapai, 1281:4.
En-šukru, s. Aku-šenni, 1281:12.
Ḫamanna, f. Hunniya, 1282:29, 37.
Ḫamanna, f. Zenni, 1281:18.
Ḫanaya, s. Na[l-tukka?], 1281:1.
Ḫaniku, s. [Ta]i-šenni, 1282:30.
Ḫaniku, f. Ar-tešup, 1282:30.
Ḫašip-paralla, s. Paliya, 1282:33.
Ḫulukka, s. Zinnaya, 1281:5.
Ḫunniya, s. Ḫamanna, 1282:29, 37.
Ili-iddina (AN.SUM-na), 1281:23.
Itḫ-apu, s. Taena, 1281:6.
Itḫ-apu, f. Šummiya, 1281:11.
Ithip-šarri, s. Tae, 1281:13.
Kûbi-šarri, s. Tae, 1281:10.
Mušte-[ ], 1282:35.
Nai-tilla, 1282:3, 8, 11, 15, 20.
Nimkiya, s. Arrumpa, 1282:31, [40].
Paliya, f. Hašip-paralla, 1282:33.
^{f}Paššišše, 1281:24.
Pu[ḫi-šenni], f. Teḫip-tilla, 1282:2.
Puḫiya, s. Šukriya, 1281:15.
Purn-apiḫe, f. Sîn-dayyān (^{d}EŠ.DI.KU$_5$), 1281:14.
Purni-tura, f. Bêliya (EN-*ya*), 1281:8.
Sîn-dayyān (^{d}EŠ.DI.KU$_5$), s. Purn-apiḫe, 1281:14.
Šellapai, f. En-šaku, 1281:4.
Šepiya, *nukarribum*, 1281:9.
Šukriya, f. Puḫiya, 1281:15.
Šummiya, s. Itḫ-apu, 1281:11.
Tae, f. Itḫip-šarri, 1281:13.
Tae, f. Kûbi-šarri, 1281:10.
Taena, f. Itḫ-apu, 1281:6.
[Ta]i-šenni, f. Ḫaniku, 1282:30.
[Ta]i-šenni, g.f. Ar-tešup, 1282:30.
Tarmi-tilla, s. Teḫip-šarri, 1281:16.
Taya, scribe, s. Apil-sîn, 1282:34, 39.
Taya, s. Arip-šarri, 1282:23, 35.
Taya, f. ^{d}UTU.ANDUL, 1281:19.
Teḫip-šarri, f. Tarmi-tilla, 1281:16.
Teḫip-tilla, 1281:25.
Teḫip-tilla, s. Pu[ḫi-šenni], 1282:2, [6], 13, 14, 22.
Tupkiya, f. Ziliya, 1282:[24], 40.
Turašaya, s. Ari- ? , 1281:3.
^{d}UTU.ANDUL, s. Taya, 1281:19.
Uzukke, 1282:8.
Wantip-šarri, 1282:4, 9, 12, 16, 20.
Zenni, s. Ḫamanna, 1281:18.
Zike, f. Ar-zizza, 1282:23, 36.
Ziliya, s. Tupkiya, 1282:[24], 40.
Zinniya, f. Hulukka, 1281:5.

Geographical Names

Arrapḫa, 1282:5.
[Ki?-x]-zilakku,1282:10.

FLP 1281

OBVERSE

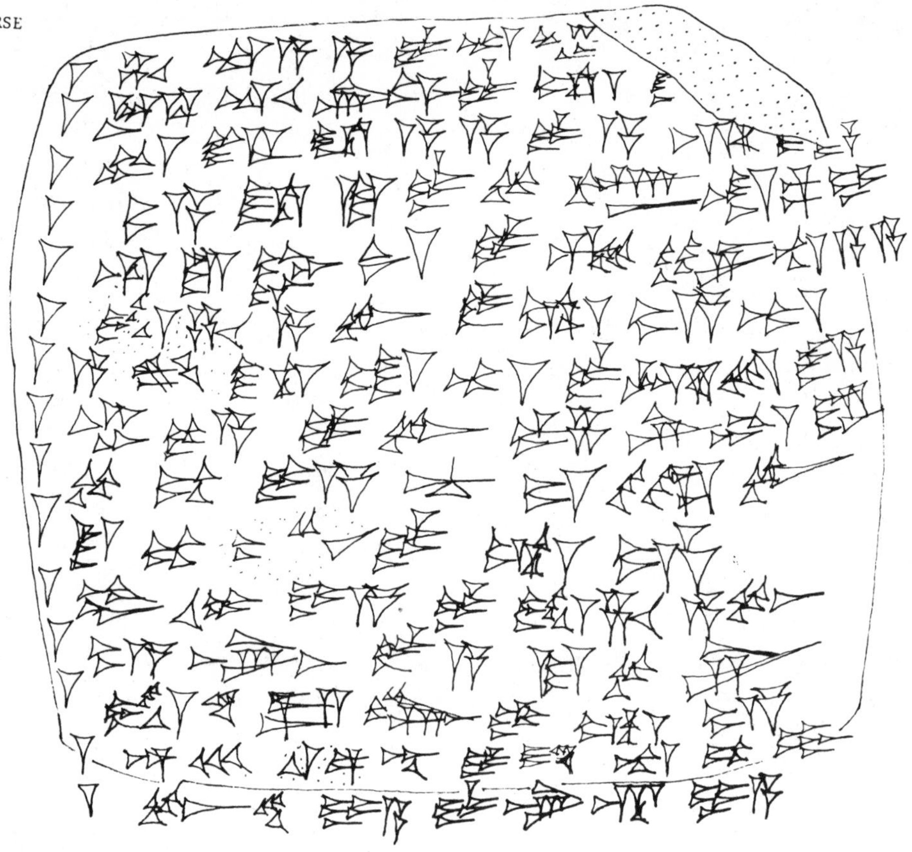

REVERSE

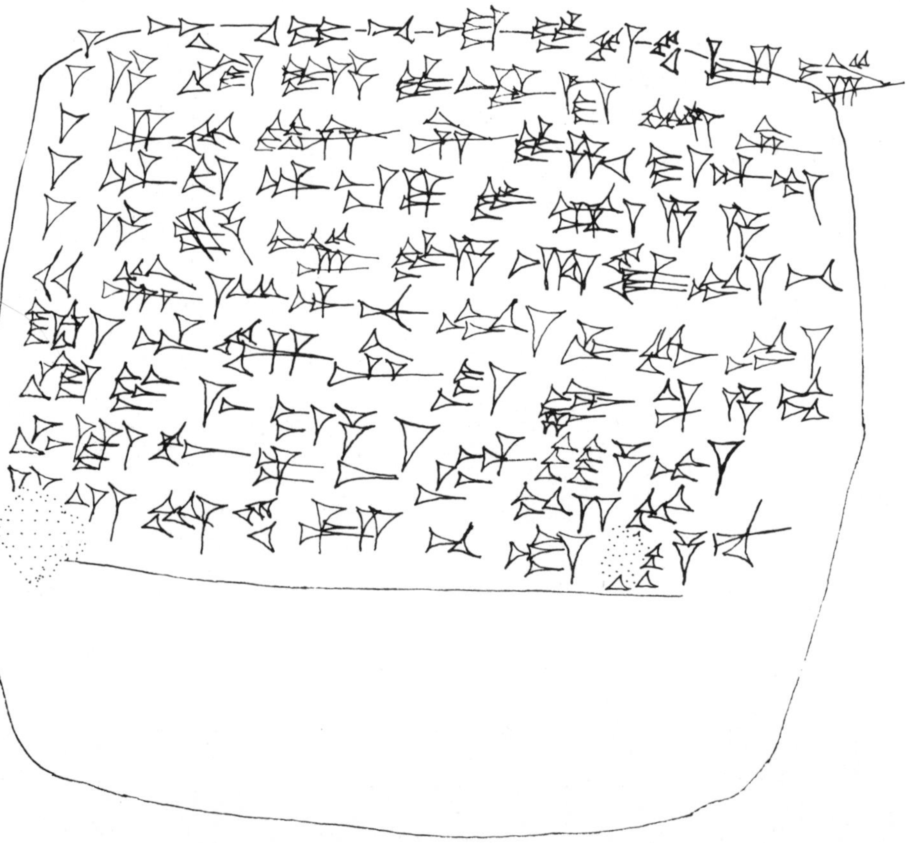

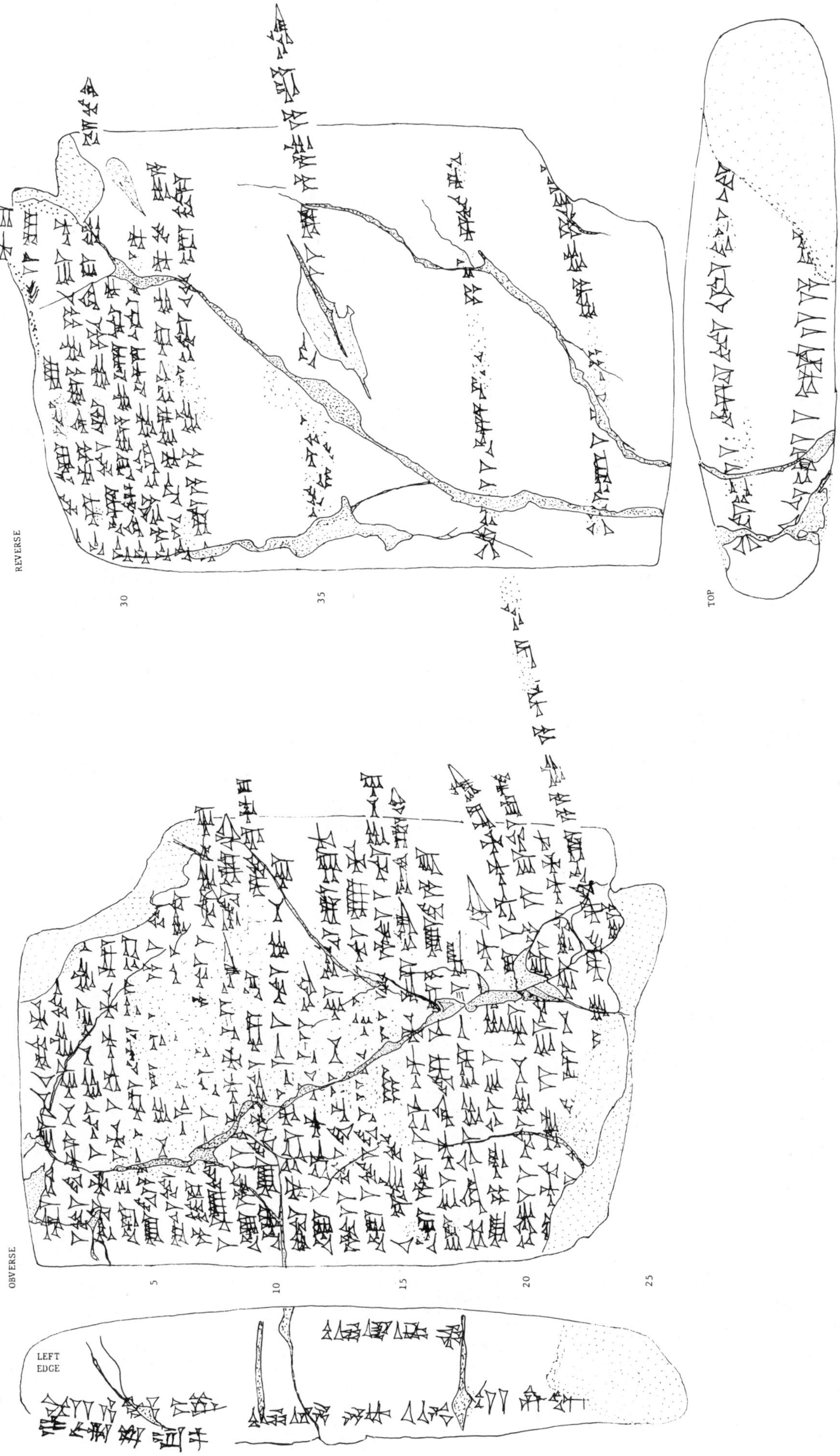

FLP 1282

AN INDEX TO THE UGARITIC PASSAGES
IN THE *UGARITIC TEXTBOOK*

Barry J. Beitzel

Preface

In scope, this index is intended to include the *Ugaritic Textbook* in its entirety with the exception of Chapter Nineteen (the Glossary) and the Glossary addenda listed on pages 550-556.

All entries within a given text are sequent; and where a reference encompasses more than one line, it is given preference over a single-line entry. Thus for example, if in Text 68 there is a reference for lines 15 *and* 16 (listed in this index 15-16), and a separate reference for line 15, the former reference is listed first. All references are to the obverse unless otherwise stipulated.

The author wishes to express his gratitude to Dr. David I. Owen, Professor at the Dropsie University, at whose suggestion and under whose supervision this project was undertaken.

Abbreviations

*	before UT reference number this indicates that the passage is quoted in UT. Otherwise the passage is simply referred to but not quoted.
[+]	entire text referred to.
≠	text number
beg.	beginning
f.	footnote of appropriate section in UT.
l.e.	left edge.
n.	Special note listed in the main body of the paragraph.
pass.	passim
rev.	reverse
Supp.	*Supplement to the Ugaritic Textbook*, pp. 549ff. Not to be confused with *Supplement: Texts 2001-2123*, pp. 1*ff. The latter is referred to in this index as *Supplement.*
u. e.	upper edge
UT	*Ugaritic Textbook*

text line	UT reference
a: [+][1]	2.2 [thrice]
[+]	16
[+]	17.1
[+]	17.2.VII
b: [+]	2.2 [twice]
[+]	16
[+]	17.1
[+]	17.2.VII
c: [+]	2.2 [twice]
[+]	16
[+]	17.1
[+]	17.2.X
1-299	2.2
1: [+]	2.2
[+]	17.1
[+]	17.2.II
2	9.34
3	8.61
9-10	7.25
10	*4.17
10	*7.56
10	*7.57
12	21 [p. 159][2]
13	21 [p. 159]
17	21 [p. 159]
18	21 [p. 159]
20	7.32
21	21 [p. 159]
1: 22	21 [p. 159]
2-5	4.27
2: [+]	2.2
[+]	6.12
[+]	16
[+]	17.1
[+]	17.2.II
4	9.20
9	21 [p. 159]
10	21 [p. 159]
12-18	18
12	21 [p. 159]
14	9.15
14	21 [p. 159]
15	*9.15
16	*13.31
17-21	21 [p. 346]
17	*9.44
17	*13.31
17	21 [p. 159]
18	*9.38
18	21 [p. 159]
19	9.20
19	21 [p. 159]
20	9.20
21	8.52
23	*9.15
2: 23	12.2
23	21 [p. 159]
24	*9.15
25	*9.44
25	13.31
26	8.61
27-28	*9.52
28	8.3
28	*8.14
28	21 [p. 159]
29	8.52
30	8.52
30	21 [p. 159]
31	21 [p. 159]
32	21 [p. 159]
33	13.31
34	13.31
3: [+]	2.2
[+]	2.2f.[3]
[+]	16
[+]	17.1
[+]	17.2.II
1	4.10
2	4.10
3	4.17
4	4.17
7	4.10 [twice]
12	8.8
13	21 [p. 160]
15	4.10
16	4.10
22	21 [p. 160]
23	4.10
24	8.8
38	7.13
40	4.10
41	*8.8
43	7.31
45	*5.36
45	*7.52
45	*13.105
52	*13.93
54	21 [p. 160]
4: [+]	2.2
[+]	16
[+]	17.1
[+]	17.2.VIII
10	4.12
30	4.12
36	4.12 [twice]
47	8.61
48	8.61
49	4.12
53	4.12
58	4.12 [twice]
4: 62	8.54
5: [+]	2.2
[+]	16
[+]	17.1
[+]	17.2.II
2	4.17
7	*13.93
10	4.10
12	*8.72
13	4.10
26	*6.32
26	*7.15
26	*13.93
6: [+]	2.2
[+]	4.23
[+]	4.27
[+]	16
[+]	17.1
[+]	17.2.I
3	4.18
4	4.18
5	4.18
8	5.3
10	21 [p. 161]
13	21 [p. 161]
15	*8.3
18	4.17
19	4.17 [twice]
19	21 [p. 161]
22	4.17
23	21 [p. 161]
34	5.3
7: [+]	2.2
[+]	4.23f.
[+]	16
[+]	17.1
[+]	17.2.VIII
8: [+]	2.2
[+]	16
[+]	17.1
[+]	17.2.I.
2	7.15
4	8.47
5	*9.7
5	*13.67
5	*9.49f.
5	21[4]
9: [+]	2.2
[+]	16
[+]	17.1
[+]	17.2.II
2	*7.9
10	21 [p. 162]
11	4.10 [twice]
11	*4.22

text line	UT reference
9: 11	*5.21
11	21 [p. 162]
12	4.10 [twice]
13	4.10
14	4.10
16	4.10
16	21 [p. 162]
17	4.10
17	21 [p. 162]
10:[+]	2.2
[+]	4.27
[+]	16
[+]	17.1
[+]	17.2.VI
5	21 [p. 162]
6	9.6
11:[+]	2.2
[+]	4.27
[+]	16
[+]	17.1
[+]	17.2.VI
side	21 [p. 162]
12:[+][5]	2.2
[+]	16[6]
[+]	17.1
[+]	17.ln.[7]
[+]	17.2.VI[6]
1	*7.14
1	*8.72
2	*7.42
2	13.96
3	4.10
4	21 [p. 163]
5	*7.14
5	7.14f.
5	*7.32
7	*7.14
7	*8.72
8	*7.42
8	13.96
14	*7.12[6]
14	*7.41[6]
14	*7.42[6]
13:[+]	2.2
[+]	4.27
[+]	13.106
[+]	16
[+]	17.1
[+]	17.2.III
[+]	21 [p. 163]
5	*9.15
5	*12.3
6	9.6f.
7	6.2
8	6.2

text line	UT reference
13:rev. 2	6.2
rev. 3	*9.15
rev. 3	*12.3
rev. 5	4.27f.
14:[+]	2.2
[+]	16
[+]	17.1
[+]	17.2.II
15:[+]	2.2
[+]	16
[+]	17.1
[+]	17.2.VI
16:[+]	2.2
[+]	16
[+]	17.1
[+]	17.ln.
[+]	17.2.VI
8	21 [p. 163]
17:[+]	2.2
[+]	16
[+]	17.1
[+]	17.2.II
3	4.19
10	21 [p. 163]
18:[+]	2.2
[+]	4.27
[+]	13.106
[+]	16
[+]	17.1
[+]	17.2.III
1-2	*10.10
2	*9.20
17-18	*10.10[8]
17	*5.19
17	*11.10
19-22	10.4
19	4.10
19:[+]	2.2
[+]	16
[+]	17.1
[+]	17.2.II
3	4.13
8-12	17.1
12	7.7
14	7.7
15	7.7
16	4.17
16	*7.7
16	*8.4
16	13.94
17	*8.4
20:[+]	2.2
[+]	13.106
[+]	16
[+]	17.1

text line	UT reference
20:[+]	17.2.III
3	*12.5
21:[+]	2.2
[+]	13.106
[+]	16
[+]	17.1
[+]	17.2.III
22:[+]	2.2
[+]	16
[+]	17.1
[+]	17.2.II
9	*7.2
9	21 [p. 164]
10	7.41
23:[+]	2.2
[+]	16
[+]	17.1
[+]	17.ln.
[+]	17.2.II
7	*7.2 [twice]
7	21 [p. 164]
9	7.41
9	8.52
24:[+]	2.2
[+]	16
[+]	17.1
[+]	17.2.X
9	21 [p. 165]
25:[+]	2.2
[+]	16
[+]	17.1
[+]	17.2.VI
26:[+]	2.2
[+]	16
[+]	17.1
[+]	17.2.III
9	9.54
27:[+]	2.2
[+]	16
[+]	17.1
[+]	17.2.X
28:[+]	2.2
[+]	16
[+]	17.1
[+]	17.2.VIII
rev. 5	4.27f.
29:[+]	2.2
[+]	16
[+]	17.1
[+]	17.2.VI
1	7.7
2	7.7
3	*7.7
3	13.94
30:[+]	2.2

text line	UT reference
30:[+]	16
[+]	17.1
[+]	17.2.VI
31:[+]	2.2
[+]	16
[+]	17.1
[+]	17.2.VIII
32:[+]	2.2
[+]	13.106
[+]	16
[+]	17.1
[+]	17.2.III
end	4.27f.
33:[+]	2.2
[+]	16
[+]	17.1
[+]	17.2.II
34:[+]	2.2
[+]	16
[+]	17.1
[+]	17.ln.
[+]	17.2.VIII
35:[+]	2.2
[+]	16
[+]	17.1
[+]	17.2.VIII
36:[+]	2.2
[+]	16
[+]	17.1
[+]	17.2.VI
37:[+]	2.2
[+]	16
[+]	17.1
[+]	17.2.X
38:[+]	2.2
[+]	16
[+]	17.1
[+]	17.2.VI
39:[+]	2.2
[+]	16
[+]	17.1
40:[+]	2.2
[+]	16
[+]	17.1
[+]	17.2.X
41:[+]	2.2
[+]	16
[+]	17.1
[+]	17.2.II
2	7.33
3	21 [p. 166]
4-5	*7.31
42:[+]	2.2
[+]	16
[+]	17.1

text line	UT reference
42:[+]	17.2.II
43:[+]	2.2
[+]	16
[+]	17.1
[+]	17.2.III
[+]	21 [p. 163]
3	4.27f.
44:[+]	2.2
[+]	16
[+]	17.1
[+]	17.2.II
45:[+]	2.2
[+]	16
[+]	17.1
[+]	17.ln.
[+]	17.2.VIII
46:[+]	2.2
[+]	16
[+]	17.1
[+]	17.2.X
47:[+]	2.2
[+]	16
[+]	17.1
[+]	17.2.II
48:[+]	2.2
[+]	16
[+]	17.1
[+]	17.ln.
49:[+]	2.2
[+]	6.2
[+]	16
[+]	17.1
[+]	17.ln.
[+]	17.2.I
49:I: 2	9.33
2	*13.54
4-5	10.14
4	*9.48
4	13.37
6-8	*9.10
6-8	*9.52
7	*9.61
11-15	*13.63
11	*11.10
13-15	*12.3
13	*13.25
14	*13.25
15	*11.5
16-17	12.6
18	*6.17
18	*7.7
18	*9.40
19	*9.52
20	*9.15
20	*9.40

text line	UT reference
49:I: 20	*11.10
21	*9.12
25	*9.29
25	*13.57
26	*9.40
26	*11.10
28-29	*11.10
28-29	*13.33
29	*9.52
29	10.4
30	*10.10
31-32	*9.15
31-32	*9.52
31-33	*9.61
31-33	*13.146
31-34	12.4
32-33	*9.52
34	*9.9
34	*13.35
49:II:[+]	4.27f.
6-8	10.9
6	*4.23
7	*4.23
7	5.17f.
8	*4.23
12	*5.19
12	*9.20
13-14	*6.33
13-14	*9.15
13-14	*9.34
13	*9.29
13	*12.5
13	*13.57
14	*12.5
19-20	10.10
19-20	*13.116
19	*9.52
19	*13.25
21-23	*13.57
21-23	*13.111
22	*4.22
23	*8.13
24	*9.42
25	*9.7
26-27	*10.11
26	*8.5
26	*9.15
28-29	10.9
28-30	*13.110
28	*4.23
29	*4.23
29	5.17f.
31-32	*10.4
31-35	*9.11
32-33	*9.52

text line	UT reference
49:II:34	*8.5
36	9.52
49:III:2-3	*12.3
3	*13.3
4	*13.75
5	*5.39
6-7	*9.11f.
6-7	*13.117
6-8	*13.59
49:III:6	8.3f.
8-9	*12.3
8	*9.54
8	*13.65
10-21	18
12-13	*9.11f.
12-13	*9.15
12-13	*9.49
12	*9.12
13	*9.12
14	*9.7
15	10.10
16	9.15
18-19	9.11f.
18-19	*13.32
18	*9.9 [twice]
18	*9.11
19	*6.6
20-21	*12.3
20	*9.54
22	*11.5
22	13.113
23	*12.6
49:IV:27	5.40
28-29	*12.5
30	*9.4
30	*9.15
31-32	*9.48
31-32	10.14
31	13.37
36	*12.6
38	5.40
39-40	*12.5
44	*9.35
44	*13.32
46	*12.6
49:V:[+]	4.25
1	*9.34f.
2	*10.4
3	*10.4
4	*9.10
5-6	10.11
7-8	10.11
8-9	*7.15
11-15	13.25
12-15	*10.13
12-16	*13.25
12	*9.60
49:V: 14	*9.60
15-16	*8.5
15	4.25
16	4.25
20	*9.9
20	9.10
49:VI:12-13	*9.50
13	4.13
14	*9.7
14	*9.45
14	*9.48
16-22	*13.114
17-20	*9.44
17-21	10.9
23	*9.21
24-25	*9.33
26	13.118f.
27-29	*13.109
28	*4.6
28	13.9
49:VI:30-31	*13.57
50: [+]	2.2
[+]	4.27f.
[+]	16
[+]	17.1
[+]	17.2.VIII
51: [+]	2.2
[+]	4.25
[+]	6.2
[+]	16
[+]	17.1
[+]	17.2.I
51:I: [+]	4.27f.
13-14	*13.2
20-21	*13.32
20-21	*13.44
20-29	18
20	11.10
21	*6.21
21	9.21
24	9.52
24	*10.10
24	*13.67
26-27	4.25
26-27	*13.67
26-30	*13.112
28-29	4.25
28-29	*13.100
28	*7.42
29	4.23
29	*7.43
31-42	13.22
31	*6.25
31	*7.43
34-37	*9.43
35	4.13
35	13.97
51:I: 38	*6.21
38	*9.48
39	*9.6
41	*8.8f.
51:II:3	*9.23
5	9.52
8-9	*13.116
8-9	13.136
8-11	13.58
8	*13.25
9	13.97
10-11	*9.36
12	*9.26
12	10.4
12	*13.34
13-14	*9.17
21-23	13.58
21	12.5
51:II:22	*9.7
23	*9.7
26-27	*9.17
28-29	*9.8
29	9.17
51:III:8	21 [p. 237]
12	9.11f.
13-35	18
13	*5.21
13	*9.48
14-16	*13.58
14	*9.52
14	*13.25
16	*6.17
16	*9.52
17-21	*7.9
17	7.6
17	*9.6
21	*12.3
22	8.8
23-26	13.58
25-26	*9.15
27	*9.52
28-29	13.58
28-30	*12.5[8]
30-31	13.58
30-32	*9.7
30-32	*12.5
30	*9.45
30	*9.52
31	*9.52
32	*9.52
33-35	*9.15
41	*9.35
43-44	11.6
43	*11.8
51:IV:8-10	*9.4f.
8-32	18
8	13.32

text line	UT reference
51:IV:9-15	*13.58
10	*9.50
13-14	*9.11f.
13	8.61
14-15	10.10
16-17	*8.61
16	4.8
16	*9.38
16	*13.25
16	*13.52
20-21	10.14
20	11.10
20	13.37
23-24	*9.10
25-26	*10.10
26	*9.39
27-28	*12.3
27	*9.17
27	*9.60
29	*9.41
31-32	*13.162
31	12.5
32	*9.6
32	*9.7
32	*9.51
32	12.5
33	*9.7
33	*9.27
34	*9.7
34	*9.27
35-37	*13.141
35	*9.20
35	*13.100
36-38	*10.5
36	*9.20
37-38	17.4
37	11.6
37	11.8
38-39	*9.36
44	*13.5
44	*13.74
48-57	18
50	*12.9
50	*13.7
52-57	*13.115
58	*6.24
59	*12.1
59	*13.57
60	*12.1
60	*13.57
61	12.3
62	*9.31
62	*10.9
51:V: 63	*10.9
65	*13.25 [twice]
72-73	*9.36

text line	UT reference
51:V: 74	*9.31
74	9.31
74	10.10
77-79	*9.15
77-79	17.13
77	*11.10
78	*5.26
79	*6.21
80-81	*9.20
80-81	*17.9
81	*8.7
82-83	*9.4f.
82	*9.8
84-85	10.14
84	13.37
87-88	9.4f.
87	*9.8
88-89	*13.26
88-89	*13.112
88-98	18
89	*9.7
89	*9.48
93-95	17.13
94	*5.26
95-97	*9.20
100-102	*9.15
100-102	17.13
100	*6.17
100	*11.10
101	5.26
102	*6.17
103	4.27f.
103	*9.31
104-105	*9.31
106-107	*12.3
106	*9.7
107-108	*8.13
107-108	*10.16
107-108	*13.103
107-108	13.136
107	4.5
108	*8.13
108	*9.31
109-110	*9.48
109-110	*10.10
109	*5.36
114	*9.36
116	*9.36
117	*10.16
121-122	*12.6
121	*9.20
123-124	9.18
126	*12.4
51:VI:2	*13.32
4	*9.21
4	12.6

text line	UT reference
51:VI: 5-6	13.136
5-9	*9.18
8-9	13.136
13	*5.21
13	9.48
17	*9.36
22-23	10.4
22-23	*13.116
22	*9.31
24-33	*7.44f.
24-33	13.113f.
24	*12.7
26	4.13
29	*9.34f.
32-33	*9.57
32-33	*10.5
36-38	*13.117
36	*9.52
36	*13.25
38	*9.7
40-41	*13.25
41-42	4.5
42-43	*8.3
44-46	13.25
44	*13.25
47-48	*13.25
47-54	8.8
47-54	*13.25
47-54	*13.115
48	8.8
50	8.8
50	21 [p. 172]
51	*13.10
52	8.8
54	8.8
55	*9.52
57-58	*8.13
57	*8.72
58-59	11.6
58	*9.52
58	*11.8
51:VII:9-12	*7.69
9	*7.35
9	*13.91
11	*7.37
12	*7.38
17-19	*10.4
17-19	13.136
17	10.4
21-22	*9.4f.
21-22	13.58
23	*9.16
23	*13.35
25-27	*13.136
25	*9.15
26	10.4

text line	UT reference
51:VII:36	*8.7
37	*9.12
38-39	12.5
41	5.3
42	*11.5
45	*9.9
47-49	*9.10
49-50	*7.64
49-50	*10.13
49-50	*13.72
49-52	*9.10
49-52	*13.68
50	4.13
52-53	9.17
52-53	*13.51
53	21 [p. 172]
51:VIII:1-2	*9.19
1-4	10.14
1	*11.10
1	13.37
5-6	*10.13
5-8	*13.58
5	*8.5
5	*9.20
6	8.5
7-8	*9.48
7-8	*10.4
8-9	*10.4
10-11	*9.48
10-11	10.16
10-11	*11.10
10	13.37
12-13	8.13
15-16	*9.15
15-16	*12.4
15-18	*9.19
15-18	*13.36
17	*12.4
19	*8.13
20	*9.15
22-23	*9.7
24-26	4.25
26-32	*13.54
26-32	*13.58
26	10.10
29-32	*10.10
29-32	*13.139
52: [+]	2.2
[+]	4.27
[+]	16
[+]	17.1
[+]	17.2.I
1-15	18
1	*9.9
1	*9.10
6	*6.31

text line	UT reference
52: 6	*9.20 [twice]
6	*10.5
6	*13.53
8-9	*13.109
8-9	17.3
8	8.61
8	*9.48
8	17.1
12	9.31
13	8.61
15	8.75
16	*9.49
19	*7.16
19	8.8
20	7.15
21-22	9.10
21	9.9
23	*9.9
23	*9.10
24	*9.23
26	*9.23
28	8.61
31	*8.5
31	13.97
32-33	*9.50
32	*9.50
32	*12.7
33-35	10.9
33	*8.8
33	*9.34f.
34	*9.29
35-76	18
37	*9.37
37	13.58
38	*9.55
38	*11.1
39	*7.4
39	*9.15
39	*9.17
39	*12.3
39	*13.51[9]
39	*13.148
40	*9.37
41	*12.7
42-43	12.3
42	*13.2
42	Supp.[10]
43	*9.15
43	*9.23
43	*12.6
44-45	*9.42
44	*9.23
44	*9.53
45	*7.4
45	*13.2
46	*12.7

text line	UT reference
52: 47-48	*12.7
47	*13.100
48	*13.2
49	*9.44
50	*6.10
50	*8.72
50	*10.9
50	13.15
51	*10.5
52	*9.31
52	*9.48
53	*9.7
53	*13.2
54	9.14
55	*6.10
59	*9.31
59	*10.5
61	*9.23
61	*10.5
63-64	*12.2
63	*4.7
64	*4.7
64	*8.16
64	*11.3
65	*8.16
65	*9.48
67-68	*9.15
67-68	*12.3
67-68	*13.116
67	*7.16
68-71	*6.3
68-71	*13.57
68	*9.29
69	*9.29
69	*12.6
70	*9.20
70	*9.29
71-72	*13.59
71	*9.29
74	*13.3
53: [+]	2.2 [thrice]
[+]	16
[+]	17.1
54: [+]	2.2 [twice]
[+]	4.13
[+]	4.27f.
[+]	13.106
[+]	13.106f.
[+]	16
[+]	17.1
[+]	17.2.III
[+]	18
1-3	*10.10
1	8.77
7	*9.7
10-11	*10.14

text line	UT reference
54: 16-18	*11.2
16	*6.29
16	13.84
17	*6.29
17	*13.68
18	*9.50
55: [+]	2.2
[+]	4.27f.
[+]	9.28
[+]	16
[+]	17.1
[+]	17.2.V
pass.	*10.4f.
4	*9.41
5	9.28
5	10.4
6	8.75
7	9.28
7	10.4
8	8.43
8	*9.50 [twice]
9	*7.63
9	*9.28
9	10.4
10	*9.28
27	4.13
56: [+]	2.2
[+]	4.27f.
[+]	7.63
[+]	9.28
[+]	16
[+]	17.1
[+]	17.2.V
pass.	*10.4f.
17	4.13
17	*12.3
18	4.13
18	*9.50
19	*9.50
20-22	10.4
20	*9.28
21	*12.3
22	9.28
23	*12.3
57: [+]	2.2
[+]	3.6
[+]	4.3
[+]	4.26 [twice]
[+]	16
[+]	17.1
[+]	17.2.X
2	*5.1
9	5.1
11	*5.1
58: [+]	2.2
[+]	16
[+]	17.1

text line	UT reference
58: [+]	17.2.VII
59: [+]	2.2
[+]	16
[+]	17.1
[+]	17.2.VII
1-2	*10.10
60: [+]	2.2
[+]	16
[+]	17.1
[+]	17.2.VIII
4	4.9
6	4.9
7	4.9
12	4.9
18	4.9
30	4.21
36	4.21
37	4.21
61: [+]	2.2
[+]	16
[+]	17.1
[+]	17.2.VIII
1	4.27f.
62: [+][11]	2.2.
[+]	16
[+]	17.1
[+]	17.ln. [thrice]
[+]	17.2.I
4	*4.23[12]
4	*5.3
5	*4.23[12]
7-8	10.4
7	*8.14
7	*9.48[12]
8-10	*13.33
8	*9.48[12]
9	*12.3
10-11	*11.5[12]
10	*9.52[12]
12	*9.21[12]
12	10.10[12]
13-14	*13.33
14-15	*9.17[12]
14-15	*13.51[12]
14-18	*6.17
14	10.10[12]
15-18	10.4
18-19	*7.36[12]
18-19	*9.15
18	*11.8
20	*7.36[12]
22	*7.36[12]
24	*7.36[12]
42	11.10
52	4.27f.
53	*13.2
54-55	*12.1

text line	UT reference
62: rev.53-57	*9.23
63: [+]	2.2
[+]	16
[+]	17.1
[+]	17.2.VI
[+]	17.2f.
1	7.17
3	7.17
64: [+]	2.2
[+]	16
[+]	17.1
[+]	17.ln.
[+]	17.2.VI
2	4.13
8	*8.52
9	*8.52
18	21 [p. 177]
19	21 [p. 177]
25	8.52
26	8.52
27	8.52
28	8.52
29	8.52
30	8.52
40	8.58
41	8.58
65: [+]	2.2
[+]	16
[+]	17.1
[+]	17.2.VI
2	7.13
3	7.12
5	7.28
6	7.12
8	7.13
8	7.25
10	7.13
10	8.52
11	7.12
66: [+]	2.2
[+]	16
[+]	17.1
[+]	17.2.VI
67: [+]	2.2
[+]	6.2
[+]	16
[+]	17.1
[+]	17.2.I
67:I: 1-2	*8.58
1-2	*12.3
2	*9.52
3	*7.15
3	*8.7
5	5.3
5	*9.9
5	9.10

text line	UT reference
67:I: 6-8	10.4
6	5.3
6	*9.48
9	*13.25
9	13.37
10	*10.14
11	*9.12
12-14	*13.105
12	*13.2
19-20	*7.9
19-20	*10.4
20	*6.6
20	*9.9
22-23	21 [p. 178]
24-25	*13.29
24-25	13.141
25	*4.22
67:II:6-7	*13.57f.
6	*4.5
8-9	*10.10
9	*9.20
9	*13.53
10-11	*13.108
12	*13.2
12	*13.71
13	*13.25
13	13.37
14-15	10.16
15-16	*8.13
16-17	*9.12
16	*9.15
21	*21 [p. 178]
67:III:12	*9.9
67:IV:3	7.41
15-16	11.6
15	*11.8
67:V:5-6	*13.32
5	*6.17
6	*11.8
7-8	*13.108
8-9	7.15
8-9	7.16f.
8-11	*10.14
11	5.42
11	13.37
12	10.16
13-14	*9.20
13	*8.5
13	*13.58
14-15	*9.48
14-15	*10.4
14	8.5
14	*13.58
14	13.97
15-16	*9.31

text line	UT reference
67:V:15-16	*10.4
15	*13.58
16-17	12.3
17-18	13.32
17-20	*13.58
17	*13.25
17	21 [p. 179][4]
17	21 [p. 426][4]
18-19	10.4
18	4.8
19-20	*10.14
19-21	*7.69
19	*9.7
20-21	*13.91
20	*6.8f.
20	7.36
20	*10.10
21	*7.37
21	*10.10
22	*8.54f.
22	*9.48
67:VI:5-7	*10.10
5-25	18
5	*9.7
5	*13.25
8-9	*9.23
8	10.10
8	*13.25
9	*9.50
9	*13.25
10	*13.25
11-14	*10.11
11	11.10
14-16	*10.10
15-16	17.4
16-17	*9.52
16	9.12
19	9.12
20	*5.3
23-25	*12.8
23-25	*13.166
23	9.50
24-25	*8.14
25-26	*11.10
25	*9.9
25	*10.4
26	*6.32
26	*9.49
27	*6.32
68: [+]	2.2
[+]	16
[+]	17.1
[+]	17.2.I
5	*9.44
5	*11.3
6	*10.5

text line	UT reference
68: 6	*13.35
6	*13.159
6	21 [p. 180]
7-8	*9.16
7-8	*13.35
7-29	18
7	*8.13
7	*9.7
7	*10.15
7	13.57
8-9	*11.10
8-9	*13.168
8	*9.52
10	*6.26
10	*13.32
10	*13.75
11-12	*13.2
11	*6.14
11	*8.5
11	8.8
11	*9.15
11	*13.81
12-13	10.11
12	*4.6
12	*8.49
12	13.9
13-14	*9.33
13	*13.54
14-15	*9.49
15	*13.32
16-17	9.49
16-17	*10.7
16	*13.32
17-18	*12.4
17	4.13
18	8.8
18	*9.15
19	*6.14
19	*13.2
19	*13.81
20-21	*9.33
21-22	4.25
21-22	9.49
22-23	*9.43
23-24	*13.128
24-25	*9.49
24-25	*10.7
24-25	13.32
25-26	*9.43
25-26	10.10
25-26	*12.4
25-26	*13.112
28	*9.15
69: [+]	2.2 [twice]
[+]	16

text line	UT reference
69: [+]	17.1
[+]	17.2.II
1-3	9.52
1	*13.68
2	*10.10
3	*10.10
70: [+]	2.2 [twice]
[+]	16
[+]	17.1
[+]	17.2.II
1-3	9.52
1	*13.68
71: [+]	2.2
[+]	16
[+]	17.1
[+]	17.2.II
72: [+]	2.2
[+]	16
[+]	17.1
[+]	17.2.II
73: [+]	2.2
[+]	16
[+]	17.1
[+]	17.2.II
3	4.9
rev.3	4.27f.
74: [+]	2.2
[+]	3.6
[+]	4.3
[+]	4.26 [twice]
[+]	16
[+]	17.1
[+]	17.2.II
75: [+]	2.2
[+]	5.1 [twice]
[+]	5.3
[+]	5.5 [twice]
[+]	5.7 [thrice]
[+]	5.7f. [twice]
[+]	16
[+]	17.1
[+]	17.2.I
75:I: [+]	4.27f.
12-13	*9.15
12-13	10.4
12	*5.7
14	*5.7
14	*9.20
14	*9.48
16-17	8.54
16	*8.8
19	*9.20
19	*9.48
21-22	*10.16
29	8.8
75:I: 30-33	*10.4f.
30-33	10.9.
30	*8.5
30	*13.2
34	*9.49
36-37	*9.10
36-37	*13.112
37	5.7
40	9.7
40	10.4
41	4.13 [twice]
75:II:[+]	4.27f.
33	4.15
33	*5.5
34	*5.5
36	*5.5
39	*8.5
45	*7.15
45	7.16f.
46	7.16
49-50	*13.91
49-51	*7.69
49	7.15
49	7.36
50	*7.37
51-52	13.25
53-54	9.26
54-55	13.25
54	*9.7
54	*11.10
76: [+]	2.2
[+]	16
[+]	17.1
[+]	17.2.I
76:I: 12	*6.17
12	*9.53
76:II: 3	*9.15
6-7	*13.152[8]
6	*6.8f.
6	*9.6
6	*13.25
8-9	10.16
8	13.37
10	*13.31
11	*9.10
11	*13.31
13	*9.44
13	*13.31
14	*9.10
14	*9.44
14	*13.31
16	8.8
16	*10.7
17	6.8f.
17	*9.56
76:II: 18	*10.10
20	*8.8
20	*9.54
20	*13.28
21	13.69
22	13.69
23	*9.50
24-25	*9.50
28	4.10
76:III:3-4	10.10
5	*9.12
10	*12.1
30-31	*11.5
30	*9.52
33	*9.11
36-37	*10.10
38	*9.15
77: [+]	2.2
[+]	4.9
[+]	4.25
[+]	4.27
[+]	5.1 [twice]
[+]	5.3
[+]	5.5 [twice]
[+]	5.7
[+]	5.11 [twice]
[+]	16
[+]	17.1
[+]	17.2.I
[+]	18
1	8.61
1	*9.9
1	*9.50
3	*10.4
4	*5.21
5	*9.48
7	*12.7
11	*9.20
17	*9.48
18-19	*13.100
19	*9.9
20-21	*7.43
20-21	*13.105
20-21	*13.108
21-22	*5.11
21	*9.9
22-23	*13.116
22	*9.9
23-24	*9.52
23-24	*13.113
25-26	*13.101
26	8.54
27	*9.35
27	*13.45
30	*9.36

text	line	UT reference
77:	31	12.9
	32-33	*11.10
	32	*10.14
	33-37	*13.112
	34	*9.50
	36-37	*10.10
	37-38	*13.69
	38	*5.17
	39	*9.50
	40	*9.50
	44	5.11
	45-46	*10.4
	45-46	*12.7
	45-47	*13.116
	45-47	*13.169
	45	4.25
	45	5.5
	46	4.25
	47	4.25
	50	*8.73
78:	[+]	2.2 [twice]
	[+]	17.1
79:	[+]	2.2 [twice]
	[+]	17.1
80:	[+]	2.2
	[+]	16
	[+]	17.1
	[+]	17.2.VI
	2	4.12
	4	4.12 [twice]
81:	[+]	2.2
	[+]	7.2
	[+]	16[8]
	[+]	17.1
	[+]	17.2.VI
82:	[+]	2.2
	[+]	7.2
	[+]	16
	[+]	17.1
	[+]	17.2.VI
83:	[+]	2.2
	[+]	16
	[+]	17.1
	[+]	17.2.VI
	13	7.13
84:	[+]	2.2
	[+]	16
	[+]	17.1
	[+]	17.2.VI
85:	[+]	2.2
	[+]	16
	[+]	17.1
	[+]	17.2.VI
	4	5.3
	15	7.17
86:	[+]	2.2
	[+]	16
	[+]	17.1
	[+]	17.2.VI
87:	[+]	2.2
	[+]	16
	[+]	17.1
	[+]	17.2.VI
88:	[+]	2.2 [twice]
	[+]	16
	[+]	17.1
89:	[+]	2.2
	[+]	13.86
	[+]	13.106
	[+]	16
	[+]	17.1
	[+]	17.2.III
	[+]	18
	1-4	*10.10
	1-4	*13.106f.
	3	*9.20
	5	6.15
	6-11	*7.68
	6	10.10
	9	12.1
	10	*11.5
	11	13.25f.
	12-15	*10.14
	13	*6.29
	13	13.84
	14	*9.50
	15	*6.15
90:	[+]	2.2
	[+]	16
	[+]	17.1
	[+]	17.2.VI
	5-7	*7.42
	7	7.41
91:	[+]	2.2
	[+]	16
	[+]	17.1
	[+]	17.2.VI
92:	[+]	2.2
	[+]	16
	[+]	17.1
	[+]	17.1f.
	[+]	17.ln.
	[+]	17.2.VI
	1	*7.6
	1	7.28
	2	7.16
	3	*7.6
	4	7.12
	5	7.12
	6	7.11
92:	7	7.14
	8	*7.6
	9	7.32
	13	7.14
	16	7.11
	17	*7.6
93:	[+]	2.2
	[+]	16
	[+]	17.1
	[+]	17.1f.
	[+]	17.ln.
	[+]	17.2.VI
	6	*7.19
	6	7.32
	6	13.92
	7	7.12
	7	7.19
	8	7.14
	8	7.19
	10	*7.6
	10	*7.19
	10	7.25
	10	13.92
	12	7.19
	13	7.12
	13	7.19
	14	*7.9
	15	7.19
94:	[+]	2.2
	[+]	4.10
	[+]	16
	[+]	17.1
	[+]	17.2.X
95:	[+]	2.2 [twice]
	[+]	13.86
	[+]	13.106
	[+]	13.106f.
	[+]	16
	[+]	17.1
	[+]	17.2.III
	[+]	18
	1-4	10.10
	1	*6.9
	2	*9.20
	4	6.15
	5	*6.9
	5	10.10
	6	*11.5
	7	*9.7
	7	13.25f.
	10-12	*6.32
	10	*6.9
	10	*10.14
	10	*11.3
	13	11.10

text	line	UT reference
95:	13	12.1
	14	*9.50
	14	*11.3
	15-18	10.14
	15	*6.9
	16	*6.29
	16	13.84
	17	*9.50
	18	6.15
96:	[+]	2.2
	[+]	4.12
	[+]	16
	[+]	17.1
	[+]	17.2.VI
97:	[+]	2.2
	[+]	16
	[+]	17.1
	[+]	17.ln.
98:	[+]	2.2
	[+]	16
	[+]	17.1
	[+]	17.2.VI
	1	7.9
	2	7.9
	4	7.9
	4	21 [p. 185]
	5	7.9
99:	[+]	2.2
	[+]	16
	[+]	17.1
	[+]	17.2.VI
	12	*7.41
100:	[+]	2.2
	[+]	13.106
	[+]	16
	[+]	17.1
	[+]	17.2.III
	1	*13.97f.
	4	*12.1
	7	*8.3
101:	[+]	2.2
	[+]	13.106
	[+]	16
	[+]	17.1
	[+]	17.2.III
	3	*11.3
102:	[+]	2.2 [twice]
	[+]	16
	[+]	17.1
	[+]	17.2.IX
103:	[+]	2.2 [twice]
	[+]	16
	[+]	17.1
	[+]	17.2.IX
	5	4.11
104:	[+]	2.2 [twice]
	[+]	16
	[+]	17.1
	[+]	17.2.IX
105:	[+]	2.2 [twice]
	[+]	16
	[+]	17.1
	[+]	17.2.IX
	2	4.12
	3	4.12
	8	4.12
	rev.2	4.12
	rev.8	4.12
	rev.10	4.12
106:	[+]	2.2
	[+]	16
	[+]	17.1
	[+]	17.2.VIII
	8	4.27f.
107:	[+]	2.2 [twice]
	[+]	4.23f.
	[+]	16
	[+]	17.1
	[+]	17.ln.
	[+]	17.2.II
108:	[+]	2.2
	[+]	7.2
	[+]	16
	[+]	17.1
	[+]	17.2.VI
	[+]	18
	1	8.52
	2	8.52
	8	8.52
109:	[+]	2.2
	[+]	4.30
	[+]	12.1
	[+]	16
	[+]	17.1
	[+]	17.2.VI
	1-2	*8.56
	1	4.13
	1	8.8
	3-10	4.10
	3	4.30
	3	*7.9
	3	13.15
	4	4.10
	4	*7.13
	4	8.52
	5	4.10
	5	*7.13
	6	4.10
	6	4.30
	6	*7.13
	7	*7.25
109:	7	8.8f.
	8	*7.13
	9	4.10
	9	4.30
	9	*7.3
	10	4.10
	10	4.30
	10	*7.13
110:	[+]	2.2
	[+]	16
	[+]	17.1
	[+]	17.2.VI
	1	7.14
	2	*7.22
	3	*7.24
	4	*7.24
	5	7.16
	6	*7.39
	7	*7.24
	8	7.14
	9	*7.22
	11	4.12
	11	*7.24
	12	*7.26
111:	[+]	2.2
	[+]	13.87
	[+]	16
	[+]	17.1
	[+]	17.2.VI
	[+]	18
	1	7.56
	2	*7.3
	3	*7.3
	4	4.20
	4	7.56
	4	8.52
	5	*7.56
	6	*7.3
	7	*7.3
112:	[+]	2.2
	[+]	4.28
	[+]	16
	[+]	17.1
	[+]	17.2.VI
	1	*7.18
	3	7.16
	5	7.7
	8	7.7
	9	7.12
	10	*7.18
	11	8.52
	14	7.12
	15	*7.18
113:	[+]	2.2
	[+]	4.29

text line	UT reference
113: [+]	7.2
[+]	16
[+]	17.1
[+]	17.2.VI
2	8.53
8	8.52
11	8.52
12	8.52
16	21 [p. 188]
18	8.52
20	8.52
27	8.52
28	8.52
29	4.10
29	*8.67
30	4.10
37	4.10
49	8.52
51	4.10
55	4.10
57	8.52
63	8.7
64	4.10
64	8.7
72	4.10
74	*8.16
114: [+]	2.2
[+]	16
[+]	17.1
[+]	17.2.VI
2	8.7
3	8.7
4	8.30f.
6	*8.16
8	4.12
9	4.12
10	4.12
115: [+]	2.2
[+]	7.2
[+]	16
[+]	17.1
[+]	17.2.VI
4	8.30f.
5	8.52
8	8.30f.
12	8.7
13	8.7
14	*8.16
17	7.55f.
116: [+]	2.2
[+]	16
[+]	17.1
[+]	17.2.VI
[+]	18
1-3	*8.7
116: 2	10.4
4-6	*7.39
117: [+]	2.2
[+]	13.106
[+]	16
[+]	17.1
[+]	17.2.III
[+]	18
5-6	*13.25f.
7-8	*9.15
9	10.14
9	*11.3
11-13	10.14
11	*11.3
13	*9.50
13	10.10
18	*9.50
118: [+]	2.2
[+]	16
[+]	17.1
[+]	17.2.IV
[+]	17.5
pass.	*4.31
pass.	*8.75
12	4.10 [twice]
15	9.60
16	4.10
16	8.77
19	7.42f.
19	21 [p. 190]
20	4.10
20	*7.31
20	7.42f.
20	21 [p. 190]
25-26	*9.48
25-26	*10.10
25	*13.68
26	4.10
26	*8.72
27-28	*7.41
28	4.10
29-30	*7.41
31-32	*7.41
32	4.10
33-34	*7.41
33	4.10
33	21 [p. 190]
35-38	21 [p. 190]
39	4.10
119: [+]	2.2
[+]	8.12
[+]	12.1
[+]	16
[+]	17.1
[+]	17.2.VI
119: 1-17	18
3	4.12
3	7.7
4	8.77
5	*7.9
7	*7.7
7	*7.9
7	*8.72
7	13.15
8	*7.9
10	*7.7
11	*7.7
11	*7.9
13	*8.65
16	*7.6
16	*8.72 [twice]
17	7.13
18	*7.9
18	*8.72
18	13.15
19	*7.7
19	*7.9
20	*7.7
20	*7.9
22	*7.9
29	7.31
29	*10.4
29	11.9
120: [+]	2.2
[+]	16
[+]	17.1
[+]	17.2.VI
2	*7.41
4	*7.41
5	*8.16
6	*7.4
6	*8.5
7	*7.41
7	13.92
8	7.32
8	13.92
9-10	*7.34
13	7.31
14	7.31
15-16	*7.33
15-16	13.96
121: [+]	2.2 [twice]
[+]	17.1
[+]	17.ln.
[+]	17.2.I
[+]	17.2f. [twice]
121:I:[+]	16
5	*10.4
121:II:4	*9.52f.
4	*10.10

text line	UT reference
121:II:5-6	*13.58
5	*9.15
6	8.8
6	*9.52
6	*10.10
9	8.8
10	*9.10
10	9.27
122: [+]	2.2
[+]	16
[+]	17.1
[+]	17.ln.
[+]	17.2.I
[+]	17.2f. [twice]
pass.	*6.6f.
2	9.10
2	*9.50
5	11.10
123: [+]	2.2
[+]	16
[+]	17.1
[+]	17.ln.
[+]	17.2.I
pass.	*6.6f.
9	*9.50
19	9.50
124: [+]	2.2
[+]	16
[+]	17.1
[+]	17.ln.
[+]	17.2.I
8	8.7
12-14	*13.134
12	*9.7
12	*11.10
12	*12.1
13	*6.26
13	*7.3
13	*8.7
14	*8.7
20	8.58
21-22	*9.15
21	*9.12
23-24	*9.15
23-24	*10.4
23	*9.12
24	*11.9
25	*7.44
25	*10.4
25	10.4
25	*12.7
125: [+]	2.2
[+]	16
[+]	17.1
[+]	17.2.I
2	*10.9

text line	UT reference
125: 10	*11.8
10	*13.101
14-15	*13.161
14	*9.15
14	*10.4f.
15-16	*10.9
15	*8.74
15	*12.4
20-21	*9.31
20-23	*13.164
20	*11.8
20	*12.5
22	*12.2
23	*9.54
24	*9.52
25-26	*10.10
25-26	*12.4
25	*12.4
26-28	*9.10
26-28	*13.123
27	4.13
27	8.6f.
29	*7.72
30	10.10
31	*10.10
31	*11.10
31	*12.4
33	*9.7
33	*12.3
33	*13.25
33	*13.27
36	4.5
39	*7.72
46	11.10
51	9.6f.
51	9.7
53	*9.60
53	*12.3
75	*9.15
81-82	*6.29
81-82	13.58
84-85	13.58
84	*7.6
85	7.12
85	*12.3
98-99	*9.15
99	*8.74
100-101	*10.9
100	11.9
101	11.10
102	*10.9
102	*11.10
105	*12.2
112	*5.20
126: [+]	2.2

text line	UT reference
126: [+]	16
[+]	17.1
[+]	17.2.I
126:III: 9	8.9
12	*9.7
13-15	*10.5
13-15	13.25
13-15	*13.125
126:IV: 3	*13.25
4-5	*13.53
4	*9.50
5	8.8
9	8.8
10	4.13
126:V:8	*7.66
9	*7.66[8]
9	21 [p. 50]
10-11	*9.27f.
10-12	*10.4f.
10-12	*13.150
10-21	*6.33
10-21	*11.4
10	*12.5[8]
12-13	*10.4f.
12-13	*12.4
12-13	*13.5
12	*8.58
13	9.52
14-15	*9.27f.
14-15	*10.4f.
14-15	*13.150
14	*12.5[8]
15	*8.58
16	*10.4f.
16	*12.4
16	*13.5
17-18	*9.27f.
17-18	*10.4f.
17-18	*13.150
17	*7.73
17	*9.35
17	*12.5[8]
18	*8.58
18	*9.59
19-20	*7.73
19	*10.4f.
19	*12.4
19	*13.5
20-21	*9.27f.
20-21	*10.4f.
20-21	*13.150
20	*9.35
20	*12.5[8]
21	*8.58
21	*9.59

text line	UT reference
126:V: 22	9.52
22	*10.4f.
22	*12.4
22	*13.5
24-25	*9.48f.
24	*9.48
25-26	*9.33
26	*13.32
28	*9.10
49	*9.20
127: [+]	2.2
[+]	16
[+]	17.1
[+]	17.2.I
1	*8.50
2	*8.50
2	*9.15
2	*9.20
2	9.38
3	*9.27
3	*11.9f.
4	9.10
5	9.10
6	*9.10
7	*9.10
10-12	17.11f.
10	*9.11
10	*10.5
11-12	*9.26
11-12	*10.10
11-12	*13.105
11-12	*13.155
13	*8.50
13	9.38
14-24	18
16	12.6
17-18	*13.59
17-18	*13.67
18	*9.9
19-20	*13.32
19	9.15
20-21	*9.4f.
20-21	13.23
20-21	*13.58
20-21	*13.67
20-21	*13.138
21-22	*7.44
21-22	*12.7
22-24	*13.126
23	9.48
25	9.50
25	*10.10
25	11.10
26	*6.17
26	*9.48
27-28	10.10

text line	UT reference
127: 27-29	*13.140
28-29	10.10
28	*9.20
29-30	*13.58
30	*9.48
32-34	13.58
32	*13.25
33-34	*13.132
33	*9.50
33	*12.4
34	*8.16
34	*12.4
37-38	*9.11
37-38	*10.11
37-38	*13.142
39-40	*10.13
39-40	*13.121
39-57	18
41	*9.21
41	12.6
42	*9.33
42	*9.48
42	*13.54 [twice]
42	*13.58
43-44	9.58
47-50	*13.133
47	*8.16
47	*9.59
48-50	*10.8
48-50	*13.33
48	*10.10
49	*9.38
49	*12.4
52-54	*9.11
52-54	*10.11
54-57	*13.124
55	*12.6
59	*8.62
l.e.[13]	*8.52
l.e.	*13.2
128: [+]	2.2
[+]	16
[+]	17.1
[+]	17.2.I
128:I:[+]	4.27f.
3	5.36
5	*10.10
6	8.8
128:II:[+]	4.27f.
8	21 [p. 195]
11	9.52
13-16	*9.16[8]
14-16	13.35
15	8.58
16-18	*10.4

text line	UT reference
128:II:16-18	*13.149
16-28	18
18	*9.27
21-22	*11.9
21-23	*13.58
21-23	*13.68
21-23	*13.151
21	*12.6
22	*9.38
23-24	*13.137
23	10.10
24	*7.54
25-28	*13.158
26-27	*9.23
28	*9.38
128:III:13	11.10
14	*8.7
16	*6.13
16	*8.73
16	*9.35
16	*13.21
16	*13.32
17-19	*9.15
17-19	*13.127
17-25	18
18-19	*10.10
20-21	*9.48
20-21	*10.10
20-21	*13.144
22-25	*10.9
22	*7.15
22	*12.7
23	*9.44
24	11.10
25-26	*9.36f.
25-26	*13.122
28	*9.21
28	*9.60
28	11.10
29	7.73
29	12.2
128:IV:4-6	13.58
14-16	13.32
15-16	*9.15
15-16	*13.131
17-18	*9.38
17-18	*10.13
17-18	*13.160
19-20	*8.72
21	*9.14
21	*9.15
21	11.9f.
24-25	*10.4
24-25	*13.33
24-25	*13.154
27	*9.52

text line	UT reference
128:V: 7-8	*13.33
10	*9.52
18	*9.26
18	9.52
19	4.5
20	11.3
24	*9.48
128:VI: 4	*9.52
6-7	*10.9
129: [+]	2.2
[+]	16
[+]	17.1
[+]	17.2.I
17	*12.4
20	11.3
130: [+]	2.2
[+]	16
[+]	17.1
[+]	17.2.I
131: [+]	2.2
[+]	16
[+]	17.1
[+]	17.2.I
132: [+]	2.2
[+]	16
[+]	17.1
[+]	17.2.I
133: [+]	2.2
[+]	16
[+]	17.1
[+]	17.2.I[8]
134: [+]	2.2
[+]	16
[+]	17.1
[+]	17.2.II
9	8.4
135: [+]	2.2
[+]	16
[+]	17.1
[+]	17.2.I
136: [+]	2.2
[+]	16
[+]	17.1
[+]	17.2.I
137: [+]	2.2
[+]	2.2f.
[+]	16
[+]	17.1
[+]	17.2.I
15	*12.4
16	*13.53
16	21 [p. 197]
17-41	18
17	*13.2
17	*13.105
137: 19	*13.25
20	4.13
21	12.3
23	*10.10
24-25	*12.5
25	*10.10
27	*9.14
27	*10.10
28	*5.38
29	*9.14
29	*10.10
29	*13.33
32	*9.47
33-34	*13.105
34	21 [p. 198]
35	21 [p. 198]
36	*13.2
37	*13.2
38	4.13
38	*13.25 [twice]
40	4.8
43	*13.25 [twice]
138: [+]	2.2
[+]	2.2f.
[+]	13.86
[+]	13.106
[+]	16
[+]	17.1
[+]	17.ln.
[+]	17.2.III
3	4.13
3	*6.15
7-8	10.14
10-11	*11.10
12	*6.6
13	*6.6
15-16	*6.15
15	5.19
18-19	*6.15
18-19	*13.97
18	5.19
139-172	1.8
139:(=1184)(=401)	2.2
(=1184)(=401)	16
140:(=1185)(=320)	2.2
(=1185)(=320)	16
141: (=1187)	2.2
[+]	16
[+]	17.ln.
[+]	17.2.X
142: (=1183)	2.2
[+]	16
[+]	17.1
[+]	17.ln.
[+]	17.2.X
143: (=1162)	2.2
[+]	16
[+]	17.1
[+]	17.ln.
[+]	17.2.X
144: (=1154)	2.2
[+]	16
[+]	17.1
[+]	17.ln.
[+]	17.2.II
145: (=1103)	2.2
[+]	16
[+]	17.1
[+]	17.ln.
[+]	17.2.VI
146: (=1104)	2.2
[+]	16
[+]	17.1
[+]	17.ln.
[+]	17.2.VI
147: (=1041)	2.2
[+]	16
[+]	17.1
[+]	17.ln.
[+]	17.2.VI
148: (=1105)	2.2
[+]	16
[+]	17.1
[+]	17.ln.
[+]	17.2.VI
149: (=1057)	2.2
[+]	16
[+]	17.1
[+]	17.ln.
[+]	17.2.VI
150: (=1058)	2.2
[+]	16
[+]	17.1
[+]	17.ln.
[+]	17.2.VI
3	4.12
11-17	7.2f.
151: (=1072)	2.2
[+]	16
[+]	17.1
[+]	17.ln.
[+]	17.2.VI
152: (=1073)	2.2
[+]	16
[+]	17.1
[+]	17.ln.
[+]	17.2.VI
153: (=1078)	2.2
[+]	16
[+]	17.1

text line	UT reference
153: [+]	17.ln.
[+]	17.2.VI
154: (=1074)	2.2
[+]	16
[+]	17.1
[+]	17.ln.
[+]	17.2.VI
155: (=1075)	2.2
[+]	16
[+]	17.1
[+]	17.ln.
[+]	17.2.VI
156: (=1148)	2.2
[+]	16
[+]	17.1
[+]	17.ln.
[+]	17.2.VI
11	4.12
12	4.12
157: (=1149)	2.2
[+]	16
[+]	17.1
[+]	17.ln.
[+]	17.2.VI
158: (=1150)	2.2
[+]	16
[+]	17.1
[+]	17.ln.
[+]	17.2.VI
159: (=1176)	2.2
[+]	16
[+]	17.1
[+]	17.ln.
[+]	17.2.VI
2	*7.3
3	*7.3
6	*7.4
160: (=1177)	2.2
[+]	16
[+]	17.1
[+]	17.ln.
[+]	17.2.VI
161: (=1178)	2.2
[+]	16
[+]	17.1
[+]	17.ln.
[+]	17.2.VI
162: (=1068)	2.2
[+]	16
[+]	17.1
[+]	17.ln.
[+]	17.2.VI
163: (=1027)	2.2
[+]	16
[+]	17.1
163: [+]	17.ln.
[+]	17.2.VI
164: (=1119)	2.2
[+]	16
[+]	17.1
[+]	17.ln.
[+]	17.2.VI
165: (=1168)	2.2
[+]	16
[+]	17.1
[+]	17.ln.
[+]	17.2.VII
166: (=1163)	2.2
[+]	16
[+]	17.1
[+]	17.ln.
[+]	17.2.VII
167: (=1169)	2.2
[+]	16
[+]	17.1
[+]	17.ln.
168: (=1182)	2.2
[+]	16
[+]	17.1
[+]	17.ln.
[+]	17.2.X
1	21 [p. 201]
169: (=1026)	2.2
[+]	16
[+]	17.1
[+]	17.ln.
[+]	17.2.VI
1-15	18
rev.1-14	18
170: (=1040)	2.2
[+]	16
[+]	17.1
[+]	17.ln.
[+]	17.2.VI
8	*13.46
171: (=1100)	2.2
[+]	16
[+]	17.1
[+]	17.ln.
172: (=1145)	2.2
[+]	16
[+]	17.1
[+]	17.ln.
[+]	17.2.VI
173: [+]	16
[+]	17.1
[+]	17.2.II
58	21 [p. 203]
300-399	2.2
300: [+]	2.2
300: [+]	7.2
[+]	16
[+]	17.1
[+]	17.2.VI
2	*8.64
3	*10.4
5	*8.70
9	8.49
10	4.12
11	*8.67
13	8.77
15	8.77
16	*8.64
17	4.12
18	*8.63
25	8.77
28	*8.65
rev.2	*8.65
rev.4	8.52
rev.8	8.3f.
rev.11	*8.16
rev.14	8.58
rev.14	8.77
rev.15	8.52
rev.17	8.52
rev.19	8.52
rev.21	8.58
rev.24	*8.65
301: [+]	2.2
[+]	7.2
[+]	16
[+]	17.1
[+]	17.2.VI
301:I: 4	8.52
14	*8.69
301:II: 1	8.52
4	8.58
5	8.52
7	8.60
13	8.58
17	8.52
302: [+]	2.2
[+]	16
[+]	17.1
[+]	17.2.VI
303: [+]	2.2
[+]	16
[+]	17.1
[+]	17.2.VI
304: [+]	2.2
[+]	16
[+]	17.1
[+]	17.2.VI
12	*8.62
305: [+]	2.2

text line	UT reference
305: [+]	16
[+]	17.1
[+]	17.2.VI
1	4.12 [twice]
4	*7.6
306: [+]	2.2
[+]	16
[+]	17.1
[+]	17.2.VI
1-2	*12.4
1-2	*13.7
1-2	13.74
1	6.27
14	*7.16
307: [+]	2.2
[+]	7.2
[+]	16
[+]	17.1
[+]	17.2.VI
1	8.58
8	*8.69
308: [+]	2.2
[+]	13.88
[+]	16
[+]	17.1
[+]	17.2.VI
pass.	*7.4
19	*8.63
20	*7.12
20	*13.105
24	*8.62
309: [+]	2.2
[+]	16
[+]	17.1
[+]	17.2.VI
9	8.58
27	8.52
310: [+]	2.2
[+]	16
[+]	17.1
[+]	17.2.VI
3	7.35
5	4.12
6	7.35
7	7.31
8	*7.18
9	*7.18
10	7.14
311: [+]	2.2
[+]	16
[+]	17.1
[+]	17.2.VI
3	4.12
3	8.52
5	8.52

text line	UT reference
311: 6	8.52
7	8.52
12	4.12
312: [+]	2.2
[+]	16
[+]	17.1
[+]	17.2.VI
313: [+]	2.2
[+]	16
[+]	17.1
[+]	17.2.VI
7	8.77
314: [+]	2.2
[+]	16
[+]	17.1
[+]	17.2.VI
8	*8.68
12	*8.65
15	*8.66
rev. 8	8.52
rev. 11	8.52
315: [+]	2.2
[+]	16
[+]	17.1
[+]	17.2.VI
316: [+]	2.2
[+]	16
[+]	17.1
[+]	17.2.VI
317: [+]	2.2
[+]	7.8
[+]	16
[+]	17.1
[+]	17.2.VI
1	*7.8
3	*7.8
4	7.8
318: [+]	2.2
[+]	16
[+]	17.1
[+]	17.2.VI
319: [+]	2.2
[+]	16
[+]	17.1
[+]	17.2.VI
[+]	17.2.X
1	*8.72
2	*8.65
6	*8.64
320: [+]	cf. ≠140
[+]	3.1
[+]	17.ln.
2	4.10
3	4.10
321: [+]	2.2 [twice]

text line	UT reference
321: [+]	4.20
[+]	4.27f.
[+]	8.12
[+]	13.87
[+]	16
[+]	17.1
[+]	17.2.VI
321:I: 1	8.52f.
2	*7.9 [twice]
3	*7.9
4	*7.3
19	8.52
26	*7.9
27	*7.9
29	*7.9
31	8.58
31	8.60
35	*8.68
37	8.49
40	*8.69
45	8.52
46	8.58
321:II: 2	8.2
3	8.58
4	8.49
6	8.2
24	8.49
25	8.60
30-33	17.1
41	*8.69
43	*8.63
45	7.12
45	*8.69
321:III: 4	*8.65
9	*8.62
10	8.58
17	*8.69
19	8.60
20	8.15
26	*8.63
33	*8.62
38	8.3f.
41	*8.72f.
45	*8.68
321:IV: 5	7.72
6	*8.59
8	8.58
15	*8.72f.
322: [+]	2.2
[+]	16
[+]	17.1
[+]	17.2.VI
322:I: [+]	17.ln.
3	*8.63
322:II: 2	*8.19

text line	UT reference
322:II: 4	8.58
5	*8.65
10	5.3
322:V: 2	*8.62
4	*8.62
322:VI: 2	8.2
7	*8.65
323: [+]	2.2
[+]	16
[+]	17.1
[+]	17.2.VI
323:III: [+]	17.ln.
8	8.58
9	*8.66
323:IV: 10	*8.68
324: [+]	2.2
[+]	7.2
[+]	16
[+]	17.1
[+]	17.ln.
[+]	17.2.VI
325: [+]	2.2
[+]	16
[+]	17.1
[+]	17.2.VI
end	4.27f.
326: [+]	2.2
[+]	7.2
[+]	16
[+]	17.1
[+]	17.2.VI
327: [+]	2.2
[+]	16
[+]	17.1
[+]	17.2.VI
5	8.52
7	8.52
8	8.52
rev. 2	*8.66
328: [+]	2.2
[+]	16
[+]	17.1
[+]	17.2.VI
329: [+]	2.2
[+]	16
[+]	17.1
[+]	17.2.VI
2	9.6f.
14	10.17
15	10.17
17	10.17
18	10.17
330: [+]	2.2
[+]	16
[+]	17.1

text line	UT reference
330: [+]	17.2.VI
331: [+]	2.2
[+]	16
[+]	17.1
[+]	17.2.VI
332: [+]	2.2
[+]	16
[+]	17.1
[+]	17.2.VI
333: [+]	2.2
[+]	16
[+]	17.1
[+]	17.2.VI
334: [+]	2.2
[+]	16
[+]	17.1
[+]	17.2.VI
335: [+]	2.2
[+]	16
[+]	17.1
[+]	17.2.VI
400-499	2.2
400: [+]	2.2
[+]	7.2
[+]	16
[+]	17.1
[+]	17.2.VI
400:I: 14	*8.69
22	8.52
23	7.58f.
23	*8.63
side	*8.75
400:II: 3	8.69
400:III: 1	8.52
400:VI: 16	8.49
401: [+]	cf. ≠139
[+]	17.ln.
500-599	2.2
500: [+]	1.7f.
[+]	2.2 [twice]
[+]	3.6 [twice]
[+]	4.3
[+]	16
[+]	17.1
[+]	17.2.X
[+]	20
501: [+]	1.7f.
[+]	2.2 [twice]
[+]	3.6 [twice]
[+]	4.3
[+]	16
[+]	17.1
[+]	17.2.X
[+]	20
502: [+]	17.1

text line	UT reference
502: [+]	20
[+]	21 [p. 3]
503: [+]	20
[+]	21 [p. 3]
[+]	22
614: [+]	Supp.
1001:1189	13.1
1001:[+]	2.2 [twice]
[+]	16
[+]	17.1
[+]	17.2.I
3	21 [p. 214]
4	*9.50f.
4	12.3
5	9.38
5	*9.53
5	*11.7
5	12.3
5	12.4
6	*9.53
8	*6.19
8	*8.18f.
8	*12.4
9	*9.52
9	*9.53 [twice]
9	*10.4
9	21 [p. 214]
10	*9.49
10	*10.4
10	*10.10
11	9.39
16	*9.49
16	*10.7
19	9.54
22	*9.49
24	*9.49
rev. 2	*10.10
rev. 3	*9.48
rev. 4	*9.54
rev. 5	10.13f.
rev. 7	8.8
rev. 7	*9.48f.
rev. 9	*9.50
rev. 12	*9.52
rev. 13	4.13 [twice]
rev. 13	*13.62
rev. 13	*13.108
1002:[+]	2.2
[+]	16
[+]	17.1
[+]	17.2.I
13	*6.6f.
15	9.7f.
36	*9.9
37	9.48f.

text line	UT reference
1002:38	*6.3
38	13.57
41	*6.3
41	*9.9
41	13.57
42	*6.1f
42	*6.3
42	9.7
42	*9.52
42	13.57
49	*6.1f.
49	*6.3
49	9.6
50	13.57
52	*9.9
62	*6.6
62	12.3
62	12.4
62	*13.78
1003:[+]	2.2
[+]	16
[+]	17.1
[+]	17.2.I
5-7	*9.15
5-7	*13.117
5	*8.5
7	*8.5
8-9	*13.103
8	*9.24
8	*12.4
1004:[+]	2.2
[+]	16
[+]	17.1
[+]	17.2.II
1-22	10.10
1005-1023	13.106
1005:[+]	2.2
[+]	16
[+]	17.1
[+]	17.2.III
2-4	*10.9
4	5.24
5	*10.12
8-9	*13.46
9-11	*8.48
9	*6.22
10	5.24
10	*6.22
11	*6.22
12	*6.30
12	*9.2
12	*12.4
13-15	*13.47
13	*6.22
14	5.24
1005:15	*10.12
1006:[+]	2.2
[+]	16
[+]	17.1
1-2	*9.48
1-3	*13.46
1	*6.22
2	*9.52
12-19	*9.5
12	*9.3
16-17	13.7
17	*9.3
1007:[+]	2.2
[+]	16
[+]	17.1
[+]	17.2.III
7	*9.52
1008:[+]	2.2
[+]	10.17
[+]	16
[+]	17.1
1	*6.22
1	*13.49
2	*13.49
4-5	*13.49
4	*9.48
10	*6.32
11-12	*13.49
11	*6.17
14	*13.49
16-17	13.14
17	*9.2
1009:[+]	2.2
[+]	16
[+]	17.1
1-12	13.49
12-13	*6.30
12-13	13.14
13	*9.2
14	*6.22
1010:[+]	2.2
[+]	16
[+]	17.1
[+]	17.2.X
[+]	18
4-8	*12.1
4	*9.9f.
4	*12.5
5-6	*12.5
9-10	*10.13
9	*7.12
12	10.13
13	*7.9
13	10.13
15	*7.7
1010:16	10.13
21	7.35
1011:[+]	2.2
[+]	16
[+]	17.1
[+]	17.2.III
1012:[+]	2.2
[+]	16
[+]	17.1
[+]	17.2.III
2	*6.6f.
2	21 [p. 218]
3	*6.6f.
3	11.5
3	21 [p. 218]
19	*9.48
24	*7.42
25-26	*10.13
25-29	*12.1
27	*9.50
27	*13.26
28	12.1
29	*10.10
32	*6.22
32	*7.42
33-36	*13.46
34-35	*10.14
34	21 [p. 218]
35	*6.22
38	*7.42
1013:[+]	2.2
[+]	16
[+]	17.1
[+]	17.2.III
8	*11.3
9	*11.3
12	*11.3
16-18	*9.5
17	*13.29
19-20	*9.27
21	4.13
21	*9.19
1014:[+]	2.2
[+]	16
[+]	17.1
[+]	17.2.III
1-6	18
1015:[+]	2.2
[+]	16
[+]	17.1
[+]	17.ln.
[+]	17.2.III
[+]	18
4-5	*4.5
6-8	*13.65

text line	UT reference
1015:7	*4.5
7	12.3f.
8	10.10
9-10	*10.4
9-10	*11.10
9	*9.50
10-11	*10.1f.
10	*4.5
11	*5.22
11	*14.12
14	*11.3
16-17	*6.29
19	*10.14
1016:[+]	2.2
[+]	16
[+]	17.1
[+]	17.2.III
1017:[+]	2.2
[+]	16
[+]	17.1
[+]	17.2.III
4	*6.6
5	*9.38
6	7.15
6	*7.56
1018:[+]	2.2
[+]	16
[+]	17.1
[+]	17.2.III
2	4.10
17-18	*10.10
17	10.10
17	12.1 [twice]
19	10.10 [twice]
21	10.10 [twice]
22	*6.26
1019:[+]	2.2
[+]	16
[+]	17.1
[+]	17.2.III
4	4.20
6	*10.8
7-8	*13.46
9-10	*6.18
10	21 [p. 220]
12-16	*13.79
1020:[+]	2.2
[+]	16
[+]	17.1
[+]	17.2.III
3	*4.5
3	*9.53
5	9.53f.
1021:[+]	2.2

text line	UT reference
1021:[+]	16
[+]	17.1
[+]	17.2.III
1-3	*13.50
1	*9.48
3	*9.48
4	*9.24f.
6-7	*13.57
6	*9.29
8	*9.52
13	*4.5
13	12.3f.
16	10.14
1022:[+]	2.2
[+]	16
[+]	17.1
[+]	17.2.III
3	*9.9
7	6.32
8	6.32
1023:[+]	2.2
[+]	16
[+]	17.1
[+]	17.2.III
5	9.38
1024:[+]	2.2
[+]	16
[+]	17.1
[+]	17.2.VI
1	*6.27
3	4.12
8	21 [p. 220]
25	*7.39
26-27	*6.27
rev. 1-2	*10.4
rev. 4-5	*8.10
rev. 4	7.10
rev. 4	*7.16
rev. 5	*7.19
rev. 6	6.27
rev. 7	*7.19
rev. 7	*7.21
rev. 8	6.27
rev. 8	*10.4
rev. 9	*7.22
rev. 9	7.25
rev. 10	*8.10
rev. 11	*8.10
rev. 22	7.25
1025:[+]	2.2
[+]	16
[+]	17.1
[+]	17.2.VI
[+]	18
3	*7.40

text line	UT reference
1025:4	*9.2
5	*7.40
6	*9.2
1026:[+]	2.2
[+]	16
[+]	17.1
1027:[+]	2.2
[+]	16
[+]	17.1
1028:[+]	2.2
[+]	16
[+]	17.1
[+]	17.ln. [twice]
[+]	17.2.VI
1	*7.13
1	7.18
2	*7.23
4	7.11
5	7.18
6	7.17
7	7.18
8	7.15
9	*7.39
10	*7.39
12-13	*7.40
13-14	*13.68f.
1029:[+]	2.2
[+]	16
[+]	17.1
[+]	17.ln.
[+]	17.2.VI
[+]	18
1	7.17
5	*7.29
7	*7.23
9	7.12
12	4.12
13	*7.27
14-16	*13.68f.
14	*7.40
1030:[+]	2.2
[+]	16
[+]	17.1
[+]	17.ln.
[+]	18
3	7.18
7	4.12
7	*7.38
8	*7.40
10	*7.40
1031:[+]	2.2
[+]	16
[+]	17.1
[+]	17.2.VI
10	*7.23

text line	UT reference
1031:13	4.12
16-17	*7.40
1032:[+]	2.2
[+]	16
[+]	17.1
[+]	17.2.VI
[+]	18
1033:[+]	2.2
[+]	16
[+]	17.1
[+]	17.2.VI
9	6.25
1034:[+]	2.2
[+]	16
[+]	17.1
[+]	17.2.VI
1035:[+]	2.2
[+]	16
[+]	17.1
[+]	17.2.VI
4-5	12.4
4	*6.27
5	4.13
5	*6.27
13	21 [p. 223]
rev. 1	21 [p. 223]
rev. 10	21 [p. 223]
1036:[+]	2.2
[+]	16
[+]	17.1
[+]	17.2.VI
12	21 [p. 223]
1037:[+]	2.2
[+]	16
[+]	17.1
[+]	17.2.VI
1038:[+]	2.2
[+]	16
[+]	17.1
[+]	17.2.VI
1039:[+]	2.2
[+]	16
[+]	17.1
[+]	17.2.VI
22	21 [p. 166]
1040:[+]	2.2
[+]	16
[+]	17.1
[+]	17.2.VI
1041:[+]	2.2
[+]	16
[+]	17.1
[+]	17.2.VI
1042:[+]	2.2
[+]	16
1042:[+]	17.1
[+]	17.2.VI
1043:[+]	2.2
[+]	16
[+]	17.1
[+]	17.2.VI
1044:[+]	2.2
[+]	16
[+]	17.1
[+]	17.2.VI
1045:[+]	2.2
[+]	5.1 [twice]
[+]	16
[+]	17.1
[+]	17.2.VI
2	5.32
3	5.32
4	5.25
4	5.31
6	5.34
7	5.31
8	5.25
13	5.32
1046:[+]	2.2
[+]	16
[+]	17.1
[+]	17.2.VI
8	8.60
12	*8.68
1047:[+]	2.2
[+]	16
[+]	17.1
[+]	17.2.VI
10	4.10
11	4.10
16	4.12
17	4.10
18	4.10
19	4.10
20	4.10
21	4.10
25	21[p. 225]
1048:[+]	2.2
[+]	16
[+]	17.1
[+]	17.2.VI
1049:[+]	2.2
[+]	16
[+]	17.1
[+]	17.2.VI
1050:[+]	2.2
[+]	16
[+]	17.1
[+]	17.ln. [twice]
[+]	17.2.VI
1050:3	7.15
3	*10.4
6	7.11
8	7.11
9	7.11
1051:[+]	2.2
[+]	16
[+]	17.1
[+]	17.ln.
[+]	17.2.VI
3	10.4
4	10.4
1052:[+]	2.2
[+]	16
[+]	17.1
[+]	17.2.VI
1-9	10.4
1	8.64
1053:[+]	2.2
[+]	16
[+]	17.1
[+]	17.2.VI
1	*10.15
2	10.15
3	10.15
1054:[+]	2.2
[+]	16
[+]	17.1
[+]	17.2.VI
1	4.24
1055:[+]	2.2
[+]	16
[+]	17.1
[+]	17.2.VI
1	*8.68
8-10	*7.39
1056:[+]	2.2
[+]	16
[+]	17.1
[+]	17.ln.
[+]	17.2.VI
1057:[+]	cf. ≠149
1058:[+]	cf. ≠150
1059:[+]	2.2
[+]	16
[+]	17.1
[+]	17.2.VI
1	8.46
7	3.1
1060 A: [+]	2.2
[+]	16
[+]	17.1
[+]	17.2.VI
12	8.70
1060 B: [+]	2.2

text line	UT reference
1060 B: [+]	16
4	8.70
6	8.70
7	8.53
1061:[+]	2.2
[+]	16
[+]	17.1
[+]	17.2.VI
1	*7.9
2	7.9
3	21 [p. 227]
8	5.30
15	7.9
1062:[+]	2.2
[+]	16
[+]	17.1
[+]	17.2.VI
8	*7.13
10	*7.12
12	*7.18
20	4.9
1063:[+]	2.2
[+]	16
[+]	17.1
[+]	17.2.VI
1	*8.69
1064:[+]	2.2
[+]	16
[+]	17.1
[+]	17.2.VI
1065:[+]	2.2
[+]	16
[+]	17.1
[+]	17.2.VI
1066:[+]	2.2
[+]	16
[+]	17.1
[+]	17.2.VI
3	8.62
1067:[+]	2.2
[+]	16
[+]	17.1
[+]	17.2.VI
1068:[+]	2.2
[+]	16
[+]	17.1
[+]	17.2.VI
1069:[+]	2.2
[+]	16
[+]	17.1
[+]	17.2.VI
1070:[+]	2.2
[+]	16
[+]	17.1

text line	UT reference
1070:[+]	17.2.VI
1071:[+]	2.2
[+]	16
[+]	17.1
[+]	17.2.VI
5	9.6
1072:[+]	cf. ≠151
1073:[+]	cf. ≠152
1074:[+]	cf. ≠154
1075:[+]	cf. ≠155
1076:[+]	2.2
[+]	16
[+]	17.1
[+]	17.2.VI
1	10.4
3	11.4f.
3	13.110f.
4	11.4f.
4	13.110f.
5	11.4f.
5	13.110f.
6	11.4f.
6	13.110f.
1077:[+]	2.2
[+]	16
[+]	17.1
[+]	17.2.VI
2	4.10
5	4.10
7	4.10
8	4.10
9	4.10
1078:[+]	cf. ≠153
1079:[+]	2.2
[+]	13.75
[+]	16
[+]	17.1
[+]	17.2.VI
[+]	18
2	13.75
3	*7.10
3	*13.75
6	*7.10
6	13.75
9	13.75
11	13.75
13	13.75
15	13.75
1080:[+]	2.2
[+]	16
[+]	17.1
[+]	17.2.VI
1	8.52
3	8.52

text line	UT reference
1080:5	8.52
11	8.52
12	8.52
15	8.52
1081:[+]	2.2
[+]	16
[+]	17.1
[+]	17.2.VI
4	7.22
12	4.13
16	4.13
16	*9.9f.
18	7.24
21	7.22
1082:[+]	2.2
[+]	16
[+]	17.1
[+]	17.2.VI
pass.	*7.5
1	*10.13
2	*7.5
3	*7.5
4-22	10.13
4	*7.5
5	*7.5
5	*8.62
6-9	*7.5
8	21 [p. 230]
10	*7.5
11	*7.5
18	*7.5
21	*7.5
22	*7.5
rev. 4-9	10.13
rev. 4	*7.5
rev. 8	*4.22
rev. 10	*7.5
1083:[+]	2.2
[+]	7.20 [twice]
[+]	16
[+]	17.1
[+]	17.2.VI
1	7.24
2	8.54
2	*9.2
2	*9.7
3	10.14f.
4	7.21
5	*10.14f.
8	*7.25
10	*7.23
12	*7.13
14	*7.25
1084:[+]	2.2

text line	UT reference
1084:[+]	16
[+]	17.1
[+]	17.2.VI
[+]	18
1	*13.73
2	*12.4
2	*13.73
6	*7.41
9	*7.40
11	*7.39
12	*5.22
25	*7.41
27	*13.45
1085:[+]	2.2
[+]	16
[+]	17.1
[+]	17.2.VI
1086:[+]	2.2
[+]	16
[+]	17.1
[+]	17.2.VI
1087:[+]	2.2
[+]	16
[+]	17.1
[+]	17.2.VI
1	*7.22
1088:[+]	2.2
[+]	16
[+]	17.1
[+]	17.2.VI
11-15	4.22f.
1089:[+]	2.2
[+]	16
[+]	17.1
[+]	17.2.VI
[+]	18
3	*8.52
5	*8.46
7	*8.52
8	*8.46
9	8.8
10	*8.52
1090:[+]	2.2
[+]	16
[+]	17.1
[+]	17.2.VI
[+]	18
1-2	*8.72
1	*10.4f.
3	*10.4f.
4-5	*8.56
4	*8.52
8	*8.52
13	*8.52
text line	UT reference
1091:[+]	2.2
[+]	16
[+]	17.1
[+]	17.2.VI
1092:[+]	2.2
[+]	16
[+]	17.1
[+]	17.2.VI
8	9.52
1093:[+]	2.2
[+]	16
[+]	17.1
[+]	17.2.VI
1094:[+]	2.2
[+]	16
[+]	17.1
[+]	17.2.VI
1	*7.41
1095:[+]	2.2
[+]	16
[+]	17.1
[+]	17.2.VI
3	*8.22
3	21 [p. 233]
1096:[+]	2.2
[+]	16
[+]	17.1
[+]	17.2.VI
2	*7.40
2	*8.22
1097:[+]	2.2
[+]	16
[+]	17.1
[+]	17.2.VI
1-2	*10.4
1098:[+]	2.2
[+]	4.24
[+]	16
[+]	17.1
[+]	17.2.VI
1-27	18
1	*5.13f.
2	7.22
6	4.24
29	7.22
33	7.22
44	*9.52
1099:[+]	2.2
[+]	16
[+]	17.1
[+]	17.2.VI
3	*8.52
8	21 [p. 234]
8	Supp.
text line	UT reference
1099:15	8.71
25	*8.9
27	4.14
28	4.14
32	*8.9
35	4.14
1100:[+]	2.2
[+]	16
[+]	17.1
[+]	17.2.VI
1	*8.7
1	*8.72
2	*8.8
2	*8.72
3	*8.74
8	8.13
1101:[+]	2.2
[+]	16
[+]	17.1
[+]	17.2.VI
1102:[+]	2.2
[+]	16
[+]	17.1
[+]	17.2.VI
1103:[+]	cf. ≠145
1104:[+]	cf. ≠146
1105:[+]	cf. ≠148
1106:[+]	2.2
[+]	16
[+]	17.1
[+]	17.2.VI
1	*10.4
4	*8.72
8	8.75
14	7.27
57	*10.4
58	*9.53
60	*9.53
1107:[+]	2.2
[+]	16
[+]	17.1
[+]	17.2.VI
[+]	18
5-8	*13.80
6-7	*10.5
7	9.13
8	9.13
8	*9.49
12-13	*10.4
1108:[+]	2.2
[+]	16
[+]	17.1
[+]	17.2.VI
1-2	*10.4[8]

text line	UT reference
1108:1-8	10.4
1	7.18
3	7.13
4	7.11
5	7.14
6	7.18
6	*17.1
7	7.12
8	7.18
8	*10.4
9	*17.1
1109:[+]	2.2
[+]	16
[+]	17.1
[+]	17.2.VI
1	5.16
4	*5.16
1110:[+]	2.2
[+]	16
[+]	17.1
[+]	17.2.VI
[+]	18
1111:[+]	2.2
[+]	13.75
[+]	16
[+]	17.1
[+]	17.2.VI
3	4.13
8	*6.26
8	*13.75
9	8.46
10	7.22
11	*8.46
12	*13.75
1112:[+]	2.2
[+]	16
[+]	17.1
[+]	17.ln.
[+]	17.2.VI
14	*8.75
19	4.13
1113:[+]	2.2
[+]	16
[+]	17.1
[+]	17.2.VI
11	4.13
1114:[+]	2.2
[+]	16
[+]	17.1
[+]	17.2.VI
1115:[+]	2.2
[+]	16
[+]	17.1
[+]	17.2.VI
1-5	10.4

text line	UT reference
1116:[+]	2.2
[+]	16
[+]	17.1
[+]	17.2.VI
1117:[+]	2.2
[+]	16
[+]	17.1
[+]	17.2.VI
4	21 [p. 237]
12	4.24 [twice]
15	4.24
17	4.24
18	*4.24
18	*9.2
19	*4.24
20	*4.24
20	*9.2
1118:[+]	2.2
[+]	16
[+]	17.1
[+]	17.2.VI
3	21 [p. 237]
4	*5.13f.
1119:[+]	cf. ≠164
[+]	17.1
[+]	17.2.VI
1120:[+]	2.2
[+]	16
[+]	17.1
[+]	17.2.VI
1121:[+]	2.2
[+]	16
[+]	17.1
[+]	17.2.VI
[+]	18
1-5	*10.17
1	*6.26
2	*6.26
2	*10.4
3	*6.13
4	*6.13
5	*6.13
6-7	*13.7
6	*7.9
8	*7.8
9-10	*6.24
1122:[+]	2.2
[+]	16
[+]	17.1
[+]	17.2.VI
1-2	*9.24
2	9.52
2	*10.4
3	*7.8
4	9.52

text line	UT reference
1122:6	*9.52
8	9.53
1123:[+]	2.2
[+]	16
[+]	17.1
[+]	17.2.VI
[+]	18
4	7.8
5-6	8.75
7	*7.8
9-10	*7.7
1124:[+]	2.2
[+]	16
[+]	17.1
[+]	17.2.VI
[+]	18
1125:[+]	2.2
[+]	16
[+]	17.1
[+]	17.2.VI
rev. 3	4.9
1126:[+]	2.2
[+]	16
[+]	17.1
[+]	17.2.VI
[+]	18
2	8.41
5	7.26
1127:[+]	2.2
[+]	16
[+]	17.1
[+]	17.2.VI
[+]	18
5	*7.22
9	*8.6
13	*7.14
15	8.44
1128:[+]	2.2
[+]	16
[+]	17.1
[+]	17.2.VI
[+]	20
16	*8.13
20	*8.4
21	*8.4
26	4.14
28	*4.31
28	*7.41
30	*7.42
31	*7.24
1129:[+]	2.2
[+]	16
[+]	17.1
[+]	17.2.VI
1	12.4

text line	UT reference
1129:8	6.24
8	*6.26
9	4.13
9	*6.26
11	*6.24
11	6.24
11	*7.7
1130:[+]	2.2
[+]	16
[+]	17.1
[+]	17.2.VI
11-12	*4.25
1131:[+]	2.2
[+]	4.12 [twice]
[+]	7.20
[+]	16
[+]	17.1
[+]	17.2.VI
4-6	*7.26
4	7.27
5	4.12
6	4.12
6	7.27
7	7.14
7	7.26
8	*7.40
9	4.12
1132:[+]	2.2
[+]	16
[+]	17.1
[+]	17.2.IV
1133:[+]	2.2
[+]	16
[+]	17.1
[+]	17.2.VI
1134:[+]	2.2
[+]	16
[+]	17.1
[+]	17.2.IV
[+]	18
1	8.40
1135:[+]	2.2
[+]	16
[+]	17.1
[+]	17.2.VI
7	*6.27
7	*9.48
1136:[+]	2.2
[+]	16
[+]	17.1
[+]	17.2.VI
1137:[+]	2.2
[+]	16
[+]	17.1
[+]	17.2.VI

text line	UT reference
1137:4	8.63f.
1138:[+]	2.2
[+]	16
[+]	17.1
[+]	17.2.VI
1	*7.9
1	10.4
2	10.4
3	10.4
1139:[+]	2.2
[+]	16
[+]	17.1
[+]	17.2f.
1140:[+]	2.2
[+]	16
[+]	17.1
[+]	17.2.VI
2-13	7.7
1141:[+]	2.2
[+]	16
[+]	17.1
[+]	17.2.VI
1	7.8
4	7.7
1142:[+]	2.2
[+]	16
[+]	17.1
[+]	17.2.VI
1143:[+]	2.2
[+]	16
[+]	17.1
[+]	17.2.VI
1	4.10
1	*7.41
1	10.14f.
2	*8.5
3	4.10
3	10.14f.
7	4.10
8	10.14f.
9	4.10
10	10.14f.
10	21 [p. 241]
11	4.10
12	4.10
12	10.14f.
13	4.10
1144:[+]	2.2
[+]	7.20
[+]	16
[+]	17.1
[+]	17.2.VI
5	*5.1
6	7.24
1145:[+]	cf. ≠172

text line	UT reference
1146:[+]	2.2
[+]	16
[+]	17.1
[+]	17.2.VI
5	3.1
5	*8.9
12	3.1
12	8.13
13	3.1
13	8.13
1147:[+]	2.2
[+]	16
[+]	17.1
[+]	17.2.VI
1	8.8
1148:[+]	cf. ≠156
1149:[+]	cf. ≠157
1150:[+]	cf. ≠158
1151:[+]	2.2
[+]	16
[+]	17.1
[+]	17.2.VI
6	*8.46
1152:[+]	2.2
[+]	16
[+]	17.1
[+]	17.2.VI
3	8.32
4	8.46
rev. 9	6.32
1153:[+]	2.2
[+]	16
[+]	17.1
[+]	17.2.VI
2	5.34
3	*5.17f.
3	5.34
4	8.23
5	*9.53
1154:[+]	cf. ≠144
4	5.34
6	5.34
7	5.34
1155:[+]	2.2
[+]	16
[+]	17.1
[+]	17.ln.
[+]	17.2.VI
1-2	*10.4
1-3	*13.48
2	4.22
3	5.3f.
3	8.65
3	*9.2
6-8	*10.4

text line	UT reference
1155:6	*5.16
6	*9.24
6	*9.47
1156:[+]	2.2
[+]	16
[+]	17.1
[+]	17.2.VI
1	13.48
2	*4.22
3	*9.2
1157:[+]	2.2
[+]	16
[+]	17.1
[+]	17.2.VI
3	4.22
4	4.22
5	*7.37
1158:[+]	2.2
[+]	16
[+]	17.1
[+]	17.2.X
1159:[+]	2.2
[+]	16
[+]	17.1
[+]	17.2.X
1160:[+]	2.2
[+]	16
[+]	17.1
[+]	17.2.II
1	4.22f.
3	4.22f.
5	*4.22f.
1161:[+]	2.2
[+]	16
[+]	17.1
[+]	17.2.VI
[+]	18
1	*8.34
1	*8.58
2-3	*10.4[13]
2	*6.26
2	*9.3
5	*6.29
5	*8.36
6	*6.26
6	*9.36
8	4.27
8	*6.4
8	*6.4f.
9	4.27
9	*6.4f.
9	*9.3
9	*9.36
10	*4.27
11	*4.27

text line	UT reference
1162:[+]	cf. ≠143
1163:[+]	cf. ≠166
1164:[+]	2.2
[+]	16
[+]	17.1
[+]	17.2.VII
1165:[+]	2.2
[+]	16
[+]	17.1
[+]	17.2.VII
1166:[+]	2.2
[+]	16
[+]	17.1
[+]	17.2.VII
1167:[+]	2.2
[+]	16
[+]	17.1
[+]	17.2.VII
1168:[+]	2.2
[+]	16
[+]	17.1
[+]	17.2.VII
1169:[+]	2.2
[+]	16
[+]	17.1
[+]	17.2.VII
1170:[+]	2.2
[+]	16
[+]	17.1
[+]	17.2.VII
1171:[+]	2.2
[+]	16
[+]	17.1
[+]	17.2.VII
1172:[+]	2.2
[+]	16
[+]	17.1
[+]	17.2.VII
1173:[+]	2.2
[+]	16
[+]	17.1
[+]	17.2.VII
2-3	8.8
1174:[+]	2.2
[+]	16
[+]	17.1
[+]	17.2.VII
1175:[+]	2.2
[+]	16
[+]	17.1
[+]	17.2.VII
1	8.49
2	*8.49
1176:[+]	cf. ≠159
1177:[+]	cf. ≠160

text line	UT reference
1178:[+]	cf. ≠161
1179:[+]	2.2
[+]	16
[+]	17.1
[+]	17.2.VI
2	7.8
3	7.8
4	*7.8
5	*7.8
7	*7.8
1180:[+]	2.2
[+]	16
[+]	17.1
[+]	17.2.VI
1181:[+]	2.2
[+]	16
[+]	17.1
[+]	17.2.VI
side	7.8
1182:[+]	cf. ≠168
1183:[+]	cf. ≠142
1184-1189	4.12f.
1184:[+]	cf. ≠139
[+]	18
1185:[+]	cf. ≠140
3	4.12
6	4.12
1186-1189	3.1
1186:[+]	2.2
[+]	16
[+]	17.1
[+]	17.2.X
1187:[+]	2.2
[+]	16
[+]	17.1
[+]	17.2.X
1188:[+]	2.2
[+]	16
[+]	17.1
[+]	17.2.X
1189:[+]	2.2 [twice]
[+]	3.5 [thrice]
[+]	16
[+]	17.1
[+]	17.2.X
[+]	17.14f.
2001-2123	17.1
2001-2123	Supplement[14]
2001:[+]	17.1f.
[+]	17.2.I
2002:[+]	17.2.I
4	21 [p. 3*][15]
2003:[+]	17.2.I
2004:[+]	17.2.II
2005:[+]	17.2.II

text line	UT reference
2006:[+]	17.ln.
[+]	17.2.II
2007:[+]	17.2.II
2008:[+]	17.2.III
2009:[+]	17.2.III
12	*21 [p. 85]
14	21 [p. 155]
u.e. 2	*21 [p. 157]
2010:[+]	17.2.III
2011:[+]	17.2.VI
32	21 [p. 5*]
2012:[+]	17.2.VI
2013:[+]	17.2.VI
2014:[+]	17.2.VI
2015:[+]	17.2.VI
2016:[+]	17.ln.
[+]	17.2.VI
2017:[+]	17.2.VI
2018:[+]	17.2.VI
2019:[+]	17.2.VI
2020:[+]	17.2.VI
2021:[+]	17.2.VI
2022:[+]	17.2.VI
2023:[+]	17.2.VI
2024:[+]	17.2.VI
2025:[+]	17.2.VI
2026:[+]	17.2.VI
2027:[+]	17.2.VI
2028:side	*17.1
[+]	17.2.VI
2029:[+]	17.2.VI
2030:[+]	17.2.VI
2031:[+]	17.2.VI
2032:[+]	17.2.VI
2033:[+]	17.2.VI
2034:[+]	17.2.VI
2035:[+]	17.2.VI
2036:[+]	17.2.VI
2037:[+]	17.2.VI
2038:[+]	17.2f.
2039:[+]	17.2.VI
2040:[+]	17.2.VI
2041:[+]	17.2.VI
2042:[+]	17.2.VI
2043:[+]	17.2.VI
2044:[+]	17.2.VI
2045:[+]	17.2.VI
2046:[+]	17.2.VI
2047:[+]	17.2.VI
2048:[+]	17.2.VI
2049:[+]	17.2.VI
2050:[+]	17.2.VI
2051:[+]	17.2.VI
2052:[+]	17.2.VI

text line	UT reference
2053:[+]	17.2.VI
2054:rev. 25	*17.1
[+]	17.2.VI
2055:[+]	17.2.VI
2056:[+]	17.2.X
2057:[+]	17.2.X
2058:[+]	17.2.IV
rev.frag.b.:2	21 [p. 17*]
2059-2093[16]	17.2.III
2059-2113	17.1f.
2059:[+]	17.1f.
23	21 [p. 157]
2063:6	21 [p. 19*]
2066:[+]	17.2.VI
2067:[+]	17.2.VI
16	21 [p. 20*]
2068:[+]	17.2.VI
2069-2073	17.2.VI
2072:7	21 [p. 21*]
2074:[+]	17.2.VI
2075:[+]	17.2.VI
[+]	21 [p. 285]
2076:[+]	17.2.VI
2077:[+]	17.2.VI
2078:[+]	17.2.VI
2079:[+]	17.2.VI
2080-2082	17.2.VI
2083:[+]	17.2.VI
2084:[+]	17.2.VI
2085:[+]	17.2.X
2086:[+]	17.2.VI
2087:[+]	17.2.VI
2088:[+]	17.2.VI
2089:[+]	17.2.VI
2090:[+]	17.2.VI
19	21 [p. 24*]
2091-2095	17.2.VI
2093:2	17.1
2096:[+]	17.ln.
[+]	17.2.X
2097:[+]	17.2.X
2098:[+]	17.2.VI
2099:[+]	17.2.VI
2100-2102	17.2.VI
2100:18	17.1
2103:[+]	17.2.VI
2104:[+]	17.2.VI
2105:[+]	17.2.VI
2106:[+]	17.2.VI
2107:[+]	17.2.IV
2108:[+]	17.2.VI
2	21 [p. 28*]
2109:[+]	17.2.VI
2110:[+]	17.2.X

text line	UT reference
2111:[+]	17.2.VI
2113:[+]	17.2f.
25	17.1
30	17.1
2114-2123	17.ln.
2114:[+]	17.2.III
2115:[+]	17.2.III
2116:[+]	17.2.X
2117:[+]	17.2.VI
2118:[+]	17.2.VI
9	21 [p. 30*]
2124-2172	21 [twice]
2124:6	21[17]
2127:b:4	21[17]
2127:b:5	21[17]
2137:5	*21[17]
2162:B:5	*21[17]
2163:II:7	21[17]
RS 15.37:1	8.14
RS 15.37:9	8.14
RS 16. 129: 3	8.14
RS 16. 129: 6	8.14
RS 16. 129: 11	8.14
RS 16. 129: 14	8.14
RS 22. 05:[+]	3.6
RS 22. 05:[+]	5.1
RS 66. 29. 96:[+]	Supp.Addendum
RS 66. 29. 101: beg.	Supp.Addendum
"Hippic text c":[+]	10.4f.
[+]	13.61f.
[+]	17.2.V
Aqht:[+]	2.2
[+]	16
[+]	17.1
[+]	17.2.I
I Aqht I:[+]	2.2f.
[+]	6.2
2	4.23
13-14	9.44
15-16	*9.54
16-17	*9.48
16	11.10
19-20	11.10
29	9.60
30	*10.4
31	9.52[8]
32	*10.13
34-35	*10.4
34	*9.52
35	4.23
37	4.23
38	11.10
39	9.52

text line	UT reference
I Aqht I:40-42	*13.68[8]
40-42	*13.147
41	4.23
41	*9.53
41	21 [p. 125]
42-44	*7.16
42-44	*13.116
42	*7.15
43-44	17.3
43	7.6
43	*13.105
44-46	*12.4
44	*13.6
44	17.3
50-52	*17.8
50-53	13.58
53-54	*13.117
53	*6.26
53	17.4[8]
54-55	13.32
54	*6.26
55-56	*17.8
57-58	*11.5
57-58	*13.38
57-58	*13.163
57	*5.20
57	*9.11
58	*5.20
59-60	10.10
59	*6.17
59	*9.10
65-66	9.44
66	*9.34f.
67	10.4
70-71	*9.44
72-73	9.44
74	10.4
75-76	13.58
75	10.5
75	*13.35
76	*9.60
79	*7.68
82-83	*7.59
82	4.25
82	*9.34
83	4.25
86	13.85
90	12.6
91	9.50
108	*5.27
109	*9.9
109	10.15
110-111	*6.17
110-111	*13.32
110-111	*13.78
I Aqht I:111	4.13
112	4.14
112	13.32
113	10.5
113	*13.35
114-115	*13.58
115	*6.4
116	*6.13
117	*8.3
117	*12.4
117	*13.5
117	*13.108
118	*9.10
119	*9.10
120	*9.14
120	*9.20
120	*9.52
120	*9.53
120	10.4
123	*5.27
124	*9.9
124	*10.15
125-126	*6.17
126-127	13.32
129	*6.4
130	*9.52
131	*8.3
131	*12.4
132	*9.10
133-134	*9.51
133	*9.10
134-135	*10.4
134	*9.53
134	*13.108
136-186	18
137-138	*6.4
137	*5.27
138	*9.9
139-140	*12.3
139-140	*13.32
139-140	*13.170
139	*5.27
140-141	*6.17
140-141	13.32
141	4.14
141	*13.35
143	*6.4
144	*9.52
145-146	*10.5
145	*8.3
147	*6.17
147	8.43
147	10.4
148-150	*12.3
148-150	*13.117
I Aqht I:148-150	*13.153
148	*13.113
150	*10.13
150	*13.78
151	*6.17
151	*8.3
151	*9.14
151	*9.38
154	*8.3
154	*8.56
154	*10.12f.
154	*11.1
154	*11.1f.
154	*13.105
154	17.3
155-156	*13.58
156-158	9.53
159-160	9.44
159-160	12.4
159-160	*13.148
159	10.4
160	4.10
161-162	*11.1f.
161-162	17.3
161	*8.3
161	*10.12f.
161	*11.1
162-163	*13.58
162	4.10
163	*9.52
167	*11.10
170-172	13.58
170	*4.24
170	4.25
170	*13.148
171-172	*9.7
171-172	*9.23
171-172	*9.52
171-172	*13.129[8]
171	4.25
172	4.25
172	*9.38
172	10.4
173-175	*10.10
175-177	*10.11
176-177	*10.4
176-177	*10.12
176-178	*7.53
176-178	*9.52
176-178	*13.33
176	8.3
179-180	*10.4
183	*9.52
190	*9.52
191-192	*13.53

text line	UT reference
I Aqht I:194-195	*13.35
194-195	13.58
194-195	*13.67
194	*9.12
194	9.24
195	*9.12
195	9.24
196	*9.9
196	*9.23
200	5.42
201	9.23
202	*9.35
202	*9.52
206	21 [p. 246]
207	*9.50
207	*10.4
208	*5.39
213	*9.50
213	*13.25
214	*9.12
214	*9.50
214	*13.25
215	*13.53
215	*13.58
216-217	*13.58
216	*10.4
216	13.116f.
217	*6.17
218	*9.12
218	13.116f.
220-221	*13.68
II Aqht I: 14	*9.52
15	*13.59
16	*10.4
19-20	*13.74
21	*12.4f.
22-23	*13.117
24-25	*9.16
24-25	10.10
26-27	*13.116
26	*9.50
28	*9.48
37-38	*9.54
46	*9.48
II Aqht II: pass.	*8.13
10-11	*9.15
10-12	*13.113f.
11	*5.39
11	10.10
12-13	*9.11
12-14	*9.11f.
12-14	*13.32
12-31	18
13	*6.6
14	*6.6
II Aqht II: 14	*10.10
15	*6.6
19-23	*9.23
19	6.6f.
21	6.6f.
24-25	*13.38
24	*9.61
25-26	*13.58
26	9.61
26	*10.4
27-29	*11.10
28	*8.13
32-34	*9.38
32-40	*7.44f.
32-40	13.113f.
32	*12.7
39	*9.7
39	*10.5
II Aqht V: pass.	13.51
3	*9.38
4-21	18
5	11.10
6	*13.31
7-8	*13.130
7	*6.27
7	*13.75
9	10.4
10-11	*8.61
10-11	*13.117
11	*9.32
12-13	*9.38
12-13	*12.7
12-13	*13.117
13-15	11.10
15	*9.17
15	11.5
15	13.51
15	*13.113
16-20	*13.58
16	13.113
19-20	*9.52
19-20	*13.143
19	*9.38
20	*6.4
20	*9.20
20	13.18
21-22	*9.15
21-22	13.32
21-22	13.113
22	8.54
23-24	10.10
26-27	*9.11
26-28	*13.156
26	10.4
27-28	*10.10
II Aqht V: 28	11.10
29	*9.38
29	13.18
31-32	13.25
31-33	*10.11
31-33	*13.117
31	*9.7
31	*13.25
32	*13.25
II Aqht VI: 10	10.4
16	*9.21
17	*9.47
19	5.33
22	*8.6
24	*6.8
25	5.33
26-40	18
26	*9.47
27-28	13.58
28-29	*10.14
28-29	*13.117[8]
28	*9.38
31	*9.50
32-33	*9.54
34	*12.4
35	*6.33
35	*12.5
36-37	21 [p. 399]
36	*6.33
36	8.75
36	*12.5
37	13.97 [twice]
38	*9.9
38	*9.27
39	13.32
43-44	*8.8
43	*10.4
43	13.35
45	*8.73
46-47	10.14
46	11.10
48-49	9.52
III Aqht: 3	5.3[18]
9	*12.5
11	*9.12
12	*12.6
17	*9.9
17	*13.32[18]
20	*9.15
20	*9.35f.
21-22	*9.35
21	4.12
22-23	*7.65
22-23	*10.13
22	*5.38

text line	UT reference
III Aqht: 22	*7.9[18]
23	*7.68
24-25	*9.10
24-26	10.9
26	4.11
26	*10.5
27-37	18[18]
27	*13.32[18]
28-29	10.9
29	4.11
29	4.13
29	*12.3[18]
30-31	*9.15
30-31	*10.13
33-34	7.65
33-34	*10.13
33	5.38
34	*7.68
36	*9.7
36	*9.8[18]
36	*9.10
36	*13.25[18]
III Aqht rev.:11-12	*13.10
12	*11.5
14	*5.3
14	*10.5
15	*9.12
16	*9.7
16	*13.25
16	*13.27
20	13.37
22	*9.8
23	*9.21
IV Aqht: [+]	2.2
Krt: [+]	2.2
[+]	14.12
[+]	16
[+]	17.1
[+]	17.2.I
8-9	*17.9
9	*7.16
12-13	*13.35
12	*13.22
13	*13.22
14	*13.25
16-21	*7.55
16	*7.58
17	*7.59
18	*7.60
19	*7.61
20	*7.62
24	*12.7
26-27	*9.26
26	*9.61
26	10.4

text line	UT reference
Krt: 27	*9.52
28-29	10.9
28	*9.34
29	*8.56
29	*11.1
30	*7.60
30	*11.1
31	*9.52
31	*10.4
32-33	10.4
36	*5.39
37-38	*13.56
38-39	*13.64
38-39	*13.83
39	*9.52
40	4.13
60-62	*9.26
60-62	*13.56
60	*9.52
62-66	*13.54
62	*9.34
62	*13.58
63	*5.39
63	*13.58
64	*5.39
65	*13.58
66	*13.58
67	*13.58
68	*8.13
73-74	*9.52
73	*9.20
74-75	11.8
74-80	17.12
74	*9.20
74	*13.53
74	13.97
75-77	13.58
75	*8.3
75	*9.20
75	*9.44
75	*13.101
76	*5.39
77-79	*13.116
77	*9.48
79-80	*9.61
79-80	*10.11
79-81	*9.48
79-83	*13.67
80-82	*10.10
80-83	13.58
80-84	17.11
82	8.9
85	*9.10
87	*9.10

text line	UT reference
Krt: 89	*7.11
89	*7.41
89	*7.43
90-91	*10.6
90	*12.4
90	*13.74
91	4.10
91	*12.4
91	*13.74
92-95	7.70
96	*13.25
97-98	9.27
99-100	9.27
100-101	*8.72
100	9.40
100	9.48f.
102	10.10f.
103-105	*13.157
103	*5.39
104	4.27
105	8.3
106-107	13.95
106-108	*7.44
107-108	*12.7
107-109	*13.34
107	*11.5
108-109	*9.52
108-109	*10.10f.
109	4.13
112	8.8
113	4.22
113	*5.33
114-119	7.44f.
114	*8.8f.
114	9.35
115	4.13
118-119	7.44
118-119	*12.7
118	*11.5
120	*5.37
124	*9.49
124	*10.14
126-134	13.58
126	14.4
128	*7.6
128	*7.11
130-131	*11.5
131-133	*13.108
134	*8.72
135	*13.2
136	*5.36
137	*5.36
138	14.4
141	8.8
142	6.27

text	line	UT reference
Krt:	142	*12.1
	142	*13.72
	143	8.54
	143	*9.48
	144	*5.28
	145	6.27
	149	*9.51
	150-151	10.4
	150	*9.48
	152-153	10.10
	156-157	*9.33
	156-158	*10.12
	156-175	18
	157-160	*13.58
	157	5.39
	157	*11.1
	158	*11.1
	158	*13.105
	159-161	*7.67
	159	*9.46
	159	10.4
	161	*8.13
	165	9.52
	166-167	11.6
	166-167	*11.8
	166-170	*13.25
	166	13.97
	167	*8.3
	167	*13.101
	168	*5.39
	169	*9.48
	171	4.10
	172-175	17.11
	173	8.9
	189	*8.72
	189	9.40
	189	*9.48
	191	*5.39
	191	10.10f.
	192-194	*10.9
	194-196	7.44f.
	194-209	13.113f.
	194-211	18
	194	*9.12
	195-196	*10.2
	196	*11.5
	199	11.2f.
	203-204	*9.46
	203-204	*12.3
	203-205	*13.45
	203-205	*13.167
	203-206	*13.32
	203	8.54
	204-205	*9.61
	204	*9.2
Krt:	205-206	*7.71
	205-206	*11.5
	205	4.13
	206	*9.48
	207-209	7.44f.
	207	*9.12
	207	*9.49
	209	*10.2
	209	*10.4
	209	*11.5
	210-211	*8.72
	210-211	*9.52
	210-211	*10.10f.
	215	8.8
	216	4.22
	216	*5.33
	217	*8.8f.
	217	*9.35
	221	*11.5
	223	*5.37
	234	4.10
	274-275	*11.5
	282	*13.82
	286	*8.8
	288-292	*13.70
	288-300	18
	290	*5.28
	291	13.69
	296	*13.69
	298-299	4.22
	300-301	*9.14f.
	301-303	*10.14
	301	11.10
	301	13.37
	303-304	*9.12
	303	*9.15
	304	*6.10
ʻnt I:	[+]	2.2 [twice]
	[+]	16
	[+]	17.1
	[+]	17.2.I
	2-4	*13.25
	4-5	*13.25
	4	*13.52
	5	*6.17
	7	*8.4
	7	*8.72
	8-9	*13.25
	8-9	*13.52
	8	*8.13
	9	*6.17
	11	*7.9
	13	*8.72
	18	*13.52
	21	10.4
ʻnt I:	22-23	*9.47
ʻnt II:	3	*7.9
	4	*7.9
	5-6	*12.7
	5-7	*9.33
	5-41	18
	5	4.25
	6	4.25
	7-8	*9.15
	7	*8.5
	9-10	*13.2
	9-10	*13.16
	9	*10.15
	13-15	*9.53
	13	*8.6
	17	*12.7
	18	*8.8
	20-22	*9.30
	20	8.5
	22	*8.7
	23-24	*9.33
	23-24	*13.165
	23	*9.11
	23	*11.10
	24-27	*9.52
	25-26	*9.10
	27-28	*9.53
	29	*9.33
	29	*12.3
	30-31	*9.30
	30-31	*9.48
	30	*8.5
	30	*10.7
	32-33	*13.116
	32-35	*13.135
	32	4.25
	32	21 [p. 253]
	33	4.25
	33	5.33
	36	8.8
	38-39	*13.11
	39	17.4
	40-41	*13.68
ʻnt III:	2	10.10
	3-5	*13.109
	6-9	13.54
	6-9	13.58
	7	*6.4
	9	5.33
	12	*9.20
	12	10.4
	16	*9.15
	16	*10.14
	17-18	*12.4
	17-18	*13.4

text line	UT reference
‘nt III:17-19	*13.112
17-28	18
19	*7.73
21	4.8
23-25	*9.48
23	*13.68
25-26	*9.52
25	9.52
28	4.27f.
29	*9.60
29	*12.3
32-50	18[19]
33	*12.5
34	*6.29
35-37	13.35
35-38	*13.58
43-44	*9.48
43	*9.33
44	*9.20
44	*10.5
46	4.10 [twice]
‘nt IV:45	*10.5[8]
46-47	*10.11
46	*6.16f.
47	4.10
48-50	9.44
48	*6.29
49	*9.15
75-76	*7.71
75-76	13.32
77	*13.25
77	21 [p. 35]
79-80	7.9
80	*10.15
81	*11.10
81	13.37
83	*9.50

text line	UT reference
‘nt IV:84-85	13.25
84	*9.38
85-86	*9.50
85-86	13.136
85	4.5
87	17.4
89	*9.36
‘nt V:10-11	13.32
11	*9.31
11	*10.10
29	*9.19
32-33	*13.10
32-33	*13.32
32-41	18
32	*9.38
32	*9.49f.
33-35	7.16f.
33	*11.5
35	*13.25
36	*6.33
36	*12.5
39	*10.14
40-41	*13.74
40	*6.11
40	*13.2
41	4.7
41	*12.4
44-45	*13.120
45	4.13
46	*12.4
46	*12.9
‘nt VI:7	4.10
8	4.10
9-23	18
11	4.10
11	8.61

text line	UT reference
‘nt VI: 11	*9.52
12-13	*10.16
12	13.37
13	5.42
14-15	*4.6
14-16	*13.145
15	13.9
18-20	*9.39
18-22	13.58
18-23	*13.54
18	5.27
19	4.16
19	4.25
20	4.25
20	*6.4
21-22	10.10
21-23	*13.109
21	13.139
22	*9.20
‘nt pl. ix:II:[+]	16
18	21 [p. 255]
22	9.15
23	10.16
‘nt pl.ix:III:[+]	16
14	4.8
14	4.10
16	*9.52
‘nt pl.x:IV: [+]	16
2	11.5
12	4.10 [twice]
16	9.7
24	6.16f.
‘nt pl.x:V: [+]	16
8	4.11
17	4.10
25	4.11

Footnotes

[1] Designation for entire text.
[2] Chapter twenty-one (Additions and Corrections) is organized according to the page numbers in UT. Thus this entry refers to a correction on page 159.
[3] Designation when the entry is made in a footnote to the paragraph in UT.
[4] A corrected error in chapter twenty-one.
[5] Sometimes listed as 12+97 in UT.
[6] Listed as 12+97 in UT.
[7] Special note listed in the main body of the paragraph.
[8] Printing error in UT.
[9] Translated elsewhere in UT.
[10] Designation for *Supplement to the Ugaritic Textbook*, pp. 549ff.
[11] Sometimes listed as 62I in UT.
[12] Listed as 62I in UT.
[13] Printing error in the sentence containing reference.
[14] Designation for *Supplement: Texts 2001-2123*, pp. 1*ff.
[15] Designation for the pagination of *Supplement: Texts 2001-2123* and for its additions and corrections, cf. UT, p. 544.
[16] Should this entry read 2059-2065? Cf. Addition entries for texts between 2065 and 2093 and note the designation of these texts in 17.1.
[17] See under special new words, UT, p. 544.
[18] *obverse* not noted in UT.
[19] lines 45-50 are actually the first part of ʿnt IV.

INDEXES

Subject Index

abonimation 83
acrobatics 156f
adoption, real-estate 99f
adoption of daughters 99f
alabaster 95
allophone 175
Amarna letters 96f
animals, innocence or guilt 83, 89[13]
Aqht legend 71-80
arrow, as sexual symbol 73f
aspect 167, 175
Babylonian Chronicle 149
banishment 84, 87
Base-ring I & II wares 93
basic rules for sequence of tenses 173ff
bathing, ritual 84
bestiality 81ff
bezel, scaraboid 94[39]
Black Slip II wares 93
Black topped Ware 184, 186, 198
blood guilt, automatic 81
bound morpheme 170f[11]
bow, as sexual symbol 73f
breakup of composite phrase 57f
bride 86f
broad-room structure 6f
bronze 29, 31ff
calf, golden 151ff
  fabrication of 153[10]
  at Tell Dan 153[10]
causal *beth* 57
cedar 31
champlevé enameling 116[15]
chariot 30f, 94
chiasmus 172
chronology 17[2]; 19[25]; 22[62]; 23[82], 24[95,97]
Çıradere Ware 204
cloisonné inlay technique 111[15]
colophon 86
composite phrase 54
consecutive tenses 168ff
  same as simple ones 175
  uses of 169
copper 29ff, 32, 34ff, 18, 19, 26, 92
court declarations, at Nuzu 226ff
court procedure, at Nuzu 223ff
cylinder seals
  Old Babylonian in Crete 20
  Middle Babylonian & Syrian in Thebes 26[116]ff
Cypriote Sea 58
dance 157ff
dative suffix 54f[9]
dativus commodi 54
daughters adopted as sons 99ff
debt bondange 147
dependent clause
  consec. tense vb. introducing 171
desert sanctuary 6
detestable act 83
diachronic study 168, 175
diplomacy 91ff, 96f
divorce 86
dowry 86f
earring, Egyptian 117[22]
ebony 94
eggs, ostrich 94
elders, village 86
elephants' tusks 93
Eliashiv ostraca 3[19]
enclitic *-m* 58
exchange tablets, at Nuzu 226ff
faience 94, 95
  Egyptian 91
fancy furniture 94
fidi liquid 93
flood, universal 120
frescoes
  Cretan & Western Asiatic 22
frog-shaped beads 94[43]
fruitstands 184, 185
future tense
  simple future 167, 168, 175
  waw future 168
games, ritual 157ff
gemination 168
gender discord 56[21]
genealogies 119ff
glass 94, 95
glyptics 94
gold 31, 94, 95

hearths 182, 188
Heavy Black Burnished Ware 185, 186, 198
Hebrew slave 146
hierodule 213[3], 220[68]
Hieroglyphic Hittite seals 26[123]
hieros gamos 213, 214[11], 216, 217[48], 222[85]
Homeric Age 120
homosexuality 81ff
horns of consecration 22[66]
horses 30ff, 93, 94
hunting metaphor 54[6]
Hurrian personal names in Linear A 23[78]
idioms 56f
imperfect tense 167, 175
incest 81f
infinitive absolute 56
infixed *-t-* conjugation 55, 58
ingots, copper 29ff. 92[8]
Intermediate Ware 204
ius primae noctis 216
ivory 31f, 94
jewelry 94
  Achaemenian 109ff
  Akkadian 111
  Egyptian 110, 111[22]
  Lydian 113
  Median 109, 114
  Neo-assyrian 109, 112
  Neo-Babylonian 112, 113
  Neo-Sumerian 111
  Scythian 109
  Sumerian Early Dynastic 110, 111
  Syro-Palestinian 111, 112
  Urartian 113, 114
Kamares pottery 19[23]
lapis lazuli
  imports to Crete 20
law code, or Hammurabi 215
lead 34
legitimate Yahwistic sanctuary 3
levirate marriage 82
Linear A 23[70 ff], 34f
Linear B 23[82f]
linens 94
LXX 54, 57
mankind, families of 120
merchants 95
messenger-merchants 96, 97
messengers 95, 97
metaphor
  hunting 54[6]
  military 54
miners, Egyptian 6
mining at Apliki 92[8]
misogyny 78
morphology 56
n- prefix in Egyptian 212
n- prefix in Semitic 208f
myth, meaning of 78ff
Nations, Table of 119ff
negation
  and rules of sequence of tenses 171, 173
Negro 30
neutron activation 181
New Year festival 149
oaths, vassal 144[10]
obsidian trade 181
oil 94
  of *Apoupa* 93
  Cypriote 93
ointments 94
one-room sanctuary 7
opium 94
Orion 73[10]
ostrich eggs 94f
ox 94
palaces, Crete & Western Asia 22
palaeography, Hittite 90[26]
past tense 167
  simple past 168, 175
  waw past 168
Peoples of the Sea 27
perfect tense 167, 175
poetic structures outside normal sequence 171ff
poetic structures, rewritten as prose 172[16]
pottery 30, 33, 35
  Cypriote 91
  Minoan 19[23], 20; 22
  Mycenaean 24; 25
precative perfect 54
preformative *t* 55
prepositions 53
punishments for incest 84
purification rite 84f
"real estate adoption" 99f
Red-Black Burnished Ware 182, 187, 189

Reserved Slip Ware 183, 184
rings, finger 94
Sabbatical year 143, 147, 148, 149
Sammeltafel 86
scapegoat 84, 86f
scarabs 35f, 95
scriptio defectiva 53
scriptio plena 54
seafaring 58
Sea Peoples 32, 34f, 121
See also: Peoples of the Sea
seals 35f
Semitic words and names
in Linear A 23[74]ff
in Linear B 23, 24[85]
shekel 34
shema 128
ship building, Cypriote 92
silver 30f, 92[7], 94
simple tenses 168ff
sister marriage 81f
slaves, manumission of 144ff
sodomy 81ff
suffix, double-duty 54
swords and daggers 17, 22
synchronic study 168, 175
Tabernacle 1, 4, 5, 6, 7, 8
Table of Nations 119ff
Targum of Job 55
Targum Pseudo-Jonathan 148
temple at Arad 1, 3, 5, 6, 7, 8
temple, Solomonic 1ff
tenses 167, 175
tin 21, 31
trade, Late Bronze Age 91ff
triple-duty preposition 57
Vulgate 56, 57[24]
waw consecutive, origin of 175
weights 34ff
White Painted Pendant Line Style Ware 93
White Painted Ware 10, 11, 12, 13ff
White Painted VI Ware 93
White Slip 11
White Slip I & II Wares 93
wilderness sanctuary 6
wood, Cypriote 92
woman, nature of 78
Yale Hittite fragment YBC 3991 84
yiphil causative 56
yiphil infinitive absolute 56

Personal Names

Abbabashti 111
Adada, s. of Ur-sukkala 132
Adapa 124
Aḥiram 57
Allala 131, 132
Amar-Suena 133, 134[27]
Amenhotep II 30
Amenophis III 24
Amenophis IV 36
Apoolodorus 121
ar-Rāzī 127, 128, 129, 130
as-Suyūṭī 128, 129
Astronoe 76f
aṭ-Ṭabarī 129
Ay 30
az-Zamakhsharī 127, 128, 129, 130
Berossus, *Babyloniaca* 124f
Cadmus 220
Constantine 219
Dada 130
Dakusene 23[78]
Danane 23[78]
Darius inscription 109[9]
David 3, 6, 7
Eli 6
Esarhaddon 121
Gilgamesh 76f
Gudea 134[27]
Guzana 135, 136, 137
Ham 122
Hammi-Idrap of Yaraquh 26
Hammurapi of Babylon 17[2]; 20; 21[45]
Hannah 6
Hellenos 123
Herodotus 119, 121
Hezekiah 3[22]
Homer 120
Hophra (pharaoh) 145

Iapetos 123f
Ibbī-Sin 135, 137
Ibn Abbās 129
Ibn Manẓur 129, 130
'Ikrimah 129
Iškun-Ea 135, 136
Japheth 119f
genealogies of 119ff
in Gen. 10 119ff
Jehoiachin 144
Jeroboam 7
Kadumane 23[78]
Khian 22
Korah 3
Kupanu 23[78]
Kurbilag, f. of Iškun-Ea 137
Lú-Enki 136[53]
Lugal-melam 133
Lú-Nanna 135ff
Makawete 23[78]
Meremoth 2
Merneptah 121
inscriptions of 121
Muhammad 128, 129, 130
Namzitara 132, 133, 134
Naram-Sin of Eshnunna 20
Nebuchadnezzar 144
Noah 120
Pashhur 3
Pliny 121
Plotinus 128
Puḫišenni, s. of Turišenni 100
Ramesses II 30
Ramesses III 31, 121
inscriptions of 121
ar-Rāzī 127, 128, 129, 130
Rekhmirē 32
Sargon of Akkad
and Kaptara 19
Shalmanezer III 31
Shamshi-Adad I 18
Sharrum-bani 137
Sheplarpak of Elam 20; 21[45]
Shishak 3[19]
Shulgi 133
Shu-Sin 131ff
^{D}Šu-^{D}Sin-nu-urma-ti-is-su
Shu-Sîn-nūr-matishu 137
Solomon 3[19]
Strabo 121
Stratonice 75
Sukiriteseya 23[78]
as-Suyūṭī 128, 129
aṭ-Ṭabarī 129
Teḫiptilla, s. of Puhishenni 100
^{f}Tulpunnaya 100[4]
Turishenni, f. of Puḫishenni 100
Umani 135, 136
Ur-Nanibgala 132, 133
Ur-nig̃ara 132
Ur-nig̃u 131, 132
Ur-saga 133
Ur-sukkala 131, 132
^{f}Winnirki 100
az-Zamakhsharī 127ff
Zedekiah 144ff
Zelophehad, daughters of 100
Zimri-Lim 18, 19, 20, 21, 22

Divine Names

Adonis 75, 77, 219
Ahuramazda 110, 113, 114
Allah 127, 128, 129, 130
Anaitis (Anahita) 222
Anath 72ff, 157, 217, 219
Anubis 76
Aphrodite 58, 219ff
Asherah 218, 219
Assur 110
Astarte 217, 219, 221
Attis 75, 77, 78[38]
Baal 130
Bata 76, 77
Dakuna 23[78]
Dido 221
Dionysos 159
Dumuzi (cf also Tammuz) 214
Elkunirsha 76[30]; 77[35]
Eshmun 76ff
Hephaestus 58
Il 130
Inanna 214
Ishtar 214, 215, 74
Mari ritual of 152[9]
festival of 158
Isis 221[84]
Kombabos 75ff
Kothar 58
Kushar-wa-Khasis 21[53-54]
^{d}Mar-du$_{10}$-edin-an-na 134

dMar-TU 134
Min 217
Nanibgal 133[18]
Nergal 32
Ptah 21[53]
Qudshu 217, 218, 219
Resheph 26[120]; 27[125]; 32; 217
Sin 110
Tammuz (cf Dumuzi) 214, 218
Tanit 221
Venus 219

Modern Scholars

Aberbach, H. 151[2]
Aharoni, Y. 1ff
Albright, W.F. 36[53]; 151[2]; 157; 121; 130; 216
Alkim, U. 187, 188
Alp, S. 83
Alt, A. 8
Amiran, R. 182, 183, 185
Andersen, F.I. 157
Astour, M.C. 214[13]; 220[71]
Aström, L. 33
Aström, P. 36; 37
Bailey, L. 151[3]; 153[10]
Barrelet, M.-Th. 157
Beer, G. 157[30]
Beyerlin, 151[1-2]; 154[12]
Biggs, R. 214[12]; 215[25]
Birkeland, H. 129
Braidwood, R. 189
Brinkman, J.A. 29
Brown, G.H. 183, 184
Buchholz, H. 29[3]; 31
Burney, C.A. 182, 183, 186
Busink, Th.A. 1ff
Cadogan, G. 30, 35
Caquot, A. 156[20]
Caskey, J. 29[2]; 34[40]
Cassuto, V. 151[4]; 152
Catling, H.W. 30[13], 31ff; 35; 37
Chapman, S. 116[1]
Coats, G. 151
Cornford, F. 156[24]
Cross, F.M. 6
Dale, A.H. 158[37]; 159[38]
de Vaux, R. 35; 151[3]; 154[11]; 155[20]
De Vries, C.E. 156[25]
Diamant, S. 188
Diehl, E. 159[39]
Dikaios, P. 30[5+14]; 31; 33
Dossin, G. 152
Driver, S.R. 154[44]
Edgerton, W.F. 122
Eissfeldt, O. 151[1]; 153[10]
Fahd, Toufic 130
Finkelstein, J.J. 215[27]; 216
Forrer, E. 89[17]
French, D.H. 183
Friedrich, J. 83, 84
Gadd, C.J. 215
Gardiner, E.N. 156[26]
Goetze, A. 83, 88, 90[21-22]; 156[24]
Gordon, C.H. 41, 29, 34ff, 82, 83, 99, 120[5], 123[30], 126[44], 128, 130, 156[20], 213, 222
Güterbock, H.G. 89[17]
Hallo, W.W. 214[7]
Harrison, J. 156[24]
Herzfeld, A. 109
Hoffner, H.A. 81ff, 94[44], 116[1], 135[41], 158[33], 213[1], 222[85]
Hyatt, J.P. 152
Jacobsen, Th. 158[33], 214[9], 216[28]
Karageorghis, V. 12, 33[30], 36[53]
Kaufman, Y. 151[3]
Köhler-Baumgartner 157
Kuschke, A. 2, 7
Labat, R. 158[35]
Lacheman, E.R. 99f
Lambert, W.G. 134, 214[10], 215, 216
Landsberger, B. 156[22], 158ff, 214, 216
Lane, W.W. 127, 129, 130
Laroche, E. 39ff, 86, 87, 88, 90[31]
Latte, K. 156[24]
Lawler, L. 158f
Lehming, S. 151[2]
Lewy, I. 151
Linder, E. 34
Loewenstamm 151[4]
Marinatos, Sp. 34
Mazar, B. 3[23]
Mellaart, J. 182, 183, 187
Merrillees, R.S. 37
Michalowski, P. 136[53]
Muhly, J. 29[4], 35, 36
Neiman, D. 119ff
Nicoll, A. 159[41]
North, M. 152, 153[10]
Noth, M. 2
Orthmann, W. 185
Otten, H. 88
Parrot, A. 153[10]
Pedersen 152
Phillip, A. 155[19]
Porada, E. 116, 117[26]
Pritchard, J. 218
Rainey, A. 219
Redford, D. 155[15]
Reinach, T. 159[38]
Reuveni, A. 118
Römer, W. 158[33]
Rosenthal, F. 129
Ross, J. 155
Rowley, H.H. 154[11], 155[21]
Rutter, J. 188
Sasson, J. 35[47], 135[46], 151[3]
Schaeffer, C. 32, 153[10]
Schmid, H. 152[5]
Schult, H. 2
Sjöberg, A. 158[33]
Skinner, J. 119, 122
Smith, S. 214[11]
Soggin, S. 155[18]
Smolar, L. cf. Aberbach, H.
Speiser, E.A. 119
Stewart, J.R. 10
Vagnetti, L. 29[3]
Van Loon, M. 184
Von Rad, G. 122
Watson, P.L. 151[4]
Webster, T. 159[38]

Wegner, M. 156[26]
White, E.F. 156[25]
Whybray, R. 157
Wilcke, C. 158[33]
Willets, R. 159[39]
Wilson, J. 122
Wright, G.E. 121
Yadin, Y. 156[20]
Yamauchi, E. 213ff
Yeivin, S. 1[5], 3[22]
Young, W.J. 116[1 and 9]
Zaccagnini, C. 33[31], 34[42], 35[46]

Geographic & Ethnic Names

Achaeans cf. Mycenaeans
Adiyaman 186
Aegean 33ff, 120, 121, 122
Aegean Basin
  and the Near East 17ff
Aegean Sea 120, 122
Aflak 202
Africa 119
Ağzıkarahan S.W. 202
Ahlatlibel 198
Akhera, Cyprus 12
Aksaray 202
Alaca Hüyük 183, 184f, 190, 204
Alalakh 1, 22, 24, 111
Alashiya 18, 92[2], 121[13], 121
Alişar Hüyük 183, 184, 186, 190, 194, 196, 204
Amas 198
Ambelico 10
Amorites 135
Amuq Plain 182, 184, 187, 188, 189
Amuq Plain Simple Ware 184
Amurru 18
Anatolia 222
Ankara 183, 185
Anti-Taurus 198
Apliki, mining at 92[8]
Arabia 120, 122
Arad 1, 3[19 and 21], 4ff
Aram 120
Armenia 122, 222
Arpachshad 120
Ashkenaz 120, 122
Asia 119
Asia, Central 120
Askalon 219[64]
Aškuza 121
Assur (city) 111, 114
Assyria 121
Assyrian 121
Assyrians
  trade with Cappadocia 18
Athenian civilization 119
Athens
  Acropolis hoard 26
Ayia Irini, Kea 29, 34
Ayia Paraskevi 11
Azerbaijan (Iranian) 188
Babylonia 121
Bactria 116[9]
Baghdad 31
Balikh River 188
Battal II 204
Bethel 7
Beth-Shan 6, 30
Beth Yerah, cf. Khirbet Kerak
Beycesultan 185, 190
Beydeğirmeni 198
Black Sea 122
Büyük Güllücek 183, 185, 190, 200
Büyük Kale Tepe Harmandalı 202
Byblos 17, 18, 19[23], 117[20], 219
Canaan 120
Canaanites 121
Cape Gelidonya 29ff
Caphtor 19, 20, 21, 22, 25f
Cappadocia 18
Cappadocian Ware 204
Carthage 221
Caspian 189
Çatal Hüyük-'Amuq 189
Çatal Hüyük West-Çumra 185
Central Anatolia, pottery of 182, 183ff, 194ff
    Büyük Güllücek type wares 185, 200
    Early Chalcolithic 185
    Cappadocian ware 204
    Çıradere Ware 204
    Early Bronze I 184, 194-97
    Early Bronze II 186, 202
    Early Bronze III 186, 204

Chorasmia 116[9]
Cilicia 188
Çimeliyeniköy 202
Cimmeria 122
Cnossus 22, 23[82]
Corinth 220
Crete 17ff, 30, 34, 36, 58
Cush 120
Cyclades 34
Cyprus 17, 18, 19, 23, 25, 26, 30ff, 121, 219f
  Hyksos presence in 182
  Middle Cypriote Period 182
Cythera 19, 20, 21, 24, 219f
Dan 7
Danuna 121[18]
Deve Hüyük 113
Dhahab 189
Diyarbakır 188
Dodanim 120
Dodona 121
Drehem 136, 137
Eastern Anatolia, pottery
  Early Bronze I-II 182, 183, 184, 186, 187, 192
  Early Bronze III 186, 204
Eber 122
Ebla 18[18]
Eğriköy 204
Egypt 120, 216ff
  and the Aegean 17, 22, 23, 24
Elazığ 183, 184, 186, 187
Elbistan Plain 184, 187
Elemenli Hüyük 185, 190
Elishah 120, 121
Emirilyas 198
Enkomi 30ff, 34[41]
Ephesus 220[68]
Erimi 10
Ernis 192
Eryx 221
Eshnunna 20, 21, 137
Eskiyapar 184
Ethiopia 122
Europe 119
Fethiye 204
Gâvur Hüyük 204
Gaziantep 187, 188
Gelidonya, Cape 19[22], 26, 29ff
Gimmiraya 121
Gomer 121, 122
Greece 34ff, 120, 122
Habur River 188
Hacafer Tepe 202
Hacıbektaş, cf. Suluca Karahüyük
Hadhramawt 122
Halab (Aleppo) 18
Ham 119, 120, 122
Hankendi 192, 204
Harran 188
Has Hüyük 184
Hazarmaveth 122
Hazor 1, 6
Heliopolis (Baalbek) 219
Hellas 122
Hellenes 120
Hinsor 192
Hopnik Çayı 188
Hurrians 85, 182
Hyksos 182
Hyksos period 19, 22
Indian Ocean 122
Ionia 119
Iran 120, 122
Iranian 122
Iraq 29
Islahiye 187
Israel 120, 182
Javan 120, 122
Jericho 189
Jerusalem, siege of 144
Joktan 120
Jordan 182, 188
Judaidah 189
Kamir Blur 118[49]
Kaptara (cf. also Capthor) 19, 20
$^{m\bar{a}t}$*Kabtu-ri* (^{KUR}DUGUD-*ri*) 25f
Kara Elbistan 198
Karahüyük (Elbistan) 204
Karaoğlan 198
Karavenk 204
Karipli Büyük Hüyük 202, 204
Karnak 30
Karpass Peninsula 182
Kayseri 183, 184
Keban Dam 183, 189
Keftiu 23, 34

Kemi, "Black Land" of Egypt 122
Khirbet Kerak
  architecture 182, 188
  pottery 182, 187
  problem of foreign relations 181ff
Kiledere 202
Kimmerioi 121
Kirkuk 224[9] ff
Kırşehir 202
Kittim 3[22], 120
Kızılırmak 185
Kizzuwatna 85
Knidos 30
Kom el Hetan 24[99]
Könk 192, 204
Konya Plain 185
Korucu Tepe 184
Köşk Pınar 186, 198
Kouklia (Cyprus) 116[15]
Kültepe-Kayseri 184, 186, 189, 190, 204
Kush 122
Lachish 6, 9
Latakia (Laodicea) 18
Laurium silver mines 19[31]
Lebanon 182, 188
Libya 119
Lud (son of Shem) 120
Madai 120, 122
Magog 120
Ma'hadu 18
Malatya 183, 186, 187, 188
Maraş 187, 188
Mar-dú 134ff
Mari 18, 19, 20, 21, 22
MAR.TU 134
Medinet Habu 31
Megiddo 2, 3, 9, 10, 11, 12
Memphis
  a residence of Kushar-wa-Khasis 21
  in Linear B personal name 23[83]
Meshech 120
Mesopotamia 18, 19, 20, 22[66], 24, 214ff
  arrival of Sumerians in 182
Milia tombs 9, 12
Minet el-Beida 18, 25
Minoan 36
Minoan civilization
  Early Minoan 17[3]
  Middle Minoan 17, 18, 19, 20[36], 21, 22, 23
  Late Minoan 22[68]
Minoan Language 21, 22, 23
Minoans 19, 21
Mizraim 120
Mycenae Shaft Graves 182
Mycenaean Greek, cf. Linear B
Mycenaeans 23, 24, 25, 26, 27, 31, 33ff
Nakhichevan lug 183
Neirab 112[39]
Nevşehir 186, 202
Niğde 183, 186
Nimrud 31ff
Nippur 131ff
Norşun Tepe 183[16]
Nubia 122
Ömerhanlı 202
Orontes estuary 18
Oxus treasure 114
Palestine 34, 36, 95, 218ff
Paphos 220
Pasargadae 114, 115
Peloponnese 19, 24
Persepolis 109, 113, 114
Persia 120
Philia 10
Phoenicia 219
Phoenician 34[42], 35f, 53, 54, 55
Phoenicians 121
Pınarbaşı (Kayseri Vil.) 184
Poskoflu 198
Put 120
Pylos 23[82]
Pyrgi inscription 58
Qal'at er-Rûs 18[14]
Qalparunda 31
Qatna 24
Qumran 53ff
Qyzqypan 116[14]
Ras Shamra 11, 96
Rawwafah 6
Rhodes 121
Riphath 120
Russia, southern 120
Samanköy 204
Saracık 204
Sarafand 35
Sardinia 29, 31, 121
Sardis 113, 114
Scythia 122
Şeriflikoçhisar 185
Shechem 2, 3

Shem 119, 120, 122
Shiloh 6, 7[43]
Sicca Veneria 221
Sicily 221
Simurrum 135, 136, 137
Sinaranu 25
Skythoi 121
Spain 121
Suluca Karahüyük-Hacıbektaş 184
Sumerians, arrival in Mesopotamia 182
Susa 109, 112, 114, 115, 137
Syria 17, 18, 19ff, 34, 182, 188, 219
Syrians 17ff, 30ff
Syro-Mycenean art 24f
Tabara el Akrad 190
Tarshish 120, 121
Tarsus 184, 186, 190
Ta'yinat 1, 2, 8, 189
Tepecik-Elazığ 183
Tell Beit Mirsim 10, 31
Tell Brak 22[66]
Tell el-'Ajjul 9, 12, 111
Tell Sūkās 18[14]
Tell Ta'yinat 1, 2, 8, 189
Tepe Sialk 112
Thebes (Egyptian) 30
Thebes (Boeotian) 23[82], 26[116]ff, 27, 35, 220
Thera 34
Timna' 6
Timna Valley 33
Tiras 120, 121
Togarmah 120
Totak 185, 190
Trans-Caucasus
  architecture 182
  chronology 183[13]
  pottery 182, 183, 186, 187
  terminology 183[13]
Tubal 120
Tülüntepe 204
Tuz Gölü 183, 185
Tyrrhenioi 121
Tyrsenioi 121
Ugarit (Ras Shamra) 11, 17-27, 96
Ugnim 135, 136
Ulukışla N. 202
Unqi 31
Urfa 188
Yanık Tepe 182, 185, 188
Yaraquh 26[121]
Yaycı 192
Yazıhüyük Küçük Tepe 202
Yorghan Tepe 224[9]ff
Yozgat 183
Zimudar 136
Ziwiye 109

Akkadian Texts Cited

AB I p. 130, lines 47-54 74
AfO Beiheft 9, p. 99, rev 55-56 74
AfO 8, pp 17-26, rev v 12-13 74
AOTU 1, 120:31 153[10]
ARMT 13, 2:9 153[10]
Babylonian Chronicle 149
R. Biggs, TCS 2 (1967), no. 18:3-4 74
BWL, 192:18 157
Codex Hammurapi §40 215[23]
  §117 148[21]
  §137 90[37], 215[23]
  §142 90[37]
  §§144-6 215[23]
  §§154-8 82, 89[20]
  §§178-82 215[23]
  §187 215[23]
  §§192-3 215[23]
EA 7:18 97[78]
  7:50-52 97[78]
  9:46-47 97[78]
  15:7-22 97[79]
  16:35-52 97[79]
  17:46-53 97[80]
  19:71-73 97[80]
  28:17-24 97[80]
  33:9-11 96[59]
  33:16 92[3]
  33:18 92[5]
  33:19-26 97[62]
  33:25 97[62]
  33:27-32 96[62]
  34:9-15 96[59]
  34:16-19 96[57]
  34:18 92[5]

EA 34:20 94[28]
34:21 94[29 and 32]
34:22 93[17]; 94[30]
34:22-3 94[31]
34:24 94[33]
34:25 94[31]
34:28 94[28]
34:42-46 96[62]
34:47 94[31]
34:50 93[13]
35: 92, 94, 96, 97
36: 92[5 and 11]
37: 93, 94, 96, 97
38: 96, 97
39: 96[62]; 97
40: 92, 93, 94, 97
41:14f 97[81]
44:2 97[74]
Erra Epic, iv 55f 74
Gilgamesh Epic, I, iv 1-41 82[8]
IV 34-36 216
Gilgamesh VI 76
Gilgamesh Epic, VI 165 216
VII iv 15 157
JEN 14:15 229
25:20 229
47:19 224
105: 230[20]
106: 230[20]
131: 226[16]
JEN 152: 226[16]
157: 226[16]
160: 100
260: 226[16]
266: 226[16]
281:4 224
361: 226[17]
373: 226[17]
399: 226[17]
459:18 230
507:11 224
510:6 225
514:12 224
662: 227[18]
668: 226
699: 226[17]
JENu 529a: 226[16]
KAI 1:2 57
26:12f 56
214:1-2 57
KAV 92:42 19
RA 23 3:37 225
23 7:24 229
23 52: 230[21]
23 59: 230[20]
35 2-3: 152[9]
RS 16.238:10 (PRU 3, 107f) 25f
Syria 20 107 153[12]
TCL 9 15 226[17]
9 44:21 229

Arabic Texts Cited

Qur'an 127, 128, 129, 130
Qur'an, Surah 112 127

Biblical Texts Cited

Gen 1:5 172
2:18ff 89[2]
:24 169
5: 125
10: 119ff
11:27-12:3 61
11:27-25:11 61
12:10-13:1 61
14:1-24 62
15:5-6 171
Gen 16:12 154
17:6 63
19:14 155
:31-35 82
20:1-18 61[15]
21:9 154f
:10 154
21:23 63[21]
23:1-20 62
24:1-67 62
Gen 25:1-11 62
:12-18 61
:19-34 61
25:19-29 61
26:1-35 61
:8 152
27:16f 169
:22f 173
:30 170f[11]
28:1-9 64

Gen 28:10-22 62
:20-22 62
31:13 62[19]
33:1 62[16]
35:11 63
:16-20 62
:21-26 62
:27-29 62
36:1-37:1 61
37:2-36 61
37:2-50:26 61
38: 64, 82
:15 218
:21f 218
39:14 155
42:1-38 61
46:1 62[17]
48:1-22 62
50:1-14 62
:15-21 62
:22-26 62

Ex 5:3 62[17]
12:1-42 174[21]
:8 172f
:11 173
:14 172f
:17 173
13:3 145
:14 145
:18 170
:18f 169
14:4 170
:6 172f
:28 173
15:19 170
:26 145
20:2 145
21:1-11 145f
:2 145, 146, 148[24]
:3 145
:4 145
:5 145
:7 145, 146, 148
:7-11 146
:11 145
:16 146
:18 173
21:26f 145

Ex 22:2 147, 148
22:17 71[2]
26:16-17 4
:31ff 4
:34 4
27:1 (Hb) 4
30:1ff 4
:18 4
32: 151ff

Lev 16:20ff 84
18:23 81
19:18f 170
20:15f 81
:23 82
25:8-10 149
:10 147
:35f 147
:39 147
:47-54 147
26:5 170
:34f 143
:43 143

Num 4:14 219
5:11ff 151[4]
11:30f 170
25:1-3 218
27: 100

Deut 4:23 145
5:2 145
:3 145
:6 145
6:4 128
:12 145
:18 145
7:8 145
8:14 145
9:9 145
:16 153[10]
12:25 145
:28 145
13:6 145
:11 145
:19 145
15: 145, 146f
:1 146
:8 147
:9 146

Deut 15:12 145, 146, 148,[24]
:12-18 146, 147
:13 145, 146
:13f 146[16]; 147
:15 146, 147
:17 146, 147
:18 145, 146
16:12 146[16]
17:2 145
20:16 71[2]
21:9 145
23:17f 218, 219
:19 81
24:18 146[16]
:22 146[16]
27:14 54
:26 145
28:25f 145
:69 145
29:11 145
:13 145
:21 145
:24 145
31:10ff 146, 147, 149
:16 145
32:15 170[8]
33:12 55

Judg 16:25 154
21:21 157[31]

1 Sam 1:7 7
:9 6, 7
:24 155
2:22 218
3:3 7
10:5 54[6]
:10 54[6]
21:12b 158
29:5 158

2 Sam 2:12-17 156[20]
6: 155
:17 6, 7
13: 82

1 Kings 6:2 1
:3 7
:16-20 2
:16 7
:17 7

1 Kings 6:19 7
12:28 7
14:23-24 218
15:12 218
22:46 218

2 Kings 4:1 147
:1-7 147f
23:6f 218
25:1 144

1 Chron 13:8 155[18]
15: 155
16: 155

2 Chron 3:3 4[27]
6:13 4
36:13 144[10]
:21 143

Neh 5:1-13 149
:5 147
8:2 149
9:1 149
10:32 149

Job 5:3f 56[16]
6:9 55
7:13 57[24]
9:12
16:12 208
19:15 55
:17 57
29:16 55[9]
:20 73
38:37 56
39:3 54[6]

Ps 19:2 56
74:13 208[12]
88: 157
109:19 153[10]
127:4f 73
149:3 158

Prov 7:10f 58
22:7 147

Eccles 5:4 57[24]
:5 63[20]

Song 7:1 158

Is 5:13 54
14:13 58
:30 56
:31 56
24:18 54[6]
:19 208
27:2 157
29:5 54
33:1 55
:3 53f
37:19 56
47:1 57
50:1 147
:6 55
59:13 56
61:1f 147
63:16 56

Jer 13:27 218
17:1 54
:4 147
26:1 149[32]
27:1 149[32]
:3 149[32]
:12 149[32]
:16-22 149[32]
28:1 149[33]
30:20a 57f
31:3 158
34: 143ff
:6 144[6]
:7 144
:8ff 144, 146
:18f 144

Jer 34:9 145
:10 145, 146
:11 144, 146
:13 145, 146
:14 145, 146
:20 145
:21f 144
37:5-11 144
39:1 144
49:34 149[32]
52:4 144

Lam 3:22 55
:27 57
4:17 144[11]

Ezek 16: 218
17:11-18 144
23:37-41 218
24:1-2 144
30:20f 145
46:17 147

Hos 4:14 218
13:2 54

Amos 2:6 147
:7f 218
8:6 147

Hab 3:10 54

Zech 12:10 57
14:9 128

Ecclus 6:8 57
26:12 73

1 Macc. 121

Dead Sea Texts Cited

IQIs[a] 37:19 56
47:1 57[25]

IQIs[a] 63:13 56
:16 56

IIQTgJb 19:15 55

New Testament Texts Cited

Gal 4:29 154
1 Cor 6: 221

Talmudic Texts Cited

Bab. Talm., Ta'anith 121
Rosh Hashanah 8b-9b 149[34]
Ta'anith 29b 149[29]
Nedarim 61a 149[34]
Arakhin 11b 149[29]
Bab. Talm., Arakhin 12a-b 149[34]
18b 148[26]
32b 149[34]
Niddah 48a 148[26]
Pal. Talm., Kiddushin 1:2 148[26]

Midrashic Texts Cited

Mekilta d.R.Y., Mishpaṭim I, 249 148[26]
Sifra, Behar, II, 6, 107b 148[26]
Sifrei, Re'eh, §111-112, 97a-b 148[26]

Classical Texts Cited

Apollodorus, Library 121
Athenaus of Naucrates, Deipnosophists, 1:15 159[41]
Augustine, City of God, IV:10 219
Bacchylides of Keos 159
Diodorus Siculus, IV:83 221[82]
Herodotus, I:93 222
I:105 219[64]
I:181f 214[9], 217
I:199 216, 220
II:60 217[49]
II:126 217
Homer, Hymn to Pythian Apollo 159[41]
Homer, Iliad 36, 120, 121
Iliad, XVIII:593-605 159
Odyssey 120, 121
Odyssey, IV:17-19 159[41]
VII:262ff 159[41]
VIII:288 220
:362 220
Josephus, Antiquities, XVIII:65-80 221
Juvenal, IX:24 221[84]
Lucian, De Dea Syria, 6 219
19-27 75f
Lucian, The Dance, 16 159[40]
Ovid, Fasti, IV:223-244 75
Metamorphoses, X:708-716 75
Pausanius, I:xiv:6 220[64]
Photius, Bibliotheca Migni, CIII, 1303f 76
Pindar 159
Plato, Ion. 534C 159
Pliny, Historia Naturalis 121
Plutarch, Lives, Numa, XIII:3-7 156[24]
Plutarch, Quaest. Convi. IX:152 159[41]
Pratenas of Phlius 159[30]
Strabo, II:xiv:6 222
VI:ii:5 221
VIII:vi:20 220
XII:iii:36 222
XVI:i:20 216
XVII:i:6 217
Tacitus, Histories, II:i:2 220
Thaletas of Gortyn 159
Xenodemus 159[41]
Xenophon, Anabasis, VI:1 156[24]
Symposium 159

Egyptian Texts Cited

Eb. 101, 18-20 (= Gr. Med. 855q) 212
Eb. 41, 10-11 (= Gr. Med. 204d) 212
Kom el-Hetan, List E_n 24[99]
Pap. Anastasi IV, pl. 15, 2-4 93[14]
pl. 17, 7-9 93[14] and [17]
Pap. Leiden I 343, VI:2-6 211
Sm. 2, 20 212

Hittite Texts Cited

Hittite law §98 90[31]
§§187-8 82, 84
§189 87
§194 222[85]
§196 89[18]
§199 82
§§199-200A 82, 84
Hukk. §29 87
IBoT II 117 iii 1-3 87
iv 1-3 87, 90[41]
KBo V 3 iii 28ff 87
VI 2 ii 57 89[17]
XII 38 92[12]
38 i 5ff 94[44]
115 90[25]
KBo XII 115 rev 1-5 87[41]
XXI 33+ 51[86]
35 obv i 4, 11 88
KUB XIII 2 iii 9ff 89[19]
14 90[23]
XXX 34 iv 15ff 90[24]
67:7-9 84, 90[25]
XXXII 40 + 49a + KBo XXI 33 +, 51[86]
XLI 11 rev 2ff 85ff
ZA 33, p. 98, lines 25-29 74
Bo 2968 obv 5-10 84, 89[17]
6464: 11-14 84
254/d ii 1 and 15 90[25]
827/z 1-9 87
YBC 3991 84

Sumerian Texts Cited

CBS 9178 134[39]
9766 131, 132
UM 29-13-268 134
UNC 7 135
YBC 2401 135[41]
4672 136[53]
7149 136[53]
3 NT 299 133[18]

Ugaritic Texts Cited

UT 49: v 19 151[4]
ii 31-37 151[4]
ii 37 209
51: vii 15f 57f
vii 47-49 58
52: 143
:61 58[29]
67: vi 12-14 57
125:25f 55[9]
128: iii 25f 63
132:1ff 82[6]
137:12 209
UT 607:3 58
2056: 34
1 Aqht I 16 71[2]
120 208
134 208
IV 206 80
2 Aqht I 17-19 57
VI 26f 71[2]
3 Aqht IV 13 71[2]
27 71[2]
Krt 62

Akkadian Words Cited

anzillu 83, 89[16]
assinnu 82, 215[27]
aššabu 229
bābu 229
ekallu 7[46], 49
elēlu 157f
entu 215[23]
gayatu 94[44]
ḫarimtu 215, 222[85]
ištarītu 214[15], 215
kaptaru 22[56]
katappu 20[32]
keppû 158
kezertu 215[27], 222[85]
kīmē 225
kiṣallu 158
kulmašītu 214[15], 215
kulu'u 82
lišānšu 226[16]ff
massiku 153[10]
mēlultu 158
lelulu 158, 158[3]
mīšaru 143, 148[22], 149[27]
mummelu 158[33]
nadānu 226[15], 229
nadītu 215
nukaribbu 224, 225
parāru 208[7]
parīsu 94[44]
passu 158
peḫû 226[12]
pilpilû 82
pûḫ 226[12]
qadištu 214, 215
rābiṣu 97[67 and 68]
raqādu 158
raqqidu 153[3]
rēš šarruti 149[31-32]
saḫiptu 215[26]
sâru 158
sinnišānu 82
sirrimu 51[88]
šamḫatu 215[27]
šugītu 215[26]
šulmānu 96[62]
šupêlu 226[12]
šupe'ultu 226[12]ff
tēlītu 215[26]
tudittu 85ff
ṭuppat pūḫāti 226[12]
ṭuppi šupe'ulti 226f[12]ff
(w)ardu 135[42]
zakû 226[15], 229
zammiru 158[33]
zikru 215[23]

Arabic Words Cited

'anfara "frighten away" 208
faḫid "clan" 54[6]
fāra "be roused, throb" 209, 210
nafara "disperse, scatter" 208
nafrat "escape" 208
'ḤD 127, 128, 130
al-'iḫlaṣ 127, 130
ar-raḥmān 127, 130
'ijmā' 129, 130
ka'bat 130
ṢMD 127, 128, 129, 130

Aramaic Words Cited

npr "flee" 208[18]

Egyptian Words Cited

inb (liquid) 93
ḥmt nṯr 217
ḥnrwt 217
mrt 217
np3 212
np3p3 212
nṣf 34
p3 209ff
qdt 34
sp3 212
zp3 212

Greek Words Cited

hyporkhēma 158ff
malakos 81
paizein 154, 154[13]
stasimon 158[37]

Hebrew Words Cited

'iyyîm 121
'iyyê haggôyîm 120, 121
'al 173
'ēl 62[19]
'ēl šadday 62[19]
'ûlam 1, 2, 7
'amhōtay 55
b^e^ "from" 57
biṭnî "her womb" 57
bêt'ēl 62[19]
b^e^*tôk* 7
dbr 2
d^e^*bîr* 1, 2, 6, 7, 8
d^e^*rôr* 147
hêkal 1-8
hāmôn "army" 54
hōmīyyāh "turbulent" 58
hrg "to slay" 56
w^e^ "and" 168 et passim
zbḥ 154
zônāh 218
zônôt 218
ḥebel "band, herd" 54[6]
hištaḥ^a^*wōt* 154
ḥwl 157
ḥll 158
ḥannōt "supplication" 57
ḥpp "to surround" 55
ḥāqar "to investigate" 55
ḥāraš "to carve" 54
yṣ' 171[11]
yāṣā' l^e^*ḥopšî* 145
yrh "to show" 55
kî "indeed" 55
kôk^e^*bê 'ēl* 58
keleb 81
kālāh "to be exhausted" 55
killāh 171[11]
kātab "to engrave" 54
lāhem "for them" 54
lô' 173
mûg "to melt" 56
nāmôg "to melt" 56[20]
mrmmtk 54
m^e^*yabbêm* 82
m^e^*tê rā'āb* "men of the Hungry One" 54
m^e^*tîm* "soldiers" 54
maṣṣebāh 3
mkr 146
m^e^*ḥōlāh* 154, 157ff
massēkāh 153[10]
ngš (Hiphil) 154
nkr "to recognize" 56
nš' b "to take from" 57[24]
ntn "to give" 56
swr "to turn aside" 55
sōrāret "aggresive" 58
'ēdāh "assembly" 58
'edût 90[30]
ha'alôt 'ôlôt 154
'innûg 157[30]
'nh 154, 157
'annôt (Pi''el) 154, 157ff
paḥad "pack" 54[6]
pārar "to shake, tremble" 208
ṣhq 154ff
qr' "to call" 58
qôl rām "a loud voice" 54
q^e^*dēšîm* 81, 218
q^e^*dēšôt* 218
rēšît mamlākāh 149
rûᵃḥ taḥnûnîm 57
rām "loud voice" 54
šillaḥ ḥopšî 145
š^e^*miṭṭāh* 146, 147[20], 148[25]
ša'ar "gate" 56
šōreš "offspring" 56
tebel 81
tabnît "shape" 54
tôledôt 61
tāmam "to be terminated" 55
tannôt 157

Hittite Words Cited

annaneka- 88
appezzi- "low-ranked person" 87
ašuša- 90[40]
ḫaššatar 87
ḫurkel 82f
iwaru 86f
iwarwannai- 86
iwarwatar 86
anda kariya- 85, 86, 90[36]
TÚG *kariulli-* 90[36]
MÍ*karšant-* 88
kattan (= GAM-*an*) 90[26]
kiššan 90[26]
kutrueššar 85, 90[30]
memianzi 90[26]
mulatar 83
nakkuš "noxa" 90[31]
nakkušša- 85[31]
neka- 88
pennianzi 90[27]
tallai- 90[39]

Hurrian Words Cited

ambašši- 85

Latin Words Cited

carmen saliare 156[24]
ludō 154
salii 156[24]
sodales 156

Minoan Words Cited

kumina 23[75]
kunisu 23[74]
samuku 23[75]
sasame 23[75]
yane 23[75]

Mycenaean Words Cited

aikupitiyo 23
arasiyo 23
kito 24[85]
kumino 24[85]
kuruso 24[85]
misarayo 23
ponikiyo 24
rita 24[85]
sasama 24[85]
teoyo doero 220[66]

Sumerian Words Cited

GIŠAGA 89[17]
an-zil 89[16]
e-ne-di/du$_{11}$ 158[33]
ki-e-ne-di 158
é-gal > *ekallu* > (Heb) *hêkal* 7[46]
ensí 131, 132, 133, 134
**ere* 135, 136
mí*kar-kid* 88, 222[85]
ki-ága 132, 133
LÚ.KU 229
LUKUR 215
mí-é-ge$_4$*-a* 85, 86
MÍ.SUḪUR.LÁ 222[85]
MUŠEN ḪUR-RI 85
ni$_x$ = NIGÌN 132
NU.GIG 214
PA (unit of measure) 94[44]
RA 90[26]
sa-a 94[44]
sukkal-mah 137
šakkana 136[49]
še-sa-a 94[44]
šu-bar 133
Ú-tu 229
u$_4$ . . *a* 135, 136

Syriac Words Cited

'apar "put to flight" 208
n^e*par* "run away" 208

Ugaritic Words Cited

'idrp 26[120]
bn ym "son(s) of the sea" 58
bn "son" 56
b "because of" 57
ḥwy 71[2]
ḥkpt 23[83]
-y (3rd sg suff) 54
yn 23[76]
yṯb l "to sit upon" 57

kṯr-w-ḫss 21[54]
khnm 219
l 71[2]
nhrm "ocean currents" 58
-nm (pl suff) 54
npr "birds, fowl" 209
srr "be rebellious" 58
ʿdt "confluence" 58
bnm ʿdt "son of the confl." 58
ʿdt thmtm "confl. of Upper & Lower Flood" 58
pr "take flight" 208
prpr (prop. name) 208
qdšm 219
qrʾ "to call" 58
rm "sound" 54
šrš "offspring" 56
tp "drum" 54
ṯʿ 63
ṯġrt "gates" 56[21]

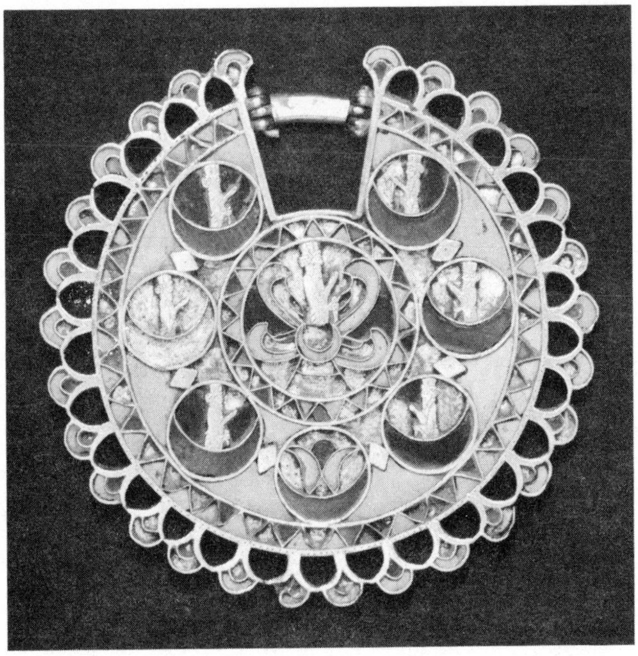

a

Boston Earring — Obverse
Courtesy Museum of Fine Arts, Boston

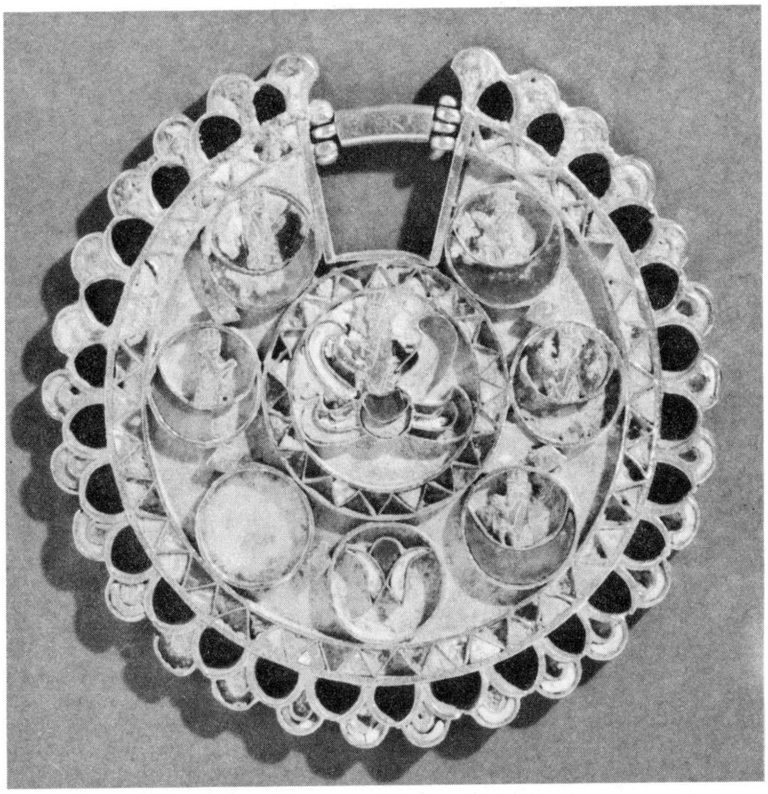

b

Boston Earring — Reverse (uncleaned)
Courtesy Museum of Fine Arts, Boston

a: UNC 7

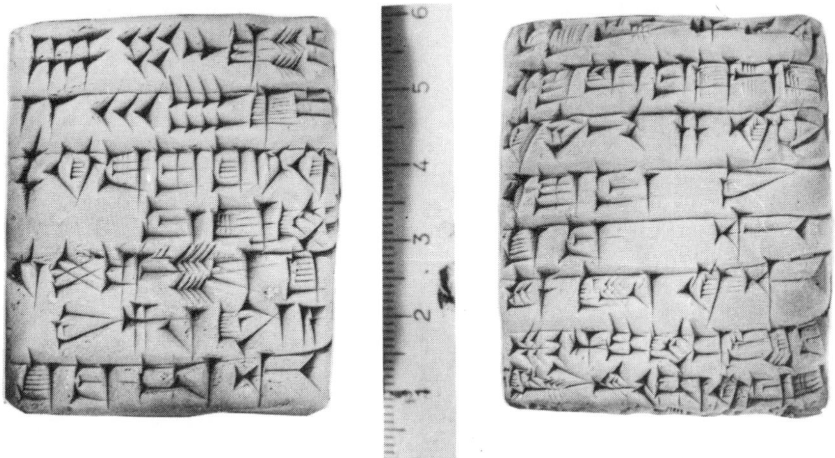

obv. rev.

b: FLP 1281

obv.

bottom

rev.

FLP 1282

obv.

rev.

top

left edge